LR-DI

Mantra

for

CAT

by
Gautam Puri

Includes
CAT 2019 Solved Paper (Slot-1)

CL MEDIA (P) LTD.

Edition : 2020

ISBN : **978-93-89718-61-4**

Typeset by : *CL Media DTP Unit*

Administrative and Production Offices

Published by : **CL Media (P) Ltd.**

A-45, Mohan Cooperative Industrial Area,
Near Mohan Estate Metro Station,
New Delhi - 110044

Marketed by : **G.K. Publications (P) Ltd.**

A-45, Mohan Cooperative Industrial Area,
Near Mohan Estate Metro Station,
New Delhi - 110044

For product information :

Visit ***www.gkpublications.com*** or email to ***gkp@gkpublications.com***

Preface

Dear Students,

It is no surprise that competition in CAT is increasing every other day which makes it inevitable for aspirants to become good in each of the three sections, one of which is LR-DI which has become quite tough in the past couple of years and is the toughest of the three sections. It is against this backdrop, that [illegible]**antra for CAT** is a must for systematic and comprehensive preparation [illegible] has been designed by including a theme based learning that revolves around different concepts with diverse applications. The end of your journey, with this book, will be an enriching learning experience.

Our integrated thematic methodology driven by latest research has been involved in this book to enhance your learning. Practice exercises on all the possible topics of LR-DI have been incorporated to reinforce the conviction in the ability of aspirants. Our pedagogy experience coupled with extensive research has lent credence to our conviction that learning is at its very best when concept based understanding and applications go hand in hand.

To enhance your learning and assimilation of relevant concepts, we have also included numerous sets of LR-DI from past years' CAT exams as well.

At the end of each module, we expect the students to:

(i) Master each topic by solving all possible types of questions.

(ii) Quickly and effectively apply relevant concepts to different types of question in a time-bound examination scenario.

(iii) Develop long-lasting skills by imbibing each concept that is clearly covered through a module.

Armed with the latest tools for success, along with your diligence and positive attitude, you have begun your march towards success. Have faith in yourself!

"*The woods are lovely, dark and deep,*
But I have promises to keep,
*And **miles to go before I sleep,***
*And **miles to go before I sleep***"

- Robert Frost

Contents

Introduction to Data Interpretation

DATA REPRESENTATION

Introduction

A major part of a manager's daily routine is to analyze data. The amount of data that a manager comes across is mind-boggling, to say the least. Financial data as in P&L sheet, cost sheets, marketing and sales data, divided across product groups and further across quarters and years, compared with previous years' figures; competition and market information of market shares, value wise and volume wise; data on productivity; data on performance appraisal; data on each and every process that you can imagine. There exists an entire department in most companies, MIS (Management Information Systems), which generates and managers every conceivable data that one can imagine.

For a manager to gather worthwhile information from this overwhelming amount of data, the data needs to be presented in a lucid and concise manner. Duplicating data has to be avoided and at the same time no detail has to be lost out. The data representation should immediately be able to provide the overall scenario and also should be sufficient to compute any detailed information. This is where data representation plays a very important role.

While there can be any number of ways a data can be represented, in this chapter we will look at the standard ones only.

Learning Objectives

By the end of the chapter, you should be able to

1. Understand the various standard ways of representing data.
2. Understand how certain types of data are more suited to a particular form of data representation.

Tables

A table is one of the simplest and the most convenient tools used for summarizing data. In a table, data is systematically arranged in columns and rows. All the columns and the rows have a particular heading that defines the information contained in the respective columns and rows. The column and the row heading may also define the units of measurements, if any. While a tabular data can offer a lot of information, it lacks a pictorial representation and hence it may demand some time (and calculations) to give an idea of the overall scenario.

Annual Sales of 2-wheelers in India, 2000 – 2004

Type	Number of vehicles sold in year (in '000s)				
	2000	**2001**	**2002**	**2003**	**2004***
Mopeds	580	490	450	380	330
Scooters	520	640	720	680	830
Motorcycles	460	540	750	840	930
Total	1560	1670	1920	1900	2090

* Figures for 2004 are projected numbers

While reading a table, or for that matter any representation of data, it is imperative that you read everything about the data i.e. the heading for the data, the column headings, any foot notes, units of the data, etc. and not giving just a cursory glance to the actual numbers.

For example on reading the head note of the data, it should be kept in mind that the data is about sales and not production. Thus any information on production cannot be assumed or derived from this unless further data or piece of information in the form of text is given.

Another point to note is that the figures correspond only to India and only to 2-wheelers and not to any other kind of automobile. The units suggest that the sale of mopeds in the year 2000 is not 580 but 580000.

The column heading should have made it clear that the data refers to the number of vehicles and not the revenue generated through sales (a very common mistake would have been to assume 580 as Rs. 580,000). The actual number of mopeds sold in 2004 is NOT 330. This is clear as the figures for 2004 are projections and not the actual, as stated in the foot-note.

Line graph

The data given in the table, on previous page, could have also been represented in a line graph as follows:

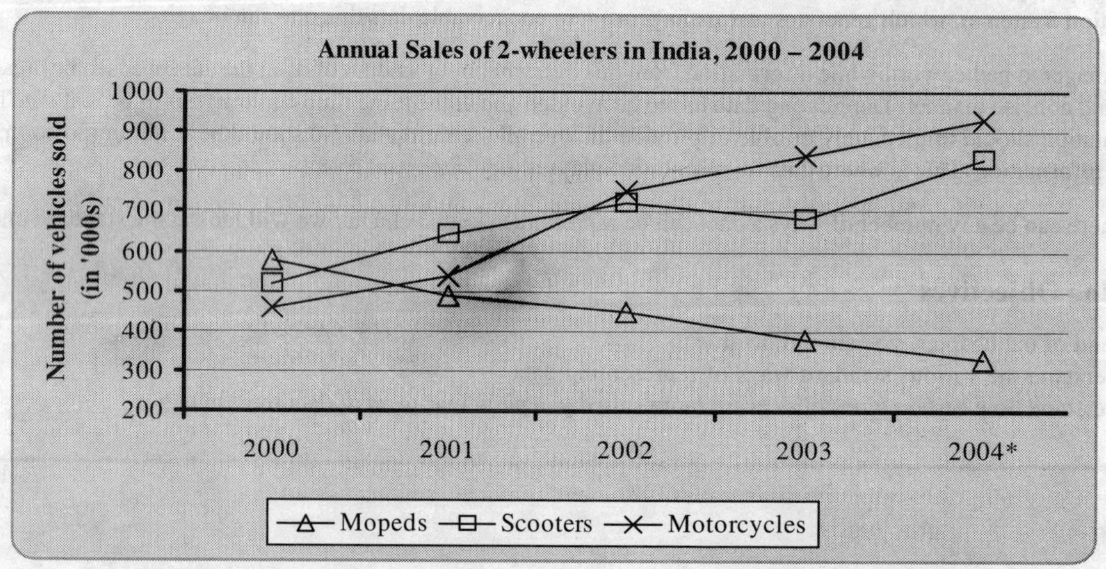

* Figures for 2004 are projected numbers

What a line graph achieves over a table is that it is a pictorial representation and hence can give an immediate overall picture of trend. Thus it is very obvious that the sales of mopeds have continuously decreased over the period whereas the sales of motorcycles have shown the highest growth rate over the period. Not only this, it is also immediately clear that the highest growth rate in any year, by any product group, is shown by motorcycles in the period 2001-2002 as the line is the steepest in this period. What is lost out in the process is the accuracy as one would have to ascertain the value of any point looking at the scale of the Y axis. However the actual values could also be mentioned in the same graph adding accuracy although it will make the graph look more cluttered. Apart from these differences, any minute information that could be calculated using the data in table or this data in line graph remains the same because the underlying data remains the same. Thus all questions that could have been asked on the tabular data can also be asked on this representation.

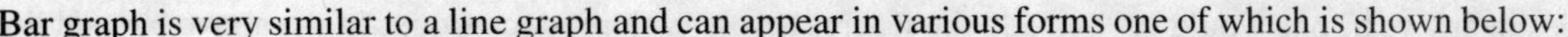

Bar graph

Bar graph is very similar to a line graph and can appear in various forms one of which is shown below:

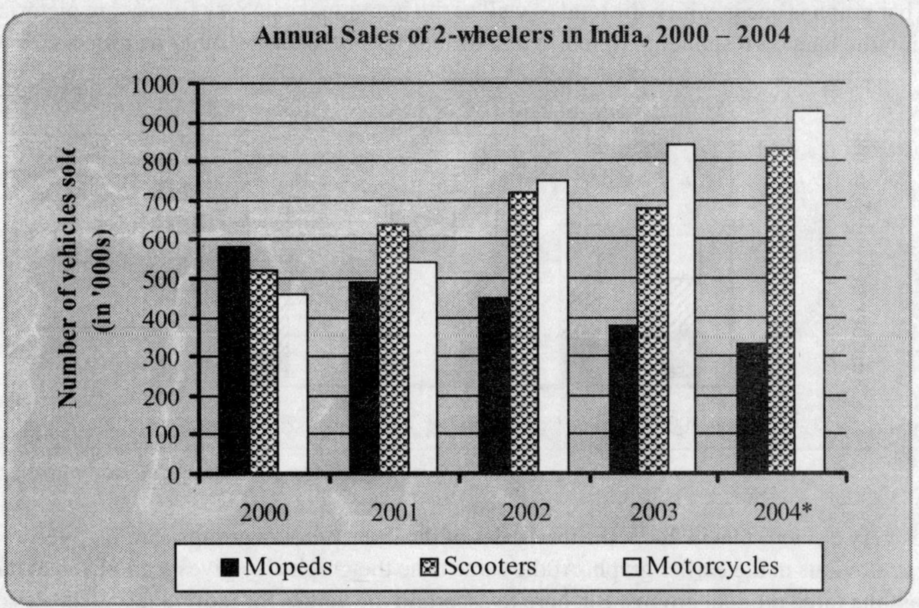

* Figures for 2004 are projected numbers.

This type of graph is more correctly called a column chart rather than a bar chart. As the underlying data is exactly the same as in the tabular data and in the line graph, there is no information lost and any of the three representations can be used interchangeably. Lest you start wondering why then are there so many varied ways of representations, a moments glance can help you understand that this type of graph is more visually appealing when we have to compare the sales across product groups in any particular year whereas the line graph was more visually appealing for the growth rates or trends across years for a particular product group.

Please note that in such a graph, it is only the height of the bar that matters and the width of the bar does not hold any significance. An exactly similar representation can also be given with horizontal bars as follows:

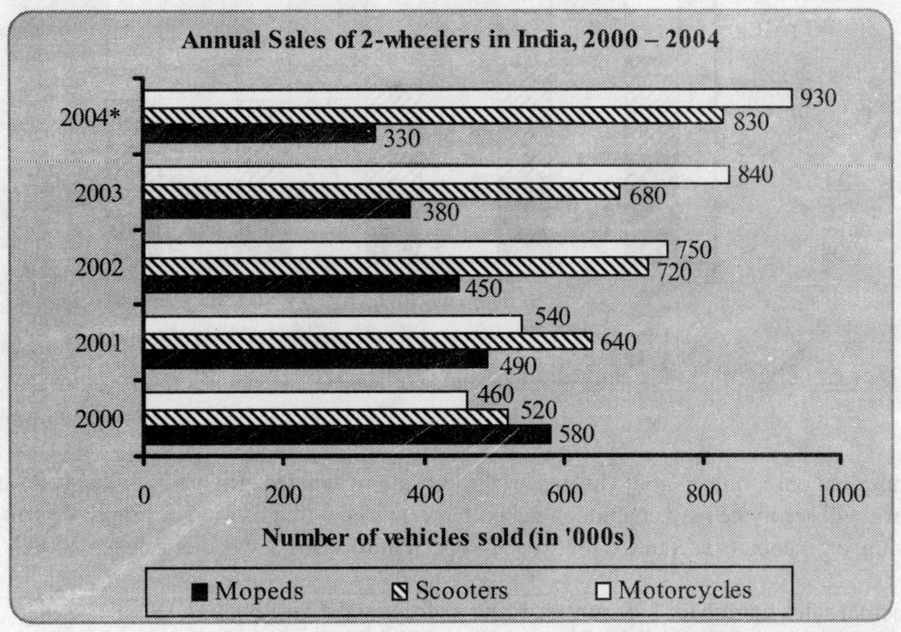

* Figures for 2004 are projected numbers

Cumulative Bar Graph

To calculate the total sales in any year, one would need to add the figures across each product groups in the above bar and line graph. A cumulative bar graph is one in which the total as well as the individual category figures are pictorially represented. This is achieved by stacking the bars corresponding to individual categories one over the other as follows:

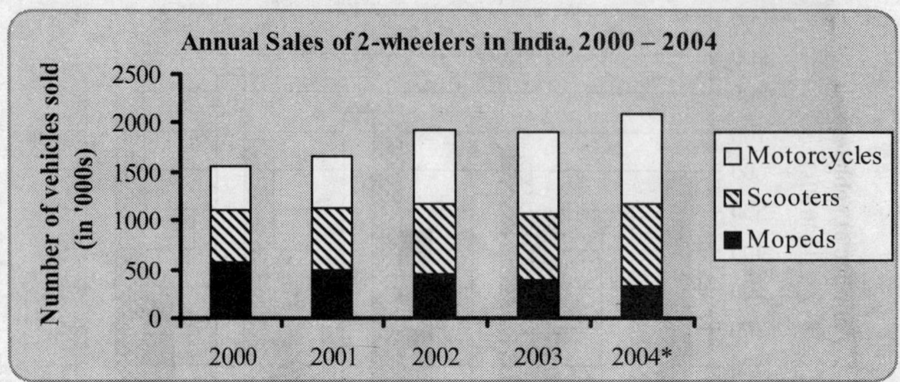

* Figures for 2004 are projected numbers.

Thus, here it becomes very obvious that in 2003, the total sales of the three product groups, cumulatively, was lower than that in 2002 which was not so obvious in the earlier graph. At the same time the graph also gives a good visual idea of the distribution of the total sales across the three product groups. But here to ascertain the values for individual categories one needs to do some subtraction. Thus the sales of scooters in 2000 is not 1100 as the bar of scooters ends at 1100 but is 1100 – 600 = 500.

An intellectually stimulating graph (and often used to add difficulty to the questions asked) is a cumulative bar graph of not the sales figures but that of the percent share of each product group, as shown:

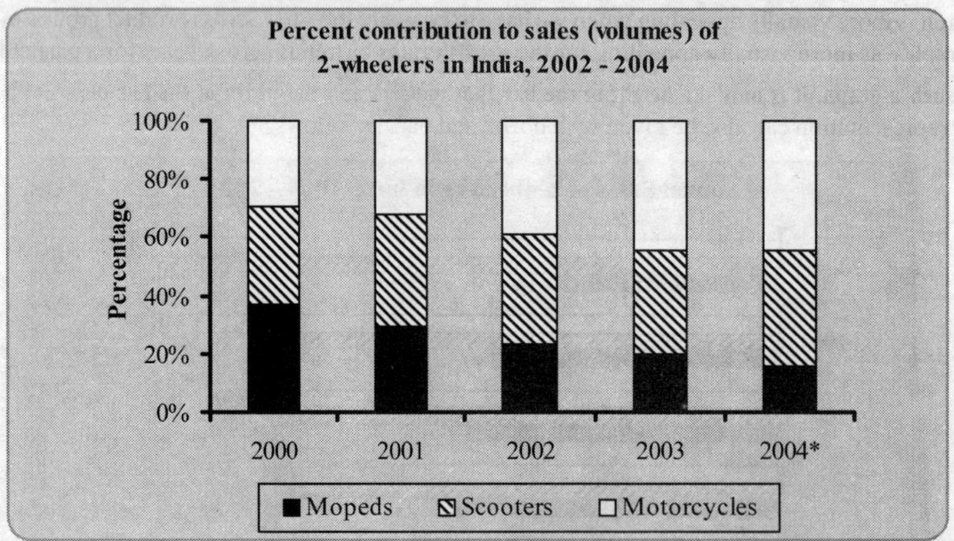

* Figures for 2004 are projected numbers.

An immediate and important observation should be that all the bars are of same length (and obviously so as all the bars represent a total of 100%). As we will see in the next chapter on data interpretation, with this kind of graph, we can get just an idea of the share of a product group, e.g. scooters accounted for 70 – 38 = 32% of the total 2-wheeler sales in 2000.

We cannot infer the actual sales figures for 2000 unless some additional data is given.

Pie chart

The cumulative bar graph of the percent contribution of each category introduced the idea of a percent share of the total. A more appropriate graph to depict this is the pie chart. The name itself suggests that this graph basically shows the manner in which an entire pie is divided among different groups.

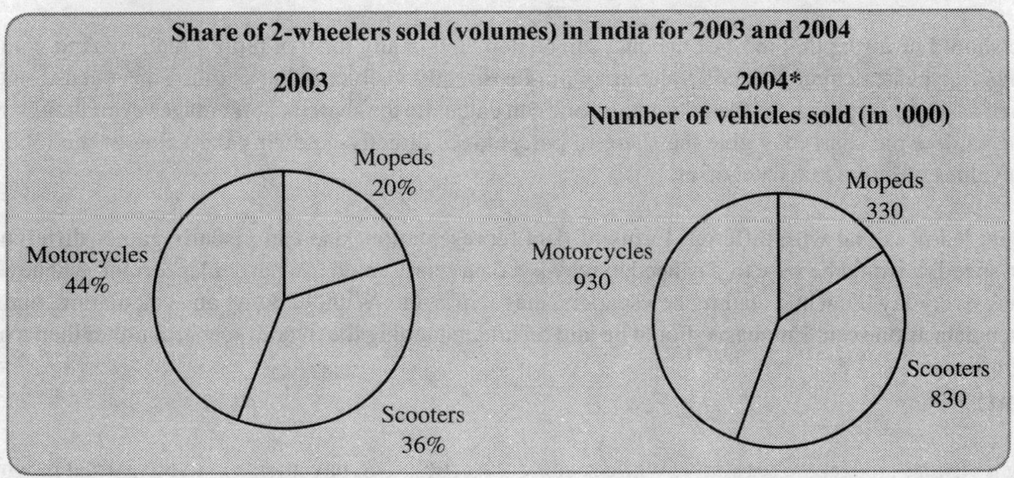

* Figures for 2004 are projected numbers

Thus, when using pie-charts, each pie generally corresponds to a particular year. Also worth noting is that the pie on the left has just the percentages whereas the pie on the right has the actual sales figures given. Thus for the year 2003, we cannot find the actual sales figures as the total value of the pie (cumulative sales of the three product groups) is not known for 2003. But for 2004, we can calculate the expected share of each product group in percentage as we can sum the individual figures to know the total sales of 2-wheelers.

Pie charts are easier to compare the share of various product groups, visually. Thus it is very clear just by visual observations that the share of mopeds has declined at the expense of an increase in share of scooters, with the share of motorcycles remaining almost the same.

Combination graphs

Any of the above types of graphs can be combined to form a combination graph. An example of a combination graph is shown below. The line graph shown has additional data of the average price of a product group.

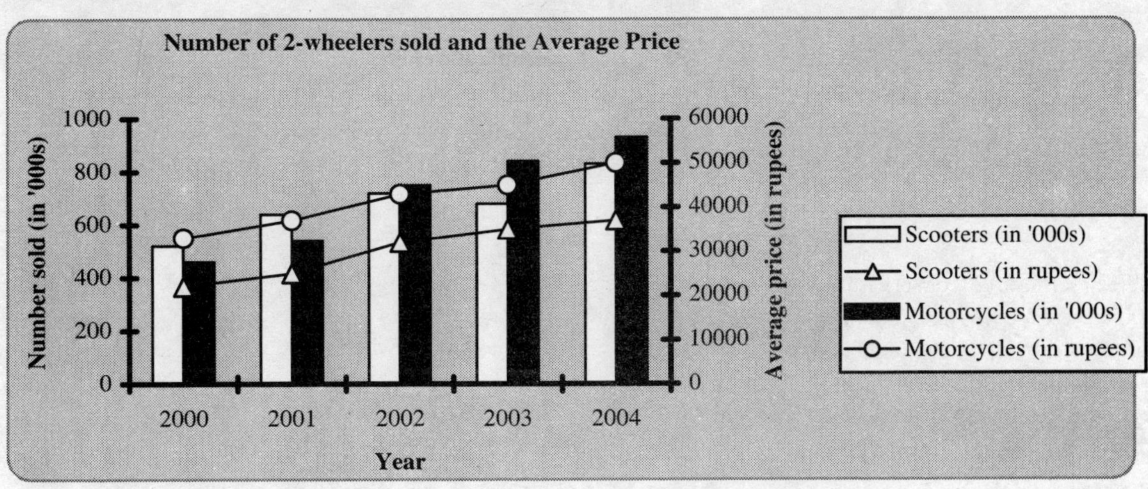

In this chapter we have discussed only the standard types of data representation. Data can be represented in many more unusual ways (in the past, CAT papers have had a variety of data representation styles, many of which were unfamiliar). We will come across these unusual types throughout the study material. Irrespective of the type of graph, if one reads the instructions, head notes and foot notes carefully, one can very easily decipher the graphs.

Learning Outcomes:

By now, one should be aware that most of the data can be depicted in any form of representation. And with any form of representation, one can calculate a detail which may not be directly visible on the graph. Thus even if data is given in tabular form or as a line graph, say of the sales value, one can calculate the share in percentages even though it is not given directly. And while a pie chart may give the share in percentages directly, knowing the value of the total pie, one can calculate the values of individual categories.

Another aspect learnt is that with different forms of data representation, one can visually gather different inferences. Thus, to gain speed, it would be wise to pay heed to why is a data represented in a particular format, whenever one comes across a data in everyday life while reading newspapers, magazines, etc. Without doing any calculation, one should try to gather as much data as one can. Emphasis should be laid on understanding the overall scenario rather than a minute detail.

Assignment:

Start reading a business magazine regularly. While reading the articles, do pay attention to the format in which facts and figures are given. Take a particular data set and then represent the same data in various other standard forms of representation. See what sort of hurdles you face while representing the data from one form to another.

Assume any five values e.g. sales of a company for five consecutive years. On an Excel sheet, fill in these values and then plot different types of graphs. Excel offers all the standard types of graphs and sub-graphs and would give you a clear understanding of the various types of graphs.

CONCEPTS OF DATA INTERPRETATION

Introduction

Data is just like loads of ammunition with you. It can come to your aid or else may overwhelm you in a negative sense. Just as a tool is just as good as the craftsman, data it self is of no use unless we can interpret it meaningfully to gather valuable information.

Though the interpretation would depend on the actual data given, this chapter tackles some of the general interpretations that you will come across in most of the data sets.

Learning Objectives

- Difference between Growth and Growth rates
- Growth rate in Line graphs.
- Market Share : Value wise and Volume wise
- Simplifying two pie charts

Growth Rates

Consider the following data :

Snapshot of ABC Corporation, (1999 – 2003)

All figures are in Rs. Lacs

	1999	2000	2001	2002	2003
Sales	200	240	290	320	350
Profit	40	50	55	70	50

Note: Profit = Sales – Costs

Growth refers to just the increase in the underlying value. Thus growth in sales from 1999 to 2000 would be 240 – 200 i.e. Rs. 40 lacs. And growth in sales over the entire period would be 350 – 200 i.e. Rs. 150 lacs.
Growth rate refers to the percentage increase. Thus while reading a question one must make a distinction between the growth and growth rate.

Thus the growth rate of sales in 2000 would be $\frac{240-200}{200}\times 100 = 20\%$. Unless other wise stated in the question growth would be over the previous year and the base would be the previous year's value.

Similarly growth rate in sales over the period 1999 – 2003 would be $\frac{350-200}{200}\times 100 = 75\%$

Annual Growth Rate

There are two ways in which annual growth rates, over a period of time, can be calculated viz. the Simple Annual Growth Rate (also called average annual growth rate) and the Compounded Annual Growth Rate (CAGR).
If the initial value is P and the final value is A after n time periods then the two growth rates are defined as

Simple growth rate = $\frac{A-P}{P}\times 100\times \frac{1}{n}$

Compounded growth rate $= \left(\left(\frac{A}{P}\right)^{1/n} - 1\right) \times 100$

The two formulae come straight from the theory of simple and compound interest.
It is important to note that n is the time periods and not the number of years. i.e. if we are considering the growth from 1999 to 2000, it is just one annual time period and not two.

Thus the simple annual growth rate of sales of ABC Corp over the period 1999 to 2003 will be $\frac{75\%}{4} = 18.75\%$ i.e. the growth rate over the period divided by the number of time periods. Once again attention is drawn to the fact that though 1999 to 2003 is 5 years, the time period is just 4 i.e. 1999-2000, 2000-2001, 2001-2002 and 2002-2003. If one is still unsure, just think if growth is to be found over two successive years, say in 2000 over 1999, would one divide the growth rate by 2?

The compounded annual growth rate of sales of ABC Corp over the period 1999 to 2003 will be

$$\left(\left(\frac{350}{200}\right)^{\frac{1}{4}} - 1\right) \times 100 = \left(\left(\frac{7}{4}\right)^{\frac{1}{4}} - 1\right) \times 100 \cong \left(\left(\frac{2.64}{2}\right)^{\frac{1}{2}} - 1\right) \times 100 \cong \left(\sqrt{1.32} - 1\right) \times 100 \cong (1.148 - 1) \times 100 = 14.8\%$$

As in the case of SI and CI, unless the question specifically mentions compounded annual growth rate, we will calculate simple annual growth rate. But for case of population and increase/decrease in monetary value of asset, it will be CAGR always.

Profit Percentages

What is the profit percentage of ABC Corp in the year 1999?

The profit percentage is not $\frac{40}{200} \times 100 = 20\%$. Please recollect profit percentage is always as a percentage of Cost Price. In this case the cost will be 160 and the profit percentage will be 25%.

What is the percentage change in profit percentage in the year 2003 over that in 2002.

Profit percentage in 2002 $= \frac{70}{250} \times 100 = 28\%$

Profit percentage in 2003 $= \frac{50}{300} \times 100 = 16.66\%$

Thus percentage change in profit percentage in the year 2003 over that in the year 2002

$$= \frac{16.66 - 28}{28} \times 100 = \frac{-11.33}{28} \times 100 = -40.5\%$$

Calculations would be simpler if we just took the ratio of profit percentage as: $\frac{16.66}{28} = \frac{\frac{100}{6}}{28} = \frac{100}{168} = 0.595$ i.e. a decrease of 40.5%

Remember, the percentage change in profit percent is not $16.66\% - 28\% = -11.33\%$. The profit percentage has decreased by 11.33 percentage points and by 40.5 percent.

Growth rates in Line graph

Consider the following line graph

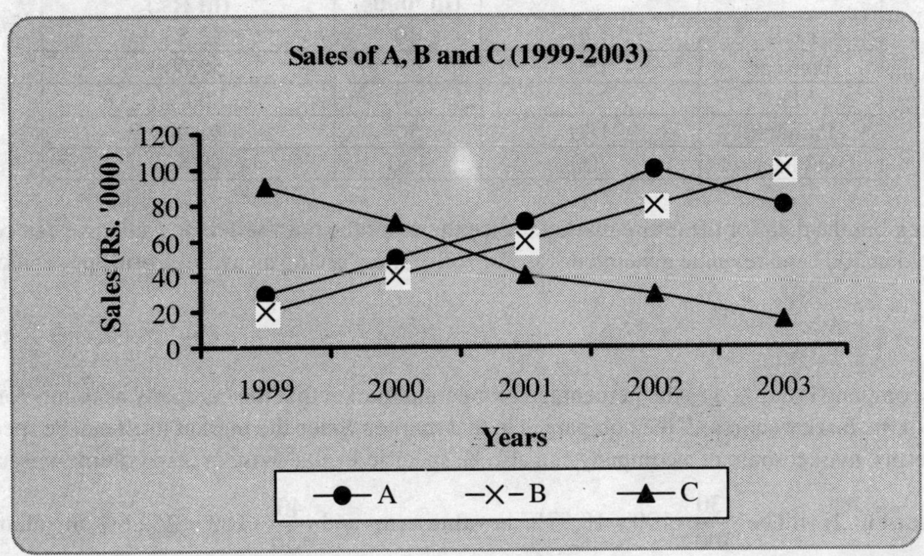

The growth rate is related to the slope of a line. Yet the relation is not really as simple as steeper the line, higher is the growth rate. Few points worth understanding in the above graphs are

1. Though the sales of B is a straight line, i.e. the slope of each segment is same across all years, the growth rate is not the same in all years. The same slope simply means that the sales grows by a constant amount each year, in this case by 20 every year. But the growth rate keeps decreasing every year as the base value keeps increasing.
2. Though the slope of the line depicting sales of A and B is same for 1999 to 2001, their growth rates are not the same. Again in this case too, the actual growth of sales is same but the base value is different.
3. Though the line representing sales of A in 2001-02 is steeper, 2002 is not the year with highest growth rate of sales of A. The highest growth rate of sales of A occurs in year 2000.
4. Similarly, though the line segment of sales of C is steepest (in downward direction) in 2000-2001, the year with highest growth rate (in negative sense) is in the year 2003 which is a 50% decline.

While in most of the cases, the steepest line will mean the highest growth rate, it is not always so. It would always pay, to spend a moment getting an idea of the base value over which the growth occurs to get the right answer.

Market Share : Value and Volume

Sales figures can either be in value terms (in Rs. or $ or similar value units) or in volume terms (in nos. or kgs or similar volume units). E.g. consider the following data:

Sales of PCs in India (2003)

Company	Sales (in Rs. cr.)	Sales (in '000s)
LCH	130	40
Pomqac	150	30
MBI	240	30
Pinnacle	180	50

Assume these are the only sellers in India.

The value-wise sales and the volume-wise sales are linked together with the average price per unit. E.g. in the above case the data says that LCH has sold 40,000 PCs and earned a revenue of Rs. 130 cr. Thus the average price per PC sold will be $\frac{130\times10^7}{40,000}$

i.e. Rs. 32,500

Thus, Sales in value terms = (Sales in volume terms) × (Price/unit)

Thus for the above data, we can actually calculate price per unit for all the companies and the data will now look like

Company	Sales (in Rs. cr.)	Sales (in '000s)	Avg. Price/unit (in Rs.)
LCH	130	40	32,500
Pomqac	150	30	50,000
MBI	240	30	80,000
Pinnacle	180	50	36,000
Total Market	700	150	46,666

The last row is nothing but the data for the entire market. Since these are the only sellers in India, we can conclude that in India 150,000 PCs were sold in 2003 and revenue generated was Rs. 700 cr, thus giving an average price per unit of Rs. 46,666.

Market Share

Market share of any company is defined as the percentage of the total market that the company accounts for. The total market is nothing but the sum of the market shares all the companies in that market. Since the market itself can be specified in either value terms or in volume terms, market share of a company can also be specified value-wise or also volume-wise.

Thus the market share of LCH will be $\frac{130}{700}\times 100 = 18.57\%$ in value terms and $\frac{40}{150}\times 100 = 26.66\%$ in volume terms. This means is that all though LCH sells 26.66% of the total number of PCs sold in India, it accounts for only 18.57% of the total revenue of the entire PC market.

Thus the market share for all the companies can be calculated as

Company	Mkt Share of value	Mkt. share of volume	Avg. Price/unit
LCH	18.57%	26.66%	32,500
Pomqac	21.42%	20%	50,000
MBI	34.28%	20%	80,000
Pinnacle	25.71%	33.33%	36,000
Total Market	100%	100%	46,666

An important aspect to understand is that companies which have a higher price/unit than the industry wide average price/unit (Rs. 46,666) e.g. Pomqac and MBI, both have a higher market share in value terms and a lower market share in volume whereas companies which have a lower average price/unit than the industry wide average price/unit have a higher volume share but lower value share. And this should be obvious too as a company which sells less number of units but yet makes more money would be doing so because it would have been selling the units at a higher price. In fact there is a deeper relation and just based on the market share (value and volume) one can also deduce by what percentage is a company's price per unit higher or lower than the industry average.

$$\text{Sales of LCH}_{\text{value}} = \text{Total sales}_{\text{value}} \times \text{Market share of LCH}_{\text{value}}$$

Similarly, $\text{Sales of LCH}_{\text{volume}} = \text{Total sales}_{\text{volume}} \times \text{Market share of LCH}_{\text{volume}}$

Dividing the two, we get

$$\frac{\text{Sales of LCH}_{\text{value}}}{\text{Sales of LCH}_{\text{volume}}} = \frac{\text{Total sales}_{\text{value}}}{\text{Total sales}_{\text{volume}}} \times \frac{\text{Market share of LCH}_{\text{value}}}{\text{Market share of LCH}_{\text{volume}}} \text{ i.e.}$$

$$\text{Price / unit of LCH} = \text{Price / unit of Market} \times \frac{\text{Market share of LCH}_{\text{value}}}{\text{Market share of LCH}_{\text{volume}}} \text{ i.e.}$$

$$\frac{\text{Price / unit of LCH}}{\text{Price / unit of Market}} = \frac{\text{Market share of LCH}_{\text{value}}}{\text{Market share of LCH}_{\text{volume}}}$$

Thus if numerator of RHS is higher than denominator, price per unit of the company will be higher than the industry average and vice-versa.

To assess, what we have just learnt, check if you can answer the questions following the data:

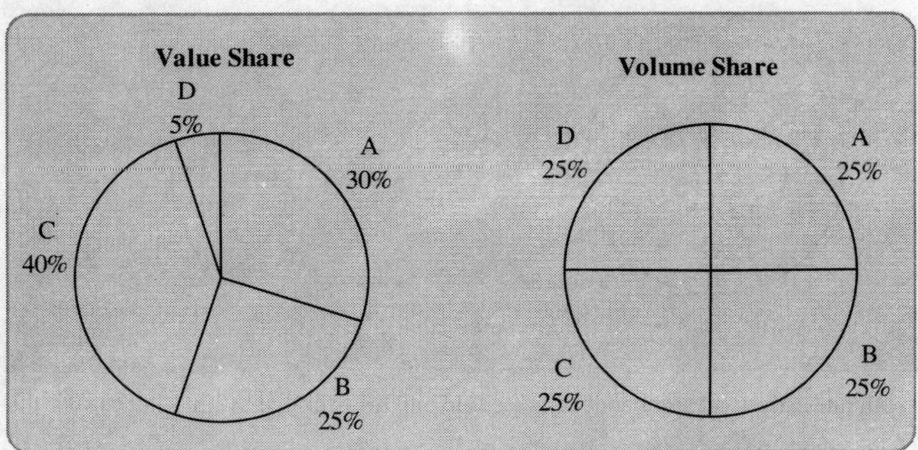

Value and Volume share of A, B, C and D in 2003

1. For the year 2003, rank the four companies in decreasing order of price/unit.
2. By what percentage is the price/unit of company C higher than the average price per unit of the industry in the year 2003?
3. What is the ratio of the price per unit of company A to that of company B in the year 2003?

Solutions: The questions should have been solved orally and one must have just done the following observations in mind.

1. The ratio of value share to volume share for A, B, C and D are 1.2, 1, 1.6 and 0.2 and thus the order in decreasing order of price/unit would be C, A, B and D
2. The ratio of value share to volume share of company C is 1.6 and this means the price/unit of company C is 60% more than the average price per unit of the market.
3. The required ratio is simply 1.2 : 1 i.e. 6 : 5

If these oral calculations are not clear, assume the total market is of Rs. R and of V units. For each company now calculate the value and volume sales and then the price per unit. You will realize that you are basically calculating the ratio of value and volume shares.

Simplifying two pies

Consider the pie chart given in the first chapter. The pie chart is reproduced here with the same data.

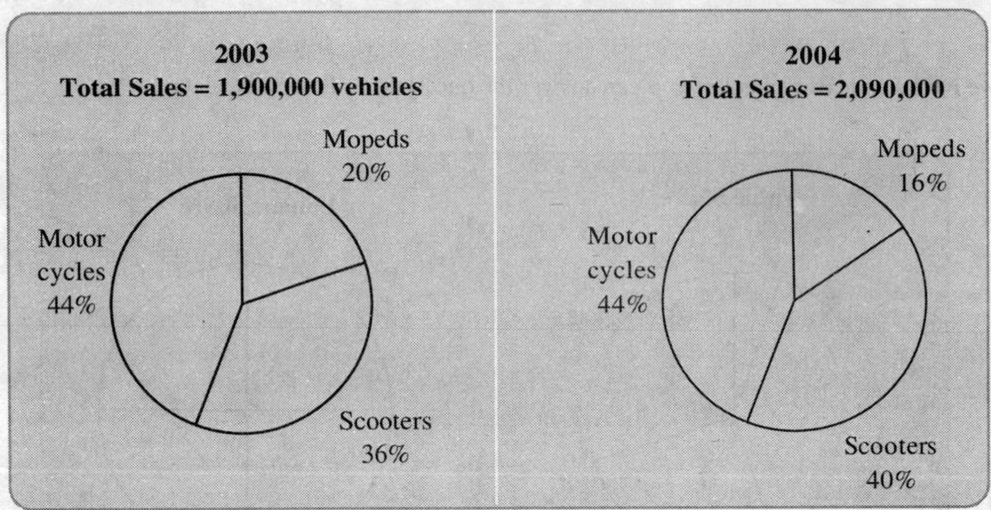

If we calculate the growth rate in the total number of vehicles sold in 2004 over that in 2003, we can use this data very effectively for further questions. In this case the growth rate is $\frac{209}{190} = 1.1$ i.e. a growth rate of 10%. Now each of the percentage figures of the right hand pie chart could be increased by 10% and then all the figures in percentages appearing in both the pies would be as a percent of 1,900,000 and comparison of sales across the two years would be easier.

To clarify further, in 2004, sales of scooters were 40% of 2,090,000 which is same as 40% of $1.1 \times 1,900,000$ i.e. 44% of 1,900,000. Thus in questions, say , what is the ratio of the number of scooters sold in 2004 to the number of mopeds sold in 2003, one can mentally think that scooters sold in 2004 is 44% of 1,900,000 and mopeds sold in 2003 is 20% of 1,900,000 and thus the ratio is 44 : 20 i.e. 11 : 5. Another example, what is the percentage increase in the number of scooters sold in 2004 over those sold in 2003?

Here one just needs to find the percentage increase between 36 and 44 i.e. a percentage increase of $\frac{8}{36}$ i.e. $\frac{2}{9}$ i.e. 22.22%

Thus in pie charts where there are two pies given, showing the same data over two different time periods, calculating the percentage increase in the size of the pie can help us in ignoring the actual value of the pies while comparing two sectors or calculating the growth rate of individual sectors over the time period.

Learning Outcomes:

To effectively tackle Data Interpretation questions, the prime skill needed is that of gathering information from raw data. Even before you start worrying of calculations and speed, adequate attention has to be given to understanding the data. Read everything about the data – the title, headings, units, footnotes, etc. before moving to questions. This way, you should have a fair idea of the expected questions simply by analyzing the data. If this is not so, your understanding of the data is not complete. Do few questioning about the data and only when you have understood the data fully, attempt the questions.

While reading the questions, take appropriate pauses, referring back to the data while reading the questions to gather the relevant numbers and thus proceed. Do not read the question mechanically at one go and then look for relevant data. Both reading and identify relevant data has to happen simultaneously.

1

CHAPTER

Tables

SOLVED EXAMPLES

Directions for examples 1 to 4: Answer the questions on the basis of the information given below.

The table given below shows the per capita CO_2 emission and populations of six countries during the period 2013-2016. The total CO_2 emission (in million tonnes) of the world in 2013, 2014, 2015 and 2016 was 30700, 31433, 32155 and 32042 respectively.

Country	Per Capita CO_2 emission (in tonnes)				Population (in millions)			
	2013	2014	2015	2016	2013	2014	2015	2016
China	4.4	4.4	4.9	5.2	1314	1321	1326	1350.8
Germany	9.8	9.8	-	9.6	81.6	82.4	80.5	81.4
India	0.3	0.3	0.4	0.4	1095	1129	1140	1166
Japan	1.1	1.1	1	1.3	124.6	126.1	127.2	127.6
Russia	0.9	0.9	0.9	1	138.8	140.2	141.2	142.6
USA	0.2	0.2	0.2	0.2	298.4	301.4	304	306.5

1. The CO_2 emission of China was approximately what percent of the total CO_2 emission of the world during the given period?

(1) 10 (2) 20 (3) 12 (4) 28

2. The CO_2 emission of Russia and Japan put together was approximatelyn what percent of that of India and USA put together during the given period?

(1) 60 (2) 45 (3) 75 (4) 70

3. If the CO_2 emission of Germany was 2.4% of the total CO_2 emission of the world during the given period, then what was the per capita CO_2 emission (in tonnes) of Germany in 2015?

(1) 7 (2) 10 (3) 9 (4) 8

4. The total CO_2 emission by which country was second lowest in 2014

(1) Germany (2) Russia (3) India (4) Japan

For examples 1 to 4:

1. 2 The total CO_2 emission (in million tonnes) of the world during the given period

= 30700 + 31433 + 32155 + 32042 = 126330

The total CO_2 emission (in million tonnes) of China during the give period

= 4.4 × (1314 + 1321) + 4.9 × 1326 + 5.2 × 1350.8 = 25115.56

Hence, the required percentage $= \frac{25115.56}{126330} \times 100 \approx 20.$

1.2 TABLES

2. 1 The total CO_2 emission (in million tonnes) of Russia and Japan put together

= [0.9 × (138.8 + 140.2 + 141.2) + 1 × 142.6] + [1.1 × (124.6 + 126.1) + 1 × 127.2 + 1.3 × 127.6] = 1089.3

The total CO_2 emission (in million tonnes) of India and USA put together

= [0.3× (1095 + 1129) + 0.4 × (1140 + 1166)]+ [0.2 × (298.4 + 301.4 + 304 + 306.5)] =1831.66

Hence, the required percentage $= \frac{1089.3}{1831.66} \times 100 \approx 60.$

3. 4 Let the per capita CO_2 emission (in tonnes) of Germany in 2015 be 'x'.

$\therefore$ 9.8 × (81.6 + 82.4) + 80.5 × x + 9.6 × 81.4 $= \frac{2.4}{100} \times 126330$

$\Rightarrow x \approx 8.$

4. 2 It is clear from the table that the lowest emission of CO_2 is by USA and the second lowest is by Russia.

Directions for examples 5 to 8: Answer the questions on the basis of the information given below.

The following table provides partial information about the composition of six different alloys namely A, B, C, D, E and F. Each of these six alloys contains the five different elements namely Zinc, Tin, Lead, Copper and Nickel. An alloy G, the composition of which is not given in the table, contains alloys A, B and C in the ratio 2 : 1 : 3. It is also known that in alloy G, tin, lead and copper are present in an equal quantity.

Alloy	Zinc	Tin	Lead	Copper	Nickel
A	10%	40%			10%
B	25%	15%	50%	5%	5%
C	15%		20%		35%
D	20%	25%	15%	30%	10%
E	5%	50%	25%	5%	15%
F	40%	10%	5%	30%	15%

5. Find the percentage of copper in alloy A.

(1) $\frac{95}{9}$ (2) $\frac{95}{3}$ (3) $\frac{25}{9}$ (4) $\frac{25}{3}$

6. If an alloy X, which contains 15% nickel, at least 15% zinc and at most 20% copper, is to be made, how many combinations of exactly two of the six mentioned alloys can be used to make it?

(1) Three (2) Four (3) Five (4) Two

7. Which of the following can be a value of the ratio in which alloys A, E and F need to be mixed to get at least 12% lead in the resulting mixture?

(1) 4 : 1 : 1 (2) 2 : 1 : 3 (3) 1 : 2 : 3 (4) 1 : 2 : 4

8. If an alloy Z, which contains at least 8.25% nickel, is to be made by using the alloys mentioned in the table, the percentage of alloy B in alloy Z cannot be more than

(1) 95.46% (2) 83.12% (3) 97.24% (4) 89.16%

For examples 5 to 8:

The given information can be tabulated as:

	Zinc	Tin	Lead	Copper	Nickel
A	10%	40%	(x) %	(40 – x)%	10%
B	25%	15%	50%	5%	5%
C	15%	(y) %	20%	(30 – y)%	35%
D	20%	25%	15%	30%	10%
E	5%	50%	25%	5%	15%
F	40%	10%	5%	30%	15%

5. 2 In alloy G, the percentage of:

$$\text{Tin} = \left(2 \times \frac{40}{6} + 1 \times \frac{15}{6} + 3 \times \frac{y}{6}\right) = \frac{3y + 95}{6}$$

$$\text{Lead} = \frac{2x + 110}{6}$$

$$\text{Copper} = \frac{175 - 2x - 3y}{6}$$

Now, $(3y + 95) = (2x + 110) = (175 - 2x - 3y) \Rightarrow x = \frac{25}{3}$ and $y = \frac{95}{9}$

Therefore, the percentage of copper in alloy A $= (40 - x) = \left(40 - \frac{25}{3}\right) = \frac{95}{3}$.

6. 4 There are two possible ways in which the alloy X can be formed. The possible combinations are (E and F) and (B and C).

7. 3 The percentage of lead in A, E and F is $\frac{25}{3}$%, 25% and 5% respectively.

By checking options:

Option (1): Percentage of lead in the mixture $= \frac{1}{6}\left(4 \times \frac{25}{3} + 1 \times 25 + 1 \times 5\right) = \frac{95}{9}\% < 12\%$

Option (2): Percentage of lead in the mixture $= \frac{1}{6}\left(2 \times \frac{25}{3} + 1 \times 25 + 3 \times 5\right) = \frac{85}{9}\% < 12\%$

Option (3): Percentage of lead in the mixture $= \frac{1}{6}\left(1 \times \frac{25}{3} + 2 \times 25 + 3 \times 5\right) = \frac{110}{9}\% > 12\%$

Option (4): Percentage of lead in the mixture $= \frac{1}{7}\left(1 \times \frac{25}{3} + 2 \times 25 + 4 \times 5\right) = \frac{235}{21}\% < 12\%$

Hence, option (c) is the correct answer.

8. 4 Since the percentage of nickel in alloy B and alloy Z is 5% and 8.25% respectively, in order to maximize the percentage of B in Z, we need to choose alloy in which the percentage of nickel is greater than 8.25% and also the maximum among the given alloys. So, we need to choose alloy C.

Let the percentage of alloy B in alloy Z be 'x'%.

$\therefore 5x + 35(1 - x) = 8.25 \Rightarrow x = 89.16\%$

Directions for examples 9 to 12: Answer the questions on the basis of the information given below.

An FMCG company, planning to produce potato chips of three different flavours, namely Mint, Chilly and Cream, conducted a survey among 1000 people in each of the three market segments Metros, Towns and Villages. In the survey, all the participants were requested to select exactly one of the four options out of P, Q, R and S given in the survey response sheet. One of the options out of the four was for not liking any of the three varieties of chips, and each of the other three was for liking a different variety of chips out of the three. The following table represents the responses recorded during the survey.

	P	Q	R	S
Market Segment Villages	95	390	135	380
Market Segment Metros	180	405	230	185
Market Segment Towns	210	220	220	350

As the brand manager of the company, who compiled the data, knew which option indicated which flavour, he derived the following conclusions from the given table.

I. In towns, as many as 22% of all the participants did not like any of the three flavours.

II. The total number of participants who selected Chilly flavour, differed from the total number of participants who selected Cream flavour by 100.

9. If it was in villages where the minimum number of participants liked Mint flavour, then which of the following can be definitely concluded?

(1) It was in Metros where the maximum number of participants liked Chilly flavour.

(2) It was in Metros where the minimum number of participants liked Cream flavour.

(3) It was in Villages where the maximum number of participants liked Chilly flavour.

(4) It was in Villages where the minimum number of participants did not like any of the three flavours.

10. If Cream flavour was liked by the minimum number of participants in all the three market segments put together, then which of the following statements is definitely false?

(1) Out of the participants who liked Chilly flavour in the three market segments, the minimum number belonged to villages.

(2) Out of the participants who liked Mint flavour in the three market segments, the minimum number belonged to metros.

(3) Out of the participants who did not like any of the three flavours in the three market segments, the minimum number belonged to villages.

(4) Out of the participants who did not like any of the three flavours in the three market segments, the maximum number belonged to metros.

11. In towns, if the number of participants who liked Mint flavour was the minimum, then which of the following is definitely true?

(1) In villages, the number of participants who liked neither Chilly flavour nor Cream flavour was 280.

(2) In towns, the number of participants who liked neither Mint flavour nor Cream flavour was 570.

(3) In metros, the number of participants who liked neither Chilly flavour nor Mint flavour was 635.

(4) In towns, the number of participants who liked neither Chilly nor Cream flavour was 430.

12. A maximum of how many of the following five statements can simultaneously be true?

I. In Villages, 135 participants did not like any of the three flavours.

II. In Towns, 210 participants liked Cream flavour.

III. In Metros, 185 participants liked Chilly flavour.

IV. In Towns, 220 participants liked Cream flavour.

V. In Metros, 180 participants liked Mint flavour.

(1) 4 (2) 3 (3) 2 (4) 5

For examples 9 to 12: The total number of participants in the surveys conducted in each of the three market segments is 1000. The exact number of participants selecting the four options, across the three market segments is given in the following table.

Market Segments	P	Q	R	S	Total
Villages	95	390	135	380	1000
Towns	210	**220**	**220**	350	1000
Metros	180	405	230	185	1000
Total	**485**	**1015**	**585**	**915**	3000

The two observations made by the brand manager, hold true only for the following four cases.

Possible Cases	P	Q	R	S
Case I	Cream	Rejected All	Chilly	Mint
Case II	Chilly	Rejected All	Cream	Mint
Case III	Mint	Chilly	Rejected All	Cream
Case IV	Mint	Cream	Rejected All	Chilly

9. 4 If the statement given in the problem is true, then the selection of option P, in the survey form, must indicate that the participant had liked the Mint flavour, the least. Accordingly, either Case III or Case IV could be true and the two flavours-(Chilly & Cream) must be indicated by the two options-(Q & S) but their exact order cannot be concluded. Further, selection of option R, in the survey form, indicated that the participant had rejected all the three flavours. Hence none of the options (1) or (2) or (3) can definitely be concluded but option (4) can definitely be concluded.

10. 3 If the statement given in the problem is true, then option P given in the survey form must indicate Cream flavour. Accordingly, only Case I is valid. Statement given in option (3) is definitely false as the minimum number belonged to the market segment, Towns.

11. 4 From the problem statement. We can conclude that option P in the survey form, indicates Mint flavour. Accordingly, options Q and S could indicate Chilly and Cream flavours. Option R indicated rejection of all the three flavours. Note that, in any of the given market segments, the number of participants who selected neither option P nor Q is the sum of the number of participants who selected either option R or options S. Each of the five answer options can be verified. Option (4) is correct.

12. 1 From each of the five given statements, we can make the following conclusions:

Statement	Conclusion
I	R indicated rejection of all the flavours.
II	P indicated selection of Cream flavour.
III	S indicated selection of Chilly flavour.
IV	Either Q or R indicated selection of Cream Flavour.
V	P indicated selection of Mint flavour.

Statements I, III, IV and V can simultaneously be true. Hence option (a) is the correct answer.

Directions for examples 13 to 17: Answer the questions based on the table given below.

The following table shows the business details of a company named ABC India Pvt. Ltd.

Vertical	Category	Annual sales (in Rs.)	Margin	Number of employees	Annual salary per employee (in Rs.)
Software	Inhouse	0.2 crore	23	25	20000
	Export	1.5 crore	47	15	100000
Hardware	Inhouse	0.4 crore	31	40	15000
	Export	2 crore	52	40	80000

$$\text{Margin} = \frac{\text{Profit}}{\text{Sales}} \times 100.$$

13. If the salary of each hardware inhouse employee is increased by 50%, what is the new margin percentage of the company? (All other factors remain the same)

(1) 21.5% (2) 27% (3) 35.59% (4) 45.9%

14. If the annual salary per employee of software inhouse employee is made equal to the annual salary per employee of hardware inhouse employees, what is the percentage increase in the software inhouse margin?

(1) 8.75% (2) 29.25% (3) 6.25% (4) 27.17%

15. If in each vertical category the annual sales increases by 15%, what is the total profit of the company? (The margin remains the same)

(1) Rs. 2.45 crore (2) Rs. 1.91 crore (3) Rs. 2.2 crore (4) Data insufficient

16. If the Software as well as Hardware exports of the company increases by 20% and the total inhouse business is closed then what is the over all change in the profit of the company? (The margin remains the same)

(1) 17.9 lacs (2) 35.8 lacs (3) 34.9 lacs (4) 17 lacs

17. The company plans to train the software inhouse employees and the training expenditure per employee will be Rs. 9200. What will be the new margin percentage in software inhouse division if the company goes with the training plan?

(1) 50% (2) 11.5% (3) 46% (4) Cannot be determined

13. 4 Net profit of company A in software inhouse = Rs. 0.046 crore, software export = Rs. 0.7 crore, hardware inhouse = Rs. 0.124 crore, hardware export = Rs. 1.04 crore.

∴ Total profit = Rs. 1.91 crore

Salary of hardware inhouse executives is increased by 50% that is by Rs. 7,500.

Increase in total salary is Rs. 7500 × 40= Rs. 0.03 crore

∴ New net margin = Rs. 1.88 crore

So, margin percentage $= \frac{1.88}{4.10} \times 100 = 45.9\%$

14. 4 Net decrease in cost = (20000 – 15000) × 25= Rs. 1.25 lakh
Earlier net profit = Rs. 4.6 lakh
New net profit = (Rs. 4.6 + Rs. 1.25)= Rs. 5.85 lakh

$$\left(\frac{\frac{5.85}{20}}{\frac{4.6}{20}}-1\right)\times 100=\frac{1.25}{4.6}\times 100=27.17\%$$

15. 3 Profit of company A in software inhouse = 23% of (115% of 0.2 crore) = Rs. 5.29 lacs
Profit of company A in software export = 47% of (115% of 1.5 crore) = Rs. 81.08 lacs
Profit of company A in hardware inhouse = 31% of (115% of 0.4 crore) = Rs. 14.26 lacs
Profit of company A in hardware export = 52% of (115% of 2 crore) = Rs. 119.6 lacs
Hence, the total profit = Rs. 220.23 lacs ≈ Rs. 2.2 crores

16. 1 Increase in profit = 47% of (20% of 1.5 crores) + 52% of (20% of 2 crore) = 0.141+ 0.208 = 0.349 crores = Rs. 34.9 lacs
Decrease in profit due to closing of inhouse business = 23% of 0.2 crore + 31% of 0.4 crore = (0.046 + 0.124) crore = 0.17 crore = Rs. 17 lacs.
Net increase in profit = 34.9 – 17 = Rs. 17.9 lacs.

17. 2 Before the training program, the profit of company A in software inhouse = Rs. 0.046 crores = 4.6 lacs
Now, profit = 4.6 lacs – (9200 × 25) = 2.3 lacs

So, the new margin percentage $= \frac{2.3}{20}\times 100 = 11.5\%$

Directions for examples 18 to 20: Answer the questions on the basis of the information given below.

The following table gives the details of the account statement of Raj's account in HDCF bank during the period January 2017 to April 2017. It is also known that the balance in the account as on December 31, 2016 was Rs 18000.

Date	Details	Debit	Credit	Balance
10-Jan	By Cash	NA	12000	30000
30-Jan	By CHQ 456789	NA	15000	45000
31-Jan	To ATM Withdrawal	15000	NA	30000
17-Feb	To CHQ 123456		NA	5635
23-Feb	TO POS PUR	1085	NA	4550
28-Feb	By Cash	NA	16730	21280
11-Mar	To ECS	6380	NA	
24-Mar	To Cash	14000	NA	
31-Mar	By CHQ 127128	NA	66800	67800
23-Apr	By Cash	NA	11922	79800
30-Apr	To IB TFR	31716	NA	48084

The bank offers an interest of 0.5% on monthly basis on the Average Monthly Balance(AMB). The interest, the details of which is not shown in the given account statements, is credited in the account on the last day of each month, after the completion of all transactions for that day.

$$\text{Average Monthly Balance (AMB)} = \frac{\text{Sum of the balances at the end of each day of a month}}{\text{No. of days in the month}}$$

18. What was the total balance in the account at the end of April 30?

(1) Rs 48084 (2) Rs 48384 (3) Rs 48434 (4) Rs 48344

19. During the given period, what was the average monthly interest credited in Raj's account?

(1) Rs 663 (2) Rs 165.75 (3) Rs 331.50 (4) Rs 350

20. What was the amount of the cheque that was debited in Raj's account on 17th February?

(1) Rs 24365 (2) Rs 24635 (3) Rs 24500 (4) Rs 25500

For examples 18 to 20:

1. AMB in January $= \frac{18000 \times 9 + 30000 \times 20 + 45000 \times 1 + 30000 \times 1}{31}$ = Rs. 27,000

Interest for the month of January $= \frac{27000 \times 6 \times 1}{12 \times 100}$ = Rs. 135

Balance at the end of January = 30000 + 135 = Rs. 30,135

2. AMB in February $= \frac{30135 \times 16 + 5635 \times 6 + 4550 \times 5 + 21280 \times 1}{28}$ = Rs. 20,000

Interest for the month of February $= \frac{20000 \times 6 \times 1}{12 \times 100}$ = Rs. 100

Balance at the end of February = 21280 + 100 = Rs. 21,380

3. AMB in March $= \frac{21380 \times 10 + 15000 \times 13 + 1000 \times 7 + 67800 \times 1}{31}$ = Rs. 15,600

Interest for the month of March $= \frac{15600 \times 6 \times 1}{12 \times 100}$ = Rs. 78

Balance at the end of March = 67800 + 78 = Rs. 67,878

4. AMB in April $= \frac{67878 \times 22 + 79800 \times 7 + 48084 \times 1}{30}$ = Rs. 70,000

Interest for the month of April $= \frac{70000 \times 6 \times 1}{12 \times 100}$ = Rs. 350

Balance at the end of April = 48084 + 350 = Rs. 48,434

18. 3 Balance at the end of April 2017 is Rs. 48,434.

19. 2 Total interest earned during the given period = 135 + 100 + 78 + 350 = Rs. 663

Average Interest earned $= \frac{663}{4}$ = Rs. 165.75.

20. 3 Cheque amount deducted on 17th February = 30135 – 5635 = Rs 24,500.

PRACTICE EXERCISE – 1

Directions for questions 1 to 3: Answer the questions on the basis of the information given below.

The following table shows data related to equity shares issued by five public sector companies on July 27, 2017.

Company	Number of equity shares (crores)	Current market share price (Rs.)	Percentage of equity shares held by the government
BEL	8	60	75%
BML	3.64	15	60%
BHL	24.48	150	62.5%
BPL	30	175	66.7%
BCL	1.515	350	80.0%

1. If the government disinvested 20% of its stake in BEL and 25% in BML at the given market prices, the amount of revenue generated by the government through the disinvestment was.
   (1) Rs. 80.19 crore (2) Rs. 96.55 crore (3) Rs. 72 crore (4) Rs. 109.65 crore
2. The government disinvested its entire stake in BPL at a price of Rs. 125 per share. What would have been the additional revenue generated by the government had it done the given disinvestment at the given market price?
   (1) Rs. 1,800.4 crore (2) Rs. 1,000.5 crore (3) Rs. 500.4 crore (4) Rs. 500.6 crore
3. If the share price of BCL fell to Rs. 300 on July 28, 2017, then what was the decline in the total value of BCL's shares held by the government over that of the previous day?
   (1) Rs. 50.6 crore (2) Rs. 55.6 crore (3) Rs. 60.6 crore (4) Rs. 65.6 crore

Directions for questions 4 to 6: Answer the questions on the basis of the information given below.

Following table shows the number of movies released in Jollywood as on August 15, 2017.

Name of genre	Action	Romance	Drama	Patriotic	Thriller
Total number of movies	192	250	300	77	216

The following table gives data related to hit and flop status of Jollywood movies, released during the given period, including that of a Jollywood star named STS.

Name of genre	**Action**	**Romance**	**Drama**	**Patriotic**	**Thriller**
Hit movies as a percentage of total number of movies	37.5	36	33.33	28.56	44.44
Hit movies by STS as a percentage of total number of movies by STS	50	60	16.66	50	66.66
Flop movies by STS as a percentage of total number of flop movies	10	6.25	12.5	20	5

Additional information with reference to the two tables given above is as follows:

– Every movie that releases in Jollywood belongs to exactly one of the five genres, Action, Romance, Drama, Patriotic and Thriller.

– Every movie that releases in Jollywood falls in exactly one of the two categories, Hit and Flop.

4. The total number of STS's hit movies, during the given period, across the three genres Drama, Patriotic and Thriller put together was
   (1) 28 (2) 70 (3) 32 (4) Cannot be determined
5. What percentage of the total movies released during the given period across the five genres were flop movies?
   (1) 62.89 (2) 61.72 (3) 63.28 (4) 64.19
6. For how many genres, was the number of STS's hit movies at least 50% of his flop movies?
   (1) 1 (2) 2 (3) 3 (4) 4

Directions for questions 7 to 9: Answer the questions on the basis of the information given below.

Chintamani, who is a renowned investor, was looking at the investments that he had made a year ago. He had invested in 6 companies belonging to 3 sectors – Telecom, Insurance and Retail – with two companies in each sector. The following table shows the share prices of the 6 companies that Chintamani bought on June 5, 2016 in the years 2016 and 2017 on the same date. It is also known that he bought shares of each company in a multiple of 10.

Company	Share prices as on 5th June 2016 (Rs.)	Share prices as on 5th June 2017 (Rs.)
A	150	230
B	500	575
C	200	320
D	400	440
E	800	900
F	175	245

7. If the shares that witnessed the top two absolute changes in their prices belonged to Telecom sector, while the shares that witnessed the bottom two absolute changes in their share prices belonged to Insurance sector, what was the approximate percentage change in the combined share price value of the two Retail companies during the given period?

(1) 20% (2) 24% (3) 30% (4) 40%

8. If Chintamani purchased a total of 60 shares belonging to 4 out of the six companies, then the maximum possible percentage return that he could realise on these 60 shares during the given period was

(1) 41% (2) 32% (3) 36% (4) 37%

9. If shares that witnessed the highest and lowest percentage change in their prices belonged to Telecom sector, then what was the percentage change in the combined share price value of the two Telecom companies during the given period?

(1) 26.67% (2) 35.66% (3) 40.33% (4) 45.33%

Directions for questions 10 to 13: Answer the questions on the basis of the information given below.

The table given below shows the production of some agricultural crops in a country named Indiana in the years 2010-11 and 2011-12.

Crop	Targeted production for 2011-12 (in MT)	Production for 2011-12 (in MT)	% increase in production over 2010-11
Food grains	162.7	160.4	25
Oil seeds	18.9	16.2	18
Sugarcane	20.5	22.5	35
Cotton	14.7	18.9	32
Jute	12.3	14.8	16

10. The production of Food grain (in MT) in 2010-11 was nearly

(1) 130 (2) 128 (3) 134 (4) 135

11. The crop whose production in 2011-12 showed the maximum deviation from the targeted production, witnessed the percentage deviation of

(1) 31.4 (2) 30.2 (3) 19.8 (4) 28.6

12. If there was an increase of 4.5 MT in the production of Sugarcane in 2012-13 over that of the previous year, what was the simple annual growth rate in the production of Sugarcane from 2010-11 to 2012-13?

(1) 25% (2) 26% (3) 31% (4) 28%

13. If Oil seeds production in 2019-20 was 24.4 MT, what was the simple annual growth rate in the production of Oil Seed from 2011-12 to 2019-20?

(1) 6.3 (2) 6.9 (3) 7.2 (4) 5.7

Directions for questions 14 to 17: Answer the questions on the basis of the information given below.

Fortune1000 is a list of top thousand companies in America ranked in the descending order of their annual revenues – rank 1 for highest revenue, rank 2 for the second highest revenue and so on. The following table shows all the companies in the state of Virginia (a state in America) that belonged to the Fortune1000-2013 along with their rank, revenues and the city in which they are based.

Company	Rank	Revenues ($ millions)	City
Advance Auto Parts	478	4,616.50	Roanoke
Amerigroup	676	2,835.10	Virginia Beach
Brink's	641	3,067.60	Richmond
CACI	932	1,755.30	Arlington
Circuit City Stores	215	11,597.70	Richmond
Dollar Tree Stores	532	3,969.40	Chesapeake
Dominion Resources	140	16,524.00	Richmond
DynCorp	867	1,967.00	Falls Church
Freddie Mac	50	44,002.00	McLean
Gannett	302	8,033.40	McLean
General Dynamics	92	24,212.00	Falls Church
Genworth Financial	227	11,029.00	Richmond
LandAmerica Financial	522	4,015.90	Glen Allen
Markel	739	2,519.00	Glen Allen
NVR	371	6,156.80	Reston
Owens & Minor	418	5,533.70	Mechanicsville
SLM	284	8,751.20	Reston
Smithfield Foods	217	11,506.80	Smithfield
Sprint Nextel	53	43,531.00	Reston
Universal	573	3,511.30	Richmond

14. The revenue of how many companies in Virginia was greater than that of Universal?

(1) 14 (2) 15 (3) 16 (4) 17

15. If the companies given in the table were to be ranked for the state of Virginia i.e. rank 1 for the highest revenue in the state, then which company would hold rank 10?

(1) Gannett (2) SLM (3) Owens & Minor (4) NVR

16. If the companies given in the table were to be ranked for each city i.e. rank 1 for the highest revenue in that city, which of the following two companies would hold the same rank?

(1) DynCorp and Markel

(2) Gannett and Genworth Financial

(3) Brink's and Amerigroup

(4) Dollar Tree Stores and SLM

17. What was the Fortune1000-2013 rank of US Airways Group, a company from some other state in America, with the annual revenue of $ 11, 557 million?

(1) 84 (2) 216 (3) 880 (4) Cannot be determined

Directions for questions 18 to 21: Answer the questions on the basis of the information given below.

In a flower shop, eight different varieties of flowers namely D, E, F, G, H, I, J and K are sold. The following table provides the information about the number of flowers of each variety available in the shop at the beginning of day on five different days – Day 1 through Day 5.

Flowers	day 1	day 2	day 3	day 4	day 5
D	241	204	208	191	186
E	189	199	261	225	210
F	207	276	179	184	211
G	213	182	228	216	192
H	185	197	241	219	235
I	214	254	233	191	182
J	183	211	239	245	190
K	227	194	178	257	220

18. On day 4, all the flowers of varieties G, H, I, J and K were found to be damaged. A magician generated new flowers equal in number to the total number of damaged flowers. The new flowers generated by the magician were of varieties D, E and F and the number of new flowers of each variety generated by the magician is the same. Find the total number of flowers of variety D available in the flower shop on day 4.

(1) 567 (2) 371
(3) 376 (4) 382

19. If T denotes fifty percent of the total number of available flowers of varieties D and I on day 1, day 2 and day 3 taken together, W denotes eighty percent of the total number of available flowers of varieties D and I on day 4 and day 5 taken together and M denotes twenty percent of the total number of available flowers of varieties D and I on day 4 and day 5 taken together, then find the value of (T – M + 2W).

(1) 1726 (2) 1727
(3) 1728 (4) 1729

20. One "Garland" consists of 4, 6 and 3 flowers of varieties F, G and H respectively and one "Bouquet" consists of 6 flowers such that the flowers in any bouquet is either of variety F only or G only or H only. If the maximum possible number of Garlands was made at the end of day 5 using all the available flowers from day 1 to day 5, and the remaining flowers were used to make maximum possible number of bouquets, then find the total number of so formed garlands and bouquets put together over the period of five days.

(1) 286 (2) 313
(3) 265 (4) 327

21. The total number of flowers of varieties I, J and K formed what percentage of the total number of flowers of all varieties put together over the given period?

(1) 31.24% (2) 37.87%
(3) 39.33% (4) 35.67%

Directions for questions 22 to 24: Answer the questions on the basis of the information given below.

Larry has a huge collection of shirts. The shirts with him are of four brands namely Caterpillar, Diesel, Lacoste and Dockers. The color of the shirts with him is either black or white. Out of the shirts with him, Larry has bought only few of them, whereas the rest have been gifted to him by six of his friends namely Anjana, Ravneet, Urvashi, Heena, Simar and Sarah. Larry does not know the exact number of shirts gifted to him but he knows that the number of white shirts of each brand gifted to him by each of his mentioned friends is at least 3 and at most 18. Further, the number of black shirts of each brand gifted to him by each of his mentioned friends is at least 7 and at most 25.

Larry asked his mother to help him determine the number of shirts gifted to him by each of his mentioned friends. In turn Larry's mother provided him with the information listed in the table given below.

	Number of Shirts							
	Caterpillar		Diesel		Lacoste		Dockers	
	Black	White	Black	White	Black	White	Black	White
Anjana	> 9	< 4	> 17	> 8	< 11	< 7	< 23	> 10
Ravneet	> 18	< 6	< 24	< 9	> 10	> 12	> 14	< 10
Urvashi	< 21	> 10	> 14	< 7	< 19	> 9	> 10	< 12
Heena	> 15	< 9	> 19	< 6	< 21	< 13	< 18	< 5
Simar	> 9	< 4	< 19	> 14	< 8	< 5	> 12	> 12
Sarah	< 15	< 9	> 20	< 7	< 8	> 14	> 23	< 5

22. Out of the white shirts gifted to Larry by Ravneet, Heena and Sarah the number of white shirts of brand Caterpillar is definitely less than the number of white shirts of brand(s)

(1) Diesel (2) Dockers (3) Lacoste (4) Both (2) and (3)

23. If the total number of shirts with Larry is 750 and the total number of shirts bought by him is the same as the total number of shirts gifted to him by Anjana, then the total number of shirts with Larry that are neither bought by him nor gifted to him by Anjana is at least

(1) 501 (2) 499 (3) 495 (4) 496

24. If the total number of shirts of each of the mentioned brands gifted to Larry by Urvashi and Simar is the same, then which of the following can be the total number of shirts gifted to Larry by Urvashi and Simar put together?

(1) 184 (2) 192 (3) 196 (4) 158

Directions for questions 25 to 28: Answer the questions on the basis of the information given below.

	A	B	C	D	E	F
A	1	3	5	2	5	3
B	3	1	2	4	3	5
C	5	2	1	5	4	3
D	2	4	5	1	1	2
E	5	3	4	1	1	2
F	3	5	3	2	2	1

Among 6 variables A, B, C, D, E and F, given in the table, only two kinds of arithmetic operations named 'Pontiplication' (denoted by '×') and 'Civision' (denoted by '÷') are allowed. From the table given above, we can find the result of 'Pontiplication' or 'Civision' between any two variables by the following rules:

Rule I: 'Pontiplication' of B and D denoted by BD is the product of the first number in the row of B and the number common to the row of B and the column of D.

For example, $BD = B \times D = 3 \times 4 = 12$.

Rule II: Similarly the Civision of B and D denoted by $\frac{B}{D}$, is the ratio of the first number in the row of B to the number common to the row of B and the column of D.

For example, $\frac{B}{D} = B \div D = 3 \div 4 = 0.75$.

Rule III: Neither 'Pontiplication' nor 'Civision' is defined between the same variable. For example, (B × B) or (B ¸ B) is not defined.

In the following questions, X and Y denote two distinct variables out of A, B, C, D, E and F.

25. The minimum possible value of (2XY – YX) is

(1) 0 (2) –5 (3) –10 (4) –15

26. The sum of all the possible values of XY is

(1) 284 (2) 300 (3) 312 (4) 328

27. The number of possible cases in which the value of X ¸ Y is not less 1 is

(1) 18 (2) 20 (3) 22 (4) 24

28. If the possible values of $\left[XY + YX - \frac{X}{Y}\right]$, where Y divides X completely, are arranged in decreasing order, which is the second highest distinct value?

(1) 11 (2) 15 (3) 23 (4) 29

Directions for questions 29 and 30: Answer the questions on the basis of the information given below.

The following chart shows the results of an experiment conducted to check the presence of Ca, Mg and P ions in 6 different brands of toothpastes. The following table shows the quantity used for conducting the experiment, amount of Ca, Mg and P ions present, and the recommended quantity of toothpaste to be used per brushing for each of the six types of toothpaste.

Toothpaste	Quantity used (in grams)	Ca ions (in mg)	Mg ions (in mg)	P ions (in mg)	Recommended use per brushing (in grams)
Colgate	200	24	8	32	1.25
Pepsodent	100	10	6	14	1.00
Babool	300	27	18	40	1.60
Promise	200	22	11	27	1.40
Sensoform	100	11	5	13	0.80
Close-up	200	25	9	24	1.10

Based on the experiment results, toothpastes were categorised as follows:

Excellent	If percentage of Ca ions is the highest and percentage of Mg ions is the least as compared to other toothpastes
Good	If percentage of Ca ions is the highest and percentage of P ions is the least as compared to other toothpastes
Average	If percentage of P ions is the highest and percentage of Mg ions is the least as compared to other toothpastes
Poor	If percentage of Mg ions is the highest and percentage of Ca ions is the least as compared to other toothpastes

It is known that 1 grams = 1000 mg.

29. If Colgate is taken as reference, then what would be the percentage saving in usage of Sensoform per month if a person uses it as recommended? (Assume that the number of brushings per month with all the pastes is same.)

(1) 36% (2) 66.6% (3) 40% (4) None of these

30. In how many of the given toothpastes is the percentage of Ca ions more than that of Mg ions and P ions taken together?

(1) 0 (2) 1 (3) 3 (4) 4

Directions for questions 31 to 34: Answer the questions on the basis of the information given below.

The table given below shows the data related to the average marks scored by boys and girls in primary and secondary classes of a school during the period 2011-2017. It also gives the average marks of all the boys and girls, studying in primary and secondary classes for the same period.

Years	Primary		Secondary		Total	
	Boys	Girls	Boys	Girls	Boys	Girls
2011	40	54	54	62	48	58
2012	72	80	60	68	64	72
2013	60	76	68	70	62	74
2014	94	96	90	98	92	97
2015	58	60	76	80	64	62
2016	50	60	80	90	70	76
2017	64	80	76	90	70	84

31. In 2011, which of the following could be the total number of boys studying in either primary or secondary classes of the school?

(1) 14 (2) 22

(3) 17 (4) 24

32. Which of the following statements is definitely true?

(1) The total number of boys in the years 2012 and 2013, put together, was greater than the total number of girls in the years 2013 and 2014, put together.

(2) The total number of boys in all the given years, put together, was greater than the total number of girls in the years 2012 and 2013, put together.

(3) The total number of students in primary classes in the years 2011 and 2012, put together, was lesser than the total number of students in secondary classes in the years 2011 and 2012, put together.

(4) None of these.

33. If the average marks score by all the students in the years 2015 and 2016 was 63 and 72 respectively, and the number of boys studying in secondary classes in the year 2015 was equal to the number of boys studying in the primary classes in the year 2016, then which of the following statements is definitely true?

(1) The total number of students in 2015 was equal to that in 2016.

(2) The total number of students in 2015 was 40% more than the total number of students in 2016.

(3) The total number of students in 2015 was 20% less than the total number of students in 2016.

(4) The total number of students in 2015 was 33.33% more than the total number of students in 2016.

34. If the average marks of all the students in 2017 was 80 and the number of boys in secondary classes was 500, then the total number of students in 2017 was

(1) 4560 (2) 3620

(3) 4200 (4) 3500

Directions for questions 35 to 38: Answer the questions on the basis of the information given below:

The following table gives details related to the number of runs scored by four players – Kemp, Kallis, Klusener and Kevin – in four different tournaments – Standard Bank Series, Afro-Asia Cup, Natwest Series and Benson & Hedges Series. However, the names of the players are disguised as P, Q, R, S and the names of the tournaments are disguised as A, B, C, D, not necessarily in the same order.

	P	Q	R	S
A	225	300	250	350
B	250	325	275	400
C	275	250	300	125
D	300	275	200	200

It is also known that:

- The total number of runs scored by the 4 players, put together, in Afro-Asia Cup was greater than that in the other three tournaments.
- The absolute difference between the total runs scored in Afro-Asia Cup and Benson & Hedges Series and the total runs scored in Natwest Series and Standard Bank Series by the 4 players was 100.
- When the total runs scored scored by individual players in the four tournaments, put together, are arranged in descending order (from top to bottom), Kevin and Kemp occupy the top two positions.

35. What can be said regarding the following two statements?

Statement X: Kallis's 2nd highest score was in Natwest Series.

Statement Y: The absolute difference between the highest individual scores in Afro-Asia Cup and Standard Bank Series was 100.

(1) If Statement X is true, then Statement Y is necessarily true.
(2) Statement X is false and Statement Y is true.
(3) Statement X is false but Statement Y may be true.
(4) Both Statements X and Y are necessarily false.

36. What can be said regarding the following two statements?

Statement X: Klusener's highest score was in Natwest Series.

Statement Y: Kallis's second lowest score was in Standard Bank Series.

(1) If one of the statements is false, then the other is definitely false.
(2) If Statement X is true, then Statement Y is necessarily false.
(3) If Statement Y is true, then Statement X is necessarily false.
(4) Both Statements X and Y are true independently.

37. What can be said regarding the following statements?

Statement X: Kevin's lowest score was in Benson & Hedges series.

Statement Y: Kemp's highest score was in Afro-Asia Cup.

(1) Statement X may be false but Statement Y is necessarily true.
(2) Statement Y may be false but Statement X is necessarily true.
(3) Both Statement X and Statement Y are necessarily true.
(4) Both Statements X and Y may be false together.

38. What can be said regarding the following two statements?

Statement X: The total runs scored by Kevin in the four tournaments, put together, was highest.

Statement Y: The number of runs scored by Kemp in the Natwest Series was highest.

(1) If statement X is true, then statement Y is necessarily true.
(2) If statement Y is true, then statement X is necessarily false.
(3) If statement Y is true, then statement X is necessarily true.
(4) If statement Y is false, then statement X is necessarily true.

Directions for questions 39 to 42: Answer the questions on the basis of the information given below.

Five companies were vying with each other in their bid to take-over Mittal Steel, the largest steel-maker of the world. The companies initially offered a price per share of Mittal Steel which is termed as 'offer price'. The offer prices of the respective companies as on 1st February 2017 morning was as follows:

Sl.No	Name of the Company	Offer price in Rs. as on 1st Feb 2017
1	Tata Steel	594
2	JK Steel	592
3	Essar Steel	591
4	Modi Steel	596
5	Nippon Steel	598

The bidding process continued for six days from 1st to 6th February. During this period, all the companies followed a simple rule for revising their offer prices.

I. If the closing price of the share of a particular company on Bombay Stock Exchange (BSE) on any day was higher than the previous day's closing price, the offer price was revised upwards the next day by Rupee 1/- per share.

II. If the closing price of the share of a particular company on BSE on any day was lower than the previous day's closing price, the offer price was revised downwards by Rs. 2 per share the next day.

III. Each day, the offer prices of the companies were revised starting with the first revision on 2nd February and the final revision on 6th February.

The Table below shows the closing share prices on BSE for the 5 companies mentioned. Data for the closing price of Tata Steel on 3rd February and of Modi Steel on 2nd February are not available.

Sl.No	Name of the Company	Closing Share Price in Rs. as on					
		31/01/2016	1/2/2017	2/2/2017	3/2/2017	4/2/2017	5/2/2017
1	Tata Steel	519	520	527.5		527	522
2	JK Steel	703	700	690	695	700	705
3	Essar Steel	248	250	253	255	260	265
4	Modi Steel	858		865	867	870	867
5	Nippon Steel	154	150	154	156	158	153

Following additional information is available:

A. For Tata Steel, the number of days on which the share price increased was one more than the number of days on which the share price decreased, during the given period. Also, the share price of Tata Steel neither decreaed nor increased on two consecutive days.

B. The share price of Modi Steel increased on 4 days and decreased on 1 day, during the given period.

39. Mittal Steel was taken over by the company that offered the maximum offer price as on 6th February. Identify the company that was successful in taking over Mittal Steel.

(1) Tata Steel

(2) Modi Steel

(3) Essar Steel

(4) Nippon Steel

40. Which group of companies had the same absolute change in the offer price on 6th February with respect to 1st February?

(1) Tata, JK and Nippon Steel

(2) Tata and JK Steel

(3) JK and Nippon Steel

(4) Tata and Nippon Steel

41. Had the bidding concluded on 5th February, and companies with the top two offer prices not showed interest in taking over the company, which company could have taken over Mittal Steel?

(1) Modi Steel

(2) JK Steel

(3) There will be a tie between Tata Steel and Essar Steel

(4) Tata Steel

42. Only those companies with an offer price of more than Rs. 595 on 4th February were considered for further participation. How many companies were not eligible for making bid on 6th February?

(1) 3 (2) 4 (3) 1 (4) 2

Directions for questions 43 to 46: Answer the questions on the basis of the information given below.

In a city there are ten Police patrolling jeeps for providing security to the residents. Each patrolling jeep has three policemen viz. one Inspector, one Constable and one Driver. Each patrolling jeep has a wireless system to make calls to other patrolling jeeps. Codes are required to activate the wireless system which are different for Inspectors, Constables and Drivers. Four patrolling jeeps receive every call made by an Inspector, two patrolling jeeps receive every call made by a Constable and one patrolling jeep receives every call made by a Driver. The patrolling jeeps can make or receive calls to / from other patrolling jeeps only. The following table provides information about the number of received and dialed calls by each patrolling jeep at the end of a particular day.

Police Patrolling jeep No.	No. of Received Calls	No. of Dialed Calls
1	6	5
2	15	3
3	7	2
4	9	6
5	6	1
6	8	3
7	10	2
8	9	1
9	7	4
10	5	3

43. If Police Patrolling jeep No. 2 had received calls from only three Police Patrolling jeeps, then what could be the lowest possible number of Police Patrolling jeeps from which Police Patrolling jeep No. 7 received calls?

(1) 6 (2) 4 (3) 3 (4) 2

44. What could be the maximum possible number of calls that can be made by the Constables?

(1) 19 (2) 16 (3) 13 (4) 10

45. If the total number of calls made by all the Inspectors was not less than the total number of calls made by all the Constables and the total number of calls made by all Constables was not less than the total number of calls made by the all the Drivers, then what was the minimum number of calls that could have been made by the Drivers?

(1) 6 (2) 4 (3) 2 (4) 8

46. If the total number of calls made by all the Inspectors was not less than the total number of calls made by all the Constables and the total number of calls made by all Constables was not less than the total number of calls made by the all the Drivers, then what was the maximum number of calls that could have been made by the Drivers?

(1) 10 (2) 8 (3) 6 (4) 4

Directions for questions 47 to 49: Answer the questions on the basis of the information given below.

The table given below shows the closing prices (in Rs.) of the stocks of six Indian banks viz. Axis Bank, BOB, ICICI Bank, HDFC, PNB and SBI, on the days on which trading happened on a stock exchange from April 16, 2017 to May 15, 2017.

Date \ Bank	AXIS Bank	BOB	ICICI Bank	HDFC	PNB	SBI
16-Apr-17	1363	681	1079	663	740	2183
17-Apr-17	1377	676	1099	660	748	2245
18-Apr-17	1429	688	1123	674	767	2300
22-Apr-17	1441	699	1148	698	781	2327
23-Apr-17	1445	693	1161	689	779	2288
25-Apr-17	1503	709	1177	690	786	2335
26-Apr-17	1486	699	1145	689	772	2288
29-Apr-17	1475	699	1153	695	785	2274
30-Apr-17	1493	699	1164	682	768	2264
2-May-17	1516	712	1172	693	769	2299
3-May-17	1475	699	1130	681	744	2214
6-May-17	1460	700	1143	676	739	2226
7-May-17	1504	705	1164	688	748	2257
8-May-17	1490	692	1158	697	749	2255
9-May-17	1454	700	1153	690	783	2291
10-May-17	1470	703	1165	703	771	2294
11-May-17	1472	703	1168	703	773	2306
13-May-17	1452	690	1149	693	758	2278
14-May-17	1468	704	1147	689	766	2293
15-May-17	1509	728	1191	715	822	2383

47. Which of the six banks recorded the maximum increase in its closing stock price on a day over any of the preceding days during the given period?

(1) SBI

(2) HDFC

(3) ICICI

(4) AXIS Bank

48. On which date did the closing stock price of ICICI Bank record the maximum increase over that of the previous day during the given period?

(1) 18th April

(2) 15th May

(3) 23rd April

(4) 6th May

49. Which of the six banks recorded the maximum percentage increase in its closing stock price over the given period?

(1) PNB

(2) AXIS Bank

(3) ICICI

(4) BOB

Directions for questions 50 to 52: Answer the questions on the basis of the information given below.

The table given below shows the data related to a few key financial indicators for fourteen European countries in the FY 2016-17.

Country	Inflation (%)	Long-term interest rate (% p.a.)	Debt to GDP ratio (in %)	Fiscal-deficit (as a % of GDP)
Austria	2.2	3.4	70.2	4.8
Belgium	3.4	3.9	100.8	4.8
Cyprus	2.2	4.6	61.1	5.7
Denmark	2.2	3	46.6	4.6
Estonia	2.4	5.7	7.7	1.7
Finland	1.1	3.1	45.4	3.4
France	1.5	3.3	83.5	8
Germany	1.9	2.9	74.8	4.5
Italy	1.4	4.6	118	5.1
Latvia	1.2	7.5	48	8.6
Malta	1.7	4.4	72	3.8
Netherlands	1.1	3.1	64.6	5.6
Poland	2.4	5.9	53.9	7.3
Portugal	1.1	6.5	83.2	7.3

50. If the Fiscal-deficit of France was x Euros, which was 50% more than that of Belgium, then what was the Debt (in Euros) of Belgium in FY 2016-17?

(1) 13x

(2) 7x

(3) 14x

(4) 6.5x

51. The countries with the Long-term interest rate less than 4% per annum, Debt to GDP ratio less than 60% and Fiscal-deficit not more than 4.6% were given a AAA rating. The number of countries rated AAA among the fourteen in FY 2016-17 was

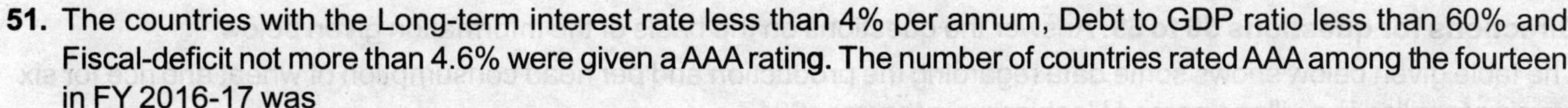

(1) 0

(2) 1

(3) 2

(4) None of these

52. If the GDP (in Euros) of Finland was 50% more than that of Italy, then by what percent was the Fiscal-deficit (in Euros) of Italy more/less than that of Finland in FY 2016-17?

(1) 0

(2) 1.5

(3) 0.5

(4) Cannot be determined

Directions for questions 53 to 55: Answer the questions on the basis of the information given below.

The table below gives information regarding the number of candidates who appeared in CEE, an exam conducted for selection of Probationary Officers in 10 banks, and the number of candidates who were finally selected for the post by the banks. The exam was conducted in 2014 for the first time. A candidate could not reappear for the exam during the given period after getting selected once. It is also known that no two banks ever selected the same candidate for the post in a year.

	2014	2015	2016	2017
Total	559232	593456	642965	691584
AB	112	124	104	119
IOB	76	84	92	97
OBC	345	496	221	245
BB	239	117	179	381
PNB	715	225	468	159
BOI	224	72	802	415
PSB	1092	948	732	645
BOM	510	713	196	240
SB	468	749	217	69
CB	698	1534	1149	1358

53. The number of candidates who appeared at least two times for the exam during the given period cannot be more than

(1) 541803 (2) 1236421 (3) 752863 (4) 1193558

54. If a candidate kept on appearing for the exam till he/she was selected by one of the banks, how many candidates appeared in all the years during the given period?

(1) 541803 (2) 554753 (3) 531803 (4) Cannot be determined

55. How many banks selected at least 0.05% of the appearing candidates each year during the given period?

(1) 0 (2) 1 (3) 2 (4) 3

Directions for questions 56 to 59: Answer the questions on the basis of the information given below.

The table given below shows some data regarding the production and per head consumption of wheat and rice for six farming families in a village named Hoshiarpur in the year 2017.

Surplus = Production – Consumption

Family	Number of members	Wheat Produced (in kg)	Rice Produced (in kg)	Per head consumption of wheat (in kg)	Per head consumption of rice (in kg)
Sharma's	6	600	520	91.2	83.2
Sen's	4	440	260	100.8	60
Srivastava's	7	800	560	108.4	78.4
Sehgal's	8	600	640	74.4	75.2
Srinivasan's	5	480	500	80	96.8
Suri's	7	520	460	63.2	64

56. For how many families was the surplus of Wheat and Rice together greater than 73.5 kg?

(1) 1 (2) 2 (3) 0 (4) 3

57. A relative of Sehgal's family joined it at the beginning of the year 2017 and stayed till the end of the year. If the amount of wheat consumed by the relative was 68 kg, by what amount must the family have reduced its per head consumption of wheat to meet the requirement with the produced quantity only?

(1) 7.10 kg (2) 7.43 kg (3) 7.90 kg (4) None of these

58. What was the total combined surplus of wheat and rice of all the families put together at the end of the year?

(1) 296 kg (2) 404.8 kg (3) 411.6 kg (4) None of these

59. Price of rice and wheat are Rs. 20 and Rs. 10 per kg respectively. How many families earn more amount by selling the surplus of rice then that by the selling the surplus of wheat at the end of the year?

(1) 1 (2) 2 (3) 3 (4) 4

Directions for questions 60 to 63: Answer the questions on the basis of the information given below.

The total electricity production of five thermal power plants in India in year 2016-17 is given in the table below. Capacity utilization for any power plant is the percentage of maximum capacity, of that power plant, which is used for power production.

Maximum capacity (100%) = Capacity utilization (In %) + Unutilized production (In %)

Power Plant	Capacity Utilization	Unutilized production (In MW units)	Number of units sold as a percentage of maximum capacity
A	93%	595	89%
B	88%	750	87%
C	92.50%	750	90%
D	86%	1190	85%
E	81%	1805	80%

	Production Cost (In Rs. / kw units)	Selling Price (In Rs. / Kw units)
A	2.1	3.4
B	2.25	3.2
C	2.0	2.9
D	2.35	3.0
E	2.2	2.8

Total cost of production = Units Produced (in Kw) × Production Cost (in Rs. / Kw units)

Total Revenue = Units Sold (in Kw) × Selling price (in Rs. / Kw units)

$$\text{Profitability} = \left(\frac{\text{Revenue} - \text{Cost}}{\text{Cost}}\right) \times 100\%$$

60. In the given year, if capacity of power plant B had 12.5% of the total power capacity of India, and thermal power capacity of India is 95% of its total power capacity. The total capacity of these 5 thermal power plants was what percentage of the total thermal power capacity of India?

(1) 91.92% (2) 85.5% (3) 77.73% (4) 90%

61. Which of the following represents the decreasing order of units sold by the given 5 power plants?

(1) E > C > D > A > B (2) C > E > A > D > B (3) E > C > A > D > B (4) C > A > E > B > D

62. Which power plant had the third highest profitability?

(1) A (2) C (3) D (4) B

63. Which of the following statements is true?

(1) The power plant with the lowest percentage capacity utilization sold minimum number of units.

(2) The power plant with the second highest per unit selling price sold minimum number of units.

(3) The power plant B had the second lowest capacity.

(4) The total capacity of E was more than 10,000 MW units.

Directions for questions 64 to 67: Answer the questions on the basis of the information given below.

The BCCI has devised a grade system for cricket players. The players will be placed in four grades, I to IV. The more the points, the better the grade. Grades are assigned based on points, awarded on the basis of performance considering certain parameters. The following information gives relation between points and grades:

A player with points more than 15000 is assigned Grade I.

A Player with points between 10001 to 15000, both inclusive, is assigned Grade II.

A Player with points between 5000 to 10000, both inclusive, is assigned Grade III.

A Player with points less than 5000 is assigned Grade IV.

The following table gives partial information regarding the parameters that are taken into account for awarding points for a few Indian players. Blank cells indicate missing data.

Player	Runs	Wickets	Catches	Centuries	5 wicket-haul
Ganguly	10000	50			
Tendulkar		80	80	25	5
Sehwag		40	50	10	4
Laxman	3000	0	60		
Dravid	8000	0		12	
Zaheer	1000		50		8
Kumble	1500	300	75	0	14

For the grading system,

1 run = 1 point, 1 wicket = 20 points, 1 catch = 3 points

In addition, there is a bonus point system as well:

1 century = 50 bonus points, one 5-wicket haul = 50 bonus point.

Additional information given below is available to fill up the blank cells.

I. Tendulkar has scored more runs than Ganguly.

II. Dravid has scored more runs than Sehwag.

III. Kumble has taken the highest number of wickets, which is twice the number of wickets taken by Zaheer.

IV. Dravid has taken the highest number of catches.

V. Number of catches taken by Laxman is equal to half the number of catches taken by Dravid.

64. Laxman is in Grade

(1) II (2) III (3) IV (4) Cannot be determined

65. If it is given that the total points of Ganguly is greater than that of Tendulkar, the number of centuries scored by Ganguly cannot be less than

(1) 31 (2) 29 (3) 30 (4) 35

66. The number of players who can be in grade IV cannot be more than

(1) 3 (2) 4 (3) 2 (4) 1

67. If Sehwag is in Grade II, the number of runs scored by Sehwag could not be less than

(1) 8351 (2) Sehwag cannot be in Grade II

(3) 8350 (4) None of these

PRACTICE EXERCISE – 2

Directions for questions 1 to 4: Answer the questions on the basis of the information given below.

Production at a cloth manufacturing plant involves the following stages:

W — Warehouse; A — Cutting; B — Rolling; C — Bleaching; D — Accumulating ; E — Charging (Input)

The sequence of working for a unit of product is E–D–C–B–A. After this, the unit gets stored in the warehouse as the final product. Transfer between different stages of production takes negligible time. Transfer of the semi-processed units between any two stages of production occurs at the end of 1-hr shift, and 1-hr is the processing time during each stage. Final products are transferred out of warehouse only at end of day i.e. at 4 : 00 p.m. The warehouse can store any number of units i.e. it does not have capacity constraint. Following is the work capacity of cloth manufacturing plant during different shifts of the day:

Shift time	E	D	C	B	A
10:00 a.m.–11:00 a.m.	2	6	4	1	1
11:00 a.m.–12:00 noon	6	1	6	6	3
12:00 noon–1:00 p.m.	4	5	2	3	4
1:00 p.m.–2:00 p.m.	2	2	2	5	2
2:00 p.m.–3:00 p.m.	5	5	5	1	5
3:00 p.m.–4:00 p.m.	3	4	6	2	4

At 10:00 a.m., A, B, C, D and E stages have 1, 1, 4, 6 and 2 units respectively. There are no units kept in the warehouse at 10 : 00 a.m. 'Outstanding' is defined as the number of unfinished units at any stage of production which cannot be processed due to capacity constraint. If capacity permits, the outstanding of any shift can be processed during the next shift.

1. What is the maximum possible number of final products that can be stored in the warehouse at 3 : 00 p.m.?
   (1) 12 (2) 15
   (3) 11 (4) 13
2. Which stage of production will encounter 'Outstanding' for the first time?
   (1) A (2) B
   (3) C (4) D
3. Had there been only two stages of production namely E and D, what would have been the maximum possible number of final products that can be stored in the warehouse at 4 : 00 p.m.? (D is the final stage of production and at 10 : 00 a.m., E and D have 2 and 6 units of product respectively.)
   (1) 22 (2) 23
   (3) 21 (4) Cannot be determined
4. Had there been only two stages of production namely B and A, what would have been the maximum possible number of final products that can be stored in the warehouse at 2 : 00 p.m.? (A is the final stage of production and B is the input, with 1 unit of product at each stage at 10 : 00 a.m.)
   (1) 8 (2) 13
   (3) 10 (4) Cannot be determined

Directions for questions 5 to 8: Answer the questions on the basis of the information given below. The following table gives the break-up of marks across various topics in an examination called KAT for the period of six years from 2012 to 2017. In each of these years, the questions were asked from the given topics only. The examination is conducted once a year.

S. No.	Topic	2012	2013	2014	2015	2016	2017
1	Algebra	11	12	8	7	9	13
2	Analogies	5	5	10	5	8	5
3	Analytical Reasoning	20	30	15	24	15	10
4	Arithmetic	5	11	9	8	5	12
5	Comprehension	30	25	20	15	15	25
6	Data Interpretation	30	20	15	15	35	25
7	Data Sufficiency	10	4	13	3	15	2
8	Fill in the blanks	10	8	7	10	10	5
9	Geometry	9	11	5	15	6	9
10	Mathematical Reasoning	25	15	30	16	10	10
11	Modern Maths	6	5	11	4	0	2
12	Number System	8	7	7	11	9	6
13	Parajumbles	8	7	0	10	5	20
14	Sentence Correction	8	5	15	7	8	6

5. For how many years, were the marks allotted to geometry questions lesser than those allotted to analogies as well as arithmetic?

(1) 1 (2) 2 (3) 3 (4) None of these

6. Which topic accounted for the second lowest number of marks over the given period?

(1) Arithmetic (2) Parajumbles (3) Analogies (4) Modern Maths

7. Which year's paper had the maximum number of total questions during the given period?

(1) 2012 (2) 2013 (3) Both (a) and (b) (4) Cannot be determined

8. How many of the topics witnessed positive and negative growth rates for 2014 and 2015 respectively?

(1) 5 (2) 6 (3) 8 (4) None of these

Directions for questions 9 to 12: Answer the questions on the basis of the information given below.

The following table gives the brand-wise percentage distribution of certain categories of cars sold in India in 2017.

	Small	Midsize	MUV	Sedan	SUV
Tata	25	25	50	12.5	40
Maruti	30	15	30	7.5	6
Hyundai	24	20	10	15	12
Honda	15	33.33	8.33	40	16
BMW	0	6.66	1.66	20	8

The following table shows category-wise percentage distribution of given brands of cars.

	Tata	Maruti	Hyundai	Honda	BMW
Small	25	50	40	18.75	0
Midsize	15	12.5	20	25	16
MUV	30	25	10	6.25	4
Sedan	10	8.33	20	40	64
SUV	20	4.16	10	10	16

Note: These may not be the only brands of car in the given categories.

9. If Hyundai sold 6000 Midsize cars in India in 2017, then the number of SUV cars sold by the brand which had the second highest share in SUV category could not be more than

(1) 3600 (2) 4200 (3) 4500 (4) None of these

10. What was the ratio of the number of Honda Sedans sold to the number of Midsize cars sold in India in 2017?

(1) 15 : 8 (2) 8 : 15 (3) 3 : 10 (4) 6 : 5

11. If BMW sold 25000 cars in India in 2017, then what was the number of Sedans sold by the brand which has the smallest share in that category?

(1) 1200 (2) 4000 (3) 6000 (4) Cannot be determined

12. Revenue earned by Maruti from Small cars was what percentage of the revenue earned by Honda from Sedans?

(1) 111.1% (2) 112.5% (3) 87.5% (4) Cannot be determined

Directions for questions 13 to 16: Answer the questions on the basis of the information given below.

The following table shows the information related to population and a few other parameters for 5 states of India for the year 2017.

States	Population (In Lakhs)	Rural population (In %)	Literacy Rate (In %)	No. Of women per 1000 men
P	720	40	50	920
Q	400	70	55	914
R	420	55	45	970
S	350	64	44	958
T	640	30	60	990

13. In rural region of state P, all women i.e. 188 Lakh are literate and all men are illiterate. The literacy rate among urban men in state P is atleast

(1) 40% (2) 0% (3) 4% (4) None of these

14. If the literate population, staying in urban area, of each state is maximum possible, then in how many states urban population can be 100% literate?

(1) 2 (2) 1 (3) 3 (4) More than 3

15. In each state 10% of rural population migrates to urban areas of the same state.If this migrant population is illiterate then which state will have lowest literacy rates in its urban areas?

(1) Q (2) R (3) S (4) Cannot be determined

16. If 70% of literate population of each state lives in urban areas, then which state has the lowest percentage of literacy in rural areas?

(1) Q (2) R (3) S (4) Cannot be determined

Directions for questions 17 to 20: Answer the questions on the basis of the information given below.

The tables below show the fare structure and the average number of passengers who travel per day for a bus service connecting villages A, B, C and D.

Fare per passenger (Rs.)

Source \ Destination	A	B	C	D
A	-	15	18	16
B	15	-	8	20
C	18	8	-	13
D	16	20	13	-

Number of passengers per day

Source \ Destination	A	B	C	D
A	-	30	35	15
B	25	-	42	16
C	23	12	-	5
D	5	10	14	-

A passanger who wants to travel by using the given bus service, can buy a ticket between any two of the given stations only. It is also known that a commuter has to buy a ticket at the boarding station.

17. At which station is the collection the maximum?

(1) A (2) B (3) C (4) D

18. What is the total daily collection (in Rs.) on the route B–C–D–C–B ?

(1) 579 (2) 679 (3) 779 (4) 879

19. If the fare is charged at a rate 40p per km along all the routes except BD, along which it is 60p per km, what is the approximate length (in km) of the route BDAC?

(1) 118 (2) 138 (3) 158 (4) 177

20. A revenue inspector residing in village C travels to villages A, B and D in that order, on regular basis. His pattern of travel is such that he travels to only one village each day and returns to his home village at the end of the same day. What are his expenses on bus fare in the month of September 1999 considering he does not travel on Sundays? It is further known that 31st July is a Sunday and the inspector travelled to village D on 30th September.

(1) Rs. 580 (2) Rs. 666 (3) Rs. 780 (4) Data inconsistent

Directions for questions 21 to 24: Answer the questions on the basis of the information given below.

The following table shows the details of various mutual fund schemes available in the market. The returns indicate the average return over the given time period (1-year or 3-year) in rupee terms.

Scheme	Assets (Rs. in crore)	Return 1-year	Return 1-year SIP	Return 3-year	Best 1-year return	Worst 1-year return
HSBC Equity	1108.3	93.36	60.99	—	195.44	93.33
Reliance Growth	493.76	80.29	52.21	50.74	229.36	–56.73
Franklin India Prima	629.32	69.87	46.53	56.01	217.85	–47.60
DSPML Opportunities	604.39	68.88	39.59	36.68	166.83	–44.87
Franklin India Bluechip	1668.93	67.6	34.55	32.91	199.42	–36.54
Birla Dividend Yield Plus	433.74	61.67	27.97	—	146	60.81
Templeton India Growth	367.04	61.06	29.69	30.04	152.23	–39.49
Reliance Vision	658.62	59.69	26.59	56.12	212.39	–47.82
HDFC Equity	993.65	57.55	28.78	38.98	179.39	–40.23
HDFC Top 200	605.03	56.03	28.94	36.71	154.57	–38.98

According to the directives of SEBI, the scheme (among those given above), having the highest ratio of the difference between Best 1-year return and Worst 1-year return to the assets of that scheme, will be given a gold medal. The second-best ratio holder scheme gets a silver medal. The schemes having the worst two ratios will be barred from doing any business in future.

21. How many schemes are there with assets of more than Rs. 500 crore and the ratio of Best 1-year return to Return 1-year more than 2?

(1) 5 (2) 6 (3) 7 (4) 8

22. Based on the SEBI's directive, which scheme will get the gold medal?

(1) Reliance Growth (2) Franklin India Prima
(3) HSBC equity (4) Reliance Vision

23. Based on the SEBI's directive, which scheme will get the silver medal?

(1) Templeton India Growth (2) Reliance Vision
(3) DSPML Opportunities (4) HDFC Top 200

24. Based on the SEBI's directive, which two schemes will be barred from doing any business in future?

(1) HSBC Equity and Franklin India Blue-chip
(2) Birla Dividend Yield Plus Franklin India Blue-chip
(3) HSBC Equity and HDFC Equity
(4) None of these

Directions for questions 25 to 28: Answer the questions on the basis of the information given below.

Brass alloy is made by mixing copper and zinc in a certain proportion. The following table shows the information related to four alloy – copper used in each alloy was of a different quality, quantity and price, whereas zinc used in each alloy was of the same quality and price @ Rs 150/kg. In none of the alloy, Weight of zinc is more than the weight of copper.

	Weight of copper (in Kg)	Rate of copper (in Rs/Kg)	Weight of zinc (in Kg)	Rate of brass (in Rs/Kg)
Alloy 1	12	90	W	A
Alloy 2	16	60	X	B
Alloy 3	18	75	Y	C
Alloy 4	20	102	Z	D

Price of brass alloy per kg = (weight of copper × rate of copper + weight of zinc × rate of zinc)/(weight of copper + weight of zinc)

It is also known that W, X, Y, Z, A, B, C and D are natural numbers.

25. How many values can B take ?

(1) 3 (2) 4 (3) 5 (4) More than 5

26. Which of the following statement(s) is/are true?

i. 'A' is definitely less than 'C'

ii. Whenever 'W' is more than 'Z', 'A' is not less than any possible value of 'C'

iii. When 'W' and 'Z' are equal, 'A' and 'D' can also be equal

iv. 'Z' can take 3 values

(1) Only iv (2) Only iv & ii (3) Only ii & iii (4) Only ii

27. If equal weights of Alloy 1 and Alloy 2 are melted together to form a new alloy, then which of the following is not a possible price of the new alloy (in Rs/Kg)?

(1) 105 (2) 96 (3) 90 (4) None of these

28. Which of the following value(s) is/are possible for more than one out of A, B, C and D?

(1) 102 (2) 120 (3) 118 (4) (1) and (2) both

Directions for questions 29 to 32: Answer the questions on the basis of the information given below.

The following Table gives the number of students across six different classes of Pune Modern School in the years 2016 and 2017.

Class	Students in the year 2016	Students in the year 2017
V	100	125
VI	75	82
VII	68	65
VIII	60	57
IX	45	50
X	34	47

It is also known that:

i. New students join the school only in class V.

ii. No student leaves the school before passing out class X.

iii. The students who fail in a class in a year will study in the same class next year.

29. What was the maximum possible number of students who joined the school in 2017?

(1) 100 (2) 76 (3) 75 (4) None of these

30. In 2016, which of the following was not a possible pass percentage of class VI?

(1) 60% (2) 16% (3) 58.66% (4) More than one of these

31. In 2016, if the number of students who passed in class VI was more than the number of students who failed in class IX, then what was the minimum pass percentage of class VIII?

(1) 46.66% (2) 48.33% (3) 53.33% (4) None of these

32. In 2016, if the pass percentage in class IX was 60%, then what was the pass percentage of class V?

(1) 33.33% (2) 67% (3) 58% (4) None of these

Directions for questions 33 to 36: Answer the questions on the basis of the information given below.

The table below gives the marks scored by six candidates of an engineering college in four subjects – Digital systems, Analog systems, Power electronics and Microprocessors. Each subject is assigned a Credit as mentioned in bracket along with the subject name as shown in the table below.

Subject / Student	Digital systems (4)	Analog systems (2)	Power electronics (3)	Microprocessors (6)
Arihant	78	34	63	72
Gopal	67	65	81	51
Nitin	75	61	77	58
Saurabh	31	47	49	78
Prabhakar	55	62	62	49
Gaurav	42	46	92	44

The grade assigned to a student in a subject is based on the marks scored by him in that subject and each grade is assigned a distinct point. The following tables show the relation between 'marks and grade', and 'grade and points'.

Marks(M)	Grade
$M \geq 80$	A
$65 \leq M < 80$	B
$50 \leq M < 65$	C
$40 \leq M < 50$	D
$M < 40$	E

Grade	Points
A	5
B	4
C	3
D	2
E	1

The CGPA of a student is calculated using the following formula:

$$\text{CGPA} = \frac{\Sigma[\text{Credit(Subject S)} \times \text{Points Received(subject S)}]}{\Sigma \text{ Credits}}$$

("S" represents a subject out of the four subjects)

33. The names of the two students who got the same CGPA are

(1) Nitin and Arihant (2) Gaurav and Prabhakar

(3) Prabhakar and Saurabh (4) No two students got the same CGPA

34. Who got the highest CGPA?

(1) Nitin (2) Arihant (3) Saurabh (4) None of these

35. Except the student who got the highest CGPA among these six students, everybody applied for rechecking and each one of them got their marks increased in one or more subjects. One of them got 'k' more marks in total, after rechecking, and his CGPA became the highest. What is the smallest possible value of k?

(1) 4 (2) 7 (3) 6 (4) 5

36. What was the CGPA of Gaurav?

(1) 2.66 (2) 2.6 (3) 2.4 (4) 2.56

Directions for questions 37 to 40: Answer the questions on the basis of the information given below.

Rahul has a total of 80 coins and these coins are made up of different metals among platinum, gold, silver, bronze, copper and aluminium. Denominations of platinum and gold coins are multiple of 25 (in paise) and that of coins made up of other metals are multiple of 5 (in paise). The range of denominations of these coins and the breakup of total coins are given in the tables below.

Variety	Range of denomination (In Paise)
Platinum	(200,500]
Gold	[100,200]
Silver	[75,100)
Bronze	[50,75)
Copper	[25,50)
Aluminium	[1,25)

[x, y) means all the numbers between x and y, including x and excluding y.

Variety	Number of coins (in %)
Platinum	5
Gold	15
Silver	20
Bronze	20
Copper	30
Aluminium	10

37. Total value of silver and bronze coins with Rahul can exceed the value of platinum and gold coins with him by at most

(1) 720 paise (2) 620 paise (3) 540 paise (4) 450 paise

38. Rahul had atleast one copper coin each of all possible denominations and total value of all these copper coins is Rs. 9.60. What is the maximum number of 45 paise copper coins that he could have?

(1) 18 (2) 17 (3) 16 (4) 15

39. If government allows use of only those coins in market whose value (in paise) is multiple of 25, then what can be the maximum value of coins that Rahul can use in the market?

(1) Rs. 70 (2) Rs. 84 (3) Rs. 78 (4) Rs. 72

40. What is the maximum number of coins of denominations lying between 25 and 50 paise, both inclusive, with Rahul?

(1) 32 (2) 48 (3) 40 (4) 24

Directions for questions 41 to 44: Answer the questions on the basis of the information given below.

A company launched four types of products – software inhouse, software export, hardware inhouse and hardware export recently. The following table shows the figures related to sum of the key business parameters for the company in 2017.

Company A 's business details

Business	Annual sales (in Rs.)	Margin percentage	Number of employees	Annual salary per employee (in Rs.)
Software Inhouse	0.2 crore	23	25	20000
Software Export	1.5 crore	47	15	100000
Hardware Inhouse	0.4 crore	31	40	15000
Hardware Export	2 crore	52	40	80000

Total cost of any business for year

$$= \text{Annual sales} - \text{Annual sales} \times \frac{\text{Margin}}{100} = \text{Other cost} + \text{Salary paid to the employees}$$

41. For which business was the salary as a percentage of total cost least?

(1) Software inhouse (2) Software export
(3) Hardware inhouse (4) Hardware export

42. Had the everage salary of Software Inhouse employee been equal to that of Hardware Inhouse employee and other costs remain the same, by what percent would have been the margin of Software Inhouse more than its actual margin?

(1) 8.75% (2) 29.25%
(3) 6.25% (4) 27.17%

43. In 2018, if the total annual sales of the company increases by 15%, and the salary of the employees increases by 12.5%, what is total margin of the company?

(1) Rs. 2.45 crore (2) Rs. 1.91 crore
(3) Rs. 1.88 crore (4) Data insufficient

44. In 2018, if total cost of Hardware Export increases by 15%, by what per cent should salary be reduced so that margin percentage of Hardware Exports remains the same as it was in 2017?

(1) 45% (2) 25%
(3) 30% (4) 15%

Directions for questions 45 to 48: Answer the questions on the basis of the information given below.

Citrus Mobile Ltd. launched a new model "Orange" in April, 2017. For the mobile, which was sold exclusively online, the bookings started on April1, 2017 and ended on September 30, 2017. The model had only one variant at a fixed price. There were three modes of booking – premium booking, which were delivered in the same month at 5% premium i.e. one had to pay 105% of the price of the mobile; normal bookings, which were delivered in next month i.e if booking was done in Xth month, it was delivered in (X + 1)th month without any extra charges; and discounted bookings, which were delivered in next to next month, i.e if booking was done in Xth month, it was delivered in (X + 2)th month, at 2% discount i.e. one had to pay 98% of the price of the mobile. The payment for all kind of deliveries was done in the month of booking. In every month, except April, exactly one-fifth of the bookings were normal bookings.

The following table gives the number of bookings and the number of deliveries for the given period.

Month	April	May	June	July	August	September	October	November
No. of bookings	1240	1060	820	900	1100	1360	0	0
No. of deliveries	0	888	953	924	1080	1080	790	765

45. For how many moths premium collected was more than discount given?

(1) 2 (2) 3
(3) 4 (4) 5

46. In which month was the number of premium bookings as a percentage of total bookings highest?

(1) August (2) September
(3) May (4) July

47. How many Orange mobiles booked in June were delivered in August?

(1) 532 (2) 538
(3) 496 (4) 512

48. In how many months did number of discounted bookings constitute not more than half of total bookings in that month?

(1) 1 (2) 2
(3) 3 (4) 4

Directions for questions 49 to 52: Answer the questions on the basis of the information given below.

On the occasion of Diwali, Pranav bought gifts from ten shops namely Sh1, Sh2, Sh3, ... Sh10. These shops are located in four different areas – Andheri, CP, NFC and Gurgaon. Pranav bought only four types of gifts from these shops – wallet, watch, perfume and pens. Table 1 gives the number of gifts of each type bought from these gift shops and Table 2 gives the number of gifts of each type bought from the four areas.

Shops	Watch	Wallet	Perfume	Pen
Sh1	0	1	0	1
Sh2	2	1	0	0
Sh3	1	3	1	1
Sh4	1	0	0	2
Sh5	1	0	1	1
Sh6	3	1	0	1
Sh7	0	0	1	1
Sh8	1	2	0	1
Sh9	2	1	0	2
Sh10	0	1	2	1

Areas	Watch	Wallet	Perfume	Pen
Andheri	5	2	1	2
CP	3	1	0	4
NFC	2	3	2	2
Gurgaon	1	4	2	3

49. Sh7 is located in

(1) Andheri (2) NFC

(3) Gurgaon (4) Cannot be determined

50. Which of the following groups of shops are not located in Andheri?

(1) Sh6 and Sh2 (2) Sh6 and Sh7

(3) Sh2 and Sh9 (4) More than one of the above

51. Which area definitely has only 2 of these shops?

(1) Andheri (2) Gurgaon

(3) CP (4) None of these

52. Which of the following shops is located in Gurgaon ?

(1) Sh1 (2) Sh4

(3) Sh8 (4) More than one of the above

Directions for questions 53 to 56: Answer the questions on the basis of the information given below.

The table given below shows the information related to the postpaid plans offered by three different mobile service providers – Airtel, Vodafone and Idea. The rent and the CLIP charges are payable on a monthly basis, unless otherwise mentioned, whereas charges for all calls – STD or local – are payable in rupees per minute. The SMS rates are given in rupees per SMS. A person is considered to be on roaming when he is outside of his state. The roaming rental is applicable only when a person uses roaming services.

	All Charges in rupees		
	Airtel	**Vodafone**	**Idea**
RENTAL	150	175	100
CLIP	50	75	75
INCOMING CALLS	Free	Free	Free
STD CALLS	2.65	3	3
LOCAL CALLS TO			
GSM PHONE	1.5	1.5	1
LANDLINE PHONE	3	2	2
CDMA PHONE	2.5	2	2.5
SMS			
LOCAL	1	1	1
NATIONAL	2	2	1.5
INTERNATIONAL	5	5	3
ROAMING			
RENT	50 per month	100 per month	1.5 per day
INCOMING CALLS	2	3	2.5
OUTGOING CALLS	2	3	2.5
SMS (ANYWHERE)	2	2	2

53. A sales manager travels for 10 days in a month outside his state. In this period, on an average, he receives 6 calls of 1 min each per day and he makes 2 calls of 1 min each per day. He does not use the SMS facility during this period. Based on this observation, he wants to minimize his mobile expenses for these 10 days. Which one of the three given mobile service providers should he choose?

(1) Idea
(2) Airtel
(3) Vodafone
(4) Any one between Airtel and Idea

54. If all the service providers decide to charge the same amount for all calls, both local and STD, and all SMS, which mobile service provider should a person, who does not go outside his state, choose?

(1) Idea
(2) Airtel
(3) Vodafone
(4) Any one of the given 3 service providers

55. Ajay, who does not go outside of his state, has a budget of Rs. 1,500 per month for mobile phone expenses. He makes local calls for an equal amount of time to GSM, landline and CDMA phones. If he does not make any STD calls or sends any SMS, which mobile service provider will give him service to make calls for maximum amount of time?

(1) Airtel
(2) Vodafone
(3) Idea
(4) Either (2) or (3)

56. Idea comes up with a new scheme in which it waives off CLIP charges if a customer is on roaming for 7 or more days in a month. If Ram, who uses Idea mobile services, receives the same number of calls every day of 1 min each and does not use outgoing calls facility or SMS facility while on roaming then what is the maximum number of calls that he can receive everyday such that his incoming call charges while on roaming does not exceed Rs. 75. (Assume he is on roaming for 10 days in a month)

(1) 3
(2) 4
(3) 2
(4) Not possible

Directions for questions 57 to 60: Answer the questions on the basis of the information given below.

The following table provides partial information about the composition of six different alloys namely A, B, C, D, E and F. Each of these six alloys contains the five different elements namely Zinc, Tin, Lead, Copper and Nickel. An alloy G, the composition of which is not given in the table, contains alloys A, B and C in the ratio 2 : 1 : 3. It is also known that in alloy G, tin, lead and copper are present in an equal quantity.

Alloy	Zinc	Tin	Lead	Copper	Nickel
A	10%	40%			10%
B	25%	15%	50%	5%	5%
C	15%		20%		35%
D	20%	25%	15%	30%	10%
E	5%	50%	25%	5%	15%
F	40%	10%	5%	30%	15%

57. Find the percentage of copper in alloy A.

(1) $\frac{95}{9}$ (2) $\frac{95}{3}$ (3) $\frac{25}{9}$ (4) $\frac{25}{3}$

58. If an alloy X, which contains 15% nickel, at least 15% zinc and at most 20% copper, is to be made, how many combinations of exactly two of the six mentioned alloys can be used to make it?

(1) Three (2) Four (3) Five (4) Two

59. Which of the following can be a value of the ratio in which alloys A, E and F need to be mixed to get at least 12% lead in the resulting mixture?

(1) 4 : 1 : 1 (2) 2 : 1 : 3 (3) 1 : 2 : 3 (4) 1 : 2 : 4

60. If an alloy Z, which contains at least 8.25% nickel, is to be made by using the alloys mentioned in the table, the percentage of alloy B in alloy Z cannot be more than

(1) 95.46% (2) 83.12% (3) 97.24% (4) 89.16%

Directions for questions 61 to 64: Answer the questions on the basis of the information given below.

The table given below shows the total population, ratio of the number of males and females, literacy rate and number of literate females in eight different states of India for the year 2015.

Name	Population (in lakh)	Male : Female	Literacy rate	Number of literate females (in lakh)
Bihar	570	3 : 2	70%	199
Odisha	360	5 : 4	80%	120
UP	605	7 : 4	60%	180
Jharkhand	340	9 : 8	65%	95
Assam	425	14 : 11	84%	167
MP	510	10 : 7	90%	169
Kerala	240	5 : 3	95%	80
Karnataka	320	9 : 7	85%	102

The table given below shows the age-wise percentage break up of males and females separately in these eight states taken together in the same year.

Age group(x)	Male	Female
x ≤ 25 years	60%	55%
25 < x ≤ 40	20%	20%
40 < x ≤ 60	10%	15%
60 < x ≤ 75	5%	7%
x > 75 years	5%	3%

61. The approximate value (in lakhs) of the average number of literate males in the eight states taken together was

(1) 184 (2) 186 (3) 187 (4) 188

62. What percentage (approximately) of total population of all the eight states taken together was illiterate?

(1) 21.21 (2) 23.23 (3) 25.25 (4) 33.33

63. A state having at least 75% female literacy rate is placed in 'Group A' by HRD ministry of India. How many states, out of the eight states, are placed in 'Group A'?

(1) 6 (2) 5 (3) 4 (4) 3

64. By what approximate percentage was the number of total males in the age group '$25 < x \le 40$' greater than the number of total females in the same age group for the eight states taken together?

(1) 41.58 (2) 39.09 (3) 46.63 (4) 37.14

ANSWER KEYS

PRACTICE EXERCISE – 1

1. (1)	**2.** (2)	**3.** (3)	**4.** (1)	**5.** (3)	**6.** (4)	**7.** (2)	**8.** (1)	**9.** (1)	**10.** (2)
11. (4)	**12.** (3)	**13.** (1)	**14.** (1)	**15.** (4)	**16.** (1)	**17.** (2)	**18.** (1)	**19.** (2)	**20.** (4)
21. (2)	**22.** (3)	**23.** (4)	**24.** (1)	**25.** (4)	**26.** (3)	**27.** (2)	**28.** (4)	**29.** (1)	**30.** (1)
31. (1)	**32.** (3)	**33.** (4)	**34.** (4)	**35.** (3)	**36.** (1)	**37.** (3)	**38.** (3)	**39.** (2)	**40.** (1)
41. (3)	**42.** (1)	**43.** (4)	**44.** (1)	**45.** (2)	**46.** (3)	**47.** (1)	**48.** (2)	**49.** (1)	**50.** (3)
51. (3)	**52.** (1)	**53.** (2)	**54.** (4)	**55.** (3)	**56.** (4)	**57.** (3)	**58.** (3)	**59.** (2)	**60.** (4)
61. (2)	**62.** (4)	**63.** (2)	**64.** (3)	**65.** (3)	**66.** (1)	**67.** (2)			

PRACTICE EXERCISE – 2

1. (4)	**2.** (4)	**3.** (2)	**4.** (1)	**5.** (1)	**6.** (3)	**7.** (4)	**8.** (1)	**9.** (3)	**10.** (2)
11. (4)	**12.** (4)	**13.** (4)	**14.** (3)	**15.** (4)	**16.** (3)	**17.** (1)	**18.** (2)	**19.** (1)	**20.** (2)
21. (3)	**22.** (1)	**23.** (1)	**24.** (1)	**25.** (3)	**26.** (3)	**27.** (4)	**28.** (4)	**29.** (2)	**30.** (1)
31. (2)	**32.** (4)	**33.** (2)	**34.** (4)	**35.** (1)	**36.** (2)	**37.** (3)	**38.** (3)	**39.** (1)	**40.** (3)
41. (2)	**42.** (4)	**43.** (4)	**44.** (1)	**45.** (2)	**46.** (1)	**47.** (2)	**48.** (1)	**49.** (1)	**50.** (3)
51. (3)	**52.** (4)	**53.** (2)	**54.** (1)	**55.** (3)	**56.** (1)	**57.** (2)	**58.** (4)	**59.** (3)	**60.** (4)
61. (1)	**62.** (2)	**63.** (1)	**64.** (1)						

EXPLANATIONS

PRACTICE EXERCISE – 1

1. Total cost of BEL shares = 8 crore × 60

= Rs. 480 crore.

Government holding $= \frac{75}{100} \times 480 =$ Rs. 360 crore.

Disinvestment (20%) $= \frac{20}{100} \times 360 =$ Rs. 72 crore.

Total cost of BML shares = 3.64 × 15

= Rs. 54.6 crore.

Government holding

$= \frac{60}{100} \times 54.6 =$ Rs. 32.76 crore.

Disinvestment (25%)

$= \frac{25}{100} \times 32.76 =$ Rs.8.19 crore

Hence, the total revenue generated

= 72 + 8.19 = Rs. 80.19 crore.

2. The required difference $= (175 - 125) \times \frac{66.7}{100} \times 30$

= Rs. 1,000.5 crore.

3. The price of BCL shares fell to Rs. 300.

Loss on each share = Rs. 50

∴ Fall in the value of shares held by the government

$= 50 \times \frac{80}{100} \times (1.515) =$ Rs. 60.6 crore

For questions 4 to 6:

Considering the Action genre:

Total number of hit movies $= \frac{37.5}{100} \times 192 = 72$

∴ Total number of flop movies = 192 – 72 = 120.

Number of flop movies by STS $= \frac{10}{100} \times 120 = 12$

Now, 50% of the movies of STS are hit and the rest 50% flop.

Number of hit movies by STS = 12

∴ Total number of movies by STS = 12 + 12 = 24.

Similarly, we can determine these values for other genres. The whole information has been summarized in the table below.

Genre	Action	Romance	Drama	Patriotic	Thriller	Total
Total	192	250	300	77	216	1035
Total number of hit movies	72	90	100	22	96	380
Total number of flop movies	120	160	200	55	120	655
Number of flop movies by STS	12	10	25	11	6	64
Number of hit movies by STS	12	15	5	11	12	55
Total number of movies by STS	24	25	30	22	18	119

4. Number of hit movies by STS which belonged to one of three genres Drama, Patriotic or Thriller

= 5 + 11 + 12 = 28.

5. Number of flop movies as a percentage of total number of movies across all five genres

$= \frac{655}{1035} \times 100 = 63.28\%.$

6. The number of hit movies by STS is at least 50% of the number of flop movies by STS in all genres, except Drama.

For questions 7 to 9: The absolute and percentage variation in the prices of the shares over the given period are as follows :

Company	Share prices as on 5th June 2016	Share prices as on 5th June 2017	Absolute variation	% variation
A	150	230	80	53.3%
B	500	575	75	15.0%
C	200	320	120	60.0%
D	400	440	40	10.0%
E	800	900	100	12.5%
F	175	245	70	40.0%

7. The two Telecom companies showed the highest absolute change in the value of the share prices. Therefore C and E must be the two Telecom companies. Also, the two Insurance companies showed the lowest absolute change in the value of the share prices. Therefore D and F must be the two Insurance companies. Hence, that A and B must be the two Retail companies.

Percentage change $= \frac{(805 - 650)}{650} = \left(\frac{155}{650}\right) \times 100$

= 24% (approx.)

8. Chintamani had purchased 60 shares across 4 companies and we need to calculate the maximum percentage return. This would have been possible if he had purchased 30 shares giving the maximum percentage return i.e. of company C and minimum 10 shares each of the remaining 3 companies providing the next higher percentage returns i.e 10 shares each of companies A, F and B.

Initial Value of shares purchased

30 × 200 = Rs. 6000

10 × 150 = Rs. 1500

10 × 175 = Rs. 1750

10 × 500 = Rs. 5000

Total Value = Rs. 14250

Final values of the shares purchased

30 × 320 = Rs. 9600

10 × 230 = Rs. 2300

10 × 245 = Rs. 2450

10 × 575 = Rs. 5750

Total value = Rs. 20100

Therefore percentage change = $\frac{(20100-14250)}{14250}$

= 41%

9. One of the two Telecom companies showed the highest percentage change in the value of the share prices and the other Telecom company showed the lowest percentage change in the value of the share prices. Therefore the two Telecom companies are C and D.

Initial combined share price = 200 + 400 = Rs. 600

Final combined price = 320 + 440 = Rs. 760

Percentage change = $\frac{(760-600)}{600}$ = 26.66%.

10. Food grain production in 2010-11

$= \frac{160.4}{(100+25)} \times 100 = 128.32.$

11. From the table, it can be noted that Cotton showed the maximum deviation in its production compared to the targeted production and the percentage deviation was

$\left[\frac{18.9-14.7}{14.7}\right] \times 100 = 28.57\%$

12. Production of Sugarcane in 2011-12 = 22.5 MT

Production of Sugarcane in 2012-13

= 22.5 + 4.5 = 27 MT

Production of Sugarcane in 2010-11

$= 22.5 \times \left(\frac{100}{100+35}\right) = 16.67$ MT

Hence, the simple annual growth rate

$= \left(\frac{27-16.67}{16.67}\right) \times \frac{1}{2} \times 100 = 30.98 \approx 31\%.$

13. Production of Oil seeds in 2019-20 = 24.4 MT

Production of Oil seeds in 2011-12 = 16.2 MT

Hence, the simple annual growth rate

$= \left(\frac{24.4-16.2}{16.2}\right) \times \frac{1}{8} \times 100 = 6.3\%$

For questions 14 to 17:

State Rank	Company	Rank	Revenues ($ millions)	City
1	Freddie Mac	50	44,002.00	McLean
2	Sprint Nextel	53	43,531.00	Reston
3	General Dynamics	92	24,212.00	Falls Church
4	Dominion Resources	140	16,524.00	Richmond
5	Circuit City Stores	215	11,597.70	Richmond
6	Smithfield Foods	217	11,506.80	Smithfield
7	Genworth Financial	227	11,029.00	Richmond
8	SLM	284	8,751.20	Reston
9	Gannett	302	8,033.40	McLean
10	NVR	371	6,156.80	Reston
11	Owens & Minor	418	5,533.70	Mechanicsville
12	Advance Auto Parts	478	4,616.50	Roanoke
13	LandAmerica Financial	522	4,015.90	Glen Allen
14	Dollar Tree Stores	532	3,969.40	Chesapeake
15	Universal	573	3,511.30	Richmond
16	Brink's	641	3,067.60	Richmond
17	Amerigroup	676	2,835.10	Virginia Beach
18	Markel	739	2,519.00	Glen Allen
19	DynCorp	867	1,967.00	Falls Church
20	CACI	932	1,755.30	Arlington

14. Universal was ranked 15 in Virginia state. Thus, 14 companies were above it.

15. NVR held rank 10.

16. DynCorp in Falls Church and Markel in Glen Allen had the same rank and it was 4.

17.

6	Circuit City Stores	215	11,597.70
7	Smithfield Foods	217	11,506.80

Hence, US Airways Group, with the revenues of $11,557 billion, must have been ranked 216.

18. Total numbers of flowers that were damaged

= 216 + 219 + 191 + 245 + 257 = 1128

So, number of new flowers of variety D that were generated by the magician is $\frac{1128}{3} = 376$. Therefore, total number of flowers of variety D available on day 4 is 191 + 376 = 567.

19. Aggregate number of flowers of varieties D and I on day 1, 2, and 3 = 241 + 214 + 204 + 254 + 208 + 233 = 1354.

Therefore, T = 0.5 × 1354 = 677

Aggregate number of flowers of varieties D and I on day 4 and 5 = 191 + 186 + 191 + 182 = 750

Therefore, W = 0.8 × 750 = 600

Also, M = 0.2 × 750 = 150

So, T – M + 2W = 677 – 150 + 2 × 600 = 1727

20. Maximum possible number of Garlands is determined by the number of flowers of variety G, because the number of flowers of variety G is least among the mentioned varieties. Maximum possible number of garlands is $\left[\frac{1031}{6}\right] = 171.$

Number of flowers of varieties F, H and G used in making the garlands is (4 × 171) = 684, (3 × 171) = 513 and (6 × 171) = 1026 respectively.

So, the number of flowers of varieties F, G and H left unused are 373, 5 and 564.

Maximum possible number of Bouquets made

$\left[\frac{373}{6}\right] + \left[\frac{5}{6}\right] + \left[\frac{569}{6}\right] = 62 + 0 + 94 = 156$

Therefore, total number of Garlands and Bouquets = 171 + 156 = 327

21. Aggregate number of flowers of varieties I, J and K in the given five days is 1074, 1068 and 1076 respectively.

Aggregate number of flowers of these three given varieties = 3218.

Aggregate number of flowers of all the varieties across all the five days = 8497

Hence, percentage required

$= \frac{3218}{8497} \times 100 = 37.87\%.$

22. The following table lists down the range of the total number of white shirts of each brand gifted to Larry by his mentioned friends.

	Number of white shirts			
	Caterpillar	**Diesel**	**Lacoste**	**Dockers**
Ravneet	3 - 5	3 - 8	13 - 18	3 - 9
Heena	3 - 8	3 - 5	3 - 12	3 - 4
Sarah	3 - 8	3 - 6	15 - 18	3 - 4
Total	**9 - 21**	**9 - 19**	**31 - 48**	**9 - 17**

Since, the maximum possible number of white shirts of brand Caterpillar gifted to Larry is less than the minimum possible number of white shirts of brand Lacoste gifted to Larry, therefore the number of white shirts of brand Caterpillar gifted to Larry is definitely less than the number of white shirts of brand Lacoste gifted to Larry.

23. The following table lists down the range of the number of white and black shirts of each brand gifted by Anjana to Larry

Caterpillar		Diesel		Lacoste		Dockers	
Black	**White**	**Black**	**White**	**Black**	**White**	**Black**	**White**
10 - 25	3	18 - 25	9 - 18	7 - 10	3 - 6	7 - 22	11 - 18
68 - 127							

Given that the number of shirts bought by Larry is same as the total number of shirts gifted to him by Anjana.

Therefore, at least 750 – 2 × 127 = 496 shirts are there with Larry that are neither bought by him nor gifted to him by Anjana.

Alternate method:

Let the number of shirts bought by Larry be x.

⇒ Number of shirts gifted by Anjana = x

⇒ Number of shirts neither bought by him nor gifted by Anjana = 750 – 2x = an even number.

Only option (4) is an even number.

24. The following table lists down the range of the total number of shirts of each brand gifted to Larry by his mentioned friends.

	Number of Shirts							
	Caterpillar		Diesel		Lacoste		Dockers	
	Black	White	Black	White	Black	White	Black	White
Urvashi	7 - 20	11 - 18	15 - 25	3 - 6	7 - 18	10 - 18	11 - 25	3 - 11
Simar	10 - 25	3	7 - 18	15 - 18	7	3 - 4	13 - 25	13 - 18
Total	**17 - 45**	**14 - 21**	**22 - 43**	**18 - 24**	**14 - 25**	**13 - 22**	**24 - 50**	**16 - 29**
	31 - 56		**40 - 67**		**27 - 47**		**40 - 79**	

We can conclude from the table that the range of the total number of shirts of each brand gifted to Larry is 40 to 47.

So, the range of the total number of shirts gifted to Larry will be (40 × 4 to 47 × 4) = (160 to 188)

Only, option (1) lies within the permissible range.

For questions 25 to 28:

From the given table, we can calculate the following results:

AB = 3, AC = 5, AD = 2, AE = 5, AF = 3

BA = 3 × 3 = 9, BC = 6, BD = 12, BE = 9, BF = 15

CA = 25, CB = 10, CD = 25, CE = 20, CF = 15

DA = 4, DB = 8, DC = 10, DE = 2, DF= 4

EA = 25, EB = 15, EC = 20, ED = 5, EF = 10

FA = 9, FB = 15, FC = 9, FD = 6, FE = 6

25. While checking all the possibilities, we see that

2AC – CA = 10 – 25 = – 15 and

2AE – EA = 10 – 25 = – 15, gives the minimum value.

26. The sum of all the values of XY taken together
= 18 + 51 + 95 + 28 + 75 + 45 = 312

27. Following are the possibilities for (X, Y) such that $\frac{X}{Y} \geq 1$

(X, Y) = (B, A) (B, C) (B, E), (C, A), (C, B) (C, D) (C, E) (C, F), (D, A), (D, E), (D, F), (E, A), (E, B), (E, C), (E, D), (E, F),(F, A), (F, C), (F, D), (F, E)

Total 20 ways.

28. The following are the only possibility considering the fact that Y completely divides X;

$BA + AB - \frac{B}{A} = 9 + 3 - 1 = 11$

$BE + EB - \frac{B}{E} = 9 + 15 - 1 = 23.$

$CA + AC - \frac{C}{A} = 25 + 5 - 1 = 29.$

$CD + DC - \frac{C}{D} = 25 + 10 - 1 = 34.$

$DA + AD - \frac{D}{A} = 4 + 2 - 1 = 5.$

$DE + ED - \frac{D}{E} = 2 + 5 - 2 = 5.$

$DF + FD - \frac{D}{F} = 4 + 6 - 1 = 9.$

$EA + AE - \frac{E}{A} = 25 + 5 - 1 = 29.$

$ED + DE - \frac{E}{D} = 5 + 2 - 5 = 2.$

$FA + AF - \frac{F}{A} = 9 + 3 - 1 = 11.$

$FC + CF - \frac{F}{C} = 9 + 15 - 1 = 23.$

Clearly, the second highest value is 29.

29. Colgate used per brushing = 1.25 g
Sensoform used per brushing = 0.8 g

Percentage saving per brushing = $\frac{1.25 - .8}{1.25} \times 100$

$= \frac{0.45}{1.25} \times 100 = 36\%.$

30. Since, the comparison is to be done separately for each toothpaste, we can directly add the Mg ions and P ions from the table and compare it with Ca ions. From the table, it is clear that there is no toothpaste for which Ca ions are more than Mg ions and P ions put together.

31. Let the number of boys in primary and secondary class be b_1 and b_2.

$\Rightarrow 40 \times b_1 + 54 \times b_2 = 48 \times (b_1 + b_2)$

$\Rightarrow \frac{b_1}{b_2} = \frac{3}{4}$

Thus, $b_1 + b_2$ should be a multiple of 7 and the only possible option is (1) i.e. 14.

32. To see which of the statements is definitely true, we have to check each and every option one by one.

Option (1): Let the number of boys in primary and secondary class in the year 1997 be b_1 and b_2 respectively and in the year 1998 be b_3 and b_4. Similarly, the girls for the same be g_1, g_2, g_3 and g_4. From the given table, we can only find the values of $\frac{b_1}{b_2}, \frac{b_3}{b_4}, \frac{g_1}{g_2}$ and $\frac{g_3}{g_4}$ but there is no way to find the value of $(b_1 + b_2 + b_3 + b_4)$ or $(g_1 + g_2 + g_3 + g_4)$ or to compare these two quantities.

Hence, nothing can be said about the total number of boys and total number of girls in the given years.

Option (2): With the same logic applied in option (1) we cannot say anything about the total number of boys for all the years and the total number of girls for all the years put together.

Option (3): With the same convention used in option (a) for the years 1997 and 1998, we assume the same for the years 1996 and 1997 respectively.

$\Rightarrow \frac{b_1}{b_2} = \frac{3}{4}, \frac{b_3}{b_4} = \frac{1}{2}, \frac{g_1}{g_2} = \frac{1}{1}$ and $\frac{g_3}{g_4} = \frac{1}{2}$

$\Rightarrow b_1 < b_2;\ b_3 < b_4;\ g_1 = g_2$ and $g_3 < g_4$

$\Rightarrow b_1 + b_3 + g_1 + g_3 < b_2 + b_4 + g_2 + g_4$

Hence, statement in option (c) is definitely true.

33. Let the number of boys in primary and secondary class in the year 2000 be B_1 and B_2 respectively and in the year 2001 be B_3 and B_4 respectively.

Similarly, the number of girls in primary and secondary class in the year 2000 be G_1 and G_2 respectively and in the year 2001 be G_3 and G_4 respectively.

In 2000:

$58B_1 + 76B_2 = 64(B_1 + B_2) \Rightarrow 2B_2 = B_1$

$60G_1 + 80G_2 = 62(G_1 + G_2) \Rightarrow 9G_2 = G_1$

$64(B_1 + B_2) + 62(G_1 + G_2) = 63(B_1 + B_2 + G_1 + G_2)$

$\Rightarrow B_1 + B_2 = G_1 + G_2$

Total number of students in 2000 = $B_1 + G_1 + B_2 + G_2$
$= 6B_2$

Following the same logic as in the year 2000 for the year 2001:

Total number of students in 2001 = $B_3 + G_3 + B_4 + G_4$
$= \frac{9B_3}{2}$

Given that the number of boys studying in secondary classes in the year 2000 is equal to the number of boys studying in the primary classes in the year 2001.

$\Rightarrow B_2 = B_3$

$$\therefore \frac{\text{Total number of students in 2000}}{\text{Total number of students in 2001}} = \frac{6B_2}{\frac{9B_3}{2}} = \frac{12}{9} = \frac{4}{3}$$

Therefore, the total number of students in 2000 is 33.33% more than the total number of students in 2001.

34. Let the number of boys in the primary and in the secondary classes in the year 2002 be 'x' and 'y' respectively.

Let the number of girls in the primary and in the secondary classes in the year 2002 be 'z' and 'w' respectively.

For boys: $64x + 76y = 70(x + y) \Rightarrow x = y$

For girls: $80z + 90w = 84(z + w) \Rightarrow 2z = 3w$

For all the boys and girls:

$70(x + y) + 84(z + w) = 80(x + y + z + w)$

$\Rightarrow 2(z + w) = 5(x + y) = 10x \Rightarrow 3w + 2w = 10x$

$\Rightarrow w = 2x$ and $z = 3x$

Given that y = 500.

Therefore, x = 500, z = 1500 and w = 1000.

Total number of students in the primary and in the secondary classes in the year 2002 = x + y + z + w = 3500.

For questions 35 to 38:

	P	Q	R	S	Total Runs in the Tournament
A	225	300	250	350	1125
B	250	325	275	400	1250
C	275	250	300	125	950
D	300	275	200	200	975
Total Runs by Player	1050	1150	1025	1075	

From the additional information,

- B is Afro-Asia Cup.
- C is Benson & Hedges Series and A and D could be either Natwest Series or the Standard Bank Series.
- (Kevin and Kemp) are (Q and S) and (Kallis and Klusener) are (P and R) in any order.

35. Kallis is either P or R. P's second highest score (275) is in Benson & Hedges series and R's second highest score (275) is in Afro Asia Cup.

Thus, Statement X is definitely false.

Highest individual score in Afro Asia cup = 400. A or D could be Standard Bank series. If D is Standard Bank Series, difference would be 100.

Hence, Statement Y could be true.

36. Klusener = P or R. Natwest Series = A or D.

According to Statement X, Klusener = P and Natwest Series = D. Hence, Standard Bank Series = A and Kallis = R.

Thus, Statement Y is true.

Hence, if one of these statements becomes false, other automatically turns false.

37. Kevin = Q or S. In both the cases, Kevin's lowest score is in Benson & Hedges Series. Thus, Statement X is definitely true.

Kemp = Q or S. In both the cases, Kemp's highest score is in Afro Asia Cup. Thus, Statement Y is definitely true.

Both Statement X and Statement Y are necessarily true.

38. If statement X is true than Q is Kevin and S is Kemp, but nothing can be said regarding statement Y.

If statement Y is true than A is Natwest series, D is Standard Bank Series and S & Q are Kemp and Kevin respectively. Now Kevin has the highest runs in all the four tournaments, hence statement X is necessarily true.

For questions 39 to 42:

1. The number of days for which Tata Steel's share witnessed an increase was one more than the number of days on which it witnessed a decrease. Therefore in 5 consecutive days, there were 3 increments and 2 decrements. But if the price would have been higher than 527.5 on 3rd February, then there would have been 3 consecutive increments and 2 consecutive decrements. Therefore, the share price on 3rd February was lower than the price on 2nd February and even lower than Rs. 527.
2. Also, since the price of Modi steel increased on 4 days and decreased on 1 day, therefore the share price would have increased on 1st February because there is already a decrease from 4th to 5th February.

Based on 1 and 2 above, the following is the offer price of the companies from 1st February to 6th February.

S.N.	Name of the Company	Industry	Group	Offer price of the Companies					6th February 2017
				1/2/2017	2/2/2017	3/2/2017	4/2/2017	5/2/2017	
1	Tata Steel	Steel	Tata	594	595	596	594	595	593
2	JK Steel	Steel	JK	592	590	588	589	590	591
3	Essar Steel	Steel	Essar	591	592	593	594	595	596
4	Modi Steel	Steel	Modi	596	597	598	599	600	598
5	Nippon Steel	Steel	Nippon	598	596	597	598	599	597

Based on the above table, all the questions can be answered.

39. Modi Steel had the highest offer price of Rs.598 as on February 6th.

40. Tata Steel, JK Steel and Nippon Steel each had a price difference of Rs. 1 per share on 6th February as compared to 1st February.

41. As on 5th February, the highest price offers were from Modi Steel and Nippon Steel and therefore these two companies dropped out. That means the next highest bid was Rs. 595 which indicates a tie between Essar Steel and Tata Steel.

42. As on 4th February, only two companies had an offer price that is higher than Rs.595, which happened to be Modi Steel and Nippon Steel. Therefore the remaining 3 companies were not eligible for further participation.

For questions 43 to 46:

Let the total number of dialed calls by all the Inspectors, Constables and Drivers be x, y and z respectively.

By the problem, total number of dialed calls from all the Patrolling jeeps = 30.

Thus, $x + y + z = 30$…(i)

Total number of calls received by all the Patrolling jeeps = 82.

$\Rightarrow 4x + 2y + z = 82$…(ii)

Solving (i) and (ii), we get $3x + y = 52$.

Thus, the following cases are possible:

Cases	Possible values			Total
	x	y	z	
1	11	19	0	30
2	12	16	2	30
3	13	13	4	30
4	14	10	6	30
5	15	7	8	30
6	16	4	10	30
7	17	1	12	30

43. By the question, jeep number 2 received calls from jeep numbers 1, 4 and 9.

Assuming that no calls made from jeep numbers 1 and 4 were by a driver, it can be observed that jeep 7 could have received calls only from two jeeps viz. jeep 1 and jeep 4.

44. From the table above, the maximum possible number of calls that can be made by the Constables is 19.

45. By the information given in the question only Case 3 and Case 4 are possible. Thus, minimum possible number of calls that can be made by the Drivers is 4.

46. By the information given in the question only Case 3 and Case 4 are possible. Thus, maximum possible number of calls that can be made by the Drivers is 6.

47. From the given data, it can be observed that the maximum increase in the closing stock price on a day over any of the preceding days was for SBI and it was equal to2383 – 2183 = 200.

48. The closing stock price of ICICI bank recorded the maximum increase in its value over the previous day on 15th May, 2013 and it was equal to 1191 – 1147 = 44.

49. PNB recorded the maximum percentage increase in its closing stock price during the given period and it was equal to $\left(\frac{822-740}{740}\right)\times 100 = 11.08\%$.

50. Let the GDP of Belgium be y Euros.

$\therefore y \times \frac{4.8}{100} \times 1.5 = x \Rightarrow y = \frac{100}{7.2}x$

Hence, the debt (in Euros) of Belgium

$= \frac{100.8}{100} \times \frac{100}{7.2}x = 14x.$

51. Two countries, viz. Denmark and Finland, were rated AAA.

52. Let the GDP (in Euros) of Italy be x.

Therefore, the GDP (in Euros) of Finland = 1.5x.

The fiscal-deficit of:

Italy = 0.051x

Finland = 0.034 × 1.5x = 0.051x.

Hence, the required percentage = 0.

53. In the years 2014, 2015, 2016 and 2017, the total numbers of candidates who got selected as officers were 4479, 5062, 4160 and 3728 respectively.

In 2014, the total number of candidates not selected = 559232 – 4479 = 554753. Let's assume that all 554753 candidates appear for CEE again – 550593 in 2015 and 4160 in 2016.

The number of fresh candidates in 2015 = 593456 – 550593 = 42863. Let's assume that all 5062 selections in 2015 happen from among the 550593 reappearing candidates. This way, all 42863 fresh candidates from 2015 become eligible to reappear and, let's assume, that they do so in 2017.

The number of fresh candidates in 2016 = 642965 – 4160 = 638805. Let's assume that all 4160 candidates selected in 2016 were those who had earlier appeared in 2014. This way, all 638805 fresh candidates from 2016 become eligible to reappear and, let's assume, that they do so in 2017.

Hence, the total number of candidates who appeared for the exam at least twice during the given period = 550593 + 4160 + 42863 + 638805 = 1236421.

Alternate method:

We can also say, directly by the method given above, that the answer would be 593456 + 642965 = 1236421.

54. As we do not have any information about the number of attempts taken by selected candidates in getting through, we are not in a position to determine this.

55. Only 2 banks - PSB and CB - satisfy the given criterion.

For questions 56 to 59: The given information can be tabulated as shown below.

Family	Number of members	Production (in kg)		Per head consumption (in kg)		Total consumption (in kg)		Surplus (in kg)		
		Wheat	Rice	Wheat	Rice	Wheat	Rice	Wheat	Rice	Total
Sharma's	6	600	520	91.2	83.2	547.2	499.2	52.8	20.8	73.6
Sen's	4	440	260	100.8	60	403.2	240	36.8	20	56.8
Srivastava's	7	800	560	108.4	78.4	758.8	548.8	41.2	11.2	52.4
Sehgal's	8	600	640	74.4	75.2	595.2	601.6	4.8	38.4	43.2
Srinivasan's	5	480	500	80	96.8	400	484	80	16	96
Suri's	7	520	460	63.2	64	442.4	448	77.6	12	89.6

56. There were three families whose surplus of Wheat and Rice together was more than 73.5 and those families were Sharma's Srinivasan's and Suri's.

57. The required reduction = 74.4 – (600 – 68)/8 = 7.9 kg.

58. The required surplus = 73.6 + 56.8 + 52.4 + 43.2 + 96 + 89.6 = 411.6 kg.

59. Price of rice per kg is double as that of wheat. Sen's and Sehgal's family earned more amount by selling the surplus of rice.

For questions 60 to 63:

	Total Capacity (n MW units)	Units Sold (In MW units)
A	8,500	7,565
B	6,250	5,437.50
C	10,000	9,000
D	8,500	7,225
E	9,500	7,600

60. Total capacity of India = $6{,}250 \times \frac{100}{12.5}$

= 50,000 MW units

Thermal capacity of India = 95% of total capacity

= 47,500 MW units

Total capacity of these five power plants = 42,750 MW units

Required percentage = $\frac{42{,}750}{47{,}500} \times 100 = 90\%$.

61. The correct order is C > E > A > D > B

62. Profitability can be compared by comparing the ratio of total revenue to total cost.

Profitability for A = $\frac{(89\% \text{ of TC}) \times 3.4}{(93\% \text{ of TC}) \times 2.1} = \frac{89 \times 3.4}{93 \times 2.1}$

= 1.549.

where TC is the total capacity of that power plant.

Same values of others are

B → 1.406, C → 1.4108

D → 1.2617, E → 1.257

So, B has the third highest ratio and hence third highest profitability.

63. Only statement 'b' is true.

64. Laxman has scored 3,000 runs and has taken 60 catches. He has not taken any wickets. If we assume that he has scored all his runs in centuries, then the maximum points earned by him will be 4680 (Runs = 3,000, Catches = 180, Centuries = 30 × 50 = 1,500).

Hence, his grade is IV.

65. In order to minimize the number of centuries scored by Ganguly, the total number of runs scored by Tendulkar has to be the least possible i.e. 10,001 and the number of catches and five wicket-haul taken by Ganguly have to be the maximum possible.

Minimum number of points of Tendulkar

= 10,001 + 80 × 20 + 80 × 3 + 25 × 50 + 5 × 50 = 13,341

The maximum number of catches taken by Ganguly can be 119, as the number of catches taken by Dravid, who has taken the maximum number of catches, is 120, and that of five wicket-haul can be 10.

Maximum number of points of Ganguly with zero centuries

= 10,000 + 50 × 20 + 119 × 3 + 10 × 50 = 11,857

As the total number of points of Ganguly is more than that of Tendulkar, the total number of points of Ganguly has to be at least 13,342.

The additional points required for Ganguly i.e. (13,342 – 11,857) = 1485 will come in the form of bonus point through centuries. As each century fetches 50 points, to earn 1485 points the number of centuries required is 30.

66. Maximum number of points of Laxman = 3000 + 30 × 50 + 60 × 3 = 4680.

Therefore, Laxman is in grade IV.

The other players whose total points could be less than 5000 are Sehwag and Zaheer.

Hence, a maximum of three players could be in grade IV.

67. Sehwag could score a maximum of 7,999 runs and has taken 50 catches. He has taken 40 wickets and taken 4 five wicket hauls. He has scored 10 centuries.

The maximum points that he could have = 9649

(Runs = 7,999, Catches = 150, Centuries = 500, Wickets = 800, 5 wicket haul = 200)

Hence, he cannot be in grade II.

PRACTICE EXERCISE – 2

1. The following table illustrates the production of finished product from 10 am to 3 pm:

Time	Number of products
10 – 11:00	1
11:00 – 12:00	1
12:00 – 1:00	4
1:00 – 2:00	2
2:00 – 3:00	5
	13

Hence, the required answer is 13.

2. The following will be the structure of flow internally:

	E	D	C	B	A	Output
10:00	2	6	4	1	1	
11:00	6	②	6	4	1	1

Since work-capacity of D is not adequate at 11:00 to process this, D is the answer.

3. By using the same logic used in the previous questions, the required answer comes out to be 23.

4. By using the same logic used in the previous questions, the required answer comes out to be 8.

5. One year only in 2014.

6. The least marks was constituted by modern maths. The next least one was analogies.

7. Marks per question is not given.

Hence total number of questions cannot be determined.

8. Number of topics that experienced positive growth rate in 2000 over the previous year = 5 (analogies, data sufficiency, mathematical reasoning, modern maths, sentence correction).

Each one of them had a negative growth rate in 2015.

9. Midsize cars makes 20% of Hyundai sales and SUV makes 10% of this, so sales of Hyundai SUV is 3000. Hence, total SUV sales is 20000.

These 5 brands make up to 82% of SUV sale so if the rest of 18% sale is by a single brand then it has the second highest share.

10. Let the total Honda sale be x

Sales of Honda Sedan will be 0.4x

Sales of Honda midsize will be 0.25x

In midsize, Honda share is 33.33%, hence total midsize sale will be 0.75x

So, required ratio is 0.4x : 0.75x = 8 : 15.

11. In Sedan category, 5% of total sales is made by others which can be further divided also.

Hence, we do not know the share of the smallest brand in Sedan category.

12. Since, we do not know the price of a car of any category for any of the brand. Hence, the revenues cannot be compared.

13. In state P, male population and female population is 375 lakhs and 345 lakhs respectively; urban population and rural population is 432 lakhs and 288 lakhs respectively.

Literacy rate among urban male will be least under the conditions shown below.

Urban region (432 lakh)

275 lakh men — 157 lakh women literate

15 lakh literate — 260 lakh illiterate

Rural region (288 lakh)

188 lakh 100 lakh

literate womenilliterate men

So the number of literate women in urban area would be 157 lakhs and remaining 15 lakhs literates are male. Which means 260 urban males are illiterate.

Hence, the literacy rate among urban male

$$= \frac{15}{275} \times 100 = 5.45\%.$$

14. In state P, 60% population is urban. So even if whole literate population i.e. 50% live in urban area, 10% urban population will still remain illiterate.

In state Q, 30% population is urban which can all be literate because 55% population is literate.

Similarly, it is true for R and S but not for T.

15. Since we do not know the breakup of literate people between rural and urban areas for any state, data is insufficient to answer this question.

16. Literacy rate of rural area in each state = (0.3 × (literacy rate)/ % of rural population) × 100%

Which will be lowest for state S.

17. By observation, options (c) and (d) can be eliminated. Thus compare only A and B.

Collection at station A = 15 × 30 + 18 × 35 + 16 × 15 = Rs. 1320.

Collection at station B = 15 × 25 + 8 × 42 + 20 × 16 = 375 + 336 + 320 = Rs. 1031.

18. Collection on (BC + CD + DC + CB)
= 42 × 8 + 5 × 13 + 14 × 13 + 12 × 8
= 336 + 65 + 182 + 96 = Rs. 679.

19. $\text{Distance} = \dfrac{\text{fare per passenger}}{\text{fare per passenger per km}}$

$BD = \dfrac{20}{0.60} = 33.3$

$DA = \dfrac{16}{0.40} = 40.0$

$AC = \dfrac{18}{0.40} = 45.0$

⇒ Total distance is 118 km approximately.

20. From the question, 31st July are a Sunday.

Thus, 1st September are a Thursday.

∴ 4th, 11th, 18th and 25th September was Sunday.

Thus, the inspector must have travelled to the villages on (30 – 4)
= 26 days.

His expenses for the first 24 days
= 16(18 + 8 + 13) = Rs. 624.

∴ Total expenses in September 1999
= Rs. [624 + 2 (8 + 13)] = Rs. 666.

21. Reliance Growth, Birla Dividend Yield Plus and Templeton India Growth do not fit. Hence, the required number of companies is 7.

22. The required scheme was Reliance Growth.

23. Templeton India Growth was 2nd best and it was 0.52.

24. The schemes with bottom two values of the required ratio are HSBC Equity (0.09) and Franklin India Blue-chip (0.14).

For questions 25 to 28:

The possible values of A, B, C and D for different values of W, X, Y and Z respectively are –

Alloy 1 W	Alloy 1 A	Alloy 2 X	Alloy 2 B	Alloy 3 Y	Alloy 3 C	Alloy 3 Z	Alloy 3 D
3	102	2	70	7	96	4	110
4	105	4	78	9	100	10	118
6	110	8	90	12	105	12	120
8	114	14	102			20	126
12	120	16	105				

25. B can take 5 values.

26. Statements (ii) and (iii) are true.

27. If 18kg of each are melted together then the price of the new alloy will be Rs. 90/kg. If 20kg of each are melted together then the price of the new alloy will be Rs. 96/kg. If 24kg of each are melted together then the price of the new alloy will be Rs. 105/kg. So all of these values are possible.

28. 102 and 120 are possible values.

For questions 29 to 32:

Let the number of students who joined school in 2011 be "x". So 125 – x students failed in class V in 2010 and 100 – (125 – x) = x – 25 students of class V passed in 2010. Similarly values for each year will be –

Class	Students in the year 2016	Students who failed in 2016 in same class	Students who passed in 2016 in previous class	Students in the year 2017
V	100	125 – x	x (new joinees)	125
VI	75	107 – x	x – 25	82
VII	68	97 – x	x – 32	65
VIII	60	86 – x	x – 29	57
IX	45	76 – x	x – 26	50
X	34	78 – x	x – 31	47

Number of students who passed in class X will be 34 – (78 – x) = (x – 44)

So minimum value of x will be 44 because x – 44 ≥ 0.

29. Maximum possible number of students who joined the school in 2017 will be 76 because 76 – x ≥ 0.

30. The minimum and maximum number of students from class VI who passed in 2016 is 12 & 44 respectively and hence the corresponding pass percentages will lie between 16% and 58.66%.

31. This means (x – 32) > (76 – x) ⇒ x > 54. So lowest pass percentage for class VIII will be –
(55 – 26)/60 ×100% = 48.33%.

32. If pass percentage in class IX is 60% that means 27 students passed and x = 58. So pass percentage in class V will be (58 – 25)/100 × 100% = 33%.

For questions 33 to 36:

CGPA of all the students are as follows:

Gopal = 57/15 = 3.8

Nitin = 52/15 = 3.47

Arihant = 51/15 = 3.4

Gaurav = 39/15 = 2.6

Prabhakar = 39/15 = 2.6

Saurabh = 38/15 = 2.53

33. Gaurav and Prabhakar got the same CGPA.

34. Gopal got the highest CGPA.

35. Nitin will get highest CGPA with minimum increase if he gets 5 more marks in Digital systems and 3 more marks in Power electronics, making it 8 in total.

Arihant will get the highest CGPA with minimum increase in marks if he gets 2 more marks in Digital systems and 2 more marks in Power electronics, making it 4 in total.

For others the minimum marks needed to have highest CGPA will be much more than these values.

36. The CGPA of Gaurav was 2.6.

For questions 37 to 40:

Variety	Number of coins
Platinum	4
Gold	12
Silver	16
Bronze	16
Copper	24
Aluminium	8

37. Difference will be maximum when all the silver and bronze coins are of maximum possible denomination, i.e 95ps & 70Ps respectively and platinum and gold coins are of minimum possible denomination i.e 225Ps & 25Ps respectively.

$\therefore$ Difference = (16 × 95 + 16 × 70) – (4 × 225 + 12 × 100) = 540ps.

38. Total amount with Rahul in Copper coins is 960ps and the denominations possible are 25, 30, 35, 40 & 45. To maximise the number of 45ps coins

Either, (i) have only one coin of each except 25ps & 45ps. Let the number of 25ps coins be "a" and number of 45ps coins be "d".

So, 25a + 30×1 + 35 × 1 + 40 × 1 + 45 × d = 960 ; 5a + 9d = 171

Maximum possible value of 'd' is 14

Or, (ii) have only one coin of each except 25ps, 30ps & 45ps. Let the number of 30ps coins be 'b'.

Hence, d = 24 – (2 + a + b) = 22 – a – b; and we have to minimize (a + b)

So, 25a + 30b + 35 + 40 + 45(22– a – b = 960; 4a + 3b = 21

(a + b) will be minimum when a = 3 & b = 3 and hence d = 16.

39. Rahul will have the maximum possible amount when he will have coins of highest possible denominations of each variety. Let the total amount with him in that case be T.

T(in Rs) = 4 × 5 + 12 × 2 + 16 × 0.75 + 16 × 0.50 + 24 × 0.25 = Rs. 70.

40. He can have 24 copper coins and 16 bronze coins (of 50ps each).

41.

Business	Salary (Rs. in lakhs)	Total cost (Rs. in lakhs)
S I	5.0	15.4
S E	15.0	79.5
H I	6.0	27.6
H E	32.0	96.0

So the salary as a percentage of total cost was the least for SE.

42. Net decrease in cost = Net increment in the margin = (20000 – 15000) × 25 = Rs. 1.25 lakh

Earlier net margin = Rs. 4.6 lakh

Required percentage = $\frac{1.25}{4.6} \times 100 \approx 27.17\%$.

43. Nothing is given said about the other costs. Hence, the question cannot be answered.

44. Cost of hardware export = Rs. $2\left(1-\frac{52}{100}\right)$ crore

= Rs. 0.96 crore

Total salary = Rs. 80000 × 40 = Rs. 0.32 crore

Cost of hardware increases by 15% that is by Rs. 0.144 crore.

So salary should be reduced by Rs. 0.144 crore.

$\therefore$ Percentage by which the salary should be reduced is $\frac{0.144}{0.32} \times 100 = 45\%$.

For questions 45 to 48:

All the deliveries made in November were for bookings done in September, and one-fifth of total booking in September, that is 272, were delivered in October. Hence remaining 323 were delivered in the same month. Similarly we can find for the remaining months.

Months \ Booking	Premium	Normal	Discounted
April	0	617	623
May	271	212	577
June	118	164	538
July	183	180	537
August	362	220	518
September	323	272	765
October	0	0	0
November	0	0	0

45. Premium is 2.5 times the discount, so the month for which premium bookings is more than 0.4 times the number of discount bookings, premium collected will be more than the discount given. And this is true for months of May, August and September.

46. This value is highest for the month of August

47. 538 orange mobiles booked in June were delivered in August.

48. Required month is August.

For questions 49 to 52:

Allocation of shops to the areas is as follows –

Andheri – Sh2, Sh6, Sh7

CP – Sh4,Sh9

NFC – Sh3, Sh5

Gurgaon – Sh1, Sh8,Sh10

49. Sh7 is located in Andheri.

50. Sh9 is not located in Andheri.

51. Two shops are located in CP.

52. Sh1 and Sh8 are located in Gurgaon.

53. The roaming rental is Rs.50 for Airtel and Rs.15 for Idea for 10 days. A total of 80 calls are received or made during these 10 days. Given a call difference of Re. 0.50 between Airtel and Idea, the additional call charges for Idea is Rs. (80 × 0.5) i.e. Rs. 40. Hence Airtel is cheaper by Rs. 5 for the roaming period.

54. Rent plus CLIP is lowest for Idea among the three service providers.

55. Budget = Rs. 1,500.

Subtracting the rental and CLIP charges, the available balance for the three service providers is given in the table below:

Airtel	Hutch	Idea
1300	1250	1325

Since the total charges of one local CDMA call, one local GSM call and one landline call put together for Idea, Airtel and Vodafone is Rs. 5.5, Rs. 5.5 and Rs. 7 respectively and the amount left after rental and CLIP charges is the maximum for Idea, the plan offered by Idea would be the best choice for him.

56. In order to maximize the number of calls received during 10 days while on roaming, he should received as many calls as he can at an expense of Rs. 75.

∴ Number of calls which he can receive in 10 days

$$= \frac{75}{2.5} = 30.$$

⇒ Number of call which he can receive everyday

$$= \frac{30}{10} = 3.$$

Hence, Ram can receive a maximum of 3 calls everyday of 1 minute each while ensuring his roaming bill does not exceed Rs. 75.

For questions 57 to 60:

The given information can be tabulated as:

	Zinc	Tin	Lead	Copper	Nickel
A	10%	40%	(x) %	(40 – x)%	10%
B	25%	15%	50%	5%	5%
C	15%	(y) %	20%	(30 – y)%	35%
D	20%	25%	15%	30%	10%
E	5%	50%	25%	5%	15%
F	40%	10%	5%	30%	15%

57. In alloy G, the percentage of:

$$\text{Tin} = \left(2 \times \frac{40}{6} + 1 \times \frac{15}{6} + 3 \times \frac{y}{6}\right) = \frac{3y + 95}{6}$$

$$\text{Lead} = \frac{2x + 110}{6}$$

$$\text{Copper} = \frac{175 - 2x - 3y}{6}$$

Now, $(3y + 95) = (2x + 110) = (175 - 2x - 3y)$

$$\Rightarrow x = \frac{25}{3} \text{ and } y = \frac{95}{9}$$

Therefore, the percentage of copper in alloy A

$$= (40 - x) = \left(40 - \frac{25}{3}\right) = \frac{95}{3}.$$

58. There are two possible ways in which the alloy X can be formed. The possible combinations are (E and F) and (B and C).

59. The percentage of lead in A, E and F is $\frac{25}{3}$%, 25% and 5% respectively.

By checking options:

Option (1): Percentage of lead in the mixture

$$= \frac{1}{6}\left(4 \times \frac{25}{3} + 1 \times 25 + 1 \times 5\right) = \frac{95}{9}\% < 12\%$$

Option (2): Percentage of lead in the mixture

$$= \frac{1}{6}\left(2 \times \frac{25}{3} + 1 \times 25 + 3 \times 5\right) = \frac{85}{9}\% < 12\%$$

Option (3): Percentage of lead in the mixture

$$= \frac{1}{6}\left(1 \times \frac{25}{3} + 2 \times 25 + 3 \times 5\right) = \frac{110}{9}\% > 12\%$$

Option (4): Percentage of lead in the mixture

$$= \frac{1}{7}\left(1 \times \frac{25}{3} + 2 \times 25 + 4 \times 5\right) = \frac{235}{21}\% < 12\%$$

Hence, option (3) is the correct answer.

60. Since the percentage of nickel in alloy B and alloy Z is 5% and 8.25% respectively, in order to maximize the percentage of B in Z, we need to choose alloy in which the percentage of nickel is greater than 8.25% and also the maximum among the given alloys. So, we need to choose alloy C.

Let the percentage of alloy B in alloy Z be 'x'%.

$\therefore$ 5x + 35(1 – x) = 8.25 $\Rightarrow$ x = 89.16%

For questions 61 to 64: The following table can be made:

Name	Population (in lakh)	Male (in lakh)	Female (in lakh)	Total Literate (in lakh)	Literate Males (in lakh)	Literate females (in lakh)
Bihar	570	342	228	399	200	199
Odisha	360	200	160	288	168	120
UP	605	385	220	363	183	180
Jharkhand	340	180	160	221	126	95
Assam	425	238	187	357	190	167
MP	510	300	210	459	290	169
Kerala	240	150	90	228	148	80
Karnataka	320	180	140	272	170	102

61. The average of literate males (in lakhs) across 8 states

$$= \frac{200 + 168 + 183 + 126 + 190 + 290 + 148 + 170}{8} \approx 184.$$

62. The total number of illiterate people = 783

Total population = 3370

Required percentage = $\frac{783}{3370} \times 100 \approx 23.23.$

63. There were six such states that had female literacy rate of at least 75% and those states were Bihar, Odisha, UP, Assam, Kerala and MP.

64. Total number of males in the age group $25 < x \leq 40$

$= 1975 \times \frac{20}{100}$

Total number of females in the age group $25 < x \leq 40$

$= 1395 \times \frac{20}{100}$

Required percentage = $\frac{(1975 - 1395) \times \frac{20}{100}}{1395 \times \frac{20}{100}}$

= 41.58%.

Line Graph

SOLVED EXAMPLES

1.

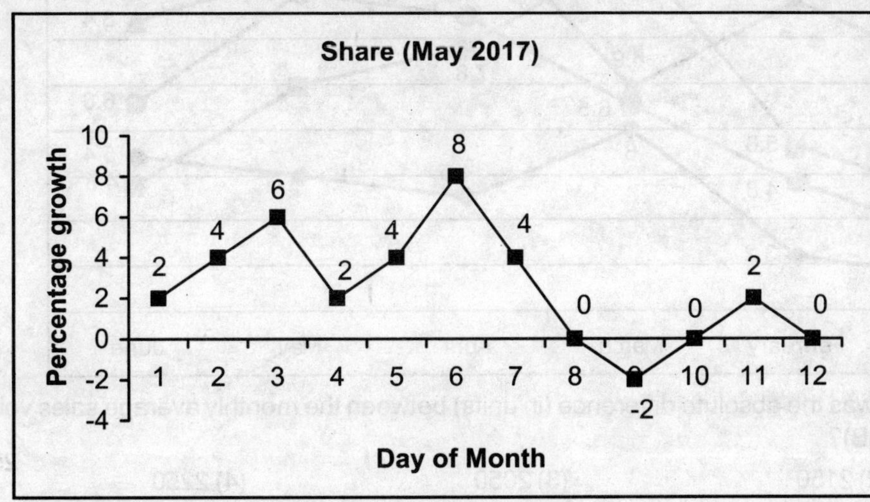

The above graph represents the percentage growth in the value of a share in a stock market over a period of 12 days. Its value on day 0, the day on 7which it was issued, was Rs.30. Which of the following statements is definitely true?

(1) The maximum value of the share was on day 6.

(2) The minimum value of the share was on day 9.

(3) The value of share on day 6 was greater than that on day 9.

(4) The maximum and the minimum value of share was on day 8 (or day 7) and day 0 respectively.

For example 1:

1. 4 The percentage growth in the value of the share was maximum on day 6.

This does not mean that the absolute value of the stock is maximum on day 6.

On day 7, the value of stock was 4% greater than that on day 6.

Hence, option (1) is incorrect.

Even though the value of the stock witnessed a decrease of 2% on day 9, the value of the stock was still more than that on day 0.

Hence, option (2) is incorrect.

Suppose, the value of the stock on day 6 was 'a', then the value of the stock on day 9 will be (1.04 × 0.98)a (approx 1.01a).

Hence, option (3) is incorrect.

The maximum value of the stock was on day 7 or day 8. This is because the value of the stock has witnessed a increase for 7 consecutive days.

The minimum value of the stock was on day 0.

2.2 LINE GRAPH

Directions for examples 2 to 4: Answer the questions on the basis of the information given below.

Slipkart is the only online retail store that sells mobiles of Fotorola in India. Fotorola launched four different models – Foto E, Foto G (8GB), Foto G (16GB) and Foto X – in India in January 2017. The line graph given below shows the online sales volume (in 000's) of the four mobiles phones in India in the last 6 months.

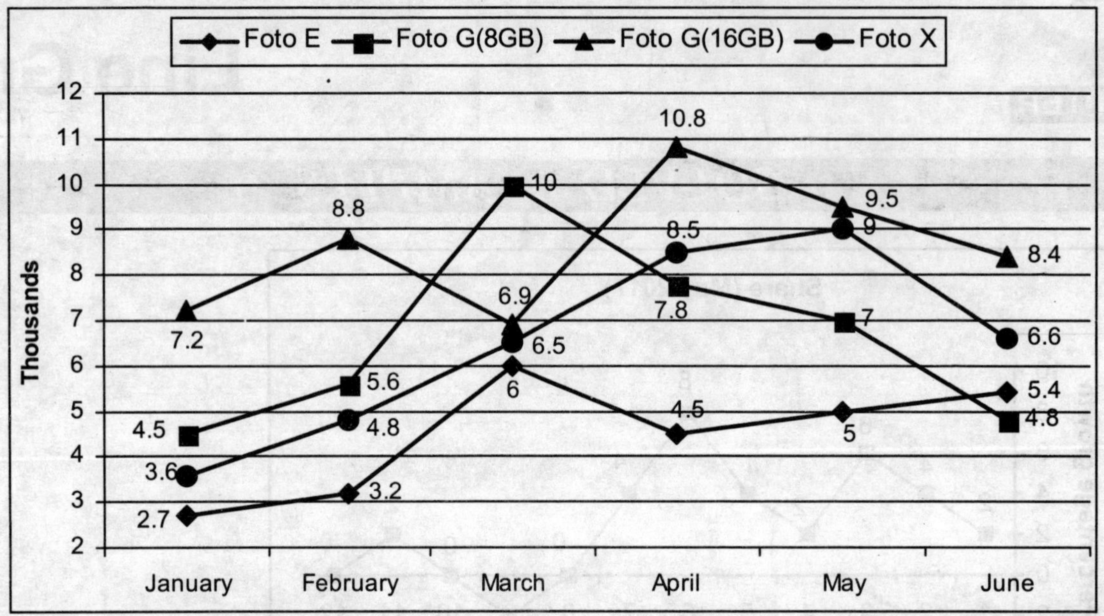

2. During the given period, what was the absolute difference (in units) between the monthly average sales volume of Foto E and that of Foto G (8GB)?

(1) 4300 (2) 2150 (3) 2050 (4) 2250

3. In 2017, if the simple average growth rate of Foto X from July to December is estimated to be the same as that from January to June and the estimated sales of Foto X in July is the same as that in June, find the estimated sales volumes (in units) of Foto X in December.

(1) 12100 (2) 9600 (3) 11550 (4) Cannot be determined

4. What was the maximum growth rate in the sales volume of any mobile in any month over that of the previous month?

(1) 87.5% (2) 56.5% (3) 78.57% (4) 85.71%

For examples 2 to 4:

2. b During the given period, the average monthly sales of: Foto E

$$= \frac{2700 + 3200 + 6000 + 4500 + 5000 + 5400}{6} = \frac{26800}{6}$$

$$\text{Foto G (8GB)} = \frac{4500 + 5600 + 10000 + 7800 + 7000 + 4800}{6} = \frac{39700}{6}$$

$$\text{Hence, the difference} = \frac{39700}{6} - \frac{26800}{6} = \frac{12900}{6} = 2150 \text{ units.}$$

3. 1 The growth in the sale of Foto X from January to June = 6600 – 3600 = 3000 units.

$$\therefore \text{ Percentage growth} = \frac{3000}{3600} \times 100 = \frac{250}{3}\%$$

$$\therefore \text{ Sales in December} = 6600 + \frac{250}{3}\% \text{ of } 6600 = 12{,}100 \text{ units.}$$

4. 1 The maximum growth was shown by Foto E from the month of February to March and it was equal to

$$\frac{6000 - 3200}{3200} \times 100 = 87.5\%.$$

Directions for examples 5 and 6: Answer the questions on the basis of the information given below.

The graphs below show the runs scored and the wicket taken by a famous all rounder named Puneet in a recently concluded bilateral ODI series, consisting of 5 matches, between Industan and Falistan. It is also known that he participated in all the five matches of the series.

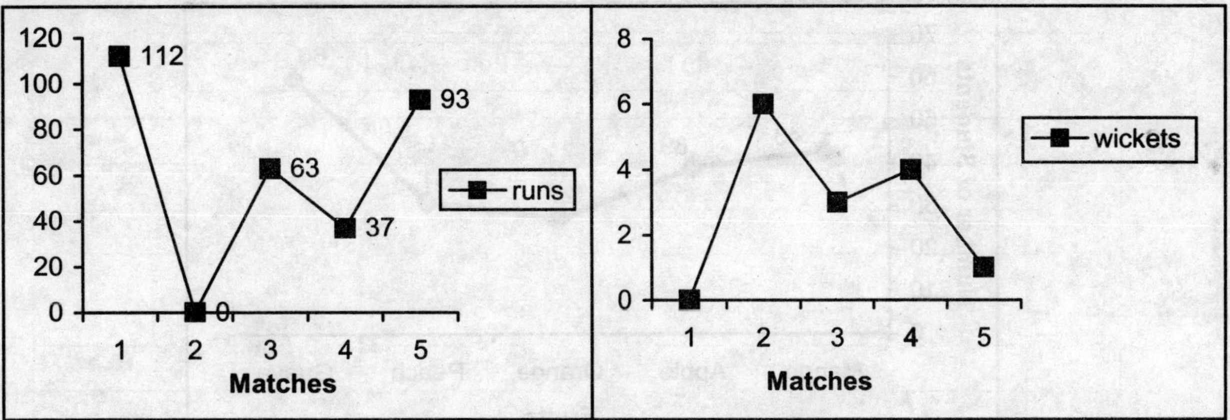

It is also known that in a point-system, every wicket is awarded 10 points and for the first 20 runs the batsman gets 2 points. Thereafter, every 10 runs earn 4 points to the batsman.

$$\text{Batting average} = \frac{\text{Total runs scored}}{\text{Total number of times he was out}}$$

5. In the series, if the batting average of Puneet was more than 75 and less than 150, how many times did he remain not out?

(1) 1 (2) 2

(3) Either (1) or (2) (4) Cannot be determined

6. In the series, if Puneet gave away 16.71 runs for every wicket that he took, what was the average number of runs given by him per match?

(1) 46.8 (2) 43.5

(3) 45.2 (4) 44.7

For examples 5 and 6:

5. 3 Total runs scored by Puneet in the tournament = 305

Number of times Puneet can be out = 1, 2, 3, 4 or 5

$\therefore$ Possible batting averages= $\frac{305}{1}, \frac{305}{2}, \frac{305}{3}, \frac{305}{4}$ or $\frac{305}{5}$ = 305, 152.5, 101.66, 76.25 or 61

So, the averages in the given range are 101.66 and 76.25, when he was out for 3 and 4 times respectively. Hence, he can be not out either 1 or 2 times.

6. 1 Total wickets taken by Puneet in the series = 14

Hence total runs given by Puneet = (16.71 × 14)

So, runs given per match = $\frac{16.71 \times 14}{5} \approx 47.$

2.4 LINE GRAPH

Directions for examples 7 to 11: Answer the questions on the basis of the information given below.

In a class of 200 students, 200 fruits, belonging to five different varieties namely Mango, Apple, Orange, Peach and Guava, were distributed such that each student got exactly 1 fruit. The following line graph provides information about the number of students who received a mango, an apple, an orange, a peach and a guava.

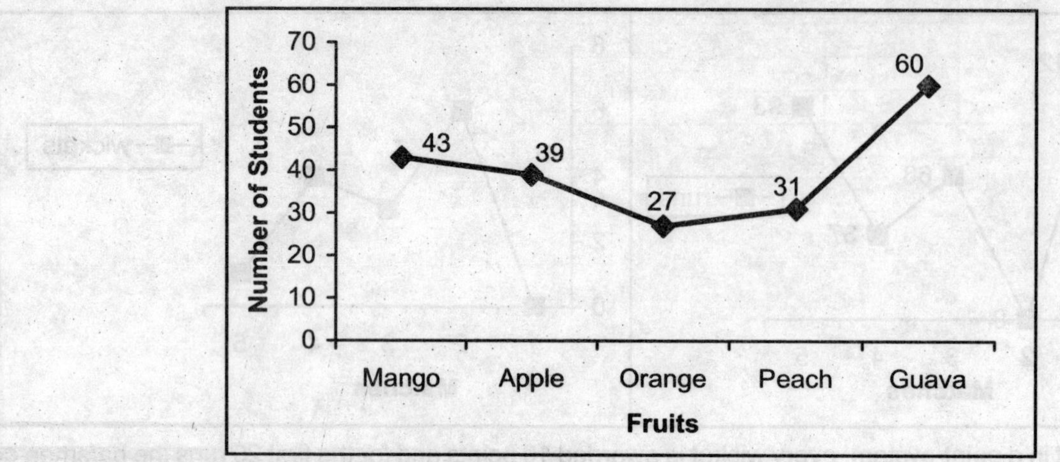

The students exchanged the fruits among themselves and after the completion of exchanges, it was noted that no child had the same variety of fruit that he/she had earlier, and each student has exactly one fruit. After the completion of exchanges, the following observations were made:

- Out of the students who initially had a mango, the number of students who ended up with an apple, orange, peach and guava was 8, 11, 13 and 11 respectively.
- Out of the students who initially had an orange, the number of students who ended up with a mango and an apple was 3 and 16 respectively.
- Out of the students who initially had a peach, the number of students who ended up with a mango was 8.
- Out of the students who initially had a guava, the number of students who ended up with a peach was also 8.

7. After the completion of exchanges, out of the students who initially had a guava, at least how many students must have a mango eventually?

(1) 18 (2) 19 (3) 20 (4) 21

8. After the completion of exchanges, if out of the students who initially had an apple, the number of students who ended up with a guava was the maximum possible, then at most how many of those student who had an orange after exchanges had a guava initially?

(1) 16 (2) 17 (3) 18 (4) 19

9. After the completion of exchanges, if out of the students who initially had an apple, 7 have an orange, then, what was the maximum number of students who initially had a guava and end up with an orange?

(1) 9 (2) 8 (3) 10 (4) 6

10. Out of the students who initially had an apple, what was the maximum number of students who ended up with either a mango or an orange after the exchange?

(1) 10 (2) 11 (3) 8 (4) 7

11. If out of the students who initially had a peach, 22 end up with a guava after the exchange, and out of the students who initially had an apple 14 end up with a guava, then what was the number of students who initially had an orange and ended up with a guava?

(1) 13 (2) 15 (3) 10 (4) Data inconsistent

For examples 7 to 11:

	Mango	Apple	Orange	Peach	Guava	Total
Mango	0	8	11	13	11	**43**
Apple	w	0	z	10 – y	29+y–w–z	**39**
Orange	3	16	0	y	8 – y	**27**
Peach	8	x	11–w–z–x	0	12 + w + z	**31**
Guava	32 – w	15 – x	5 + w + x	8	0	**60**
Total	**43**	**39**	**27**	**31**	**60**	

From the table we get the following inequalities:

$0 \le w \le 11$

$0 \le x \le 11$

$0 \le y \le 8$

$0 \le z \le 11$

$x + w + z \le 11$

$w + z - y \le 29$

7. 4 From the above table, out of the students that originally had a guava, the number of students now having a Mango is '32 – w'. Maximum possible value of w is 11.

Therefore minimum possible value of $32 - w = 32 - 11 = 21$.

8. 1 Out of the students that originally had apple, the number of students now having a guava is $29 + y - w - z$.

Maximum possible value of $29 + y - w - z$ is 37 when $y = 8$, $w = z = 0$.

Out of the students that now have an orange, the number of students that originally had a guava is $5 + w + x$.

Maximum possible value of $5 + w + x$ is 16, i.e. at $x = 11$(maximum possible value of $x = 15$).

9. 1 By the question, $z = 7$.

Required to find:

Maximum value of $5 + w + x$

From the afore-mentioned inequalities $w + x + z \le 11$

$\Rightarrow w + x \le 4$

$\therefore$ Required value $= 5 + 4 = 9$.

10. 2 The question asks for maximum value of $w + z$

From the afore-mentioned inequalities $w + x + z \le 11$

If $x = 0$, then $w + z \le 11$.

Thus, maximum value of $w + z = 11$.

11. d By the question,

$12 + w + z = 22$ and $29 + y - w - z = 14$

$\Rightarrow w + z = 10$ and $w + z - y = 15$

$\Rightarrow y = -5$, which is not possible.

Thus, the data is inconsistent.

2.6 LINE GRAPH

Directions for examples 12 to 15: Answer the questions on the basis of the information given below.

The graph given below shows data related to milk production (in million tonnes) in India during the period from 1995-96 to 2016-17. (1 tonne = 1000 kg)

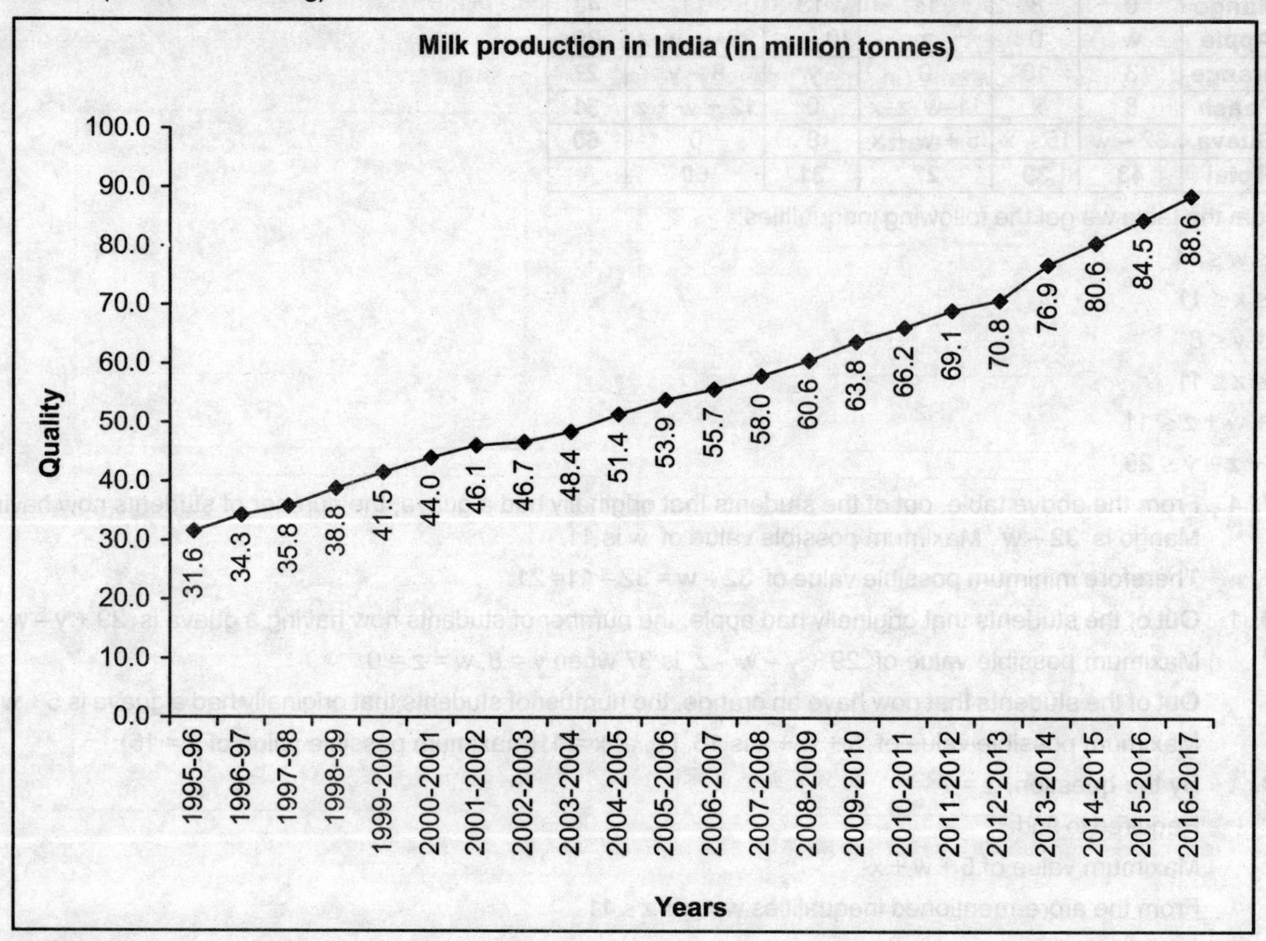

12. In 2008-09, India exported 22% of its total milk production and that was equal to 17% of the world milk export in that year. What was the world milk export (in million tonnes) in 2009-10?

(1) 78.42 (2) 7.842 (3) 784.2 (4) Cannot be determined

13. If price of milk in 2000-01 was Rs. 12 per kg, then the value of total milk produced in India in the same year was

(1) Rs. 52.8×10^{10} (2) Rs. 528×10^{10} (3) Rs. 5.28×10^{10} (4) Cannot be determined

14. Total milk production in India during the period from 1995-96 to 2001-02 as a percentage of total milk production in India during in the period from 1999-2000 to 2012-13 was closest to

(1) 35% (2) 54% (3) 62% (4) 13%

15. In how many years during the period from 1995-96 to 2012-13 was the production of milk in India more than 46.5 million tonnes?

(1) 11 years (2) 10 years (3) 12 years (4) Cannot be determined

For examples 12 to 15:

12. 4 Since the quantity of export of milk for the year 2009-10 is not known.
Hence, the answer cannot be determined.

13. 1 The required value = $44 \times 10^6 \times 10^3 \times 12$ = Rs. 52.8×10^{10}.

14. 1 Milk production in India from 1995-96 to 2001-02 = 272.1 million tonnes
Total production from 1999-2000 to 2012-13 = 776.3 million tonnes

$\therefore$ The required percentage change $= \frac{272.1}{776.2} \times 100 \approx 35.$

15. 1 By observation, the required number of years comes out to be 11.

PRACTICE EXERCISE – 1

Directions for questions 1 to 4: Answer the questions on the basis of the information given below.

Four athletes – Lewis, Pat, Carlos and Stan – competed in four races – R1, R2, R3 and R4. Each race was of 200m. The following graphs show time (in small) taken by the four athletes in the given races.

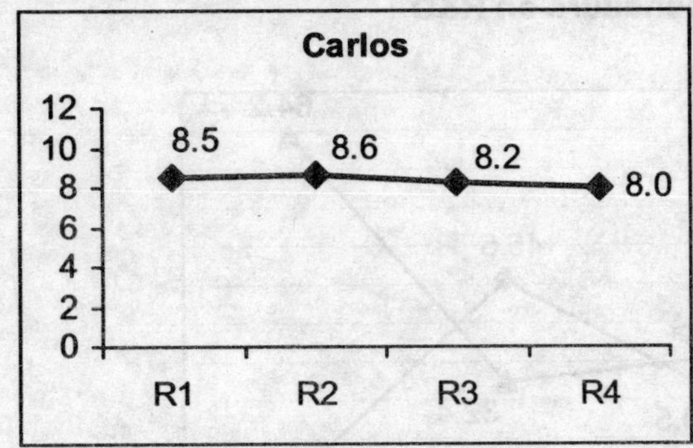

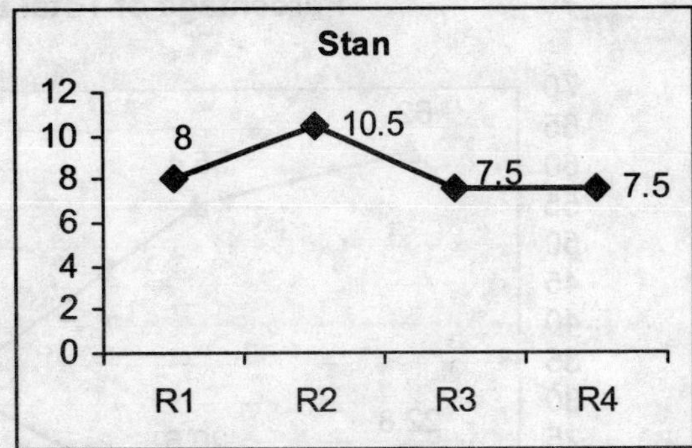

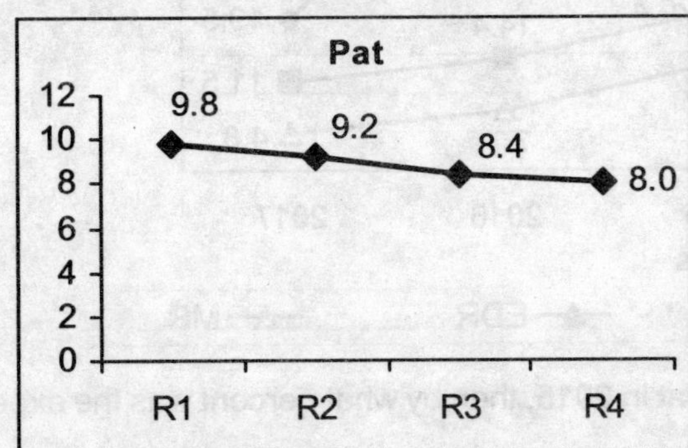

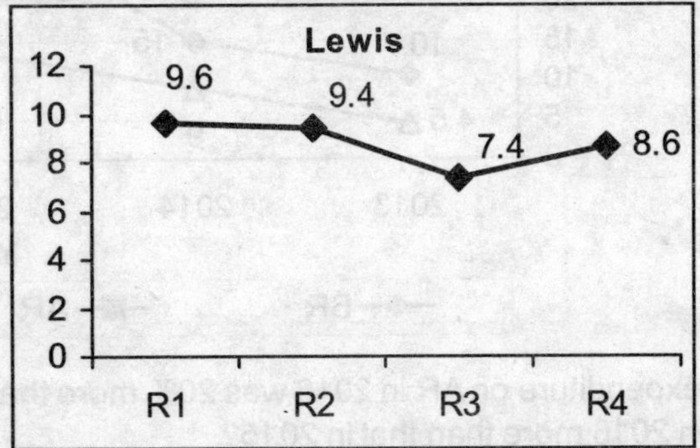

- Consistency Variation(CV) for an athlete = (Maximum time taken in a race out of the 4 races – Minimum time taken in a race out of the 4 races)/ Average time taken in the 4 races
- Performance Enhancement (PE) for an athlete = (Time taken in the first race – time taken in the last race)/ time taken in the first race
- Consistency Index (CI) is the inverse of CV

1. Who had the highest CI?

(1) Carlos (2) Pat (3) Stan (4) Lewis

2. Whose average of speeds for the four races was the highest?

(1) Pat (2) Lewis (3) Carlos (4) Stan

3. Who had the highest PE?

(1) Pat (2) Stan (3) Carlos (4) Lewis

4. Each of the four athletes was sponsored by a different company out of Nike, Puma, Rolex and Adidas. Their choice of athlete was based on their performance in the four races. Nike sponsored the athlete with the highest consistency index. Rolex sponsored the athlete whose least time taken in a race out of the four races was lower than that of any other athlete. Adidas sponsored the athlete whose average of speeds was the maximum in the four races. And the fourth athlete was sponsored by Puma. Who was sponsored by Puma?

(1) Carlos (2) Lewis (3) Stan (4) Pat

2.8 LINE GRAPH

Directions for questions 5 to 7: Answer the questions on the basis of the information given below.

The line graph given below shows the percentage break-up of the Gross Domestic Expenditure on four areas - Basic Research (BR), Applied Research (AR), Experimental Development Research (EDR) and Miscellaneous Research (MR) – of Research and Development (R&D) activity by a country in the period 2013-17.

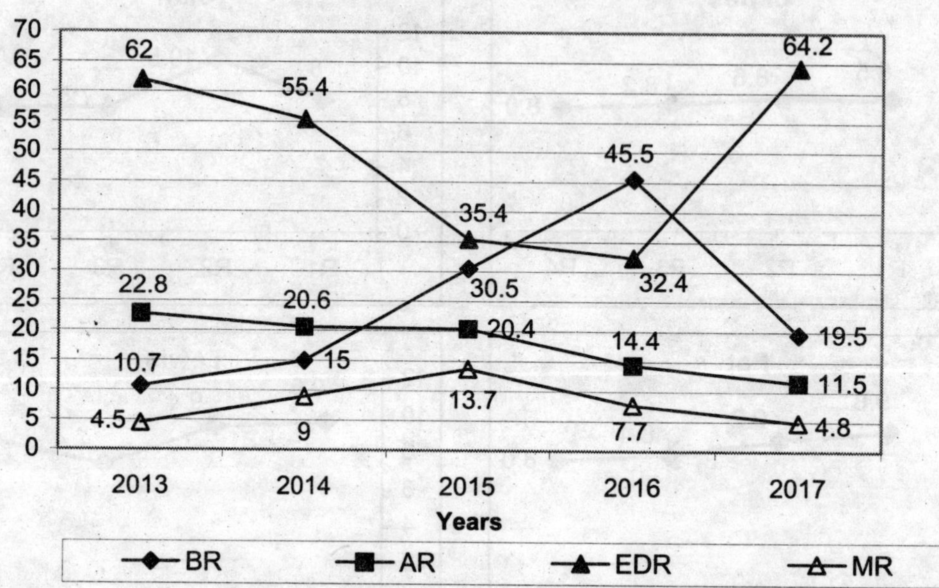

5. If the expenditure on AR in 2016 was 20% more than that in 2015, then by what percent was the expenditure on EDR in 2016 more than that in 2015?

(1) 55.6 (2) 50.4 (3) 66.5 (4) 45.8

6. If the expenditure on R&D was equal in all the years during the given period, then how many areas witnessed a continual increase in expenditure during the given period?

(1) 3 (2) 1 (3) 2 (4) 0

7. If the absolute difference between the expenditures on BR and AR in 2016 was $46.65 mn and that in 2017 was $16 mn, then the total expenditure on R&D in 2017 was what percent more than that in 2016?

(1) 25.00 (2) 33.33 (3) 66.67 (4) 35.00

Directions for questions 8 to 10: Answer the questions based on the line graphs given below.

The following line graphs give the land area under paddy cultivation and wheat cultivation and the respective production during the period 2012-17.

Yield is defined in terms of tonnes per hectare.

Land utilization is defined in terms of hectare per tonne.

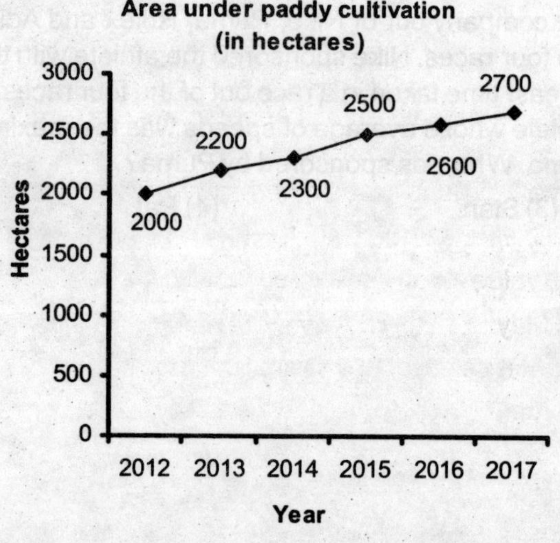

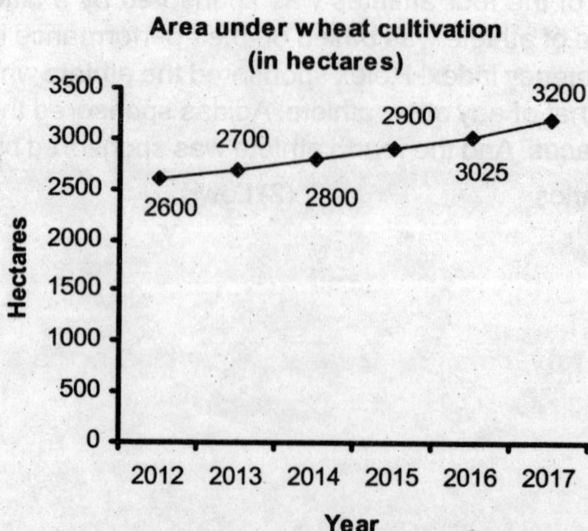

8. In which year was the land utilization the minimum?

(1) 2014 (2) 2015 (3) 2016 (4) 2017

9. What was the approximate percentage increase in the yield of wheat from 2012 to 2016?

(1) 50 (2) 42.85 (3) 28.57 (4) 57.14

10. If the land under paddy in 2018 was 5% more than that in 2017 and the production of paddy in 2018 was 1,75,000 tonnes, then the yield of paddy in 2018 was what percentage more/less than that in 2017?

(1) 1.2% more (2) 0.12% less (3) 1.2% less (4) 0.12% more

Directions for questions 11 to 15: The graph below shows the end of the month market values of 4 shares for the period from January to June. Answer the following questions based on this graph.

[CAT 1991]

11. Which share showed the greatest percentage increase in market value in any month during the entire period?

(1) A (2) B (3) C (4) D

12. In which month was the greatest absolute change in market value for any share recorded?

(1) March (2) April (3) May (4) June

13. In which month was the greatest percentage increase in market value for any share recorded?

(1) February (2) March (3) April (4) May

14. An individual wishes to sell 1 share of C and 1 share of D to buy 1 share of A at the end of a month. At which month-end would the individual's loss from this decision, due to share value changes, be the most?

(1) February (2) March (3) April (4) June

15. An individual decides to sell 1 share of C and 1 share of D to buy 1 share of A at the end of the month. What can be the individual's greatest gain from this decision, due to share value change

Directions for questions 16 to 20: Study the following graph and answer questions that follow. The x – axis denotes the years from 1983 to 1991.

[CAT 1991]

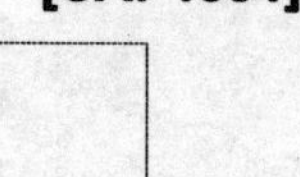

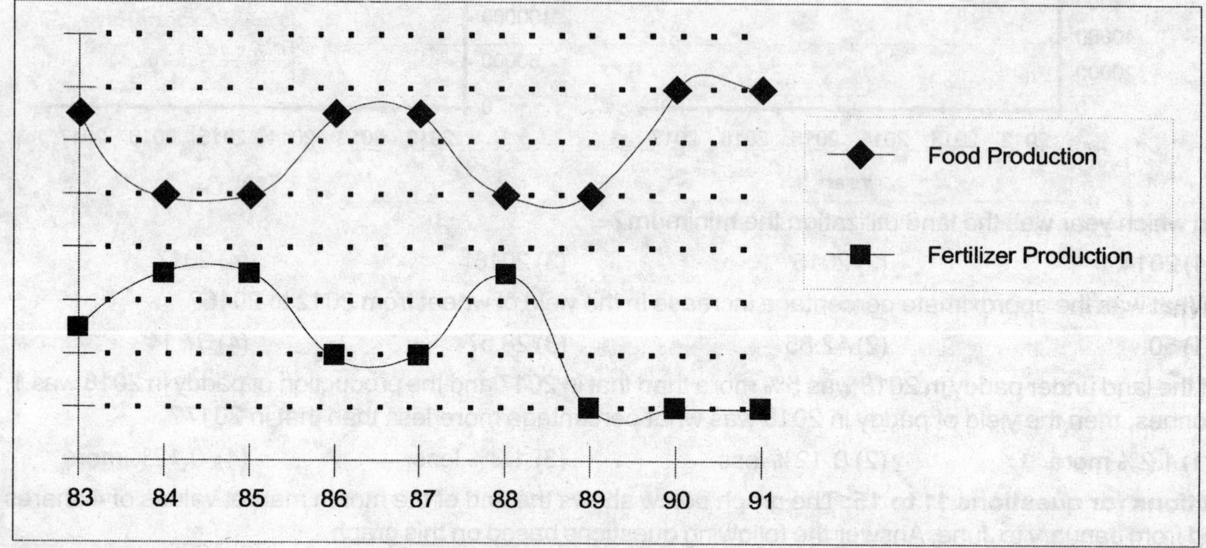

16. The sum of food and fertilizer production has shown a constant value for how many years?

(1) None of the years (2) 2

(3) 4 (4) 5

17. If in 1988, the sum of the food and fertilizer production was 170 million tonnes, the value of food production must have been (approximately, in million tonnes) ...

(1) 90 (2) 70

(3) 100 (4) Insufficient data

18. From its apparent behaviour, the food production in year 1992 can be expected to ...

(1) go up (2) go down

(3) remain the same as previous year. (4) nothing can be said.

19. Going according to previous trends, one can say that the Fertilizer Production has shown an anomalous behaviour in which year?

(1) 1985 (2) 1984

(3) 1991 (4) 1989

20. A scholar observed that if the production of fertilizers in 1989 had been the same as that in 1988, then the total fertilizer production for all the given years would have been 450 million tonnes. Using this information, and knowing that the food production has been plotted on the same scale, one may say that the food production in 1983 was (approximately, in million tonnes) ...

(1) 80 (2) 130

(3) 105 (4) Cannot be determined

Directions for questions 21 to 24: Study the graph below and answer the questions that follow.

[CAT 1993]

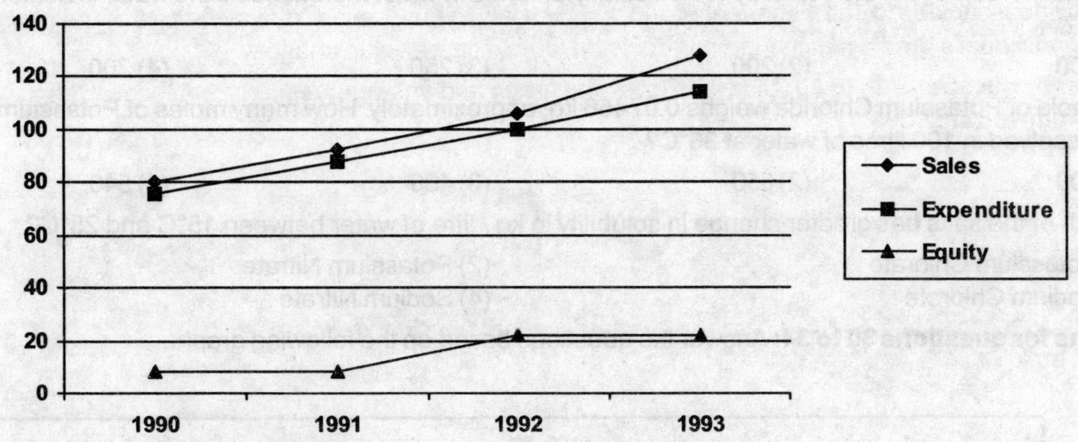

Profit is defined as Sales - Expenditure

21. In which year is the profit per rupee of equity the highest?

(1) 1991 (2) 1992 (3) 1993 (4) 1990 and 1991

22. The simple annual growth rate in sales was the highest between the years?

(1) 1990–91 (2) 1991–92 (3) 1992–93 (4) 1990–92

23. In which year is the sales per rupee of expenditure the lowest?

(1) 1990 (2) 1991 (3) 1992 (4) 1993

24. In which year is sales per rupee of equity the highest?

(1) 1990 (2) 1991 (3) 1992 (4) 1994

Directions for questions 25 to 29: Answer the questions on the basis of the information given below.

[CAT 1994]

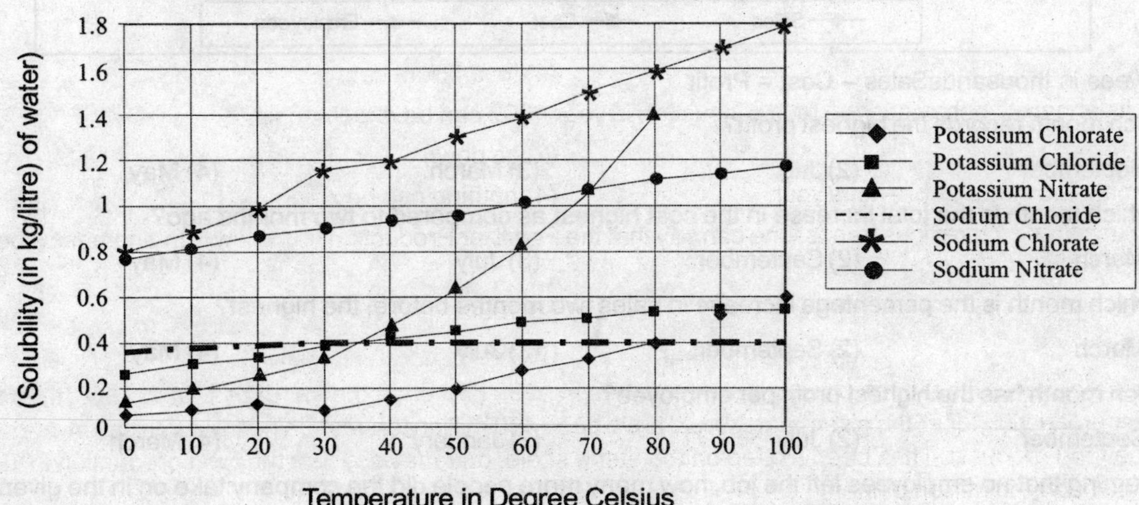

25. Which of the following salts has greatest solubility?

(1) Potassium Chlorate at 80°C.
(2) Potassium Chloride at 35°C.
(3) Potassium Nitrate at 39°C.
(4) Sodium Chloride at 85°C.

26. Approximately, how many kg of Potassium Nitrate can be dissolved in 10 litres of water at 30°C?

(1) 0.04 (2) 0.4 (3) 4 (4) 0.35

27. By what percentage is the solubility of Potassium Chlorate in water increased as the water is heated from 30°C to 80°C?.

(1) 100 (2) 200 (3) 250 (4) 300

28. If 1 mole of Potassium Chloride weighs 0.07456 kg, approximately. How many moles of Potassium Chloride can be dissolved in 100 litres of water at 36°C?

(1) 700 (2) 650 (3) 480 (4) 540

29. Which of the salts has greater change in solubility in kg / litre of water between 15°C and 25°C?

(1) Potassium Chlorate (2) Potassium Nitrate
(c) Sodium Chlorate (4) Sodium Nitrate

Directions for questions 30 to 34: Answer the questions based on the following graph.

[CAT 1996]

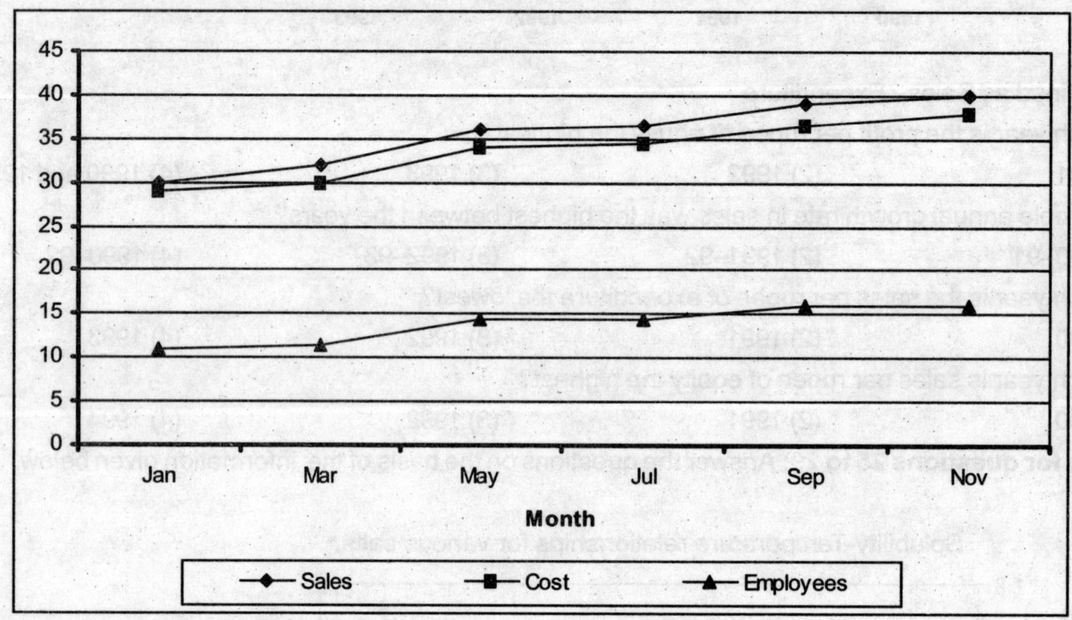

Employees in thousandsSales – Cost = Profit

30. Which month records the highest profit?

(1) September (2) July (3) March (4) May

31. In which month is the total increase in the cost highest as compared to two months ago?

(1) March (2) September (3) July (4) May

32. In which month is the percentage increase in sales two months before, the highest?

(1) March (2) September (3) July (4) May

33. Which month has the highest profit per employee?

(1) September (2) July (3) January (4) March

34. Assuming that no employees left the job, how many more people did the company take on in the given period?

(1) 4,600 (2) 5,000 (3) 5,800 (4) 6,400

Directions for questions 35 to 39: Answer the questions based on the following information.

[CAT 1996]

The first table gives the percentage of students in MBA class, who sought employment in the areas of finance, marketing and software. The second table gives the average starting salaries of the students per month, (rupees in thousands) in these areas. The third table gives the number of students who passed out in each year.

First table

	Finance	Marketing	Software	Others
1992	22	36	19	23
1993	17	48	23	12
1994	23	43	21	13
1995	19	37	16	28
1996	32	32	20	16

Second table

	Finance	Marketing	Software
1992	5450	5170	5290
1993	6380	6390	6440
1994	7550	7630	7050
1995	8920	8960	7760
1996	9810	10220	8640

Third table

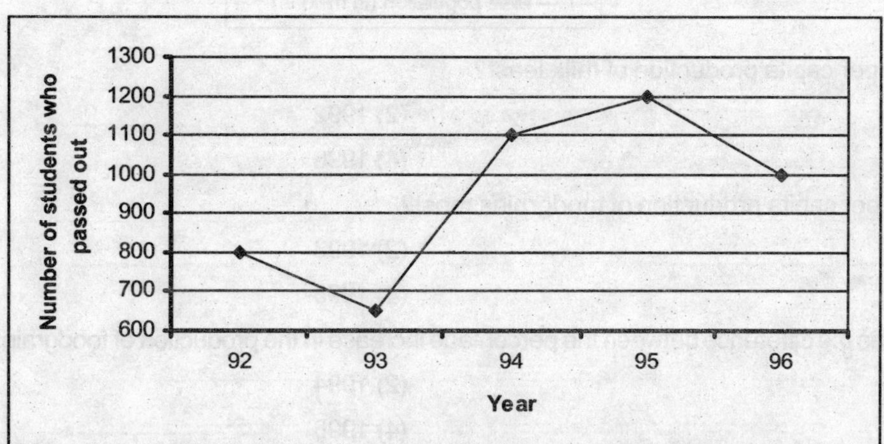

35. The number of students who get jobs in finance is less than the students getting marketing jobs, in the 5 years, by

(1) 826 (2) 650

(3) 750 (4) 548

36. What is the percentage increase in the average salary of finance from 1992 to 1996?

(1) 60% (2) 32%

(3) 96% (4) 80%

37. The average annual rate at which the initial salary offered in software increases is

(1) 21% (2) 33%

(3) 15.9% (4) 65%

38. What is the average monthly salary offered to a management graduate in 1993?

(1) Rs. 6,403 (2) Rs. 6,330

(3) Rs. 6,333 (4) Cannot be determined

39. In 1994, students seeking jobs in finance earned ___ more than those opting for software (per annum).

(1) Rs. 43 lakh (2) Rs. 33.8 lakh

(3) Rs. 28.4 lakh (4) Rs. 38.8 lakh

2.14 LINE GRAPH

Direction for questions 40 to 45: Answer the questions based on the following graph.

The graph given below shows the quantity of milk and food grains consumed annually along with female and male population (in millions). Use the data to answer the questions that follow.

[CAT 1997]

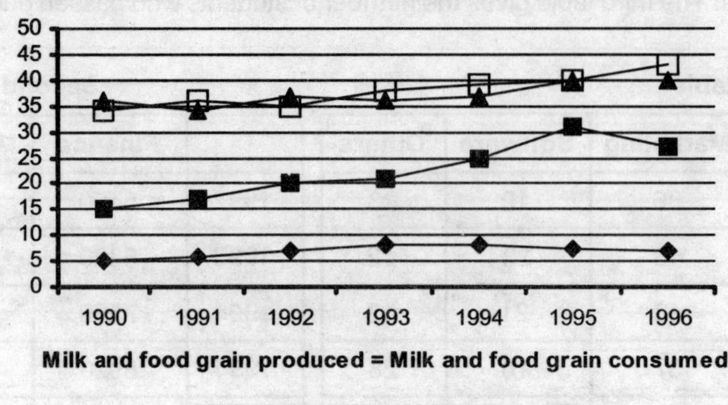

Milk and food grain produced = Milk and food grain consumed

40. When was the per capita production of milk least?

(1) 1990 (2) 1992

(3) 1994 (4) 1996

41. When was the per capita production of foodgrains most?

(1) 1992 (2) 1993

(3) 1994 (4) 1995

42. In which year was the difference between the percentage increase in the production of foodgrains and milk maximum?

(1) 1993 (2) 1994

(3) 1995 (4) 1996

43. If milk contains 320 calories and foodgrains contain 160 calories, in which year was the per capita consumption of calories highest?

(1) 1993 (2) 1994

(3) 1995 (4) 1996

44. If one gallon milk contains 120 g of a particular nutrient and one tonne of foodgrains contains 80 g of the same nutrient, in which year was the availability of this nutrient maximum?

(1) 1993 (2) 1994

(3) 1995 (4) 1996

45. Referring to the above question, in which year was the per capita consumption of this nutrient highest?

(1) 1993 (2) 1994

(3) 1995 (4) 1996

Directions for questions 46 to 50: Answer the questions based on the following information.

[CAT 1998]

Ghosh Babu has a manufacturing unit. The following graph gives the cost for various number of units. Given: Profit = Revenue – Variable cost – Fixed cost. The fixed cost remains constant up to 34 units after which additional investment is to be done in fixed assets. In any case, production cannot exceed 50 units.

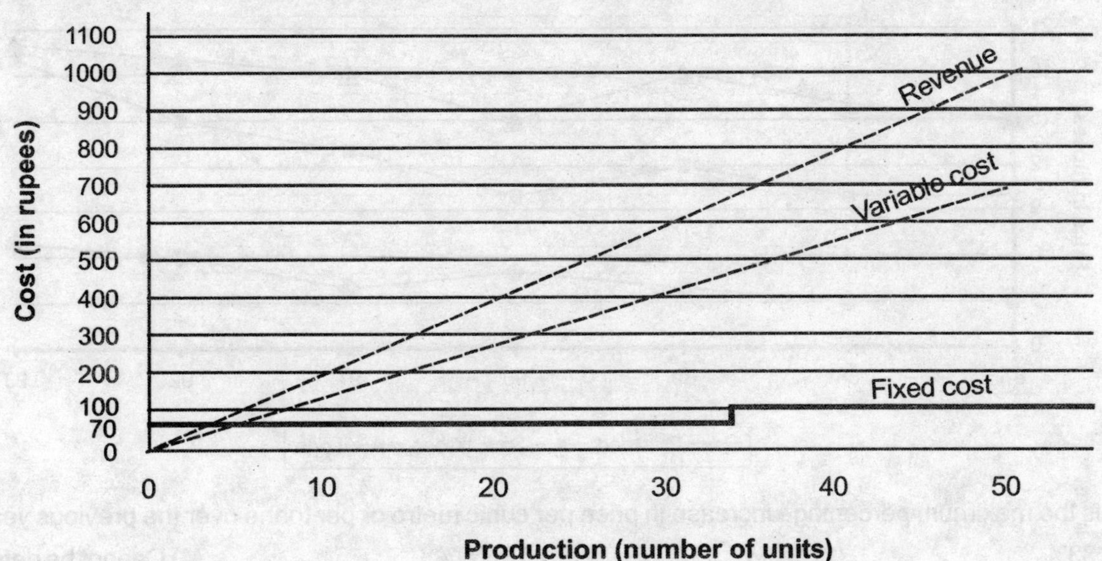

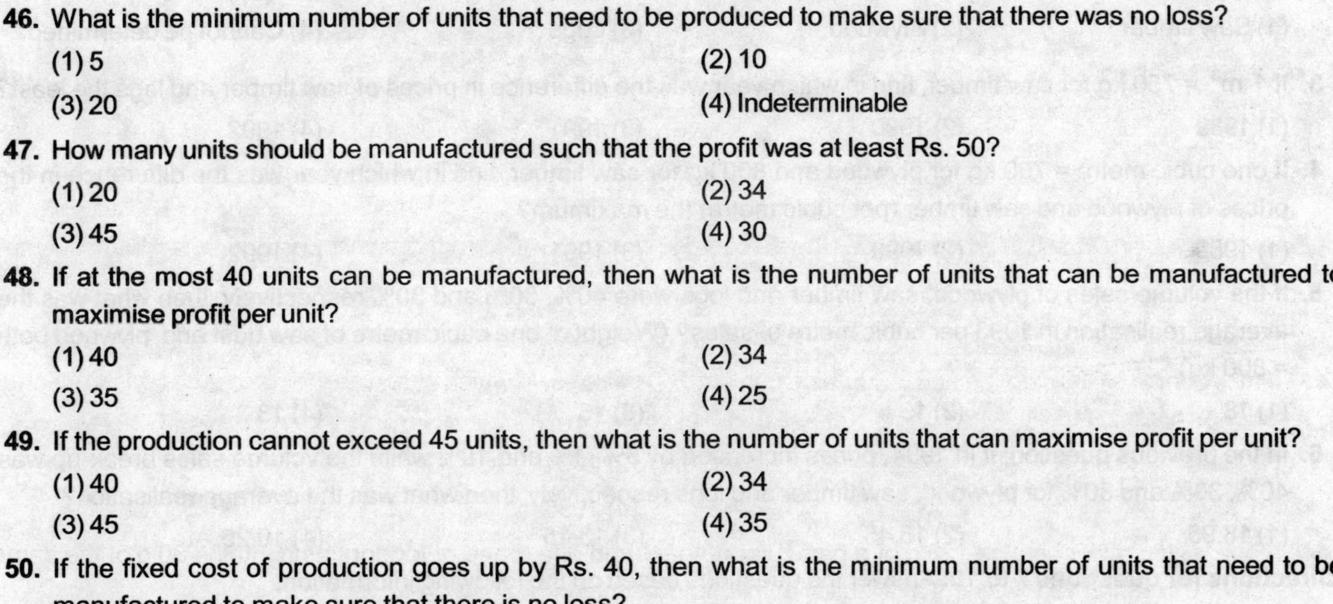

46. What is the minimum number of units that need to be produced to make sure that there was no loss?

(1) 5 (2) 10
(3) 20 (4) Indeterminable

47. How many units should be manufactured such that the profit was at least Rs. 50?

(1) 20 (2) 34
(3) 45 (4) 30

48. If at the most 40 units can be manufactured, then what is the number of units that can be manufactured to maximise profit per unit?

(1) 40 (2) 34
(3) 35 (4) 25

49. If the production cannot exceed 45 units, then what is the number of units that can maximise profit per unit?

(1) 40 (2) 34
(3) 45 (4) 35

50. If the fixed cost of production goes up by Rs. 40, then what is the minimum number of units that need to be manufactured to make sure that there is no loss?

(1) 10 (2) 19
(3) 15 (4) 20

PRACTICE EXERCISE – 2

Direction for questions 1 to 6: Answer the questions based on the following information.

[CAT 1998]

In the following chart, the price of logs shown is per cubic metre and that of plywood and saw timber is per tonne.

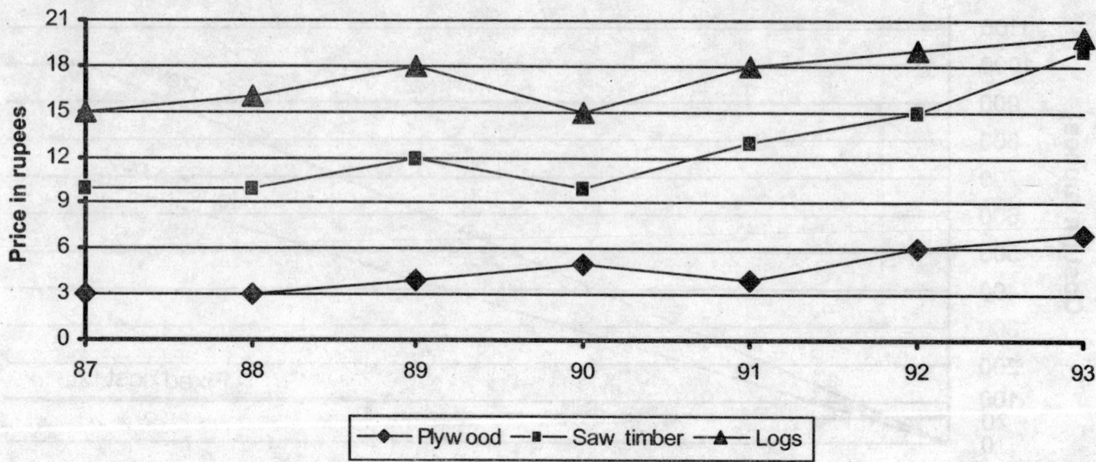

1. What is the maximum percentage increase in price per cubic metre or per tonne over the previous year?

(1) 33.33% (2) 85% (3) 50% (4) Cannot be determined

2. Which product shows the maximum percentage increase in price over the period?

(1) Saw timber (2) Plywood (3) Logs (4) Cannot be determined

3. If 1 m^3 = 750 kg for saw timber, find in which year was the difference in prices of saw timber and logs the least?

(1) 1989 (2) 1990 (3) 1991 (4) 1992

4. If one cubic metre = 700 kg for plywood and 800 kg for saw timber, find in which year was the difference in the prices of plywood and saw timber (per cubic metre) the maximum?

(1) 1989 (2) 1990 (3) 1991 (4) 1992

5. If the volume sales of plywood, saw timber and logs were 40%, 30% and 30% respectively, then what was the average realisation in 1993 per cubic metre of sales? (Weight of one cubic metre of saw dust and plywood both = 800 kg)

(1) 18 (2) 15 (3) 16 (4) 13

6. In the previous question, if in 1994, prices increased by 5%, 1% and 10% while the volume sales break-up was 40%, 30% and 30% for plywood, saw timber and logs respectively, then what was the average realisation?

(1) 18.95 (2) 16.45 (3) 13.15 (4) 10.25

Directions for questions 7 to 10: Answer the questions based on the following information.

[CAT 1999]

In each of the following questions, a pair of graphs F(x) and F1(x) is given. These are composed of straight- line segments, shown as solid lines, in the domain $x \in (-2, 2)$.

Choose the answer as

(1) if F1(x) = –F(x)

(2) if F1(x) = F(–x)

(3) if F1(x) = –F(–x)

(4) if none of the above is true

7.

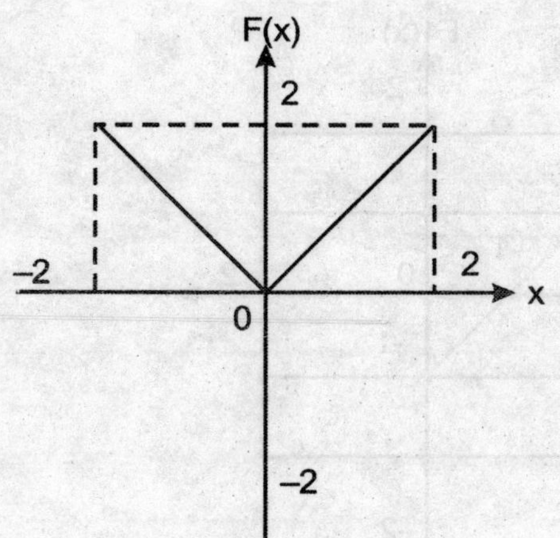
F(x)
2
–2
2
x
0
–2

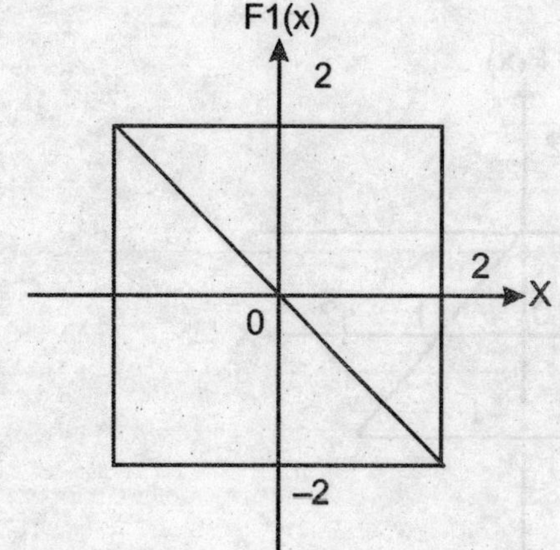
F1(x)
2
2
X
0
–2

8.

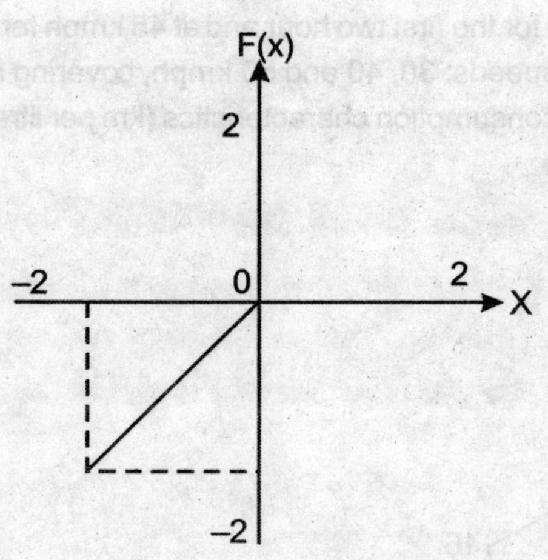
F(x)
2
–2
0
2
X
–2

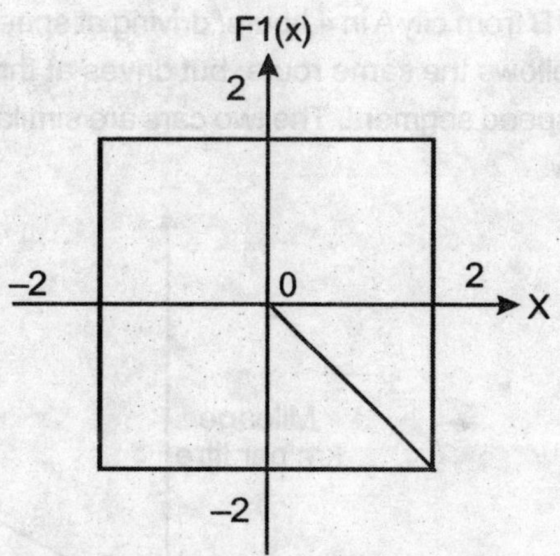
F1(x)
2
–2
0
2
X
–2

9.

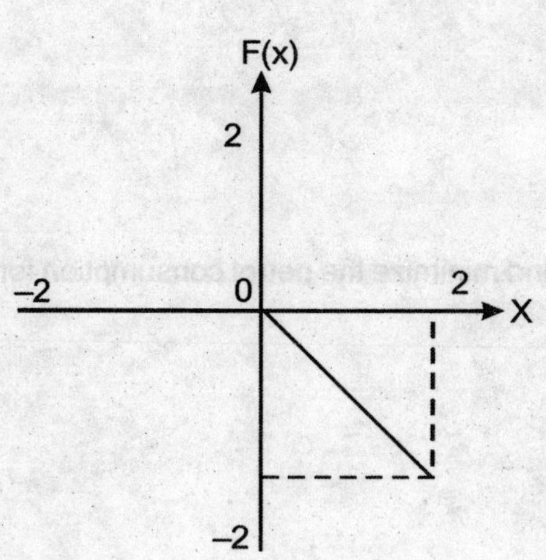
F(x)
2
–2
0
2
X
–2

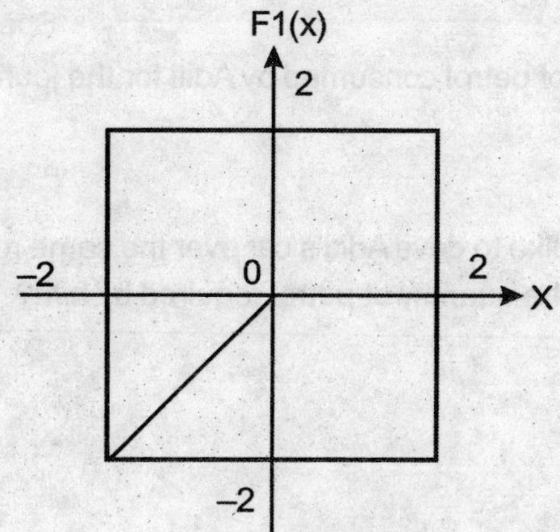
F1(x)
2
–2
0
2
X
–2

10.

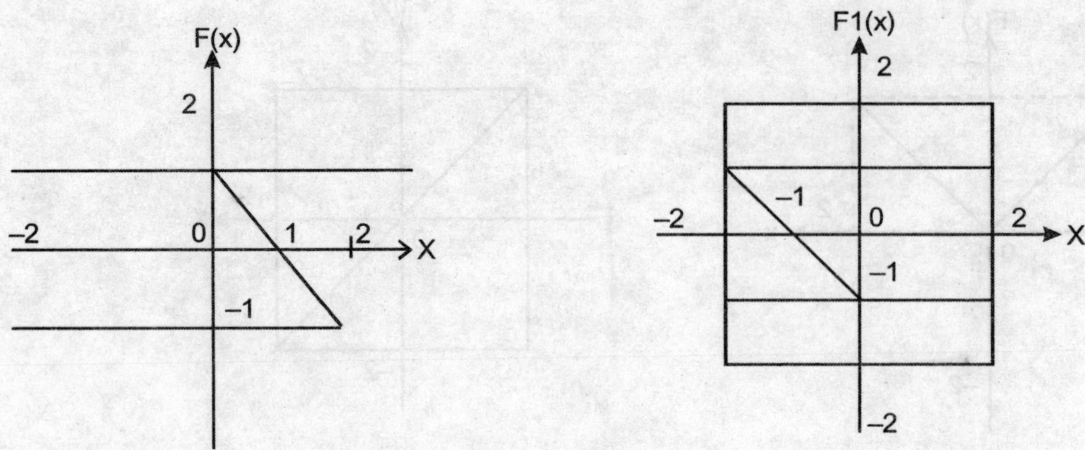

Directions for questions 11 and 12: Answer the questions based on the following information.

[CAT 1999]

Rajiv reaches city B from city A in 4 hours, driving at speed of 35 kmph for the first two hour and at 45 kmph for the next two hours. Aditi follows the same route, but drives at three different speeds: 30, 40 and 50 kmph, covering an equal distance in each speed segment. The two cars are similar with petrol consumption characteristics (km per litre) shown in the figure below.

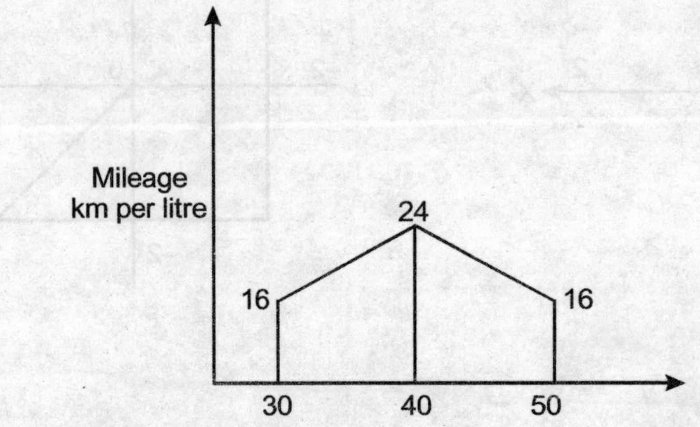

Speed km per hour

11. The quantity of petrol consumed by Aditi for the journey is

(1) 8.3 l
(2) 8.6 l
(3) 8.9 l
(4) 9.2 l

12. Zoheb would like to drive Aditi's car over the same route from A to B and minimize the petrol consumption for the trip. What is the quantity of petrol required by him?

(1) 6.67 l
(2) 7 l
(3) 6.33 l
(4) 6.0 l

Directions for questions 13 to 16: Answer the questions based on the following information.

[CAT 1999]

The figure below represents sales and net profit in Rs. crore of IVP Ltd. for five years from 1994-95 to 1998-99. During this period the sales increased from Rs. 100 crore to Rs. 680 crore. Correspondingly, the net profit increased from Rs. 2.5 crore to Rs. 12 crore. Net profit is defined as the excess of sales over total costs.

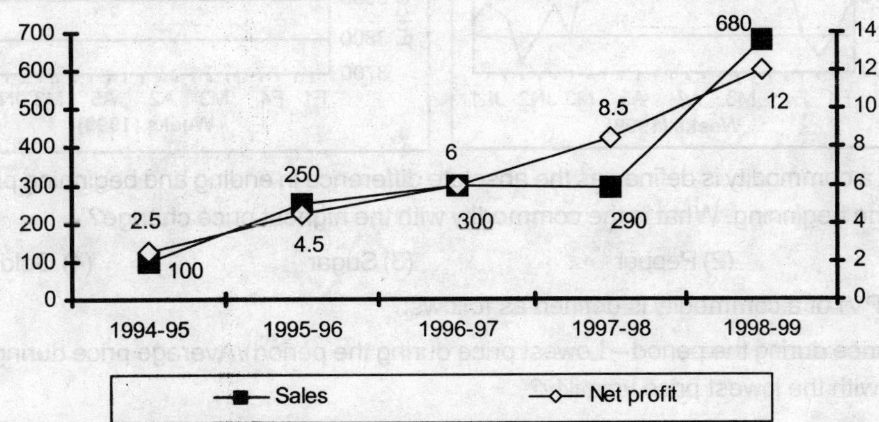

13. The highest percentage of growth in sales, relative to the previous year, occurred in

(1) 1995-96 (2) 1996-97 (3) 1997-98 (4) 1998-99

14. The highest percentage growth in net profit, relative to the previous year, was achieved in

(1) 1998-99 (2) 1997-98 (3) 1996-97 (4) 1995-96

15. Defining profitability as the ratio of net profit to sales, IVP Ltd., recorded the highest profitability in

(1) 1998-99 (2) 1997-98 (3) 1994-95 (4) 1996-97

16. With profitability as defined in question 137, it can be concluded that

(1) profitability is non-decreasing during the five years from 1994-95 to 1998-99.

(2) profitability is non-increasing during the five years from 1994-95 to 1998-99.

(3) profitability remained constant during the five years from 1994-95 to 1998-99.

(4) None of the above

Directions for questions 17 to 20: Answer the questions based on the following information.

[CAT 1999]

These questions are based on the price fluctuations of four commodities — arhar, pepper, sugar and gold during February-July 1999 as described in the figures below.

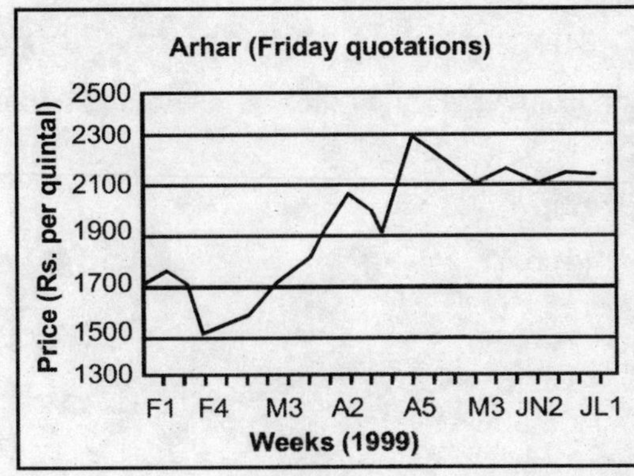

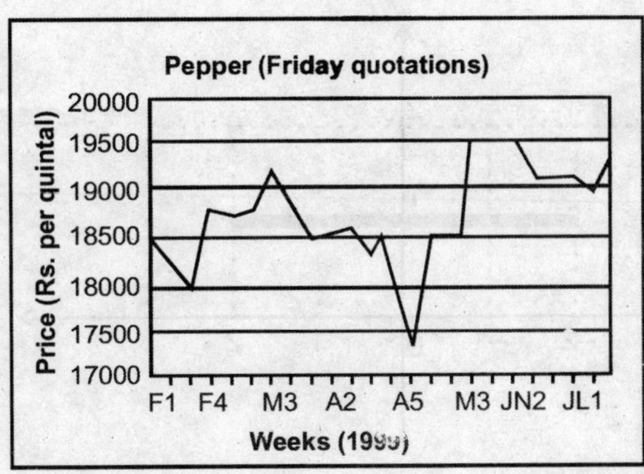

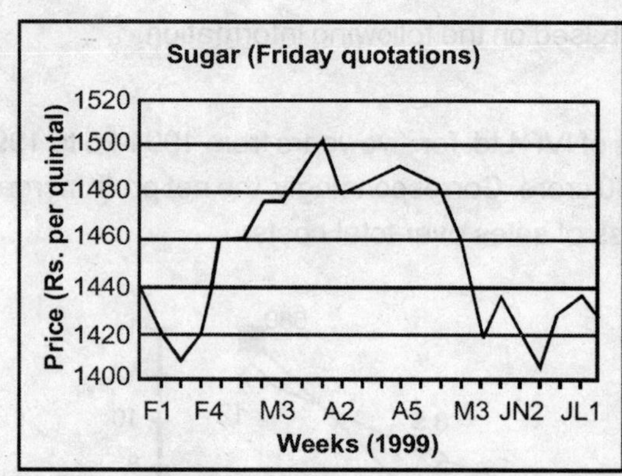

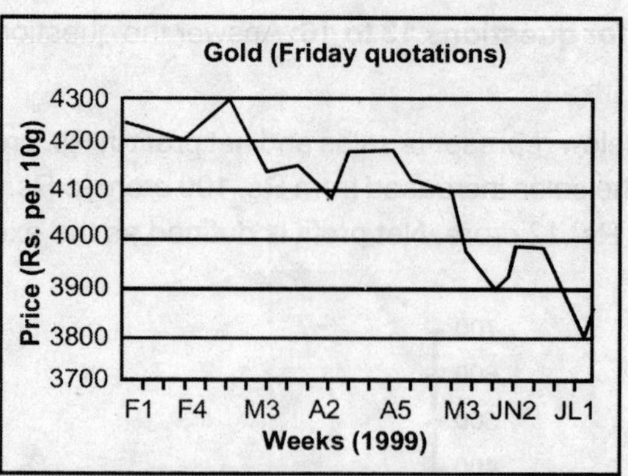

17. Price change of a commodity is defined as the absolute difference in ending and beginning prices expressed as a percentage of the beginning. What is the commodity with the highest price change?

(1) Arhar (2) Pepper (3) Sugar (4) Gold

18. Price volatility (PV) of a commodity is defined as follows:

PV = (Highest price during the period – Lowest price during the period)/Average price during the period. What is the commodity with the lowest price volatility?

(1) Arhar (2) Pepper (3) Sugar (4) Gold

19. Mr X, a fund manager with an investment company invested 25% of his funds in each of the four commodities at the beginning of the period. He sold the commodities at the end of the period. His investments in the commodities resulted in

(1) 17% profit (2) 5.5% loss (3) No profit, no loss (4) 5.4% profit

20. The price volatility(PV) of the commodity with the highest PV during the February-July period is approximately equal to

(1) 3% (2) 40% (3) 20% (4) 12%

Directions for questions 21 to 23: Given below are three graphs made up of straight line segments shown as thick lines. In each case choose the answer as

(1) if $f(x) = 3 f(-x)$

(2) if $f(x) = -f(-x)$

(3) if $f(x) = f(-x)$

(4) if $3f(x) = 6 f(-x)$, for $x \geq 0$

[CAT 2000]

21.

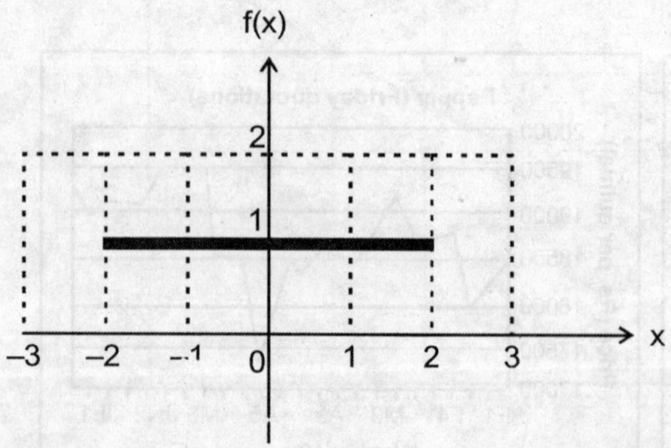

22.

23.

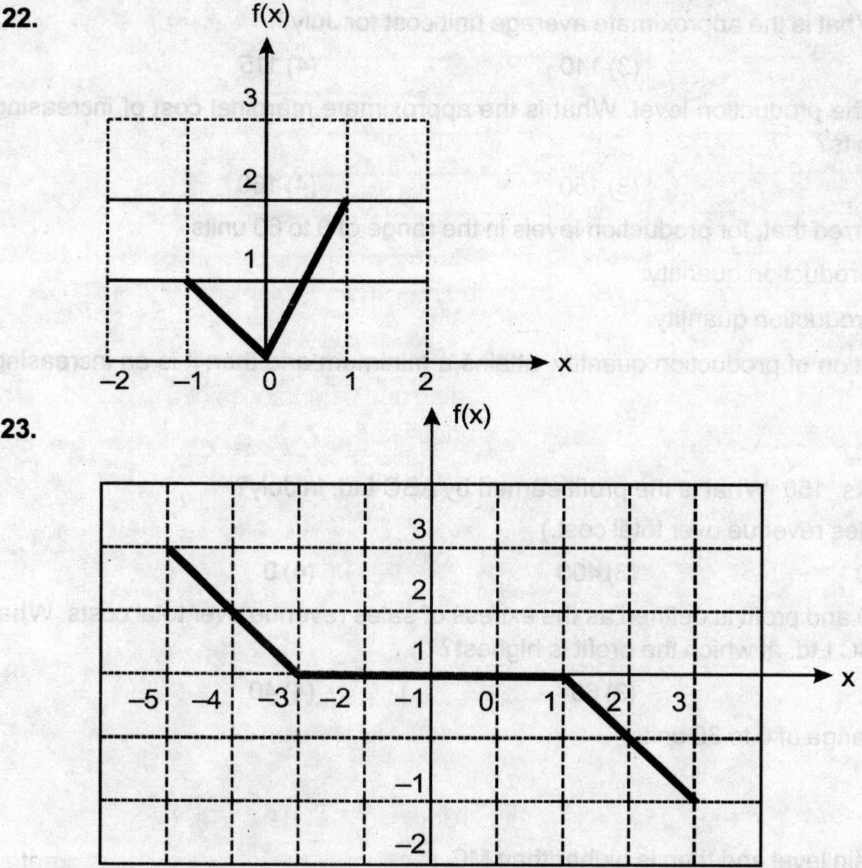

Directions for questions 24 to 29: Answer the questions based on the following information.

[CAT 2000]

ABC Ltd. produces widgets for which the demand is unlimited and they can sell all of their production. The graph below describes the monthly variable costs incurred by the company as a function of the quantity produced. In addition, operating the plant for the first shift results in a fixed monthly cost of Rs. 800. Fixed monthly costs for second shift operation is estimated at Rs. 1,200. Each shift operation provides capacity for producing 30 widgets per month.

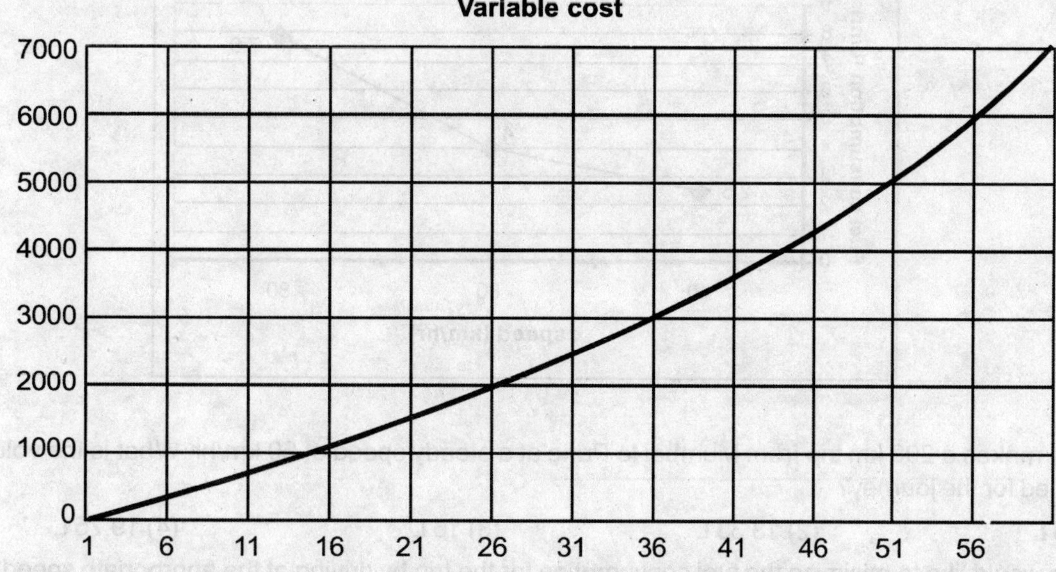

Note: Average unit cost, AC = $\frac{\text{Total monthly costs}}{\text{Monthly production}}$ and marginal cost, MC is the rate of change in total cost for unit change in quantity produced.

24. Total production in July is 40 units. What is the approximate average unit cost for July?

(1) 3,600 (2) 90 (3) 140 (4) 115

25. ABC Ltd. is considering increasing the production level. What is the approximate marginal cost of increasing production from its July level of 40 units?

(1) 110 (2) 130 (3) 150 (4) 160

26. From the data provided it can be inferred that, for production levels in the range of 0 to 60 units,

(1) MC is an increasing function of production quantity.

(2) MC is a decreasing function of production quantity.

(3) initially MC is a decreasing function of production quantity, attains a minimum and then it is an increasing function of production quantity.

(4) None of the above.

27. Suppose that each widget sells for Rs. 150. What is the profit earned by ABC Ltd. in July? (Profit is defined as the excess of sales revenue over total cost.)

(1) 2,400 (2) 1,600 (3) 400 (4) 0

28. Assume that the unit price is Rs. 150 and profit is defined as the excess of sales revenue over total costs. What is the monthly production level of ABC Ltd. at which the profit is highest?

(1) 30 (2) 50 (3) 60 (4) 40

29. For monthly production level in the range of 0 to 30 units,

(1) AC is always higher than MC.

(2) AC is always lower than MC.

(3) AC is lower than MC up to a certain level and then is higher than MC.

(4) None of the above.

Directions for questions 30 and 31: Answer the questions based on the following information.

[CAT 2001]

The petrol consumption rate of a new model car 'Palto' depends on its speed and may be described by the graph below.

30. Manasa makes a 200 km trip from Mumbai to Pune at a steady speed of 60 km/hr. What is the volume of petrol consumed for the journey?

(1) 12.5 L (2) 13.33 L (3) 16 L (4) 19.75 L

31. Manasa would like to minimize the fuel consumption for the trip by driving at the appropriate speed. How should she change the speed?

(1) Increase the speed (2) Decrease the speed

(3) Maintain the speed at 60 km/hr (4) Cannot be determined

Directions for questions 32 to 35: Answer the questions on the basis of the information given below.

[CAT 2003 Leaked)

The length of an infant is one of the measures of his/her development in the early stages of his/her life.

The figure below shows the growth chart of four infants in the first five months of life.

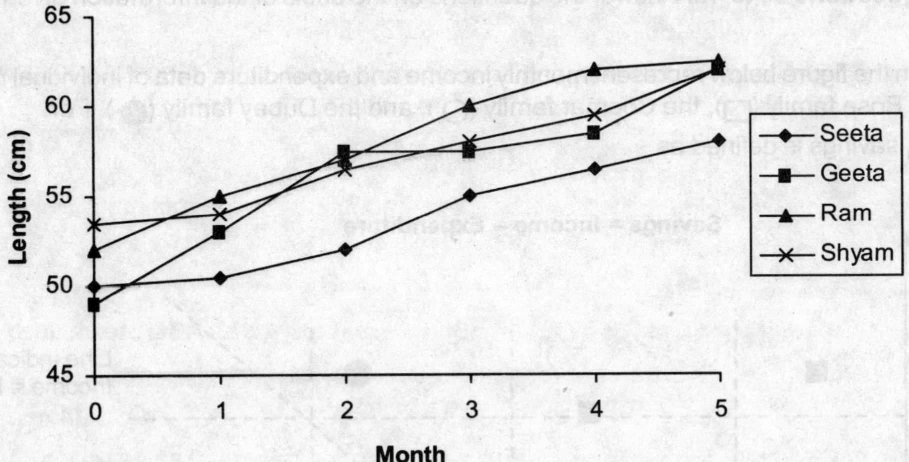

32. After which month did Seeta's rate of growth start to decline?

(1) Second month (2) Third month (3) Fourth month (4) Never

33. Who grew at the fastest rate in the first two months of life?

(1) Geeta (2) Seeta (3) Ram (4) Shyam

34. The rate of growth during the third month was the lowest for

(1) Geeta (2) Seeta (3) Ram (4) Shyam

35. Among the four infants, who grew the least in the first five months of life?

(1) Geeta (2) Seeta (3) Ram (4) Shyam

Directions for questions 36 to 38: Answer the questions on the basis of the data presented in the figure below.

[CAT 2003]

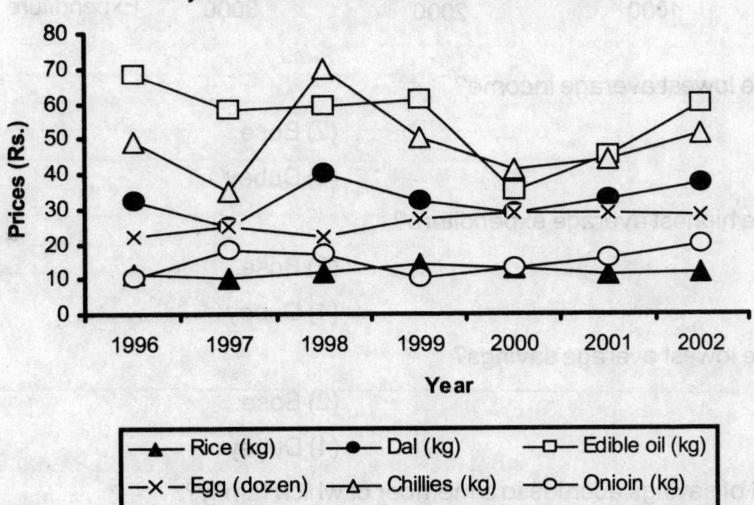

36. During 1996-2002, the number of commodities that exhibited a net overall increase and net overall decrease, respectively, were

(1) 3 and 3 (2) 2 and 4 (3) 4 and 2 (4) 5 and 1

37. The number of commodities that experienced a price decline for two or more consecutive years is

(1) 2 (2) 3 (3) 4 (4) 5

38. For which commodities did a price increase immediately follow a price decline only once in this period?

(1) Rice, edible oil and dal (2) Egg and dal (3) Onion only (4) Egg and onion

Directions for questions 39 to 42: Answer the questions on the basis of the information given below.

[CAT 2004]

The data points in the figure below represent monthly income and expenditure data of individual members of the Ahuja family (■), the Bose family (□), the Coomar family (○), and the Dubey family (●). For these questions, savings is defined as

Savings = Income – Expenditure

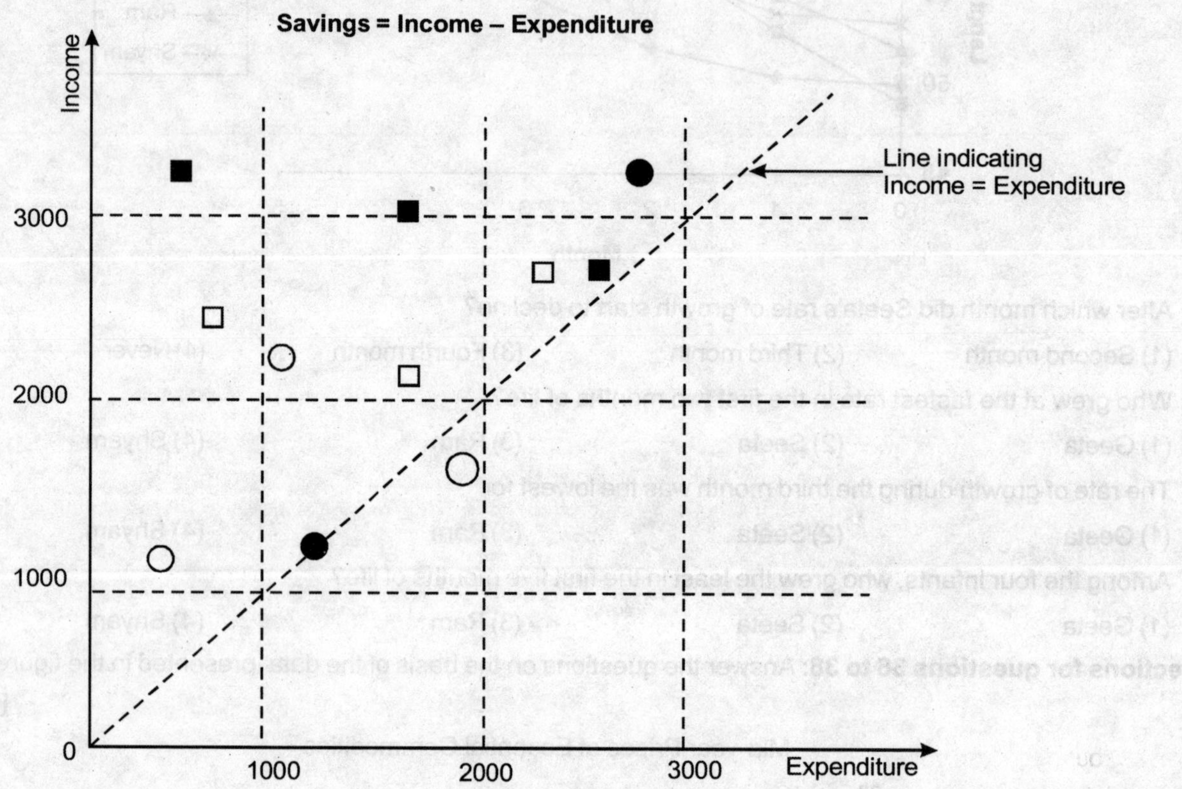

39. Which family has the lowest average income?

(1) Ahuja (2) Bose

(3) Coomar (4) Dubey

40. Which family has the highest average expenditure?

(1) Ahuja (2) Bose

(3) Coomar (4) Dubey

41. Which family has the lowest average savings?

(1) Ahuja (2) Bose

(3) Coomar (4) Dubey

42. The highest amount of savings accrues to a member of which family?

(1) Ahuja (2) Bose

(3) Coomar (4) Dubey

Directions for questions 43 to 45: Answer the following questions based on the information given below:

[CAT 2008]

Telecom operators get revenue from transfer of data and voice. Average revenue received from transfer of each unit of data is known as ARDT. In the diagram below, the revenue received from data transfer as percentage of total revenue received and the ARDT in US Dollars (USD) are given for various countries.

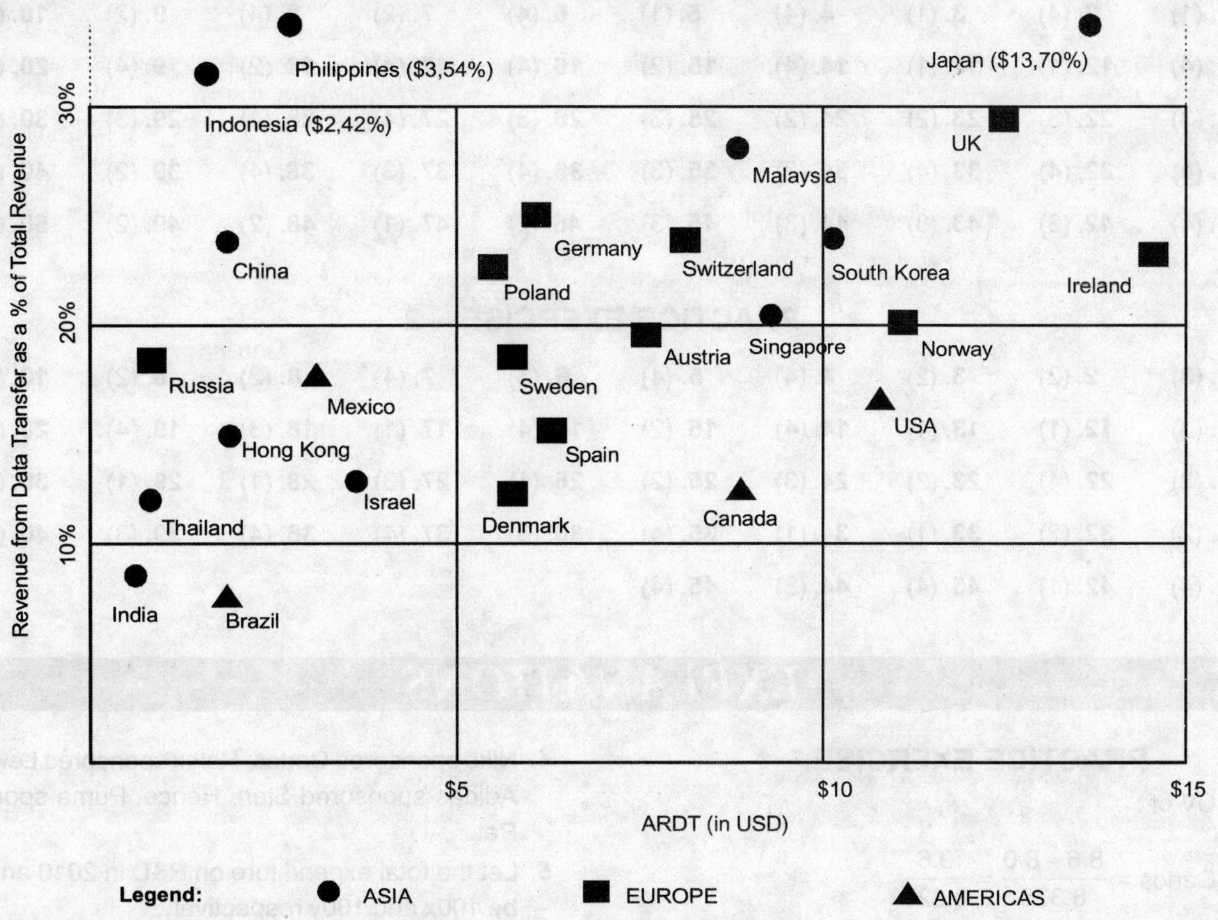

43. It was found that the volume of data transfer in India is the same as that of Singapore. Then which of the following statements is true?

(1) Total revenue is the same in both countries.

(2) Total revenue in India is about 2 times that of Singapore.

(3) Total revenue in India is about 4 times that of Singapore.

(4) Total revenue in Singapore is about 4 time that of India.

44. It is expected that by 2010, revenue from data transfer as a percentage of total revenue will triple for India and double for Sweden. Assume that in 2010, the total revenue in India is twice that of Sweden and that the volume of data transfer is the same in both the countries. What is the percentage increase of ARDT in India if there is no change in ARDT in Sweden?

(1) 400% (2) 550%

(3) 800% (4) 950%

45. If the total revenue received is the same for the pairs of countries listed in the choices below, choose the pair that has approximately the same volume of data transfer.

(1) Philippines and Austria (2) Canada and Poland

(3) Germany and USA (4) UK and Spain

ANSWER KEYS

PRACTICE EXERCISE – 1

1. (1)	**2.** (4)	**3.** (1)	**4.** (4)	**5.** (1)	**6.** (4)	**7.** (2)	**8.** (4)	**9.** (2)	**10.** (3)
11. (4)	**12.** (1)	**13.** (1)	**14.** (4)	**15.** (2)	**16.** (4)	**17.** (4)	**18.** (2)	**19.** (4)	**20.** (4)
21. (3)	**22.** (3)	**23.** (2)	**24.** (2)	**25.** (3)	**26.** (3)	**27.** (4)	**28.** (4)	**29.** (3)	**30.** (1)
31. (4)	**32.** (4)	**33.** (4)	**34.** (2)	**35.** (3)	**36.** (4)	**37.** (3)	**38.** (4)	**39.** (2)	**40.** (1)
41. (4)	**42.** (3)	**43.** (3)	**44.** (3)	**45.** (3)	**46.** (2)	**47.** (1)	**48.** (2)	**49.** (2)	**50.** (2)

PRACTICE EXERCISE – 2

1. (3)	**2.** (2)	**3.** (2)	**4.** (4)	**5.** (4)	**6.** (3)	**7.** (4)	**8.** (2)	**9.** (2)	**10.** (3)
11. (3)	**12.** (1)	**13.** (1)	**14.** (4)	**15.** (2)	**16.** (4)	**17.** (1)	**18.** (3)	**19.** (4)	**20.** (2)
21. (3)	**22.** (4)	**23.** (2)	**24.** (3)	**25.** (2)	**26.** (1)	**27.** (3)	**28.** (1)	**29.** (1)	**30.** (2)
31. (2)	**32.** (2)	**33.** (1)	**34.** (1)	**35.** (4)	**36.** (3)	**37.** (4)	**38.** (4)	**39.** (3)	**40.** (4)
41. (4)	**42.** (1)	**43.** (4)	**44.** (3)	**45.** (4)					

EXPLANATIONS

PRACTICE EXERCISE – 1

1. CV of :

$$\text{Carlos} = \frac{8.6-8.0}{8.325} = \frac{0.6}{8.325}$$

$$\text{Stan} = \frac{10.5-7.5}{8.375} = \frac{3}{8.375}$$

$$\text{Pat} = \frac{9.8-8.0}{8.85} = \frac{1.8}{8.85}$$

$$\text{Lewis} = \frac{9.6-7.4}{8.75} = \frac{2.2}{8.75}$$

Carlos has the lowest CV and hence the highest CI.

2. Average of speeds of Carlos is

$$= \frac{1}{4}\left[\frac{200}{8.5}+\frac{200}{8.6}+\frac{200}{8.2}+\frac{200}{8.0}\right] \simeq 24\,\text{m/s}$$

Similarly, Average speed of other three athletes can be calculated. The highest average is of stan. i.e. 24.3 m/s.

3. PE is highest for Pat and it equal to,

$$\left(\frac{9.8-8.0}{9.8}\right) = 0.18.$$

4. Nike sponsored Carlos, Rolex sponsored Lewis and Adidas sponsored Stan. Hence, Puma sponsored Pat.

5. Let the total expenditure on R&D in 2010 and 2011 be 100x and 100y respectively.

$\therefore$ $14.4y = 1.2 \times 20.4x \Rightarrow y = 1.7x.$

Hence, the required percentage

$$= \frac{32.4y - 35.4x}{35.4x} \times 100$$

$$= \frac{32.4 \times 1.7x - 35.4x}{35.4x} \times 100$$

$= 55.6.$

6. It is clear from the graph that none of the four areas of R&D witnessed a continual increase in the expenditure during the given period.

7. Let the total expenditure on R&D in 2011 and 2012 be \$100x mn and \$100y mn.

$\therefore$ $45.5x - 14.4x = 46.65 \Rightarrow x = 1.5$

and $19.5y - 11.5y = 16 \Rightarrow y = 2$

Hence, the required percentage

$$= \frac{2-1.5}{1.5} \times 100 = 33.33.$$

8. Collective land utilization for the year 2012

$$= \left[\frac{2000}{126000} + \frac{2600}{182000}\right] = \left[\frac{1}{63} + \frac{1}{70}\right]$$

Similarly, Collective land utilization for the year 2013

$$= \left[\frac{1}{60} + \frac{1}{72.1}\right]$$

Collective land utilization for the year 2014

$$= \left[\frac{1}{60} + \frac{1}{80}\right]$$

Collective land utilization for the year 2015

$$= \left[\frac{1}{59} + \frac{1}{90}\right]$$

Collective land utilization for the year 2016

$$= \left[\frac{1}{62} + \frac{1}{100}\right]$$

Collective land utilization for the year 2017

$$= \left[\frac{1}{62.5} + \frac{1}{100.5}\right]$$

It is apparent that the land utilization is the minimum for the year 2017.

9. Yield of wheat in 2012 = $\frac{182000}{2600}$ = 70 tonnes/hectare

Yield of wheat in 2016 = $\frac{302500}{3025}$ = 100 tonnes/hectare

$\therefore$ The percentage increase = $\frac{100-70}{70} \times 100$

= 42.85.

10. Land area for paddy increased by 5% in 2017-18 and production of paddy increased to 1,75,000 tonnes.

$\therefore$ Increased land area = 2835

Yield for 2018 = $\frac{175000}{2835}$ = 61.73

Yield for 2017 = 62.5

Hence, the percentage decrease = $\frac{0.77}{62.5} \times 100$

= 1.2.

For questions 11 to 15:

The values of the graph can be tabulated as given below:

	A	% Change	B	% Change	C	% Change	D	% Change
Jan	100	–	70	–	60	–	40	–
Feb	95	–5%	72	2.85%	55	-8.33%	50	25%
Mar	115	21%	74	2.77%	60	9.09%	50	–
Apr	105	–8.7%	76	2.70%	69	15%	41	–18%
May	100	–4.7%	78	2.63%	60	–13%	44	7.31%
Jun	110	10%	80	2.56%	55	-8.33%	45	2.27%

11. As it is seen the highest % increase is for D in Feb. viz.25%.

12. The greatest absolute change in the market value for any share recorded is 20 i.e. for share "A" for month of March = 115 – 95 = 20.

13. The greatest percentage change in any share was recorded for share D for the month of February viz. 25%.

14.

	C	D	Total Earning	A	Gain/ Loss
Jan	60	40	100	100	–
Feb	55	50	105	95	+10
Mar	60	50	110	115	–5
Apr	69	41	110	105	+5
May	60	44	104	100	+4
Jun	55	45	100	110	–10

Hence, the maximum loss due to share value changes is 10 for the month of Jun. Hence the answer is (4).

15. Again referring to the above table it can be seen that the individual's highest gain is Rs.10.

For questions 16 to 20:

Students please note that the values on the Y-axis are not given. For the sake of convenience let us assume that one step on y-axis is 'x' and starting value be k.

Years	Food production	Fertilizer production
83	6.5 + k	2.5x + k
84	5 + k	3.5x + k
85	5 + k	3.5x + k
86	6.5 + k	2x + k
87	6.5 + k	2x + k
88	5 + k	3.5x + k
89	5 + k	x +
90	7x + k	x + k
91	7x + k	x+ k

16. If you see, for each year from 1984 to 1988 sum of food and fertilizers = 8.5x + 2k

Hence, it is constant for 5 years.

17. Fertilizers production in 1988 = 3.5x + k

Food production in 1988 = 5x + k

As per the given information

8.5x + 2 k = 170

Value of x and k cannot be determined.

18. The graph of food production shows an alternate increase and decrease in every 1 to 2 years. Hence looking at the trend of the graph in 1990 and 1991, it can be expected that the graph will go down in 1992.

19. It is clear that the graph for fertilizer production remains constant for two consecutive years. But it breaks this trend in 1989 as it has a value lower than its value in 1988.

20. If the fertilizer production in 1989 had been the same as that in 1988, its value for 1989 would have been 3.5x + k.

Hence total fertilizer production according to our values would have been (2.5x + k + 3.5x + k + 3.5x + k + 2x + k + 2x + k + 3.5x + k + 3.5x + k + x + k + x + k) = 22.5x + 9k. As per the given information 22.5x + k = 490

Value of x and k cannot be determined.

For questions 21 to 24: The given graph can be represented in the following table:

Company	Sales (1)	Expend. (2)	Profit (3)=(1)–(2)	Equity (4)	Pro/Equ (3)/(4)	Sal/Equ (1)/(4)	Sal/Exp (1)/(2)	Growth Rate Sales
1990	80	76	4	8	0.5	10	1.05	
1991	92	88	4	8	0.5	**11.5**	**1.04**	15%
1992	106	100	6	22	0.27	4.82	1.06	15.21%
1993	128	114	14	22	**0.64**	5.82	1.12	**20.75%**

21. It is clear that the profit per rupee of equity is highest for 1993 viz. 0.64.

22. The simple annual growth rate in sales is maximum for the year 1992-93 viz. 20.75%.

23. Sales per rupee of the expenditure is lowest for the year 1991 viz. 1.04.

24. Sales per rupee of equity is highest for 1991 viz. 11.5

25.

Option	Description	Solubility
(a)	Potassium Chlorate at 80°	0.4
(b)	Potassium Chloride at 35° C	0.4
(c)	Potassium Nitrate at 39° C	**0.48**
(d)	Sodium Chloride at 85° C	0.4

Hence (3) is the correct answer.

26. At 30°C, solubility of potassium nitrate is 0.38 kg./lt. Hence in 10 litres 3.8 kg.($\approx$4 kg) of potassium nitrate can be dissolved.

27. Percentage increase in solubility of potassium chlorate $= \dfrac{(0.4-0.1)\times 100}{0.1} = 300\%$.

28. Solubility of potassium chloride at 36°C = 0.4 kg./lt. Hence the amount of Potassium chloride that can be dissolved in 100 lt. at 36°C = 40 kg.

$$\text{Number of moles} = \frac{40}{0.07456} \approx \frac{40}{0.075} = 533.$$

As we have approximated 0.07456 as 0.075 and 540 is closest to 533, it should be correct answer.

29. From the graph it can be seen that between 15°C &25°C, solubility of sodium nitrate, potassium chloride, sodium chloride, is almost constant. It can clearly seen from graph that solubility of sodium chlorate is maximum.

30. By observation gap between the Cost and the Sales is the highest in September. Thus, the highest profit is recorded in September.

31. By observation difference between the Cost in March and May is the highest. Thus, in May total increase in Cost is the highest as compared to two months ago.

32. By observation difference between the Cost in March and May is the highest. Also, the Sales in March is less as compared to the following months. Thus, in May percentage increase in sales two months before the highest.

33. By observation increase in the number of employees from January to March is the less than the increase in profit from January to March. Thus, profit per employee is the highest in March.

34. From January to November the number of employees that company takes = (16 – 11) × 1000 = 5000.

35.

Year	Number of students employed	Number of students employed from finance	Number of students employed from marketing
1992	800	0.22 × 800 = 176	0.36 × 800 = 288
1993	640	0.17 × 650 = 110.5	0.48 × 650 = 312
1994	1100	0.23 × 1100 = 253	0.43 × 1100 =473
1995	1200	0.19 × 1200 = 228	0.37 × 1200 = 444
1996	1000	0.32 × 1000 = 320	0.32 × 1000 = 320
		1087.5	1837

$\therefore$ Difference in number of students employed from finance and marketing = 1837 – 1087.5 = 749.5 $\approx$ 750.

36. Percentage increase in the average salary of finance

$$= \frac{9810 - 5450}{5450} \times 100 = 80\%$$

37. Average annual rate at which the initial salary offered in software increases

$$= \frac{1}{4}\left[\frac{(8640 - 5290)}{5290} \times 100\right] = 15.83\% \approx 15.9\%$$

38. As we don't have any information about the average monthly salary offered to 'Others', we cannot determine the answer.

39.

Year	Number of candidates employed from finance	Number of candidates employed from software
1994	0.23 × 1100 = 253	0.21 × 110 = 231

Difference in the amount earned = 253 × 7550 – 231 × 7050 = 1910150 – 1628550 = Rs. 2.81 lakh per month = Rs. 33.8 lakh per annum.

40.

Year	Male population	Female population	Total	Per capita production
1990	34	36	70	5/70 = 0.071
1992	35	37	72	7/72 = 0.09
1994	39	37	76	7.6/76 = 0.1
1996	43	40	83	7/83 " 7/84 = 0.08

From the table, it is clear that in 1990, the per capita production of milk was least.

41. We can prepare a similar kind of table that we prepared for previous question. This table prepared is for food grains.

Year	Total population	Per capita production
1992	72	20/72 = 0.27
1993	74	22/74 = 0.297
1994	76	25/76 " 25/75 = 0.33
1995	80	31/80 " 30/80 = 0.375

Hence, per capita production of foodgrains was maximum in 1995.

42. Percentage increase in production of food

Year	Production of foodgrains	% increase = X	Production of milk	% increase = Y	X – Y
1992	20		7		
1993	22	2/20 = 10%	8	1/7 = 14.2%	–4.28%
1994	25	3/22 = 13.6%	7.5	–0.5/8 = –6.2%	19.8%
1995	31	6/25 = 24%	6.8	-0.7/7.5 = –9.3%	33.3%
1996	27	– 4/31 = – 12.9%	7	0.2/6.8 = 2.9%	15.8%

From the last table, it is clear that in 1995, the difference between percentage increase in production of foodgrains and percentage increase in production of milk was maximum.

43.

Year	Per capita consumption of milk = A	Calories consumed = X(X = 320x A)	Per capita consumption of foodgrains = B	Calories consumed = Y(Y = 160 x B)	X + Y
1993	0.11	35.2	0.28	44.8	80
1994	0.1	32	0.33	52.8	84.8
1995	0.093	29.76	0.37	59.2	88.96
1996	0.08	25.6	0.33	52.8	78.4

From the last column of the table, it is clear that the per capita consumption of calories was highest in 1995.

44.

Year	Production of milk = A	Availability of nutrient= 120A =X	Production of foodgrains = B	Availability of nutrient= 80B =Y	X +Y
1993	8	960	22	1760	2720
1994	7.5	900	25	2000	2900
1995	6.8	816	32	2560	3376
1996	7	840	27	2160	3060

Clearly, from the table, availability of nutrient is maximum in1995.

45.

Year	Total population	Per capita consumption of nutrient
1993	74	2720/74 = 36.75
1994	76	2900/76 = 38.15
1995	80	3376/80 = 42.2
1996	83	3060/83 = 36.86

From the table, it is clear that the per capita consumption is maximum in 1995.

46. Profit = Revenue – Variable Cost – Fixed Cost = Revenue – (Variable Cost + Fixed Cost). If we consider (Fixed Cost + Variable cost) as total cost, then as long as the revenue is higher than the total cost, there is a profit. In case the revenue is less than the total cost there would be a loss. If we are to compile the data given in the question it would be as follows:

Production	Fixed cost (Rs.)	Variable cost (Rs.)	Total cost (Rs.)	Revenue (Rs.)	Profit /loss (Rs.)
9	70	126	196	180	–16
10	70	140	210	200	–10
12	70	168	238	240	+2
20	70	280	350	400	+50
30	70	420	490	600	+110
40	100	560	660	800	+140
50	100	700	800	1,000	+200

Thus, we can say that at a production of 12 units, there is a profit of Rs. 2. Above 12 units there is always a profit and below 12 units there is loss. Hence, to make sure there is no loss, one has to manufacture a minimum of 12 units.

* The answer is clearly not indeterminable, it should be 12 units, but among the options given the one closest to it is 10 units.

47. It can be seen that at 20 units there is a profit of Rs. 50. Below this the profit will reduce. Hence, to ensure that the profit is at least Rs. 50, then 20 units have to be manufactured.

48. Let us verify for the given options.

Production	Fixed cost (Rs.)	Variable cost (Rs.)	Total cost (Rs.)	Revenue (Rs.)	Profit/loss (Rs.)	Profit/unit (Rs.)
25	70	350	420	500	+80	3.20
34	70	476	546	680	+134	3.94
35	100	490	590	700	+110	3.14
40	100	560	660	800	+140	3.50

Hence, we can see that to maximise profit per unit, we need to manufacture 34 units.

49. Extending the above table for 45 units, we get

Production	Fixed cost (Rs.)	Variable cost (Rs.)	Total cost (Rs.)	Revenue (Rs.)	Profit/loss (Rs.)	Profit/unit (Rs.)
45	100	630	730	900	+170	3.77

Thus, it can be figured out that still he has to manufacture 34 units.

50. Referring to the table in question 163, we can see that if the fixed cost increases by Rs. 40, the profit will reduce by Rs. 40. Hence, we can see that at 10 units he will make a loss of Rs. 30 and at 20 units he will make a profit of Rs. 10. Hence, the answer has to be between (2) and (3). Let us verify for them:

Production	Fixed cost (Rs.)	Variable cost (Rs.)	Total cost (Rs.)	Revenue (Rs.)	Profit/loss (Rs.)
15	110	210	320	300	–20
19	110	266	376	380	+4

Thus, we see that to make sure there is no loss, he has to manufacture 19 units.

PRACTICE EXERCISE – 2

1. The data can be represented in the following table.

	Plywood		Saw timber		Logs	
	Price	% increase	Price	% increase	Price	% increase
87	3	–	10	–	15	–
88	3	–	10	–	16	6.67%
89	4	33.33%	12	20%	18	12.5%
90	5	25%	10	–	15	–
91	4	–	13	30%	18	20%
92	6	50%	15	15.38%	19	5.55%
93	7	16.66%	19	27%	20	5.26%

Thus, we can see that the maximum increase is 50%.

2.

	Price in 1987	Price in 1993	Percentage increase
Plywood	3	7	133.33%
Saw timber	10	19	90%
Logs	15	20	33.33%

Thus, we see that the maximum percentage increase over the period is shown by plywood.

3. Since the price of saw timber is given in rupees per tonne and that of log is given in rupees per cubic metre, we cannot compare the two. Hence, using the given conversion, let us convert the price of saw timber in per cubic metre. The table will be as follows:

(**Note:** 1 tonne = $\frac{4}{3}$ = 1.33 cubic m)

Year	Saw timber (Price in Rs./tonnes)	Saw timber (Price in Rs./cubic metres)	Logs price in (Rs./cubic metres)	Difference in price
1989	12	9	18	9
1990	10	7.50	15	7.50
1991	13	9.75	18	8.25
1992	15	11.25	19	7.75

Thus, we see that the difference is least in the year 1990.

4. As in the previous table, we can draw a similar table for saw timber and logs.

(**Note**: One tonne of plywood = $\frac{10}{7}$ cubic m = 1.43 cubic m and one tonne of saw timber = $\frac{5}{4}$ cubic m = 1.25 cubic m.

Year	Saw timber (Price in Rs./ tonnes)	Saw timber (Price in Rs./cubic metres)	Plywood (Price in Rs./ tonnes)	Plywood (Price in Rs./cubic metres)	Difference in price
1989	12	9.60	4	2.80	6.80
1990	10	8.00	5	3.50	4.50
1991	13	10.40	4	2.80	7.60
1992	15	12.00	6	4.20	7.80

Hence, it can be seen that the difference is maximum for 1992.

5. Note that one tonne = $\frac{4}{3}$ m^3 = 1.33 m^3, for both plywood and saw timber.

In 1993, price of logs = Rs. 20 per cubic metre.

Price of plywood = $\left(\frac{7}{1.33}\right)$ = Rs. 5.26 per cubic metre.

And price of saw timber = $\left(\frac{19}{1.33}\right)$ = 14.28 per cubic metre.

Now the sales volume of plywood, saw timber and logs are in the ratio 4 : 3 : 3. So the average realisation per cubic metre of sales is indeed the weighted average.

This is given as

$$\frac{[(4 \times 5.26) + (3 \times 14.28) + (3 \times 20)]}{(4 + 3 + 3)}$$

= Rs. 12.4

= Rs. 13 (Approximately)

6. The only change would be the accounting for price increase. This is given as

$$\frac{(4\times 5.26\times 1.05)+(3\times 14.28\times 1.01)+(3\times 20\times 1.10)}{(4+3+3)}$$

= Rs. 13.15

7. The graph F(x) represents the function F(x) = | x |, where x is any real number.

The graph of F1(x) represents the function F1(x) = – x, where x is any real number.

None of the given relationships are satisfied by these two functions.

Alternate solution:

F1(–2) = 2 = F(–2) and F1(2) = –2. But F(2) = 2.

So the correct option is (4).

8. $F(x)=\begin{cases}0 & \text{when } x\geq 0\\ x & \text{when } x<0\end{cases}$ and $F1(x)=\begin{cases}-x & \text{when } x>0\\ 0 & \text{when } x\leq 0\end{cases}$

Therefore, replacing x by (–x) in above functions, we get

$F(-x)=\begin{cases}0 & \text{when } x\leq 0\\ -x & \text{when } x>0\end{cases}$ and $F1(-x)=\begin{cases}x & \text{when } x<0\\ 0 & \text{when } x\geq 0\end{cases}$

Clearly, F1(x) = F(–x), hence, option (b) is the correct choice.

Alternate solution:

F1(-2) = 0 = F(2) and F1(2) = –2 = F(–2).

So the correct option is (b), i.e. F1(x) = F(–x).

9. $F(x)=\begin{cases}0 & \text{when } x\le 0\\ -x & \text{when } x>0\end{cases}$ and $F1(x)=\begin{cases}x & \text{when } x<0\\ 0 & \text{when } x\ge 0\end{cases}$

Therefore, replacing x by (–x) in above functions, we get

$$F(-x)=\begin{cases}0 & \text{when } x\ge 0\\ x & \text{when } x<0\end{cases} \text{ and } F1(-x)=\begin{cases}-x & \text{when } x>0\\ 0 & \text{when } x\le 0\end{cases}$$

Clearly, F1(x) = F(–x), hence, option (b) is the correct choice.

Alternate solution:

F1(–2) = –2 = F(2) and F1(2) = 0 = F(–2).

So the correct option is (2), i.e. F1(x) = F(–x)

10. $F(x)=\begin{cases}1-x & \text{when } 0\le x<2\\ 1 & \text{when } -2<x<0\end{cases}$ and

$$F1(x)=\begin{cases}-1-x & \text{when} -2<x<0\\ -1 & \text{when } 0\le x<2\end{cases}$$

Therefore, replacing x by (–x) in above functions, we get

$$F(-x)=\begin{cases}1+x & \text{when } -2<x<0\\ 1 & \text{when } 0\le x<2\end{cases} \text{ and}$$

$$F1(-x)=\begin{cases}-1+x & \text{when } 0\le x<2\\ -1 & \text{when } -2<x<0\end{cases}$$

$$\therefore\ -F(-x)=-\begin{cases}1+x & \text{when } -2<x<0\\ 1 & \text{when } 0\le x<2\end{cases}$$

$$=\begin{cases}-1-x & \text{when} -2<x<0\\ 1 & \text{when } 0\le x<2\end{cases}=F1(x)$$

Hence, option (3) is the correct option.

Alternate solution:

F1(2) = –1 = F(2) and F1(–2) = 1 = F(–2).

So the correct option is (3), i.e. F1(x) = – F(–x).

11. Distance between A and B = (35 × 2) + (45 × 2) = 160 km.

Distance covered by Aditi in each speed segment

$$=\frac{160}{3}$$

Hence, total petrol consumed

$$=\left(\frac{160}{3}\times\frac{1}{16}\right)+\left(\frac{160}{3}\times\frac{1}{24}\right)+\left(\frac{160}{3}\times\frac{1}{16}\right)=8.9\text{ l}$$

12. For minimum petrol consumption, Zoheb should drive at 40 kmph, petrol consumption = $\frac{160}{24}$ = 6.67 l.

13. From the graph, we know the percentage growth in sales are:

	Previous sales	Current sales	Difference	Percentage
1995-96	100	250	150	150%
1996-97	250	300	50	20%
1997-98	300	290	-10	–3.33%
1998-99	290	680	390	134.5%

It is but obvious from the above table that the maximum percentage increase relative to previous year occurred in 1995-96.

Alternative method:

The sales witnessed highest growth in 1995-96 and it was equal to $\frac{250-100}{100}\times 100=150\%$.

14. From the graph, we can again calculate the growth in profits.

	Previous profit	Current profit	Difference	Percentage
1995-96	2.5	4.5	2	80%
1996-97	4.5	6	1.5	33.33%
1997-98	6.0	8.5	2.5	41.66%
1998-99	8.5	12	3.5	41.2%

The highest percentage growth in net profit relative to the previous year was achieved in 1995-96.

Alternative method:

The net profit witnessed highest growth in 1995-96 and it was equal to $\frac{4.5-2.5}{2.5}\times 100=80\%$.

15.

	Net profit	Net sales	Ratio
1994-95	2.5	100	0.025
1995-96	4.5	250	0.02
1996-97	6	300	0.02
1997-98	8.5	290	0.03
1998-99	12	680	0.018

The profitability is maximum for 1997-98.

16. It may be seen that profitability does not follow a fixed pattern as the first three statements try to generalize the profitability. They are not applicable.

17. The price changes for each commodity are as follows.

	Ending	Beginning	Difference	Percentage
Arhar	2125	1700	425	25
Pepper	19275	18525	750	4
Sugar	1435	1440	5	–0.3
Gold	3820	4250	330	7.8

The highest price change from the graph and the above is definitely for Arhar.

18. The price volatility for each individual.

	Highest price	Lowest price	Difference	Average price	PV
Arhar	2300	1500	800	1900	0.42
Pepper	19500	17350	2250	18425	0.12
Sugar	1500	1410	90	1455	0.062
Gold	4300	3800	480	4050	0.12

The price volatility for sugar is least, hence answer choice is (3).

Note: Average price can be calculated by highest price, lowest price, ending and beginning price.

19. Let us assume Mr X invested Rs. 100 in each commodity.

	Price increase percentage	Income on Rs. 100
Arhar	25	25
Pepper	4	4.0
Sugar	–0.3	–0.3
Gold	–7.8	–7.8
		21.5

$\therefore$ His income is Rs. 21.5 on Rs. 400.

$\therefore \frac{21.5}{400} \times 100 = 5.4\%$ profit

20. As per the table in question 18, the maximum PV is around 40%.

For questions 21 to 23:

In graphs, the horizontal line x represents the values of x and the vertical line represents y, where y = f(x). For different values of x, we get the corresponding values of f(x).

21. From the graph, x = 2

$\Rightarrow$ f(2) = 1 and x = –2 $\Rightarrow$ f(–2) = 1

Thus, f(2) = f(–2). Hence, f(x) = f(–x)

22. From the graph, x = 1 $\Rightarrow$ f(1) = 2 and x = –1

$\Rightarrow$ f(–1) = 1

Thus, f(1) = 2f(–1)

Hence, 3f(x) = 6f(–x)

23. From the graph, x = 4

$\Rightarrow$ f(4) = –2 and x = –4 $\Rightarrow$ f(–4) = 2

Thus, f(4) = –f(–4)

Hence, f(x) = –f(–x)

24. Cost in shift operation = 800 + 1200 = Rs. 2,000

Variable cost for 40 units = Rs. 3,600

Approximate average unit cost for July

$= \frac{3600 + 2000}{40} = \text{Rs. } 140.$

25. The only change for change of production from 40 to 41 is the variable cost which is Rs. (3730 – 3600) = Rs. 130.

26. As the graph is an increasing function graph, MC always increases with increase in the number of units produced.

27. Total sales revenue = Rs. (150 × 40) = Rs. 6,000

Total production cost = Rs. (3600 + 2000)

= Rs. 5600.

So profit = Rs. 400.

28. Profit is highest when there is no second shift.

29. For production level in the range of 0 – 30 units, AC is always greater than Rs. 100 whereas MC is always less than or equal to Rs. 100.

30.

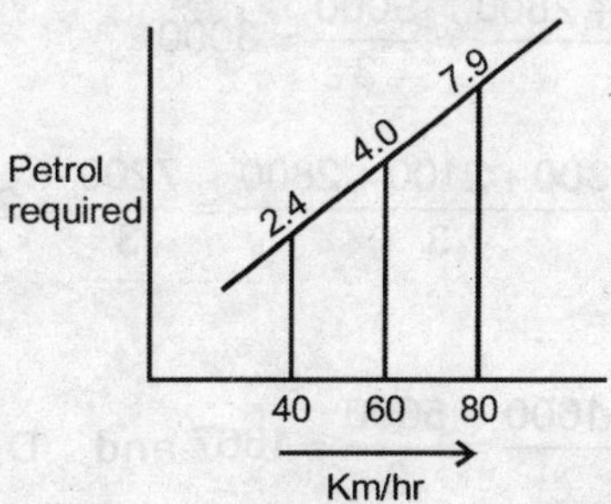

60 km/hr is travelled in 4 L petrol (from the graph).

$\therefore$ 1 L is required for 15 km, i.e. for 15 km, 1 L petrol is required.

For 200 km, $\frac{200}{15}$ = 13.33 L is required.

31. The fuel consumption at various speeds would be

$$\frac{200}{40} \times 2.5 = 12.5\text{L}$$

$$\frac{200}{80} \times 7.9 = 19.75\text{ L}$$

$$\frac{200}{60} \times 4 = 13.33\text{ L}$$

If Manasa travels at 40 km/hr, the total consumption would be 12.5 L. Hence Manasa has to decrease the speed.

32. It is evident from the graph that Seeta's growth rate decreased from third month as this is the first time the slope has decreased.

33. Geeta grew at the fastest rate in the first two months (the slope of the line in this period is steepest for Geeta).

34. Geeta grew the lowest in the third month (during this period, the slope was least for Geeta).

35. Seeta increased by 7 cm on 50 cm and Shyam by 7 cm on 53 cm. Hence, Shyam grew least.

For questions 36 to 38: Based on observation only.

36. By observation, 4 commodities namely Chillies, Onion, Egg and Dal showed a net overall increase and the remaining two , namely Edible Oil and Rice showed a net overall decrease.

37. Except Edible Oil, all the other five commodities experienced a price decline for two or more consecutive years.

38. Egg and Onion shows a price rise immediately after a price decline only once in this period.

39. Average incomes of Ahuja family

$$= \frac{3200+3000+2800}{3} = \frac{9000}{3} = 3000;$$

$$\text{Bose family} = \frac{2300+2100+2800}{3} = \frac{7200}{3} = 2400;$$

Coomar family =

$$\frac{1200+2200+1600}{3} = \frac{5000}{3} \approx 1667 \text{ and Dubey}$$

$$\text{family} = \frac{1200+3200}{2} = \frac{4400}{2} = 2200.$$

Hence, Coomar family has the lowest average income.

40. The average expenditures (approximately) for the families:

$$\text{Ahuja} = \frac{700+1700+2700}{3} \approx 1733;$$

$$\text{Bose} = \frac{800+1750+2300}{3} \approx 1617;$$

$$\text{Coomar} = \frac{500+1100+1900}{3} \approx 1167 \text{ and}$$

$$\text{Dubey} = \frac{1200+2800}{2} = 2000.$$

Hence, Dubey family has the highest average expenditure.

41. The average savings (approximately) for the families:

$$\text{Ahuja} = \frac{2500+1300+100}{3} = 1300;$$

$$\text{Bose} = \frac{1500+350+500}{3} \approx 783;$$

$$\text{Coomar} = \frac{700+1100+300}{3} = 700 \text{ and}$$

$$\text{Dubey} = \frac{0+400}{2} = 200.$$

Hence, Dubey family has the lowest average savings.

42. The savings of a person is maximum if he/she has high income but less expenditure. From the graph, a member of Ahuja family has Rs.3200 as income and Rs.700 as expenditure. Hence, he/she will have the maximum savings among all.

43. Let volume of data transfer in India = Volume of data transfer in Singapore = x

For INDIA:

ARDT for India ≈ \$1 (approx)

∴ Revenue from data transfer = \$x (approx)

$$\frac{\text{Revenue from data transfer}}{\text{Total Revenue}} \times 100 = 9\% \text{ (approx)}$$

$$\Rightarrow \text{Total Revenue} \simeq \frac{x}{9} \times 100 \text{ (approx)}$$

For SINGAPORE:

ARDT = \$9 (approx)

∴ Revenue from data transfer = \$9x (approx)

$$\frac{\text{Revenue from data transfer}}{\text{Total Revenue}} \times 100 = 20.5\% \text{ (approx)}$$

$$\Rightarrow \text{Total Revenue} = \frac{9x}{20.5} \times 100 \text{ (approx)}$$

$$\frac{\text{Total Revenue for Singapore}}{\text{Total Revenue for India}} = \frac{\frac{9x}{20.5} \times 100}{\frac{x}{9} \times 100} \approx 4 \text{ (approx)}$$

44. Let total revenue of Sweden in 2010 = x

Therefore total Revenue of India in 2010 = 2x

For Sweden in 2010:

ARDT = $6

Revenue from data transfer = 2 × 18% of x

$\therefore$ Volume of data transfer = $\dfrac{2 \times 18\% \text{ of } x}{6}$

For India in 2010:

Let ARDT = y

Revenue from data transfer = $3 \times 9\%$ of 2x

$\therefore$ Volume of data transfer = $\dfrac{3 \times 9\% \text{ of } 2x}{y}$

Therefore $\dfrac{2 \times 18\% \text{ of } x}{6} = \dfrac{3 \times 9\% \text{ of } 2x}{y} \Rightarrow y = \$9$

Therefore % change in ARDT of India

$= \dfrac{9-1}{1} \times 100 = 800\%$

45. For UK:

$\dfrac{\text{Revenue from Data transfar}}{\text{Total Revenue}} \times 100 = 30\% (\text{approx})$

Revenue from Data transfer

$= \dfrac{30}{100} \times \text{Total Revenue}$

ARDT = $ 13 (approx)

$\therefore$ Volume of Data transfer

$= \dfrac{30}{100} \times \dfrac{\text{Total Revenue}}{13}$

$\approx \dfrac{3}{130} \times \text{Total Revenue}$

For Spain:

$\dfrac{\text{Revenue from Data transfar}}{\text{Total Revenue}} \times 100 = 15\% (\text{approx})$

ARDT = 6.5 (approx)

$\therefore$ Volume of Data transfer

$= \dfrac{15}{100} \times \dfrac{\text{Total Revenue}}{6.5}$

$\approx \dfrac{3}{130} \times \text{Total Revenue}$

Similarly, we can check the other options and easily see that the volume of data transfer is NOT the same for given pair countries.

CHAPTER

3

Pie Chart

SOLVED EXAMPLES

Directions for examples 1 to 3: Answer the questions on the basis of the information given below.
Traditionally, pens have been of two types – Ink and Ball point. However, in the last few years, a new type of pen named 'Thin Nib' has gained acceptance. In 2017, the ratio of the sales volumes of the three types of pens, in the given order, in India was 7 : 12 : 1. The total sales volume of the three types of pens put together was 100 crore and that of the sales value of the three types of pens put together was Rs. 150 crore.
Pie chart-1 shows the distribution of the sales volume for Ball Point pens of seven brands. Pie chart-2 shows the distribution of the sales value for Ball Point pen of the seven brands.

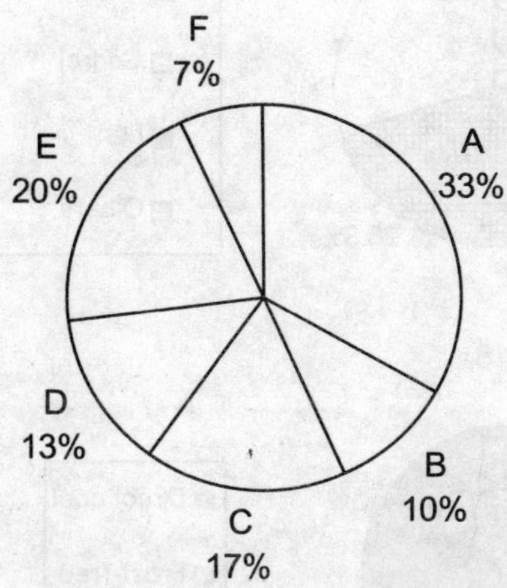

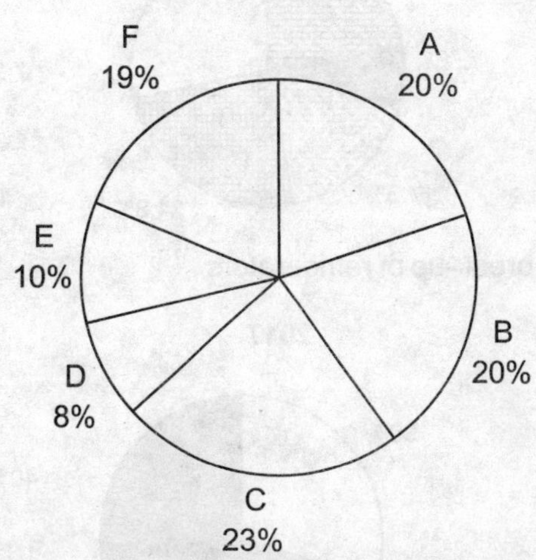

It is also known that only aforementioned brands of Ball Point pens were in the market in India in 2017 and each of these brands sold all of its Ball Point pens at the same price.

1. In India, which brand sold its Ball Point pen at the maximum price in the given year?
(1) B (2) D (3) C (4) F

2. In India, the total sales volume of Ball Point pens of brand E and half of brand B put together was _____% of the total sales volume of Ball Point pens in the given year?
(1) 75% (2) 20% (3) 25% (4) 30%

3. If a pie chart for the total sales volume of the three types of pen put together in India in the given year is drawn, then what would be the angle (in degree) subtended by the sales volume of Chinese Ink pens in the pie chart if Chinese Ink pens constituted 15% of the total sales of Ink pens?
(1) 17.8 (2) 18.9 (3) 17.9 (4) 19.8

For examples 1 to 3:

1. 4 The brand having the highest value of the ratio of the sales value to that of the sales volume must have sold its pens at the maximum price. We can see from the two pie charts that this ratio was the maximum for F.

2. 3 The percentage $= 20 + \frac{10}{2} = 25\%$.

3. 2 Angle subtended by ink pens in pie chart $= \frac{35}{100} \times 360 = 126°$

Hence, the angle subtend by the chinese ink pens $= \frac{15}{100} \times 126 = 18.9°$.

3.2 PIE CHART

Directions for examples 4 to 6: Answer the questions on the basis of the information given below.

The data given below represents the market share details for refrigerators in India.

Volumewise distribution of market share of frost-free refrigerators

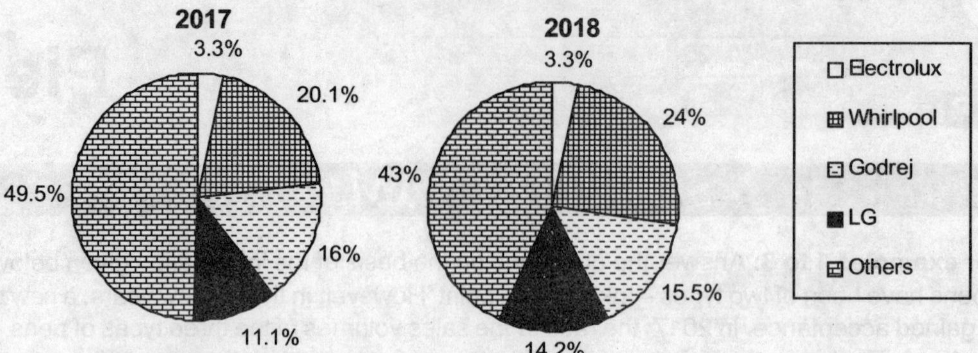

Volumewise distribution of market share of direct-cool refrigerators

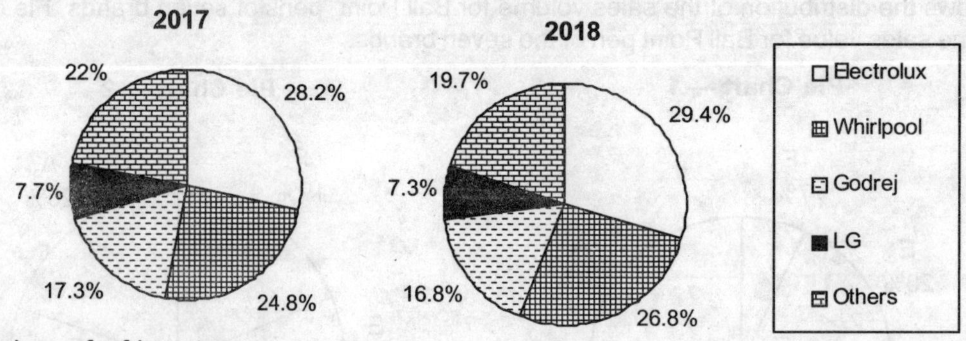

Total market break-up of refrigerators

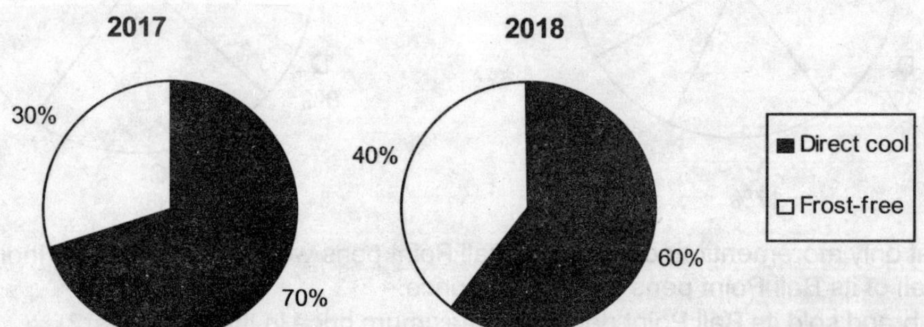

In 2017, the total market size of refrigerators was 7,50,000 units and in 2018, the market size grew by 10%.

4. In 2017, the per unit price of frost-free refrigerators was twice that of direct-cool refrigerators and the per unit price of direct cool refrigerators of Godrej and LG were in the ratio 1.5 : 1 . The sales revenue of Godrej was how many times that of LG in 2017?

(1) 2.7 (2) 1.8 (3) 0.37 (4) Data insufficient

5. What was the ratio of the growth rates of direct-cool to that of frost-free refrigerators in 2018 over 2017?

(1) 0.122 : 1 (2) –0.15 : 1 (3) –0.122 : 1 (4) 0.15 : 1

6. Which company registered the highest percentage growth in its sales volume of direct-cool refrigerators in 2018 over the same in 2017?

(1) Electrolux (2) Whirlpool (3) Godrej (4) LG

For examples 4 to 6:

4. 1 In 2017, the volumes of LG and Godrej are given below. Let LG direct cool unit price be x.

	Frost-free		Direct cool		Total sales
	Units	Sales	Units	Sales	
LG	24975	49950x	40425	40425x	90375x
Godrej	36000	108000x	90825	136240x	244240x

Hence, Godrej total sales than that of LG $= \dfrac{244240x}{90375x} = 2.7$ times

Alternate method:

Assume total market size of refrigerator be 100 units.

	DC = 70 units		FF = 30 units	
	Number of units	Turnover	Number of units	Turnover
Godrej	17.3% × 70 = 12.11	18.16	16% × 30 = 4.8	14.4
LG	7.7% × 70 = 5.39	5.39	11.1 × 30 = 3.33	6.66

Hence, sales turnover of Godrej to LG refrigerator in 2017 $= \dfrac{32.56}{12.05} = 2.7$

5. 3 Growth rate of direct cool $= \dfrac{495-525}{525} = -\dfrac{2}{35}$

Growth rate of frost-free $= \dfrac{330-225}{225} = \dfrac{7}{15}$

$\therefore$ Ratio $= \dfrac{-2}{35} \times \dfrac{7}{15} = -0.122:1.$

6. 2 The percentage growth in 2018 over 2017 in volume of direct cool refrigerators

	2017	2018
Electrolux	0.282 × 525000 = 148050	0.294 × 495000 = 145530
Whirlpool	0.248 × 525000 = 130200	0.268 × 495000 = 132660
Godrej	90825	0.168 × 495000 = 83160
LG	40425	0.073 × 495000 = 36135

Only Whirlpool showed positive growth.

3.4 PIE CHART

Directions for examples 7 to 9: Answer the questions on the basis of the information given below.

The following pie charts give the number of employees at UltraTech at the end of the year for the period 1999 to 2003. The charts also capture the education qualification of the employees. UltraTech does not employ people who are not atleast matriculates and once a person gets recruited, he cannot pursue further education. It is also known that no employee of the company left the job during the given period.

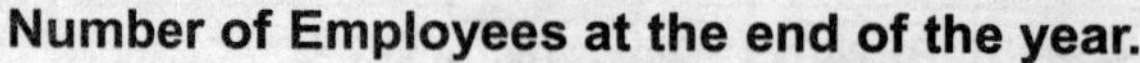

Number of Employees at the end of the year.

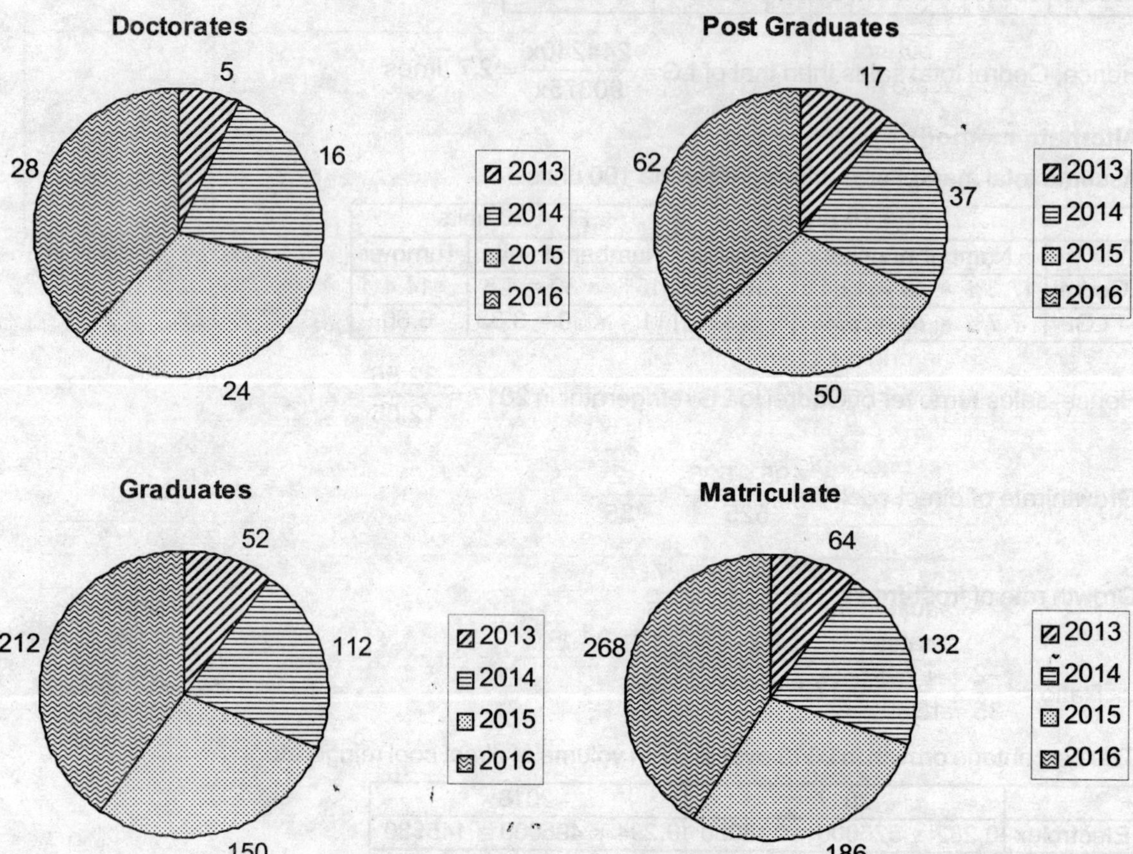

NOTE: It is necessary for a doctorate to be a post graduate, for a post graduate to be a graduate and for a graduate to be a matriculate. This means that the number of matriculates also include those who went on to do their graduation, post graduation, doctorates. Similar is the case for the numbers of graduates and post graduates.

7. How many graduates joined UltraTech in the year 2015?

(1) 38 (2) 56

(3) 62 (4) Cannot be determined

8. How many post graduates who did not continue their education to become doctorates, joined UltraTech in 2015 and 2016 put together?

(1) 14 (2) 13

(3) 12 (4) Cannot be determined

9. How many employees joined UltraTech in the year 2014?

(1) 68 (2) 91

(3) 84 (4) Cannot be determined

For examples 7 to 9:

Since the figures are cumulative (both row wise and column wise), it would have been better to construct the following table:

	Existing in 2013	Joined in 2014	Joined in 2015	Joined in 2016
Doctorates	5	11	8	4
Post Graduates but not Doctorates	12	a	b	
Graduates but not Post Graduate or Doctorates	35	c	d	
Matriculates but not Graduate, Post Graduate or Doctors	12			

The values given in the above table can easily be deduced as in any cumulative series (the value minus the preceding value).

Identifying the further values is the difficult part. Now the post graduates (including doctorates) in 2014 (including those in 2013) is 37 as given in original table. Thus 5 + 11 + 12 + a = 37 i.e. a = 9.

Similarly 5 + 11 + 8 + 12 + a + b = 50. Since we already know a = 9, we can find b = 5

Also 5 + 12 + 35 + 11 + a + c = 112. Thus c = 40.

Having found a, b, and c, one could have found d because 5 + 11 + 8 + 12 + a + b + 35 + c + d = 150 $\Rightarrow$ d = 25.

Now one can populate the entire table in a similar manner. The final table will be:

	Existing in 2013	Joined in 2014	Joined in 2015	Joined in 2016
Doctorates	5	11	8	4
Post Graduates but not Doctorates	12	9	5	8
Graduates but not Post Graduates or Doctorates	35	40	25	50
Matriculates but not Gradudates, Post Graduate or Doctorates	12	8	16	20

7. 1 The number of graduates who joined UltraTech in the year 2015 = 25 + 5 + 8 = 38.

8. 2 The number of post graduates who did not continue their education to become doctorates, that joined UltraTech in 2015 and 2016 put together = 5 + 8 = 13.

9. 1 The number of employees that joined UltraTech in the year 2000 = 132 – 64 = 68.

Directions for examples 10 to 12 Answer the questions on the basis of the information given below.

The pie charts given below show the distribution of the number of athletes sent by three countries to take part in eight different games in the recently held Olympics. The numbers of athletes sent by USA, China and Russia were in the ratio 8 : 11 : 5. It is also known that the total number of athletes sent by the three countries put together was 2400.

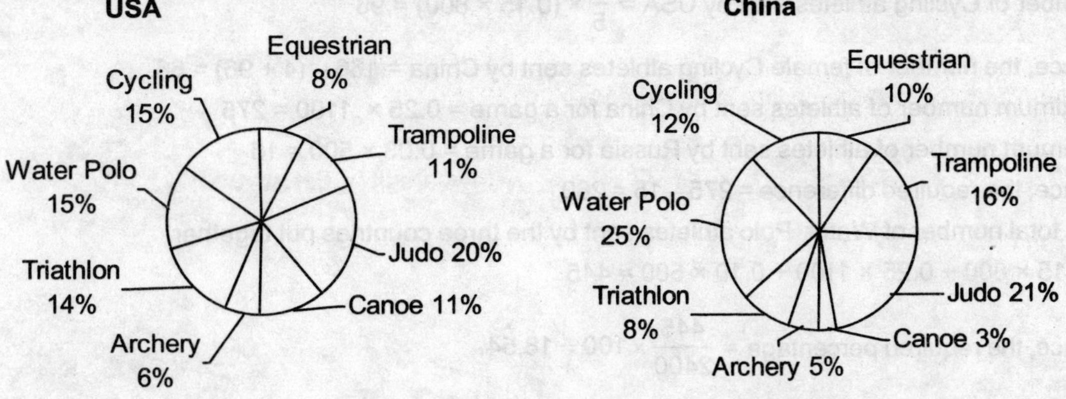

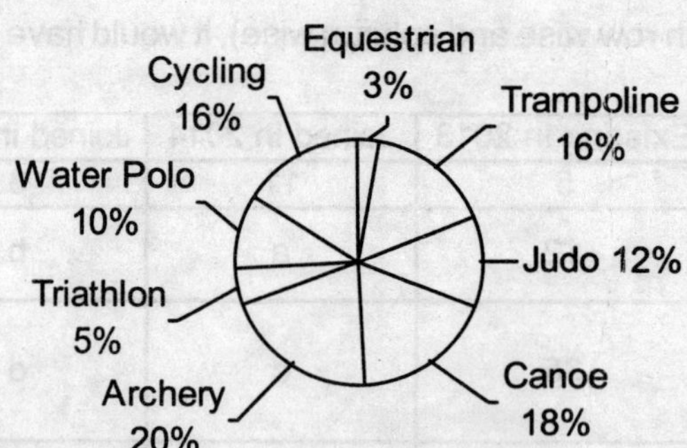

10. The female to male ratio for Cycling athletes from Russia and USA was 1 : 19 and 4 : 1 respectively. If the number of female Cycling athletes was equal to the number of male Cycling athletes for the three countries put together, then what was the number of female Cycling athletes from China?

(1) 4 (2) 96 (3) 66 (4) None of these

11. What was the absolute difference between the maximum number of athletes sent by China for a game and the minimum number of athletes sent by Russia for a game?

(1) 260 (2) 160 (3) 242 (4) 145

12. The number of Water Polo athletes constituted what percent of the total number of athletes sent by the three countries put together?

(1) 20.00 (2) 18.90 (3) 22.30 (4) 18.54

For examples 10 to 12:

The total number of athletes sent by:

$$\text{USA} = 2400 \times \frac{8}{24} = 800$$

$$\text{China} = 2400 \times \frac{11}{24} = 1100$$

$$\text{Russia} = 2400 \times \frac{5}{24} = 500$$

10. 3 Total number of Cycling athletes sent by the three countries together
$= 0.15 \times 800 + 0.12 \times 1100 + 0.16 \times 500 = 332$

Total number of female Cycling athletes sent by the three countries together = 166

Number of female Cycling athletes sent by Russia $= \frac{1}{20} \times (0.16 \times 500) = 4$

Number of Cycling athletes sent by USA $= \frac{4}{5} \times (0.15 \times 800) = 96$

Hence, the number of female Cycling athletes sent by China = 166 – (4 + 96) = 66.

11. 1 Maximum number of athletes sent by China for a game = $0.25 \times 1100 = 275$

Minimum number of athletes sent by Russia for a game = $0.03 \times 500 = 15$

Hence, the required difference = 275 – 15 = 260

12. 4 The total number of Water Polo athletes sent by the three countries put together
$= 0.15 \times 800 + 0.25 \times 1100 + 0.10 \times 500 = 445$

Hence, the required percentage $= \frac{445}{2400} \times 100 = 18.54.$

Directions for examles 13 to 16: Answer the questions on the basis of the information given below.
Pie chart 1 shows the state-wise distribution of population of Australia, which has six states – Queensland, Tasmania, Sydney, Hobart, Newland and Hampshire. Pie chart 2 shows the state-wise distribution of GDP of Australia. The states are denoted as a, b, c, d, e and f, not necessarily in same order.

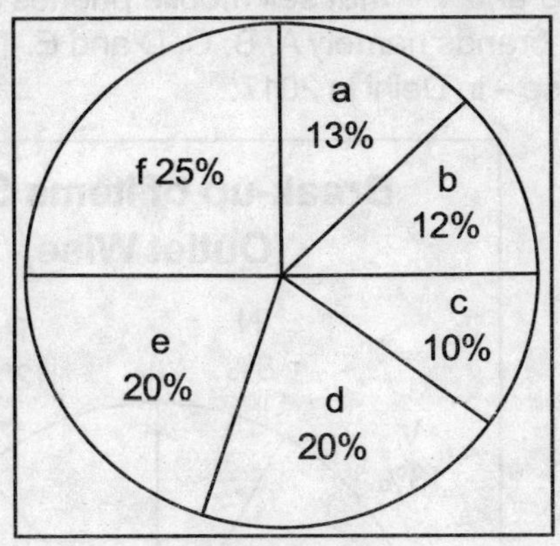

Pie Chart 1

a 15%
b 18%
c 12%
d 16%
e 21%
f 18%

Pie Chart 2

Per Capita Income(PCI) = GDP/Population
It is also known that:
(i) PCI of Newland is 10% less than PCI of Hampshire and 40% less than PCI of Tasmania.
(ii) PCI of Queensland is 30% less than PCI of Hobart.

13. If GDP of Hampshire is 24 billion dollars and population of Tasmania is 1.5 million, then what is the PCI (in dollar) of Queensland?
(1) 1050 (2) 16000 (3) 10500 (4) 15000

14. How many states have PCI higher than that of Australia?
(1) 2 (2) 4 (3) 3 (4) 1

15. If PCI of Hobart is more than that of Hampshire by $8400, then what is the PCI of Tasmania?
(1) $14000 (2) $14400 (3) $15000 (4) $16000

16. What is the PCI of Newland?
(1) 0.72 (2) 1.05 (3) 0.8 (4) Cannot be determined

For examples 13 to 16:
Let the total GDP be 100G and total population be 100P.
From the given data and information the GDP and population of different states of Australia can be tabulated as shown below.

	GDP	Population	PCI	States
a	15G	13P	1.15G/P	Sydney
b	18G	12P	1.5G/P	Hobart
c	12G	10P	1.2G/P	Tasmania
d	16G	20P	0.8G/P	Hampshire
e	21G	20P	1.05G/P	Queensland
f	18G	25P	0.72G/P	New land

13. 3 GDP of Australia = $\frac{24}{16} \times 100$ = 150 billion dollars
Population of Australia = 1.5 × 10 = 15 million.

PCI of Queensland = $1.05 \times \left(\frac{150}{15}\right) \times \frac{10^9}{10^6} = 1.05 \times 10^4 = 10500.$

14. 2 CPI of Australia = $\frac{G}{P}$
It is clear from the table, Sydney, Hobart, Tasmania and Queensland are the required states.

15. 2 (1.5 – 0.80)G/P = 8400 so 1.2G/P = $14400.

16. 4 The exact value cannot be determined because we do not know the exact value of the GDP and population of the Australia.

PRACTICE EXERCISE – 1

Directions for questions 1 to 4: Answer the questions on the basis of the information given below.

In Delhi, there were only eight outlets – N, P, Q, R, S, T, U and V – that sell mobile phones in 2017. Each of these outlets sold mobiles of one or more brands out of the five brands namely A, B, C, D and E. The following pie charts show break-up of mobiles sold – brand-wise and outlet-wise – in Delhi in 2017.

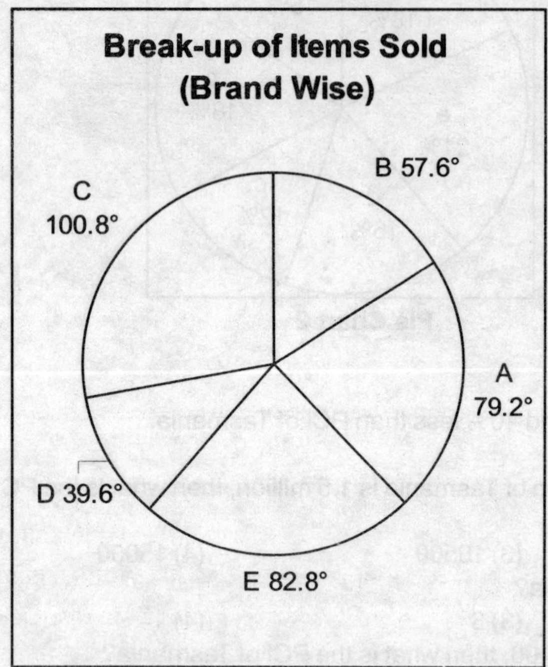

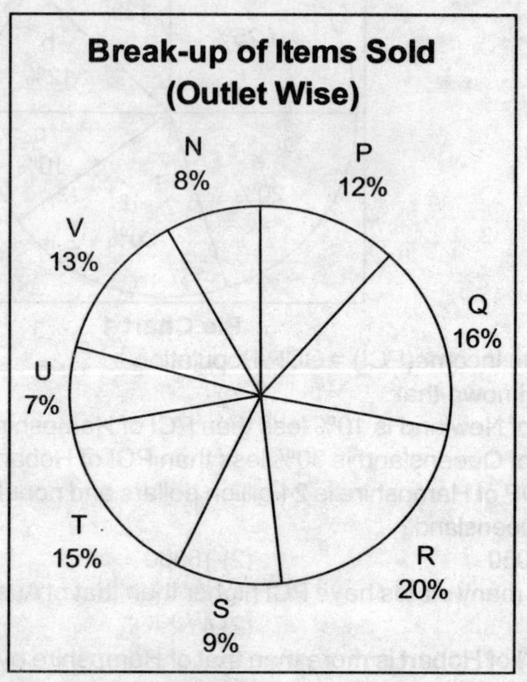

1. The number of outlets that sold mobiles of only one brand could not be more than

   (1) 7 (2) 4

   (3) 5 (4) 6

2. If R did not sell mobile of brand A, and A did not constitute more than 30% of sales of any outlets, the sales of brand A through any of the outlets as a percentage of the total sales of that outlet could not be less than

   (1) 7.77% (2) 14.2%

   (3) 5% (4) 1.4%

3. Due to some technical glitch, brand C had to recall 40% of its products sold in 2017 in Delhi. It is also known that every outlet had sold at least 10% of these defective items. If the sales of each outlet was adjusted after this recall, then, after adjustment, the share of sales of any outlet as a percentage of total sales could not be less than

   (1) 5.36% (2) 4.76%

   (3) 4.1% (4) 3.64%

4. If R sold at least 30% of the total mobiles sold of brands A and C put together, then at most what percentage of the total mobiles sold of brand B was sold by R?

   (1) 31.25% (2) 16.66%

   (3) 33.3% (4) None of these

Directions for questions 5 to 8: Answer the questions on the basis of the information given below.

ABC Ltd. is a courier company that uses three modes of transport for its services – Air, Rail and Road. The following pie charts show the distribution of the total number of couriers (Chart-1), revenue generated (Chart-2) and total cost (Chart-3) for the different modes of transport for the year 2017. Assume that the only cost involved was that incurred on transportation.

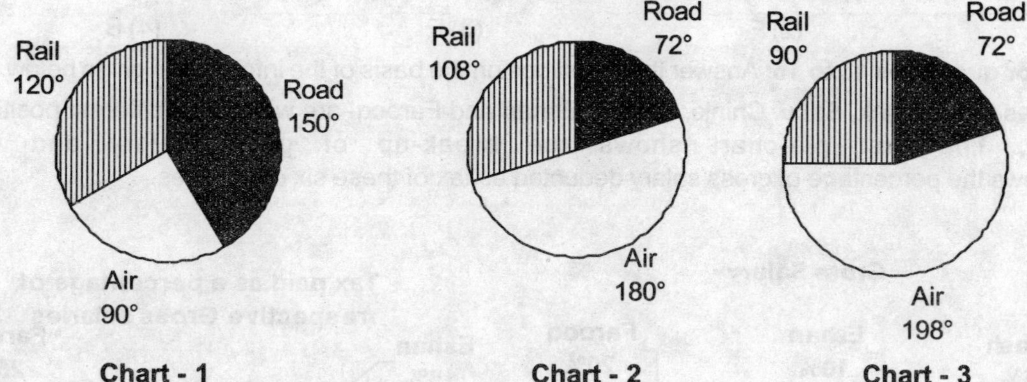

5. In 2017, if the company made a profit of 20%, what was the profit percentage on the couriers sent by Air transport?

(1) 9.09% (2) 10% (3) 32% (4) 33.2%

6. Through which mode of transportation did the company generate maximum profit in 2017?

(1) Rail (2) Road (3) Air (4) Data Insufficient

7. Which mode of transportation had the least cost of transport per courier in the year 2017 for the company?

(1) Rail (2) Road (3) Air (4) Data Insufficient

8. In 2017, if the company made neither profit nor loss, then for how many modes of transportation did the company incur loss?

(1) 0 (2) 1 (3) 2 (4) 3

Directions for questions 9 to 12: Answer the questions on the basis of the information given below.

The following pie chart gives details of the production, expenses and export of the six products manufactured by company KL Enterprises, which manufactures only the given six products, in the year 2017. In the given year, the company followed a very strict internal audit policy and any item that did not meet the specifications were rejected and disposed off. All the products exported were those manufactured in the same year itself.

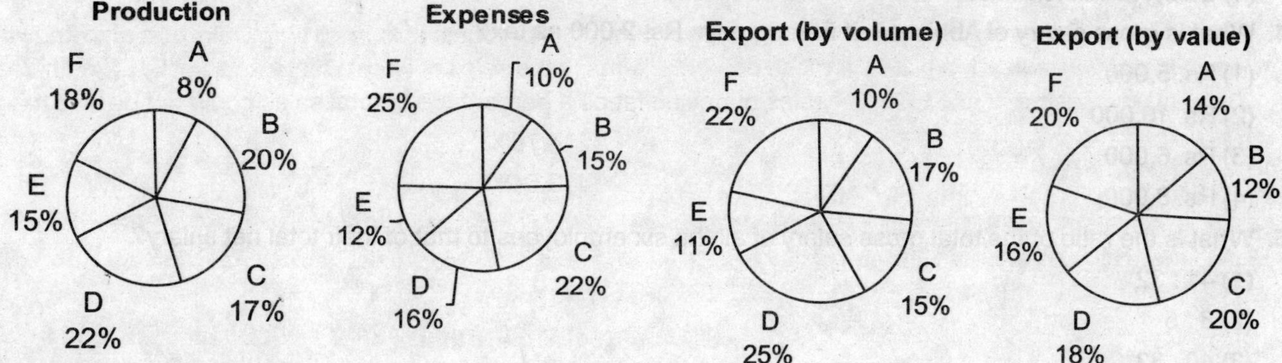

Profit = Sales – Expenses

$$\text{Profitability (\%)} = \frac{\text{Profit}}{\text{Expenses}} \times 100$$

Note: Export is the only source of sales.

9. In 2017, the products exported as a percentage of the products manufactured by the company could not be more than

(1) 73.3% (2) 81.81% (3) 80% (4) 88%

10. In 2017, if product D was a profit making product for the company, what was the maximum number of products that were loss making products for the company?

(1) 2 (2) 3 (3) 4 (4) Zero

11. The export price per unit of which product was the highest?

(1) A (2) C (3) D (4) E

12. For which product the rejection rate was maximum?

(1) C (2) F (3) E (4) B

Directions for questions 13 to 16: Answer the questions on the basis of the information given below.

Six employees – Abhishek, Babu, Chinki, Dinesh, Eshan and Farooq–are working at different positions in Geosis Technology. The first pie-chart shows the break-up of gross salary and the second pie-chart shows the percentage of gross salary deducted as tax of these six employees.

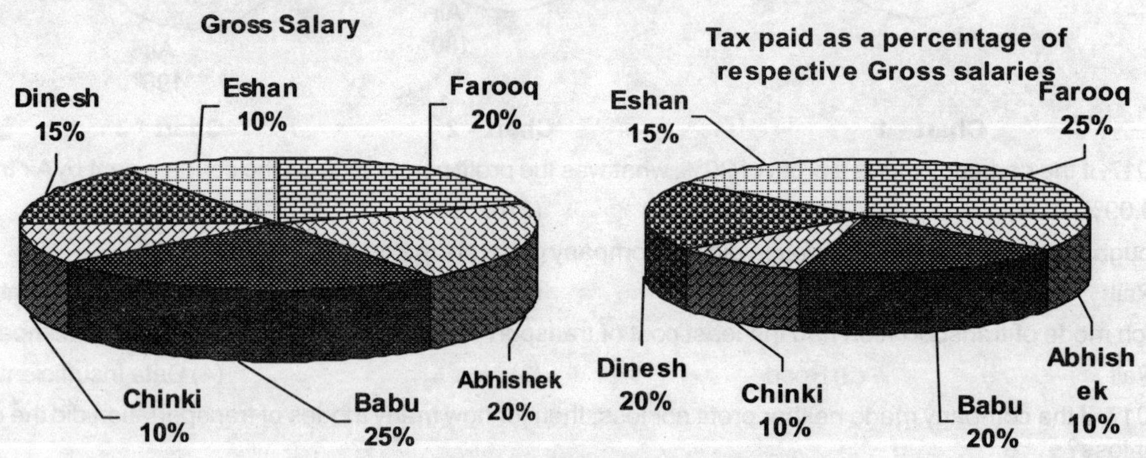

Net salary = Gross salary – Tax deducted.

13. What is the ratio of the net salaries of – Abhishek, Babu, Chinki, Dinesh, Eshan and Farooq?

(1) 36 : 40 : 18 : 24 : 17 : 30

(2) 36 : 40 : 18 : 26 : 17 : 30

(3) 36 : 40 : 9 : 18 : 17 : 30

(4) Cannot be determined

14. What is gross salary of Abhishek, if Farooq pays Rs. 2,000 as tax?

(1) Rs. 5,000

(2) Rs. 10,000

(3) Rs. 6,000

(4) Rs. 8,000

15. What is the ratio of the total gross salary of all the six employees to that of their total net salary?

(1) 41 : 32

(2) 8 : 5

(3) 40 : 33

(4) Cannot be determined

16. What is the ratio of tax collected by A, B and C put together to that by D, E and F put together?

(1) 19 : 17

(2) 17 : 19

(3) 19 : 16

(4) 16 : 19

Directions for questions 17 to 20: Refer to the pie-chart given below:

[CAT 1994]

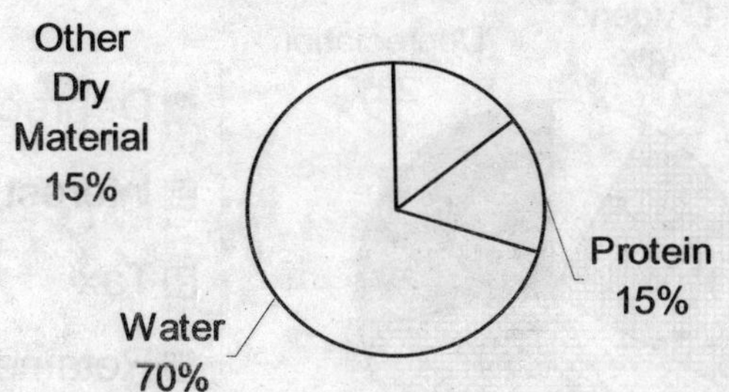

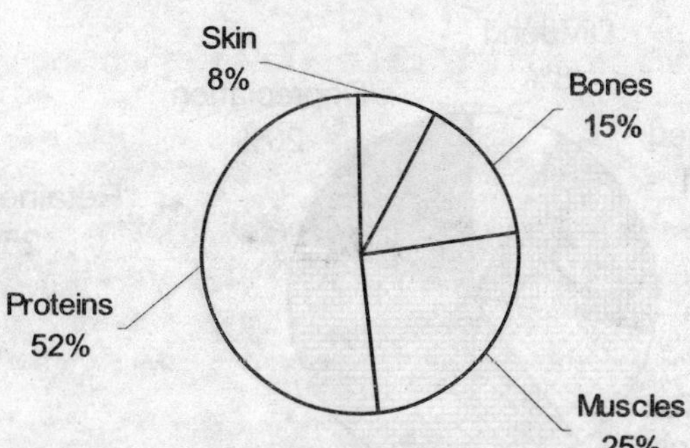

17. What fraction of (Approximately) Ghoshbabu's weight consists of muscular and skin protein?

(1) $\frac{1}{13}$ (2) $\frac{1}{30}$

(3) $\frac{1}{20}$ (4) Cannot be determined

18. Ratio of distribution of protein in muscle to the distribution of protein in skin is

(1) 3 : 1 (2) 3 : 10

(3) 1 : 3 (4) $3\frac{1}{2} : 1$

19. What percent of Ghosh Babu's body weight is made up of skin

(1) 0.15 (2) 10

(3) 1.2 (4) Cannot be determined

20. In terms of total body weight, the portion of material other than water and protein is closest to

(1) $\frac{3}{20}$ (2) $\frac{1}{15}$

(3) $\frac{85}{100}$ (4) $\frac{1}{20}$

PRACTICE EXERCISE – 2

Directions for questions 1 to 5: Answer the questions based on the following piecharts. **[CAT 1995]**

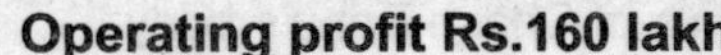

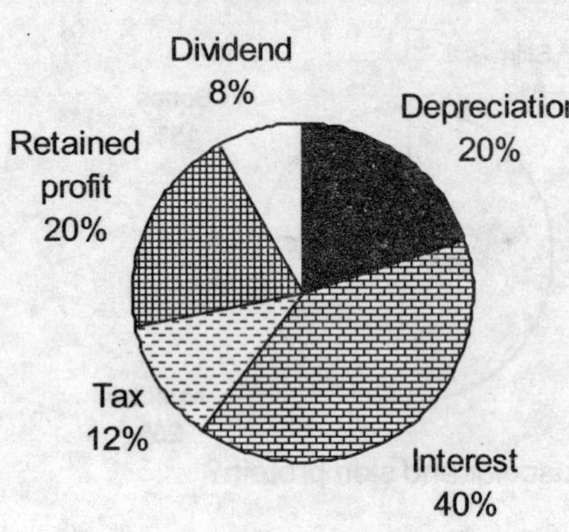

1991-92

Operating profit Rs.130 lakh

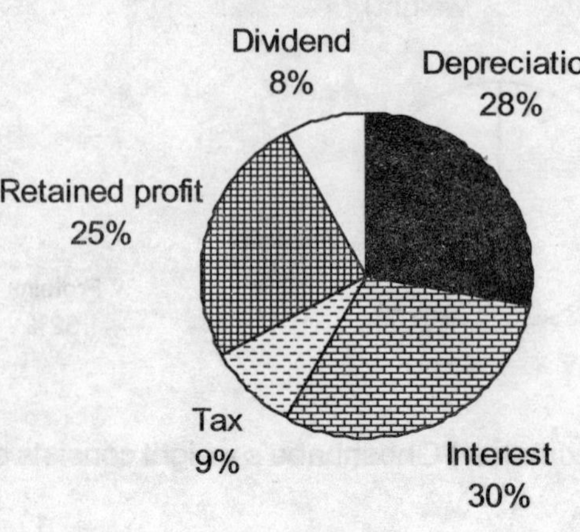

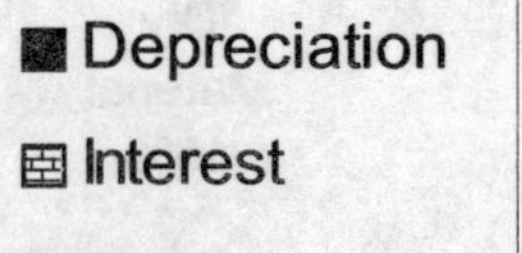

1990-91

1. The operating profit in 1991-92 increased over that in 1990-91 by

(1) 23% (2) 22%

(3) 25% (4) 24%

2. The interest burden in 1991-92 was higher than that in 1990-91 by

(1) 50% (2) Rs.25 lakh

(3) 90% (4) Rs.41 lakh

3. If on an average, 20% rate of interest was charged on borrowed funds, then the total borrowed funds used by this company in the given two years amounted to

(1) Rs.221 lakh (2) Rs.195 lakh

(3) Rs.368 lakh (4) Rs.515 lakh

4. The retained profit in 1991-92, as compared to that in 1990-91 was

(1) higher by 2.5% (2) higher by 1.5%

(3) lower by 2.5% (4) lower by 1.5%

5. The equity base of these companies remained unchange(d) Then the total dividend earning by the share holders in 1991-92 is

(1) Rs.104 lakh (2) Rs.9 lakh

(3) Rs.12.8 lakh (4) Rs.15.6 lakh

Directions for questions 6 to 9: Answer the questions based on the following information

[CAT 1999]

Consider the information provided in the figure below relating to India's foreign trade in 1997-98 and the first eight months of 1998-99. Total trade with a region is defined as the sum of exports and imports from that region. Trade deficit is defined as the excess of imports over exports. Trade deficit may be negative.

A. USA	B. Germany	C. Other EU
D. UK	E. Japan	F. Russia
G. Other East European countries	H. OPEC	I. Asia
J. Other LDCs	K. Others	

Source of imports

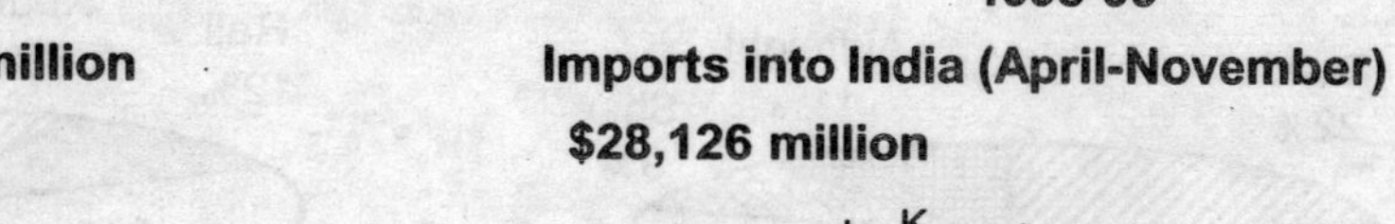

1997-98	1998-99
Imports into India $40,779 million	**Imports into India (April-November) $28,126 million**

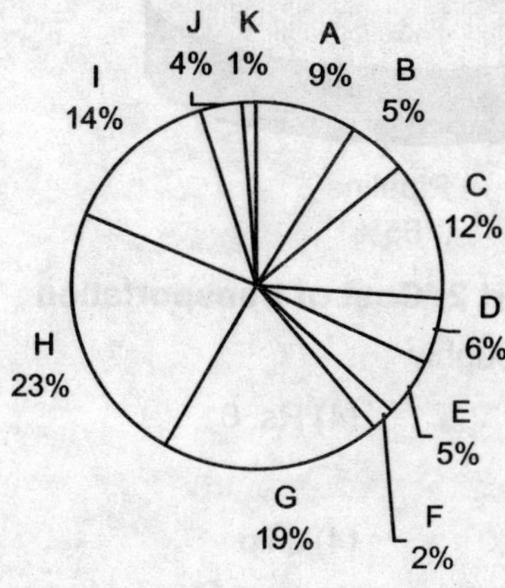

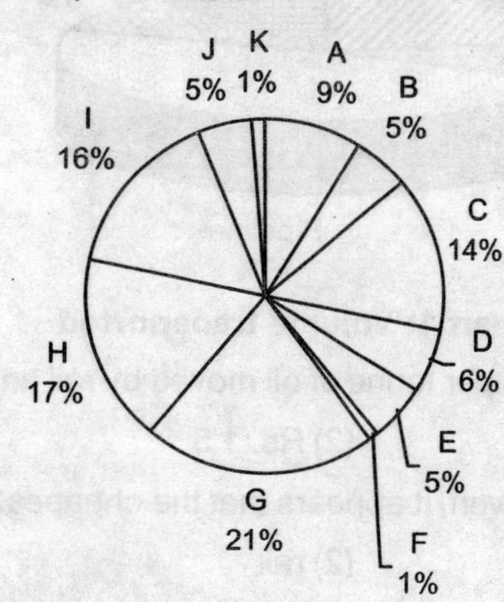

Destination of exports

1997-98	1998-99
Exports from India: $33,979 million	**Exports from India (April-November) $21,436 million**

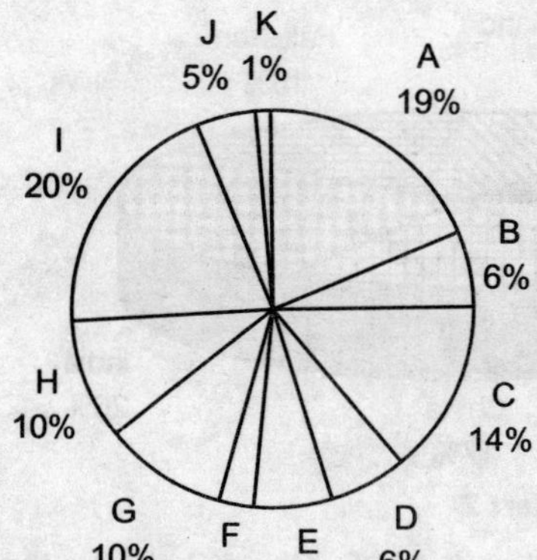

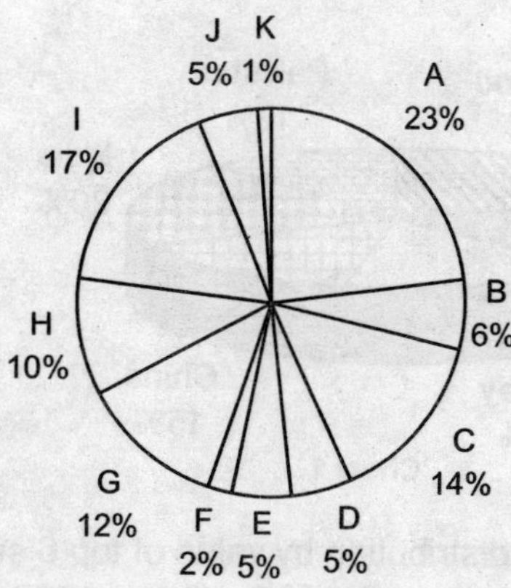

6. What is the region with which India had the highest total trade in 1997-98?

(1) USA (2) Other EU countries (3) OPEC (4) Others

7. In 1997-98 the amount of Indian exports, million US dollars, to the region with which India had the lowest total trade, is approximately

(1) 750 (2) 340 (3) 220 (4) 440

8. In 1997-98, the trade deficit with respect to India, billion US dollars, for the region with the highest trade deficit with respect to India, is approximately equal to

(1) 6.0 (2) 3.0 (3) 4.5 (4) 7.5

9. What is the region with the lowest trade deficit with India in 1997-98?

(1) USA (2) Asia (3) Others (4) Other EU countries

Directions for questions 10 to 12: Answer the questions based on the pie charts given below.

[CAT 2001]

Chart 1 shows the distribution of 12 million tonnes of crude oil transported through different modes over a specific period of time. Chart 2 shows the distribution of the cost of transporting this crude oil. The total cost was Rs. 30 million.

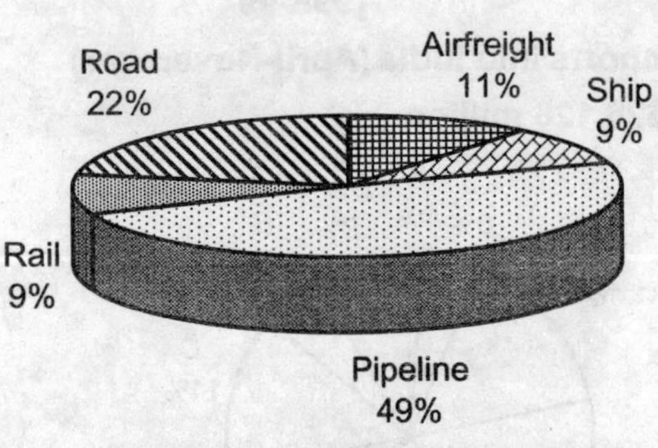

Chart 1: Volume transported

Rail 12%
Road 6%
Airfreight 7%
Ship 10%
Pipeline 65%

Chart 2: Cost of transportation

10. The cost in rupees per tonne of oil moved by rail and road happens to be roughly

(1) Rs. 3 (2) Rs. 1.5 (3) Rs. 4.5 (4) Rs. 8

11. From the charts given, it appears that the cheapest mode of transport is

(1) road (2) rail (3) pipeline (4) ship

12. If the costs per tonne of transport by ship, air and road are represented by P, Q and R respectively, which of the following is true?

(1) R > Q > P (2) P > R > Q (3) P > Q > R (4) R > P > Q

Directions for questions 13 and 14: Answer the questions based on the pie charts given below.

[CAT 2002]

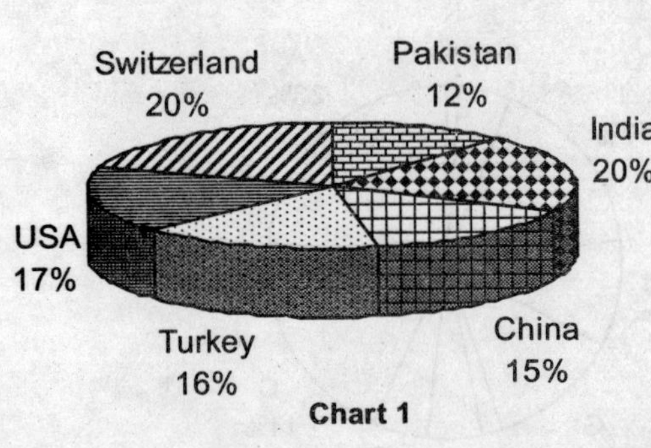

Chart 1

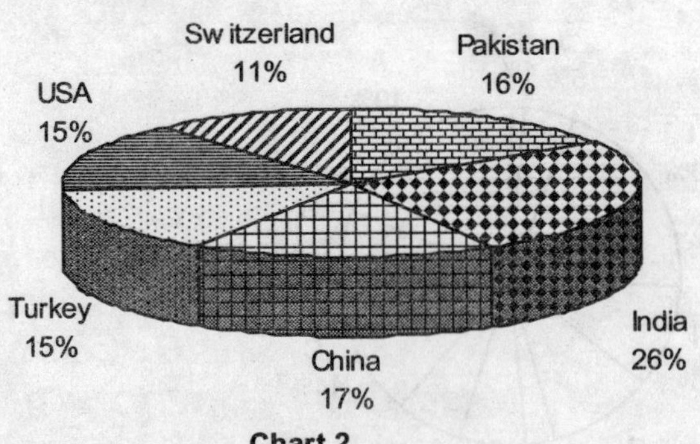

Chart 2

Chart 1 shows the distribution by value of top 6 suppliers of MFA Textiles in 1995. Chart 2 shows the distribution by quantity of top 6 suppliers of MFA Textiles in 1995. The total value is 5760 million Euro (European currency). The total quantity is 1.055 million tonnes.

13. The country which has the highest average price is

(1) USA (2) Switzerland (3) Turkey (4) India

14. The average price in Euro per kilogram for Turkey is roughly

(1) 6.20 (2) 5.60 (3) 4.20 (4) 4.80

ANSWER KEYS

PRACTICE EXERCISE – 1

1. (1)	**2.** (4)	**3.** (3)	**4.** (1)	**5.** (1)	**6.** (4)	**7.** (2)	**8.** (2)	**9.** (3)	**10.** (2)
11. (4)	**12.** (3)	**13.** (1)	**14.** (4)	**15.** (3)	**16.** (4)	**17.** (3)	**18.** (1)	**19.** (4)	**20.** (1)

PRACTICE EXERCISE – 2

1. (1)	**2.** (2)	**3.** (4)	**4.** (4)	**5.** (3)	**6.** (3)	**7.** (2)	**8.** (1)	**9.** (1)	**10.** (2)
11. (1)	**12.** (3)	**13.** (2)	**14.** (2)						

EXPLANATIONS

PRACTICE EXERCISE – 1

For questions 1 to 4:

Break-up of mobiles sold brandwise:

A-22%, B-16%, C-28%, D-11%, E- 23%

1. Following are the outlets that would sell mobile phones of only one brand:

T, N $\rightarrow$ E

P, Q $\rightarrow$ C

S, U $\rightarrow$ B

V $\rightarrow$ A or R $\rightarrow$ A

Hence, the number of required outlets is 7.

2. Let say the share of that outlet be x% in total sales. So A sells 30% through each of other outlet, leaving R as well, to minimize its share in the desired outlet. Hence A sells (22 – 0.3(100 – 20 – x)) % of its items through that outlet.

Percentage of this sale out of that outlets total sales will be = ((22 – 0.3(100 – 20 – x))/x) X 100 = (0.3 – 2/x) X 100

Which will be minimum when x is minimum, that is when its outlet U – 7%

And it will make 1.4%

3. Lets assume total sales be 100x. C's sale will be 28x and total recall will be 0.4 X 28x = 11.2x.

Now the total sales will be 100x – 11.2x = 88.8x

If the maximum recall is from outlet having least share then the impact will be maximum, that is U.

So minimum recall is from other outlets, 1.12x by each of the other 7 outlets, that is 7.84x. Hence remaining 3.36x recall will be from U. Now, share of U will be ((7x – 3.36x)/ 88.8x) X 100 % = 4.1%

4. To maximize the share of R in B sales, share of other brands should be minimized. So exactly 30% of sales of A & C is through R, that 15% of total sales. So remaining 5% is of brand R, which makes 31.25% share of B.

5. The ratio of total revenue to total cost for

Air transport = $\frac{10R}{11C}$

Where R is the revenue generated by the company. C is the total cost of the company.

If the profit% of the company is 20%, then $\frac{R}{C} = 1.2$

So, total revenue as a fraction of cost for couriers sent through Air transport = $\frac{10}{11} \times 1.2 = 1.0909$

Hence, the profit% for couriers sent through Air transport = 9.09%

6. Let the total cost be 360C and the revenue generated be 360R for ABC Ltd. in the year 2017.

Profit generated by:

Road transport = 72R – 72C.

Rail transport = 108R – 90C.

Air transport = 180R – 198C.

The profit generated is a function of R and C whose value are not known.

So the answer cannot be determined.

7. Let the total number of couriers be 360N and the total cost be 360C.

So the cost per courier for:

Road transport = $\frac{72C}{150N} = \frac{0.48C}{N}$.

Rail transport = $\frac{90C}{120N} = \frac{0.75C}{N}$.

Air transport = $\frac{198C}{90N} = \frac{2.2C}{N}$.

It is clear from the above that the road transport has the least cost of transport per courier.

8. Let the total cost be 360C and the Revenue Generated be 360R.

As 360C = 360R,

Therefore, the company incured loss for air transport.

9. Let the production be 100x and export (volume) be 100y.

As the share in export for three products (I.e. A, D and F is more than that in production but A witness the maximum change in share.)

For maximizing the export (volume) assume all volume of A is exported

$\therefore\ 8x = 10y \Rightarrow \dfrac{y}{x} = 0.8 = 80\%.$

10. Let the expenses and export by value be 100 x and 100y respectively.

As D is making profit

$\therefore\ 16x > 18y \Rightarrow x > \dfrac{9}{8}y$

Now, we can see that three products B, C and F can be in loss.

11. Let export (by volume) and export by value be 100x and 100y respectively then price per unit for all products is shown below:

$$A = \frac{14y}{10x}, B = \frac{12y}{17x},\ C = \frac{20y}{15x},\ D = \frac{15y}{25x}$$

$$E = \frac{16y}{11x},\ F = \frac{20y}{22x}$$

Hence, E has the highest price per unit.

12. Let the production and export is 100x and 100y respectively.

Rejection rate of all products is given below:

$$A = 1 - \frac{10y}{8x},\ B = 1 - \frac{17y}{20x},\ C = 1 - \frac{15y}{20x}$$

$$D = 1 - \frac{25y}{22x},\ E = 1 - \frac{11y}{15x},\ F = 1 - \frac{22y}{18x}$$

Hence, E has the maximum rejection rate.

For questions 13 to 16:

Let cumulative salary be Rs. 100. So their respective salaries will be:

	Gross Salary	Tax	Net Salary
Abhishek	20	2	18
Babu	25	5	20
Chinki	10	1	9
Dinesh	15	3	12
Eshan	10	1.5	8.5
Farooq	20	5	15

13. The required ratio = 18 : 20 : 9 : 12 : 8.5 : 15

i.e. 36 : 40 : 18 : 24 : 17 : 30

14. Tax paid by Farooq = Rs. 2,000

So, gross salary of Farooq = $2000 \times \dfrac{20}{5}$ = Rs. 8,000

(As gross salary of Farooq and Abhishek is same)

Hence, Gross salary of Abhishek = Rs. 8,000.

15. If total Gross salary be Rs. 100, then total net salary = (18 + 20 + 9 + 12 + 8.5 + 15) = Rs. 82.50

Hence, required ratio is 100 : 82.50 i.e. 40 : 33.

16. Total tax collected by A, B and C put together = 2 + 5 + 1 = 8

Total tax collected by D, E and F put together = 3 + 1.5 + 5 = 9.5

Required ratio = 8 : 9.5 = 16 : 19.

17. The skin & muscular protein totally constitutes 33% of the total proteins. The total proteins itself is 15% of the total body weight. Hence the percentage of skin & muscular protein as a fraction of the total body weight = 33% of 15% $\approx$ 5% = $\dfrac{1}{20}$.

18. Required Ratio = 25 : 8 $\approx$ 3 : 1.

19. We can determine only the percentage of skin protein in Ghosh Babu's total body weight. But there is no data given about the percentage of skin in Ghosh Babu's body.

20. Proportion of material other than water & protein in Ghosh Babu's body is $\dfrac{15}{100} = \dfrac{3}{20}$.

PRACTICE EXERCISE – 2

1. Percentage increase = $(160 - 130)\dfrac{100}{130} = \dfrac{300}{13}$ = 23%.

2. Interest in 1990-91 = 30% of 130 = Rs.39 lakh

Interest in 1991-92 = 40% of 160 = Rs.64 lakh

Hence, required difference = (64 – 39) = Rs.25 lakh

3. Total interest = (30% of 130) + (40% of 160) = (39 + 64) = Rs.103 lakh.

If this total interest is charged on borrowed funds, then (20% of borrowed funds) = 103. Hence, borrowed funds = (5 × 103) = Rs.515 lakh.

4. Retained profit in 1990-91 = (25% of 130) = Rs.32.5 lakh

Retained profit in 1991-92 = (20% of 160) = Rs.32 lakh

Hence, percentage change in retained profit

$= \dfrac{(32.5 - 32)}{32.5} = 1.5\%$ lower.

5. Total dividend earned by shareholders in 1991-92 = (8% of 160) = Rs.12.8 lakh.

6. Total trade with a region is defined as: The sum of exports and imports from that region, from the pie charts for 1997-98, we have the following sectors occupying maximum area.

	Country	Exports	Imports	Trade
H	OPEC	3397.9	9379.2	12795.1
G	East Europe	3397	7748	11145.9
K	Others	407.79	339.79	747.58
A	USA	6456	3670	10126

H – OPEC has the maximum trade.

7. From the pie chart, the region having lowest trade is K.

1% of imports + 1% of exports

∴ Indian exports are 1% of 3397.9 which is roughly 340 million USD.

8.

	Imports to India	Exports from India	Trade deficit
A	3670.11	6456.01	–2785.9
B	2038.95	2038.74	0.21
C	4893.48	4757.06	136.42
D	2446.74	2038.74	408
E	2038.95	2038.74	0.21
F	815.58	1019.37	–203.79
G	7748.01	3397.9	4350.11
H	9379.17	3397.9	5981.27
I	5709.06	6795.8	–1086.74
J	1631.16	1698.95	–67.79

So, we see that region H has highest trade deficit of approximately $6,000 million or $6 billion.

9. From the pie chart for 1997-98, we get that USA which is a region A has the lowest trade deficit.

(9% of imports – 19% of total exports)

$$\left(\frac{9}{100} \times 40779 - \frac{19}{100} \times 33979\right)$$

= $– 2785.9 million.

10. Cost in rupees of oil moved by rail and road is 18% of 30 million = 5.4 million.

Volume of oil transported by rail and road = 31% of 12 million tonnes = 3.72 million tonnes.

Cost in rupees per tonnes = $\frac{5.4}{3.72} = 1.5$ approximately.

11. From the chart, we can make out the least among road, rail, pipeline, ship by looking at the ratio of cost to volume.

Road = $\frac{6}{22}$

Rail = $\frac{12}{9}$

Pipeline = $\frac{65}{49}$

Ship = $\frac{10}{9}$

Since ratio of cost to volume for road is the lowest, it is the cheapest.

12. Ship, air and road.

Like the previous answer again look at ratio of

$\frac{10}{9}, \frac{7}{11}, \frac{6}{22}$

So $\frac{10}{9} > \frac{7}{11} > \frac{6}{22}$

Hence, $P > Q > R$

13. It can be easily observed from the two charts that Switzerland's ratio of chart 1 to chart 2 is $\frac{20}{11}$ has the highest price per unit kilogram for its supply.

14. Total value of distribution to Turkey is 16% of 5760 million Euro.

Total quantity of distribution to Turkey is 15% of 1.055 million tonnes.

So the average price in Euro per kilogram for Turkey is

$$\frac{\left(5760 \times \frac{16}{100}\right)}{\left(1055 \times \frac{15}{100}\right)} \simeq 5.6$$

Bar Graph

SOLVED EXAMPLES

Directions for examples 1 to 3: Answer the questions on the basis of the information given below.

Four countries – USA, Kenya, Russia and Australia – participated in a 4 × 400 metres relay which is an athletic track event in which each team comprises four runners, each of whom completes 1 lap of 400 metres. In the event, four runners, with one from each team, start running simultaneously from the same point on the track. As soon as the first runner from any team completes 1 lap of 400 metres, the second runner from that team starts running, from the same starting point, and this process continues till the fourth runner from the team has completed his lap. The same goes for the other teams. The winner of the event is the team whose players take the least composite times to complete the four laps. The following bar graph gives the information about the average speeds at which runners from the four teams ran to complete their laps.

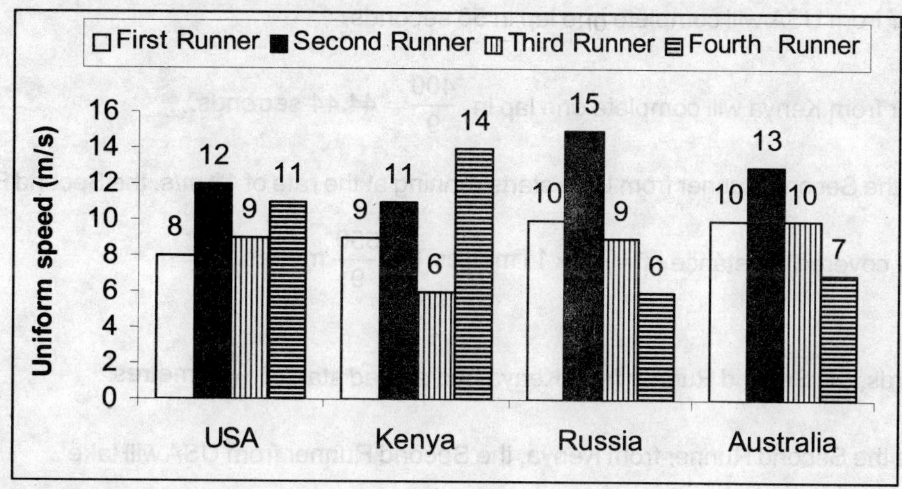

1. Which country won the event?
   (1) USA
   (2) Australia
   (3) Russia
   (4) Kenya
2. What was the shortest distance between the starting point and the point at which the second runner from USA and Kenya met?
   (1) 100 metres
   (2) 50 metres
   (3) 244.44 metres
   (4) Second runner from USA and Kenya did not meet
3. Which of the following statements is definitely true?
   (1) A runner from Australia was never behind the corresponding numbered runner from USA.
   (2) Third runner from Russia and Kenya never met during the course of the event.
   (3) Second runner from Kenya and Russia definitely met once during the event.
   (4) A runner from Kenya was always behind the corresponding numbered runner from Russia.

4.2 BAR GRAPH

For examples 1 to 3:

1. 1 The following lists down the time taken by each of the 4 mentioned countries to complete the 4 × 400 metres relay.

$$USA = \left(\frac{1}{8} + \frac{1}{12} + \frac{1}{9} + \frac{1}{11}\right) \times 400 \simeq 164 \text{ seconds}$$

$$Kenya = \left(\frac{1}{9} + \frac{1}{14} + \frac{1}{6} + \frac{1}{11}\right) \times 400 \simeq 176 \text{ seconds}$$

$$Russia = \left(\frac{1}{10} + \frac{1}{15} + \frac{1}{9} + \frac{1}{6}\right) \times 400 \simeq 178 \text{ seconds}$$

$$Australia = \left(\frac{1}{10} + \frac{1}{13} + \frac{1}{10} + \frac{1}{7}\right) \times 400 \simeq 168 \text{ seconds}$$

Hence, the USA was the winner of the relay.

2. 4 First Runner from USA will complete one lap in 50 seconds.

First Runner from Kenya will complete one lap in $\frac{400}{9} = 44.44$ seconds.

By the time the Second Runner from USA starts running at the rate of 12 m/s, the Second Runner from Kenya had already covered a distance of $= \frac{50}{9} \times 11$ metres i.e. $\frac{550}{9}$ metres.

In other words, the Second Runner from Kenya had a head start of $\frac{550}{9}$ metres.

To overtake the Second Runner from Kenya, the Second Runner from USA will take

$$= \frac{\left(\frac{550}{9}\right)}{(12-11)} = \frac{550}{9} \text{ seconds}$$

This implies that the Second Runner from USA will have to run $= \frac{550}{9} \times 12 = \frac{2200}{3} = 733.33$ metres

This is impossible because each runner can cover a maximum of 400 metres.

This implies that the Second Runners from USA and Kenya never met.

Hence, option (4) is the correct choice.

3. 2 Third Runner from Russia and Kenya did not meet as the speed of each of the corresponding runners from Russia was greater than the speed of the corresponding runner from Kenya.

Directions for examples 4 to 6: Answer the questions on the basis of the information given below.

In the election for the post of General Secretary of a university, 10 students namely P, Q, R, S, T, U, V, X, Y and Z were contesting. The university had a total of 200 students. Each student was given a sheet of paper on which he/she had to write the name(s) of the candidate(s) of his/her choice. Each student could write a maximum of three different names on a priority basis. The first name as his/her first choice, second name as his/her second choice and the third name as his/her third choice. Every student had to write at least one name on the sheet of paper. The following bar graph represents the information regarding the number of times the names of each of the 10 candidates were written on the sheets of paper.

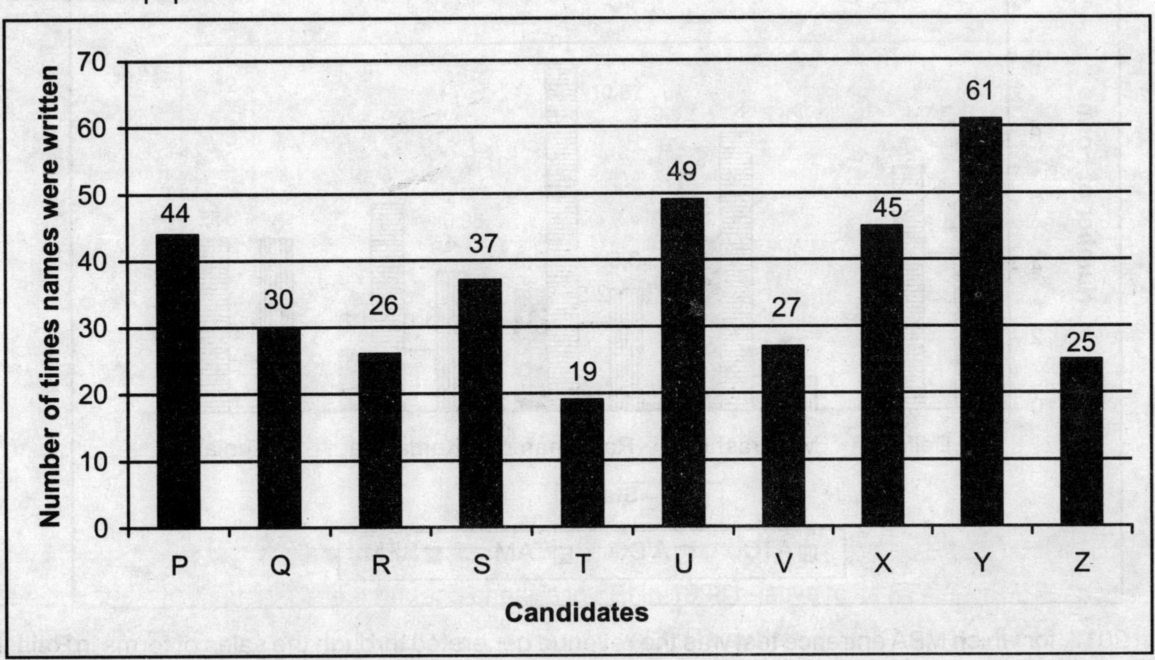

4. How many of the following are not possible values of the number of students who wrote exactly one name on their sheets?

A. 35 B. 36 C. 119 D. 109 E. 121 F. 118

(1) 1 (2) 2 (3) 3 (4) 4

5. What was the minimum possible number of students who wrote at least two names on their sheets?

(1) 80 (2) 81 (3) 82 (4) 83

6. What could be the maximum value of the sum of the number of students who wrote exactly one name and that of those who wrote exactly three names?

(1) 200 (2) 119 (3) 199 (4) 118

For examples 4 to 6:

Total number of names written on the sheets = 363

Let a, b and c denote the number of the students who wrote exactly one, two and three names on their sheets of paper respectively.

Therefore a + 2b + 3c = 363 and a + b + c = 200.

or, b + 2c = 163.

Possible Values of c: 0, 1, 2, 3 ...and goes till 81

Corresponding values of b: 163, 161, 159, 157 ... and goes till 1.

Corresponding values of a: 37, 38, 39 ... and goes till 118.

4. 4 Possible number of students who wrote exactly one name on their sheet of paper can be any number from 37 to 118. Only 109 and 118 lie within the permissible limits.

5. 3 Minimum possible number of students who wrote at least two names on their respective sheets of paper = minimum of (b + c) = 81 + 1 = 82.

6. 3 We need to minimize the students who wrote exactly two names, i.e. b = 1.
Hence, Maximum number of students who wrote 1 or 3 names = maximum value of (a + c) = 118 + 81 = 199.

4.4 BAR GRAPH

Directions for examples 7 to 10: Answer the questions on the basis of the information given below.

The following bar graph provides information about the number of forms (in 000's) sold for four different MBA entrance tests namely ATC, ATX, TAM and SFM, in 5 different states of India, in August 2017. The price at which each form of ATC, ATX, TAM and SFM was sold was Rs. 1300, Rs. 1000, Rs. 700 and Rs. 1100 respectively. Assume that these are the only five states in India where the forms of the abovementioned MBA entrance tests were sold and no other form except the forms of the mentioned tests were sold in the given states.

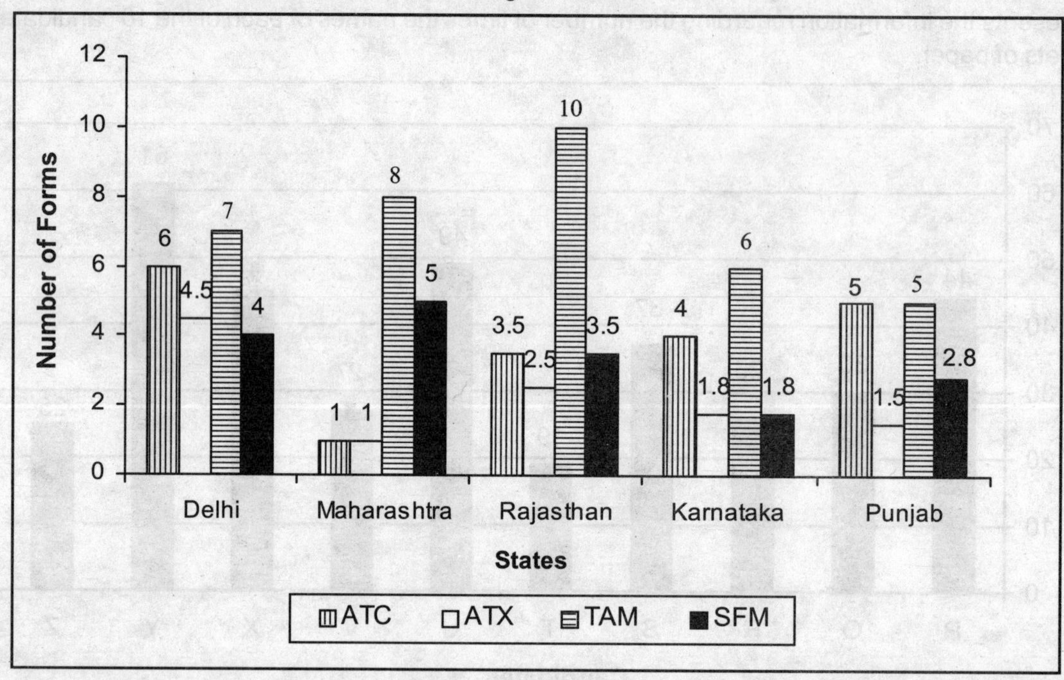

7. In August 2017, for which MBA entrance test was the revenue generated through the sales of forms in Rajasthan the second lowest?

(1) ATC (2) ATX

(3) SFM (4) TAM

8. If the number of forms sold for ATX in August 2018 increased by 25% compared to that in August 2017 and the total revenue generated through the sales of forms for the fours tests put together in August 2018 increased by 15% compared to that in August 2017, then what was the approximate percentage change in the price of an ATX form in August 2018 over that in August 2017? (Assume that the price and the number of forms sold for the mentioned tests other than ATX remained the same in August 2018.)

(1) 66 (2) 55

(3) 51 (4) 48

9. In August 2017, the percentage contribution of Delhi in the total revenue generated through the sales of forms of the fours tests put together was closest to

(1) 29% (2) 27%

(3) 41% (4) 33%

10. In August 2017, in which state(s) was the number of TAM forms sold less than 30% of the total number of forms sold for the fours tests put together in that particular state?

(1) Punjab, Delhi and Maharashtra (2) Only Maharashtra

(3) Delhi and Maharashtra (4) None of these

For examples 7 to 10:

7. 3 Percentage contribution of Rajasthan in the revenue generated by the sale of ATC forms

$= \left(\frac{3.5}{19.5}\right) \times 100 = 17.94\%$

Percentage contribution of Rajasthan in the revenue generated by the sale of ATX forms

$= \left(\frac{2.5}{11.3}\right) \times 100 = 22.12\%$

Percentage contribution of Rajasthan in the revenue generated by the sale of TAM forms

$= \left(\frac{10}{36}\right) \times 100 = 27.77\%$

Percentage contribution of Rajasthan in the revenue generated by the sale of SFM forms

$= \left(\frac{3.5}{17.1}\right) \times 100 = 20.46\%$

Hence, in August 2017, the MBA entrance test for which the revenue contribution of Rajasthan is second lowest is SFM.

Hence, option (3) is the correct choice.

8. 1 Total revenue (in thousands) generated through the sale of the forms of the mentioned tests in August 2017

= Rs.(19.5 × 1300 + 11.3 × 1000 + 36 × 700 + 17.1 × 1100) = Rs.80660.

Total revenue (in thousands) generated through the sale of the forms of the mentioned tests in August 2018

= Rs.(1.15 × 80660) = Rs.92759

Revenue generated (in thousands) through the sale of ATX forms in 2017 = Rs.11300

Revenue generated (in thousands) through the sale of ATX forms in 2018 = Rs. 11300 + Rs. 12099 = Rs.23399

Total number of ATX forms sold in August 2018 = 1.25 × 11300 = 14125

Price of an ATX form in August 2018 $= \text{Rs.}\left(\frac{23399}{14125}\right) = \text{Rs.}1656.56$

Required percentage change = 65.65%

Hence, option (1) is the correct choice.

9. 2 Required percentage contribution $= \left(\frac{6 \times 1300 + 4.5 \times 1000 + 7 \times 700 + 4 \times 1100}{80660}\right) \times 100 \approx 27.$

10. 4 Required percentage contribution in Delhi $= \left(\frac{7}{21.5}\right) \times 100 = 32.55\%$

Required percentage contribution in Maharashtra $= \left(\frac{8}{15}\right) \times 100 = 53.33\%$

Required percentage contribution in Rajasthan $= \left(\frac{10}{19.5}\right) \times 100 = 51.28\%$

Required percentage contribution in Karnataka $= \left(\frac{6}{13.6}\right) \times 100 = 44.11\%$

Required percentage contribution in Punjab $= \left(\frac{5}{14.3}\right) \times 100 = 34.96\%$

Hence, option (4) is the correct choice.

4.6 BAR GRAPH

Directions for examples 11 to 14: Answer the questions on the basis of the information given below.

There are ten boxes namely B1, B2, B3,..., B10 with Mr. Zero. Each of these ten boxes is colored with one out of the four colors namely Black, White, Yellow and Pink. The number of coins in each of these ten boxes is one of the five numbers 12, 15, 20, 25 and 30. The following bar graphs provide information about the number of boxes of the given colors and about the number of boxes that have different number of coins. It is also known that no two boxes that are colored with the same color have an equal number of coins.

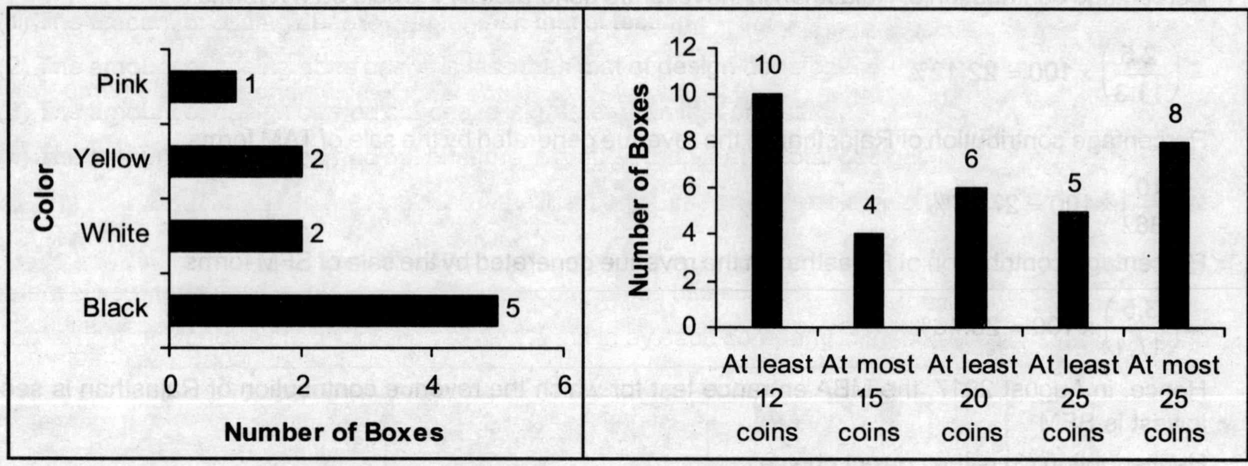

11. What is the total number of coins in all the boxes that are colored black?

(1) 102 (2) 92 (3) 95 (4) 105

12. The total number of coins in all the ten boxes put together with Mr. Zero is at most

(1) 202 (2) 207 (3) 212 (4) 222

13. If the number of coins in the box that is colored pink is 30, which of the following can be the total number of coins in all the boxes that are colored white?

(1) 45 (2) 37 (3) 42 (4) Both (a) and (b)

14. If the total number of coins in the boxes that are colored yellow is the maximum possible and the total number of coins in all the boxes put together is the least, then what is the number of coins in the box that is colored pink?

(1) 25 (2) 30 (3) 15 (4) 12

For examples 11 to 14:

The number of boxes that are colored Pink, Yellow, White and Black is 1, 2, 2 and 5 respectively.

It is also given that no two boxes that are colored with the same color have an equal number of coins.

It is also given that the number of coins in each of the ten boxes is 12, 15, 20, 25 or 30.

Also, since there are five boxes that are colored black, the number of coins in the these boxes are 12, 15, 20, 25 and 30.

From the second bar chart, it can also be observed that the number of boxes that have 30, 25, 20 and 5 or less coins is 2, 3, 1 and 4 respectively.

The derived conclusions can be tabulated as shown below:

Number of Coins	Number of Boxes
12	1 - 3
15	1 - 3
20	1
25	3
30	2

11. 1 The total number of coins in all the boxes that are colored black = 12 + 15 + 20 + 25 + 30 = 102

12. 3 The total number of coins with Mr. Zero will be maximum when there are 3 three boxes that have 15 coins each and there is only box that has 12 coins.

Therefore, the total number of coins with Mr. Zero is at most $= 1\times 12 + 3\times 15 + 1\times 20 + 3\times 25 + 2\times 30 = 212$

13. 2 We already know that the number of coins in 5 boxes that are colored Black are 12, 15, 20, 25 and 30.
Given that the number of coins in the box that is colored Pink is 30.
Total number of boxes with Mr. Zero that are colored white is 2.
The total number of coins in the boxes that are colored White can be (25 + 12 = 37), (25 + 15 = 40) and (12 + 15 = 27)
Hence, option (2) is the correct choice.

14. 4 Given that the total number of coins in the boxes that are colored Yellow is maximum possible, which means that, the total number of coins in the boxes that are colored Yellow is 25 + 30 = 55.
Also, since the total number of coins in all the boxes is the least, which means that the number of boxes in which there are 15 coins and 12 coins is 1 and 3 respectively.
So, the only possibility that is left is the box that is colored Pink has 12 coins and the two boxes that are colored White have 25 and 12 coins.

Directions for examples 15 to 18: Answer the questions on the basis of the information given below.

A manufacturing company named PXZ Pvt. Ltd.manufactures only three different types of lubricant oil namely X, Y and Z. On a given day, in the first three months of 2017, the number of bottles of each varieties of lubricants manufactured is either 2, 4 or 5. Similarly, the number of bottles of each type of lubricants sold on any given day is either 1, 2 or 3. It is also given that, on a particular day, the number of bottles of each varieties of lubricants manufactured or sold is different from the number of bottles of any other variety of lubricants manufactured or sold. The following bar graph provides the information about the number of bottles of X, Y and Z left unsold at the end of the first three months of 2017. Assume each month has 30 days and also assume that there were no bottles of X, Y or Z left unsold at the end of the year 2016.

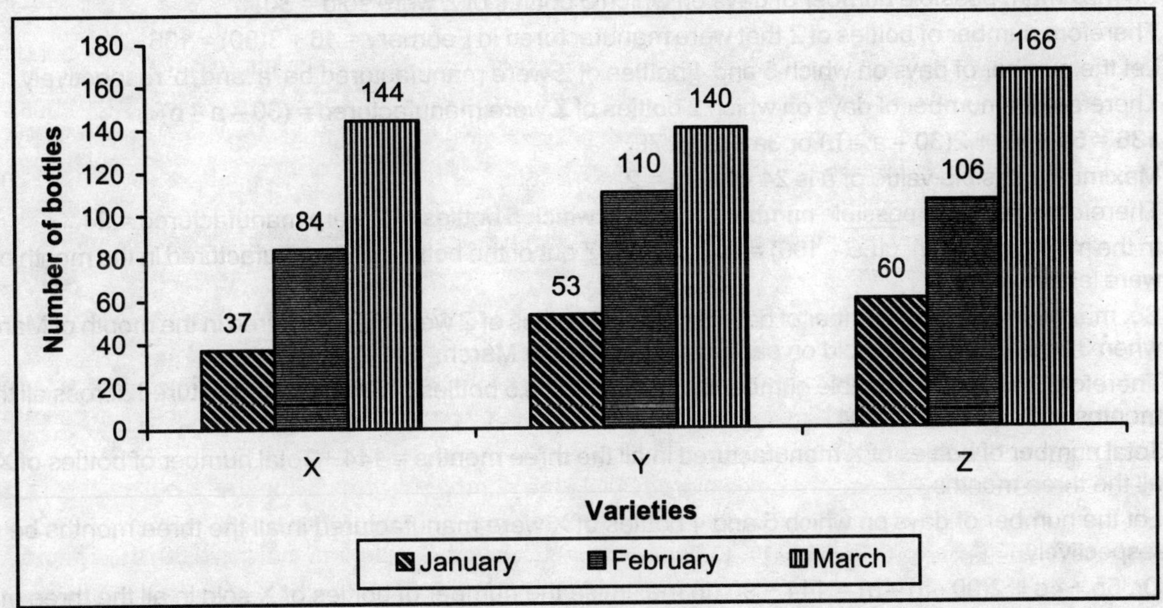

15. If the maximum possible number of bottles of Z were manufactured in January, then find the least possible number of days on which 4 bottles of Y were manufactured in January.
(1) 8 (2) 10 (3) 12 (4) 14

16. Find the maximum possible number of days on which 5 bottles of Z were manufactured over the period of three months.
(1) 78 (2) 80 (3) 82 (4) 84

17. Find the minimum possible number of days on which 5 bottles of X were manufactured over the period of three months.
(1) 0 (2) 18 (3) 16 (4) 15

18. If the ratio of the number of days on which 2, 4 and 5 bottles of Y were manufactured in February was 1 : 2 : 3 and the number of days on which 3 bottles of Y were sold in February was the minimum possible, then find the number of days on which 2 bottles of Y were sold in February.
(1) 24 (2) 23 (3) 22 (4) 21

15. 3 Number of bottles of Z left unsold at the end of January = 60.

If maximum possible number of bottles were manufactured, then maximum possible number of bottles should be sold. That means that on each of the 30 days in the month of January, 5 bottles were manufactured and 3 bottles were sold. That means 5 units of 'Y' can not be manufactured and 3 units of Y can bot be sold on any day of January.

In the month of January, let, the number of days on which 4 bottles of Y were manufactured be x, therefore the number of days on which 2 bottles of Y were manufactured = 30 – x.

Let the number of days on which 1 bottle of Y was sold be 'y', therefore the number of days on which 2 bottles of Y were sold is (30 – y). Obviously 'x' and 'y' are integers less than or equal to 30.

$53 = 4x + 2(30 - x) - y - 2(30 - y) = 2x + y$. Maximum possible value of y = 29, because if y = 30 then the value of x is not an integer.

Minimum possible value of $x = \frac{53 - 29}{2} = 12$.

16. 4 Number of bottles of Z left unsold at the end of January = 60.

Maximum possible number of days on which 5 bottles of Z were manufactured in January is 30, when the numbers of days on which 3 bottles of Z were sold = 30.

That means, (106 – 60) = 46 bottles out of the total bottles of Z, which were manufactured in February were left unsold.

Since we have to maximize the number of days on which 5 bottles of Z were manufactured, we will maximize the number of days on which 3 bottles of Z were sold.

So maximum possible number of days on which 3 bottles of Z were sold = 30.

Therefore number of bottles of Z that were manufactured in February = 46 + 3(30) = 136.

Let the number of days on which 5 and 4 bottles of Z were manufactured be 'a' and 'b' respectively.

Therefore the number of days on which 2 bottles of Z were manufactured = (30 – a – b).

$136 = 5a + 4b + 2(30 - a - b)$ or $3a + 2b = 76$.

Maximum possible value of a is 24 when b = 2.

Therefore maximum possible number of days on which 5 bottles of Z were manufactured = 24.

In the month of March, (166 – 106) = 60 bottles of Z out of the bottles of Z manufactured in the month of March were left unsold.

So, maximum possible number of days on which 5 bottles of Z were manufactured in the month of March = 30, when 3 bottles of Z were sold on each of the 30 days in March.

Therefore, maximum possible number of days on which 5 bottles of Z were manufactured across all the three months = 30 + 24 + 30 = 84.

17. 1 Total number of bottles of X manufactured in all the three months = 144 + Total number of bottles of X sold in all the three months.

Let the number of days on which 5 and 4 bottles of X were manufactured in all the three months be p and q respectively.

Or, $5p + 4q + 2(90 - p - q) = 144 + 90$ (to maximise the number of bottles of X sold in all the three months)

$3p + 2q = 54$.

Minimum value of p will be 0, when the value of q is 27.

Therefore minimum possible number of days on which 5 bottles of X were sold in all the three months = 0.

18. 3 Ratio of number of days on which 2, 4 and 5 bottles of Y were manufactured in the month of February is 1:2:3, therefore the number of days on which 2, 4 and 5 bottles of Y were manufactured is 5, 10 and 15 respectively.

Number of bottles of Y manufactured in the month of February = 2(5) + 4(10) + 5(15) = 10 + 40 + 75 = 125.

Let the number of days on which 1, 2 and 3 bottles of Y were sold in the month of February be d, e and f respectively.

Therefore, $125 - d - 2(30 - d - f) - 3f = 110 - 53$

Or, $f - d = 8$

Or, $f = 8 + d$.

Therefore on at least 8 days 3 bottles of Y were sold.

So, minimum value of 'f' is 8, and in that case d = 0.

Number of days on which 2 bottles of Y were sold in February = 30 – 8 = 22.

PRACTICE EXERCISE – 1

Directions for questions 1 to 4: Answer the questions on the basis of the information given below.

In a particular batch of an Engineering college, there are 90 students each in four different departments viz. ECE, CSE, ME and EE. The IT department has only 60 students. The following graph shows the number of students passed and failed in the English paper of the second semester examination. It also shows the number of students who applied for re-evaluation of the same paper. Only the students who initially failed in the paper, were eligible to apply for a re-evaluation. After re-evaluation, some students passed while the others could not pass even after the re-evaluation. All the failed students along with the absentees have to clear the English paper next year. The number of passed and failed students, as captured in the following bar-chart, only indicate the situation before re-evaluation. The passed and failed students taken together indicate the number of students who appeared in that paper. Difference, if any, between the total number and the appeared number of students from any department is due to the absentees.

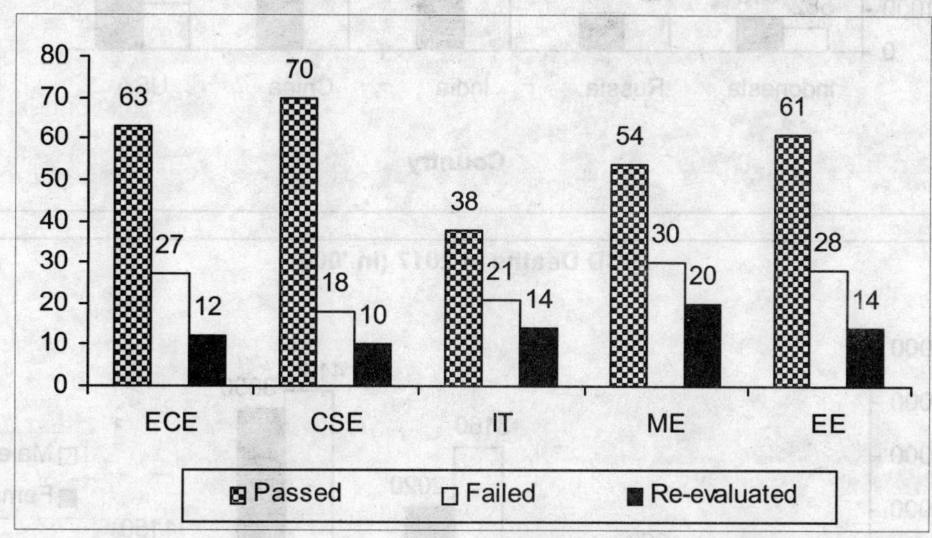

1. What was the pass percentage of all the streams taken together before re-evaluation ?

   (1) 66.5% (2) 69.3%

   (3) 64.7% (4) 68.1%

2. If less than 70% of the students who applied for re-evaluation, pass after the re-evaluation from each department, then for which department the ratio of passed students to failed students was the maximum after the re-evaluation?

   (1) ECE (2) CSE

   (3) ME (4) Cannot be determined

3. From each department, exactly 50% of the students who applied for re-evaluation failed even after re-evaluation. For which department, the percentage of failed students with respect to the total number of students is the minimum after the re-evaluation?

   (1) ECE (2) CSE

   (3) IT (4) ME

4. From each department, exactly 50% of the students who applied for re-evaluation failed even after re-evaluation. How many students from this batch will have to clear the paper next year?

   (1) 45 (2) 89

   (3) 95 (4) 99

4.10 BAR GRAPH

Directions for questions 5 to 8: Answer the questions on the basis of the information given below.

The bar graphs given below show the gender-wise deaths (in '000) due to NCDs (Non Communicable Diseases) in five countries for the years 2016 and 2017.

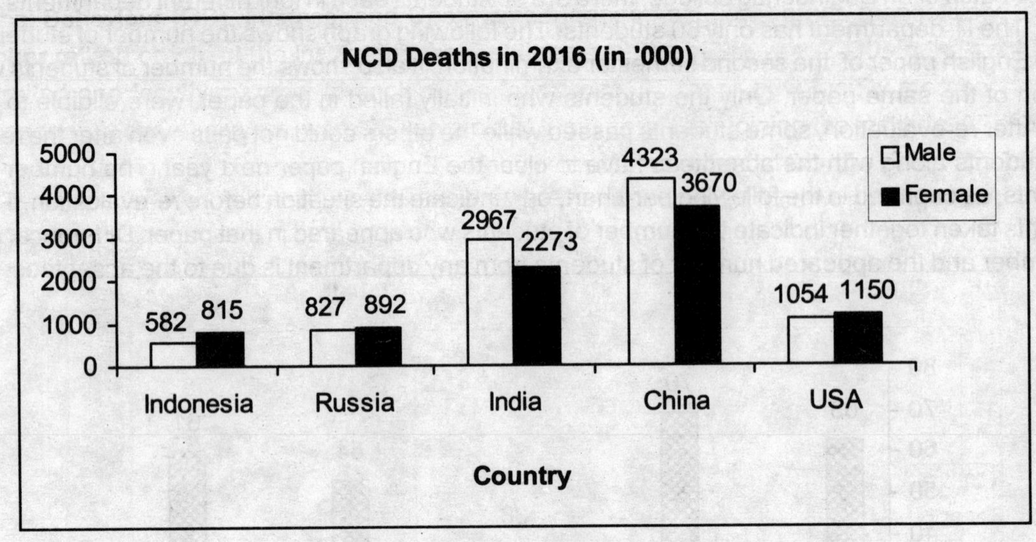

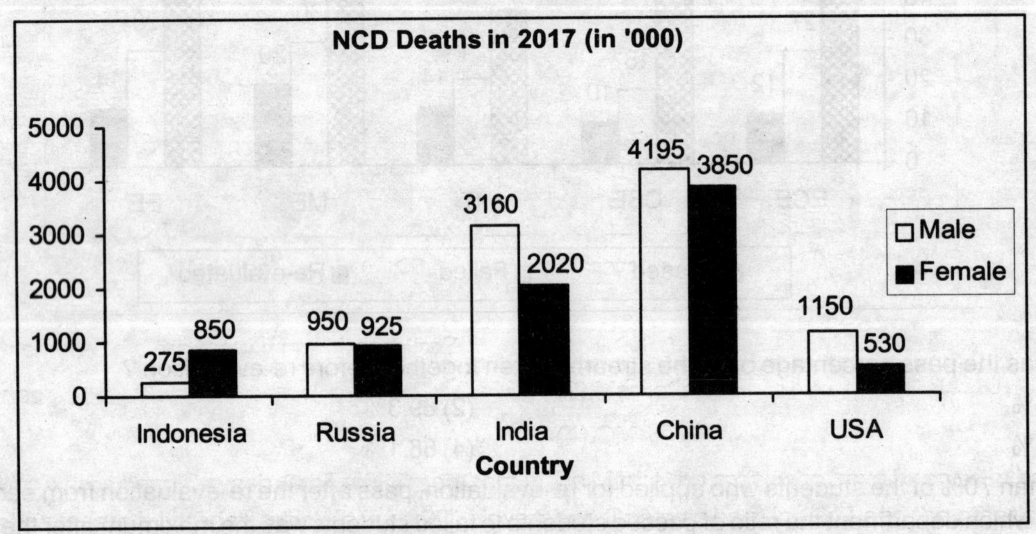

5. In how many countries was the number of deaths due to NCDs in 2016 less than that in 2017?

(1) 1 (2) 2 (3) 3 (4) 4

6. By what percent was the total number of female deaths due to NCDs in the five countries put together in 2017 more/less than that in 2016?

(1) 7.10 (2) 6.40 (3) 8.60 (4) 7.90

7. What was the absolute difference between the total number of male deaths due to NCDs in the five countries put together in 2016 and 2017?

(1) 22500 (2) 23000 (3) 24000 (4) None of these

8. For which country the percentage increase in the total number of deaths due to NCDs in 2017 as compared to 2016 was the least?

(1) China (2) USA (3) India (4) Russia

Directions for questions 9 to 11: Answer the questions on the basis of the information given below.

The bar chart given below shows the average of marks obtained by 20 students of a class in three pre-board exams–E_1, E_2, and E_3. In each of the exams, six papers on subjects–Hindi, English, Science, Maths, History and Geography–were conducted. It is also known that the maximum marks in each paper across the exams was 100 and a student needed to score at least 40% marks in a paper to pass it.

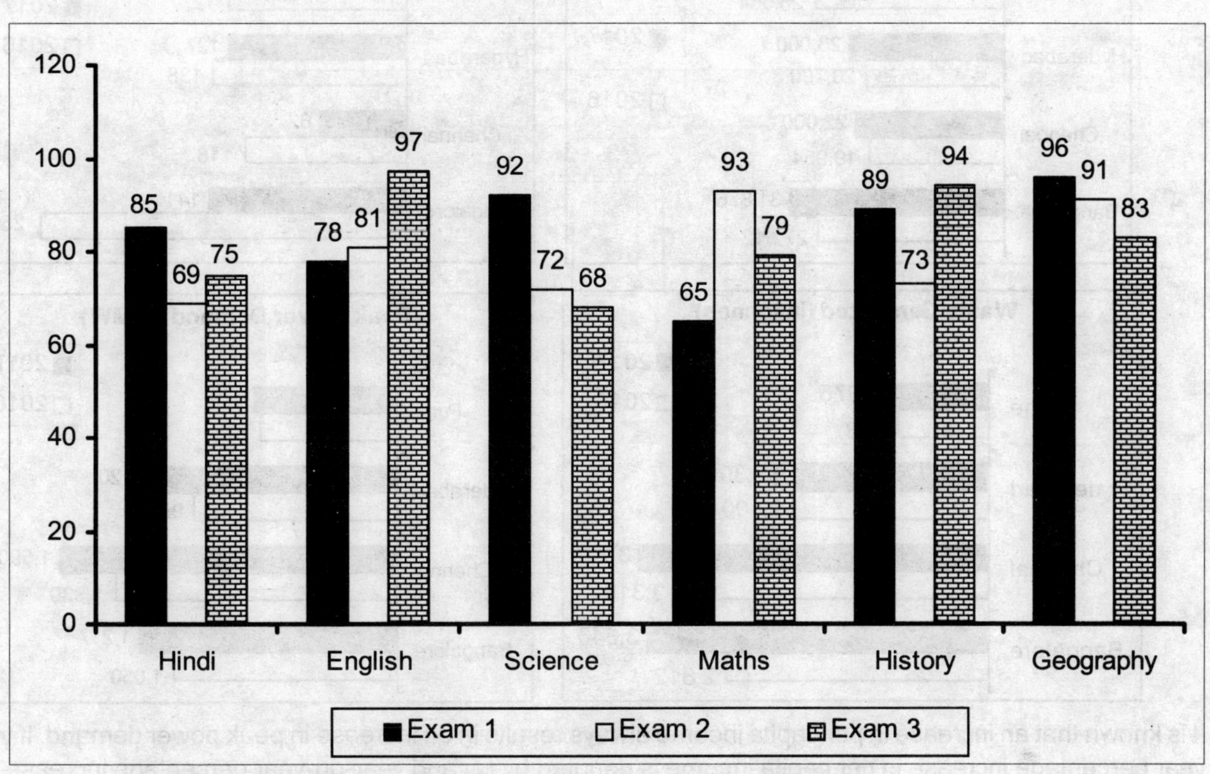

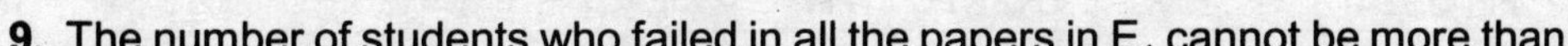

9. The number of students who failed in all the papers in E_1 cannot be more than

(1) 0 (2) 1

(3) 2 (4) 3

10. If no student failed in any of the papers in E_2, at most how many students could have scored 100 marks in at least one of the papers in E_2?

(1) 9 (2) 10

(3) 5 (4) 20

11. The number of students who scored more than 90 marks in all the papers in each of the exams cannot be more than

(1) 20 (2) 14

(3) 11 (4) Cannot be determined

Directions for questions 12 to 15: Answer the questions on the basis of the information given below.

The charts given below show the data related to a few parameters for four cities of India for 2016 and 2017.

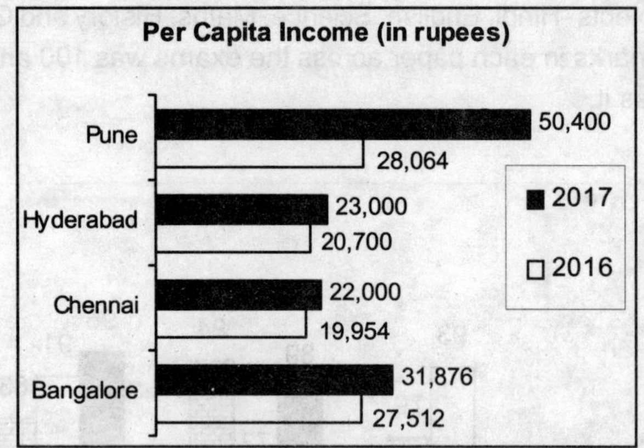

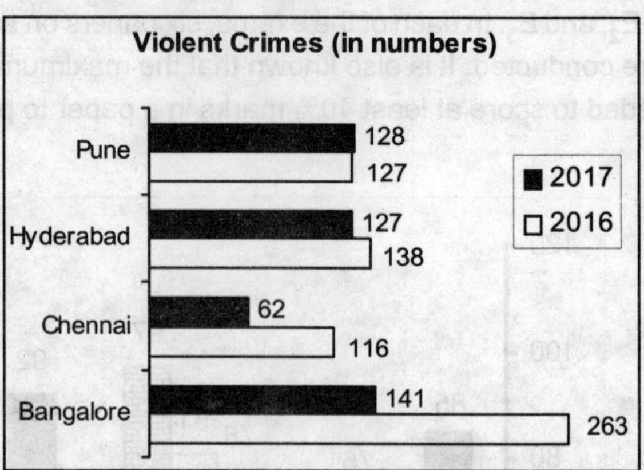

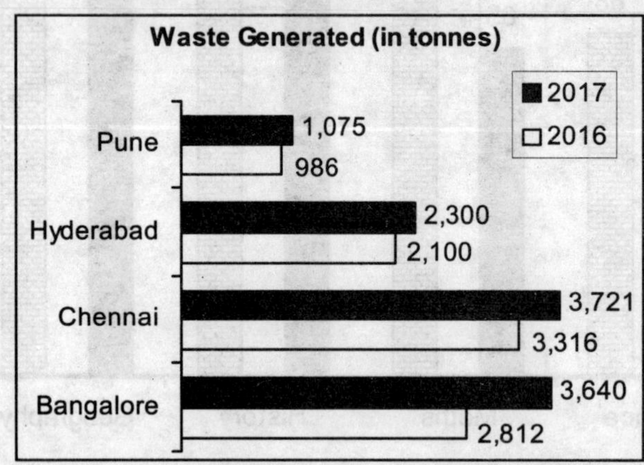

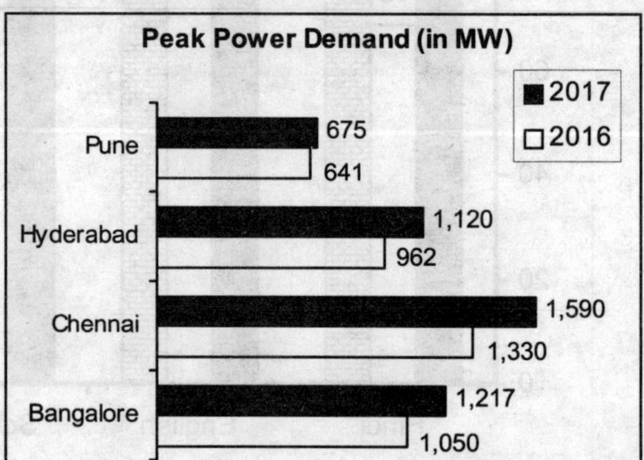

12. It is known that an increase in per capita income always results in an increase in peak power demand. If year-on-year percentage increase in per capita income is denoted by I_{PC} and year-on-year percentage increase in peak power demand is denoted by I_{PP}, for how many cities was $(I_{PC} - I_{PP})$ negative when calculated over the period of 2016 and 2017?

(1) 0 (2) 1 (3) 2 (4) 3

13. It is known that in a city each person generates the same amount of waste and for each of the four cities, percentage increase in waste generated per person in 2017 compared to that in 2016 is denoted by x. The value of x for different cities is as follows:

Bangalore : x = 4 ;

Chennai : x = 3

Hyderabad : x = 5;

Pune : x = 4

Which of the following cities witnessed maximum percentage increase in its population in 2017 over 2016?

(1) Bangalore (2) Chennai (3) Pune (4) Cannot be determined

14. Which city witnessed the maximum percentage increase in its population in 2017 over that in 2016?

(1) Bangalore (2) Pune (3) Chennai (4) Cannot be determined

15. Over the given period, the total number of violent crimes committed in Pune and Chennai put together was what percent of the total crimes committed in Hyderabad and Bangalore put together?

(1) 64.72 (2) 63.98 (3) 65.80 (4) 70.20

Directions for questions 16 to 19: Answer the questions on the basis of the information given below.

The following two graphs depict the Merchandise Exports (in billion dollars) and the growth rate of GDP over the previous year for China, Indonesia, Malaysia and Thailand from 2012 to 2016.

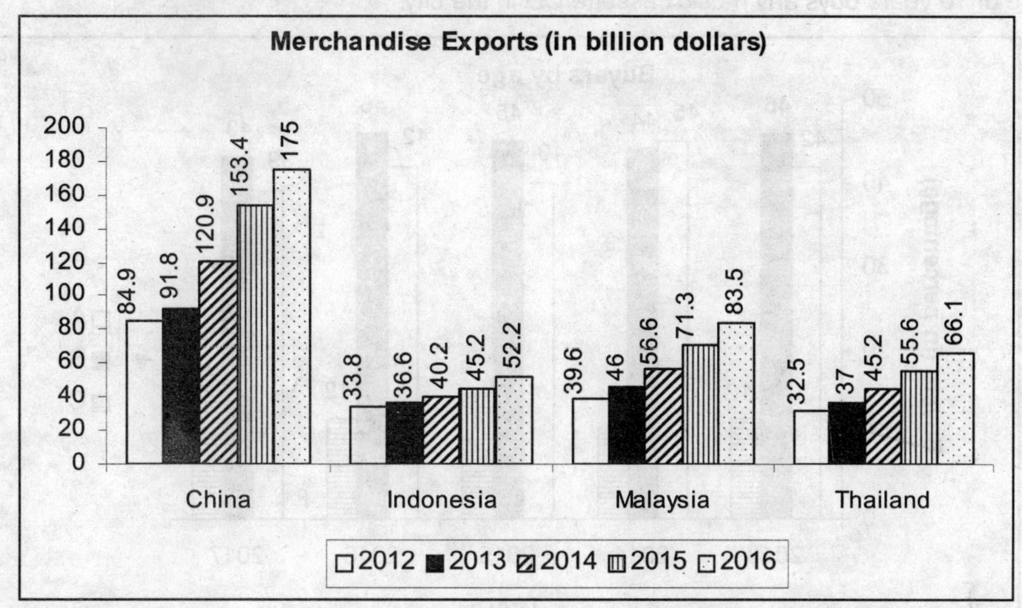

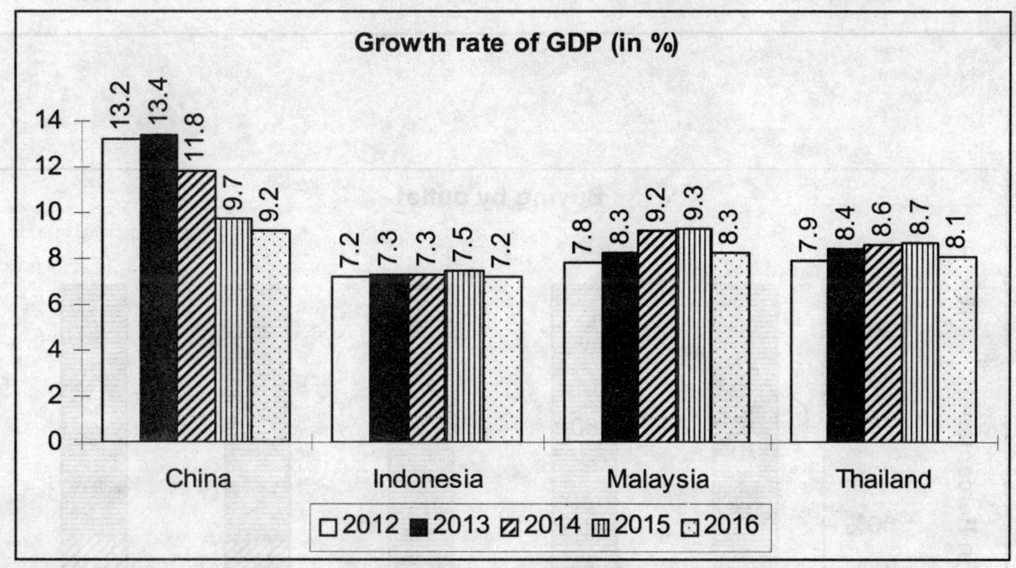

16. If the GDP of Indonesia in 2012 was \$60 billion and that of China was \$181 billion, what was the approximate difference between China's GDP and Indonesia's GDP in 2013?

(1) \$120 billion (2) \$140 billion (3) \$160 billion (4) \$180 billion

17. If the GDP of Malaysia in 2012 was \$50 billion, then the ratio of Merchandise Exports to GDP of Malaysia in 2013 with respect to that in 2012

(1) increased (2) decreased (3) remained the same (4) Cannot be determined

18. In which of the following years did Thailand have the least ratio of Merchandise Exports to GDP? (Given that GDP is always greater than exports)

(1) 2012 (2) 2013 (3) 2016 (4) Cannot be determined

19. If the GDP of Malasiya in 1992 was \$ 60 billion, find its GDP (in billion \$) in 1995.

(1) 77.56 (2) 76.24 (3) 72.35 (4) 75.56

Direction for questions 20 to 23: Answer the questions on the basis of the information given below.

The charts given below show the music cassettes/CDs buying behavior of people according to their age and their preference for different types of sales outlets in the city of Phoren during the period 2013-17. It is assumed that nobody below the age of 10 years buys any music cassette/CD in the city.

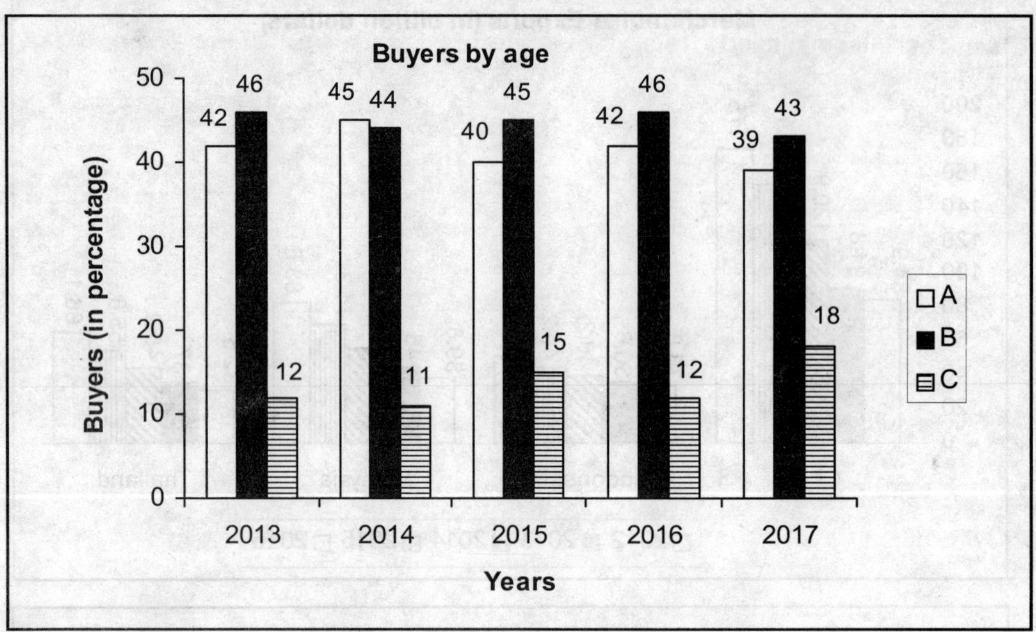

$10 \leq A < 25$
$25 \leq B < 45$
$45 \leq C$

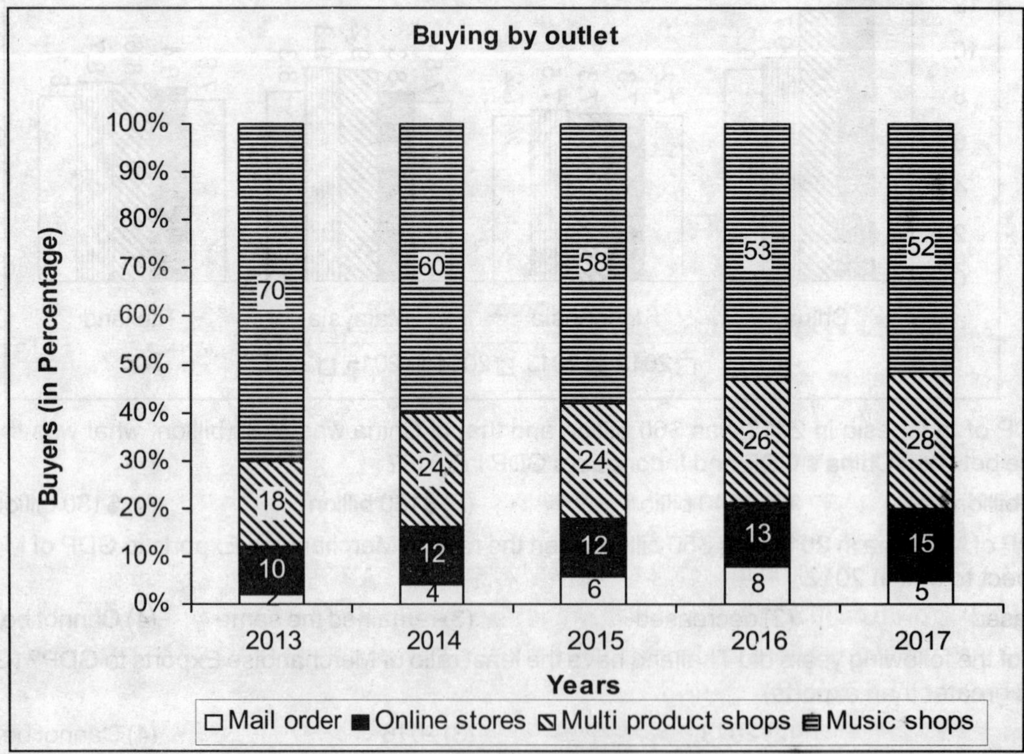

20. In 2013, if there was a total of 1000 buyers of music cassettes/CDs in the city of Phoren and the number of buyers increased by 100 every year during the given period, then what was the total number of buyers of music cassettes/CDs who were from age group C during the period 2013 to 2017?

(1) 729 (2) 789 (3) 829 (4) 879

21. By what percentage did the difference between number of buyers who bought music cassettes/CDs from mail order and those from online stores change between 2013 and 2017? (Assume the number of buyers of music cassettes/CDs remained the same for every year during this period)

(1) Decreased by 15% (2) Decreased by 25%
(3) Increased by 15% (4) Increased by 25%

22. Which type of sales outlet(s) managed to retain the number of its customers at the same level for a period of three consecutive years in the period 2013 to 2017?

(1) Multi product shops (2) Online stores
(3) Both (a) and (b) (4) Data Insufficient

23. In every age group, if the pattern of buying from various sales outlets show the same break-up as the one given for the total, then approximately what was the number of buyers in the age group B buying music cassettes/CDs from music shops in 2013? (Assume there was a total of 1000 buyers of music cassettes/CDs in the city of Phoren and the number of buyers increased by 100 every year during the given period.)

(1) 500 (2) 322 (3) 425 (4) 380

Directions for questions 24 to 27: Answer the questions on the basis of the information given below.

The bar graph given below shows the data related to the number of people visiting the famous 'Ancient Wax Museum' in Putlabad from the year 2012 to the year 2016.

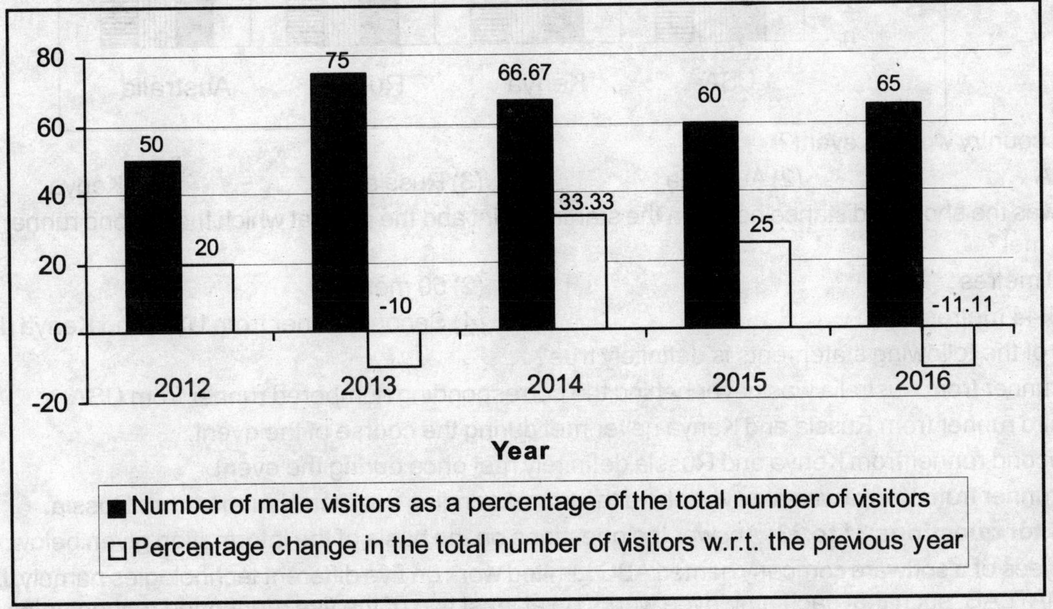

24. If the total number of visitors in the year 2016 was 46850, what was the number of female visitors in the year 2016?

(1) 28110 (2) 26236 (3) 37480 (4) None of these

25. Which of the following statements is true?

(1) The only year in the given period when the number of female visitors decreased as compared to the previous year was 2013.
(2) There was a growth of 40% in the number of male visitors from 2013 to 2014.
(3) There was a growth of 50% in the number of female visitors from 2014 to 2015.
(4) The year 2013 onwards, there was an increase each year in the number of male visitors as compared to the previous year.

26. The difference between the number of male visitors and the number of female visitors in a year is called "Gender Gap". For which of the following pairs of years is Gender Gap equal?

(1) 2013 and 2016 (2) 2014 and 2015 (3) 2013 and 2015 (4) 2014 and 2016

27. In which year was the number of male visitors the maximum?

(1) 2014 (2) 2015 (3) 2016 (4) 2017

Directions for questions 28 to 30: Answer the questions on the basis of the information given below.

Four countries – USA, Kenya, Russia and Australia – participated in a 4 × 400 metres relay which is an athletic track event in which each team comprises four runners, each of whom completes 1 lap of 400 metres. In the event, four runners, with one from each team, start running simultaneously from the same point on the track. As soon as the first runner from any team completes 1 lap of 400 metres, the second runner from that team starts running, from the same starting point, and this process continues till the fourth runner from the team has completed his lap. The same goes for the other teams. The winner of the event is the team whose players take the least composite times to complete the four laps. The following bar graph gives the information about the average speeds at which runners from the four teams ran to complete their laps.

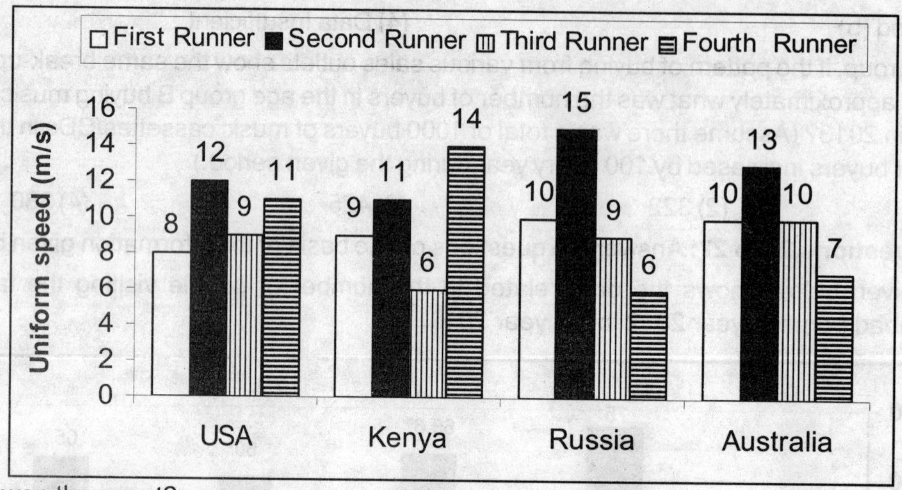

28. Which country won the event?

(1) USA (2) Australia (3) Russia (4) Kenya

29. What was the shortest distance between the starting point and the point at which the second runner from USA and Kenya met?

(1) 100 metres (2) 50 metres

(3) 244.44 metres (4) Second runner from USA and Kenya did not meet

30. Which of the following statements is definitely true?

(1) A runner from Australia was never behind the corresponding numbered runner from USA.

(2) Third runner from Russia and Kenya never met during the course of the event.

(3) Second runner from Kenya and Russia definitely met once during the event.

(4) A runner from Kenya was always behind the corresponding numbered runner from Russia.

Directions for questions 31 to 33: Answer the questions on the basis of the information given below.

The employees of a software company named ABC Limited work on five different technologies namely J2EE, C#, .Net, XML and MATLAB, such that each employee works on at least two of the five mentioned technologies. The following bar graph provides information about the number of employees working on each of the five technologies.

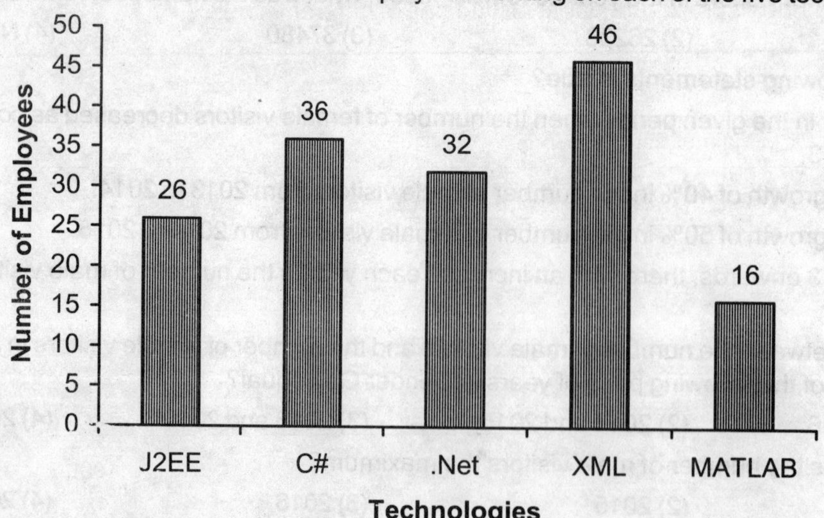

31. Find the absolute difference between the maximum and minimum possible number of employees in ABC Limited.
(1) 38 (2) 36 (3) 34 (4) 32

32. The number of employees working in the company is the minimum possible. Find the maximum possible number of employees working on exactly two different technologies.
(1) 21 (2) 22 (3) 23 (4) 24

33. The number of employees working in the company is the minimum possible. Find the maximum possible number of employees working on exactly three different technologies.
(1) 39 (2) 38 (3) 37 (4) 36

Directions for questions 34 to 36: Refer to the following Bar-chart and answer the questions that follow.

[CAT 1990]

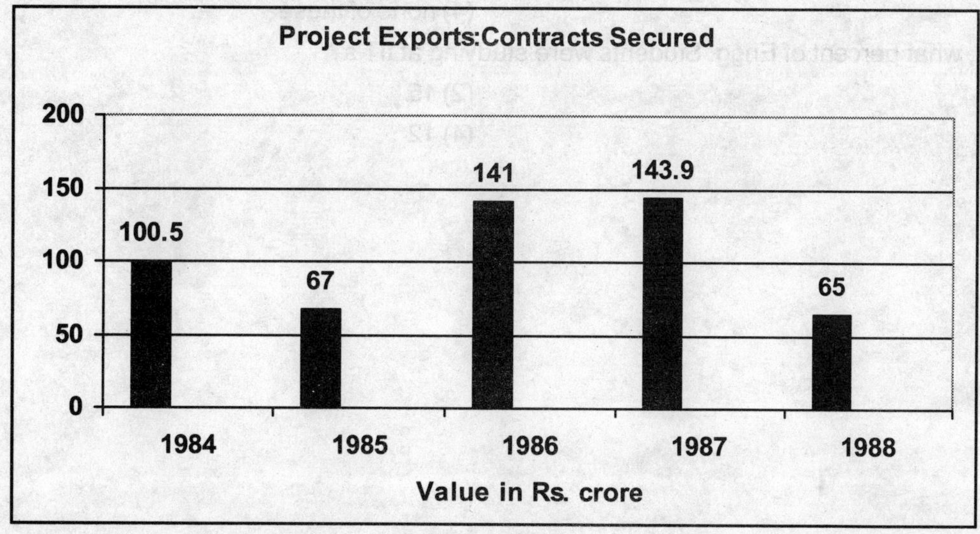

34. What is the average value of the contract secured during the years shown in the diagram?
(1) Rs. 103.48 crore (2) Rs. 105 crore (3) Rs. 100 crore (4) Rs.125.2 crore

35. Compared to the performance in 1985 (i.e. taking it as the base), what can you say about the performances in the years '84, '85, '86, '87, '88 respectively, in percentage terms?
(1) 150, 100, 211, 216, 97 (2) 100, 67, 141,144,65 (3) 150, 100, 200, 215, 100 (4) 120, 100, 220, 230, 68

36. Which is the year in which the highest percentage decline is seen in the value of contract secured compared to the preceding year?
(1) 1985 (2) 1988 (3) 1984 (4) 1986

Directions for questions 37 to 40: Answer the questions on the basis of the information given below.

[CAT 1994]

Number of Engineering Students (in hundreds) at institutions of different kinds

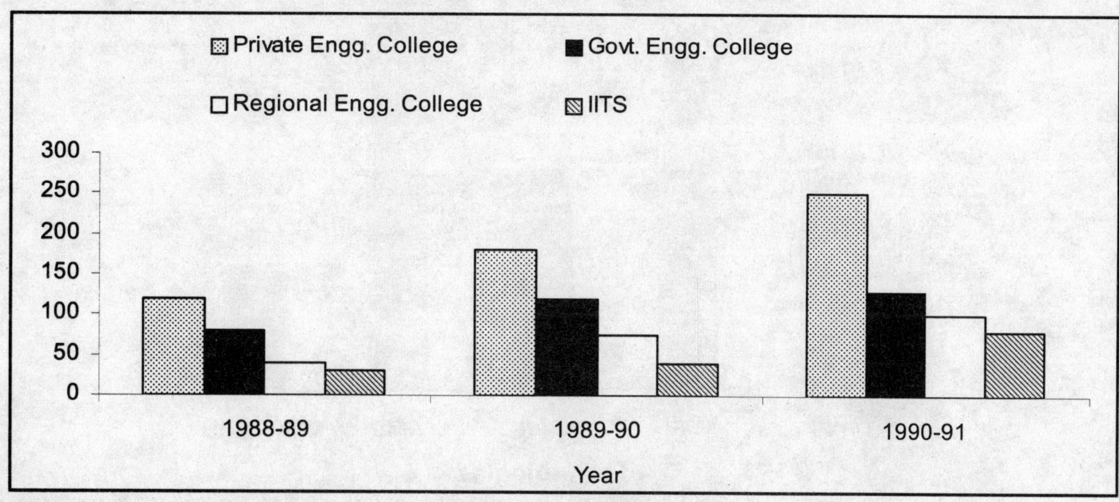

37. What was the total number of engineering students in 1989 – 90?
(1) 28500 (2) 4400 (3) 4200 (4) 42000

38. The growth rate in students of Govt. Engg. Colleges compared to that of Private Engg. Colleges between 1988-89 and 1989-90 is

(1) more (2) less

(3) equal (4) $\frac{3}{2}$

39. The total number of Engg. Students in 1991 – 92, assuming a 10% reduction in the number over the previous year, is

(1) 5700 (2) 57000

(3) 44800 (4) none of these

40. In 1990 – 91, what percent of Engg. Students were studying at IIT's?

(1) 16 (2) 15

(3) 14 (4) 12

PRACTICE EXERCISE – 2

Directions for questions 1 to 4: Answer these questions based on the data presented in the figure below.

[CAT 2000]

FEI for a country in a year, is the ratio (expressed as a percentage) of its foreign equity inflows to its GDP. The following figure displays the FEIs for select Asian countries for 1997 and 1998.

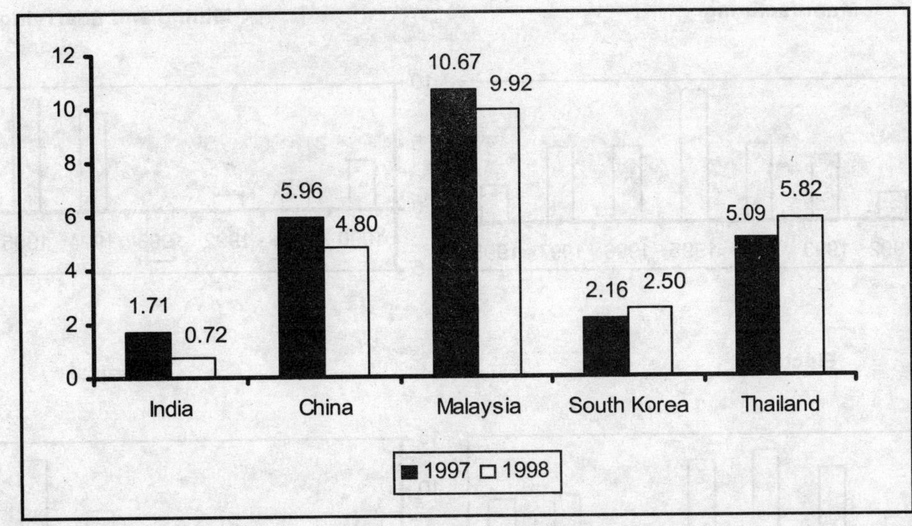

1. The country with the highest percentage change in FEI in 1998 relative to its FEI in 1997, is

(1) India (2) China (3) Malaysia (4) Thailand

2. Based on the data provided, it can be concluded that

(1) absolute value of foreign equity inflows in 1998 was higher than that in 1997 for both Thailand and South Korea.

(2) absolute value of foreign equity inflows was higher in 1998 for Thailand and lower for China than the corresponding values in 1997.

(3) absolute value of foreign equity inflows was lower in 1998 for both India and China than the corresponding values in 1997.

(4) None of the above can be inferred

3. It is known that China's GDP in 1998 was 7% higher than its value in 1997, while India's GDP grew by 2% during the same period. The GDP of South Korea, on the other hand, fell by 5%. Which of the following statements is/are true?

I. Foreign equity inflows to China were higher in 1998 than in 1997.

II. Foreign equity inflows to China were lower in 1998 than in 1997.

III. Foreign equity inflows to India were higher in 1998 than in 1997.

IV. Foreign equity inflows to South Korea decreased in 1998 relative to 1997.

V. Foreign equity inflows to South Korea increased in 1998 relative to 1997.

(1) I, III and IV (2) II, III and IV (3) I, III and V (4) II and v

4. China's foreign equity inflows in 1998 were 10 times that of India. It can be concluded that

(1) China's GDP in 1998 was 40% higher than that of India

(2) China's GDP in 1998 was 70% higher than that of India

(3) China's GDP in 1998 was 50% higher than that of India

(4) no inference can be drawn about relative magnitudes of China's and India's GDPs

4.20 BAR GRAPH

Directions for questions 5 to 10: Answer the questions based on the data given below.

[CAT 2000]

The figures below present annual growth rate, expressed as the percentage change relative to the previous year, in four sectors of the economy of the Republic of Reposia during the 9-year period from 1990 to 1998. Assume that the index of production for each of the four sectors is set at 100 in 1989. Further, the four sectors: manufacturing, mining and quarrying, electricity, and chemicals, respectively, constituted 20%, 15%, 10% and 15% of total industrial production in 1989.

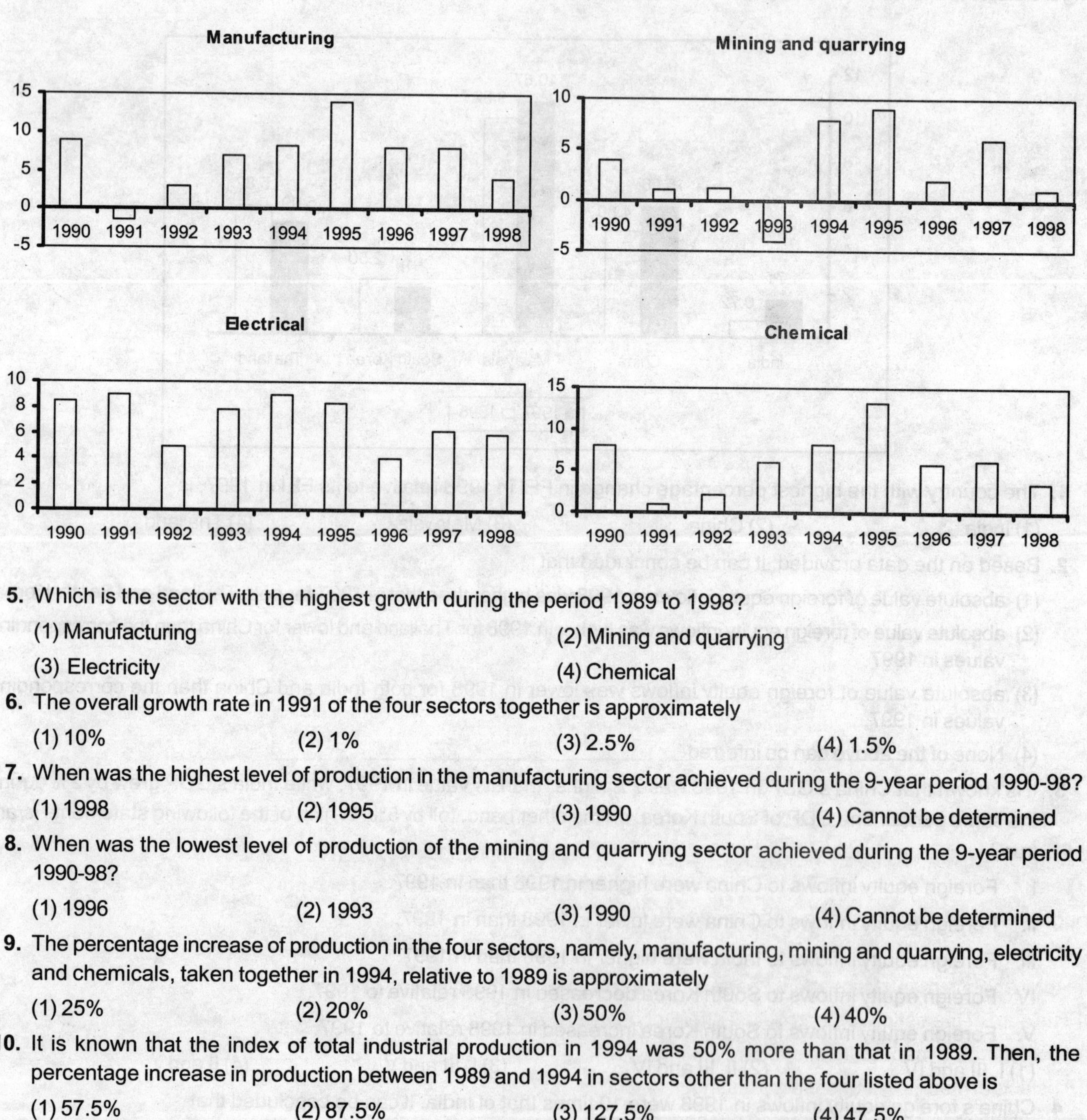

5. Which is the sector with the highest growth during the period 1989 to 1998?

(1) Manufacturing (2) Mining and quarrying

(3) Electricity (4) Chemical

6. The overall growth rate in 1991 of the four sectors together is approximately

(1) 10% (2) 1% (3) 2.5% (4) 1.5%

7. When was the highest level of production in the manufacturing sector achieved during the 9-year period 1990-98?

(1) 1998 (2) 1995 (3) 1990 (4) Cannot be determined

8. When was the lowest level of production of the mining and quarrying sector achieved during the 9-year period 1990-98?

(1) 1996 (2) 1993 (3) 1990 (4) Cannot be determined

9. The percentage increase of production in the four sectors, namely, manufacturing, mining and quarrying, electricity and chemicals, taken together in 1994, relative to 1989 is approximately

(1) 25% (2) 20% (3) 50% (4) 40%

10. It is known that the index of total industrial production in 1994 was 50% more than that in 1989. Then, the percentage increase in production between 1989 and 1994 in sectors other than the four listed above is

(1) 57.5% (2) 87.5% (3) 127.5% (4) 47.5%

Directions for questions 11 to 16: Answer the questions based on the two graphs shown below.

[CAT 2001]

Figure I shows the amount of work distribution, in man-hours, for a software company between offshore and onsite activities. Figure 2 shows the estimated and actual work effort involved in the different offshore activities in the same company during the same period. [**Note:** Onsite refers to work performed at the customer's premise and offshore refers to work performed at the developer's premise.]

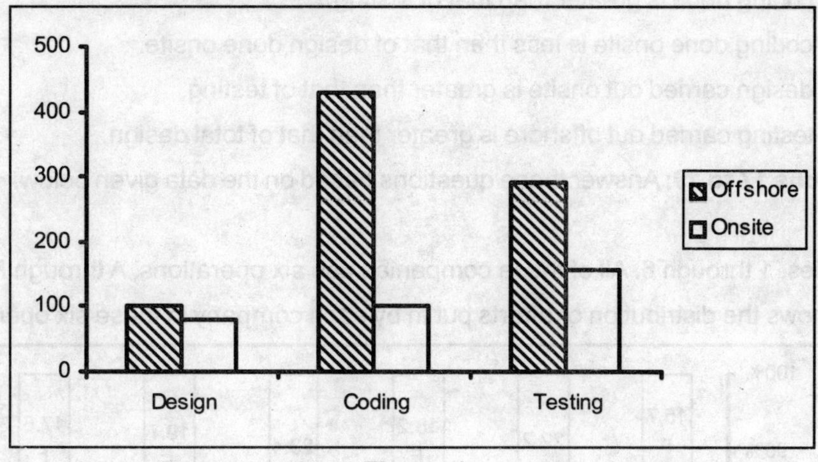

Figure 1

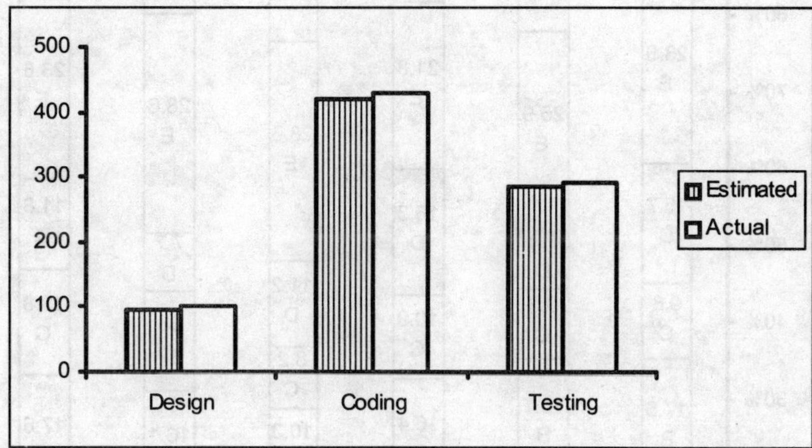

Figure 2

11. Which work requires as many man-hours as that spent in coding?

(1) Offshore, design and coding (2) Offshore coding

(3) Testing (4) Offshore, testing and coding

12. Roughly, what percentage of the total work is carried out onsite?

(1) 40% (2) 20 % (3) 30 % (4) 10 %

13. The total effort in man-hours spent onsite is nearest to which of the following?

(1) The sum of the estimated and actual effort for offshore design.

(2) The estimated man-hours of offshore coding.

(3) The actual man-hours of offshore testing.

(4) Half of the man-hours of estimated offshore coding.

14. If the total working hours were 100, which of the following tasks will account for approximately 50 hr?

(1) Coding (2) Design

(3) Offshore testing (4) Offshore testing plus design

15. If 50% of the offshore work were to be carried out onsite, with the distribution of effort between the tasks remaining the same, the proportion of testing carried out offshore would be

(1) 40% (2) 30% (3) 50% (4) 70%

16. If 50% of the offshore work were to be carried out onsite, with the distribution of effort between the tasks remaining the same, which of the following is true of all work carried out onsite?

(1) The amount of coding done is greater than that of testing.

(2) The amount of coding done onsite is less than that of design done onsite.

(3) The amount of design carried out onsite is greater than that of testing.

(4) The amount of testing carried out offshore is greater than that of total design.

Directions for questions 17 to 19: Answer these questions based on the data given below:

[CAT 2001]

There are six companies, 1 through 6. All of these companies use six operations, A through F.

The following graph shows the distribution of efforts put in by each company in these six operations.

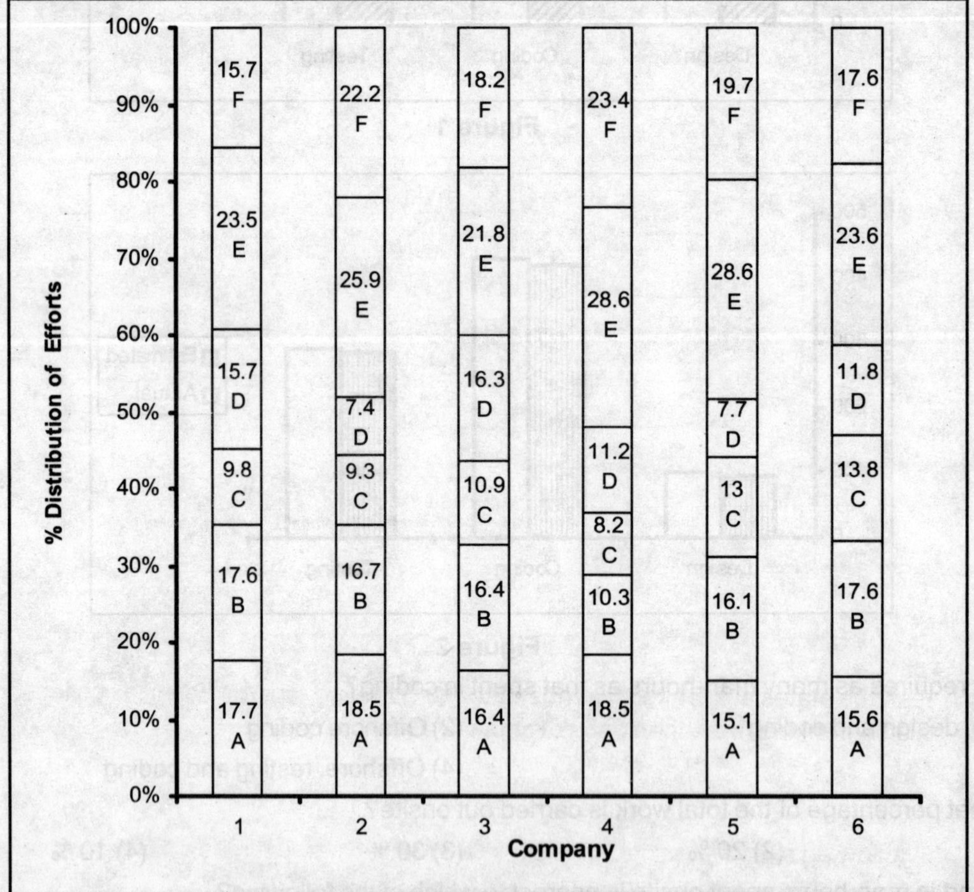

17. Suppose effort allocation is inter-changed between operations B and C, then C and D, and then D and E. If companies are then ranked in ascending order of effort in E, what will be the rank of company 3?

(1) 2 (2) 3 (3) 4 (4) 5

18. A new technology is introduced in company 4 such that the total effort for operations B through F get evenly distributed among these. What is the change in the percentage of effort in operation E?

(1) Reduction of 12.3 (2) Increase of 12.3 (3) Reduction of 5.6 (4) Increase of 5.6

19. Suppose the companies find that they can remove operations B, C and D and redistribute the effort released equally among the remaining operations. Then which operation will show the maximum across all companies and all operations?

(1) Operation E in company 1

(2) Operation E in company 4

(3) Operation F in company 5

(4) Operation E in company 5

Directions for questions 20 to 25: Answer the questions based on the chart given below.

[CAT 2002]

The chart given below indicates the annual sales tax revenue collections (in rupees in crores) of seven states from 1997 to 2001. The values given at the top of each bar represents the total collections in that year.

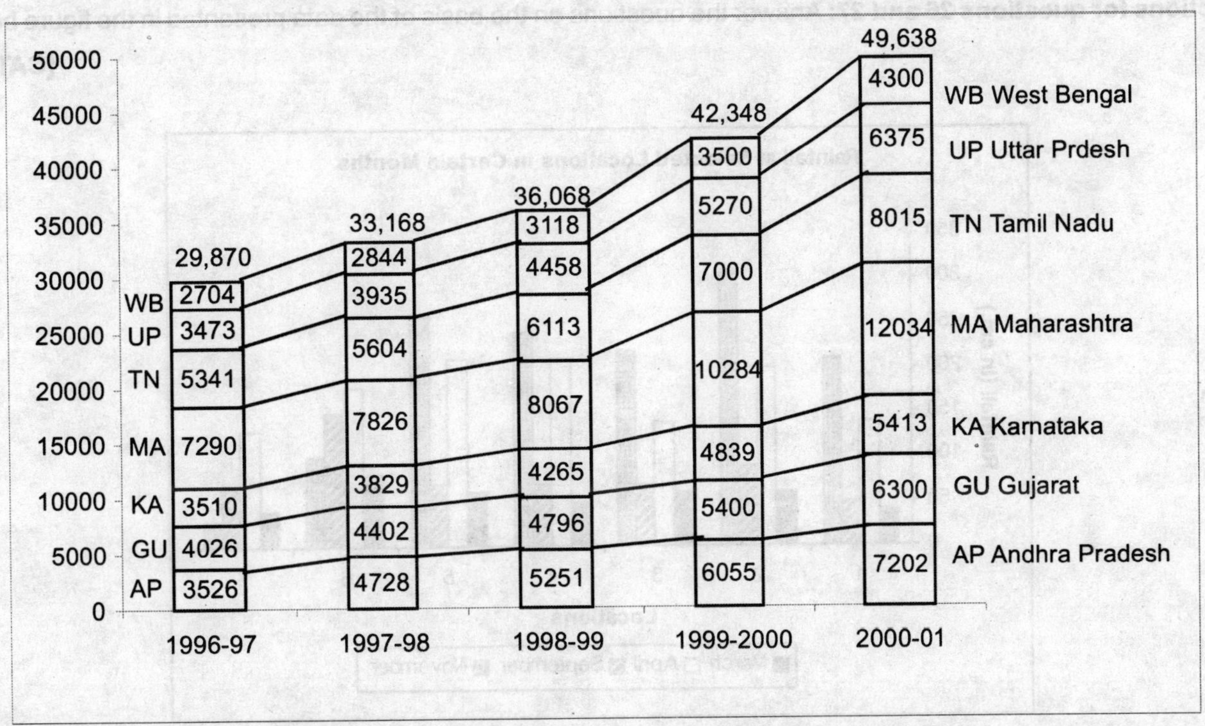

20. If for each year, the states are ranked in terms of the descending order of sales tax collections, how many states do not change the ranking more than once over the five years?

(1) 1 (2) 5

(3) 3 (4) 4

21. Which of the following states has changed its relative ranking most number of times when you rank the states in terms of the descending volume of sales tax collections each year?

(1) Andhra Pradesh (2) Uttar Pradesh

(3) Karnataka (4) Tamil Nadu

22. The percentage share of sales tax revenue of which state has increased from 1997 to 2001?

(1) Tamil Nadu (2) Karnataka

(3) Gujarat (4) Andhra Pradesh

23. Which pair of successive years shows the maximum growth rate of tax revenue in Maharashtra?

(1) 1997 to 1998 (2) 1998 to 1999

(3) 1999 to 2000 (4) 2000 to 2001

24. Identify the state whose tax revenue increased exactly by the same amount in two successive pair of years?

(1) Karnataka

(2) West Bengal

(3) Uttar Pradesh

(4) Tamil Nadu

25. Which state below has been maintaining a constant rank over the years in terms of its contribution to total tax collections?

(1) Andhra Pradesh

(2) Karnataka

(3) Tamil Nadu

(4) Uttar Pradesh

Directions for questions 26 and 27: Answer the questions on the basis of the data presented in the figure below.

[CAT 2003]

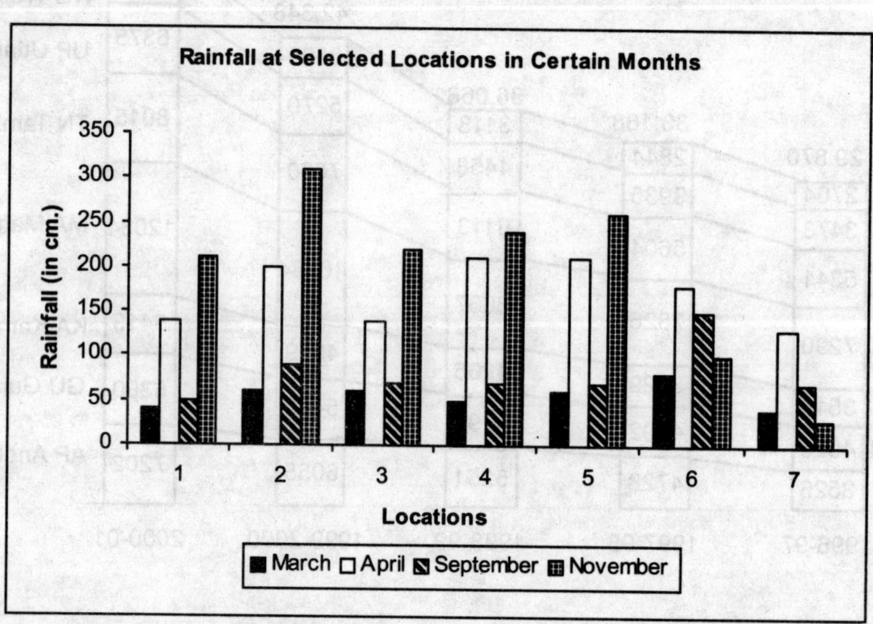

26. Which of the following statements is correct?

(1) November rainfall exceeds 100 cm in each location.

(2) September rainfall exceeds 50 cm in each location.

(3) March rainfall is lower than September rainfall in each location.

(4) None of these.

27. Locations 6 and 7 differ from all the rest because only in these two locations,

(1) April rainfall exceeds March rainfall.

(2) Peak rainfall occurs in April.

(3) November rainfall is lower than March rainfall.

(4) April rainfall is less than 200 cm.

Directions for questions 28 to 31: Answer the questions on the basis of the information given below.

[CAT 2004]

Purana and Naya are two brands of kitchen mixer-grinders available in the local market. Purana is an old brand that was introduced in 1990, while Naya was introduced in 1997. For both these brands, 20% of the mixer-grinders bought in a particular year are disposed off as junk exactly two years later. It is known that 10 Purana mixer-grinders were disposed off in 1997. The following figures show the number of Purana and Naya mixer-grinders in operation from 1995 to 2000, as at the end of the year.

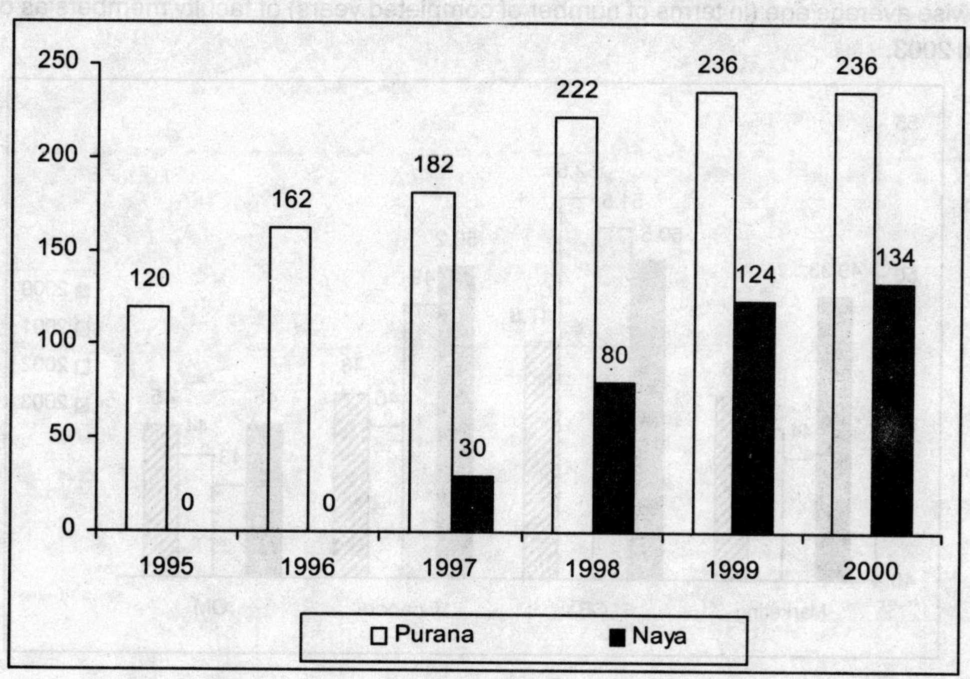

28. How many Naya mixer-grinders were purchased in 1999?

(1) 44 (2) 50 (3) 55 (4) 64

29. How many Naya mixer-grinders were disposed off by the end of 2000?

(1) 10
(2) 16
(3) 22
(4) Cannot be determined from the data

30. How many Purana mixer-grinders were disposed off in 2000?

(1) 0
(2) 5
(3) 6
(4) Cannot be determined from the data

31. How many Purana mixer-grinders were purchased in 1999?

(1) 20
(2) 23
(3) 50
(4) Cannot be determined from the data

Directions for questions 32 to 35: Answer the questions on the basis of the information given below:

[CAT 2005]

A management institute was established on January 1, 2000 with 3, 4, 5, and 6 faculty members in the Marketing, Organisational Behaviour (OB), Finance, and Operations Management (OM) areas respectively, to start with. No faculty member retired or joined the institute in the first three months of the year 2000. In the next four years, the institute recruited one faculty member in each of the four areas. All these new faculty members, who joined the institute subsequently over the years, were 25 years old at the time of their joining the institute. All of them joined the institute on April 1. During these four years, one of the faculty members retired at the age of 60. The following diagram gives the area-wise average age (in terms of number of completed years) of faculty members as on April 1 of 2000, 2001, 2002, and 2003.

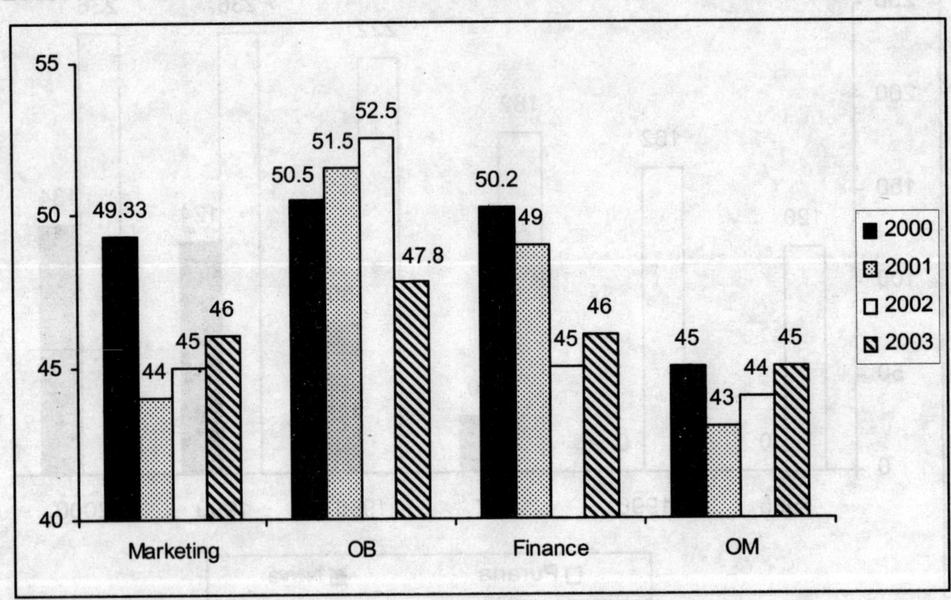

32. From which area did the faculty member retire?

(1) Finance (2) Marketing

(3) OB (4) OM

33. Professors Naresh and Devesh, two faculty members in the Marketing area, who have been with the Institute since its inception, share a birthday, which falls on 20th November. One was born in 1947 and the other one in 1950. On April 1 2005, what was the age of the third faculty member, who has been in the same area since inception?

(1) 47 (2) 50

(3) 51 (4) 52

34. In which year did the new faculty member join the Finance area?

(1) 2000 (2) 2001

(3) 2002 (4) 2003

35. What was the age of the new faculty member, who joined the OM area, as on April 1, 2003?

(1) 25 (2) 26

(3) 27 (4) 28

Directions for questions 36 to 39: Answer the following questions based on the information given below:

[CAT 2008]

The bar chart below shows the revenue received in million US Dollars (USD), from subscribers to a particular Internet service. The data covers the period 2003 to 2007 for the United States (US) and Europe. The bar chart also shows the estimated revenues from subscription to this service for the period 2008 to 2010.

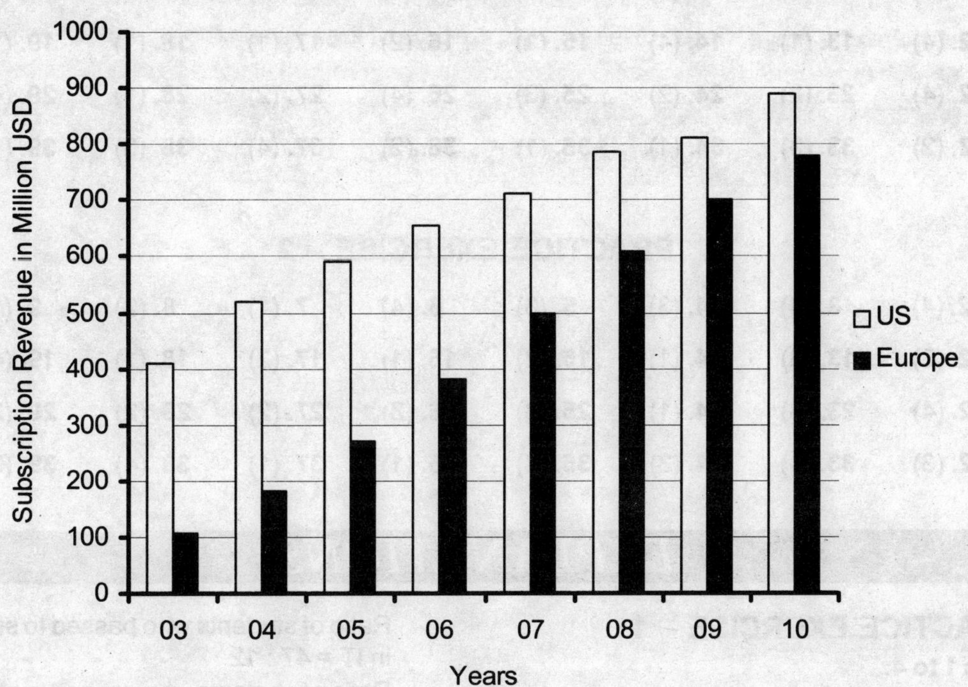

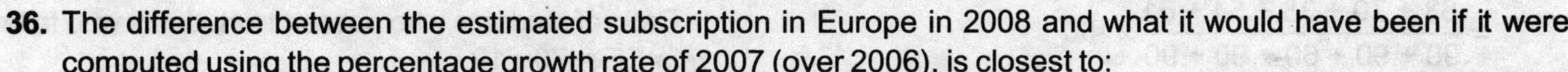

36. The difference between the estimated subscription in Europe in 2008 and what it would have been if it were computed using the percentage growth rate of 2007 (over 2006), is closest to:

(1) 50 (2) 80 (3) 20 (4) 10 (5) 0

37. In 2003, sixty percent of subscribers in Europe were men. Given that women subscribers increase at the rate of 10 percent per annum and men at the rate of 5 percent per annum, what is the approximate percentage growth of subscribers between 2003 and 2010 in Europe? The subscription prices are volatile and may change each year.

(1) 62 (2) 15 (3) 78 (4) 84 (5) 50

38. Consider the annual percent change in the gap between subscription revenues in the US and Europe. What is the year in which the absolute value of this change is the highest?

(1) 03 - 04 (2) 05 - 06 (3) 06 - 07 (4) 08 - 09 (5) 09 - 10

39. While the subscription in Europe has been growing steadily towards that of the US, the growth rate in Europe seems to be declining. Which of the following is closest to the percent change in growth rate of 2007 (over 2006) relative to the growth rate of 2005 (over 2004)?

(1) 17 (2) 20 (3) 35 (4) 60 (5) 100

ANSWER KEYS

PRACTICE EXERCISE – 1

1. (4)	**2.** (4)	**3.** (2)	**4.** (4)	**5.** (3)	**6.** (1)	**7.** (2)	**8.** (1)	**9.** (2)	**10.** (4)
11. (2)	**12.** (4)	**13.** (1)	**14.** (4)	**15.** (1)	**16.** (2)	**17.** (1)	**18.** (1)	**19.** (1)	**20.** (3)
21. (4)	**22.** (4)	**23.** (2)	**24.** (2)	**25.** (3)	**26.** (4)	**27.** (2)	**28.** (1)	**29.** (4)	**30.** (2)
31. (4)	**32.** (2)	**33.** (3)	**34.** (1)	**35.** (1)	**36.** (2)	**37.** (4)	**38.** (3)	**39.** (4)	**40.** (3)

PRACTICE EXERCISE – 2

1. (1)	**2.** (4)	**3.** (4)	**4.** (3)	**5.** (3)	**6.** (4)	**7.** (1)	**8.** (2)	**9.** (1)	**10.** (2)
11. (1)	**12.** (3)	**13.** (3)	**14.** (1)	**15.** (2)	**16.** (1)	**17.** (2)	**18.** (1)	**19.** (4)	**20.** (2)
21. (2)	**22.** (4)	**23.** (3)	**24.** (1)	**25.** (3)	**26.** (3)	**27.** (2)	**28.** (2)	**29.** (2)	**30.** (4)
31. (1)	**32.** (3)	**33.** (4)	**34.** (3)	**35.** (3)	**36.** (1)	**37.** (1)	**38.** (4)	**39.** (3)	

EXPLANATIONS

PRACTICE EXERCISE – 1

For questions 1 to 4:

1. Pass percentage of the whole batch

$$= \frac{63 + 70 + 38 + 54 + 61}{90 + 90 + 60 + 90 + 90} \times 100$$

$$= \frac{286}{420} \times 100 = 68.1\%.$$

2. Maximum number of additional students who passed from ECE is (less than 70% of 12) = 8

Maximum number of additional students who passed from CSE is (less than 70% of 10) = 6

Maximum number of additional students who passed from IT is (less than 70% of 14) = 9

Maximum number of additional students who passed from ME is (less than 70% of 20) = 13

Maximum number of additional students who passed from EE is (less than 70% of 14) = 9

Number of students who passed in ECE = 63 + 8 = 71

Number of students who passed in CSE = 70 + 6 = 76

Number of students who passed in IT = 38 + 9 = 47

Number of students who passed in ME = 54 + 13 = 67

Number of students who passed in EE = 61 + 9 = 70

Ratio of students who passed to students who failed in ECE = 71 : 19

Ratio of students who passed to students who failed in CSE = 76 : 12

Ratio of students who passed to students who failed in IT = 47 : 12

Ratio of students who passed to students who failed in ME = 67 : 17

Ratio of students who passed to students who failed in EE = 70 : 19

Clearly ratio is the maximum for CSE in this case. But if we assume that no additional student passed from CSE, then the ratio is maximum for ME department.

So correct answer is option (4).

3. Number of students who failed in ECE = 27 – 6 = 21

Number of students who failed in CSE = 18 – 5 = 13

Number of students who failed in IT = 21 – 7 = 14

Number of students who failed in ME = 30 – 10 = 20

Number of students who failed in EE = 28 – 7 = 21

Percentage of students who failed in ECE

$$= \frac{21}{90} \times 100 = 23.3\%$$

Percentage of students who failed in CSE

$$= \frac{13}{90} \times 100 = 14.4\%$$

Percentage of students who failed in IT

$$= \frac{14}{60} \times 100 = 23.3\%$$

Percentage of students who failed in ME

$$= \frac{20}{90} \times 100 = 22.2\%$$

Percentage of students who failed in EE

$= \frac{21}{90} \times 100 = 23.3\%$

∴ Minimum percentage of students who failed is from CSE.

4. Total students who failed even after applying for re-evaluation = 21 + 13 + 14 + 20 + 21 = 89

Total number of students who would appear next year = failed + absentees = 89 + (2 + 1 + 6 + 1) = 99.

For questions 5 to 8: The given data can be tabulated as shown below.

Counties	NCD deaths in 2016			NCD deaths in 2017		
	Male	Female	**Total**	Male	Female	**Total**
Indonesia	582	815	**1397**	275	850	**1125**
Russia	827	892	**1719**	950	925	**1875**
India	2967	2273	**5240**	3160	2020	**5180**
China	4323	3670	**7993**	4195	3850	**8045**
USA	1054	1150	**2204**	1150	530	**1680**
Total	**9753**	**8800**	**18553**	**9730**	**8175**	**17905**

5. In three countries, viz. Indonesia, India and USA, the number of deaths due to NCDs in 2017 was less than that in 2016.

6. Required percentage = $\frac{8800 - 8175}{8800} \times 100 = 7.10.$

7. Required difference = (9753 – 9730) × 1000 = 23000.

8. Minimum percentage increase in the total number of deaths due to NCDs in 2017 was for China.

9. We need to look only at the paper in which the average was the highest in E_1 i.e. Geography. The total marks obtained by the 20 students together in Geography paper = 96 × 20 = 1920. Not more than 1 out of 20 students could have failed in Geography with this total. So the maximum number of students who could have failed in all the papers in E_1 was 1.

10. As the average was the highest for Maths in E_2, we can infer that this was paper in which maximum number of students could have scored 100 marks.

The total marks obtained by the 20 students together in Maths paper in E_2 = 93 × 20 = 1860

We can see that 17 students could have scored 100 marks and the remaining 3 students could have scored 160 marks in total, which each of the 3 scoring at least 40 marks. Now, these 3 students could have scored 100 marks each in some other paper in E_2. So there are multiple ways in which this can be achieved.

Hence, all 20 students could have scored 100 marks in at least one of the papers in E_2.

11. We just need to look at the paper in which the average was the lowest across subjects and exams. This paper was Maths in E_1 at 65 marks.

The total marks obtained by the 20 students together in Maths paper in E_1 = 65 × 20 = 1300

So the maximum number of students who could have scored more than 90 marks in Maths in E_1 = [1300/90] = 14.

Hence, not more than 14 students could have scored more than 90 marks all the papers in each of the exams.

12.

	I_{PC}	I_{PP}
Bangalore	15.86	15.94
Chennai	10.25	19.54
Hyderabad	11.11	16.42
Pune	79.3	5.3

Obviously, $I_{PC} - I_{PP}$ is negative for 3 cities.

13. This is a question of applying successive percentage formula a + b + (ab/100) is the total increase in waste generated, where a is the increase in waste generated per person and b is the increase in total population of the city

For Bangalore,

$100 \xrightarrow{4\% \uparrow} 104 \xrightarrow{24.44\% \uparrow} 129.44$

So, increase in population = 24.44%

For Chennai,

$100 \xrightarrow{3\% \uparrow} 103 \xrightarrow{8.93\% \uparrow} 112.2$

So, increase in population = 8.93%

For Hyderabad,

$100 \xrightarrow{5\% \uparrow} 105 \xrightarrow{4.30\% \uparrow} 109.52$

So, increase in population = 4.30%

For Pune,

$100 \xrightarrow{4\% \uparrow} 104 \xrightarrow{4.8\% \uparrow} 109.02$

So, increase in population = 4.8%

Hence, Bangalore is the required city.

14. Adequate data is not available to answer this question.

15. Required percentage =

$$\frac{(128 + 127) + (62 + 116)}{(127 + 138) + (141 + 263)} \times 100$$

= 64.72.

16. China's GDP in 2013

$= 181 + 181 \times \frac{13.4}{100} = \$205.25$ billion

Indoneisa's GDP in 2013

$= 60 + 60 \times \frac{7.3}{100} = \$64.38$ billion

So the difference in their GDP in 2013

$= (205.25 - 64.38) = 140.87 \approx \$140$ billion

17. The ratio of Merchandise Exports to GDP of Malaysia in 2012 $= \frac{39.6}{50} = 0.792$ and the ratio of Merchandise Export to GDP of Malaysia in 2013

$= \frac{46}{50 \times 1.083} = \frac{46}{54.1} = 0.851$

So the ratio increased in 2013 as compared to 2012.

18. The ratios in 2012, 2013, 2016 would be

$\frac{32.5}{x}, \frac{37}{1.084 \times x}, \frac{66.1}{1.084 \times 1.086 \times 1.087 \times 1.081 \times x}.$

Obviously, the numerator has more than doubled but the denominator would not have doubled. Thus, the last ratio is the highest, i.e. in 2016 and least in 2012. If you are confused between 2012 and 2013, in 2013, the numerator surely increased by more than 8.04% and hence the ratio has increased.

19. Required answer $= 60 \times 1.083 \times 1.092 \times 1.093 = 77.56$.

20. Required number of buyers

$= 1000 \times 0.12 + 1100 \times 0.11 + 1200 \times 0.15 + 1300 \times 0.12 + 1400 \times 0.18 = 829.$

21. Number of people who buy music by mail order changed from 2% (2013) to 5% (2017). Number of people buying from online stores changed from 10% to 15%. Difference between number of people who buy music by mail order and those buying from online stores changed from (10 – 2) = 8% in 2010 to (15 – 5) = 10% in 2017. Thus the registered change was an increase of $\frac{(10-8)}{8} \times 100 = 25\%$

22. Nothing can be said about the number of customers as no data on number of buyers in any of the years is given.

23. In 2013, 46% people are from age group B. 70% people purchased from music shops. Note that in every age group the pattern of buying from various sales outlet shows the same break up as the total and the total number of buyers in 2013 was 1000. So, in 2013 the number of people in age group B buying from music shops was approximately

$\frac{46}{100} \times \frac{70}{100} \times 1000 = 322.$

For questions 24 to 27:

The data given in the bar graph can be tabulated as shown below.

Let the total number of visitors in the year 2016 be 100x.

Year	Total number of visitors	Number of male visitors	Number of female visitors
2012	120x	60x	60x
2013	108x	81x	27x
2014	144x	96x	48x
2015	180x	108x	72x
2016	160x	104x	56x

24. The total number of female visitors in the year 2016 $= 56x = 56 \times 468.50 = 26236$

25. Percentage growth in the number of female visitors from 2014 to 2015

$= \frac{72x - 48x}{48x} \times 100 = 50\%$

26. Gender Gap in the year 2014 = 96x – 48x = 48x the year 2016 = 104x – 56x = 48x

Hence, it is equal in 2014 and 2016.

27. 2015

For questions 28 to 30:

28. The following lists down the time taken by each of the 4 mentioned countries to complete the 4 × 400 metres relay.

$$USA = \left(\frac{1}{8} + \frac{1}{12} + \frac{1}{9} + \frac{1}{11}\right) \times 400 \simeq 164 \text{ seconds}$$

$$Kenya = \left(\frac{1}{9} + \frac{1}{14} + \frac{1}{6} + \frac{1}{11}\right) \times 400 \simeq 176 \text{ seconds}$$

$$Russia = \left(\frac{1}{10} + \frac{1}{15} + \frac{1}{9} + \frac{1}{6}\right) \times 400 \simeq 178 \text{ seconds}$$

$$Australia = \left(\frac{1}{10} + \frac{1}{13} + \frac{1}{10} + \frac{1}{7}\right) \times 400 \simeq 168 \text{ seconds}$$

Hence, the USA was the winner of the relay.

29. First Runner from USA will complete one lap in 50 seconds. First Runner from Kenya will complete one lap in $\frac{400}{9} = 44.44$ seconds.

By the time the Second Runner from USA starts running at the rate of 12 m/s, the Second Runner from Kenya had already covered a distance of $= \frac{50}{9} \times 11$ metres i.e. $\frac{550}{9}$ metres.

In other words, the Second Runner from Kenya had a head start of $\frac{550}{9}$ metres.

To overtake the Second Runner from Kenya, the Second Runner from USA will take $= \frac{\left(\frac{550}{9}\right)}{(12-11)}$

$= \frac{550}{9}$ seconds

This implies that the Second Runner from USA will have to run

$= \frac{550}{9} \times 12 = \frac{2200}{3} = 733.33$ metres

This is impossible because each runner can cover a maximum of 400 metres.

This implies that the Second Runners from USA and Kenya never met.

Hence, option (4) is the correct choice.

30. Third Runner from Russia and Kenya did not meet as the speed of each of the corresponding runners from Russia was greater than the speed of the corresponding runner from Kenya.

For questions 31 to 33:

Let 'x', 'y', 'z' and 'w' be the number of employees working on exactly two, exactly three, exactly four and exactly five technologies respectively and the total number of employees in ABC Limited be 'k'.

Therefore, 2x + 3y + 4z + 5w = 26 + 36 + 32 + 46 + 16 = 156 and x + y + z + w = k.

31. Since we need to maximize the number of employees in ABC Limited, we need to maximize the number of employees working on exactly two technologies.

So, if we assume that all employees work on exactly two technologies, then the number of employees $= \frac{156}{2} = 78$.

Maximum possible number of employees in ABC Limited = 78.

The minimum possible number of employees in ABC Limited has to be greater than or equal to 46.

Let us take a case as follows:

Maximum possible number of employees working on five technologies is 16. In this case extra number of employees in J2EE, C#, .Net and XML is 10, 20, 16 and 30 respectively.

Now, 16 employees can possibly work on .Net, C# and XML while 10 employees work on J2EE and XML and 4 employees work on C# and XML.

∴ Minimum possible number of employees = 16 + 16 + 10 + 4 = 46.

Thus, required difference = 78 – 46 = 32.

For questions 32 and 33: By the given condition, the number of employees working in ABC Limited is 46.

Therefore,

2x + 3y + 4z + 5w = 156 ...(i)

x + y + z + w = 46 ...(ii)

$(i) - 3 \times (ii): z + 2w - x = 18 \Rightarrow x = (z+2w) - 18$

(i) – 2 × (ii) : y + 2z + 3w = 64

$\Rightarrow y = 64 - (2z + 3w)$

32. Maximum possible value of x will be attained when (z + 2w) is maximum. Thus, we need to maximize the value of 'w', i.e. 16. Now in order to maximize the value of 'z' we need to minimize the value of 'y', which can be equal to zero.

In this case, z = 8 and (z + 2w) = (8 + 32) = 40. Maximum possible number of employees in ABC Limited who work on exactly two technologies is (z + 2w) – 18 = (40 – 18) = 22.

33. Maximum possible value of 'y' will be attained when the value of (2z + 3w) is minimum possible. It is also evident that the value of 'z' as well as 'w' should be minimum, because then only 'y' will be maximized.

Since 'x' cannot be negative, value of (z + 2w) is atleast 18. Keeping in mind this constrain, the minimum possible value of (2z + 3w) is attained when z = 0 and w = 9.

Therefore in this case the maximum possible number of employees that work on exactly three technologies is 37.

34. Required average

$= \frac{(100.5 + 67 + 141 + 143.9 + 65)}{5} =$ Rs.103.48 crore

35. The key here is figuring out that the only performance which is less than the 1985 performance is the 1988 performance. Hence the percentage corresponding to 1988 should be less than 100.

Thus we see that (3) cannot be the answer. Also (2) cannot be the answer as it shows two of the years having less than 100%.

Between options (1) and (4), the correct answer is (1), This is so because the difference between the 1985 and 1988 performance is only 2 units on 67 units. Hence percentage wise it has to be 97% and not 68%.

36. The highest percentage decline over the previous year is seen for the year 1988, as in this year the performance almost halved.

For question 37 to 40:

The data given the graph can be tabulated as given below:

College	1988-89	1989-90	1990-91
Private Engg. College	120	180	250
Govt. Engg. College	80	130	130
Regional Engg. College	40	70	100
IIT	30	40	80

37. Total number of students in 1989–90
= (180 + 130 + 70 + 40) × 100 = 42000.

38. Growth rate in number of students in Govt. Engg.

College = $\frac{(120-80)}{80}$ = 50%

Growth rate in number of students in Private Engg.

College = $\frac{(180-120)}{120}$ = 50%. Hence the growth rate is equal.

39. Total number of students in 1990–91 = (250 + 130 + 100 + 80) 100 = 56000

Hence the total number of students in 1991-92 = 0.9 × 56000 = 50400. Hence (d) is the correct answer

40. Percentage of IIT students in 1990 – 91

$= \frac{80}{560} = \frac{1}{7} = 14.28\%$

PRACTICE EXERCISE – 2

1. Percentage change in FEI in 1998 relative to 1997 for various countries is:

   For India = $\frac{(0.72-1.71)}{1.71}$ = -57.89 %

   For China = $\frac{(4.8-5.96)}{4.8}$ = –19.46%

   For Malaysia = $\frac{(9.92-10.67)}{10.67}$ = – 7.02%

   For Thailand = $\frac{(5.282-5.09)}{5.2}$ = 14.34%

   Hence, highest change (absolute) is for India.

2. Since the absolute values are not given, it cannot be calculated.

3. Assume GDP of India for 1997 to be x.

   For 1998, India's FEI = $\frac{0.72 \times 102x}{100}$ = 0.7344x

   And foreign equity inflows for 1997 = 1.71x

   For China, assume GDP as y. Then, FEI in 1998

   $= \frac{107y}{100} \times 4.8 = 5.136y$. And FEI in 1997 = 5.96y.

   For South Korea, let GDP be z.

   FEI in 1998 = $\frac{95z}{100} \times 2.5 = 2.375z$ and FEI in 1997 = 2.16z.

   FEI of India and China were lower in 1998 than in 1997, while that of South Korea was higher in 1998 than in 1997.

4. Let x be the foreign equity inflow of India. Thus, China's foreign equity inflow is 10x.

   Now in 1998, FEI in India was 0.72. Therefore,

   $0.72 = \frac{x}{\text{GDP of India}}$

   Similarly, FEI in China in 1998 was 4.8, therefore,

   $4.8 = \frac{10x}{\text{GDP of China}}$

   Hence, (GDP of China/GDP of India) = (10 × 0.72)/ 4.8 = 1.5.Thus, China's GDP is 50% higher than that of India.

5. It is clear from the given graph.

6. Let us first find out the growth in 1990 of the all four sectors. So manufacturing 9% of 20 = 1.8. Hence, 20 + 1.8 = 21.8. Similarly, for mining and quarrying it is 15.6.

   For electrical, it is 10.85 and for chemical it is 16.1. Now in 1991 there is 1% negative growth in manufacturing. So 1% of 21.8 becomes 0.218. Thus, 21.8 – 0.218 = 21.582. Similarly, for mining and quarrying it is 15.44. For electrical it is 11.88 and for chemical it is 16.21.

   Now we add the figures for 1991 of all the sectors which comes to 21.582 + 15.75 + 11.88 + 16.21 = 65.42. Now, 65.42 – 64.35 = 1.07, which comes to approximately 1.5% growth rate.

7. It is clear from the graph that manufacturing is always growing in 1992 – 98. Hence, it will reach highest level in 1998.

8. In 1990, there is 4% growth. Hence, 4% of 15 = 0.6. So weightage in 1990 becomes 15.6.

   Similarly, in 1991 it becomes 15.44, in 1992 it is 15.6, in 1993 it is 14.97, in 1994 it is 16.16.

   Hence, it can be seen that the lowest level of production was in 1993.

9. Find out the weightage for all the sectors for 1994. For manufacturing it is 25.54, for mining and quarrying it is 16, for electrical it comes out to be 14.5 and for chemical it is 19.5. The total comes to approximately 77. In 1989, it was 60. Hence, 77 – 60 = 17 which is approximately 25% increase.

10. Since the index of total industrial production in 1994 is 50% more than in 1989, it becomes 150.

Now total weightage for manufacturing, mining and quarrying, electrical and chemical in 1994 is approximately 77. So 150 – 77 = 73.

In 1989, it was 100 – 60 = 40.

So 73 – 40 = 33, which is approximately 87.5%.

11. Man-hours spent in coding is 420 + 100 = 520.

Now going by options, we see (a) is the only option.

12. Total work is approximately

(100 + 80) + (420 + 100) + (280 + 140) = 1120

On-site work = 80 + 100 + 140 = 320

Percentage of total work carried out on-site is

$\frac{320}{1120} \times 100 = 30\%$ approximately.

13. From figure the total effort in man-hours spent on-site is 320.

It is nearest to actual man-hours of offshore testing which is 280 (approximately.)

14. Total man-hours

= (100 + 80) + (420 + 100) + (280 + 140) = 1120.

Total working hours = 100

Total man working = $\frac{1120}{100} = 11.2$ or 11.

For 50 hr the total man-hours is 50 × 11 = 550 which is near to coding (420 + 100)

Hence, (1) is the answer

15. Initial offshore testing man-hours = 280.

Initial onshore testing man-hours = 140.

Final offshore testing man-hours = 280 – 50% of 280 = 140

Final onshore testing man-hours = 140 + 140 = 280.

Hence, the proportion of testing offshore $= \frac{140}{(140+280)} = 30\%$ approximately.

16.

	Design	Coding	Testing
Initially	80	100	140
Finally	$80 + \frac{100}{2} = 130$	$100 + \frac{420}{2} = 310$	$140 + \frac{294}{2} = 287$

17. On interchanging the effort allocation between operations B and C, then C and D, and then D and E we find that B takes the E's position.

Looking at the effort in B and then ranking in ascending order we find that the company 3 ranks third.

18. Total effort for operation B through F is 81.5%.

Even distribution will give effort allocation in each

operation = $\frac{81.5}{5} = 16.3\%$

$\therefore$ Change in E = 28.6 – 16.3 = 12.3%

19. Since we are given about company 1, 4, 5 in options so we will look for changes in these companies only.

Allocation of effort in B, C, D in companies 1 = 43.1

Remaining operations gets $\frac{43.1}{3} = 14.4\%$ each.

Allocation of effort in B, C, D operations of company 4 = 29.7

Remaining operation is allocated extra $\frac{29.7}{3} = 9.9\%$ each.

Allocation of effort in B, C, D operation of company 5 = 36.8

Remaining operation is allocated $\frac{36.8}{3} = 12.3\%$ each.

We see that operation E in company 5 will then show the maximum.

For questions 20 to 25:

Position of States (Rank)	Year					
	96-97	97-98	98-99	99-00	00-01	
1	MA	MA	MA	MA	MA	
2	TN	TN	TN	TN	TN	
3	GU	AP	AP	AP	AP	
4	AP	GU	GU	GU	UP	} changed
5	KA	UP	UP	UP	GU	twice
6	UP	KA	KA	KA	KA	
7	WB	WB	WB	WB	WB	

20. From above table, we can conclude that option (2) is correct.

21. On referring to the table, we can see that UP is the state which changed its relative ranking most number of times.

22. We can say directly on observing the graph that the sales tax revenue collections for AP has more than doubled from 1997 to 2001.

23. Growth rate of tax revenue can be calculated as:

(Sales tax revenue of correct year – Sales tax revenue of previous year)

For year 1997-98 $\frac{7826-7290}{7826} = 0.068$

For year 1998-99 $\frac{8067-7826}{7826} = 0.030$

For year 1999-2000 $\frac{10284-8067}{8067} = 0.274$

For year 2000-01 $\frac{12034-10284}{10284} = 0.170$

24. For increase by the same amount for 2 successive years, eliminate the options by subtracting only the last digit.

For Karnataka, increase in 2000-01 is 5413 – 4839 = 574 and increase in 1999-2000 is 4839 – 4265 = 574.

Hence, (1) is the correct option.

25. On referring to the table, we can see that Tamil Nadu has been maintaining a constant rank over the years in terms of its contribution to total tax collections.

26. March rainfall is lower than September rainfall in every location. Just check the bar graph.

27. Peak rainfall occurs in April only in locations 6 and 7.

28. Number of Naya mixer-grinders disposed off in 1999 = 20% of 30 = 6

So the number of Na ya mixer-grinders in 1999, i.e. 124 is inclusive of those mixer grinders produced in 1997 and 1998 and still in operation. The numbers are (30 – 6)= 24 and (80 – 30) = 50 respectively.

Therefore, number of new Naya mixer-grinders purchased in 1999 = 124 – (50 + 24) = 50.

29. Number of Naya mixer-grinders disposed off in 1999 = 20% of 30 = 6

Number of Naya mixer-grinders disposed off in 2000 = 20% of (80 – 30) = 10

Therefore, total number of Naya mixer-grinders disposed by end of 2000 = 6 + 10 = 16.

30. Sine information regarding the number of Purana mixer-grinders for the years prior to 1995 is not known, it cannot be ascertained as to how many of them were disposed off in 2000.

31. It is given that 10 Purana mixer-grinders were disposed off as junk in 1997. So the number of mixer-grinders in operation in 1997 must have been 162 – 10 = 152. But it is given to be 182.

∴ Number of newly purchased Purana mixer-grinder in 1997 = 182 – 152 = 30

20% of this, i.e. 6 were disposed off in 1999. So the number of mixer-grinders in operation in 1999 must have been 222 – 6 = 216. But it is given to be 236.

∴ Number of newly purchased Purana mixer-grinder in 1999 = 236 – 216 = 20.

For questions 32 to 35:

In any department in any given year, the average age ranges between 42-53 years.

(i) When a 25 year old will join, the average age will dip by a minimum of 3 years.

(ii) When a 60 year old will retire, the dip will be less compared to (i).

32. In the bar graph, one dip corresponds to the new 25 year old joinee. However, two dips in the trend implies joining of a 25 year old and the retirement of a 60 year old employee. This trait is observed only in Finance department. Hence, the faculty member who retired belonged to Finance.

33. From the graph of Marketing, it is clear that the new faculty joined in 2001.

On April 1, 2000, completed age of Professor Naresh and Devesh were 52 years and 49 years, in no particular order.

∴ Age of the third Professor on April 1, 2000

= 49.33 × 3 – (52 + 49) = 47 years

Hence, his age on April 1, 2005 was 52 years.

34. As the dip will be less in case a faculty retired compared to that when a new faculty joined in, so the new faculty member joined the Finance area in 2002.

35. For the OM area, the only dip comes in the year 2001. So the new 25 year old faculty joined in 2001. Hence, on April 1, 2003, his age will be 27 years old.

36. Subscription in Europe in 2006 = 380 Mn USD

Subscription in Europe in 2007 = 500 Mn USD

% change in 2007 $= \frac{500-380}{380} \times 100 \approx 30\%$

Therefore subscription (based upon the growth rate of 2007 over 2006) in 2008 should have been = 500 × 1.3 = 650 Mn USD (approx)

Therefore difference from the estimated subscription = 650 – 600 = 50 Mn USD (approx)

[Please note that the unit is mentioned neither in the question, nor in the options]

37. Let the total number of subscribers = 100x

Number of men = 60x

Therefore number of men in 2010 = $60x \times (1.05)^7$

= 84.42x (approx)

Number of women = 40x

Therefore, number of women in 2010 = $40x \times 1.1^7$

= 77.94x (approx)

Therefore, total number of subscribers = 84.42x + 77.94x = 162.36x

Percentage growth of subscribers

$$= \frac{162.36x - 100x}{100x} = 62.36 \text{ (approx)}$$

38. Gap in 2008 = 780 – 600 = 180 Mn USD

Gap in 2009 = 810 – 700 = 110 Mn USD

$$\text{Annual \% change} = \frac{110 - 180}{180} \times 100 = -39\%$$

Absolute change = 39% which is the highest.

Among the other options, option (3) '06-07' is closest, but it will lead to only 22% change in gap.

39. $\text{Growth rate of 2007} = \frac{500 - 380}{380} \times 100 = 31.58\%$

$$\text{Growth rate of 2005} = \frac{280 - 190}{190} \times 100 = 47.37\%$$

Therefore % change in growth rate of 2007 relative to growth rate of 2005 is

$$\frac{47.37 - 31.58}{47.37} \times 100 \approx 35\%$$

Combinational Graphs

SOLVED EXAMPLES

Directions for examples 1 to 4: Answer the questions on the basis of the information given below.

The line graph given below provides information about the production (in '000 tonnes) of eight different crops – Rice (R), Wheat (W), Pulses (P), Maize (M), Bajra (B), Jowar (J), Potatoes (PO) and Onions (O) – in India in 2013.

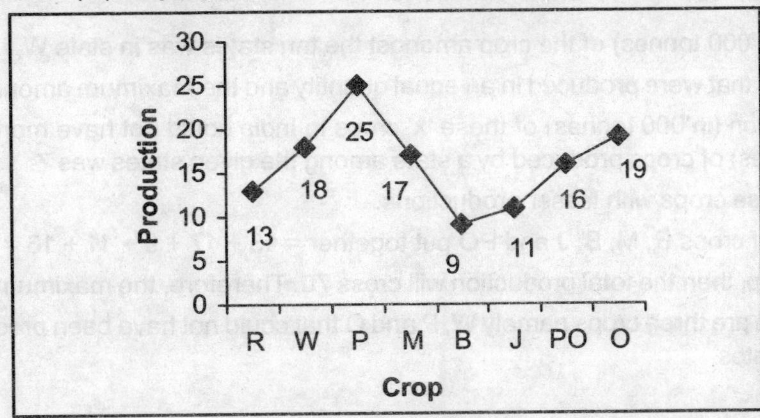

The bar graph given below provides information about the total production (in '000 tonnes) of crops across ten different states in India – Haryana(H), Uttar Pradesh(U), Punjab(P), West Bengal(W), Madhya Pradesh(MP), Gujarat(G), Tamil Nadu(T), Andhra Pradesh(A), Karnataka(K) and Maharashtra(M).

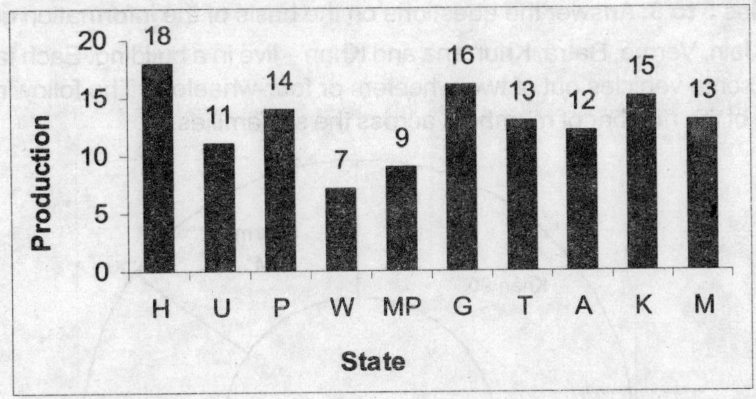

Assume that these eight mentioned crops were the only crops that were produced in India and the given ten states were the only states in India that produced the given eight crops in 2013.

1. If W, P, B and M were the only crops that were produced in H, U, P and T, then the production of P in G as a percentage of the total production of the crops G could not be more than

(1) 88.75 (2) 80.5 (3) 86.25 (4) 81.25

2. If PO and O were produced in exactly 3 states and no other crops were produced in these 3 states, then the state in which the crop PO was definitely not produced was

(1) G (2) H (3) MP (4) U

3. If the maximum possible number of crops were produced in an equal quantity (by weight) in all the given states then what was the number of crops that were not produced in an equal quantity in the given states?

(1) 4 (2) 3 (3) 5 (4) 1

4. If the maximum possible number of crops were produced in an equal quantity (by weight) in all the given states then the production (in '000 tonnes) of W in MP could not be more than

(1) 2.4 (2) 2.8 (3) 3.8 (4) 3.4

1. 4 Total production (in '000 tonnes) of the crops in states H, U, P and T put together = 18 + 11 + 14 + 13 = 56.

Total production (in '000 tonnes) of the crops in states W, P, B, M put together = 18 + 25 + 9 + 17 = 69.

Assume that the excess production (in '000 tonnes) was of crop P, which is equal to 69 – 56 i.e. 13.

Maximum production (in '000 tonnes) of crop P in state G = 13

Hence, the required percentage = $\frac{13}{16} \times 100 = 81.25$.

2. 2 The possible combinations of states where the crop PO and O could be grown are (W, A, G), (W, T, K), (W, M, K), (MP, A, P), (T, M, MP) and (U, K, MP).

So, H was definitely not the state where crop PO was grown.

For examples 3 and 4:

Minimum production (in'000 tonnes) of the crop amongst the ten states was in state W, i.e. 7.

Let the number of crops that were produced in an equal quantity and the maximum amount in the given states be 'x'.

The aggregate production (in'000 tonnes) of these 'x' crops in India could not have more than 70 as the minimum production (in'000 tonnes) of crops produced by a state among the given states was 7.

So, we need to pick those crops with lesser productions.

Aggregate production of crops R, M, B, J and PO put together = 13 + 17 + 9 + 11 + 16 = 66.

If we take one more crop, then the total production will cross 70. Therefore, the maximum possible value of 'x' is 5.

3. 2 Therefore, there are three crops namely W, P and O that could not have been produced in equal quantities in the given ten states.

4. 1 The aggregate production (in '000 tonnes) of crops R, M, B, J and PO put together in state MP = $\left(\frac{66}{10}\right) = 6.6$

So, maximum possible production (in '000 tonnes) of the crop W in state MP = 9 – 6.6 = 2.4.

Directions for examples 5 to 8: Answer the questions on the basis of the information given below:

Six families – Sharma, Jain, Verma, Batra, Khurrana and Khan – live in a building. Each family has a different number of members and owns some vehicles out of two-wheelers or four-wheelers. The following doughnut chart gives the percentage distribution of the number of members across the six families.

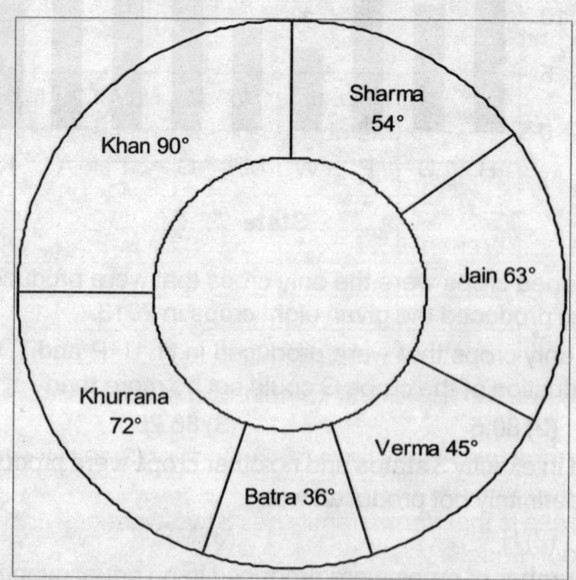

The table given below gives the number of vehicles per person for the six families.

Family	Vehicles/person
Sharma	0.67
Jain	1
Verma	0.6
Batra	1.5
Khurrana	0.375
Khan	0.4

No family has more than 20 members. No two families have the same combination of two-wheelers and four-wheelers. There is only one family that has no four-wheelers, and each family has atleast one two-wheeler. The number of four-wheelers with Batra and Jain is 2 and 4 respectively. No family has more than 9 two-wheelers.

5. The number of four-wheelers with how many families is definitely more than that of two-wheelers?
(1) 1 (2) 2 (3) 3 (4) 4

6. By what percent can the number of two wheelers with Verma family be more than that with Khan family?
(1) 75 (2) 66.66 (3) 200 (4) 33.33

7. For which family is the value of the product of the number of members and the number of vehicles the minimum?
(1) Batra (2) Verma (3) Jain (4) Sharma

8. Which family does not have any four-wheeler?
(1) Sharma (2) Verma (3) Khurrana (4) Cannot be determined

For examples 5 to 8:

Let the total number of people = 40n

So the members and vehicles can be shown as below, using the doughnut chart and the table given:

Family	Members	Vehicles
Sharma	6n	4n
Jain	7n	7n
Verma	5n	3n
Batra	4n	6n
Khurrana	8n	3n
Khan	10n	4n

Now no family has more than 20 members.

$\Rightarrow$ The number of members of Khan family ≤ 20

or $10n \leq 20$

or $n \leq 2$

Now n = 2 is not feasible as in such a case the number of vehicles owned by the Jain family will be 14 which will imply that they have 10 two-wheelers. But this is not possible as no family can have more than 9 two-wheelers.

So n = 1, we get the following table:

Family	No. of members	No. of vehicles	No. of 2 wheelers	No. of 4 wheelers
Sharma	6	4		
Jain	7	7	3	4
Verma	5	3		
Batra	4	6	4	2
Khurrana	8	3		
Khan	10	4		

Now Sharma and Khan family can have following combination of two-wheelers and four-wheelers: (1, 3), (2, 2), (3, 1), (4, 0)

Similarly the Verma and Khurrana family may have (1, 2), (2, 1) or (3, 0) two-wheelers and four-wheelers respectively.

5. 1 We could be sure only about the Jain family.

6. 3 One of the possible case is that Verma family has 3 two-wheelers and 0 four-wheelers and Khan family has 3 two-wheelers and 1 four-wheelers

So the required percentage = $\frac{3-1}{1} \times 100 = 200\%$

7. 2 Its minimum for the Verma family, i.e. 5 × 3 = 15.

8. 4 From the given data we cannot determined that which family does not own any four-wheeler.

Directions for examples 9 and 10: Answer the questions on the basis of the information given below.

Five companies – Alta Vista, Bultaco, Coleco, Dixons and Eletropaulo – are disguised as A, B, C, D and E – not necessarily in the same order. The square charts represent the percentage profit earned by the five companies in the years 2016 and 2017. In each of these charts, the numerical value of the area of each of the regions A, B, C, D and E gives the percentage profit earned by the company represented by the letter. The cumulative bar chart represents the revenue (in rupees crores) of these five companies in given years.

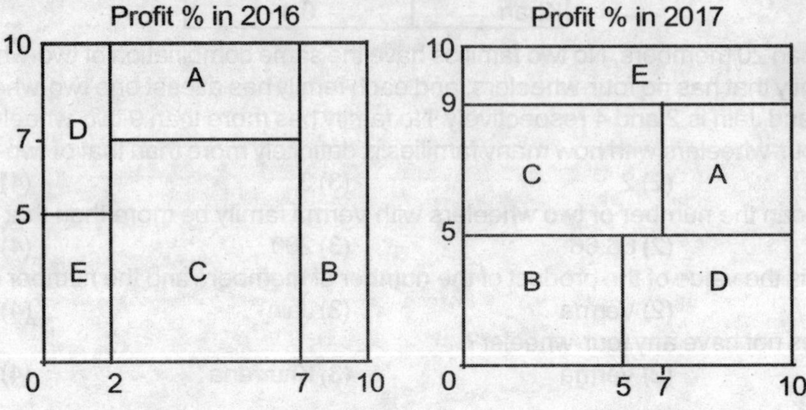

Revenue in 2016 and 2017 of five companies

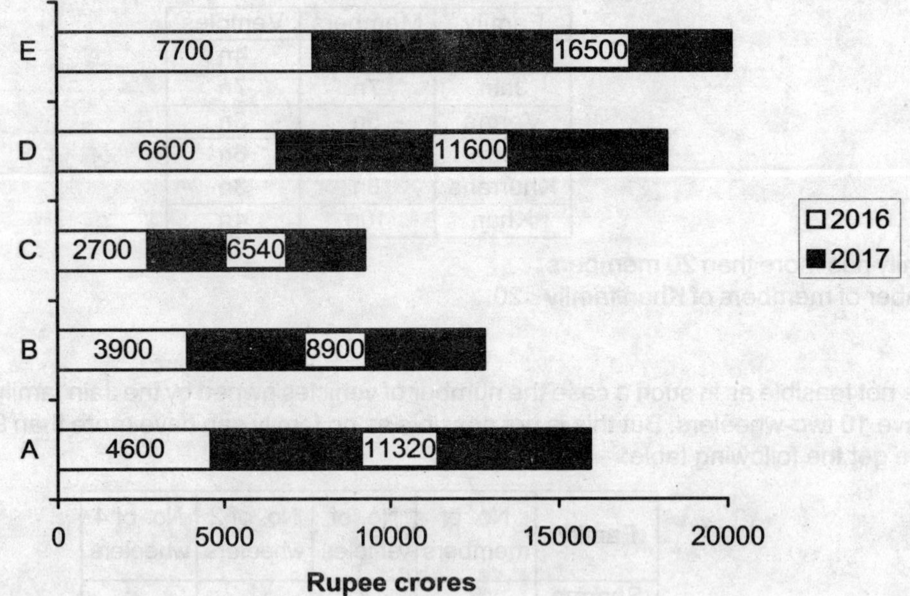

Further, it is known as:

1. Revenue = Expenditure + Profit, and Profit % = $\frac{\text{Total Profit}}{\text{Expenditure}} \times 100$.
2. Among the five companies, "Dixons" earned the minimum profit in both the years 2016 and 2017.
3. Among the five companies, Eletropaulo had the maximum difference between the profit earned in the years 2016 and 2017.

9. Among the five companies, if Coleco earned the highest profit in 2016, which company(ies) earned the second highest profit in 2016?

(1) Both Alta Vista and Bultaco
(2) Both Bultaco and Eletropaulo
(3) Both Eletropaulo and Alta Vista
(4) Alta Vista

10. Among the five companies, if Alta Vista earned the second highest profit in the year 2017, which of the following choices contains the names of the companies the profit of which could be the highest in 2017?

(1) Both Bultaco and Dixons
(2) Both Coleco and Eletropaulo
(3) Both Eletropaulo and Dixons
(4) Both Bultaco and Coleco

For examples 9 and 10:

The following table can be made:

(all figures in rupee crores)

	2016			2017		
	Revenue	Profit %	Profit	Revenue	Profit %	Profit
A	4600	15	600	6720	12	720
B	3900	30	900	5000	25	1000
C	2700	35	700	3840	28	840
D	6600	10	600	5000	25	1000
E	7700	10	700	8800	10	800

By the given information, A is Dixons and D is Eletropaulo.

9. 1 Here B is Coleco. The second highest profit in 2016 is Rs.700 crore. So both Alta Vista and Bultaco is the answer.

10. 2 Here C is Alta Vista. The highest profit earned by any Company in 2017 is Rs. 1000 crore. So, from the choices, Coleco and Electropaulo is the answer.

Directions for examples 11 to 14: Answer the questions on the basis of the information given below.

The following table gives the amount (in crores) of loan disbursed by banks in India during 2013-2017. The bank which disburses the maximum amount in a particular year is considered to be the market leader.

Name of the Bank	2013	2014	2015	2016	2017
ICICI	88	98	113	129	146
HDFC	98	118	128	138	130
CBI	47	43	53	49	58
SBI	46	53	48	59	71
Others	89	111	123	133	145

The pie-chart given below shows the distribution of the loans disbursed by all the banks that are part of others in 2017.

Constituents of others in 2017

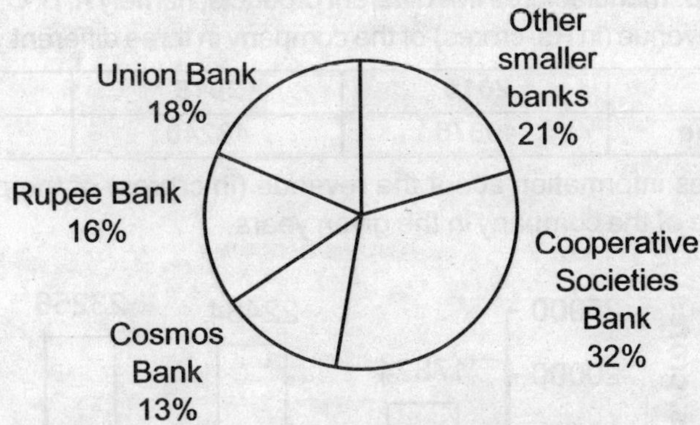

11. In 2015, all banks had the same percentage share in auto finance as their respective share in loan disbursement. By what amount was the share of HDFC Bank greater than the share of SBI, if the total auto finance market was Rs. 180 crore?

(1) Rs. 11.4 crore
(2) Rs. 13.6 crore
(3) Rs. 30.97 crore
(4) None of these

12. In 2018, if all banks retained their respective market shares as they had in 2017, the total loan disbursed by which of the following three banks put together was more than that of ICICI?

(1) CBI, SBI and Cosmos Bank
(2) CBI, Rupee Bank and Union Bank
(3) Cosmos Bank, Rupee Bank and SBI
(4) Rupee Bank, Union Bank and SBI

13. The total amount of loan disbursed by all the banks put together in 2013 was what percent of that in 2017?

(1) 61.91 (2) 72.61 (3) 88.45 (4) 66.90

14. If the share of constituents of others in 2013 was the same as that in 2017, then what was the approximate value of the ratio of the market share of other smaller banks to that of SBI in 2013?

(1) 7 : 20 (2) 2 : 5 (3) 1 : 3 (4) 3 : 7

For examples 11 to 14:

11. 3 Market share of HDFC in the loan segment (2015) = $\frac{128}{465} \times 100 = 27.53\%$

Market share of SBI in the loan segment (2015) = $\frac{48}{465} \times 100 = 10.32\%$

Difference in share = 27.53% – 10.32% = 17.21%

Auto finance market in 2015 = Rs. 180 crore

17.21% of 180 crore = Rs. 30.97 crore

12. 1 Option (1) gives 58 + 71 + 145 × 0.13 = 147.85

Option (2) gives 58 + 145 × 0.34 = 107.3

Option (3) gives 0.29 × 145 + 71 = 113.05

Option (4) gives 0.34 × 145 + 71 = 120.3

Only the option (1) gives a value which is more than the loan disbursed by ICICI.

13. 4 Total loan amount disbursed in 2013 and 2017 is 368 and 550 respectively.

The required percentage = $\frac{368}{550} \times 100 = 66.91\%$

14. 2 Market share of SBI, in 2013 = 46 crores.

Market share of other smaller banks, in 2008 = 21% of 89 = 18.69 crores.

Required ratio = $\frac{18.69}{46} \cong \frac{2}{5}$, i.e. 2 : 5.

Directions for examples 15 to 17: Answer the questions on the basis of the information given below.

A company named Tipro India Ltd. manufactures five different products, namely A, B, C, D and E. The following table gives the information about the total revenue (in Rs. crores) of the company in three different years.

Year	2014	2015	2016
Revenue	40876	48240	52624

The following bar chart provides information about the revenue (in crores) of the product that made the maximum contribution in the total revenue of the company in the given years.

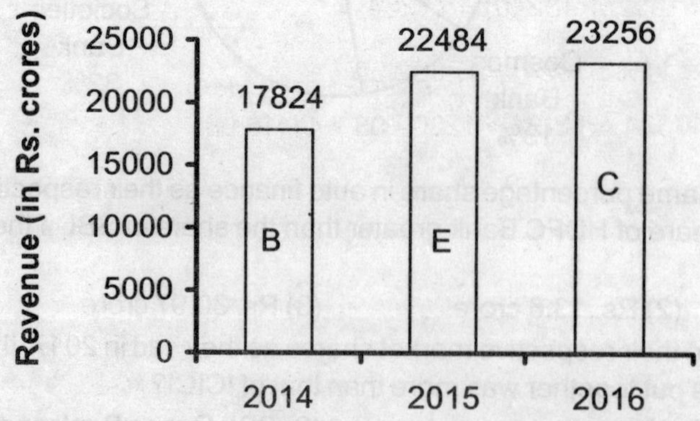

Each product made a contribution of at least 12%, 10% and 11% in the total revenue of the company in the years 2014, 2015 and 2016 respectively.

15. In 2014, what could be the minimum possible value of the absolute difference between the revenue generated through the sales of B and that through the sales of A?

(1) Rs.8472.36 crores (2) Rs.8224.64 crores (3) Rs.9422.36 crores (4) Rs.9487.36 crores

16. In each of the given years, if all the products, except the one which made the maximum contribution in the total revenue of the company in that year, made an equal percentage contribution in total revenue, then what was the percentage increase in the revenue generated through the sales of E in 2016 over that in 2014?

(1) 28.60 (2) 24.54 (3) 27.40 (4) 26.22

17. The total revenue (in Rs. crores) generated through the sales of B in the given years put together could not be more than

(1) 40987.03 (2) 41110.08 (3) 32840.50 (4) 50434.48

15. 4 The minimum possible difference between the revenue earned by B and A will be when A would have had maximum possible revenue (as B already had maximum revenue in 2014)

Each product contributed at least 12% towards total revenue in 2014.

So minimum percentage contribution by C, D and E = 12 + 12 + 12 = 36%

So the maximum revenue contribution by A

= 40876 – (17824 + 36% of 40876)

= 40876 – (17824 + 14715.36)

= 40876 – 32539.36 = Rs. 8336.64 crores

∴ The minimum possible difference = 17824 – 8336.64 = Rs. 9487.36 crores.

16. c All products (except those which contributed the maximum revenue in the given years) had an equal percentage contribution towards the total revenue.

Contribution of all the products except B in the year 2014 = 40876 –17824 = 23052

Contribution of each product except B in the year 2014 = $\frac{23052}{4}$ = 5763 crores.

Contribution of all the products except C in the year 2016 = 52624 –23256 = 29368 crores

Contribution of each product except C in the year 2006 = $\frac{29368}{4}$ = 7342 crores

∴ Percentage increase in the revenue of product E in 2016 over 2014 = $\left[\frac{(7342-5763)}{5763}\right] \times 100 = 27.40$.

17. b In order to get the required answer, the revenue generated through the sales of B should be maximised in 2015 and 2016, as it was already the maximum in 2014.

By using the logic used in explanation of **Q. 15**, we will get the maximum possible sales of B in 2015 and 2016.

The maximum possible sales of B in:

2015 = 48240 – (22484 + 3 × 10% of 48240) = 11284

2016 = 52624 – (23256 + 3 × 11% 52624) = 12002.08

Hence, the required sales = 17824 + 11284 + 12002.08 = 41110.08.

PRACTICE EXERCISE – 1

Directions for questions 1 to 4: Answer the questions on the basis of the information given below.

The following chart and table give the information about advertisement tariffs and viewership for 4 different TV channels – A, B, C and D – during the period 2015-2017.

Advertisement tariff (in rupees) per 10 seconds

	2015	2016	2017
A	100000	120000	150000
B	150000	175000	200000
C	120000	150000	180000
D	80000	100000	125000

Viewership of channels

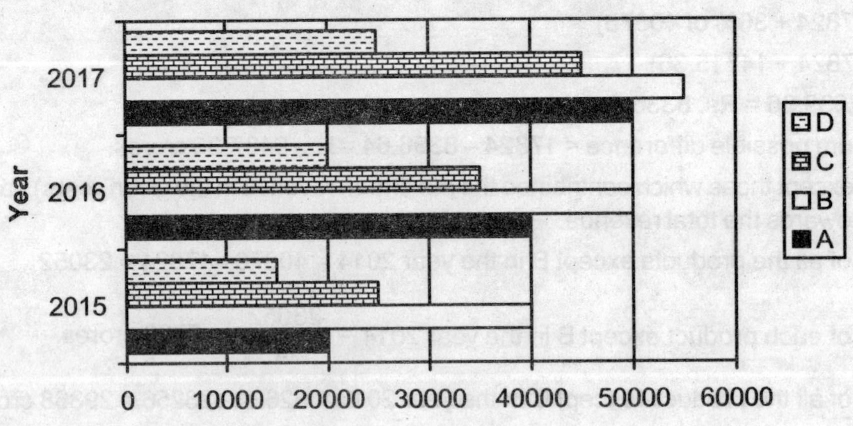

1. Had A witnessed the same growth rate in its viewership during the given period as what it was witnessed by C during the same period, by what percent its viewership in 2017 would have been less than the actual viewership in the same year?

   (1) 25% (2) 28%
   (3) 39% (4) 70%

2. Let X be the ratio of the advertisement cost per viewer for A to the average of advertisement cost per viewer for all the four channels in 2015 and the same ratio for 2017 be Y. What is the value of X : Y?

   (1) 3.28 : 1 (2) 0.88 : 1
   (3) 1.37 : 1 (4) 2.62 : 1

3. In each year from 2015 to 2017, which channel had a viewership closest to the average of the viewership of the four channels in that year? (Assume each viewer view only one channel.)

   (1) A (2) B
   (3) C (4) None of these

4. What was the advertisement cost per viewer for channel D in the year 2016?

   (1) Rs. 3.5 (2) Rs. 5
   (3) Rs. 4.3 (4) None of these

Directions for questions 5 and 6: Answer the questions on the basis of the information given below.

Each of employees working in XYZ Ltd. holds exactly one of the designation out of six designations namely Executive (E), Assistant Manager (AM), Manager (M), Senior Manager(SM), Deputy General Manager (DGM) and General Manager (GM). The following bar graph provides information about the average experience of employees across the six designations.

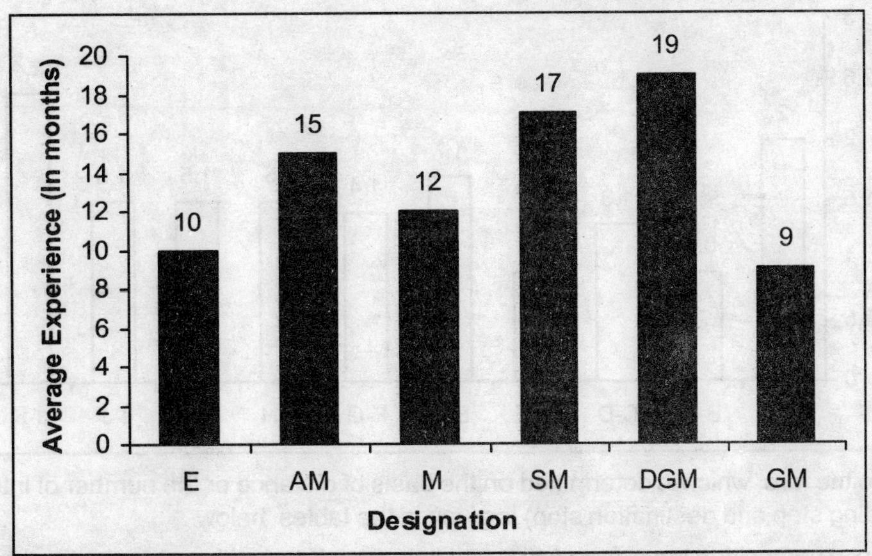

The following table gives the number of employees with experience less or more than the average experience of employees across the six designations. The average experience of employees with experience less or more than the average experience of employees for each of the six designations is an integer.

	Number of Employees	
	Less than the Average Experience	More than the Average Experience
E	16	28
AM	10	12
M	24	10
SM	8	16
DGM	4	10
GM	8	2

5. Find the absolute difference between the aggregate experience of Executives with more experience than the average experience of Executives and the aggregate experience of Executives with less experience than the average experience of Executives.

(1) 344 (2) 360

(3) 316 (4) 372

6. The average experience of DGMs with experience more than 19 months is at least

(1) 20 (2) 21

(c) 22 (4) 23

Directions for questions 7 to 10: Answer the questions on the basis of the information given below:

A bus starts from terminus A and terminates its journey at K. It stops at 9 intermediate bus stops between A and K viz. at B, C, D, E, F, G, H, I and J. Bus is the only mode of transportation available. The bar chart given below shows the distance (in km) between some pairs of bus stops.

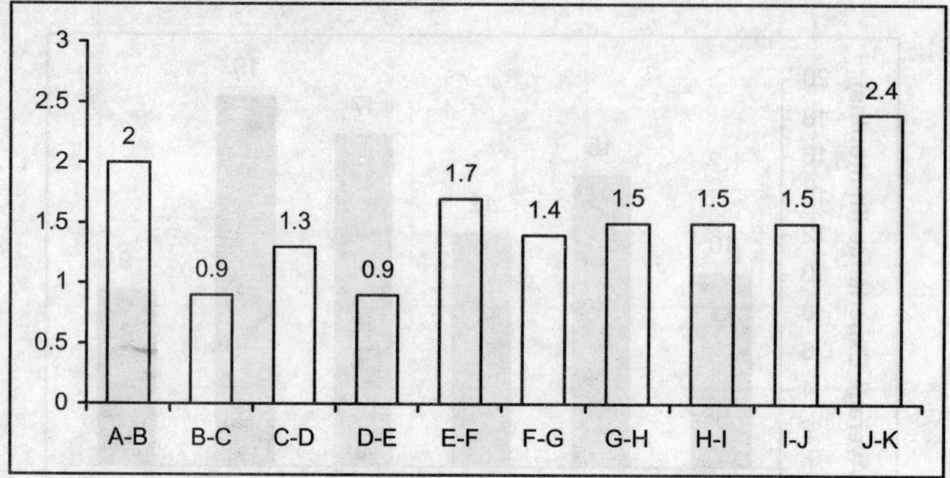

The details related to the fare, which is determined on the basis of distance or the number of intermediate bus stops (excluding the boarding stop and destination stop) is given in the tables below.

In case of a round trip, a person can travel from A to K and then from K to A without terminating his journey at K. In that case K will be considered only as an intermediate bus stop.

Distance (kms.)	Fare (Rs.)
0 to 4	3
Above 4 till 7	5
Above 7 till 10	8
Above 10 till 12	10
Above 12	16

No. of Intermediate Bus stops	Fare (Rs.)
0 - 2	3
3 - 5	5
6 - 8	8
9 - 11	14
11+	16

Fare policy is such that the fare increases according to increasing distance or increasing number of bus stops, whichever increases the fare by a larger amount. For example, if the distance covered by travelling 2 bus stops is 5 km then fare charged will be according to the distance i.e. Rs. 5. On the other hand, if for travelling 2 km the number of bus stops covered is 5 then the fare will be charged according to the number of bus stops. Anyone buying a ticket of any denomination makes full utilisation of the ticket and gets down at the point beyond which the ticket would not be valid or the bus reaches its terminus. In addition to the information given above, a person trying to minimise or maximise the fare paid, can change any number of buses.

7. What can be the minimum possible fare in which one can reach K from A?

(1) Rs. 14 (2) Rs. 11 (3) Rs. 13 (4) Rs. 12

8. If a person has Rs. 5 with him, then what can be the maximum possible number of intermediate bus stops and the minimum possible number of intermediate bus stops respectively that he can pass through while travelling from A to K?

(1) 4, 3 (2) 2, 1 (3) 1, 0 (4) 4, 2

9. Government offers a scheme on the 67th 'Independence Day' in which a person can take a round trip from A to K and then from K to A without terminating at K with a single ticket costing Rs. 16 and fare charges remain as given. What is the difference between the maximum possible fare paid (with atleast one intermediate stop for each sub-journey) to the minimum possible fare paid for the round trip? [Note: while travelling from A to K, A to F is an example of a sub-journey]

(1) Rs. 18 (2) Rs. 16 (3) Rs. 14 (4) Rs. 17

Additional information for question 10:

Due to some construction work, road between G to H is closed. Thus, buses reach H from G via route GMNOH. The distance (in km) between different bus stops in the new route is shown in the graph given below:

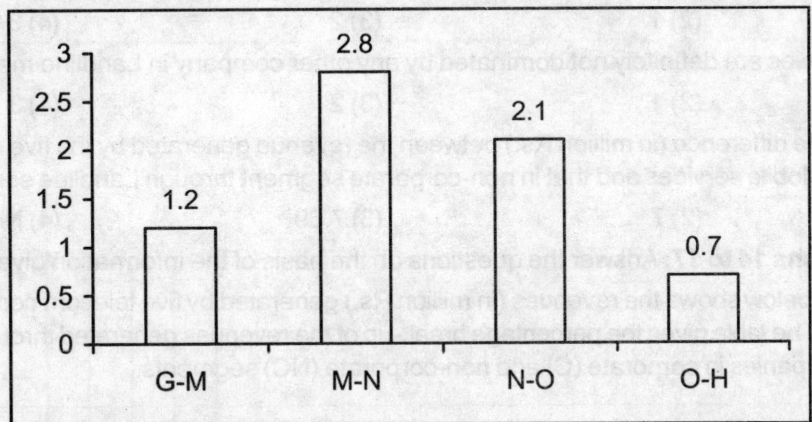

10. What is the ratio of the minimum possible fare to travel from B to I previously to the maximum possible fare to travel from C to J now (with atleast one intermediate stop for each sub-journey while travelling from C to J)? [Note: while travelling from A to K, A to F is an example of a sub-journey]

(1) 8 : 15 (2) 2 : 9 (3) 1 : 3 (4) 4 : 9

Directions for questions 11 to 13: Answer the questions on the basis of the information given below.

The line diagram given below shows the revenues (in million Rs.) generated by five telecom companies through Mobile and Landline services. The table gives the percentage break-up of the revenues generated through Mobile and Landline services of the five companies in corporate (C) and non-corporate (NC) segments.

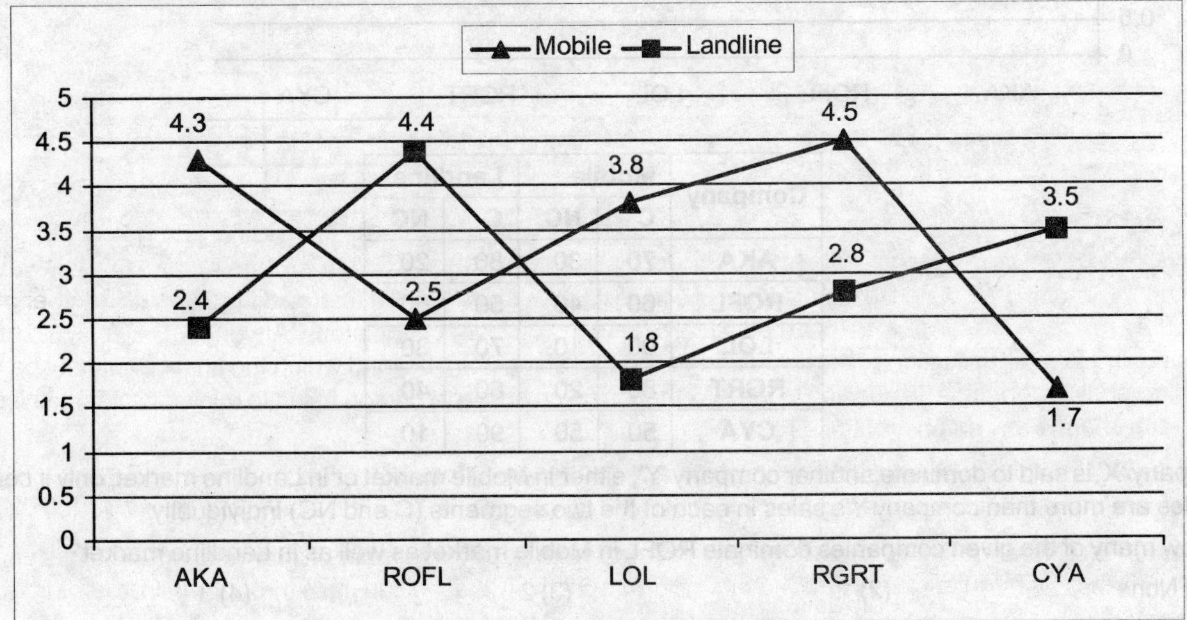

Company	Mobile		Landline	
	C	NC	C	NC
AKA	70	30	80	20
ROFL	60	40	50	50
LOL	90	10	70	30
RGRT	80	20	60	40
CYA	50	50	90	10

A company 'X' is said to dominate another company 'Y', either in Mobile market or in Landline market, only if company X's sales are more than company Y's sales in each of the two segments (C and NC) individually.

11. How many of the given companies dominate ROFL in Mobile market as well as in Landline market?

(1) 0 (2) 1 (3) 2 (4) 3

12. How many companies are definitely not dominated by any other company in Landline market?

(1) 0 (2) 1 (3) 2 (4) 3

13. What is the absolute difference (in million Rs.) between the revenue generated by the five companies in corporate segment through Mobile services and that in non-corporate segment through Landline services?

(1) 5.79 (2) 7 (3) 7.69 (4) None of these

Directions for questions 14 to 17: Answer the questions on the basis of the information given below.

The line diagram given below shows the revenues (in million Rs.) generated by five telecom companies through Mobile and Landline services. The table gives the percentage break-up of the revenues generated through Mobile and Landline services of the five companies in corporate (C) and non-corporate (NC) segments.

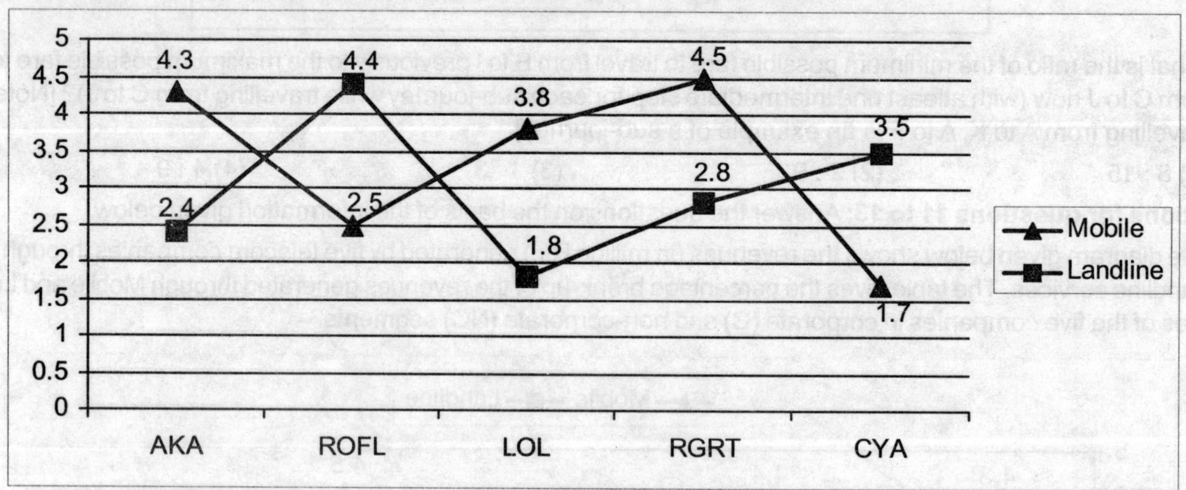

Company	Mobile		Landline	
	C	**NC**	**C**	**NC**
AKA	70	30	80	20
ROFL	60	40	50	50
LOL	90	10	70	30
RGRT	80	20	60	40
CYA	50	50	90	10

A company 'X' is said to dominate another company 'Y', either in Mobile market or in Landline market, only if company X's sales are more than company Y's sales in each of the two segments (C and NC) individually.

14. How many of the given companies dominate ROFL in Mobile market as well as in Landline market?

(1) None (2) 1 (3) 2 (4) 3

15. How many companies are definitely not dominated by any other company in Landline market?

(1) 1 (2) 2 (3) None (4) 3

16. What is the absolute difference (in million Rs.) between the revenue generated by the five companies in corporate segment through Mobile services and that in non-corporate segment through Landline services?

(1) 6.94 (2) 7.42 (3) 7.69 (4) 8.19

17. If the revenue generated by a company through mobile services is at least 150% of that generated through landline services, then that company is called a dynamic company. How many dynamic companies are there?

(1) None (2) 1 (3) 2 (4) 3

Directions for questions 18 to 21: Answer the questions on the basis of the information given below.

The following pie chart gives the distribution of the total loans disbursed by ADB in 2017 among eleven Asian countries.

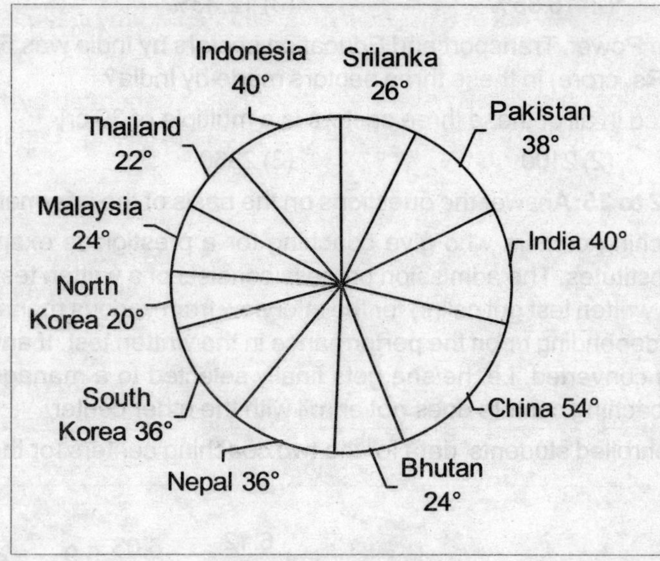

The following line graph gives the percentage contribution of loan from ADB in the total investment made in different sectors in the same year by India and China.

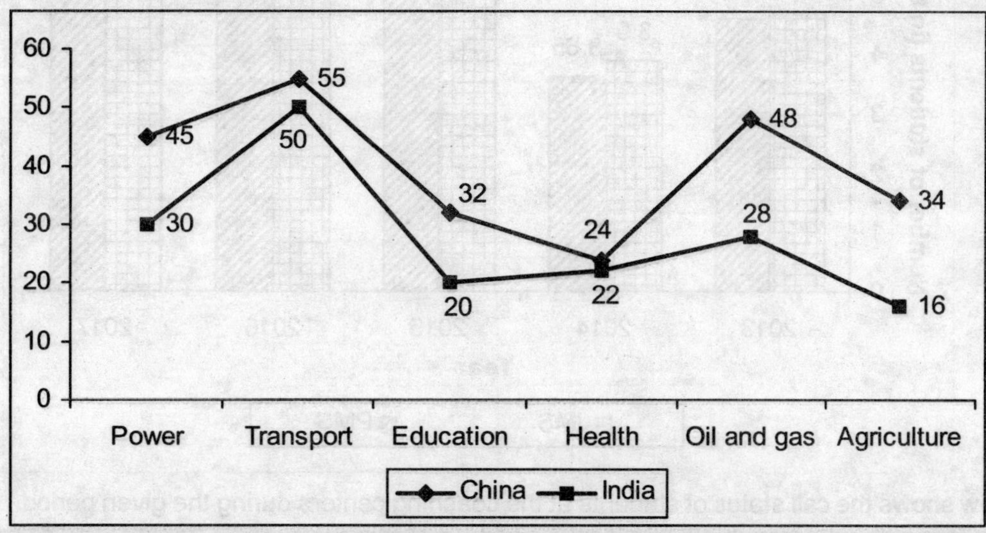

For both China and India, the loan received from ADB was utilized in the given sectors only.

18. If the total investment in Education sector in China was 60% higher than that in India, then what is the ratio of A and B, where

A : The percentage of loan from ADB invested in Education sector by China

B : The percentage of loan from ADB invested in Education sector by India

(1) 256 : 135 (2) 256 : 189 (3) 256 : 225 (4) Cannot be determined

19. The amount of loan invested in Transport sector by China was equal to 60% of the total loan given by ADB to Malaysia. The amount of loan invested in Transport sector by India was equal to 60% of the total loan given by ADB to North Korea. The total investment made in Transport sector by India was approximately what percent of that made by china?

(1) 75.76 (2) 91.67 (3) 80.80 (4) 81.81

20. If the total investments made in Education, Health and Agriculture sectors in India in 2017 was Rs. 150 cr., Rs. 120 cr and Rs. 400 cr. respectively, then the amount of ADB loan invested by India in these three sectors constitute what percentage of the total loan granted to India by ADB?

(1) 15.05% (2) 18.85% (3) 12.33% (4) 16.66%

21. The total loan invested in Power, Transport and Education sectors by India was 500 cr. What was the maximum possible investment (in Rs. crore) in these three sectors made by India?

[The loan amount invested in all of these three sectors is a multiple of 30 cr]

(1) 2000 (2) 2100 (3) 2360 (4) 2400

Directions for questions 22 to 25: Answer the questions on the basis of the information given below.

JMS and PMS are two coaching centers who give coaching for a prestigious exam named AIEA, conducted for admission to management institutes. The admission process consists of a written test followed by an interview. Only those students who clear the written test get call(s) for the interview from various management institutes. The number of calls may vary from 1 to 6 depending upon the performance in the written test. If anybody clears the interview then his/her call(s) are said to be converted, i.e. he/she gets finally selected to a management institute. A student who enrolls with one of the two coaching centers does not enroll with the other center.

The chart below shows the enrolled students' data for the two coaching centers for the period 2013 to 2017.

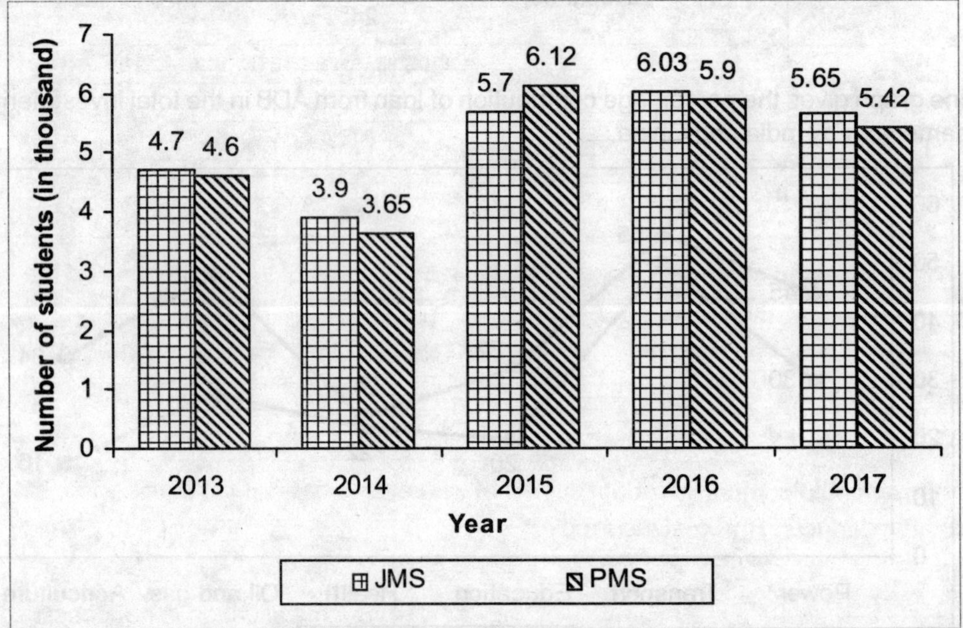

The table below shows the call status of students at the coaching centers during the given period.

Year	Total number of students who got interview call(s)		Number of students who got more than 3 interview calls		Number of students who converted their call(s)	
	JMS	PMS	JMS	PMS	JMS	PMS
2013	122	109	68	47	79	62
2014	117	119	63	62	77	81
2015	121	129	53	52	68	69
2016	112	102	62	58	75	71
2017	114	107	61	49	76	63

$$\text{Strike rate} = \frac{\text{Final number of students who converted their call(s)}}{\text{Total number of students who got calls}} \times 100$$

22. In which year the 'strike rate' of JMS was maximum?

(1) 2017 (2) 2014 (3) 2016 (4) 2013

23. For how many years during the period 2013-2017, was the 'strike rate' of PMS better than the 'strike rate' of JMS?

(1) 1 (2) 2 (3) 3 (4) Never

24. If it is assumed that all the students who got more than 3 calls, converted their calls, then in which year, during the period 2013-2017, did the maximum number of students who got 3 or less than 3 calls convert their calls, considering the students from both the coaching centers together?

(1) 2015 (2) 2017 (3) 2013 (4) 2014

25. What is the absolute difference between the average annual number of students enrolled with two coaching centers during the given 5 year period?

(1) 66 (2) 72 (3) 58 (4) 52

Directions for questions 26 to 29: Answer the questions on the basis of the information given below.

Company A and company B are two rival enterprises operating in the same market segment. Company A can adopt any one of X, Y, or Z strategy, and company B can, in turn, can adopt any one of P, Q, or R strategy. The following table gives the pay-off to company A depending on which strategy it adopts and which strategy company B adopts in response. A positive sign indicates that company A gains and company B loses, whereas a negative sign indicates company A loses and company B gains.

Pay-off to company A

Strategy that company A adopts	Strategy that company B adopts		
	P	Q	R
X	–4000	5000	–6000
Y	5800	–5200	5500
Z	–6200	4500	–6500

Further, both company A and company B incur a cost in adopting any of the strategies and the costs are given in the following table.

Cost to company A			Cost to company B		
X	Y	Z	P	Q	R
500	3000	1500	1400	200	2800

26. Which strategy should company A adopt such that whatever is company B's response, it will always make a net profit even after deducting the cost incurred?

(1) X (2) Y

(3) Z (4) Such a situation is not possible

27. If company A has very good cash flow and is aggressive, and its sole objective is to maximize the ratio of its gains to the losses of company B, which strategy should company A adopt?

(1) X (2) Y (3) Z (4) Either X or Y

28. What is the difference between the maximum gain that company B and company A can make?

(1) 500 (2) 700 (3) 12500 (4) 13200

29. Company A has to act first by choosing a strategy and then company B will respond, i.e. company B has an advantage of knowing what strategy A has adopted. In such a situation, which strategy should company A adopt such that the 'advantage' to company B is least?

('Advantage' to company B is defined as the sum of the gain of company B and the loss of company A.)

(1) X (2) Y (3) Z (4) Either Y or Z

Directions for questions 30 to 33: Answer the questions on the basis of the information given below.

The following charts represent the profile of the members of Indian Parliament, comprising two houses namely Lok Sabha and Rajya Sabha, in 2017. Each member of the Parliament belongs to exactly one of the two houses. The Lok Sabha has a total of 550 seats and the Rajya Sabha has a total of 250 seats.

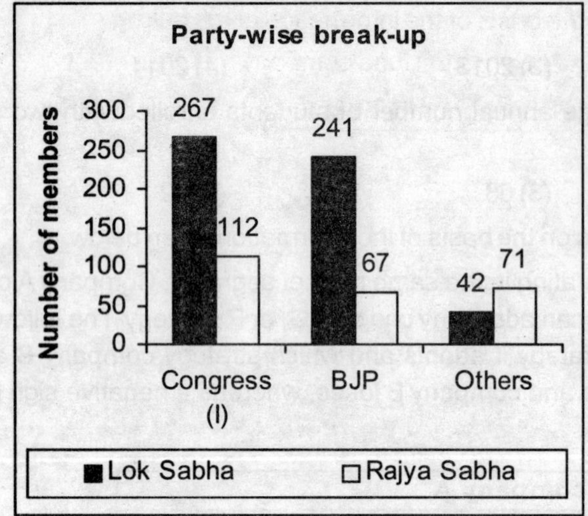

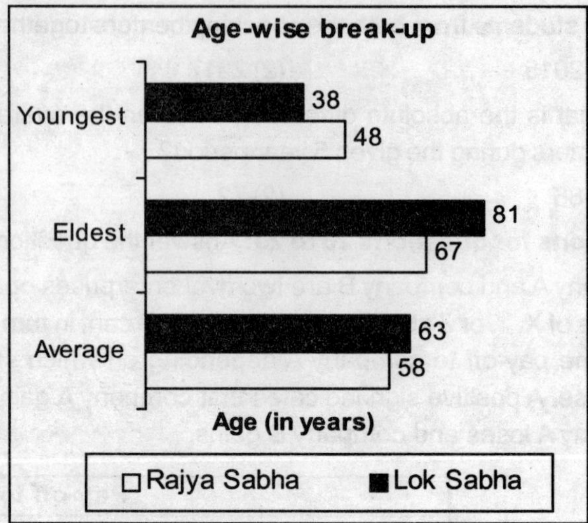

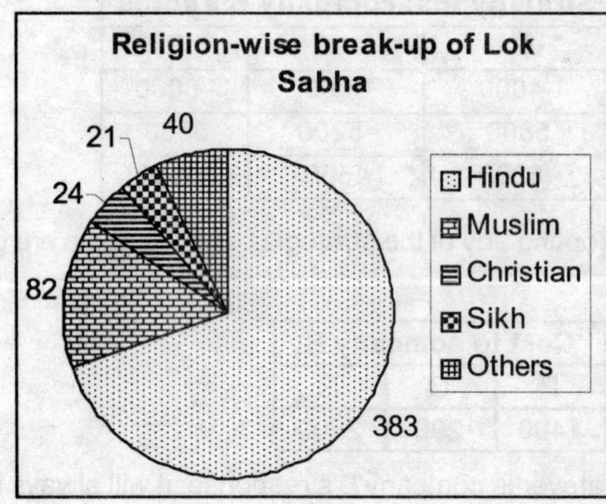

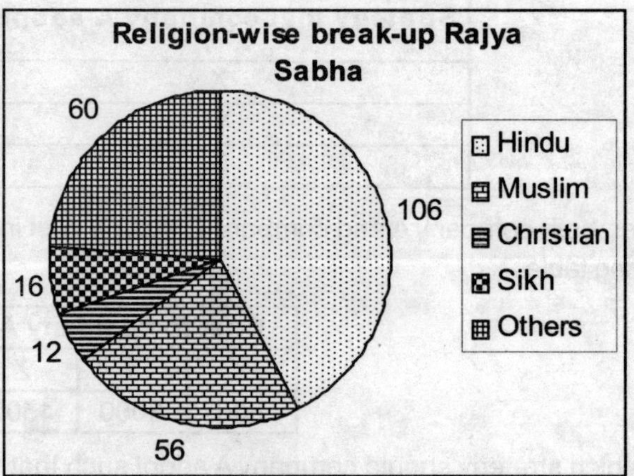

Professional and gender profile of members

Background	Lok Sabha	Rajya Sabha
Leaders	354	152
Actors	64	26
Lawyers	26	24
Doctors	12	19
Engineers	11	4
Others	83	25
Sex	**Lok Sabha**	**Rajya Sabha**
Male	398	208
Female	152	42

30. In 2017, if all lawyers and all women in the Lok Sabha voted in favour of a bill, how many more votes were required for a simple majority? (Simple majority means more than 50% members of a given house vote in favour of the bill.)

(1) 73 (2) 72 (3) 0 (4) Cannot be determined

31. What was the average age (in years) of the members of The Parliament?

(1) 61.4 (2) 57.6 (3) 63.2 (4) 60.7

32. In 2017, percentage of male members of Rajya Sabha belonging to Hindu community could not be less than

(1) 16.80% (2) 21.20% (3) 25.60% (4) 42.40%

33. What was the percentage of Congress (I) members in the parliament?

(1) 44.8% (2) 47.37% (3) 48.55% (4) 48.72%

Directions for questions 34 to 37: Answer the questions on the basis of the information given below.

The chart given below shows the sector-wise distribution of fund of a mutual fund company.

Total invested funds are worth Rs. 100 crore.

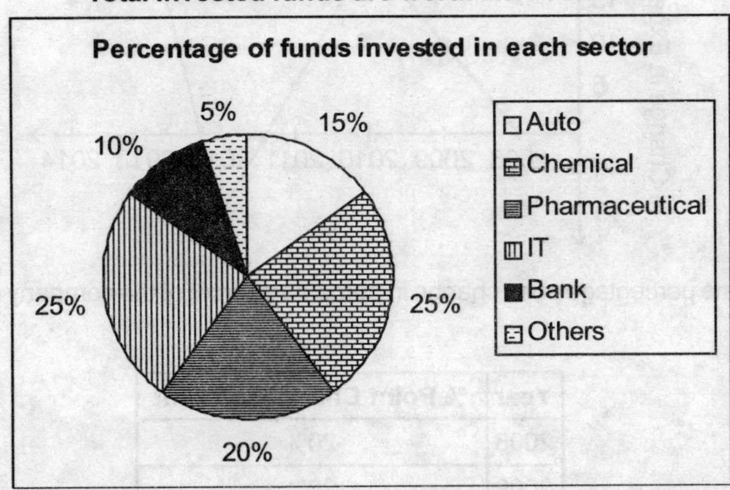

The price at which the shares of different sectors were purchased and their current market price are shown in the graph given below.

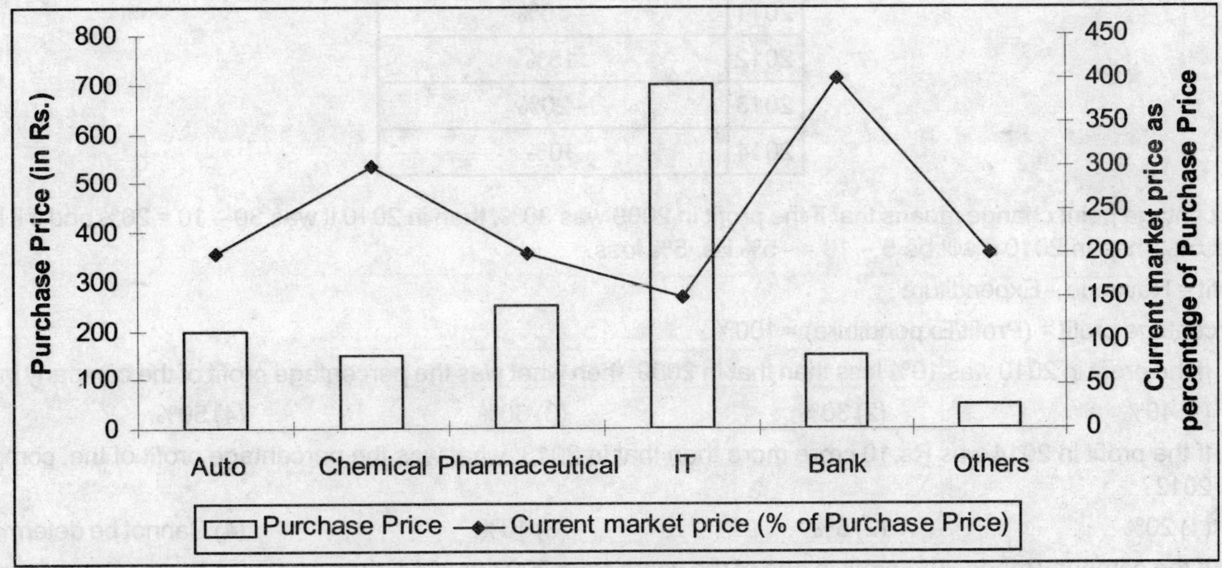

Market Capitalization = Number of Shares × Current Market Price

Market Appreciation = Number of Shares × (Current Market Price – Purchase Price)

34. Market Capitalization is highest for

(1) Chemical (2) Pharmaceutical (3) IT (4) Bank

35. For how many sectors is market Appreciation more than the average of market capitalization?

(1) 3 (2) 2 (3) 1 (4) 0

36. Total market Capitalization of the company at present is

(1) Rs. 232.5 crore (2) Rs. 222.5 crore (3) Rs. 242.5 crore (4) Rs. 200 crore

37. Number of shares is highest for

(1) Chemical (2) Pharmaceutical (3) Auto (4) Bank

Directions for questions 38 to 41: Answer the questions on the basis of the information given below.

The following graph gives the percentage change in the expenditure of a company over the previous year for the period 2008 to 2014.

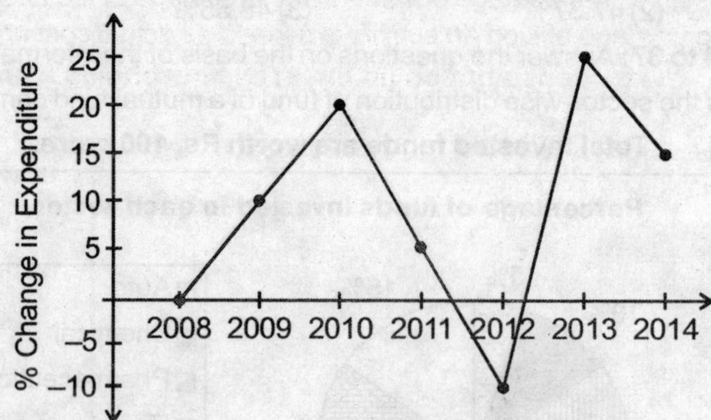

The following table gives the percentage point change in percentage profit of the company over the previous year for the time period 2008 to 2014.

Year	% Point Change in Profit
2008	20%
2009	20%
2010	–10%
2011	–10%
2012	15%
2013	–20%
2014	10%

Percentage point change means that if the profit in 2009 was 30%, then in 2010 it was 30 – 10 = 20% and if it in 2009 was 5%, then in 2010 it will be 5 – 10 = –5% i.e. 5% loss.

Profit = Revenue – Expenditure

Percentage profit = (Profit/Expenditure) × 100%

38. If the profit in 2010 was 10% less than that in 2009, then what was the percentage profit of the company in 2009?

(1) 40% (2) 30% (3) 60% (4) 50%

39. If the profit in 2014 was Rs.10 crore more than that in 2013, what was the percentage profit of the company in 2012?

(1) 20% (2) 5% (3) 10% (4) Cannot be determined

40. If the company made 20% profit in one of the years from 2007 to 2014, then what was the maximum number of years in which company did not make any profit?

(1) 4 (2) 3 (3) 2 (4) 5

41. If company made 15% loss in one of the years from 2008 to 2014, then what was the minimum number of years in which company incurred loss?

(1) 1 (2) 2 (3) 3 (4) 4

Directions for questions 42 to 45: Answer the questions on the basis of the information given below.

The pie charts given below gives the amount water consumed by two households – A and B – in the city of Chennai on various activities on July 27, 2015. However, some amount of water is wasted on each of these activities and the table given below the charts gives the wastage of water as a percentage of the total water consumed on that activity. Water consumed excluding wastage of it on an activity is defined as actual consumption.

Water consumption (in litres) by households A and B

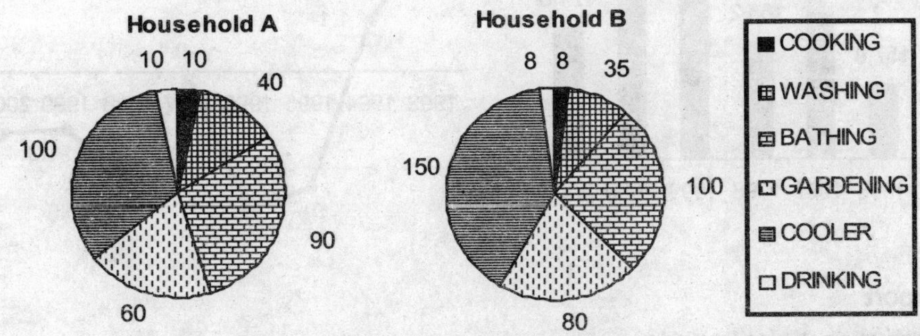

Wastage of water as a percentage of the total water consumed in each activity

Operation	A	B
Cooking	25%	25%
Washing	50%	40%
Bathing	60%	50%
Gardening	20%	40%
Cooler	10%	10%
Drinking	0%	0%

42. The actual water consumed on cooking and drinking by household A and B put together was what percentage of the total actual consumption of water by households A and B put together?

(1) 3.5% (2) 4.5% (3) 5.5% (4) 6.6%

43. The average amount of water wastage per activity by household B was greater than that by household A by

(1) 2.34 L (2) 2.38 L (3) 2.42 L (4) 2.46 L

44. The ratio of cost of water used for cooking, gardening and drinking are in the ratio 3 : 1 : 5. By what percentage was the cost of water consumed on these three activities by household B greater than by household A?

(1) 2.82% (2) 2.86% (3) 2.89% (4) 2.92%

45. The wastage of water by household A would have been exactly half the wastage of water by household B had there been no wastage of water in which of the following activities by household A?

(1) Washing, cooking, bathing

(2) Washing, gardening

(3) Washing, gardening, cooler

(4) Bathing, gardening, cooler

Directions for questions 46 to 49: Answer the questions on the basis of the information given below.

The charts given below represent the net foodgrain production and imports in India for the period 1993-2000.

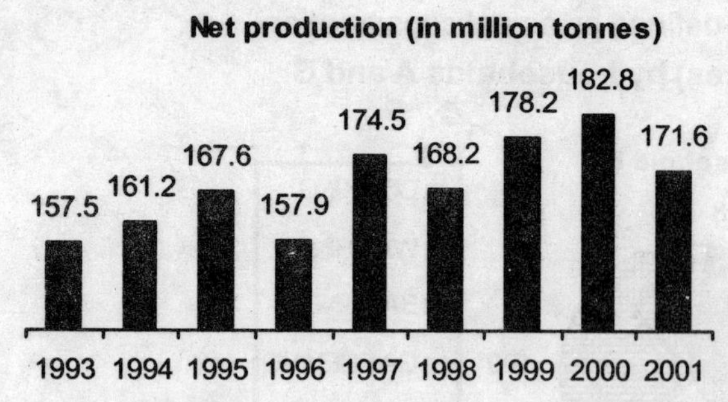

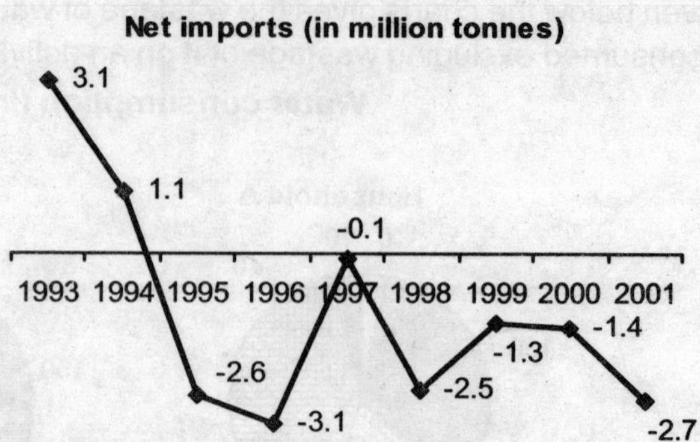

Net Import = Import – Export

Net Availability = Net Production + Net Imports

Closing Balance of Government Stock = Opening Balance + Net Addition

Net Addition = Procurement – Public Distribution.

The following charts represent the procurement of foodgrains and its distribution through public distribution system (PDS) for the period 1993-2000. The opening balance of government stock of foodgrains at the beginning of 1993 was 12.5 million tonnes.

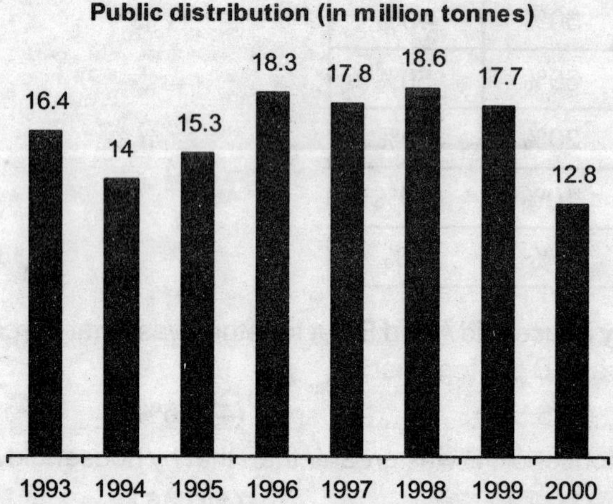

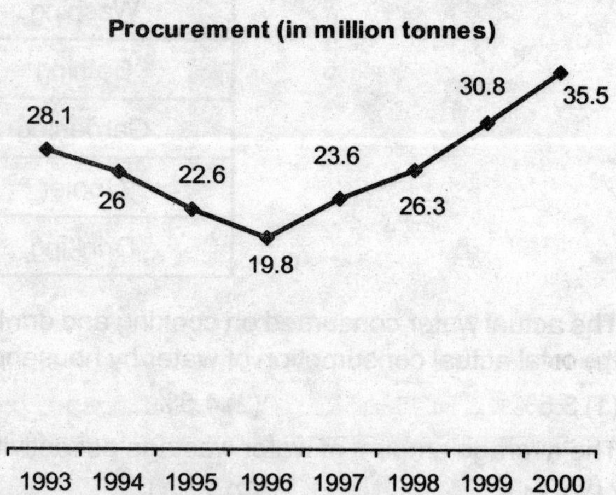

46. In which year did the net availability register the highest growth over the previous year?

(1) 1996 (2) 1997 (3) 1998 (4) 1999

47. Which year had the highest closing balance of government stock of foodgrains?

(1) 1994 (2) 1998 (3) 1999 (4) 2000

48. What was the percentage increase in procurement as a fraction of the net availability in 2000 over that in 1999?

(1) 104 (2) 10.45 (3) 12.6 (4) Data insufficient

49. Complete the table below with the best choice for A, B and C respectively amongst the alternatives.

Year	Export	Import	Magnitude of net import as a percentage of net availability
1996	12.3	A	2.00%
2000	B	16.2	C

(1) (15.4, 14.8, 0.85%) (2) (15.4, 17.6, 0.6%) (3) (9.2, 17.6, 0.77%) (4) (9.2, 17.6, 1.5%)

Directions for questions 50 to 53: Answer the questions on the basis of the information given below.

The line graph given below provides information about the production (in '000 tonnes) of eight different crops – Rice (R), Wheat (W), Pulses (P), Maize (M), Bajra (B), Jowar (J), Potatoes (PO) and Onions (O) – in India in 2013.

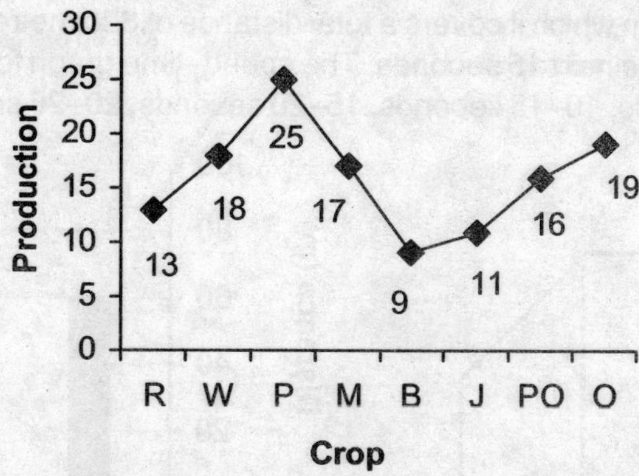

The bar graph given below provides information about the total production (in '000 tonnes) of crops across ten different states in India – Haryana(H), Uttar Pradesh(U), Punjab(P), West Bengal(W), Madhya Pradesh(MP), Gujarat(G), Tamil Nadu(T), Andhra Pradesh(A), Karnataka(K) and Maharashtra(M).

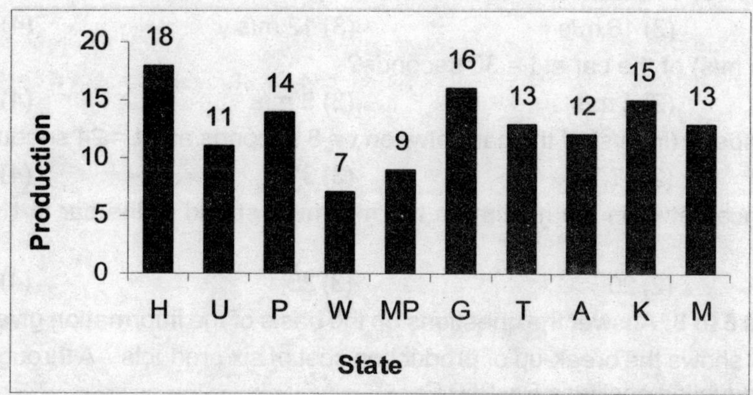

Assume that these eight mentioned crops were the only crops that were produced in India and the given ten states were the only states in India that produced the given eight crops in 2013.

50. If W, P, B and M were the only crops that were produced in H, U, P and T, then the production of P in G as a percentage of the total production of the crops G could not be more than

(1) 88.75 (2) 80.5 (3) 86.25 (4) 81.25

51. If PO and O were produced in exactly 3 states and no other crops were produced in these 3 states, then the state in which the crop PO was definitely not produced was

(1) G (2) H (3) MP (4) U

52. If the maximum possible number of crops were produced in an equal quantity (by weight) in all the given states then what was the number of crops that were not produced in an equal quantity in the given states?

(1) 4 (2) 3 (3) 5 (4) 1

53. If the maximum possible number of crops were produced in an equal quantity (by weight) in all the given states then the production (in '000 tonnes) of W in MP could not be more than

(1) 2.4 (2) 2.8 (3) 3.8 (4) 3.4

PRACTICE EXERCISE – 2

Directions for questions 1 to 4: Answer the questions on the basis of the information given below.

A car starts moving along a straight line in the North direction at t = 0 seconds. The speed–time graph for the car is given below for the first 15 seconds in which it covers a total distance of 320 metres. The bar chart given below shows the distance covered by the car in the next 15 seconds. The speed–time graph for the car is a straight line in the time intervals 0–5 seconds, 5–10 seconds, 10–15 seconds, 15–20 seconds, 20–25 seconds and 25–30 seconds.

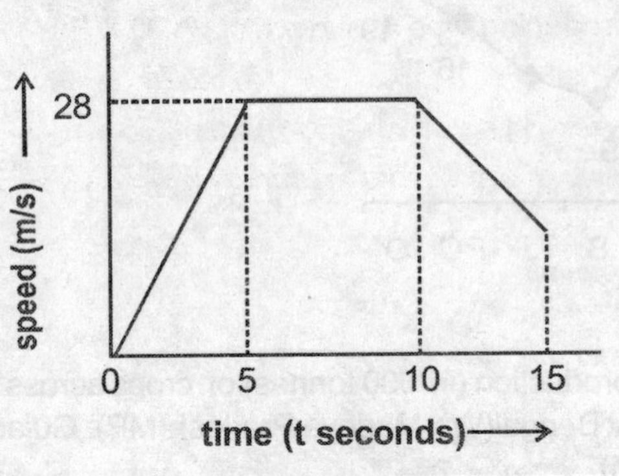

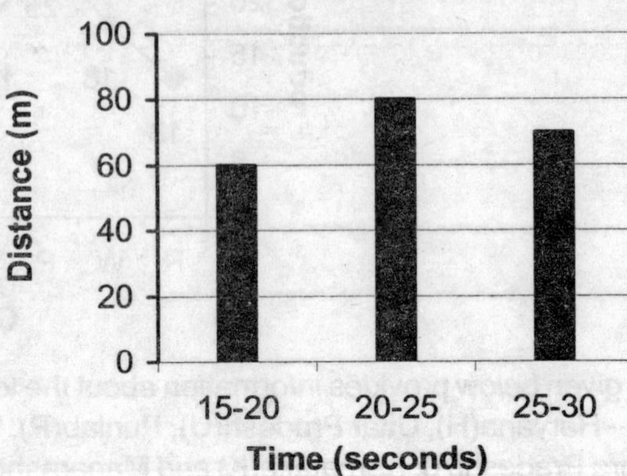

1. What is the speed (in m/s) of the car at t = 15 seconds?
   (1) 14 m/s (2) 16 m/s (3) 12 m/s (4) 10 m/s
2. What is the speed (in m/s) of the car at t = 30 seconds?
   (1) 2 m/s (2) 4 m/s (3) 5 m/s (4) 6 m/s
3. What is the average speed (in m/s) of the car between t = 8 seconds and t = 24 seconds?
   (1) 20.7 (2) 17.7 (3) 31.2 (4) 22.2
4. The absolute difference between the maximum the minimum speed of the car in t = 15 seconds and t = 30 seconds is
   (1) 10 (2) 20 (3) 25 (4) 30

Directions for questions 5 to 8: Answer the questions on the basis of the information given below.

The pie chart given below shows the break-up of production cost of six products – A through F – of Zen Private Ltd. in year 2011. The total production cost was Rs. 250 Cr.

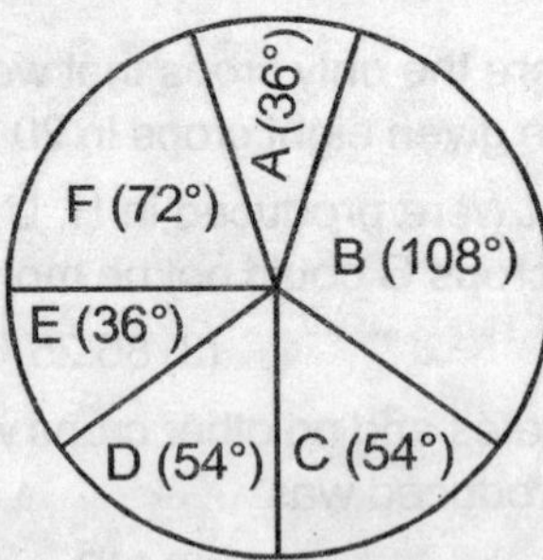

Each of the six products is produced in two varieties- Type P and Type Q. The ratio of the units produced for each product and the profit percentage on selling them is given in the table below.

Product	Ratio of production		Profit Percentage	
	Type P	Type Q	Type P	Type Q
A	3	2	15	30
B	4	3	25	20
C	5	6	15	20
D	1	1	15	10
E	5	3	25	20
F	5	4	20	15

Also for each product, the cost of production per item of Type P and Type Q varieties are in the ratio 4 : 5.

5. For how many of the six products, is the profit made on items of type Q not more than the profit made on items of type P?

(1) 3 (2) 4 (3) 2 (4) 1

6. For which product is the ratio of total profit to total production cost, the lowest?

(1) B (2) C (3) D (4) F

7. For how many products, overall profit percentage is more than 20%?

(1) 2 (2) 3 (3) 1 (4) 4

8. The nearest integer to the total cost (In Rs. Cr.) incurred in producing type A of products A, D & F is

(1) 55-24 (2) 55.31 (3) 52.31 (4) 52.24

Directions for questions 9 to 12: Answer the questions on the basis of the information given below.

The following pie-chars – I, II, III and IV give gender-wise distributions of professors in four universities – A, B, C and D respectively as on December 31, 2012.

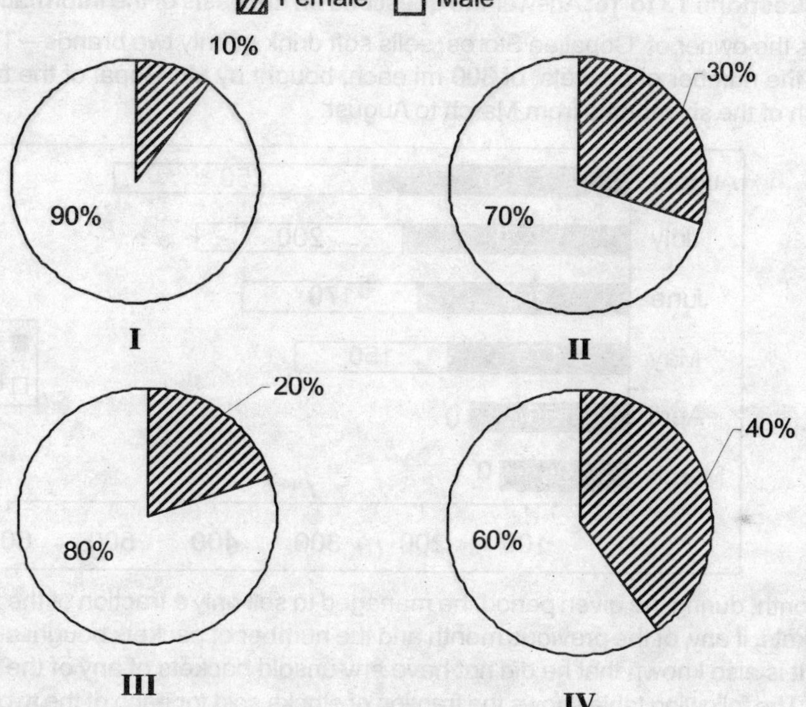

The number of female professors in the universities A, B, C and D was P, Q, R and S respectively. The following bar-graph provides information about the values of P, Q, R and S.

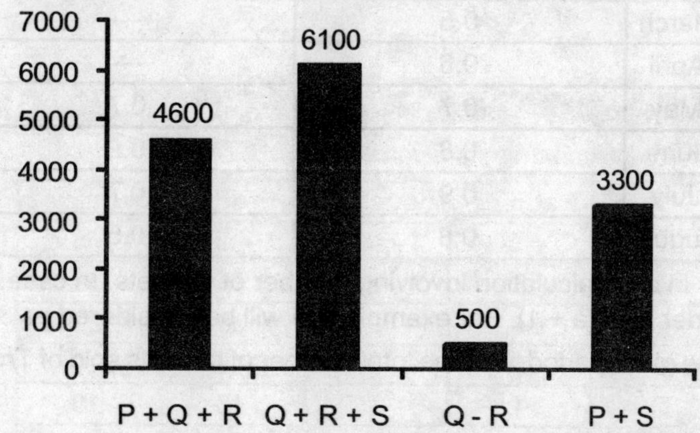

9. What was the absolute difference between the number of male professors in university A and the number of female professors in university D?

(1) 6700 (2) 6300 (3) 5700 (4) 7100

10. What was the ratio of the total number of professors in university D to the number of male professors in university C?

(1) 16 : 15 (2) 3 : 4 (3) 4 : 3 (4) 15 : 16

Additional Information for questions 11 and 12:

In 2013, a total of 2000 professors join universities A, B, C and D in the ratio 4 : 3 : 2 : 1.

11. In which of the mentioned universities, was the number of male professors as a percentage of the total number of professors in that university the maximum?

(1) B (2) C (3) A (4) Cannot be determined

12. If the total number of female professors who joined the four universities put together was equal to the number of female professors in university A after the joining, then the total number of male professors who joined the four universities put together in 2013 cannot be less than

(1) 200 (2) 300 (3) 400 (4) 800

Directions for questions 13 to 16: Answer the questions on the basis of the information given below.

Mr. Gopal, who is the owner of 'Gopaljee Stores, sells soft drink of only two brands – Trooti and Frooti. The following bar chart shows the number of packets, of 300 ml each, bought by Mr. Gopal of the two brands of soft drink, at the beginning of each of the six months from March to August.

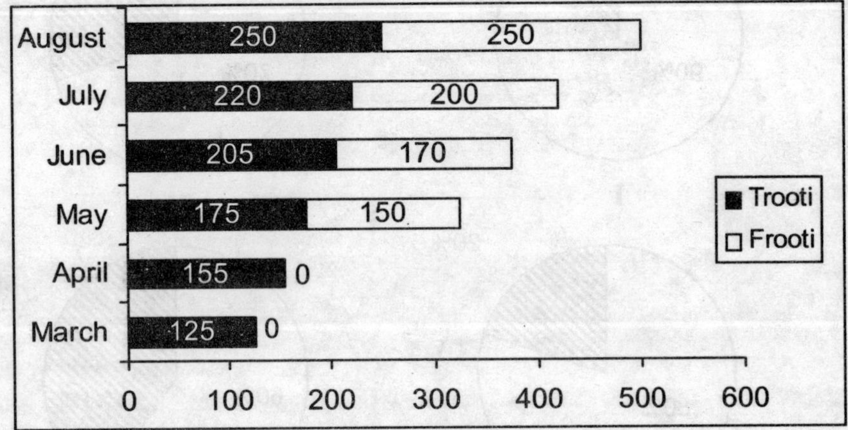

In each of the month, during the given period, he managed to sell only a fraction of the total stock, which is the sum of the left over packets, if any, of the previous month and the number of packets bought at the beginning of the month, of the two brands. It is also known that he did not have any unsold packets of any of the two brands of cold drink at the end of February. The following table shows the fraction of stocks sold for each of the two brands of cold drink during the given period.

Month	Fraction of Trooti sold	Fraction of Frooti sold
March	0.5	—
April	0.6	—
May	0.7	0.7
June	0.8	0.9
July	0.9	0.7
August	0.8	0.5

Consider the nearest integer in any calculation involving number of packets. In case, a fraction is of the form 'a·5', where 'a' is an integer, consider it as (a + 1). For example, 2.5 will be considered as 3.

13. In which month, during the given period, was the total number of packets sold of Trooti and Frooti put together the highest?

(1) July (2) June (3) August (4) Cannot be determined

14. In which month, during the given period, was the total stock of the two brands put together the highest ?

(1) June (2) August (3) July (4) Cannot be determined

15. In which month, during the given period, was the number of packets sold of Trooti the highest?

(1) June (2) August (3) July (4) Cannot be determined

16. In which month, during the given period, was the value of the ratio of the number of packets sold of Trooti in a month to the number of the packets bought at the beginning of the same month the maximum?

(1) May (2) June (3) August (4) July

Directions for questions 17 to 20: The following graph shows the value of liquor supplied by the 5 states in 1996 and the excise duty rates in each state.

[CAT 1990]

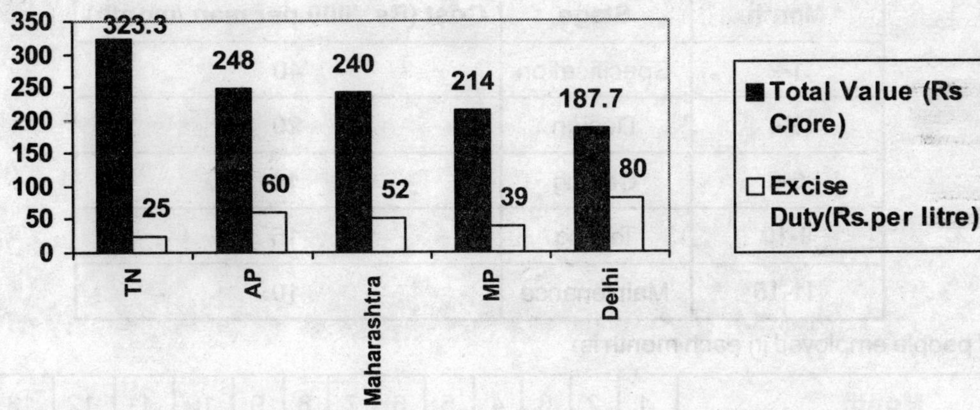

Amount of liquor supplied in Tamil Nadu Distilleries A, B, C, D, E (from bottom to top) in lakh litres.

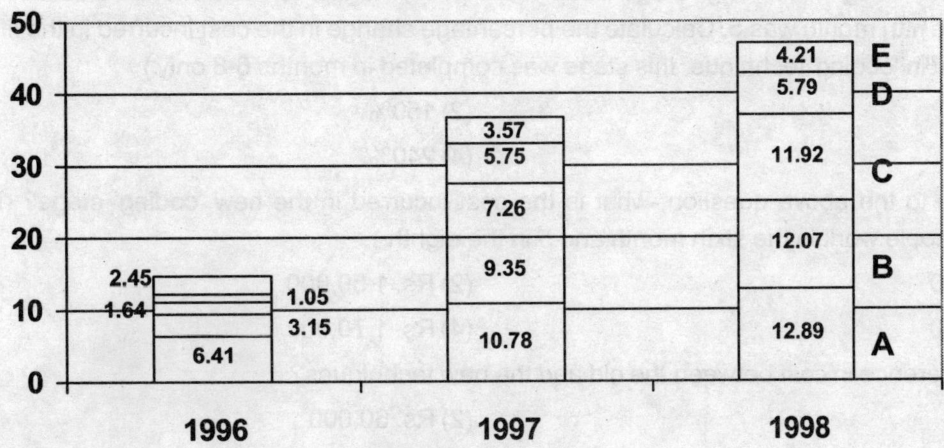

17. What is the lowest percentage difference in the excise duty rates for any two states?

(1) 12 (2) 15 (3) 20 (4) Cannot be determined.

18. Which of the five states manufactured liquor at the lowest cost?

(1) Tamil Nadu

(2) Delhi

(3) The states which has the lowest value for (wholesale price-Excise duty) per litre

(4) Cannot be determined.

19. If Excise duty is levied before the goods leave the factory (on the value of the liquor), then which of the following choices shows distilleries in ascending order of the excise duty paid by them for the year 1996? (Assume the total liquor in TN is supplied by only these 5 distilleries).

(1) ECABD (2) ADEBC (3) DCEBA (4) Cannot be determined.

20. If the Tamil Nadu distillery, with the least average simple annual growth in amount of liquor supplied in the given period had shown the same rate of growth as the one which grew fastest, what would that company's supply have been in 1998, in lakh liters?

(1) 13 (2) 15.11

(3) 130 (4) Cannot be determined.

Directions for questions 21 to 25: Answer the questions based on the following information.

[CAT 1996]

Mulayam Software Co., before selling a package to its clients, follows the given schedule.

Month	Stage	Cost (Rs. '000 per man /month)
1-2	Specification	40
3-4	Design	20
5-8	Coding	10
9-10	Testing	15
11-15	Maintenance	10

The number of people employed in each month is:

Month	1	2	3	4	5	6	7	8	9	10	11	12	13	14	15
Number of people employed	2	3	4	3	4	5	5	4	4	1	3	3	1	1	1

21. Due to overrun in 'design', the design stage took 3 months, i.e. months 3, 4 and 5. The number of people working on design in the fifth month was 5. Calculate the percentage change in the cost incurred in the fifth month. (Due to improvement in 'coding' technique, this stage was completed in months 6-8 only.)

(1) 225% (2) 150%

(3) 275% (4) 240%

22. With reference to the above question, what is the cost incurred in the new 'coding' stage? (Under the new technique, 4 people work in the sixth month and 5 in the eighth.)

(1) Rs. 1,40,000 (2) Rs. 1,50,000

(3) Rs. 1,60,000 (4) Rs. 1,70,000

23. What is the difference in cost between the old and the new techniques?

(1) Rs. 30,000 (2) Rs. 60,000

(3) Rs. 70,000 (4) Rs. 40,000

24. Under the new technique, which stage of software development is most expensive for Mulayam Software Co.?

(1) Testing (2) Specification

(3) Coding (4) Design

25. Which five consecutive months have the lowest average cost per man-month under the new technique?

(1) 1-5 (2) 9-13

(3) 11-15 (4) None of these

Direction for questions 26 to 31: Answer the questions based on the following information.

[CAT 1998]

The following bar chart gives the growth percentage in the number of households in middle, upper-middle and high income categories in the four regions for the period between 1987-88 and 1994-95.

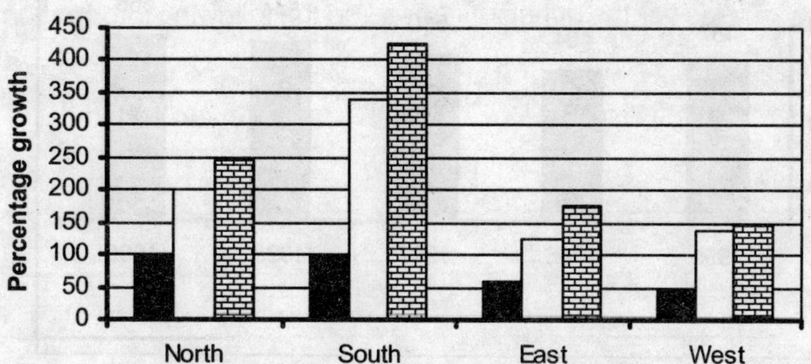

	Number of households in 1987–88 (in thousands)	Average household income in 1987–88	Growth in average household income (1994–95 over 1987–88)
Middle income	40	Rs. 30,000	50%
Upper- middle	10	Rs. 50,000	60%
High income	5	Rs. 75,000	90%

26. Which region showed the highest growth in number of households in all the income categories for the period?

(1) North (2) South

(3) West (4) None of these

27. What was the total household income in northern region for upper-middle class?

(1) Rs. 50 lakh (2) Rs. 500 million

(3) Rs. 300 million (4) Cannot be determined

28. What is the percentage increase in total number of households for the northern region (upper-middle) over the given period?

(1) 100% (2) 200%

(3) 240% (4) Cannot be determined

29. What was the average income of the high-income group in 1987-88?

(1) Rs. 75,000 (2) Rs. 25,000

(3) Rs. 2,25,000 (4) Cannot be determined

Additional direction for questions 30 and 31: The numbers of households in each category were equally distributed in all the regions.

30. The ratio of total income for the high-income category to the upper-middle class increased by how much percentage in the given period?

(1) 20% (2) 36%

(3) 25% (4) Cannot be determined

31. The average income for the northern region in 1987-88 was

(1) Rs. 37,727 (2) Rs. 37,277

(3) Rs. 35,000 (4) Cannot be determined

Directions for questions 32 to 34: Answer the questions on the basis of the following charts.

[CAT 2003]

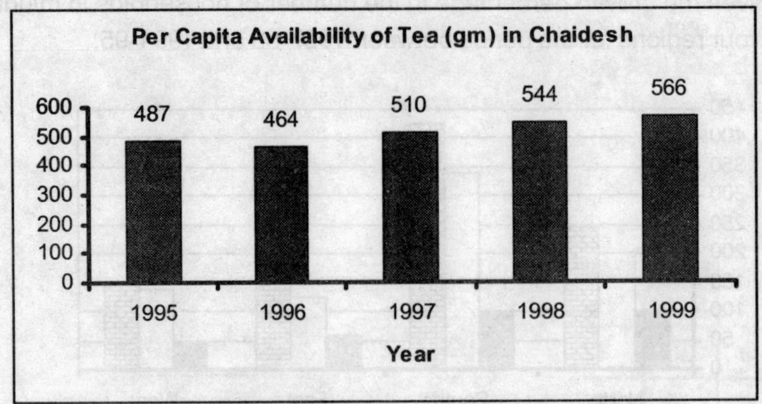

(**Note:** Availability is defined as production less export.)

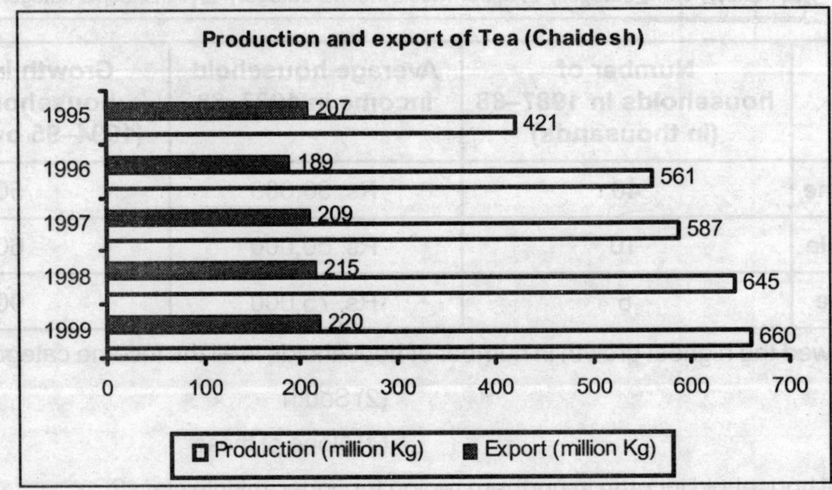

32. In which year during the period 1996-1999 was Chaidesh's export of tea, as a proportion of tea produced, the highest?

(1) 1996 (2) 1997

(3) 1998 (4) 1999

33. In which of the following years was the population of Chaidesh the lowest?

(1) 1995 (2) 1996

(3) 1997 (4) 1999

34. The area under tea cultivation continuously decreased in all four years from 1996 to 1999, by 10%, 7%, 4%, and 1%, respectively. In which year was tea productivity (production per unit of area) the highest?

(1) 1999 (2) 1998

(3) 1997 (4) 1996

Directions for questions 35 to 38: Answer the questions on the basis of the following table.

[CAT 2003]

Below is a table that lists countries region-wise. Each region-wise list is sorted, first by birth rate and then alphabetically by name of country. We now wish to merge the region-wise list into one consolidated list and provide overall rankings to each country based first on birth rate and then on death rate. Thus, if some countries have the same birth rate, then the country with a lower death rate will be ranked higher. Further, countries having identical birth and death rates will get the same rank. For example, if two countries are tied for the third position, then both will be given rank 3, while the next country (in the ordered list) will be ranked 5.

Rank	Country	Birth Rate	Death Rate	Region
1	South Africa	36	12	Africa
2	Egypt	39	13	Africa
3	Cameroon	42	22	Africa
4	Mozambique	45	18	Africa
5	Zaire	45	18	Africa
6	Ghana	46	14	Africa
7	Angola	47	23	Africa
8	Madagascar	47	22	Africa
9	Morocco	47	16	Africa
10	Tanzania	47	17	Africa
11	Ethiopia	48	23	Africa
12	Ivory coast	48	23	Africa
13	Rhodesia	48	14	Africa
14	Uganda	48	17	Africa
15	Nigeria	49	22	Africa
16	Saudi Arabia	49	19	Africa
17	Sudan	49	17	Africa
18	Algeria	50	16	Africa
19	Kenya	50	14	Africa
20	Upper Volta	50	28	Africa

Rank	Country	Birth Rate	Death Rate	Region
1	Germany (FRG)	10	12	Europe
2	Austria	12	13	Europe
3	Belgium	12	12	Europe
4	Germany (DRG)	12	14	Europe
5	Sweden	12	11	Europe
6	Switzerland	12	9	Europe
7	U.K.	12	12	Europe
8	Netherlands	13	8	Europe
9	France	14	11	Europe
10	Italy	14	10	Europe
11	Greece	16	9	Europe
12	Bulgaria	17	10	Europe
13	Hungary	18	12	Europe
14	Spain	18	8	Europe
15	USSR	18	9	Europe
16	Yugoslavia	18	8	Europe
17	Czech. Rep.	19	11	Europe
18	Portugal	19	10	Europe
19	Romania	19	10	Europe
20	Poland	20	9	Europe

Rank	Country	Birth Rate	Death Rate	Region
1	Japan	16	6	Asia
2	Korea (ROK)	26	6	Asia
3	Sri Lanka	26	9	Asia
4	Taiwan	26	5	Asia
5	Malaysia	30	6	Asia
6	China	31	11	Asia
7	Thailand	34	10	Asia
8	Turkey	34	12	Asia
9	India	36	15	Asia
10	Burma	38	15	Asia
11	Iran	42	12	Asia
12	Vietnam	42	17	Asia
13	Korea (DPRK)	43	12	Asia
14	Pakistan	44	14	Asia
15	Nepal	46	20	Asia
16	Bangladesh	47	19	Asia
17	Syria	47	14	Asia
18	Iraq	48	14	Asia
19	Afghanistan	52	30	Asia

Rank	Country	Birth Rate	Death Rate	Region
1	U.S.A.	15	9	N. America
2	Canada	16	7	N. America
3	Cuba	20	6	N. America
4	Mexico	40	7	N. America
1	Australia	16	8	Pacific
2	Philippines	34	10	Pacific
3	Indonesia	38	16	Pacific
1	Argentina	22	10	S. America
2	Chile	22	7	S. America
3	Colombia	34	10	S. America
4	Brazil	36	10	S. America
5	Venezuela	36	6	S. America
6	Guatemala	40	14	S. America
7	Peru	40	13	S. America
8	Ecuador	42	11	S. America

35. In the consolidated list, what would be the overall rank of the Philippines?

(1) 32 (2) 33 (3) 34 (4) 35

36. In the consolidated list, how many countries would rank below Spain and above Taiwan?

(1) 9 (2) 8 (3) 7 (4) 6

37. In the consolidated list, which country ranks 37th?

(1) South Africa (2) Brazil (3) Turkey (4) Venezuela

38. In the consolidated list, how many countries in Asia will rank lower than every country in South America, but higher than at least one country in Africa?

(1) 8 (2) 7 (3) 6 (4) 5

Directions for questions 39 to 42: Answer the questions on the basis of the following charts.

[CAT 2003]

The profitability of a company is defined as the ratio of its operating profit to its operating income, typically expressed in percentage. The following two charts show the operating income as well as the profitability of six companies in the financial years (F.Ys.) 2001-02 and 2002-03.

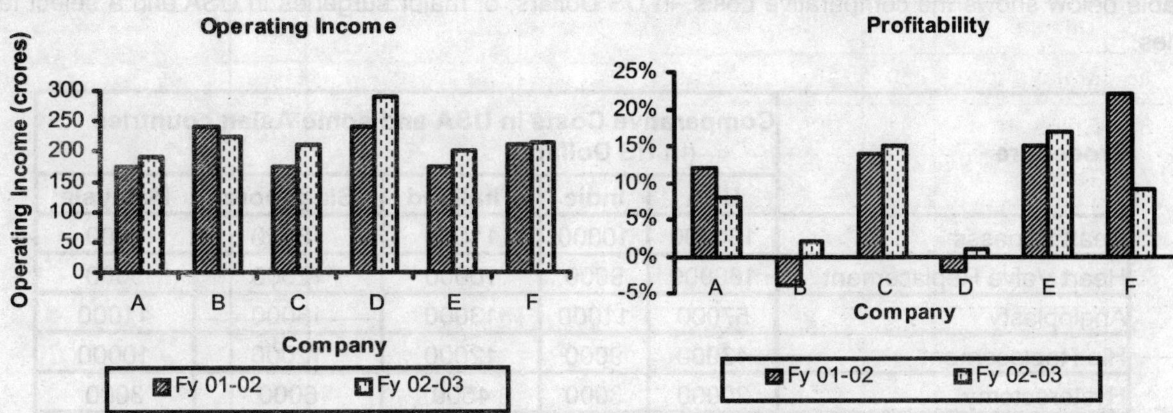

The operating profits of four of these companies are plotted against their respective operating income figures for the F.Y. 2002-03, in the third chart given below.

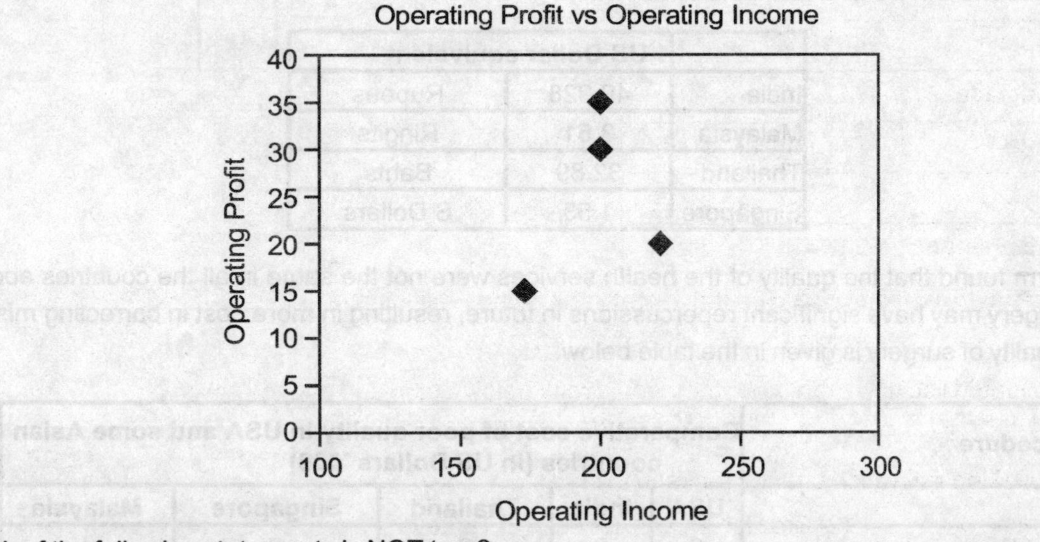

39. Which of the following statements is NOT true?

(1) The company with the third lowest profitability in F.Y. 2001-02 has the lowest operating income in F.Y. 2002-03.

(2) The company with the highest operating income in the two financial years combined has the lowest operating profit in F.Y. 2002-03.

(3) Companies with a higher operating income in F.Y. 2001-02 than in F.Y. 2002-03 have higher profitability in F.Y 2002-03 than in F.Y. 2001-02.

(4) Companies with profitability between 10% and 20% in F.Y. 2001-02 also have operating incomes between 150 crore and 200 crore in F.Y. 2002-03.

40. Which company recorded the highest operating profit in F.Y. 2002-03?

(1) A (2) C (3) E (4) F

41. What is the approximate average operating profit, in F.Y 2001-02, of the two companies excluded from the third chart?

(1) –7.5 crore (2) 3.5 crore (3) 25 crore (4) Cannot be determined

42. The average operating profit in F.Y. 2002-03 of companies with profitability exceeding 10% in F.Y. 2002-03, is approximately

(1) 17.5 crore (2) 25 crore (3) 27.5 crore (4) 32.5 crore

Directions for questions 43 to 46: Answer the following questions based on the information given below:

[CAT 2007]

The Table below shows the comparative costs, in US Dollars, of major surgeries in USA and a select few Asian countries.

Procedure	Comparative Costs in USA and some Asian countries (in US Dollar)				
	USA	India	Thailand	Singapore	Malaysia
Heart Bypasss	130000	10000	11000	18500	9000
Heart Valve Replacement	160000	9000	10000	12500	9000
Angioplasty	57000	11000	13000	13000	11000
Hip Replacement	43000	9000	12000	12000	10000
Hysterectomy	20000	3000	4500	6000	3000
Knee Replacement	40000	8500	10000	13000	8000
Spinal Fusion	62000	5500	7000	9000	6000

The equivalent of one US Dollar in the local currencies is given below:

	1 US Dollar equivalent	
India	40.928	Rupees
Malaysia	3.51	Ringits
Thailand	32.89	Bahts
Singapore	1.53	S Dollars

A consulting firm found that the quality of the health services were not the same in all the countries above. A poor quality of a surgery may have significant repercussions in future, resulting in more cost in correcting mistakes. The cost of poor quality of surgery is given in the table below:

Procedure	Comparative cost of poor quality in USA and some Asian countries (in US Dollars '000)				
	USA	India	Thailand	Singapore	Malaysia
Heart Bypasss	0	3	3	2	4
Heart Valve Replacement	0	5	4	5	5
Angioplasty	0	5	5	4	6
Hip Replacement	0	7	5	5	8
Hysterectomy	0	5	6	5	4
Knee Replacement	0	9	6	4	4
Spinal Fusion	0	5	6	5	6

43. A US citizen is hurt in an accident and requires an angioplasty, hip replacement and a knee replacement. Cost of foreign travel and stay is not a consideration since the government will take care of it. Which country will result in the cheapest package, taking cost of poor quality into account?

(1) India (2) Thailand (3) Malaysia (4) Singapore (5) USA

44. Taking the cost of poor quality into account, which country/countries will be the most expensive for knee replacement?

(1) India (2) Thailand (3) Malaysia (4) Singapore (5) India and Singapore

45. Approximately, what difference in amount in Bahts will it make to a Thai citizen if she were to get a hysterectomy done in India instead of in her native country, taking into account the cost of poor quality? (It costs 7500 Bahts for one-way travel between Thailand and India).

(1) 23500 (2) 40500 (3) 57500 (4) 67500 (5) 75000

46. The rupee value increases to Rs.35 for a US Dollar, and all other things including quality, remain the same. What is the approximate difference in cost, in US Dollars, between Singapore and India for a Spinal Fusion, taking this change into account?

(1) 700 (2) 2500 (3) 4500 (4) 8000 (5) No difference

ANSWER KEYS

PRACTICE EXERCISE – 1

1. (2)	**2.** (3)	**3.** (3)	**4.** (2)	**5.** (1)	**6.** (2)	**7.** (3)	**8.** (4)	**9.** (3)	**10.** (1)
11. (1)	**12.** (3)	**13.** (3)	**14.** (1)	**15.** (2)	**16.** (3)	**17.** (4)	**18.** (1)	**19.** (2)	**20.** (1)
21. (3)	**22.** (3)	**23.** (2)	**24.** (4)	**25.** (3)	**26.** (4)	**27.** (1)	**28.** (1)	**29.** (1)	**30.** (4)
31. (1)	**32.** (3)	**33.** (2)	**34.** (1)	**35.** (3)	**36.** (1)	**37.** (1)	**38.** (1)	**39.** (4)	**40.** (1)
41. (4)	**42.** (4)	**43.** (3)	**44.** (2)	**45.** (3)	**46.** (2)	**47.** (4)	**48.** (3)	**49.** (3)	**50.** (4)
51. (2)	**52.** (2)	**53.** (1)							

PRACTICE EXERCISE – 2

1. (2)	**2.** (2)	**3.** (2)	**4.** (2)	**5.** (2)	**6.** (3)	**7.** (2)	**8.** (2)	**9.** (3)	**10.** (4)
11. (3)	**12.** (2)	**13.** (2)	**14.** (2)	**15.** (3)	**16.** (4)	**17.** (4)	**18.** (4)	**19.** (3)	**20.** (2)
21. (2)	**22.** (1)	**23.** (2)	**24.** (4)	**25.** (3)	**26.** (2)	**27.** (4)	**28.** (2)	**29.** (1)	**30.** (2)
31. (1)	**32.** (2)	**33.** (1)	**34.** (1)	**35.** (2)	**36.** (1)	**37.** (4)	**38.** (1)	**39.** (4)	**40.** (3)
41. (1)	**42.** (4)	**43.** (3)	**44.** (1)	**45.** (4)	**46.** (2)				

EXPLANATIONS

PRACTICE EXERCISE – 1

1. Growth rate during 2015-2017 in viewership of Channel C is $\frac{45000-25000}{25000} \times 100 = 80\%$

If Channel A shows same growth rate than its viewership in 2017 would have been

$20000\left(1+\frac{80}{100}\right) = 36,000$

Actual viewership in 2017 of Channel A is 50000.

∴ It would have been less by

$\frac{50000-36000}{50000} \times 100 = 28\%$.

2. Advertisement cost per viewer for Channel A, B, C and D in 2015

$A = \frac{100000}{20000} = \text{Rs. } 5 \quad B = \frac{150000}{40000} = \text{Rs. } 3.75$

$C = \frac{120000}{25000} = \text{Rs. } 4.80 \quad D = \frac{80000}{15000} = \text{Rs. } 5.33$

$\therefore \text{Average cost} = \frac{5+3.75+4.80+5.33}{4} = \text{Rs.}4.72$

$X = \frac{5}{4.72}$

Advertisement cost per viewer for Channel A, B, C and D in 2017

$A = \frac{150000}{50000} = \text{Rs. } 3 \quad B = \frac{200000}{55000} = \text{Rs. } 3.6$

$C = \frac{180000}{45000} = \text{Rs. } 4 \quad D = \frac{125000}{25000} = \text{Rs. } 5$

$\therefore \text{Average cost} = \frac{3+3.6+4+5}{4} = \text{Rs. } 3.9$

$Y = \frac{3}{3.9}$

Hence, the required ratio = X : Y = 1.37 : 1.

3. In 2015, average viewership per channel

$= \frac{100000}{4} = 25000$

C with 25000 viewers is the closest.

In 2016, average viewership per channel

$= \frac{145000}{4} = 36250$

C with 35000 viewers is the closest.

In 2017, average viewership per channel $= \frac{175000}{4}$ = 43,750

C with 45000 viewers is the closest.

4. Advertisement cost per viewer of channel D in the year 2016 $= \frac{100000}{20000} = \text{Rs. } 5$.

5. Let 'x' and 'y' be the average experience of Executives whose experience is less and more than the average experience of all the executives.

16x + 28y = 10 (16 + 28) = 440.

⇒ 4x + 7y = 110.

Since x < 10 < y, the only value of x and y that satisfy are 3 and 14 respectively.

Required difference = 28 × 14 – 16 × 3 = 344.

6. Let 'a' and 'b' be the average experience of DGMs whose experience is less and more than the average experience of all the DGMs.

4a + 10b = 19(4 + 10) = 266.

⇒ 2a + 5b = 133.

Since a < 19 < b and we need to minimize the average experience of DGMs having experience more than 19 months, we have to maximize the average experience of DGMs having experience less than 19 months.

The minimum value of 'b' that satisfies the above equation is 21.

For questions 7 to 10:

7. Minimum possible fare is Rs.13.

This is possible in various ways. One such example is

From A to F = Rs.5

From F to J = Rs.5

From J to K = Rs.3

8. Maximum number of bus stops that can be travelled in Rs.5 = 4 (for example A-F, C-H or D-I)

Minimum number of bus stops that can be travelled in Rs.5 = 2 (from H-K).

9. If journey from A-K and from K-A is considered and fare charges remain as given then maximum fare that can be paid = Rs.30. It is possible in the following manner:

From A to C = Rs.3

From C to E = Rs.3

From E to G = Rs.3

From G to I = Rs.3

From I to K = Rs.3

From K to I = Rs.3

From I to G = Rs.3

From G to E = Rs.3

From E to C = Rs.3

From C to A = Rs.3

Minimum fare for the round trip = Rs.16 (for person taking just one ticket from A)

Thus, the required difference is 30 – 16 = Rs.14.

10. Minimum fare previously required to travel from B to I = Rs.8 (to take ticket of Rs.8 from B to I or to take Rs. 5 ticket from B to G and then Rs. 3 ticket from G to I)

Maximum fare now to travel from C to J = Rs.15. It is possible in the following manner:

From C to E = Rs.3

From E to G = Rs.3

From G to N = Rs.3

From N to H = Rs.3

From H to J = Rs.3

Hence, the required ratio is 8 : 15.

For questions 11 to 13:

The information given in the graph and table can be tabulated as shown below.

Company	Revenue (in million Rs.)					
	Mobile			Landiine		
	Total	C	NC	Total	C	NC
AKA	4.3	3.01	1.29	2.4	1.92	0.48
ROFL	2.5	1.5	1	4.4	2.2	2.2
LOL	3.8	3.42	0.38	1.8	1.26	0.54
RGRT	4.5	3.6	0.9	2.8	1.68	1.12
CYA	1.7	0.85	0.85	3.5	3.15	0.35

11. From the table it can be observed that none of the companies dominates ROFL in both the segments.

12. There are two companies which are definitely not dominated by any other company and these are ROFL and CYA.

13. The required difference (in million Rs.) = (3.01 + 1.5 + 3.42 + 3.6 + 0.85) – (0.48 + 2.2 + 0.54 + 1.12 + 0.35) = 7.69.

For questions 14 to 17:

The information given in the graph and table can be tabulated as shown below.

Company	Revenue (in million Rs.)					
	Mobile			Landline		
	Total	C	NC	Total	C	NC
AKA	4.3	3.01	1.29	2.4	1.92	0.48
ROFL	2.5	1.5	1	4.4	2.2	2.2
LOL	3.8	3.42	0.38	1.8	1.26	0.54
RGRT	4.5	3.6	0.9	2.8	1.68	1.12
CYA	1.7	0.85	0.85	3.5	3.15	0.35

14. From the table it can be observed that none of the companies dominates ROFL in both the segments.

15. There are two companies which are definitely not dominated by any other company and these are ROFL and CYA.

16. The required difference (in million Rs.) = (3.01 + 1.5 + 3.42 + 3.6 + 0.85) – (0.48 + 2.2 + 0.54 + 1.12 + 0.35) = 7.69.

17. For company AKA, LOL and RGRT the revenue generated through mobile services at least 150% of that through landline services.

18. Let the total investment in education sector by India be Rs. 'P' crore the same in China will be Rs. 1.6 P crore.

For china, 32% of 1.6 P was from ADB loans which will constitute

$$A = \frac{0.32 \times 1.6P}{\left(\frac{54}{360} \times 7200\right)} \times 100\%$$

For India,

$$B = \frac{0.2 \times P}{\left(\frac{40}{360} \times 7200\right)} \times 100\%$$

A : B = 256 : 135.

19. Amount of loan invested in transport sector by China

$$= \frac{60}{100} \times \frac{24}{360} \times 7200 \text{ cr}$$

Total investment in transport by china

$$= \frac{60}{100} \times \frac{24}{360} \times 7200 \times \frac{100}{55} = 523.63 \text{ cr}$$

Amount of loan invested in transport sector by India

$$= \frac{60}{100} \times \frac{24}{100} \times 7200 \text{ cr}$$

Total investment in transport by India

$$= \frac{60}{100} \times \frac{24}{360} \times 7200 \frac{100}{50} = 480 \text{ cr}$$

$$\text{Required percentage} = \frac{480}{523.63} \times 100 = 91.67\%.$$

20. Loan amount invested in education
= 20% of 150 = Rs 30 cr
Loan amount invested in Health
= 22% of 120 = Rs 26.4 cr
Loan amount invested in Agriculture
= 16% of 400 = Rs 64 cr

$$\text{The required percentage} = \frac{30 + 26.4 + 64}{\left(\frac{40}{360} \times 7200\right)} \times 100$$

= 15.05.

21. Total investment will be maximum when maximum loan amount is invested in education i.e. Rs. 440 cr. And Rs. 30 cr each is invested in other two sectors.

Total investment in the 3 sectors will be

$$= 440 \times \frac{100}{20} + 30 \times \frac{100}{30} + 30 \times \frac{100}{50} = \text{Rs. } 2360 \text{ cr}$$

22.

Year	Strike rate of JMS
2013	$\frac{79}{122} \times 100 = 64.75\%$
2014	$\frac{77}{117} \times 100 = 65.81\%$
2015	$\frac{68}{121} \times 100 = 56.20\%$
2016	$\frac{75}{112} \times 100 = 66.96\%$
2017	$\frac{76}{114} \times 100 = 66.67\%$

So in the year 2016 the strike rate was maximum.

23.

Year	Strike rate of JMS	Strike rate of PMS
2013	64.75%	56.89%
2014	65.81%	68.06%
2015	56.20%	53.49%
2016	66.96%	69.6%
2017	66.67%	58.89%

So from the above table it is evident that twice, i.e. in year 2014 and 2016 the strike rate of PMS was better than the strike rate of JMS.

24.

Year	Total number of students who got 3 or less than 3 calls and converted their calls			Total
	JMS		PMS	
2013	11	+	15	26
2014	14	+	19	33
2015	15	+	17	32
2016	13	+	13	26
2017	15	+	14	29

So, in the year 2014 the total number of students who got 3 or less than 3 calls and converted their calls was maximum.

25. The total number of students of JMS in 5 years was 25980 and average number of students per year was 5196. Again the total number of students of PMS in 5 years was 25690 and the average number of students per year is 5138. So the difference was 58.

For questions 26 to 29:

The net pay-off for company A (after including the cost of the strategy) is as follows:

Pay-off to company A				
		Strategy that company B adopts		
		P	Q	R
Strategy that company A adopts	X	–4500	4500	–6500
	Y	2800	–8200	2500
	Z	–7700	3000	–8000

The net pay-off for company B (after including the cost of the strategy) is as follows:

Pay-off to company B				
		Strategy that company B adopts		
		P	Q	R
Strategy that company A adopts	X	2600	–5200	3200
	Y	–7200	5000	–8300
	Z	4800	–4700	3700

(–) Represents loss in the above tables.

26. We see that irrespective of which strategy company A adopts, B can respond with a strategy such that B makes a gain. Thus, A cannot ensure that it will make a gain in any circumstances.

27. Required ratio = $\frac{4500}{5200}$

= 45 : 52.

28. The maximum gain that company B and company A can make can be see directly from the table as 5000 and 4500 respectively. Thus, the difference = 500.

29. If strategy X is selected by Company A, Company B will select strategy R to get more advantage.

In this case, advantage = 3200 + 6500 = 9700

If strategy Y is selected by Company A, Company B will select strategy Q to get more advantage.

In this case, advantage = 5000 + 8200 = 13200

If strategy Z is selected by Company A, Company B will select strategy P to get more advantage.

In this case, advantage = 4800 + 7700 = 12500.

30. Some members can be lawyers as well as women. So, we cannot find out the answer.

31. Average age = $\frac{63 \times 550 + 58 \times 250}{550 + 250} = 61.43.$

32. Minimum case is when all the Rajya Sabha female members are Hindus, i.e. 42.

So, minimum number of Hindu males is 64.

Required percentage $= \frac{64}{250} \times 100 = 25.60\%$

33. Percentage of Congress(I) members $= \frac{267+112}{550+250}$

$= \frac{379}{800} = 47.37\%$

For questions 34 to 37:

Sector	Value of Funds (in Rs. crore)	Purchase Price (Rs. Per Share)	Number of shares	Current Market Price (in Rs.)	Market Capitalization (in Rs. Crore)	Market Appreciation (in Rs. crore)
Auto	15	200	750000	400	30	15
Chemical	25	150	1666666.67	450	75	50
Pharmaceutical	20	250	800000	500	40	20
IT	25	700	357142.86	1050	37.5	12.5
Bank	10	150	666666.67	600	40	30
Others	5	50	1000000	100	10	5

34. Market capitalization is highest for chemical sector.

35. Average of market capitalization is Rs. 387500000. Market appreciation of chemical sector is more than Rs. 387500000.

36. Total market capitalization of the company is Rs. 232.5 crore.

37. Number of shares is highest for chemical sector.

For questions 38 to 41:

Let the profit % in 2008 be x%. Then profit in following years will be

Year	Profit %
2008	X%
2009	X + 20 %
2010	X + 10 %
2011	X %
2012	X + 15 %
2013	X – 5 %
2014	X + 5 %

38. Let the expenditure in 2009 be Rs y.

Profit in 2009 will be (X + 20) × y/100

Profit in 2010 will be (X + 10) × 1.2y/100

Profit in 2010 is 10% less than that in 2009, so

(X + 10) × 1.2y/100 = 0.9 × (X + 20) × y/100

Solving we will get X = 40%.

39. Let the expenditure in 2013 be Rs. Y crores.

(X + 5) × 1.15y/100 = (X – 5) × y/100 + 10

There is one equation and two variable, so value of the two variables cannot be determined uniquely

40. The number of years in which company did not make any profit will be maximum when the 20% profit was made in year 2009. In 2007, 2008, 2011 and 2013 company will not be making any profit.

41. The number of years in which company made loss will be minimum when the 15% loss occurred in 2013. In 2008, 2011, 2013 and 2014 company will be making losses.

For questions 42 to 45:

	Actual water consumed		Water wasted	
	Household A	Household B	Household A	Household B
Cooking	7.5	6	2.5	2
Washing	20	21	20	14
Bathing	36	50	54	50
Gardening	48	48	12	32
Cooler	90	135	10	15
Drinking	10	8	0	0

42. Actual water consumed in cooking in A and B

= 7.5 + 6 = 13.5 L

Actual water consumed in drinking in A and B

= 10 + 8 = 18 L

∴Total water consumed actually in cooking and drinking = 18 + 13.5 = 31.5 L

Actual consumption of water in both household

= 211.5 + 268 = 479.5 L

∴ Percentage of actual water consumed in cooking and drinking $= \frac{31.5}{479.5} \times 100 = 6.6\%$.

43. Average wastage of water per activity by household

$A = \frac{98.5}{6} = 16.41$ L

Average wastage of water per activity by household

$B = \frac{113}{6} = 18.83$ L

∴ Required difference = (18.83 – 16.41) L = 2.42 L.

44. Let the cost of water used for cooking, gardening and drinking be 3x, x and 5x respectively.

Cost of water consumed for these 3 operations by household:

$B = 3x(8) + x(80) + 5x(8) = 144x$

$A = 3x(10) + x(60) + 5x(10) = 140x$

$\therefore$ Required percentage change $= \frac{4x}{140x} \times 100 = 2.86\%$

45. Total wastage of water in household B = 113 L.

Wastage of water is household A should be 56.5 L. This means we have to stop wastage of (98.5 – 56.5) = 42 L of water. This is possible if there is no wastage of water in washing (20 L), gardening (12 L) and cooler (10 L).

46. From the first set of graphs visually it is 1997.

47. Since there is a positive net addition every year, the closing balance will be the highest in 2000.

48. In 1999, $\frac{\text{Procurement}}{\text{Net availability}} = 0.174$

In 2000, $\frac{\text{Procurement}}{\text{Net availability}} = 0.196$

Hence, percentage increase

$= \frac{0.196 - 0.174}{0.174} = \frac{0.22}{0.174} = 12.6\%$

Alternative method:

Percentage increase $= \left[\frac{\frac{35.5}{181.4}}{\frac{30.8}{176.9}} - 1\right] \times 100 \simeq 12.6\%$

49. $-3.1 = A - 12.3$

$\Rightarrow A = 9.2$

$-1.4 = 16.2 - B$

$B = 17.6$

$C = \left|\frac{1.4}{181.4}\right| < 1\%$

50. Total production (in '000 tonnes) of the crops in states H, U, P and T put together = 18 + 11 + 14 + 13 = 56.

Total production (in '000 tonnes) of the crops in states W, P, B, M put together = 18 + 25 + 9 + 17 = 69.

Assume that the excess production (in '000 tonnes) was of crop P, which is equal to 69 – 56 i.e. 13.

Maximum production (in '000 tonnes) of crop P in state G = 13

Hence, the required percentage $= \frac{13}{16} \times 100 = 81.25.$

51. The possible combinations of states where the crop PO and O could be grown are (W, A, G), (W, T, K), (W, M, K), (MP, A, P), (T, M, MP) and (U, K, MP). So, H was definitely not the state where crop PO was grown.

For questions 52 and 53:

Minimum production (in'000 tonnes) of the crop amongst the ten states was in state W, i.e. 7.

Let the number of crops that were produced in an equal quantity and the maximum amount in the given states be 'x'.

The aggregate production (in'000 tonnes) of these 'x' crops in India could not have more than 70 as the minimum production (in'000 tonnes) of crops produced by a state among the given states was 7.

So, we need to pick those crops with lesser productions.

Aggregate production of crops R, M, B, J and PO put together = 13 + 17 + 9 + 11 + 16 = 66.

If we take one more crop, then the total production will cross 70. Therefore, the maximum possible value of 'x' is 5.

52. Therefore, there are three crops namely W, P and O that could not have been produced in equal quantities in the given ten states.

53. The aggregate production (in '000 tonnes) of crops R, M, B, J and PO put together in state MP $= \left(\frac{66}{10}\right) = 6.6$

So, maximum possible production (in '000 tonnes) of the crop W in state MP = 9 – 6.6 = 2.4.

PRACTICE EXERCISE – 2

For questions 1 to 4:

In the speed-time graph:

Distance = Area under the curve

Distance covered in the first 10 seconds

$= \frac{1}{2} \times 28 \times 5 + 28 \times 5 = 210$ metres

Hence, the distance covered between t = 10 and t = 15 seconds

= 320 – 210 = 110 m

Let the speed at t = 15 seconds = V_{15}

Distance $= \frac{28 + V}{2} \times 5 = 110 \Rightarrow V_{15} = 16\text{ m/s}$

Let the speed at t = 20, 25, 30 secs be V_{20}, V_{25}, V_{30}.

From the bar chart:

Distance traveled between t = 15 seconds and t = 20 seconds = 60 m.

$= \frac{(V_{15} + V_{20})5}{2} = \frac{(16 + V_{20})5}{2}$

V_{20} = 8 m/s

Similarly,

$$\frac{(V_{20}+V_{25})5}{2} = 80 \Rightarrow V_{25} = 24 m/s$$

$$\left(\frac{V_{25}+V_{30}}{2}\right)5 = 70$$

V_{30} = 4 m/s

The complete speed–time graph for first 30 seconds can be given as:

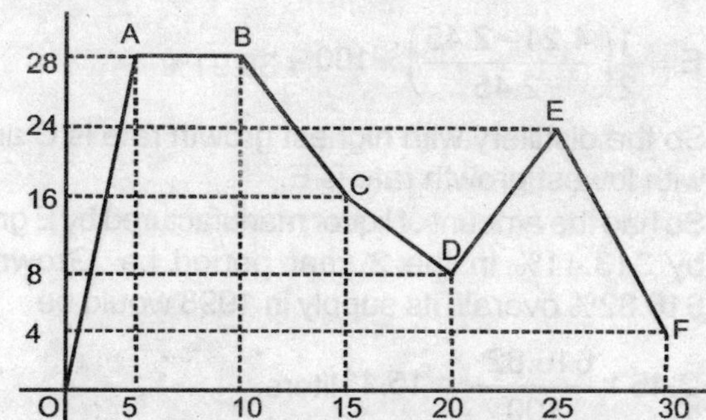

1. The speed at t = 15 seconds was 16 m/s.
2. The speed at t = 13 seconds was 4 m/s.
3. The distance travelled between t = 8 seconds and t = 10 seconds = 28 × (10 – 8) = 56 m

   The distance travelled between t = 10 seconds and t = 15 seconds = 110 m (calculated earlier)

   The distance travelled between t = 15 seconds and t = 20 seconds = 60 m (given in bar graph)

   The distance travelled between t = 20 secs and t = 24 secs:

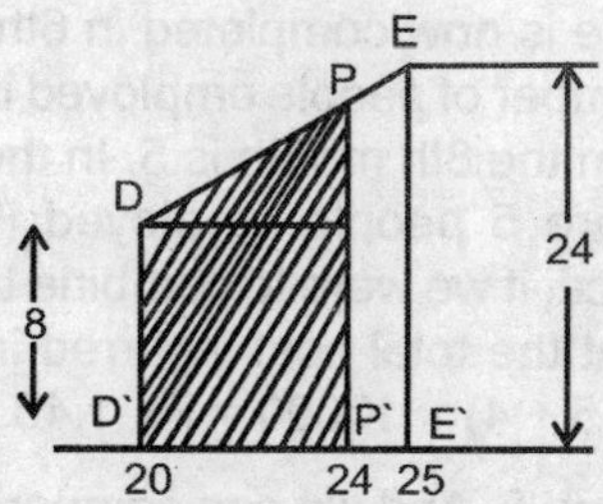

We need to find the area of DD'P'P

$$PP' = \frac{4}{5}\times(24-8)+8 = 20.8m$$

$$\text{Area DDP'P} = \frac{4\times(8+20.8)}{2} = 57.6m$$

$$\text{Average speed} = \frac{56+110+60+57.6}{24-8}$$

= 17.725 m/s

4. The required difference 24 – 4 = 20.

For questions 5 to 8:

Product	Total cost of production (In Rs. Crore)		Total profit (In Rs. Lakh)	
	Type P	Type Q	Type P	Type Q
A	13.64	11.36	204.6	340.8
B	38.71	36.29	967.8	725.8
C	15	22.5	225	450
D	16.67	20.83	250.1	208.3
E	14.3	10.7	357.5	214
F	25	25	500	375

5. The profit made on items of Type Q is not more than the profit made on items of Type P for products B, D, E and F.
6. For D, the desired ratio is lowest among all the products.
7. For A, B and E, the overall profit percentage is more than 20%.
8. Total Cost = 13.64 + 16.67 + 25 = Rs. 55.31 crore.

For questions 9 to 12:

Given that P + Q + R = 4600, Q + R + S = 6100 and P + S = 3300

2(P + Q + R + S) = (P + Q + R) + (Q + R + S) + (P + S) = 14000

P + Q + R + S = 7000

Therefore, S = 2400 and P = 900.

Also, Q – R = 500, therefore, Q = 2100 and R = 1600.

9. The absolute difference between the number of male professors in university A and the number of female professors in university D is 8100 – 2400 = 5700.
10. The ratio of the total number of professors in university D to the number of male professors in university C is 6000 : 6400 = 15 : 16.

For questions 11 and 12:

Given that 2000 professors are transferred to the universities A, B, C and D in the ratio 4:3:2:1.

Therefore, the number of professors transferred to the universities A, B, C and D is 800, 600, 400 and 200 respectively.

11. Even if we assume that all the professors that have been transferred to university A are all females and all the professors transferred to the university B, C and D are males, then also the number of male professors as a percentage of the total number of professors in university A is maximum.

12. Given that the total number of female professors that have been transferred is equal to the number of female professors in university A.
Maximum female professors that could have been transferred to university A is 800. Therefore, total number of female professors in university A = 900 + 800 = 1700.
So, the number of male professors that have been transferred to all the given four universities cannot be less than 2000 – 1700 = 300.

For questions 13 to 16: The given information can be tabulated as follows:

Month	Trooti				Frooti				Total packs sold
	Bought	Earlier stock	Total stock	Total sold	Bought	Earlier stock	Total stock	Total sold	
March	125	0	125	**63**	0	0	0	**0**	63
April	155	62	217	**130**	0	0	0	**0**	130
May	175	87	262	**183**	150	0	150	**105**	288
June	205	79	284	**227**	170	45	215	**194**	421
July	220	57	277	**249**	200	21	221	**155**	404
August	250	28	278	**222**	250	66	316	**158**	380

13. The required number was the highest in June.

14. The total stock was highest in August and it was equal to (278 + 316) i.e. 594.

15. For Trooti, the sales was highest in July.

16. Required ratio in the month of May = 183 : 175
Required ratio in the month of June = 227 : 205
Required ratio in the month of July = 249 : 220
Required ratio in the month of August = 222 : 250
Hence, ratio in the month of July is the highest.

17. The answer cannot be determined as the data for only five states is given and we don't know the excise duty rates for other states.

18. We have been given the total value in the graph, but nothing is mentioned about the amount of liquor manufactured by states other than Tamil Nadu.

19. Since Excise duty is levied on the total value of liquor produced by the 5 distilleries, this will be in the same order as the order of the amount of the liquor produced by them (as the excise duty rate remains constant). Hence the correct order is DCEBA.

20. Average simple annual growth rate of five distilleries is as follows:

$$A = \frac{1}{2}\left(\frac{12.89 - 6.41}{6.41}\right) \times 100 = 50.54\%$$

$$B = \frac{1}{2}\left(\frac{12.07 - 3.15}{3.15}\right) \times 100 = 141.58\%$$

$$C = \frac{1}{2}\left(\frac{11.92 - 1.64}{1.64}\right) \times 100 = 313.41\%$$

$$D = \frac{1}{2}\left(\frac{5.79 - 1.05}{1.05}\right) \times 100 = 225.71\%$$

$$E = \frac{1}{2}\left(\frac{4.21 - 2.45}{2.45}\right) \times 100 = 35.91\%$$

So the distillery with highest growth rate is C and with lowest growth rate is E.
So had the amount of liquor manufactured by E grown by 313.41% in the 2 year period i.e. Grown by 616.82% overall, its supply in 1998 would be

$$2.45 \times \frac{616.82}{100} = 15.11 \text{ liters.}$$

21. Originally for the fifth month, 4 people were scheduled to do coding. This would have cost them (10000 × 4) = Rs. 40,000. Now there are 5 people who are working on design in the fifth month.
The total cost for this would be (20000 × 5) = Rs.1,00,000.
Hence, percentage change in the cost incurred in the fifth month = $\frac{(100000 - 40000)}{40000} \times 100$ = 150%.

22. As given in the previous question, it can be seen that the coding stage is now completed in 6th, 7th and 8th months. Number of people employed in the 6th month is 4 and in the 8th month is 5. In the 7th month also there are 5 people employed (from previous data). Hence, if we were to combine these months, we find that the total cost incurred in the coding stage = (5 + 5 + 4) × 10000 = Rs.1,40,000.

23. The difference in the cost will arise only because of the following months: 5, 6 and 8. And we can compare the costs as given below

Month	Original scheme			New scheme		
	People	Cost per man/ month	Total cost for the month	People	Cost per man/ month	Total cost for the month
5	4	10000	40000	5	20000	1,00,000
6	5	10000	50000	4	10000	40,000
8	4	10000	40000	5	10000	50,000
Total cost			**Rs. 1,30,000**	**Total cost**		**Rs. 1,90,000**

It can be clearly seen that the difference in the cost between the old and the new technique is Rs. 60,000.

24. The cost incurred in various stages under the present scheme is as given below.

	Month	People	Cost per man/ month	Total cost for the month	Total cost for the stage
Specification	1	2	40000	80000	Rs. 2,00,000
	2	3	40000	120000	
Design	3	4	20000	80000	Rs. 2,40,000
	4	3	20000	60000	
	5	5	20000	100000	
Coding	6	4	10000	40000	Rs. 1,40,000
	7	5	10000	50000	
	8	5	10000	50000	
Testing	9	4	15000	60000	Rs. 75,000
	10	1	15000	15000	
Maintenance	11	3	10000	30000	Rs. 90,000
	12	3	10000	30000	
	13	1	10000	10000	
	14	1	10000	10000	
	15	1	10000	10000	

Hence, the most expensive stage is Design.

25. If we look at the above table again, it is clear that the average cost for 5 consecutive month period is lowest for months 11 to 15.

26. It can be seen from the graph that the southern region showed the highest growth in number of households in all the income categories for the period.

27. We only know the total number of households for all four regions combined. Nowhere have they given the region-wise break-up of this value. In the light of this, the given question cannot be answered.

28. It is very clear from the graph that the percentage increase in total number of households for the northern region for upper middle income category is 200%.

29. As seen from the table, the average income of high-income group in 1987-88 is Rs. 75,000.

30. The total income of high income category in 1987-88 is Rs. (5000 × 75000).

The total income of upper-middle class category in 1987-88 is Rs. (10000 × 50000).

Hence, the current ratio of their total incomes = 3 : 4 = 0.75

Since the number of households in each category were equally distributed in all regions, we can have the following table for high income category.

Region	Households in 1987-88	Percentage increase	Households in 1994-95
North	1250	240%	4250
South	1250	425%	6562.5
East	1250	175%	3437.5
West	1250	150%	3125
Total	5000		17375

The average household income for high-income category increased by 90%. Hence, average household income for this category in 1994-95

= (75000 × 1.9) = Rs. 1,42,500

Hence, the total income for high-income category in 1994-95 = (17375 × 142500) = Rs. 2,476 million

The same table can be drawn for upper-middle class category as follows:

Region	Households in 1987-88	Percentage increase	Households in 1994-95
North	2500	200%	7500
South	2500	340%	11000
East	2500	125%	5625
West	2500	140%	6000
Total	10000		30125

The average household income for upper-middle class category increased by 60%. Hence, the average household income for this category in 1994-95 = (50000 ×1.6) = Rs. 80,000

Hence, the total income for high-income category in 1994-95 = (30125 × 80000) = Rs. 2,410 million

Hence, the ratio of total income for these two categories in 1994-95 = $\frac{2476}{2410}$ = 1.02.

Hence, percentage increase in ratio

$$= \frac{(1.02 - 0.75)}{0.75} = 36\%$$

31. For northern region, we can draw the following table for 1987-88.

Category	Households in 1987-88	Average household income	Total income (Rs. in millions)
Middle income	10000	Rs. 30,000	300
Upper-middle	2500	Rs. 50,000	125
High income	1250	Rs. 75,000	93.75
Total	13750		518.75

Hence, the average income for northern region

$$= \frac{518.75}{13750} \times 10^6 = \text{Rs. } 37,727$$

32. Here you need to compare the ratio as which is the highest out of $\frac{189}{561}, \frac{209}{587}$ and rest of the options have equal value.

Now we can see that $\frac{209}{587}$ is greater than $\frac{189}{561}$, so 1997 has the highest ratio.

33. Population in 1995 =

$$\frac{421-207}{487} \times 1000 \text{ million} \approx 440 \text{ million}$$

Population in 1996 =

$$\frac{561-189}{464} \times 1000 \text{ million} \approx 802 \text{ million}$$

Population in 1997 =

$$\frac{587-209}{510} \times 1000 \text{ million} \approx 740 \text{ million}$$

Population in 1999 =

$$\frac{660-220}{566} \times 1000 \text{ million} \approx 777 \text{ million}$$

Hence, Chaidesh had the lowest population in 1995.

34. From 96 to 99 in each year the production has increased but the area has decreased. Therefore, the production in unit per area is highest in 1999.

For questions 35 to 38:

The table consists of sorting the different nations according to the birth rate and death rate. The only thing to remember is that if two countries have same rank (3), then next country will get (5) rank. So

rank of Philippines is 33,

rank of Spain is 17,

rank of Taiwan is 28.

In-between total 9 countries.

In consolidated list 37th country is Venezuela.

In last question, we have to check last country of South America (42, 11) and last country of Africa (50, 28). In-between there are 8 countries of Asia.

35. There are 32 nations in all the four lists which have lower birth rates than Philippines. So they are ranked higher than it. Now, three nations namely Philippines, Thailand and Colombia have identical birth rates and death rates (34 and 10 respectively). Hence, they are ranked 33rd in the consolidated list.

36. The rank of Spain is 17th overall, tied alongwith Yugoslavia. So the next country will be ranked 19th in the list. Taiwan is ranked 28th in the list. Hence, there will be (28 – 19) = 9 countries between Taiwan and Spain.

37. In the consolidated list, there are 36 countries whose birth rate doesn't exceed 35. Now looking at the countries with birth rate of 36, we see that on the basis of lower death rates, Venezuela is placed at 37th position.

38. There are 9 countries in Asia that are ranked lower than every country of South America, namely Iran, Vietnam, Korea(DPRK), Pakistan, Nepal, Bangladesh, Syria, Iraq and Afghanistan. Out of these nations, only Afghanistan is ranked below all the countries from Africa. Remaining 8 countries satisfy the given condition.

For questions 39 to 42:

Operating profit = Profitability × Operating Income

Operating profits in 2002-03 for:

$$A = \frac{8 \times 180}{100} = 14.4 \text{ crore}; B = \frac{2 \times 220}{100} = 14.4 \text{ crore};$$

$$C = \frac{15 \times 200}{100} = 30 \text{ crore}; D = \frac{1 \times 290}{100} = 2.9 \text{ crore};$$

$$E = \frac{17.5 \times 200}{100} = 35 \text{ crore}; \; F = \frac{9 \times 210}{100} = 18.9 \text{ crore}$$

Looking at the values, two companies B and D are excluded in the third graph.

39. Companies A, C and E have profitability between 10% and 20% in F.Y. 2001-02. But the operating income of C in F.Y. 2002-03 is greater than 200 crore. Hence, option (4) is the correct option.

40. E has the highest operating profit of Rs.35 crore in F.Y. 2002-03.

41. Operating profit of B in F.Y. 2001-02 =

$$\frac{(-4) \times 250}{100} = -10 \text{ crore}$$

and operating profit of D in F.Y. 2001-02

$$= \frac{(-2) \times 250}{100} = -5 \text{ crore}$$

Therefore, average operating profit for B and D in F.Y.

$$2001\text{-}02 = \frac{(-5)+(-10)}{2} \text{crore} = -7.5 \text{ crore}$$

42. Two companies C and E have profitability exceeding 10% in F.Y. 2002-03.

∴ Their average operating profit in F.Y. 2002-03

$$= \frac{30+35}{2} \text{crore} = 32.5 \text{ crore.}$$

43. The cost of angioplasty, hip replacement and a knee replacement (in US Dollars '000) in the given countries is as follows.

	India	Thailand	Malaysia	Singapore	USA
Angioplasty	11 + 5 = 16	13 + 5 = 18	11 + 6 = 17	13 + 4 = 17	57
Hip replacement	9 + 7 = 16	12 + 5 = 17	10 + 8 = 18	12 + 5 = 17	43
Knee replacement	8.5 + 9 = 17.5	10 + 6 = 16	8 + 4 = 12	13 + 4 = 17	40
Total cost	49.5	51	47	51	140

The cheapest is in Malaysia.

44.

	India	Thailand	Malaysia	Singapore
Knee replacement	8.5 + 9 = 17.5	10 + 6 = 16	8 + 4 = 12	13 + 4 = 17

Clearly, India has the highest cost for knee replacement surgery.

45. In India, total cost in US$ = 3000 + 5000 + $\frac{1500}{32.89}$

(transportation cost)

= 8456.06

In Thailand, total cost in US$ = 4500 + 6000 = 10,500

Difference in amount is 10,500 – 8456.06 = US$ 2044

≈ 67,500 Bahts

46. In India, total cost for spinal fusion in US$

$$= \frac{5500 \times 40.928}{35} = 6431.5$$

In Singapore, total cost for spinal fusion in US$ = 9000

Difference (in US$) is 9000 – 6431.5 = 2568.5

≈ 2500

6

CHAPTER

Caselet

SOLVED EXAMPLES

Directions for examples 1 to 4: Answer the questions on the basis of the information given below.

Mr. Mathew teaches students of ten different classes – A through J. The number of students in the given classes is 1 through 10 respectively. No two classes have a common student. In a particular week, he did not teach the students of exactly two out of the ten classes. In the given week, he taught students of each of the remaining eight classes on exactly three different days. He did not teach the students of any class on Sunday, and on each of the remaining six days of the week, he taught the students of exactly four different classes. The number of students taught by him on Monday, Tuesday, Wednesday, Thursday, Friday and Saturday was 18, 12, 23, 19, 32 and 25 respectively. It is also known that, in the given week, no student was absent in his/her respective class.

1. Students of which of the following classes were not taught by him in the given week?

(1) E and D (2) G and D (3) I and H (4) D and H

2. Students of which of the following classes were not taught by him on Friday of the week?

(1) F (2) I (3) G (4) None of these

3. On Saturday of the week, if Mr. Mathew did not teach students of class J but taught students of class C, then students of which of the following classes were not taught by him on two consecutive days of the week?

(1) C (2) E (3) A (4) G

4. On Saturday of the week, if Mr. Mathew did not teach students of class J but taught students of class C, then students of class F were taught on

(1) Tuesday, Friday and Saturday (2) Tuesday, Thursday and Friday

(3) Tuesday, Wednesday and Saturday (4) None of these

For examples 1 to 4:

Had Mr. Mathew taught each of the given ten classes on exactly three different days of the week, he would have taught a total of (1 + 2 + 3 + ... + 9 + 10) × 3 = 165 students.

Total number of students taught by Mr. Mathew on the six days of the week = 18 + 12 + 23 + 19 + 32 + 25 = 129

Therefore, the total number of students in the two classes that were not taught by him = $\left(\frac{165-129}{3}\right) = 12$

So, the possible pairs of the two classes that were not taught by him could be (B and J), (C and I), (D and H) or (E and G).

On Tuesday the total number of students taught by him was 12.

This is possible in two cases:

Case I: He taught the classes A, B, C and F

Case II: He taught the classes A, B, D and E

From the two cases stated above, we can definitely conclude that he taught the classes A and B.

On Friday, the total number of students taught by him was 32.

This is possible in two cases:

Case III: He taught the classes E, H, I and J.

Case IV: He taught the classes F, G, I and J.

From the two cases stated above, we can definitely conclude that he taught the classes I and J and also, he taught either class E or G.

Therefore, the two classes that Mr. Mathew did not teach were D and H.

1. 4

6.2 CASELET

2. 4 The classes taught by him on Friday were F, G, I and J. Hence, option (4) is the correct choice.

3. 1 It is given that on Saturday of the week Mr. Mathew did not teach class J but taught class C.

Since he did not teach class J on Saturday, he definitely taught class I on Saturday as on Saturday Mr. Mathew taught 25 students and only possible combination was (C, F, G, I).

Hence, he definitely taught class E on each of the three days namely Monday, Wednesday and Thursday as he did not teach class E on Friday, Saturday and Tuesday.

The possible combinations of the classes taught by him on Thursday is (E, I, C and B) or (E, A, C and J). Therefore, he definitely taught the class C on Thursday.

The only possible combination of the classes taught by him on Monday was (A, B, E and J)

The final table is given below:

Monday	Tuesday	Wednesday	Thursday	Friday	Saturday
A, B, E and J	A, B, C and F	(E, G, J and A) or (E, G, I and B)	(E, C, A and J) or (E, C, I and B)	F, G, I and J	C, I, F and G

Class C is not taught by him on two consecutive days of the week 'W'.

4. 1 By referring to the table given in the pervious question, it can be calculated that the required days were Tuesday, Friday and Saturday.

Directions for examples 5 to 7: Answer the questions based on the following information.

Four students — Rahul, Rohit, Pooja and Neha – took an exam consisting of four questions, with four options each. In the exam, each of them attempted all the questions and answered at least one question correctly, and no two of them answered the same number of questions correctly. The table given below shows the responses of the four students for the questions in the exam.

Name \ Question	1	2	3	4
Rahul	a	d	b	a
Rohit	b	c	b	b
Pooja	a	c	d	d
Neha	a	c	d	a

5. Who answered exactly two questions correctly?

(1) Rahul (2) Rohit (3) Pooja (4) Neha

6. What was the correct option for the 4th question?

(1) a (2) b (3) c (4) d

7. If the marks assigned to 1st, 2nd, 3rd and 4th questions were 1, 2, 3 and 4 respectively and there was no negative marking for a wrong answer, then who scored the second highest marks?

(1) Rahul (2) Rohit (3) Pooja (4) Neha

For examples 5 to 7:

Assume Rahul attempted all the questions correctly. No two students answer the same number of questions correctly. On checking, we find that the condition given in the previous statement does not hold. Hence, Rahul did not answer all the question correctly.

On proceeding in the similar manner, we find that Neha answered all the questions correctly.

The number of questions answered correctly by:

Rahul = 2

Pooja = 3

Rohit = 1

The correct option for the 1st, 2nd, 3rd and 4th questions were 'a', 'c', 'd' and 'a' respectively.

5. 1 Rahul answered two questions correctly.

6. 1 The correct option for the 4th question was 'a'.

7. 3 According to the given marking scheme, the marks scored by:

Rahul = 5

Rohit = 2

Pooja = 6

Neha = 10

Directions for examples 8 to 11: Answer the questions on the basis of the information given below.

Six students – John, Steve, Hans, Brown, Peter and Eddy – took an exam, with the maximum marks as 100. Each student scored a different marks and none of them scored zero marks. It is also known that:

I. The marks scored by each student, except Brown, was the squares of a natural number.
II. The marks scored by John was equal to the sum of the marks scored by two other students in the group.
III. The marks scored by Brown, Peter and Eddy were the cubes of natural numbers.
IV. The product of the marks scored by John and Peter was an odd natural number.
V. The absolute difference between the marks scored by Eddy and Steve was equal to the marks scored by one of the students, except these two, in the group.

8. The marks scored by John was equal to the sum of the marks scored by

(1) Brown and Hans (2) Steve and Eddy (3) Brown and Peter (4) Eddy and Hans

9. The ratio of the marks scored by two students in the group was 1 : 4. Who out of the two scored the lesser marks?

(1) Peter (2) John (3) Hans (4) Eddy

10. Who scored the lowest marks?

(1) Steve (2) Brown (3) Hans (4) Peter

11. What was the sum of the marks scored by Hans and Brown?

(1) 37 (2) 72 (3) 65 (4) 44

For examples 8 to 11:

Let the respective initial letters namely J, S, H, B, P and E of the boys denote the marks scored by them.

From III, B, P and E are cubes of integers. From III and I, P and E are the squares of integers as well as cubes of integers.

Now none of the scores is zero and the cubes of integers in the range 1 to 100 are 1, 8, 27, 64. Out of these, 1 and 64 are squares of integers too. So P and E are 1 and 64, not necessarily in the same order.

From IV, J × P is an odd number. Hence, both J and P have to be odd natural numbers. This implies that P cannot be 64. So P is 1 and E is 64. Therefore, B = 8 or 27.

Now, from V, 64 – S or S – 64 is equal to either J, H, B or P. From I, the possible values of S are 4, 9, 16, 25, 36, 49, 81 and 100. The respective differences between these numbers and 64 are 60, 55, 48, 39, 28, 15, 17 and 36; out of these, except 36, none is either the cube or the square of an integer. This difference has to be 36 and hence S = 100. Since P cannot be 36 as it is 1, B cannot be 36 as it is either 8 or 27 and J cannot be 36 as it is an odd natural number, H is 36.

From II, J is either 9, 25, 49, 81. Out of these only 9 (i.e., 8 + 1) is possible sum of the marks obtain by the two other boys. Hence, J = 9 and B = 8.

So, P = 1, E = 64, S = 100, B = 8, H = 36, J = 9

8. 3

9. 2

10. 4

11. 4

Directions for examples 12 to 15: Answer the questions on the basis of the information given below.

Five boys — A, B, C, D and E — went on a shopping trip. Before shopping, three of the five boys had different amounts from among Rs. 100, Rs. 300 and Rs. 400, and the remaining two of them had the same amount which was Rs. 200. While shopping, they did not lend or borrow from each other. After the shopping, it was found that each of them was left with a different amount from among Rs. 165, Rs. 95, Rs. 70, Rs. 40 and Rs. 10, not necessarily in the same order. It is also known that:

I. A started with more money than what D started with.
II. B spent Rs. 15 more than what C spent.
III. E, who spent Rs. 35, started with more money than exactly one person in the group.
IV. C started with 66.67% of the money what B started with.
V. D was left with more money than what A was left with.

12. How much money did A spend?

(1) Rs. 205 (2) Rs. 190 (3) Rs. 35 (4) Rs. 360

13. What was the position of E in ascending order of spending?

(1) 1 (2) 2 (3) 4 (4) 5

14. Who was left with Rs. 40?

(1) A (2) B (3) C (4) D

15. What was the absolute difference between the amounts spent by B and D?

(1) Rs. 160 (2) Rs. 185 (3) Rs. 180 (4) None of these

For examples 12 to 15:

Since C started with 66.67% of the money that B started with, the ratio of amounts of C and B must have been in the ratio 2 : 3 and thus C started with Rs. 200 and B with Rs. 300. Since E started with money more than just one person, E must have started with Rs. 200. Since A has more money than D, A must have started with Rs. 400 and D with Rs. 100.

B and C started with Rs. 300 and Rs. 200 respectively, and B spent Rs. 15 more than C. Hence, the difference between the amounts left with B and C should have been Rs. 85. Out of the remaining amounts, only Rs. 95 and Rs. 10 satisfy this condition. Hence, B ended with Rs. 95 and C with Rs. 10. Since E spent Rs. 35, he ended with Rs. 165. Between A and D, D ended with more than A, and hence, D ended with Rs. 70 and A with Rs. 40.

The final table is given below:

Name	Started with	Ended with	Spent
A	400	40	360
B	300	95	205
C	200	10	190
D	100	70	30
E	200	165	35

12. 4

13. 2

14. 1

15. 4

Directions for examples 16 to 18: Answer the questions on the basis of the information given below.

In each of the five consecutive years – Year 1 through Year 5 – the sports department of a school organized a game in which exactly five students participated every year. Every year, at the end of the game, the five participants were given five different ranks – 1 through 5. The number of points awarded to the participants ranked 1, 2 and 3 were 5, 3 and 1 respectively. No points were awarded to the participants ranked 4 and 5.

A total of 9 different players participated in the game over the span of five years. The following table shows the total number of points garnered by each of the nine players.

Name of the Student	Points
Aman	5
Aabhas	5
Naveen	8
Urmi	2
Sameer	5
Rashmi	6
Sanjay	4
Kanika	10
Prashant	0

In Year 1, Aman, Aabhas, Naveen, Urmi and Sameer participated in the game. In Year 2, Rashmi replaced Aman; in Year 3, Sanjay replaced Aabhas; in Year 4, Kanika replaced Naveen; in Year 5, Prashant replaced Urmi. Once a player was replaced by another player, he/she did not participate in the game in the subsequent years. It is also known that Kanika was the only participant who was awarded points in two consecutive years.

16. If Sameer was given rank 3 in Year 3, then who was given Rank 2 in Year 3?

(1) Naveen (2) Rashmi (3) Sanjay (4) Either (1) or (2)

17. At the end of the game in Year 4, the total number of points awarded to how many participants, out of those who had participated in the game at least once, was lesser than the total number of points awarded to Rashmi?

(1) 7 (2) 8 (3) 5 (4) 6

18. In Year 5, what was the ratio of the number of points awarded to Sanjay to that of Sameer?

(1) 1 : 3 (2) 3 : 1 (3) 1 : 5 (4) Cannot be determined

For examples 16 to 18:

Since, Aman participated only in Year 1 and was awarded a total of 5 points, so we conclude that Aman was given Rank 1 in Year 1.

Aabhas participated only in Year 1 and Year 2 and was awarded a total of 5 points. This possible only if he was awarded either Rank 4 or Rank 5 in Year 1 and Rank 1 in Year 2.

Naveen participated in each of the three years viz. Year 1, Year 2 and Year 3 and was awarded a total of 8 points. This is possible only if he was awarded Rank 1 in Year 3 and Rank 2 in either of the two years Year 1 and Year 2.

Kanika played only in Year 4 and Year 5 and was awarded a total of 10 points and this is possible only if she was awarded Rank 1 in Year 4 as well as Year 5.

Further, the following conclusions can be drawn

Similarly, Sanjay was awarded 1 point in one of the years and 3 points in one of the years

Also, Sameer was awarded 1 point in two of the years and 3 points in one of the years.

Rashmi was awarded 3 points in two of the years.

Urmi was awarded 1 point in two of the years.

Sanjay was awarded points only in Year 3 and Year 5 because it is given that Kanika is the only participant who was awarded points in two consecutive years.

By the same logic, Sameer was awarded points only in Year 1, Year 3 and Year 5.

Therefore, Rashmi was awarded points only in Year 2 and Year 4.

Also, Naveen was awarded points only in Year 1 and Urmi was awarded points in Year 2 and Year 4.

Now, the possible ranks awarded to each of the given participants are listed in the table given below.

	Rank 1	**Rank 2**	**Rank 3**
Year 1	Aman	Naveen	Sameer
Year 2	Aabhas	Rashmi	Urmi
Year 3	Naveen	Sanjay/Sameer	Sanjay/Sameer
Year 4	Kanika	Rashmi	Urmi
Year 5	Kanika	Sanjay/Sameer	Sanjay/Sameer

16. 3 From the table given above we can easily conclude that if Sanjay was awarded Rank 3 in Year 3, then Sanjay was awarded Rank 2, in Year 3.

17. 4 At the end of the game in Year 4, every participant except Naveen has been awarded lesser number of points than Rashmi and Prashant did not participated till then.

So, there are a total of 6 participants were awarded lesser points than Rashmi at the end of the game in Year 4.

18. 4 From the table given above, the ratio of the number of points awarded to Sanjay and Sameer could be either 1 : 3 or 3 : 1.

Hence, option (4) is the correct choice.

PRACTICE EXERCISE – 1

Directions for questions 1 to 4: Answer the questions on the basis of the information given below.

Five friends – Chris, Matthew, Shane, Graham and Greame – bought 10 cookies and distributed them among themselves such that each of them received a different number of cookies, and one of them did not get any cookie. Each of them also likes biscuits of a different brand from among Hide & Seek, Bon-Bon, Maska & Chaska, Krackjack and Good day, and a different TV show from among Sportscenter, Raw, Wrestlemania, Smackdown and Hitz. Sportscenter and Hitz are sports shows and the others are wrestling shows. No two persons like the same brand of biscuits, and the same holds true for the TV shows. Following information is also given:

I. Shane, who didn't receive any cookies, does not like a wrestling show.

II. Chris, who received more cookies than Matthew, likes Maska & Chaska.

III. The absolute difference between the number of cookies received by Shane and Chris was equal to the absolute difference between the number of cookies received by Matthew and Graham.

IV. Greame did not receive the maximum number of cookies.

V. Matthew and Shane like TV shows starting with the same letter.

VI. The person who received the maximum number of cookies likes Krackjack and a wrestling show.

VII. The persons whose names start with the same letter like TV shows of the same genre.

VIII. Greame and Shane do not like Bon-Bon and Hide & seek respectively.

1. Which of the following pairs of TV show and biscuit cannot be liked by the same person?

(1) Hitz – Maska Chaska (2) Smackdown – Good Day

(3) Raw – Bon-Bon (4) Smackdown – Bon-Bon

2. Who received the maximum number of cookies?

(1) Matthew (2) Greame (3) Graham (4) Chris

3. The show liked by Chris is

(1) Sportscenter (2) Raw (3) Hitz (4) Wrestlemania

4. What is the sum of the number of cookies received by Greame and Chris?

(1) 5 (2) 7 (3) 6 (4) 3

Directions for questions 5 to 7: Answer the questions on the basis of the information given below.

In a group of five persons – Alex, Ben, Cedric, Paul and Smith – no two persons are of the same weight. Alex is heavier than Ben, who is heavier than Cedric. Paul is heavier than Smith.

5. Which of the following is not possible?

(1) Ben is the third in descending order of weights.

(2) Alex is not the heaviest and Cedric is the lightest.

(3) Paul is heavier than Ben, and Smith is lighter than Cedric.

(4) Alex is not the heaviest, and Cedric is the third in ascending order of weights.

6. Which of the following is possible?

(1) Paul is lighter than Ben and Smith is heavier than Cedric.

(2) Smith is the heaviest.

(3) Alex is not the heaviest, and Paul is lighter than Ben.

(4) Cedric is heavier than Paul, and Smith is heavier than Ben.

7. The number of persons who are heavier than Ben cannot be more than

(1) 4 (2) 3 (3) 2 (4) None of these

Directions for questions 8 to 11: Answer the questions on the basis of the information given below.

In a wildlife survey, it was found that each of the seven jungles - A, B, C, D, E, F and G - had a dominant animal from among Zakura, Fatura, Zathura and Tandura. Each of these jungles had either 2 or 3 animals out of the given ones. It is also known that:

i. No two jungles, out of the seven, had the same set of animals.

ii. The number of jungles in which Zathura, Zakura and Fatura were present was the same. Each of these three animals was dominant from exactly 2 jungles.

iii. In all those jungles in which there were exactly two animals and Zathura was one of them, Zathura was the dominant animal.

iv. Zakura, which was not present in D, was the dominant animal of G.

v. Tandura, which was not present in G, was the dominant animal of E. Zathura was not present in E.

vi. Fatura, which was present in F along with Zakura and Zathura, was the dominant animal of F.

vii. The number of jungles in which 3 animals were present was one more than that of those in which 2 animals were present.

viii. No two jungles out of A, B and D had the same dominant animal. The number of animals in each of B and C was 2 and that in E was 3.

ix. Fatura was not present in A.

8. Which of the following statements is definitely true?

(1) Zakura was the dominant animal of A. (2) Zathura was the dominant animal of B.

(3) Zathura was the dominant animal of D. (4) More than one of the above.

9. For how many jungles, could the names of animals present in them be determined uniquely?

(1) 5 (2) 4 (3) 3 (4) 7

10. Which of the following animals was present in C but was not the dominant animal of it?

(1) Fatura (2) Zakura (3) Both (a) and (b) (4) Cannot be determined

11. The number of jungles in which Tandura was present was

(1) 3 (2) 4 (3) 5 (4) 2

Directions for questions 12 to 14: Answer the questions on the basis of the information given below.

Seth Dhanpat Ram distributed 100 notes among 7 persons namely Lalu, Malu, Salu, Dalu, Kalu, Falu and Galu, such that except Galu, everyone received the same number of notes. Galu got 5 notes less than the others. Then these persons exchanged notes as follows :

i. Lalu took 5 notes from Kalu.

ii. Dalu received notes from two of her friends.

iii. Malu gave 3 notes to Dalu and received one note from Galu.

iv. Two of them did not give any note and three of the others did not receive any note.

v. Falu was involved in only one transaction and received two notes.

vi. Lalu had 20 notes and Dalu and Falu had equal number of notes at the end of all the transactions.

vii. There were five transactions in all.

12. At the end of the fifth transaction, who had the least number of notes?

(1) Salu (2) Galu (3) Kalu (4) Salu and Kalu

13. At the end of the fifth transaction, what was the difference in the number of notes held by the person who had the maximum number of notes and the number of notes held by the person with the least number of notes?

(1) 11 (2) 12 (3) 9 (4) 8

14. Who had fewer notes than Malu?

(1) Kalu and Galu (2) Dalu and Falu

(3) Dalu, Falu and Galu (4) Salu and Dalu

6.8 CASELET

Directions for questions 15 to 18: Answer the questions on the basis of the information given below.

Twelve professionals – P, Q, R, S, T, U, V, W, X, Y, Z and F – who belong to a company named PCL India Limited – attended the 'Annual Business Review Meet 2014' at Nainital. Among the twelve professionals, P, Q, R, S, T and V were Directors, and F, U, W, X, Y and Z were Senior Executives. During the meet, they stayed in two different resorts, with six members in each, facing each other, with a room in one resort facing exactly one room in the other resort. The table given below shows the information about the room numbers in the two resorts in which the twelve professionals stayed. In the table, the room numbers in same column face each other. For example, room number 18 in Riverside faces room number 32 in Jungleview.

Resorts	Room numbers					
Riverside	20	19	18	17	16	15
Jungleview	30	31	32	33	34	35

The following are some additional information:

I. S stayed in a room the room number of which was half the room number of the room in which P stayed.

II. U, who stayed in the same resort as that of Y, stayed in a room the room number of which had exactly 2 factors.

III. Exactly four directors stayed in Jungleview, and no two directors, except P and Q, stayed in adjacent rooms.

IV. V, who stayed in the same resort in which T stayed, stayed in a room the room number of which had the maximum number of factors.

V. T and R, who did not stay in the same resort, stayed in the corner rooms. X stayed at Riverside.

VI. W did not stay in a room that was adjacent to that of any of the directors.

15. If Y stayed in Riverside, in how many different ways could they have stayed?

(1) 6 (2) 8 (3) 12 (4) 24

16. For a quiz, the 12 professional were divided into 4 groups, with 3 members each, such that each group, all of its members staying in the same resort, comprised at least one Director and at least one Senior Executive, who among the following could not be a part of the group that included T in it?

(1) V (2) U (3) P (4) R

17. Which of the following is definitely false?

(1) Y occupied room number 19. (2) Z occupied room number 34.
(3) W's room was opposite to T's room. (4) U was in room number 17.

18. If the number of professionals each of whom stayed in a room adjacent to the room of a Director on one side and a Senior Executive on the otherside was X, find the value of (12 – X).

(1) 6 (2) 7 (3) 8 (4) 9

Directions for questions 19 to 21: Answer the questions on the basis of the information given below.

In the following grid, letters A, B, C and D represent four natural numbers less than 50, with A being the greatest. Each of these letters is a multiple 5. It also known that the sum of the letters in the cells along the two diagonals in the grid is 80.

A	B	C	D
B	C	D	A
C	D	A	B
D	A	B	C

19. What is the value of (A + C + D)?

(1) 35 (2) 40 (3) 30 (4) Either (1) or (3)

20. Which of the following is a possible value of A?

(1) 35 (2) 20 (3) 30 (4) None of these

21. What is the minimum possible value of 'B' for which (A + B + C + D) is a multiple of 4?

(1) 10 (2) 20 (3) 15 (4) 5

Directions for questions 22 to 25: Answer the questions on the basis of the information given below.

Sixteen consecutive natural numbers are to be filled into a 4 × 4 square matrix shown below, such that there is one number in a cell. Four of these 16 numbers are already shown in the matrix. The remaining 12 numbers are denoted by 12 letters – A through L. The numbers are filled in such a way that the sum of the numbers in the cells in each row, each column and each diagonal of the matrix is the same. It is also known that D + E + I = 66.

15	A	B	18
C	D	E	F
G	H	I	J
27	K	L	30

22. How many numbers used for filling the matrix are numerically greater than the number denoted by C?

(1) 4 (2) 5 (3) 6 (4) Cannot be determined

23. Find the numerical value of (A + I) – (B + H).

(1) 2 (2) 1 (3) 0 (4) 3

24. If we were to construct another 4 × 4 square matrix containing 16 consecutive natural numbers having the same properties as the given matrix, then which of the following could be a possible value of the sum of the numbers in the cells in any row of this matrix?

(1) 116 (2) 144 (3) 168 (4) 170

25. What is the value of C?

(1) 22 (2) 26 (3) 25 (4) 23

Directions for questions 26 to 29: Answer the questions based on the information given below:

Four families, each of which comprises a man, his wife and their pet dog, stay in 'HINDUSTAN' colony. Further information regarding them is given below:

- The four men are Peter, Qureshi, Ramanpreet and Shyam.
- The four wives are Radha, Pamela, Jaspinder and Ameena.
- The four pets are Boxer, Jacky, Tommy and Zorro.
- Peter's pet dog is Boxer and Qureshi's pet dog is not Jacky.
- Shyam's wife is not Jaspinder.
- Pamela's pet dog is neither Boxer nor Jacky.
- Tommy is the pet dog of Ameena, whose husband is either Peter or Ramanpreet.

26. Who is the husband of Radha?

(1) Peter (2) Qureshi (3) Ramanpreet (4) Shyam

27. Boxer is the pet dog of

(1) Radha (2) Pamela (3) Jaspinder (4) Ameena

28. Pet dog of Qureshi is

(1) Zorro (2) Tommy (3) Jacky (4) Either (1) or (2)

29. How many of the following are correct combinations of man – wife – pet dog?

i. Shyam – Radha – Tommy

ii. Peter – Ameena – Boxer

iii. Qureshi – Pamela – Zorro

iv. Ramanpreet – Jaspinder – Jacky

(1) None (2) 1 (3) 2 (4) More than 2

6.10 CASELET

Directions for questions 30 to 32: Answer the questions on the basis of the information given below.

Six different birds – X_1, X_2, X_3, X_4, X_5 and X_6 – are put into three cages, with two birds in each. X_1 and X_2 are not kept in the same cage; the same holds true for pairs X_2 and X_3, X_3 and X_4, X_4 and X_5, X_5 and X_6.

30. Which of the following can be put with X_1 in one of the cages so that the pairs in the remaining two cages can not be determined uniquely?

(1) X_3 (2) X_4 (3) X_5 (4) X_6

31. If a pair of birds kept in the same cage is known, what is the probability that the other two pairs of birds kept in the remaining two cages can be determined uniquely?

(1) $\frac{2}{5}$ (2) $\frac{1}{2}$ (3) $\frac{5}{11}$ (4) $\frac{3}{5}$

32. If birds kept in one of the cages are X_2 and X_4, then which of the following pairs of birds are not kept in the same cage?

(1) X_1, X_5 (2) X_3, X_5 (3) X_1, X_6 (4) X_1, X_3

Directions for questions 33 to 35: Answer the questions on the basis of the information given below.

The following diagram, comprising six roads namely R_1, R_2, R_3, R_4, R_5 and R_6, shows the route-network of five inter-connecting cities. It is also known that traffic can flow in either direction along each of the six roads. During a journey, a person travels along each road only once.

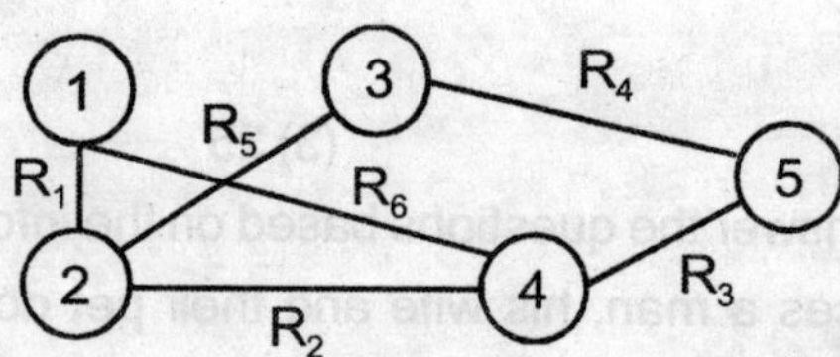

33. If a person starts from a city and wants to travel along each of the six roads, which of the following statements is necessarily true?

(1) There is no such route.

(2) She starts from from city 2 or ends at it.

(3) She ends at city 1.

(4) She definitely starts from city 5.

34. If a person starts from a city and wants to travel along each of the six roads, the number of differents routes that she can take is

(1) 4 (2) 6 (3) 8 (4) 12

35. If a person starts from a city and wants to travel along each of the six roads and she ends up in her starting city, the number of differents routes that she can take is

(1) 0 (2) 3 (3) 6 (4) 2

Directions for questions 36 to 38: Answer the questions on the basis of the information given below.

Table given below shows the month and year of birth of twelve children. Each child belongs to exactly one family from among Dahiya's, Ahuja's, Khanna's, Shrivas' and Bajpayee's. Each of the five familiees has at least two children and at most three children. The total number children with the five families is 12.

Child's age is counted in terms of number of years and months only. For example Aditya's age in May 2002 was 6 years and 2 months, irrespective of his date of birth.

Name	Month and year of Birth	
Afsana	February	**1991**
Sukrit	December	**1991**
Salim	September	**1992**
Akash	April	**1993**
Samaksh	July	**1994**
Anirudh	October	**1994**
Anjan	May	**1995**
Aditya	March	**1996**
Ansar	May	**1998**
Siddharth	October	**1998**
Sandy	June	**1999**
Sami	January	**2000**

36. If average age of children of Dahiya family in January 2001 was 6 years and 1 month, then how many of the following could belong to Dahiya family?

I. Ansar
II. Afsana
III. Anjan
IV. Samaksh
V. Siddharth

(1) 5 (2) 2 (3) 3 (4) 4

37. If with the birth of second child in Khanna family, the average age of children of Khanna family became equal to the average age of children of Ahuja family, who was the first child of Khanna family?

(1) Either Anjan or Anirudh
(2) Either Samaksh or Anjan
(3) Either Salim or Samaksh
(4) Either Salim or Aditya

38. At some instance, average age of three children of Bajpayee family was integer number of years. If names of all the children of Bajpayee family starts with the same letter, which of the following could be children of Bajpayee family?

(1) Sandy, Siddharth, Salim
(2) Akash, Anjan, Ansar
(3) Ansar, Afsana, Aditya
(4) Afsana, Ansar, Anjan

Directions for questions 39 to 42: Answer the questions on the basis of the information given below.

Ashok, Amit, Ajay, Akansh and Abhishek are five friends who live in five different cities namely Kunnamangalam, Joka, Vastrapur, Banerghatta and Prabandhnagar, not necessarily in that order. Their annual salaries (in INR) are 7,00,000, 8,00,000, 9,00,000, 11,00,000 and 13,00,000, in no particular order. Further, the following information is given:

(i) Akansh, who does not live in Banerghatta, earns a salary that is a prime number multiple of 100000.

(ii) The person who lives in Prabandhnagar is not the one whose salary is the minimum amongst the five friends.

(iii) The absolute difference between the salaries of Akansh and Ajay is the same as the absolute difference between the salaries of Ashok and Abhishek.

(iv) The salary of the person who lives in Prabandhnagar is a perfect square multiple of 1,00,000.

(v) Ajay's salary (in INR) is 1,00,000 INR more than the average salary of Akansh and Ashok.

(vi) Amit lives in the city that has the shortest name amongst the given cities.

39. If Akansh lives in Vastrapur, then what is the average salary of the persons who live in Banerghatta and Kunnamangalam?

(1) Rs. 9 lakh (2) Rs. 10 lakh (3) Rs. 12 lakh (4) Data Insufficient

40. Who lives in Prabandhnagar?

(1) Ashok (2) Amit (3) Abhishek (4) Ajay

41. If Amit and Ajay live in cities with names starting with consecutive letters, who lives in Vastrapur?

(1) Akansh (2) Amit (3) Abhishek (4) Ajay

42. If the salary of the person who lives in Banerghatta is neither maximum nor minimum, then what is the average salary of the persons who live in Kunnamanglam and Vastrapur?

(1) Rs.10.5 lakhs (2) Rs. 10 lakhs (3) Rs. 12 lakh (4) Cannot be determined

Directions for questions 43 to 45: Answer the questions on the basis of the information given below.

There are four married couples. A, B, C and D are the male members, and E, F, G and H are female members making the four couples. Each couple celebrates its marriage anniversary on a different date from among 7th, 12th, 14th and 24th, falling in different months out of March, May, October and December. Further, the following information is given:

(i) E celebrates her marriage anniversary on a date the numerical value of which is twice the numerical value of the date on which H celebrates her marriage anniversary.

(ii) The sum of the numerical values of the date and the month number of the marriage anniversary of D, is equal to the numerical value of the date of the marriage anniversary of C.

(iii) A and E are maried to each other. Only for this couple, the sum of the numerical values of date and the month number of their marriage anniversary is a prime number.

(iv) A and D celebrate their marriage anniversaries in different months starting with the same letter.

43. If G's marriage anniversary falls on 24th December, which of the following combinations of a couple and the date on which they celebrate their marriage anniversary could be correct?

(1) D-F, 7th May

(2) C-F, 12th October

(3) C-G, 24th December

(4) D-H, 7th March

44. If the sum of the numerical values of the date and the month number of marriage anniversary of F is maximum but not a perfect square, who is the husband of F?

(1) B (2) C (3) D (4) Either B or C

45. If the sum of the numerical values of the date and the month number of marriage anniversary of F is maximum but not a perfect square, what is the date on which G celebrates her marriage anniversary?

(1) 7th May (2) 12th October (3) 12th December (4) Cannot be determined

Directions for questions 46 to 49: Answer the questions on the basis of the information given below:

A new program was introduced in Yum Bee Yay course of MII, where various CEOs and mentors from the Industry come as a visiting faculty in the 3rd trimester of the course. They are:

CEO Name	**Companies**
Narayan Murthy	Infosys
Andy Grove	Intel
Kiran Deshpande	MBT
S. G. Pitroda	WorldTel
Kishor Bayani	Pantaloons

These people have been invited to teach three batches: I, II and III.

- (Narayan Murthy and Andy Grove); (Andy Grove and Kiran Deshpande); (Kiran Deshpande and S. G. Pitroda); (S. G. Pitroda and Kishor Bayani); (Kishor Bayani and Narayan Murthy) are experts in five subjects: *Leading, Following and Team Dynamics (LFTD); Strategic Management (SM); Information Technology and Systems (ITS); Services Marketing (SMkt); and International Brand Marketing (IBM)* respectively.
- There are 5 sessions in a day where all the subjects are taught daily to each batch, one subject in each session.
- Each visiting faculty comes daily for one session of each batch. They necessarily teach only the subjects they are experts in.

The partial session plan is given below:

Timings	**Batch**					
	I		**II**		**III**	
	Faculty	**Subject**	**Faculty**	**Subject**	**Faculty**	**Subject**
9:00 am - 11:00 am				ITS	Kishor Bayani	
11:00 am - 1:00 pm	Kiran Deshpande				Narayan Murthy	
2:00 pm - 4:00 pm			Andy Grove			ITS
4:00 pm - 6:00 pm	S.G.Pitroda			IBM		
6:30 pm - 8:30 pm		IBM				SM

46. In batch I, SM and ITS are taught respectively by
(1) Andy Grove and Kiran Deshpande
(2) Kiran Deshpande and S.G. Pitroda
(3) Andy Grove and S. G. Pitroda
(4) Cannot be determined

47. For batch III, IBM and SM are taught respectively by
(1) Narayan Murthy and Andy Grove
(2) Kishor Bayani and Andy Grove
(3) Narayan Murthy and Kiran Deshpande
(4) Kiran Deshpande and Kishor Bayani

48. Kishor Bayani and Narayan Murthy taught which subjects to batch I?
(1) SMkt and LFTD
(2) IBM and LFTD
(3) SMkt and IBM
(4) Cannot be determined

49. Who among the following takes the last two lectures of batch II?
(1) Narayan Murthy and Kishor Bayani
(2) Kishor Bayani and S. G. Pitroda
(3) Kiran Deshpande and Kishor Bayani
(4) Cannot be determined

Directions for questions 50 to 53 : Answer the questions on the basis of the information given below.

KAT examination was conducted in the Indus World School yesterday. The number of students who have appeared in the exam in each classroom is observed to be always a multiple of ten. Question papers are distributed from the Head-Office to all the classrooms. Number of students taking the exam in some classrooms is known. The following figure provides information about the route through which the question papers are distributed to each classroom.

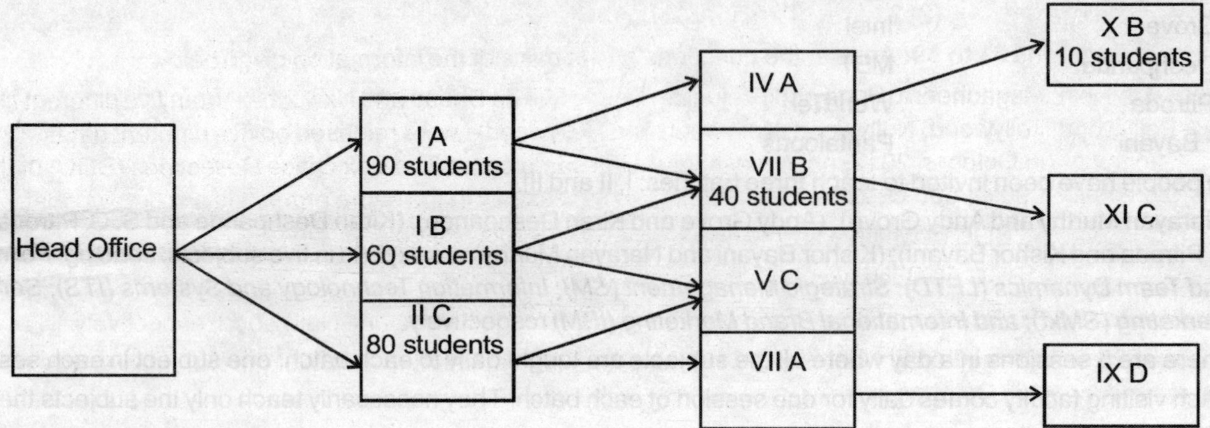

Additional Information given:

(i) Question papers from one classroom to another classroom can be passed only when question paper is distributed to every student in the previous classroom.

(ii) There are 450 question papers in the Head-Office and 150 question papers are sent through each route originating from the Head-Office.

(iii) Each and every students gets exactly one question paper.

(iv) In the end all the question papers were distributed.

50. If the number of students in classroom XI C is not less than 50 then what could be the maximum number of question papers that can come to classroom V C?

(1) 80 (2) 90 (3) 100 (4) 110

51. If the number of students in classroom IX D is least possible, then a minimum of how many students are there in classroom IV A such that number of students in classrooms XI C and V C are equal and number of students in classroom VII A is 40?

(1) 10 (2) 20 (3) 30 (4) 40

52. If time taken (in seconds) to distribute the question papers in a classroom is equal to the number of students in the classroom, then find the maximum time in which the question papers will be distributed in V C? (Assume that the time taken to travel from one classroom to other or Head-office to a classroom is negligible)

(1) 110 sec (2) 140 sec (3) 120 sec (4) 130 sec

53. If number of students taking the exam in classroom VII A is 50 then find the maximum possible number of students in classroom IV A?

(1) 60 (2) 80 (3) 50 (4) 70

Directions for questions 54 to 56: Answer the questions on the basis of the information given below.

A psychiatrist analysed the results of a test conducted to assess three personality traits—Patience, Compassion and Honesty—on five of his patients—A, B, C, D, and E. He evaluated each of the personality traits on a scale of 1 to 5 (integers only). It is also known that:

(i) Scores of no two patients were same in any of the traits.

(ii) No patient was assigned the same score in all the three traits.

(iii) Only two patients were assigned the same score in two traits.

(iv) The score of A in Compassion was equal to that of C in Honesty which was 4.

(v) The score of E in Compassion was 1 more than his score in Patience, which, in turn, was 2 less than his score in Honesty.

(vi) Neither A's nor B's score in any of the traits was 5.

(vii) The score of D in Patience was equal to that of A in Compassion, and the score of C in Compassion was the same as that of A in Honesty.

54. The score assigned to A in Patience was

(1) 2 (2) 3 (3) 5 (4) Cannot be determined

55. For which of the following pairs of traits can we be sure that no patient had the same score?

(1) Patience and Compassion (2) Compassion and Honesty

(3) Patience and Honesty (4) None of these

56. How many patients scored less than or equal to A in each of the three traits?

(1) 0 (2) 2 (3) 1 (4) 3

Directions for questions 57 to 59: Answer the questions on the basis of the information given below.

Five movies – Oblivion, Magadheera, Pride and Prejudice, Bhaag Milkha Bhaag and Nkwocha – from five different film industries – Bollywood, Tollywood, Nollywood, Kollywood and Hollywood – were released on five different dates – 2nd, 9th, 16th, 23rd and 30th – in October, 2012, not necessarily in the same order. The Box Office Collections (BOC) of the five movies were 110 cr, 90 cr, 580 cr, 200 cr and 380 cr, not necessarily in the same order. It is also known that:

(i) Bhaag Milkha Bhaag, BOC of which was 110 cr, was released on 23rd October.

(ii) Pride and Prejudice, BOC of which was 200 cr, was not from Bollywood.

(iii) The movies that were released on 2nd and 30th October were from Hollywood and Nollywood respectively.

(iv) Nkwocha was not released on 2nd October. Its BOC was equal to the sum of BOCs of the two movies that were released on 9th and 16th October.

(v) Magadheera was neither from Bollywood nor was its BOC 90 cr.

57. For how many of the five movies can the film industry be definitely determined?

(1) 2 (2) 5 (3) 3 (4) 4

58. What was the sum of BOCs of the movies that were released on 2nd and 30th October?

(1) 780 cr (2) 670 cr (3) 835 cr (4) 690 cr

59. Which movie's BOC was 580 cr?

(1) Magadheera (2) Oblivion

(3) Bhaag Milkha Bhaag (4) Nkwocha

Directions for questions 60 to 63: Answer the questions on the basis of the information given below.

A psychiatrist analysed the results of a test conducted to assess three personality traits—Patience, Compassion and Honesty—on five of his patients—A, B, C, D, and E. He evaluated each of the personality traits on a scale of 1 to 5 (integers only). It is also known that:

(i) Scores of no two patients were same in any of the traits.

(ii) No patient was assigned the same score in all the three traits.

(iii) Only two patients were assigned the same score in two traits.

(iv) The score of A in Compassion was equal to that of C in Honesty which was 4.

(v) The score of E in Compassion was 1 more than his score in Patience, which, in turn, was 2 less than his score in Honesty.

(vi) Neither A's nor B's score in any of the traits was 5.

(vii) The score of D in Patience was equal to that of A in Compassion, and the score of C in Compassion was the same as that of A in Honesty.

60. The score assigned to A in Patience was

(1) 2 (2) 3 (3) 5 (4) Cannot be determined

61. For which of the following pairs of traits can we be sure that no patient had the same score?

(1) Patience and Compassion (2) Compassion and Honesty

(3) Patience and Honesty (4) None of these

62. How many patients scored less than or equal to A in each of the three traits?

(1) 0 (2) 2 (3) 1 (4) 3

63. Whose score was the maximum in honesty?

(1) A (2) B (3) C (4) D

6.16 CASELET

Directions for questions 64 to 67: Answer the questions on the basis of the information given below.

Mr. Mathew teaches students of ten different classes – A through J. The number of students in the given classes is 1 through 10 respectively. No two classes have a common student. In a particular week, he did not teach the students of exactly two out of the ten classes. In the given week, he taught students of each of the remaining eight classes on exactly three different days. He did not teach the students of any class on Sunday, and on each of the remaining six days of the week, he taught the students of exactly four different classes. The number of students taught by him on Monday, Tuesday, Wednesday, Thursday, Friday and Saturday was 18, 12, 23, 19, 32 and 25 respectively. It is also known that, in the given week, no student was absent in his/her respective class.

64. Students of which of the following classes were not taught by him in the given week?

(1) E and D (2) G and D (3) I and H (4) D and H

65. Students of which of the following classes were not taught by him on Friday of the week?

(1) F (2) I (3) G (4) None of these

66. On Saturday of the week, if Mr. Mathew did not teach students of class J but taught students of class C, then students of which of the following classes were not taught by him on two consecutive days of the week?

(1) C (2) E (3) A (4) G

67. On Saturday of the week, if Mr. Mathew did not teach students of class J but taught students of class C, then students of class F were taught on

(1) Tuesday, Friday and Saturday (2) Tuesday, Thursday and Friday

(3) Tuesday, Wednesday and Saturday (4) None of these

Directions for question 68 to 70: Answer the questions on the basis of the information given below.

Four students — Rahul, Rohit, Pooja and Neha – took an exam consisting of four questions, with four options each. In the exam, each of them attempted all the questions and answered at least one question correctly, and no two of them answered the same number of questions correctly. The table given below shows the responses of the four students for the questions in the exam.

Question / Name	1	2	3	4
Rahul	a	d	b	a
Rohit	b	c	b	b
Pooja	a	c	d	d
Neha	a	c	d	a

68. Who answered exactly two questions correctly?

(1) Rahul (2) Rohit (3) Pooja (4) Neha

69. What was the correct option for the 4th question?

(1) a (2) b (3) c (4) d

70. If the marks assigned to 1st, 2nd, 3rd and 4th questions were 1, 2, 3 and 4 respectively and there was no negative marking for a wrong answer, then who scored the second highest marks?

(1) Rahul (2) Rohit (3) Pooja (4) Neha

Directions for questions 71 to 74: Answer the questions on the basis of the information given below.

Six students – John, Steve, Hans, Brown, Peter and Eddy – took an exam, with the maximum marks as 100. Each student scored a different marks and none of them scored zero marks. It is also known that:

I. The marks scored by each student, except Brown, was the squares of a natural number.

II. The marks scored by John was equal to the sum of the marks scored by two other students in the group.

III. The marks scored by Brown, Peter and Eddy were the cubes of natural numbers.

IV. The product of the marks scored by John and Peter was an odd natural number.

V. The absolute difference between the marks scored by Eddy and Steve was equal to the marks scored by one of the students, except these two, in the group.

71. The marks scored by John was equal to the sum of the marks scored by

(1) Brown and Hans (2) Steve and Eddy (3) Brown and Peter (4) Eddy and Hans

72. The ratio of the marks scored by two students in the group was 1 : 4. Who out of the two scored the lesser marks?

(1) Peter (2) John (3) Hans (4) Eddy

73. Who scored the lowest marks?

(1) Steve (2) Brown (3) Hans (4) Peter

74. What was the sum of the marks scored by Hans and Brown?

(1) 37 (2) 72 (3) 65 (4) 44

Directions for questions 75 to 78: Answer the questions on the basis of the information given below.

Five boys — A, B, C, D and E — went on a shopping trip. Before shopping, three of the five boys had different amounts from among Rs. 100, Rs. 300 and Rs. 400, and the remaining two of them had the same amount which was Rs. 200. While shopping, they did not lend or borrow from each other. After the shopping, it was found that each of them was left with a different amount from among Rs. 165, Rs. 95, Rs. 70, Rs. 40 and Rs. 10, not necessarily in the same order. It is also known that:

I. A started with more money than what D started with.

II. B spent Rs. 15 more than what C spent.

III. E, who spent Rs. 35, started with more money than exactly one person in the group.

IV. C started with 66.67% of the money what B started with.

V. D was left with more money than what A was left with.

75. How much money did A spend?

(1) Rs. 205 (2) Rs. 190 (3) Rs. 35 (4) Rs. 360

76. What was the position of E in ascending order of spending?

(1) 1 (2) 2 (3) 4 (4) 5

77. Who was left with Rs. 40?

(1) A (2) B (3) C (4) D

78. What was the absolute difference between the amounts spent by B and D?

(1) Rs. 160 (2) Rs. 185 (3) Rs. 180 (4) None of these

PRACTICE EXERCISE – 2

Directions for questions 1 to 4: Answer the questions on the basis of the information given below.

In a query answering module called 'Help Me', students ask their queries, which are based on four subject areas namely DI, LR, QA and VA. The queries enter the module as soon as they are asked and remain there until they are answered. All queries that are received in the first half of the day are counted as a part of that day and the ones received in the second half are counted as a part of the next day. There are four persons – Dudi, Anu, Sam and Tiru – who are responsible for answering queries. Queries are answered only in the second half of the day.

The following table gives the number of unanswered queries of the previous week, 15th to 21th May, 2015, from the four subject areas by the end of the week.

Number of unanswered queries of previous week			
DI	LR	QA	VA
24	17	48	14

The information regarding the number of new queries received in the current week, 22nd to 28th May, 2015, is given in the table below.

	DI	**LR**	**QA**	**VA**
Monday	10	2	5	2
Tuesday	12	5	2	3
Wednesday	8	2	5	0
Thursday	4	2	8	5
Friday	2	4	3	6
Saturday	4	5	1	7

- Queries based on VA are answered only by Sam.
- Tiru answers queries based on QA only. Sam answers queries on VA only.
- In the current week, if the number of queries answered by Dudi, Anu, Sam and Tiru on any day (from Monday to Saturday) are denoted by d, a, s and t respectively, then it was observed that

$6 \leq d \leq 12$

$8 \leq a \leq 18$

$5 \leq s \leq 10$

$2 \leq t \leq 15$

No query is admitted or answered on Sunday.

1. On which day of the current week could Sam answer the maximum possible number of queries?

(1) Wednesday (2) Friday (3) Saturday (4) Either Friday or Saturday

2. In the current week, if there were no pending queries of QA at the end of Saturday and only Tiru answered QA queries, the total number queries of QA that were answered on the same day when they were received could not be less than

(1) 4 (2) 3 (3) 2 (4) 1

3. Which of the following is not possible?

(1) All pending queries of the previous week could be answered by the end of Wednesday.

(2) All pending queries of the previous week could be answered by the end of Thursday.

(3) All pending queries of the previous week could be answered by the end of Friday.

(4) All pending queries of the previous week could be answered by the end of Monday.

4. On Monday, of the current week, a total of 58 queries were answered. Atmost how many of them could be of QA?

(1) 45 (2) 31 (3) 21 (4) Data inconsistent

Directions for questions 5 to 8: Answer the questions on the basis of the information given below.

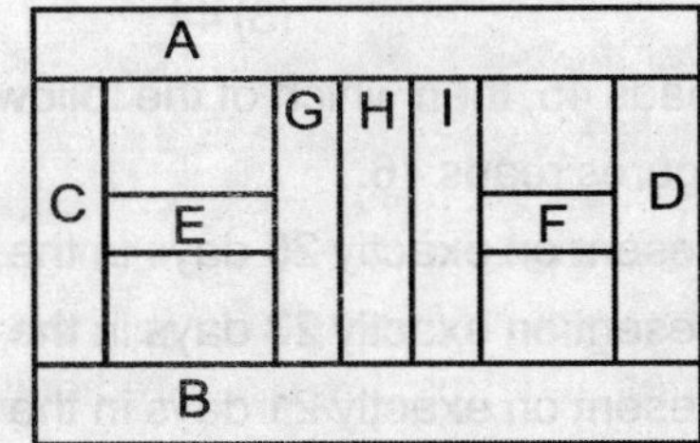

The given figure has 9 boxes labelled A, B, C, D, E, F, G, H and I respectively. Each box has a distinct single-digit natural number written on it. Two numbers, on any two adjacent boxes, are called as adjacent numbers.

Additional information :

1. The sum of the numbers on boxes G and I is less than 13.
2. The sum of the numbers on boxes adjacent to H is equal to the sum of the numbers on boxes adjacent to G.
3. The sum of the numbers on the boxes that are adjacent to the box containing 5 is 30.
4. The sum of the numbers on boxes C and D is less than 6.
5. Box E does not have the lowest number and box F does not have the highest number.
6. The sum of the numbers on boxes G and H is prime.
7. The sum of the numbers on the boxes adjacent to D exceeds the sum of the numbers on boxes adjacent to C by 6.

5. Which of the following statements is sufficient to find the number written on box C?
   (i) The sum of the numbers on boxes adjacent to F is more than the sum of the numbers on boxes adjacent to E.
   (ii) The sum of the numbers on boxes adjacent to F is less than the sum of the numbers on boxes adjacent to E.
   (1) The question can be answered by using statement (i) alone but not (ii) alone.
   (2) The question can be answered by using statement (ii) alone but not (i) alone.
   (3) The question can be answered by using either statement alone.
   (4) No more information is required.
6. For how many boxes the numbers written on them can be uniquely determined?
   (1) All of them (2) 7 (3) 3 (4) 5
7. For how many pairs of adjacent boxes, the sum of the numbers on them is 15?
   (1) 0 (2) 1 (3) 2 (4) 3
8. For how many boxes, the sum of the numbers on the boxes adjacent to them must be a prime number?
   (1) 2 (2) 3 (3) 4 (4) 5

Directions for questions 9 to 12: Answer the questions on the basis of the information given below.

Upon noticing the sudden increase in absenteeism in an office, the concerned HR manager hired a consultant to analyse the employees' attendance data. The data was regarding four employees of the company and the number of days on which they were physically present in the company in a month consisting of 30 days. The HR manager did not provide the consultant with direct information about the number of days on which these four employees were present. Instead, he chose two of the four employees at a time, added the number of days on which they had been present and collated the six numbers so obtained in a table in descending order from left to right on a sheet of paper. Just before going through the data, the consultant spilled his coffee on the sheet as a result of which the column figures numbered 3, 4 and 5 became illegible. The table, after the spilling of coffee, is shown below.

Column	1	2	3	4	5	6
Sum of the number of days on which employees were present, taken two at a time	51	49				40

For each of the employee the number of days on which he/she was absent in the given month was a distinct integer. There was no such day in the month on which all the four employees were absent.

9. Column figure numbered 5 should be:

(1) 41 (2) 42 (3) 44 (4) 45

10. If one of the illegible column figures reads 45, then which of the following is true?

(1) One of the other illegible column figures reads 46.

(2) One of the four employees was present on exactly 25 days in the month.

(3) One of the four employees was present on exactly 23 days in the month.

(4) One of the four employees was present on exactly 21 days in the month.

11. Eksa was the second employee, if the 4 employees are arranged in ascending order of the days on which they were present in the month. What could have been the maximum possible number of days on which Eksa was present?

(1) 25 (2) 24 (3) 23 (4) 22

12. When the consultant called up the HR manager and told him about the missing numbers, all that the HR manager could remember was that the column figure numbered 3 was the addition of the number of days for the two employees who were present on the maximum and the minimum possible number of days. Which of the following is column figure numbered 3?

(1) 44 (2) 45 (3) 46 (4) 47

Directions for questions 13 to 15: Answer the questions on the basis of the information given below.

The diagram given below shows the per unit Cost Price and Selling Price (in Rs.) of six items – A, B, C, D, E and F – produced by a company named Prakash & Sons in the year 2012. It is also known that the company sold all the units of the six items that it produced in the given year.

13. If the company produced A, B, C, D, E and F in the ratio 7 : 31 : 6 : 23 : 4 : 3, then the percentage profit that the company made in the year 2012 was

(1) 6.35 (2) 6.63 (3) 6.45 (4) 8.21

14. 'X' was the overall profit percentage on the profit-making items and 'Y' was the overall loss percentage on the loss-making items for the company in the year 2012. If the company produced an equal number of units of all six items, then find the sum of the values of X and Y.

(1) 68.78 (2) 82.60 (3) 42.78 (4) 90.45

15. On which of the six items did the company register the maximum loss in the year 2012?

(1) E (2) F (3) C (4) Cannot be determined

Directions for questions 16 and 17: Answer the questions on the basis of the information given below.

Each of the five persons out of Rohan, Deepak, Tripti, Sonal and Tarun completed a different number of units of work from among 200, 180, 140, 150 and 240 over a period of certain number of days. The number of days taken by Rohan, Deepak, Tripti, Sonal and Tarun to complete the mentioned units of work is 12, 10, 8, 10 and 12 days respectively. The following table provides information about the total units of work completed by each of these mentioned persons by the end of each day.

	Number of Units				
After	**Rohan**	**Deepak**	**Tripti**	**Sonal**	**Tarun**
1 day	10	12	5	20	18
2 days	22	32	15	25	20
3 days	24	50	25	40	44
4 days	40	52	50	50	48
5 days	60	84	80	65	50
6 days	68	120	96	80	95
7 days	140	140	108	100	100
8 days	148	156	140	125	112
9 days	176	172	140	140	115
10 days	180	180	140	150	120
11 days	184	180	140	150	160
12 days	200	180	140	150	240

A person is said to be more efficient than the other person only if he/she has done more number of units of work than him/her on at least seven out of the mentioned days.

16. Out of the mentioned five persons, how many persons are more efficient than exactly two persons?

(1) 4 (2) 2 (3) 1 (4) 3

17. On how many days the number of units of work completed by Sonal is more than at least one and at most two out of the mentioned persons?

(1) 5 (2) 8 (3) 6 (4) 7

Directions for questions 18 to 21: Answer the questions on the basis of the information given below.

There are three textile mills – M_1, M_2 and M_3 – in Sariska, a laidback town situated on the scenic banks of river Skirasa. The number of workers in M_1 is 30 less than that in M_2, but 20 more than that in M_3. In M_2, the number of unskilled male workers is equal to the number of unskilled female workers. The number of male workers in M_1 is equal to the number of female workers in M_3 and the number of skilled male workers in M_2 is equal to the number of unskilled female workers in M_3. Also, thrice the number of skilled male workers in M_3 is equal to the total number of unskilled male workers in M_2, which, in turn, is equal to the number of skilled female workers in M_3. The number of unskilled male workers in M_3 is 80% of the number of skilled female workers in M_1. Twice the number of unskilled male workers in M_1 is equal to the number of unskilled male workers in M_3, which, in turn, is equal to two-fifths the number of skilled female workers in M_2. It is also known that, in M_1, the number of skilled female workers is equal to the number of unskilled female workers and the total number of workers in three mills taken together is 370.

18. Which mill has the highest number of skilled male workers?

(1) M_1 (2) M_2 (3) M_3 (4) Cannot be determined

19. The number of skilled female workers in M_3 is what percentage of that in M_2?

(1) 60% (2) 40% (3) 50% (4) 70%

20. What is the absolute difference between the total number of female workers and that of the male workers in the three mills taken together?

(a) 10 (2) 20 (3) 30 (4) 40

21. The number of unskilled female workers in all the three mills together is

(1) 90 (2) 95 (3) 105 (4) 100

Directions for questions 22 to 25: Answer the questions on the basis of the information given below.

There are four companies — CCA, T & T, Birla Tea and LLL – in Udyog Nager. The following information, recorded during the FY 2014-15, is known about these four companies:

I. The local sales of LLL were eleven times the profits of T & T.

II. The sum of exports of Birla Tea and LLL is equal to half the equity base of CCA.

III. The sum of equity base of Birla Tea and the local sales of T & T is equal to five times the exports of T & T.

IV. The profit of LLL = the local sales of CCA – the exports of Birla Tea.

V. The profit of CCA is equal to the average profits of T & T and LLL.

VI. The total profit of all the companies put together was Rs. 100 crore.

VII. The local sales of Biral Tea was 1.25 times the exports of CCA.

VIII. The equity base of T & T = Total exports of all four companies – Rs. 50 crore.

IX. The equity base of LLL = 7 × (Profit of LLL + Profit of Birla Tea – Profit of T & T).

The following are some additional information regarding the four aforementioned parameters for the given companies:

1. Local sales of LLL = Rs. 110 crore
2. Equity base of CCA = Rs. 500 crore
3. Local sales of Birla Tea = Rs. 100 crore
4. Equity base of Birla Tea = Rs. 450 crore
5. Exports of T & T = Rs. 120 crore
6. Profit of Birla Tea = Rs. 40 crore
7. Exports of Birla Tea = Rs. 100 crore

22. In FY 2014-15, the equity base of LLL was

(1) Rs. 500 crore (2) Rs. 400 crore (3) Rs. 450 crore (4) Rs. 420 crore

23. In FY 2014-15, the profit of LLL was

(1) Rs. 30 crore (2) Rs. 40 crore (3) Rs. 20 crore (4) Rs. 10 crore

24. In FY 2014-15, the equity base of CCA was greater than the equity base of T & T by

(1) 10% (2) 20% (3) 25% (4) 50%

25. In FY 2014-15, the total local sales of all the four companies put together as a percentage of total equity base of all four companies put together was

(1) 36% (2) 28% (3) 32% (4) 33%

Directions for questions 26 to 29: Answer the questions on the basis of the information given below.

The Venn diagram shown below represents the past-time habits of people of age 10 years and above in five different categories - smoking, drinking, playing golf, playing cards and chewing tobacco. The numbers given in each region represent the number of people in that category. For example, 28 represents the number of people whose past-time habits are drinking and playing cards only.

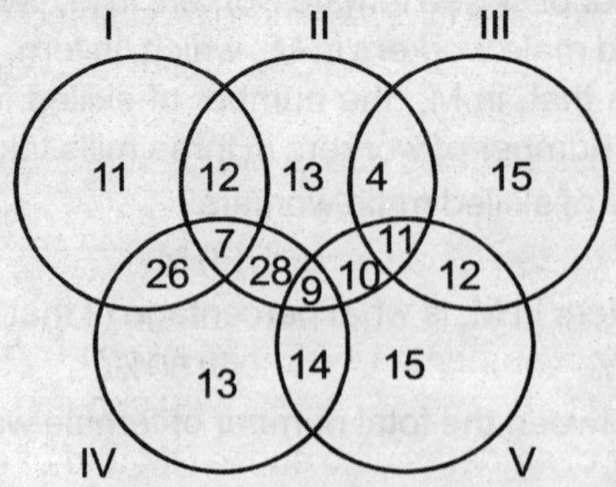

Note: All figures in 12,000s

Category I : People who smoke

Category II : People who drink

Category III : People who play golf

Category IV : People who play cards

Category V : People who chew tobacco

The pie-chart below provides additional information on further age group distribution for category IV, which holds true for each of its regions.

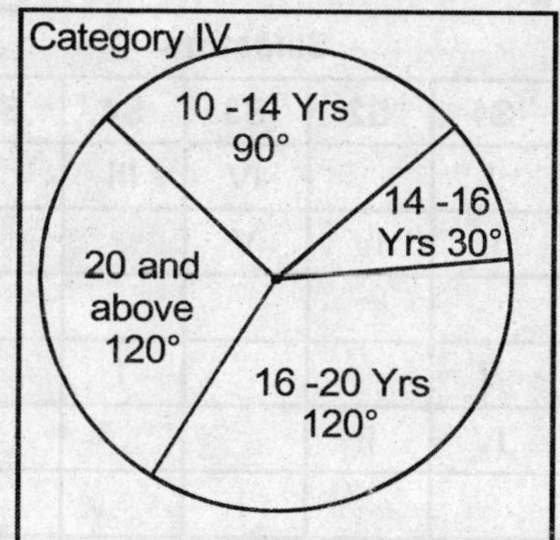

26. How many people who play cards only or play golf only belong to the age group 16-20 years ?

(1) 280000 (2) 336000 (3) 240000 (4) Data Insufficient

27. How many people who smoke and play cards belong to the age group 14-16 years ?

(1) 33000 (2) 36000 (3) 30000 (4) None of these

28. How many people who play cards and chew tobacco belong to the age group 10-14 years ?

(1) 92000 (2) 69000 (3) 72000 (4) Data Insufficient

29. If the age distribution of Category IV applies to all the five categories, then the total number of people (having these five past-time habits), who belong to the age group 20 and above, is

(1) 80000 (2) 799920 (3) 800000 (4) 670000

Directions for questions 30 to 33: Answer the questions on the basis of the information given below.

In an MBA college having 480 students, each student had to choose 3 out of 5 subjects namely Brand Management (BM), Digital Marketing (DM), Retail Marketing (RM), Consumer Behaviour (CM) and Market Research (MR). The following information is about the selection of three subjects namely BM, DM and RM by the students.

(i) Three times the number of students who chose exactly 2 of the 3 subjects was equal to the sum of the number of students who chose exactly one subject and that of those who chose exactly three subjects.

(ii) The number of students who chose both DM and RM but not BM was 16 more than that of those who chose both BM and DM but not RM.

(iii) The number of students who chose all the three subjects was at least 15.

(iv) The number of students who chose only DM was more than that of those who chose only BM.

(v) The number of students who chose both BM and DM but not RM was at least one-fifth and at most one-third that of those who chose exactly two subjects.

(vi) The number of students who chose BM was 4 less than that of those who chose RM.

(vii) The number of students who chose only RM was 6 times that of those who chose all the three subjects.

30. Students who chose only DM exceded those who chose only BM by atleast

(1) 32 (2) 13 (3) 25 (4) None of these

31. What was the maximum number of students who chose BM ?

(1) 194 (2) 211 (3) 210 (4) None of these

32. What was the minimum number of students who chose RM and exactly one out of BM and DM?

(1) 64 (2) 78 (3) 72 (4) 80

33. How many students chose atleast one among BM, DM and RM, given they had to select 3 out of 5 subjects?

(1) 450 (2) 480 (3) 432 (4) Cannot be determined

6.24 CASELET

Directions for questions 34 to 37: Answer the questions on the basis of the information given below.

Five national selectors – S_1, S_2, S_3, S_4 and S_5 – gave different grades out of I, II, III, IV and V to the cricketers on the basis of their performance in 2014.

According to the grading system, grades I, II, III, IV, and V fetch points 7,5,4,2 and 0 respectively. Grade-Average for a player is defined as the arithmetic mean of the points fetched by the grades that he was given by the selectors.

The following table gives the partial information regarding the grades, along with Grade-Average, received by a few Indian players. For example Pathan's Grade-Average is 2.8, which means the total points fetched by the grades that he was given by the selectors is 14.

Player	Selectors					Grade average
	S1	S2	S3	S4	S5	
Sehwag	I		IV	III		
Gambhir	II	IV	V			
Rahane						2.8
Uttappa	V			I		
Rohit	IV	II				3.4
Kohli			I			4
Raina	I		IV			
Dhoni	V	II				
Sachin		I				4.2
Pathan						2.8
Zaheer				II		
Harbhajan			II	II		
Ashwin		III				
Ojha						3
Umesh		II	I			

Additional Information:

(i) No selector gave grade V to Sachin and Rohit. Sachin's Grade-Average was the highest.

(ii) The Grade-Average of Sehwag was better than that of Rohit but worse than that of Kohli.

(iii) No selector gave grade I or grade V to Zaheer.

(iv) S_3 and S_5 gave the same grade to Dhoni and Ashwin. Dhoni got the same grade from S_3 and S_5.

(v) No player got grade V from more than one selector.

(vi) Three selectors gave the same grade to Uttappa.

(vii) No three selectors gave the same grade to Zaheer. The same was true for Ashwin.

34. If the Grade Average of Zaheer was better than that of Sehwag, and all the selectors, except one, gave higher grade to Zaheer than that to Sehwag, what was the grade given by S_1 to Zaheer?

(1) III (2) IV (3) II (4) Cannot be determined

35. If the Grade Average of Sehwag and Dhoni was the same, then how many different values of Grade Average were possible for Ashwin?

(1) 4 (2) 2 (3) 3 (4) 5

36. If S_3 gave higher grade than S_5 to both Sachin and Rohit, the sum of points given by S_3 to Uttappa, Sachin and Rohit can take how many different values:

(1) 5 (2) 6 (3) 4 (4) 9

37. How many different values of Grade Average are possible for Zaheer?

(1) 3 (2) 4 (3) 5 (4) 6

Directions for questions 38 to 41: Answer the questions on the basis of the information given below.

After a survey was conducted in a college to gauge how the students use their free time, the folowing observations were made:

120 students like to spend their time with girl-friends. 150 students like playing video games. 200 students like playing cricket and 170 students like watching television. 20 students like spending their time with girl-friends and playing cricket. 25 students like spending their time with girl-friends and playing video games. 25 students like watching television and playing cricket. 20 students like watching television and playing video games. 10 students like spending their time with girl-friends and watching television. 30 students like playing cricket and video games.

38. If no student has more than two interests, then how many students like playing video games or cricket but do not like watching television or spending time with their girl-friends?

(1) 230 (2) 245 (3) 225 (4) 270

39. If no student has more than two interests, then how many students like at least one out of playing video games, watching television and spending time with girl friends, but not playing cricket?

(1) 370 (2) 410 (3) 400 (4) 310

40. It is also known that the number of students who like exactly three activities is double the number of students who like all the four activities. The number of students who like any three activities, is the same for all possible combinations of three activities out of the four. Find the maximum number of students who can like all the four activities given that number of student(s) is/are an integer only.

(1) 5 (2) 4 (3) 2 (4) None of these

41. It is also known that the number of students who like exactly three activities is double the number of students who like all the four activities. The number of students who like any three activities, is the same for all possible combinations of three activities out of the four. If 79 students like to spend their time with their girl-friends only, then find the number of students who like playing cricket only.

(1) 129 (2) 139 (3) 166 (4) 183

Directions for questions 42 to 45: Answer the questions on the basis of the information given below.

Six friends decided to play a game of die, the numbers on six faces of which were from 1 to 6. They divided themselves in 3 teams – G1, G2 and G3 – with two friends in each. They played two rounds of the game. In each round, all the players threw the die once and the absolute difference (AD) between the face values obtained by the members of each team was calculated. The teams with the lowest, second highest and highest AD was declared the winner, runner up and loser respectively. The winner got 30 points, runner-up got 20 points and the loser got 10 points.

The table below shows points obtained by the teams in 2 rounds.

Teams	Points in Round 1	Points in Round 2
G1	30	30
G2	20	-
G3	10	-

Additional Data:

(i) The sum of ADs of the 3 teams in Round 1 was less than that in Round 2.

(ii) Out of 4 numbers obtained by the 2 players of G3 in two rounds, at least 2 were odd.

(iii) The sum of the four numbers obtained by the two players of G1 in the two rounds, is not a prime number.

(iv) No two friends got the same number on the die in any of the rounds. Also, no two teams had the same AD in any of the rounds.

42. If 3 players got the same value on the die, in both the rounds, what was the value on the die of the player in G2 who got the lowest value in Round1?

(1) 1 (2) 4 (3) 2 (4) Cannot be determined

43. If the same 3 players from the 3 teams got least values in their respective team in both the rounds, what is the minimum possible value of the sum of 2 values in 2 rounds for any of these 3 players?

(1) 5 (2) 4 (3) 3 (4) 2

44. For which team no player could get 4 on the die in any of the two rounds ?

(1) G3 (2) G2 (3) G1 (4) Not possible

45. Which team could definitely not get the same AD in both rounds?

(1) G1 (2) G2 (3) G3 (4) More than one of them

Directions for questions 46 to 49: Answer the questions on the basis of the information given below.

There are a total of 300 students in SRCC Hostel. Out of them 70 belong to tiger group, 85 belong to lion group and 90 belong to leopard group. Exactly 45 students belong to both tiger and lion groups, 40 students belong to both tiger and leopard groups, and 60 students belong to both lion and leopard groups.

46. If the number of students belonging to all the three groups is mean (average) of its maximum possible value and minimum possible value, how many students in the hostel do not belong to any of the three groups?

(1) 130 (2) 170 (3) 80 (4) Data insufficient

47. If the number of students belonging to all three groups is maximum possible value and tiger group starts collecting a 'Rangdari tax' from all those students who do not belong to this group at the rate of Rs. 10 per student, then what will be the amount collected by tiger group in the form of Rangdari tax?

(1) Rs. 700 (2) Rs. 2,300 (3) Rs. 1,600 (4) Rs. 900

48. If the number of students belonging to at least one of the three groups is its minimum possible value, what is the number of students who belong to only lion group?

(1) 65 (2) 20 (3) 0 (4) 55

49. If the number of students belonging to none of the three groups is maximum, how many students belong to exactly two of the three groups?

(1) 105 (2) 145 (3) 25 (4) 85

Directions for questions 50 to 53: Answer the questions on the basis of the information given below.

Seven batsmen – Ponting, Sachin, Sehwag, Gambhir, Warner, Smith and Yuvraj – played in a test match between India and Australia. The number of balls faced by them are 300, 240, 180, 160, 270, 120 and 150 not necessarily in the same order and their strike rates are 33.3%, 60%, 30%, 40%, 80%, 45% and 50% in any order.

Strike rate = (Number of runs scored/ Number of balls faced) × 100

Additional information is also given:

1. No batsman, out of the seven, scored 150 or more runs and the lowest runs scored by any of the seven batsmen was 60.
2. Ponting was the highest scorer, and either he faced the maximum number of balls or his strike rate was the highest among all.
3. The Strike rate of one of Ponting and Sachin, was twice of the other.
4. Runs scored by each of them was different, except Sehwag and Yuvraj. These two batsmen scored 60 runs each.
5. Smith scored 81 runs and Gambhir scored 108 runs.

50. What was the strike rate of Sachin?

(1) 30% (2) 40% (3) 35% (4) 45%

51. Who faced the least number of balls?

(1) Sehwag (2) Yuvraj (3) Warner (4) Either Sehwag or Yuvraj

52. Who was the second highest scorer?

(1) Gambhir (2) Warner (3) Sachin (4) Smith

53. How many runs did Warner score?

(1) 90 (2) 96 (3) 120 (4) None of these

Directions for questions 54 to 57: Answer the questions on the basis of the information given below.

A survey was conducted among 120 kids to gauge their preference for ice cream, chocolate and milkshake. It was found that the number of kids who liked at most two of these items was three times that of those who liked at least 2 of these items. The number of kids who like only chocolate was more than that of those who liked only ice cream, which, in turn, was more than that of those who liked only milkshake.

54. The number of kids who did not like either of the three items was one-fifth of those who liked exactly two items, then which of the following could be the number of kids who liked exactly one of the three items?

(1) 80 (2) 81 (3) 82 (4) 85

55. If the number of kids who did not like either of three items was less than that of those who liked only milkshake, then the number of kids who did not like any of the three items could not be more than

(1) 19 (2) 20 (3) 21 (4) 22

56. If each of the kids liked atleast one of the three items, the number of kids who liked only chocolate was 36 and the number of kids who liked ice cream was equal to that of those who liked chocolate, the number of kids who liked ice cream could not be more than

(1) 84 (2) 75 (3) 74 (4) 85

57. If each of the kids liked atleast one of the three items, the number of kids who liked only chocolate was 36 and the number of kids who liked ice cream was equal to that of those who liked chocolate, the number of kids who liked chocolate and ice cream but not milkshake could not be more than

(1) 40 (2) 39 (3) 37 (4) Cannot be determined

Directions for questions 58 to 61: Answer the questions on the basis of the information given below.

Seven candidates namely Ashok, Jitesh, Pravesh, Kalash, Ragini, Shiela and Hakim contested for the post of president of student union in Delhi University. In Round 1, if any candidate gets more than 50% of the total number of votes cast in that round, he/she is declared the winner, else top five candidates based on number of votes move to Round 2. In Round 2, if any candidate gets more than 50% of the total number of votes cast in that round, he/she is declared the winner, else top three candidates based on number of votes move to Round 3. In Round 3, the candidate who gets the maximum number of votes out of total number of votes cast in that round is declared the winner. In any round, no two candidates got the same number of votes. The table below shows the number of votes received by the candidates in Round 1 of the election.

Name of candidate	Number of votes received in Round 1
Ashok	3047
Jitesh	3112
Pravesh	3084
Kalash	3140
Hakim	3008
Ragini	3149
Shiela	3160

58. If 15000 votes were cast in Round 2, then the value of the sum of the number of votes received by the candidate who got the maximum votes and the number of votes received by the candidate who got minimum votes in that round could not be less than

(1) 3455 (2) 3752 (3) 3680 (4) 3684

59. If the winner was decided after the Round 3 and 10,000 votes were cast in each of Round 2 and Rcund 3, then total number of votes received, in the three rounds put together, by a candidate who was not the winner could not be more than

(1) 13158 (2) 13083 (3) 13082 (4) 13159

60. If 8000 votes were cast in Round 2 and 12000 votes were cast in Round 3, then the total number of votes received, in the three rounds put together, by the candidate who won the election could not be less than

(1) 7087 (2) 7009 (3) 7011 (4) 7085

61. The number of votes received, in the first two round put together, by a candidate who Reached Round 3 could not be less than

(1) 3010 (2) 3086 (3) 3087 (4) Data insufficient

Directions for questions 62 to 65: Answer the questions on the basis of the information given below.

Six friends – Hasan, Ram, Sanjay, Sunil, Alam and Govind – went to a shopping mall and each of them purchased some items. There were nine different types of items in the mall. The per unit price (in Rs.) of each of the nine items was a different integer out of 100, 200, 400, 600, 700, 900, 1100, 1200 and 1400. A total of 25 items were purchased by the six friends, and the number of items purchased by Hasan was the minimum. Alam and Govind purchased the same number of items and the number of items purchsed by Alam was more than that by Sanjay, who did not purchase 3 items. No two friends purchased the same combinations of items. It is also known that:

(i) Each friend bought at least 3 items but not more than 5 items. Also, no friend bought more than one unit of any of the nine items.
(ii) The amount spent by Hasan was Rs. 2000, which was not less than the amount spent by Govind.
(iii) Hasan did not purchase the costliest item. Alam purchased both the cheapest and the costliest items.
(iv) The amount spent by Alam was twice the amount spent by Govind. The amount spent by Sunil was average of the amount spent by Alam and Govind.
(v) An item purchased by Sunil was priced Rs. 1100. The amount spent by each of Ram and Sanjay was not more than the amount spent by Sunil.
(vi) Two units were purchased of each type of the items that were priced Rs. 100, Rs. 400 and Rs. 600.
(vii) Not more than two friends purchased 5 items each.

62. The price (in Rs.) of the item that was purchased by the maximum number of friends was
(1) 200 (2) 700 (3) 900 (4) 1100

63. The amount spent (in Rs.) by Sanjay was
(1) 2900 (2) 3000
(3) Either 2900 or 3000 (4) None of these

64. Which of the following statements is/are definitely true?
(i) The amount spent by Ram was more than that by Sanjay.
(ii) The item priced Rs. 1100 was purchased by four friends.
(1) Only (i) (2) Both (i) and (ii) (3) Only (ii) (4) Neither (i) nor (ii)

65. How many types of items were purchased by Hasan and Ram but not by Govind?
(1) 1 (2) 2 (3) 3 (4) Cannot be determined

Direction for questions 66 to 69: Answer the questions on the basis of the information given below.

Six gentlemen viz. Mr. Gupta, Mr. Pandey, Mr. Sharma, Mr. Chowbey, Mr. Haathi and Mr. Handa went to Megacity Shopping Mall for shopping. Each one of them bought exactly one item. The items bought (not necessarily in that order) were – Dress, Sweater, Camera, Telephone, Tires, Bicycle. The list price of these items (not necessarily in that order) was – Rs. 200, Rs. 1500, Rs. 300, Rs. 2000, Rs. 900 and Rs. 1200 and the price paid (after various discounts) was – Rs. 800, Rs. 600, Rs. 1200, Rs. 1000, Rs. 75 and Rs. 50. The following information is also available:

1. Mr. Gupta bought a clothing item.
2. The bicycle was bought at 50% off and its buyer's name starts with H.
3. Mr. Chowbey bought the item priced at Rs. 1500 for 4/5th of the list price.
4. The tires set was sold for Rs. 100 less than the list price.
5. The item that was sold for Rs. 50 was an article of clothing.
6. Mr. Pandey spent Rs. 400 less than that by Mr. Chowbey.
7. Mr. Haathi paid for the dress with a Rs. 100 note (value equal to 50% of the list price) and received Rs. 25 in change.
8. Mr. Gupta spent less than Mr. Sharma, who spent less than Mr. Pandey.
9. The item originally priced the highest was not sold for the highest price and the lowest priced item was not sold for the lowest amount.
10. The price paid for telephone was more than that for the Camera.

66. Who bought the Camera?
(1) Mr. Gupta (2) Mr. Pandey (3) Mr. Sharma (4) Mr. Handa

67. Who paid the highest price?
(1) Mr. Sharma (2) Mr. Handa (3) Mr. Haathi (4) Mr. Chowbey

68. What did Mr. Handa buy?
(1) The camera (2) The sweater (3) The tires (4) The bicycle

69. What was the percentage discount on the highest original price item?
(1) 70% (2) 50% (3) 25% (4) 75%

ANSWER KEYS

PRACTICE EXERCISE – 1

1. (3)	**2.** (3)	**3.** (3)	**4.** (1)	**5.** (4)	**6.** (1)	**7.** (2)	**8.** (4)	**9.** (1)	**10.** (4)
11. (1)	**12.** (2)	**13.** (1)	**14.** (1)	**15.** (2)	**16.** (4)	**17.** (3)	**18.** (3)	**19.** (4)	**20.** (2)
21. (4)	**22.** (1)	**23.** (1)	**24.** (4)	**25.** (2)	**26.** (4)	**27.** (3)	**28.** (1)	**29.** (2)	**30.** (2)
31. (2)	**32.** (4)	**33.** (2)	**34.** (2)	**35.** (1)	**36.** (1)	**37.** (3)	**38.** (4)	**39.** (4)	**40.** (3)
41. (1)	**42.** (2)	**43.** (2)	**44.** (1)	**45.** (3)	**46.** (1)	**47.** (3)	**48.** (2)	**49.** (1)	**50.** (2)
51. (2)	**52.** (4)	**53.** (3)	**54.** (4)	**55.** (4)	**56.** (1)	**57.** (3)	**58.** (2)	**59.** (4)	**60.** (4)
61. (4)	**62.** (1)	**63.** (4)	**64.** (4)	**65.** (4)	**66.** (1)	**67.** (1)	**68.** (1)	**69.** (1)	**70.** (3)
71. (3)	**72.** (2)	**73.** (4)	**74.** (4)	**75.** (4)	**76.** (2)	**77.** (1)	**78.** (4)		

PRACTICE EXERCISE – 2

1. (4)	**2.** (4)	**3.** (4)	**4.** (4)	**5.** (3)	**6.** (4)	**7.** (1)	**8.** (2)	**9.** (2)	**10.** (1)
11. (3)	**12.** (4)	**13.** (3)	**14.** (1)	**15.** (4)	**16.** (4)	**17.** (4)	**18.** (1)	**19.** (1)	**20.** (3)
21. (2)	**22.** (4)	**23.** (1)	**24.** (3)	**25.** (2)	**26.** (4)	**27.** (1)	**28.** (2)	**29.** (3)	**30.** (2)
31. (2)	**32.** (4)	**33.** (2)	**34.** (2)	**35.** (3)	**36.** (3)	**37.** (1)	**38.** (1)	**39.** (4)	**40.** (2)
41. (2)	**42.** (2)	**43.** (4)	**44.** (1)	**45.** (2)	**46.** (2)	**47.** (2)	**48.** (3)	**49.** (4)	**50.** (2)
51. (4)	**52.** (3)	**53.** (1)	**54.** (2)	**55.** (3)	**56.** (2)	**57.** (2)	**58.** (2)	**59.** (4)	**60.** (1)
61. (2)	**62.** (1)	**63.** (3)	**64.** (3)	**65.** (4)	**66.** (3)	**67.** (4)	**68.** (4)	**69.** (2)	

EXPLANATIONS

PRACTICE EXERCISE – 1

For questions 1 to 4:

From statement 1 Shane received 0 cookies. From statement 3, Shane and Chris, and Matthew and Graham can have [(0,1)(2,3)] or [(0,2)(1,3)] or [(0,3)(1,4)] cookies respectively.

Using statements 2 and 4 we can conclude that only possible case is [(0,3)(1,4)]. So Greame must have got 2 cookies.

Using statement 1 and statement 7 we can say that Graham and Greame like wrestling shows, as Shane likes a sports show and there are only two sports shows. From statement 5, Matthew likes Smackdown and Shane likes Sports Center. So Chris likes Hitz.

From statement 6 Graham likes Krackjack.

From statement 8 Greame likes Hide n Seek or Good Day. Shane likes Good Day or Bon-Bon. Matthew likes Hide n Seek or Bon-Bon or Good Day.

Name	No. of cookies	TV show	Type of Biscuit
Shane	0	Sports Center	Good Day/Bon-Bon
Matthew	1	Smackdown	Hide n Seek/Bon-Bon/Good Day
Greame	2	Raw/Wrestlemania	Hide n Seek/Good Day
Chris	3	Hitz	Maska Chaska
Graham	4	Wrestlemania/Raw	Krackjack

1. Raw – Bon Bon cannot be a matching pair, which is liked by the same person.

5. As given in the question, we can frame some relation i.e. A > B > C and P > S.

Now look at each option, (1), (2) and (3), we find that all these options are possible, now check option (4). Option (4), when Alex is not the stoutest, Paul is the stoutest. That is, Paul is No. 1 (in stoutness) Cedric cannot then be No. 3, as both Alex and Ben are above him, and hence Cedric can at best be No. 4 in the descending order (i.e. Cedric can only be No. 1 or No. 2 in the ascending order of stoutness. He cannot be No. 3 in the ascending order). Hence, which is given under this choice is not possible.

6. Similarly, check out the options as we did for previous question. Only option (1) is possible.

For questions 8 to 11:

From statement (vii), its clear that four jungles had 3 animals each and three jungles had 2 animals each.

So, the total number of animals in the five jungles put together = $(4 \times 3) + (3 \times 2) = 18$

Let the number of jungles in which Zathura, Zakura and Fatura were present be x and the number of jungles in which Tandura was present be y.

From statement (ii),

$3x + y = 18 \Rightarrow y = 3(6 - x)$

It can be noted that x = 6 is not possible; that means y = 0, which is not possible as Tandura was present in E, from statement (v). Similarly, x = 4 is also not possible, as from statements (v) and (vi), Tandura was not present in F and G.

Hence, x = 5 and y = 3.

We can also deduce from statement (ii) that Tandura was dominant in only one jungle, and from statement (v), it was E. Zakura and Fatura were the dominant animals of G and F respectively as per statements (iv) and (vi). From statements (iii) and (viii), A, B, C and D must have had Zathura, Zakura and Fatura as the dominant animal, not necessarily in that order. Also, Zathura must have been the dominant animal of jungle C.

The jungle G did not have Zathura and Fatura as the other two animals along with the dominant animal Zakura, as a combination, were present in jungle F. Hence, G had Zakura and Fatura only.

Now, its clear that Zathura was not present in jungles E and G, so it must have been present in all the other jungles and was dominant animal of jungle B. As Fatura was not present in A and Zakura was not present in D, Zakura and Fatura must have been the dominant animals of A and D respectively.

Further analysis leads to the following tables:

Jungle	Dominant animal	Other animals
A	Zakura	Zathura, Tandura
B	Zathura	Zakura/ Fatura
C	Zathura	Fatura/Zakura
D	Fatura	Zathura, Tandura
E	Tandura	Zakura, Fatura
F	Fatura	Zakura, Zathura
G	Zakura	Fatura

8. Both (1) and (2) are true.
9. The animals present cannot be determined uniquely for B and C.

For questions 12 to 14:

Let the number of notes that Galu had be x.

The number of notes with each of the remaining six persons = x + 5

$\therefore 6(x + 5) + x = 100 \Rightarrow x = 10$

So, initially Galu had 10 notes and the rest had 15 each.

The five transactions T1, T2, T3, T4, T5 are:

T1 : Kalu gave 5 notes to Lalu

T2 : Malu gave 3 notes to Dalu

T3 : Malu received 1 note from Galu

T4 : Falu received 2 notes

T5 : Dalu received some notes

By using statements (i) and (iii), it can be concluded that the number of notes after the first three transactions with Lalu, Malu, Dalu, Kalu and Galu were 20, 13, 18, 10 and 9 notes respectively.

By using statement (iv), it is apparent that Salu, Kalu and Galu did not receive any note. Now as the number of people who did not give any note was 2. It means the giver in each transaction was different.

By using statements (v) and (vi), Falu and Dalu had 17 notes in the end. Hence, Dalu must be the one who gave the two notes to Falu.

Dalu must have received one note from someone else. We know that the giver could not be Falu. It could not be Lalu either, as Lalu had to have 20 notes in the end. As we know that the givers in all the five transactions are different, Kalu, Malu and Galu are also ruled out. Hence, Salu must have given the note to Dalu.

Further analysis leads to the following table:

Persons	Initial number of notes	Notes received	Notes given	Final number of notes
Lalu	15	5	0	20
Malu	15	1	3	13
Salu	15	0	1	14
Dalu	15	3+1	2	17
Kalu	15	0	5	10
Falu	15	2	0	17
Galu	10	0	1	9

For questions 15 to 18:

From statement IV and V, it can be deduced that V stayed in room no. 30, which has the maximum number of factors out of the given room numbers, and T stayed in room no. 35. Now, from statements I and III, it can be concluded that P and Q stayed in room numbers 32 and 33 respectively, and S stayed in room no. 16. Now, it can be concluded that R stayed in room no. 20 as no two directors, except P and Q, stayed in the two adjacent rooms. From statement VI, it can be asserted that W stayed in room no. 18. From statement II, it can be concluded that U stayed in either room no. 17, 19 or 31.

The above derived conclusions can be tabulated as follows:

R		W		S		
20	19	18	17	16	15	Riverside
30	31	32	33	34	35	Jungleview
V		P	Q		T	

15. As Y stayed in Riverside, U must have also stayed in Riverside. The third person in Riverside was X. U could occupy a room in Riverside in 2 ways (room number 17 or 19). The remaining 2 people could occupy the other 2 rooms in 2 different ways. Similarly, Z and F could occupy the remaining 2 rooms in Jungleview in 2 different ways.

Therefore, the required number of ways

= 2 × 2 × 2 = 8.

16. Since R and T did not stay in the same resort, R could not be a part of the team that has T in it.

17. W's room was not opposite to T's room.

18. 8 professionals were not eligible for the lucky draw. The 4 eligible participants were P, Q, occupant of room number 19 and occupant of room number 17.

For questions: 19 to 21:

As per the given information,

$2A + 2C + 4D = 80 \Rightarrow A + C + 2D = 40$

Since, A is the largest of all the mentioned letters, A cannot be equal to 5, 10, 30 or 35.

The possible values of A are 15, 20 and 25.

19. There are three possibilities.

Case I: When A = 15.

$C + 2D = 25 \Rightarrow C = 5$ and $D = 10$.

Therefore, A + C + D = 15 + 5 + 10 = 30

Case II: When A = 20.

$C + 2D = 20 \Rightarrow C = 10$ and $D = 5$.

Therefore, A + C + D = 20 + 10 + 5 = 35

Case III: When A = 25.

$C + 2D = 15, \Rightarrow C = 5$ and $D = 5$.

Therefore, A + C + D = 25 + 5 + 5 = 35

Therefore, (A + C + D) can have two values and these are 30 and 35. Hence, option (d) is a correct answer.

20. 20 is a possible value of A.

21. In order to minimize the value of B, we have to minimize the value of (A + B + C + D). Since A + C + D = 30 or 35, therefore the minimum possible value of (A + B + C + D) which is a multiple of 4 is 40. Hence, the minimum possible value of B is 5.

For questions 22 to 25:

Since 15 and 30 are the two numbers that are already filled in the boxes of the matrix, therefore the 16 consecutive natural numbers are from 15 to 30.

Sum of these 16 numbers $= \frac{16(15+30)}{2} = 8 \times 45$

Sum of the numbers in the cells of any row or any column or any diagonal of the square matrix is $\frac{8 \times 45}{4} = 90$

Hence, A + B = 57; C + G = 48; F + J = 42; E + H = 45; D + I = 45 and K + L = 33.

Therefore, $(K, L) \rightarrow (17, 16)$ or $(16, 17)$.

Similarly, $(A, B) \rightarrow (28, 29)$ or $(29, 28)$.

Also, $E = 66 - 45 = 21 \Rightarrow H = 24$

$(C, G) \rightarrow (22, 26), (26, 22), (23, 25), (25, 23)$

$(F, J) \rightarrow (19, 23), (23, 19), (20, 22), (22, 20)$

$(D, I) \rightarrow (19, 26), (26, 19), (20, 25), (25, 20), (22, 23), (23, 22)$

In the third column, E = 21. So, B + I + L = 69

The only combination of (B, L) that satisfies without violating any condition is (28, 16).

Hence, I = 25, D = 20, K = 17, A = 29, B = 28, L = 16, H = 24 and E = 21

Now, $(C, G) \rightarrow (22, 26), (26, 22)$ and $(C, F) \rightarrow (23, 26), (26, 23)$

Hence, C = 26, G = 22, F = 23 and J = 19.

Finally the given matrix will look like as follows:

15	29	28	18
26	20	21	23
22	24	25	19
27	17	16	30

22. Since C = 26, 4 numbers are numerically greater then C.

23. (A + I) – (B + H) = 54 – 52 = 2.

24. The 16 consecutive natural numbers could be from 'n' to 'n + 15', where 'n' is a natural number.

Sum of these numbers

$= \frac{16(n+n+15)}{2} = 16n + 120.$

Sum of the numbers in the boxes of any row

$= \frac{16n+120}{4} = 4n + 30.$

Only option (4), i.e. 170 gives a integer value of n.

25. The value of C is 26.

For questions 26 to 29:

On the besis of the given information, preliminary table can be drawn as shown below:

	Radha	Pamela	Jaspinder	Ameena
Boxer				×
Zorro				×
Tommy	×	×	×	√
Jacky				×

Pamela's pet dog is neither Boxer nor Jacky. Hence, amela's dog is Zorro.

Ameena's husband is either Peter or Ramanpreet. Peter's pet dog is Boxer. Hence Ameena, owner of Tommy, cannot be the wife of Peter. Therefore, Ameena is the wife of Ramanpreet.

Pet dog of Qureshi is not Jacky. Shyam's wife is not Jaspinder.

Further analysis leads to the final table.

	Radha	Pamela	Jaspinder	Ameena	
Boxer	×	×	√	×	Peter
Zorro	×	√	×	×	Qureshi
Tommy	×	×	×	√	Ramanpreet
Jacky	√	×	×	×	Shyam

26. Husband of Radha is Shyam.

27. Boxer is the pet dog of Jaspinder.

28. Zorro is the pet dog of Qureshi.

29. Only (iii) is correct.

For questions 30 to 32:

A total of 5 different arrangements are possible

$X_1 - X_3 \quad X_2 - X_5 \quad X_4 - X_6$

$X_1 - X_4 \quad X_2 - X_5 \quad X_3 - X_6$

$X_1 - X_4 \quad X_2 - X_6 \quad X_3 - X_5$

$X_1 - X_5 \quad X_2 - X_4 \quad X_3 - X_6$

$X_1 - X_6 \quad X_2 - X_4 \quad X_3 - X_5$

30. Among the various possible arrangement shown above, there are two possible arrangements for (X_1, X_4).

31. If the pairs (X_1, X_3), (X_1, X_5), (X_1, X_6), (X_2, X_6) or (X_4, X_6) are given, then all other pairs can be determined, while if the pairs (X_1, X_4), (X_2, X_4), (X_2, X_5), (X_3, X_5) or (X_3, X_6) are given, then all other pairs can't be determined.

Therefore required probability

$$= \frac{\text{Total number of favourable cases}}{\text{Total number of possible cases}} = \frac{5}{10}$$

32. If X_2 and X_4 are kept in one cage then X_1 and X_3 cannot be kept together as in that case X_5 and X_6 will have to be paired, which violates the given condition.

For questions 33 to 35:

Only those cities that have three roads emanating from them can be start/end city.

33. All the routes which start from city 2, ends at city 4 and all the routes which start from city 4, ends at city 2.

34. Three routes starts from city 2 and city 4 each.

35. There is no such route which starts and ends at the same city.

For questions 36 to 38:

36. All of the given children can possibly be from Dahiya family.

<u>Case I</u>:

Afsana and Siddharth are from Dahiya family.

Age of Afsana in Jan 2001 = 9 years and 11 months.

Age of Siddharth in Jan 2001 = 2 years and 3 months.

Average age = 6 years and 1 month.

<u>Case II</u>:

Anjan and Samaksh are from Dahiya family.

Age of Anjan in Jan 2001 = 5 years and 8 months.

Age of Samaksh in Jan 2001 = 6 years and 6 months.

Average age = 6 years and 1 month.

<u>Case III</u>:

Afsana, Anjan and Ansar are from Dahiya family.

Age of Afsana in Jan 2001 = 9 years and 11 months.

Age of Anjan in Jan 2001 = 5 years and 8 months.

Age of Ansar in Jan 2001 = 2 years and 8 months.

Average age = 6 years and 1 month.

37. Case I: One case is possible when 1st child of Khanna family is Samaksh and second child is Sami, born in January 2000. Children of Ahuja family can be Ansar and Aditya.

Age of Aditya in January 2000 = 46 months.

Age of Ansar in January 2000 = 20 months.

Age of Samaksh in January 2000 = 66 months.

Age of Sami in January 2000 = 0 month.

$$\therefore \text{Average age} = \frac{46+20}{2} = \frac{66+0}{2}$$

Case II: Another case is possible when 1st child of Khanna family is Salim and second child is Sami, born in January 2000. Children of Ahuja family can be Akash and Sandy.

Age of Akash in January 2000 = 81 months.

Age of Sandy in January 2000 = 7 months.

Age of Salim in January 2000 = 88 months.

Age of Sami in January 2000 = 0 month.

$$\therefore \text{Average age} = \frac{81+7}{2} = \frac{88+0}{2}$$

38. Age of children as on January 2000 (in months) is given below.

Name	Age
Akash	81
Anjan	56
Ansar	20
Afsana	107
Aditya	46
Anirudh	63
Sandy	7
Siddharth	15
Salim	88
Sukrit	97
Sami	0
Samaksh	66

Now, average age of children will be integer number of years only if their age adds up to 36 months, 72 months, 108 months .... and so on.

For that to happen sum of age of children (in months) should be a multiple of 3 at any point of time.

Among the given options, only the sum of ages (in months) of Afsana, Ansar and Anjan is a multiple of 3.

For questions 39 to 42:

From statement (ii) the possibilities are

Akansh	7/9	11/13	7/11	9/13
Ajay	9/7	13/11	11/7	13/9
Ashok	11/13	7/9	9/13	7/11
Abhishek	13/11	9/7	13/9	11/7

From statement (v), Ajay's salary = 11,00,000.

$\Rightarrow$ Ashok's salary = 7,00,000 or 13,00,000.

$\Rightarrow$ Akansh's salary = 13,00,000 or 7,00,000.

Thus, the final scenario is as follows:

	Akansh	Ajay	Ashok	Abhishek	Amit
Salaries (In Rs. Lakh)	7 or 13	11	13 or 7	9	8
Cities:	K/V	B/K/V	B/K/V	Prabandhnagar	Joka

39. If Akansh, lives in Vastrapur, then Ajay and Ashok must be staying at Kunnamangalam and Banerghatta, not necessarily in that order. Their average salary in any case will be Rs. 12 lakhs or 9 lakhs. So the data is insufficient.

40. Abhishek lives in Prabandhnagar.

41. Amit lives in Joka, so Ajay must be living at Kunnamangalam. Since Akansh is not staying at Banerghatta, he must be staying at Vastrapur.

42. As person from Banerghatta did not earn maximum or minimum salary so he earns Rs.11 lakhs (from table). So average salary of persons living in Kunnamanglam and Vastrapur is $\left(\frac{13+7}{2}\right)$

= Rs.10 lakhs.

For questions 43 to 45:

From statement (i), E's anniversary date can be 14th or 24th and that of H can be 7th or 12th in that order.

From statement (ii), the anniversary date of D can be 7th May or 12th December and correspondingly C's anniversary date can be 12th or 24th.

From statement (iii), the anniversary date of A-E can be 24th May or 14th May or 14th March.

From above conclusions and statement (iv), we can conclude that A's marriage anniversary is on 14th March and D's marriage anniversary is on 7th May.

Thus, C's anniversary date comes out to be 12th. For both D and H, the marriage anniversary date comes out to be 7th May. So, they must form a couple.

Husband	A	B	C	D
Wife	E	F/G	G/F	H
Anniversary date	14	24	12	7
Month	March	Oct/Dec	Dec/Oct	May

43. Only option (2) is a possible combination.

For questions 44 and 45:

The possible anniversary dates of F can be 24th October or 24th December or 12th October or 12th December.

Among these only 24th October and 24th December gives the maximum value, in other cases sum is not maximum.

But 24th December = 24 + 12 = 36 is a perfect square.

So F's anniversary is on 24th October.

As B has his anniversary date on 24th so F is the wife of B.

44. B is the husband of F.

45. G's marriage anniversary is on 12th December.

For questions 46 to 49:

For batch I,

Andy Grove cannot take session 3 as he is busy with batch II at same time. He cannot take session 5 also, as he is not an expert in IBM. So, he will take session 1 of batch I.

For batch III,

S.G. Pitroda cannot take session 4 as he is already occupied with batch I and he cannot take session 5 as he is not an expert in SM. So, he will take session 3 of batch III.

Now, session 5 can be taken by either Kiran Deshpande or Andy Grove. If Andy Grove takes session 5 of SM, then Kiran Deshpande will have to take ITS, which is not possible as S.G. Pitroda is already scheduled for session 3 of ITS. Therefore, Kiran Deshpande will take session 5 and Andy Grove will take session 4.

Andy Grove is an expert in LFTD and SM but SM is already scheduled with Kiran Deshpande, so Andy Grove will take LFTD. Similarly, Narayan Murthy will take IBM and Kishor Bayani will take SMkt.

So the table will look like:

Session	Batch					
	I		II		III	
	Faculty	Subject	Faculty	Subject	Faculty	Subject
1	Andy Grove			ITS	Kishor Bayani	SMkt
2	Kiran Deshpande				Narayan Murthy	IBM
3			Andy Grove		S.G. Pitroda	ITS
4	S.G. Pitroda			IBM	Andy Grove	LFTD
5		IBM			Kiran Deshpande	SM

Case I: Andy Grove teaching LFTD to batch II in session 3.

If Andy Grove teaches LFTD to batch II in session 3, SM will be taken by Kiran Deshpande. But Kiran Deshpande is not available for batch II in session 2 or session 5. Thus, this case is not possible.

Case II: Andy Grove teaching SM to batch II in session 3.

Batch II:

Thus, LFTD can be taught by Narayan Murthy only. But he is with batch III in session 2. Hence, he can be with batch II in session 5 only.

⇒ IBM in session 4 will be taught by Bayani.

⇒ Pitroda teaches SMkt in session 2.

⇒ Kiran Deshpande teaches ITS in session 1.

Batch I:

IBM in session 5 can be taught by Kishor Bayani only, because Narayan Murthy is busy with batch II.

⇒ Narayan Murthy teaches LFTD in session 3.

⇒ Andy Grove teaches SM in session 1.

⇒ Kiran Deshpande teaches ITS in session 2.

⇒ S.G. Pitroda teaches SMkt in session 4.

Session	Batch					
	I		II		III	
	Faculty	Subject	Faculty	Subject	Faculty	Subject
1	Andy Grove	SM	Kiran Deshpande	ITS	Kishor Bayani	SMkt
2	Kiran Deshpande	ITS	S.G. Pitroda	SMkt	Narayan Murthy	IBM
3	Narayan Murthy	LFTD	Andy Grove	SM	S.G. Pitroda	ITS
4	S.G. Pitroda	SMkt	Kishor Bayani	IBM	Andy Grove	LFTD
5	Kishor Bayani	IBM	Narayan Murthy	LFTD	Kiran Deshpande	SM

46. In batch I, SM and ITS are taught by Andy Grove and Kiran Deshpande respectively.

47. In batch III, IBM and SM are taught by Narayan Murthy and Kiran Deshpande respectively.

48. In batch I, Kishor Bayani taught IBM and Narayan Murthy taught LFTD.

49. The last two lectures of batch II were taken by Narayan Murthy and Kishor Bayani.

50. For finding the maximum number of question papers coming to V C let us assume that number of students in XI C and IV A is minimum possible i.e. 50 and 10 respectively.

Sum of minimum number of question papers required in I A, IV A, X B and VII B = 90 + 10 + 10 + 40 = 150

Let us assume that requirement of classes I A, IV A, X B and VII B is fulfilled by 150 questions papers coming to class I A.

Hence, requirements of classes XI C and V C are to be fulfilled by question papers coming from I B.

Since class XI C can receive question papers only from class VII B, therefore 50 question papers from class I B should come to class VII B.

Maximum number of question papers that can come to V C from II C = (150 – (80 + 10 + 10)) = 50

Maximum number of question papers that can come to class V C from class I B = 150 – (60 + 50) = 40.

∴ Maximum number of question papers that can come to class V C = 50 + 40 = 90.

51. Let the number of students in each of the classes V C and XI C be 'x'.

Least possible number of students in IX D = 10

Hence total number of students in classes IV A, V C and XI C = (3 ×150) – (90 + 60 + 80 + 40 + 40 + 10 + 10) = 450 – 330 = 120

As number of students in each class is a multiple of 10

∴ x is a multiple of 10 and 2x is a multiple of 20

Hence, minimum number of students in class IV A will be when x = 50,

∴ Minimum number of students in IV A = 120 – 100 = 20.

52. Let the number of question papers going from classroom I A to classroom IV A be x.

Therefore, the number of question papers going from classroom I A to classroom VII B will be 60 – x.

Let the number of question papers going from classroom I B to classroom VII B be y and let the number of question papers going from classroom II C to classroom V C be z.

∴ The number of question papers going from classroom I B to classroom V C will be 90 – y and the number of question papers going from classroom II C to classroom VII A will be 70 – z.

Thus, the figure would be as follows:

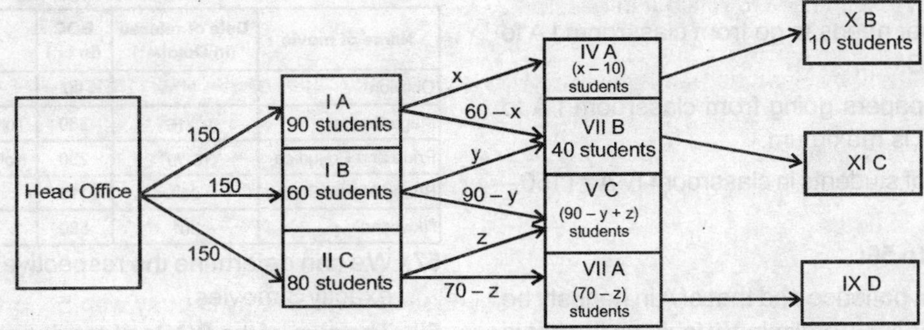

The question can be interpreted as, find the maximum number of student in classroom V C,

i.e. maximize (90 – y + z).

In order to do so, y should be minimum possible and z should be maximum possible.

Minimum number of students in classrooms VII A and IX D are 10 each.

∴ Maximum value of z = 50.

Also, minimum number of students in classrooms IV A and XI C = 10 each.

∴ Total number of students in classrooms IV A, X B, XI C and VII B combined = 70.

∴ Minimum value of y = 70 – 60 = 10.

∴ Maximum value of (90 – y + z) = 90 – 10 + 50 = 130.

53. Let the number of question papers going from classroom I A to classroom IV A be x.

Therefore, the number of question papers going from classroom I A to classroom VII B will be 60 – x.

Let the number of question papers going from classroom I B to classroom VII B be y and let the number of question papers going from classroom II C to classroom V C be z.

∴ The number of question papers going from classroom I B to classroom V C will be 90 – y and the number of question papers going from classroom II C to classroom VII A will be 70 – z.

Thus, the figure would be as follows:

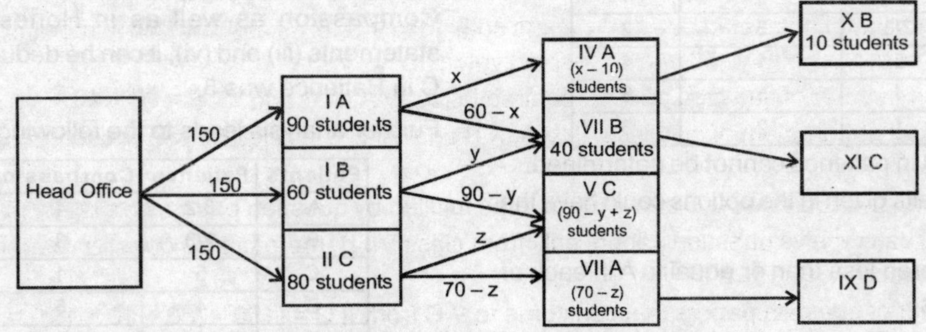

The question asks us to maximize the value of (x – 10).

By the problem, 70 – z = 50

$\Rightarrow z = 20$.

In order to maximize the value of $(x - 10)$ we must maximize the value of x.

The number of students in classroom V C = $90 - y + z = 110 - y$.

The number of question papers going from classroom I B to classroom V C = $90 - y$.

$\therefore 90 - y \geq 0$.

$\Rightarrow y \leq 90$.

$\therefore$ Maximum value of y = 90.

Thus, question papers coming from classroom I B can be distributed to all students of classrooms VII B and XI C.

Hence, no paper needs to go from classroom I A to classroom VII B.

$\therefore$ Number of papers going from classroom I A to classroom IV A is maximum.

Thus, number of students in classroom IV A = $(150 - 90) - 10 = 50$.

For questions 54 to 56:

Let the score of E in patience and that of A in honesty be x and y respectively. Now, preliminary table on the basis of the given information can be drawn as shown below.

Patients	Patience	Compassion	Honesty
A		4	y
B			
C		y	4
D	4		
E	x	x + 1	x + 2

Since scores of no two patients were same in any of the traits, the value x of must have been 1. From statements (vi) and (vii), it is obvious that the scores of B and C in Compassion could not be 5. So the score of D in Compassion as well as in Honesty was 5. From statements (iii) and (vi), it can be deduced that the score C in Patience was 5.

Further analysis leads to the following table.

Patients	Patience	Compassion	Honesty
A	3/2	4	1
B	2/3	3	**2**
C	5	1	4
D	4	5	5
E	1	2	3

54. The score of A in patience cannot be determined.

55. The pairs of traits given in the options could have the same score.

56. No patient scored less than or equal to A in each of the three traits.

For questions 57 to 59:

From statements (ii) and (iv), the BOC of Nkwocha was 580 cr. From statement (v), the BOC of Magadheera was not 90 cr, so it must have been 380 cr. Consequently the BOC of Oblivion was 90 cr.

From statement (i), Bhaag Milkha Bhaag was released on 23rd October. From statement (iv), the release dates of Magadheera and Pride and Prejudice must have been 9th and 16th October, not necessarily in that order, and those of Nkwocha and Oblivion must have been 30th and 2nd October respectively.

Using statement (iii) and previously drawn conclusions, Oblivion and Nkwocha were from Hollywood and Nollywood respectively. From statements (ii) and (v), Pride and Prejudice and Magadheera were not from Bollywood. So Bhaag Milkha Bhaag must have been from Bollywood.

From these conclusions, the following table can be drawn.

Name of movie	Date of release (in October)	BOC (in cr.)	Film Industry
Oblivion	2nd	90	Hollywood
Magadheera	9th/16th	380	Tollywood/Kollywood
Pride and Prejudice	16th/9th	200	Kollywood/Tollywood
Bhaag Milkha Bhaag	23rd	110	Bollywood
Nkwocha	30th	580	Nollywood

57. We can determine the respective film industries for exactly 3 movies.

58. The sum of the BOCs of movies released on 2nd and 30th October = (90 + 580) = 670 cr.

59. Nkwocha had BOC of 580 cr.

For questions 60 to 63:

Let the score of E in patience and that of A in honesty be x and y respectively. Now, preliminary table on the basis of the given information can be drawn as shown below.

Patients	Patience	Compassion	Honesty
A		4	y
B			
C		y	4
D	4		
E	x	x + 1	x + 2

Since scores of no two patients were same in any of the traits, the value x of must have been 1. From statements (vi) and (vii), it is obvious that the scores of B and C in Compassion could not be 5. So the score of D in Compassion as well as in Honesty was 5. From statements (iii) and (vi), it can be deduced that the score C in Patience was 5.

Further analysis leads to the following table.

Patients	Patience	Compassion	Honesty
A	3/2	4	1
B	2/3	3	**2**
C	5	1	4
D	4	5	5
E	1	2	3

60. The score of A in patience cannot be determined.

61. The pairs of traits given in the options could have the same score.

62. No patient scored less than or equal to A in each of the three traits.

63. D's score was maximum in honesty.

For questions 64 to 67:

Had Mr. Mathew taught each of the given ten classes on exactly three different days of the week, he would have taught a total of (1 + 2 + 3 + ... + 9 + 10) × 3 = 165 students.

Total number of students taught by Mr. Mathew on the six days of the week = 18 + 12 + 23 + 19 + 32 + 25 = 129

Therefore, the total number of students in the two classes that were not taught by him = $\left(\frac{165-129}{3}\right) = 12$

So, the possible pairs of the two classes that were not taught by him could be (B and J), (C and I), (D and H) or (E and G).

On Tuesday the total number of students taught by him was 12.

This is possible in two cases:

Case I: He taught the classes A, B, C and F

Case II: He taught the classes A, B, D and E

From the two cases stated above, we can definitely conclude that he taught the classes A and B.

On Friday, the total number of students taught by him was 32.

This is possible in two cases:

Case III: He taught the classes E, H, I and J.

Case IV: He taught the classes F, G, I and J.

From the two cases stated above, we can definitely conclude that he taught the classes I and J and also, he taught either class E or G.

Therefore, the two classes that Mr. Mathew did not teach were D and H.

65. The classes taught by him on Friday were F, G, I and J.

Hence, option (d) is the correct choice.

66. It is given that on Saturday of the week Mr. Mathew did not teach class J but taught class C.

Since he did not teach class J on Saturday, he definitely taught class I on Saturday as on Saturday Mr. Mathew taught 25 students and only possible combination was (C, F, G, I).

Hence, he definitely taught class E on each of the three days namely Monday, Wednesday and Thursday as he did not teach class E on Friday, Saturday and Tuesday.

The possible combinations of the classes taught by him on Thursday is (E, I, C and B) or (E, A, C and J).

Therefore, he definitely taught the class C on Thursday.

The only possible combination of the classes taught by him on Monday was (A, B, E and J)

The final table is given below:

Monday	Tuesday	Wednesday	Thursday	Friday	Saturday
A, B, E and J	A, B, C and F	(E, G, J and A) or (E, G, I and B)	(E, C, A and J) or (E, C, I and B)	F, G, I and J	C, I, F and G

Class C is not taught by him on two consecutive days of the week 'W'.

67. By referring to the table given in the pervious question, it can be calculated that the required days were Tuesday, Friday and Saturday.

For questions 68 to 70:

Assume Rahul attempted all the questions correctly. No two students answer the same number of questions correctly. On checking, we find that the condition given in the previous statement does not hold. Hence, Rahul did not answer all the question correctly.

On proceeding in the similar manner, we find that Neha answered all the questions correctly.

The number of questions answered correctly by:

Rahul = 2

Pooja = 3

Rohit = 1

The correct option for the 1st, 2nd, 3rd and 4th questions were 'a', 'c', 'd' and 'a' respectively.

68. Rahul answered two questions correctly.

69. The correct option for the 4th question was 'a'.

70. According to the given marking scheme, the marks scored by:

Rahul = 5

Rohit = 2

Pooja = 6

Neha = 10

For questions 71 to 74:

Let the respective initial letters namely J, S, H, B, P and E of the boys denote the marks scored by them.

From III, B, P and E are cubes of integers. From III and I, P and E are the squares of integers as well as cubes of integers.

Now none of the scores is zero and the cubes of integers in the range 1 to 100 are 1, 8, 27, 64. Out of these, 1 and 64 are squares of integers too. So P and E are 1 and 64, not necessarily in the same order.

From IV, J × P is an odd number. Hence, both J and P have to be odd natural numbers. This implies that P cannot be 64. So P is 1 and E is 64. Therefore, B = 8 or 27.

Now, from V, 64 – S or S – 64 is equal to either J, H, B or P. From I, the possible values of S are 4, 9, 16, 25, 36, 49, 81 and 100. The respective differences between these numbers and 64 are 60, 55, 48, 39, 28, 15, 17 and 36; out of these, except 36, none is either the cube or the square of an integer. This difference has to be 36 and hence S = 100. Since P cannot be 36 as it is 1, B cannot be 36 as it is either 8 or 27 and J cannot be 36 as it is an odd natural number, H is 36.

From II, J is either 9, 25, 49, 81. Out of these only 9 (i.e., 8 + 1) is possible sum of the marks obtain by the two other boys. Hence, J = 9 and B = 8.

So, P = 1, E = 64, S = 100, B = 8, H = 36, J = 9

For questions 75 to 78:

Since C started with 66.67% of the money that B started with, the ratio of amounts of C and B must have been in the ratio 2 : 3 and thus C started with Rs. 200 and B with Rs. 300. Since E started with money more than just one person, E must have started with Rs. 200. Since A has more money than D, A must have started with Rs. 400 and D with Rs. 100.

B and C started with Rs. 300 and Rs. 200 respectively, and B spent Rs. 15 more than C. Hence, the difference between the amounts left with B and C should have been Rs. 85. Out of the remaining amounts, only Rs. 95 and Rs. 10 satisfy this condition. Hence, B ended with Rs. 95 and C with Rs. 10. Since E spent Rs. 35, he ended with Rs. 165. Between A and D, D ended with more than A, and hence, D ended with Rs. 70 and A with Rs. 40.

The final table is given below:

Name	Started with	Ended with	Spent
A	400	40	360
B	300	95	205
C	200	10	190
D	100	70	30
E	200	165	35

PRACTICE EXERCISE – 2

1. The maximum possible value of 's' is 10. The minimum number of queries that he can answer on any day is 5. From Monday to Thursday there are 14 queries from the previous week and 10 from that week. Hence in all there are 24 queries. So there is no way he could have answered 10 queries on any day from Monday to Thursday. So he could have answered the maximum number of queries that is 10 either on Friday or on Saturday.

2. Tiru can answer in the following way:

Days	Pending	Queries asked on the day	Queries answered during the day	Remaining queries at the end of the day
Mon	48	5	15	(48 – 15) + 5 = 38
Tue	38	2	15	(38 – 15) + 2 = 25
Wed	25	5	15	(25 – 15) + 5 = 15
Thu	15	8	15	(15 – 15) + 8 = 8
Fri	8	3	8	(8 – 8) + 3 = 3
Sat	3	1	4	3 + 1 – 4 = 0

So, the required answer is 1.

3. At least two days were required to answer all the pending queries of the previous week. Hence, all the statements could be true except given in option (4).

Since, queries asked on Thursday, Friday and Saturday are less than 21 so there must be some pending queries that would be answered on Thursday, Friday and Saturday.

Hence, all pending queries cannot be answered at the end of Wednesday, Thursday and Friday.

4. Maximum number of queries that can be solved on any day = 12 + 18 + 10 + 15 = 55.

∴ The data is inconsistent.

For questions 5 to 8:

Statement (3) will be possible for the boxes which have atleast 4 adjacent boxes, i.e. for A and B or G/H/I. But since sum of numbers in C and D is less than 6, and maximum sum for G,H&I can be 7 + 8 + 9 = 24, it cannot be A or B. Because of point(1), sum of the numbers of the Boxes adjacent to H cannot be 30, as maximum sum for A and B can be 8 + 9 = 17.

From (7), number on box F exceed that by number in E by 6, since other boxes A and B are adjacent to both C and D. So sum of the numbers on boxes adjacent to I is more than that of G, and I has 5 and sum of numbers adjacent to it is 30. So A,B,H & F will have 6, 7, 8 and 9 in any order. From (1), G will be less than 8. Also from (7), E will be either 1/2/3.

From (2), sum of numbers written on the boxes I and G = sum of numbers written on the boxes H and E. The only combination possible is as follows:

A 6/9
G H I
C E 2 4 7 5 8 F D
1/3 3/1
B 9/6

5. Sum of numbers on boxes adjacent to F = (6 or 9) + (5) + (9 or 6) + (3 or 1) = 15 + 5 + (3 or 1) … (where 3 or 1 is the value for box D)
   Sum of numbers on boxes adjacent to E = (6 or 9) + (4) + (9 or 6) + (1 or 3) = 15 + 4 + (1 or 3) … (where 1 or 3 is the value for box C)
   By statement (1),
   15 + 5 + (3 or 1) > 15 + 4 + (1 or 3)
   ⇒ 1 + (3 or 1) > (1 or 3)
   This is only possible for,
   1 + 3 > 1
   ⇒ D = 3 and C = 1
   Hence, it can be solved using only statement (1)
   By statement (2)
   15 + 5 + (3 or 1) < 15 + 4 + (1 or 3)
   ⇒ 1 + (3 or 1) < (1 or 3)
   This is only possible for,
   1 + 1 < 3
   ⇒ D = 1 and C = 3
   Hence, it can be solved using only statement (2) as well.
6. The numbers written can be determined for boxes E, F, G, H and I only
7. It is not possible for any pairs of two boxes.
8. For box C – 6 + 9 + 2 = 17, for box D – 6 + 9 + 8 = 23. For box E – 4 + 1/3 = 5/7, both are prime numbers.

For questions 9 to 12:

Let a, b, c, d be the number of days on which those four employees were present.

(a > b > c > d)

⇒ a + b = 51, c + d = 40 and a + c = 49

a + b = 51 ⇒ a ≥ 26 and b ≤ 25

c + d = 40 ⇒ c ≥ 21 and d ≤ 19

a + c = 49 ⇒ a ≥ 25 and c ≤ 24

Thus, 'c' could be 21, 22, 23 or 24. Corresponding values of a, b, d would be

Cases	I	II	III	IV
a	28	27	26	25
b	23	24	25	26
c	21	22	23	24
d	19	18	17	16

But in the rightmost case IV, a < b. Thus, it may be ignored.

Cases	I	II	III
a	28	27	26
b	23	24	25
c	21	22	23
d	19	18	17

9. Column figure numbered 5 = b + d = (a + b) + (c + d) – (a + c) = 51 + 40 – 49 = 42
10. The 3rd column must be either (a + d) or (b + c). From the table above, the only way two figures can sum up to 45 is (a + d) in case II. Hence, b + c = 46. Thus, the column 3 should read 46.
11. Eksa was present on 'c' days. Maximum value of c = 23.
12. Column figure numbered 3 is (a + d). Thus, the 4th column must be (b + c). Also, since (a + d) is column figure numbered 3, a + d > b + c
    Its true only for case I.
    ⇒ (a + d) = 47.
13. Let the number of units produced of A, B, C, D, E and F be 7x, 31x, 6x, 23x, 4x, and 3x respectively.
    ∴ Required profit percentage

$$= \left(\frac{7x\times(-10)+31x\times10+6x\times(-20)+23x\times10+4x\times(-15)+3x\times(-35)}{7x\times35+31x\times30+6x\times55+23x\times45+4x\times30+3x\times70}\right)\times100$$

$= 6.45.$

14. Let the number of units produced of each of the six items be x.
    The profit-making items for the company were B and D.
    ∴ Overall profit percentage on the profit-making items

$$(X)=\left(\frac{10\times x+10\times x}{30\times x+45\times x}\right)\times100=26.67$$

The loss-making items for the company were A, C, E and F.

∴ Overall loss percentage on the loss-making items

$$(Y)=\left(\frac{10\times x+20\times x+15\times x+35\times x}{35\times x+55\times x+30\times x+70\times x}\right)\times100$$

$= 42.105$

$\therefore X + Y = 26.67 + 42.105 = 68.78.$

15. As the number of units produced of the six items is not known, we cannot determine the item on which the company registered the maximum loss in 2012.

For questions 16 and 17:

The following table provides information about the number of units of work completed on each of the twelve given days.

On the	Rohan	Deepak	Tripti	Sonal	Tarun	Total
First day	10	12	5	20	18	65
Second day	12	20	10	5	2	49
Third day	2	18	10	15	24	69
Fourth day	16	2	25	10	4	57
Fifth day	20	32	30	15	2	99
Sixth day	8	36	16	15	45	120
Seventh day	72	20	12	20	5	129
Eighth day	8	16	32	25	12	93
Ninth day	28	16	0	15	3	62
Tenth day	4	8	0	10	5	27
Eleventh day	4	0	0	0	40	44
Twelfth day	16	0	0	0	80	96

By comparing the number of units completed by each of the five persons on each of the twelve days we get the following conclusion.

Rohan is more efficient than both Tripti and Sonal.

Deepak is more efficient than both Rohan and Tripti

Tripti is more efficient than none of the mentioned persons

Sonal is more efficient than Tarun

Tarun is more efficient than both Tripti and Rohan.

16. There are three persons namely Rohan, Deepak and Tarun who are more efficient than exactly two persons.

17. On seven days namely the second, third, fourth, fifth, sixth, seventh and ninth days the number of units of work completed by Sonal is more than at least one and at most two out of the mentioned persons.

For questions 18 and 21: Let the number of workers in M1 be x.

$\therefore$ x + x + 30 + x – 20 = 370 or x = 120.

Let the number of skilled male and female workers in M1 be 'a' and 'b' respectively, and the number of skilled and that of unskilled male workers in M2 be 'c' and 'd' respectively.

Now, the given data can be tabulated as shown below.

Number of workers	Male		Female		Total
	Skilled	Unskilled	Skilled	Unskilled	
M1	a	0.4b	b	b	120
M2	c	d	2b	d	150
M3	d/3	0.8b	d	c	100

Given that,

a + 0.4b = d + c

$\therefore$ 2b = d/3 + 0.8b + 20 and 2b + d = d/3 + 0.8b + 50

Solving above euations, we get,

d = 30, b = 25, c = 40, a = 60

18. M1 has the highest number of skilled male workers.

19. The percentage = $\frac{30}{50} \times 100 = 60\%$.

20. The difference

= (a + c + d/3 + 0.4b + d + 0.8b) – (b + 2b + d + b + d + c) = (a + 1.2b + c + 4d/3) – (4d + c + 2d)

= 60 + 1.2 × 25 + 40 + 4 × 30/3) – (4 × 30 + 40 + 2 × 30) = 30.

21. Required number = b + c + d = 25 + 40 + 30 = 95.

For questions 22 to 25:

From the additional data, we can draw the following table:

Terms (Rs. in crore)	Companies			
	CCA	T & T	Birla Tea	LLL
Equity base	500	D	450	G
Local sales	A	E	100	110
Export	B	120	100	H
Profit	C	F	40	I

Using the mother data,

(I) $F = \frac{110}{11}$ = Rs. 10 crore

(II) $100 + H = \frac{500}{2} \Rightarrow H$ = Rs. 150 crore

(III) 450 + E = 5 × 120 $\Rightarrow$ E = Rs. 150 crore

(IV) I = A – 100 ... (i)

(V) $C = \frac{F + I}{2}$

$\Rightarrow$ 2C = F + I

$\Rightarrow$ 2C = 10 + I ... (ii)

(VI) C + F + I + 40 = 100

From equation (ii), we get

C + 10 + (2C – 10) + 40 = 100

$\Rightarrow$ 3C – 10 = 50

$\Rightarrow$ C = Rs. 20 crore

$\therefore$ I = Rs. 30 crore and A = Rs. 130 crore

(VII) 100 = 1.25 × B

$\Rightarrow B = \frac{100}{1.25}$ = Rs. 80 crore

(VIII) D = 80 + 120 + 100 + 150 – 50 = Rs. 400

(IX) G = 7 × (I + 40 – F)

= 7 × (30 + 40 – 10)

= 7 × 60 = Rs. 420 crore

22. Rs. 420 crore.

23. Rs. 30 crore.

24. Required percentage = $\left(\frac{500}{400}-1\right)\times 100 = 25.$

25. Total local sales of all companies
= 130 + 150 + 100 + 110 = Rs. 490 crore
Total equity base of all companies
= 500 + 400 + 450 + 420
= Rs. 1,770 crore

$\therefore$ Required percentage = $\frac{490}{1770}\times 100 \approx 28.$

26. Data insufficient as age group distribution of the people who play golf is not given.

27. People who smoke and play cards
= (26 + 7) × 12000 = 33 × 12000
Out of these, people who belong to group

14 – 16 years = $\frac{30}{360}\times 33\times 12000 = 33000.$

28. No. of people (in 12000) who play cards and chew tobacco = 14 + 9 = 23
For the age group 10 – 14 years we have

$\frac{90}{360}\times 23\times 12000 = 69000.$

29. Total no. of people = 200 × 12000
Number of people in age group 20 and above

$= \frac{120}{360}\times 200\times 12{,}000 = 800000.$

For questions 30 to 33:

Since every student has to select 3 subjects out of five, he will select at least one out of any 3 subjects. That means all 480 students selected atleast one of these 3 subjects.

Let the number of students who selected exactly one subject be S

Let the number of students who selected exactly two subject be D

Let the number of students who selected exactly three subject be T

So, S + D + T = 480

From (I), 3D = S + T; on adding D on both sides we get 4D = S + T + D = 480 and hence D = 120.

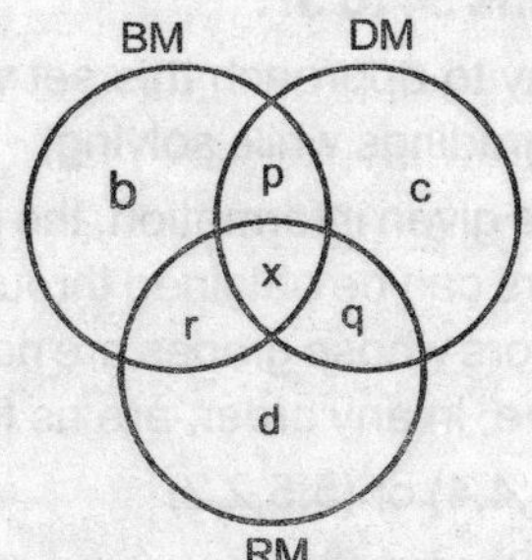

From (V), $24 \le p \le 40$ and using (II) $40 \le q \le 56$

So, p = 24 + y & q = 40 + y, where $0 \le y \le 16$

And r = 120 – (p + q) = 56 – 2y

From (VII), d = 6x

Using (VI), b + (24 + y) + (56 – 2y) + x = 6x + (56 – 2y) + (40 + y) + x – 4 ⇒ = 6x + 12

Since x is at least 15, possible values of b are 102,108,114,120...

Also, c + b + d + x = 480 – 120 = 360,

⇒ so c = 348 – 13x

As c is greater than b, possible values of c are 153, 140, 127.

Therefore, x can take only three values.

Hence, the possible values are d are 90, 96 and 102.

Final table is as follows:

x	b	c	d
15	102	153	90
16	108	140	96
17	114	127	102

30. Minimum difference is 13.

31. Number of students who chose BM = b + p + r + x = 92 – y + 7x

The above quantity will be minimum when y is maximum.

Which will be maximum when y is minimum i.e zero and x is maximum i.e 17.

So the maximum students who could select BM was 211.

32. We have to minimize (q + r) = (56 – 2y) + (40 + y) = 96 – y

When y is maximum i.e 16, we will get the minimum value = 80.

33. Since each student chose 3 out of the 5 subjects, each student must have selected at least one subjects out of BM, DM and RM. Hence, required answer is 480.

For questions 34 to 37:

(A better way to approach this set will be to use points rather than gradings while solving)

Based on the given information, the possible points for a few cricketers can be obtained through the grades given by the selectors whose grades are not shown in the table, and the same, in any order, are as follows:

Sachin- (2,4,4,4) or (5,5,2,2)

Sehwag- (5,0) or (4,2)

Uttappa- (2,2,2) or (4,4,4)

Rohit- (4,4,2)

Zaheer- (5,4,4,2) or (5,4,2,2) or (4,4,2,2)

34. The points obtained by two are tabulated below:

Name	S1	S2	S3	S4	S5	Total
Sehwag	7	2/4	2	4	4/2	19
Zaheer	2	4/5	4	5	5/4	20

35. The only possible way in which Sehwag and Dhoni can get same average is as follows-

Name	S1	S2	S3	S4	S5	Total
Sehwag	7	4/2	2	4	2/4	19
Dhoni	0	5	5	4	5	19
Ashwin		4	5		5	

Different possible ranking other two selectors can give to Ashwin (in any order) are-

(2,0), (2,2), (4,0) or (4,2).

And hence three different totals- 16,18 and 20.

36. Points which S3 can give to these players can take following values

Sachin - 4/5, Rohit- 4, Uttappa- 2/4.

37. Zaheer- (5,4,4,2,5) or (5,4,2,2,5) or (4,4,2,2,5)

Hence, three values of Grade Average are possible for Zaheer.

For questions 38 and 39:

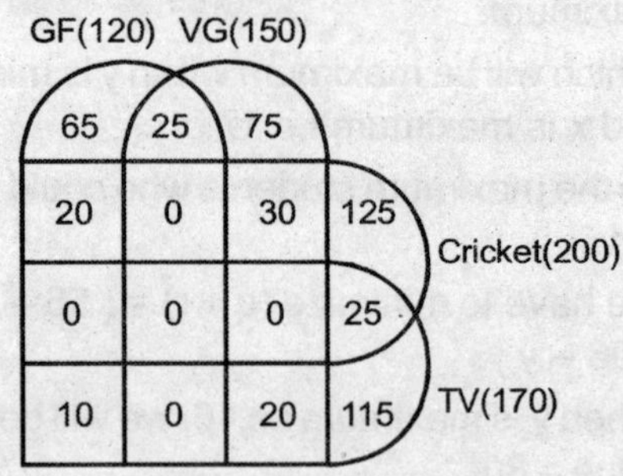

38. Number of students who like playing video games or cricket but do not like watching television or spending time with their girlfriends

= 150 + 200 – 20 – 25 – 25 – 20 – 30 = 230.

39. Number of students who like at least one out of playing video games, watching television and spending time with their girlfriends, but not playing cricket

= 65 + 25 + 75 + 10 + 20 + 115 = 310.

For questions 40 and 41:

Let the number of students who like all the four part time activities be x

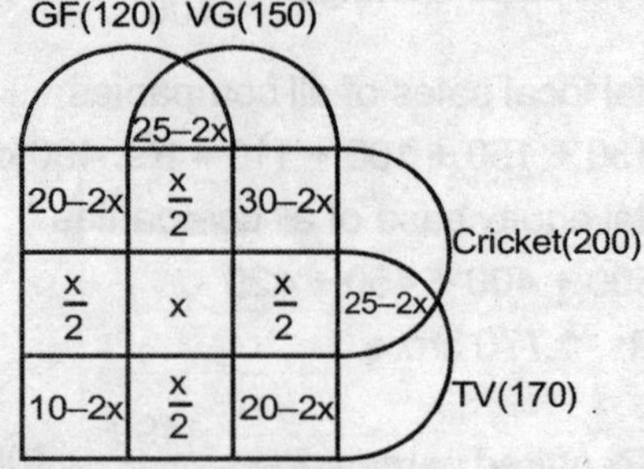

40. For x to be maximum, $10 - 2x \geq 0$

When $10 - 2x = 0$

$\Rightarrow x = 5$

When x = 5, $\frac{x}{2}$ is not an integer.

So, x should be equal to 4.

41. Total number of students who like spending time with their girlfriend $= 79 + 25 - 2x + 20 - 2x + \frac{x}{2} + \frac{x}{2} + \frac{x}{2} + x + 10 - 2x = 120$

$\Rightarrow 55 - \frac{7x}{2} = 41$

$\Rightarrow \frac{7x}{2} = 14 \quad \therefore x = 4.$

Number of students who like to play cricket only

$$= 200 - \left(25 - 2x + x + \frac{x}{2} + \frac{x}{2} + \frac{x}{2} + 20 - 2x + 30 - 2x\right)$$

= 139.

For questions 42 to 46:

Under the given conditions the possible values of Absolute Difference (AD) of 3 teams (in any order) can have 3 possibilities:

(a) 1, 2 and 4- total 7

(b) 2, 3 and 4- total 9

(c) 1, 3 and 5- total 9

As per statement (i), the AD of 3 teams is 1, 2 and 4 in round 1 and AD of G_1, G_2 and G_3 is 1, 2 and 4 respectively.

Combination (a) can be obtained in 2 ways:

(2 – 3), (4 – 6) and (1 – 5)

(4 – 5), (1 – 3) and (2 – 6)

Combination (b) can be obtained again in 2 ways:

(2 – 4), (3 – 6) and (1 – 5)

(3 – 5), (1 – 4) and (2 – 6)

Combination (c) can be obtained in only 1 way:

(3 – 4), (2 – 5) and (1 – 6)

Using the statements (ii) & (iii), we have the following possibilities:

Teams	Throws in Round 1	Throws in Round 2
G_1	(4 – 5)	(2 – 4)
G_2	(1 – 3)	(3 – 6)
G_3	(2 – 6)	(1 – 5)

Teams	Throws in Round 1	Throws in Round 2
G_1	(2 – 3)	(3 – 4)
G_2	(4 – 6)	(2 – 5) or (1 – 6)
G_3	(1 – 5)	(1 – 6) or (2 – 5)

42. The given situation realises in the following case:

Teams	Throws in Round 1	Throws in Round 2
G_1	(2 – 3)	(3 – 4)
G_2	(4 – 6)	(1 – 6)
G_3	(1 – 5)	(2 – 5)

From the table, the required value comes out to be 4.

43. For the required answer, consider the following case:

Teams	Throws in Round 1	Throws in Round 2
G_1	(2 – 3)	(3 – 4)
G_2	(4 – 6)	(2 – 5)
G_3	(1 – 5)	(1 – 6)

Lowest sum in 2 Rounds is possible for G_3, and which is 2.

44. For G_3, no player got 4 in any of 2 rounds in any of the cases.

45. In one case, G_1 got AD of 1 in both rounds. In other case, G_3 got AD of 4 in both rounds. But G_2 did not get the same AD in both the round in any case.

For questions 47 to 50:

From the given data we can draw the following Venn diagram.

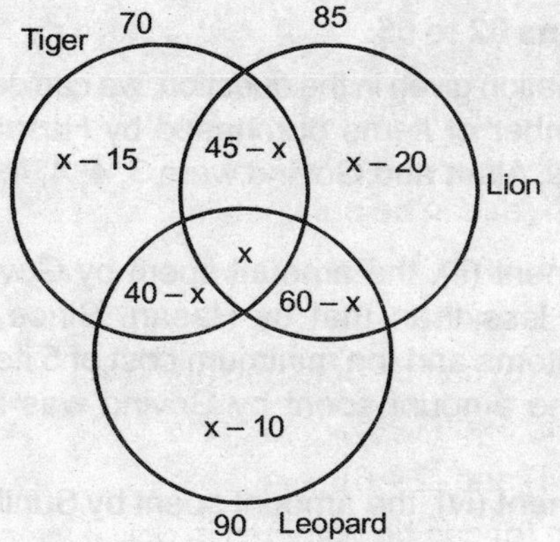

46. $x_{Max} = 40$

$x_{min} = 20$

$$\text{Mean (average)} = \frac{40+20}{2} = 30$$

$\therefore$ When x = 30, the number of students not belonging to any group = 300 – (90 + x + 10) = 300 – (100 + 30) = 170.

47. Rangdari tax = (300 – 70) × 10 = Rs. 2300.

48. Number of students belonging to atleast one group = 100 + x

The above quantity will be minimum when x is minimum i.e. 20.

Number of students belonging to only Lion group = 20 – 20 = 0

49. Number of students belonging to no group = 300 – (100 + x) = 200 – x

The above quantity will be maximum when x is minimum i.e. 20.

Number of students belonging to exactly two groups = 45 – x + 40 – x + 60 – x = 25 + 20 + 40 = 85.

For questions 50 to 53:

The given scores can be made by different combinations of balls faced and strike rate. The possible combinations for the scores given are as follows (number of balls faced, strike rate) –

Yuvraj and Sehwag - 60 runs – (120, 50%), (180, 33.3%), (150, 40%)

Smith - 81 runs – (270, 30%) , (180, 45%)

Gambhir - 108 runs – (180, 60%), (270, 40%), (240, 45%)

Strike rate of Sachin and Ponting → (30% and 60%) or (40% and 80%) in any order.

Let us suppose either Yuvraj or Sehwag had strike rate of 40% then Ponting's strike rate would have been either 30% or 60% and he must have faced 300 balls.

Hence, he can score 90 runs or 180 runs which is not possible. Hence, for Yuvraj and Sehwag the possible combinations of ball faced and strick rate are (120, 50%), (180, 33.3%) in any order.

So Smith faced 270 balls and his strike rate is 30% and Gambhir faced 240 balls with strike rate of 45%. Ponting's strike is either 40% or 80%. If Ponting's strike rate of 40%, then strike rate of Sachin would be 80% and the score made by Sachin would be more than that of Ponting, which is not possible.

Hence, strike rate of Ponting will be 80%.

Now, the following table can be made.

Player	Balls Faced	Strike rate in %	Runs
Ponting	160	80	128
Sachin	300	40	120
Gambhir	240	45	108
Warner	150	60	90
Smith	270	30	81
Yuvraj / Sehwag	180	33.3	60
Sehwag / Yuvraj	120	50	60

50. Strike rate of Sachin is 40%.

51. It can be either Sehwag or Yuvraj.

52. Sachin is the second highest scorer.

53. Warner scored 90 runs.

For questions 54 to 57:

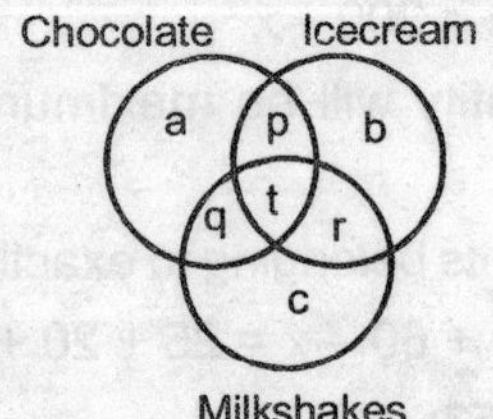

Let, the number of kids who do not like either of three = n

The number of kids who like exactly one = s

The number of kids who like exactly two = d

The number of kids who like all three= t

So, n + s + d + t = 120 – (1)

n + s + d = 3(d + t); n + s = 2d + 3t

Substituting this in (1), we get 3d + 4t = 120

40 0

36 3

32 6

. .

0 30

So, n + s = (3d + 4t)3/4 – d/4 = 90 – d/4

Range of (n + s) is 80 to 90 as 'd' decreases from 40 to 0.

54. As 'n' is one-fifth of 'd', so 'd' has to be a multiple of 5 as well, so possible values of 'd' will be 40/20/0. Possible values of (n + s) will be 80/85/90 and of 'n' will be 8/4/0 respectively. 's' can take three possible values- 72/81/90.

55. 'n' will be maximum when (n + s) will be maximum, i.e 90. And s = a + b + c, where a > b > c > n. Maximum value which 'n can take is 21.

For questions 56 and 57:

n = 0 & a = 36.

56. Kids who like ice cream is b + p + t + r, which is equal to 120 – (a + q + c) . To maximize this number minimize q & c, as "a" is given 36. maximum value that 'b' can take is 35. To minimize 'c', we should minimize 's', i.e 80. "c" will be 9.

Also kids who like ice cream is equal to kids who like chocolate, so

36 + p + t + q = b + p + t + r

36 + q = b + r, since b < a. 'q' will be zero and r = 1.

Ans is 120 – (36 + 0 + 9) = 75

57. from previous question, s = 80 so d = 40 & t = 0

b + p + t + r = 75; 35 + p + 0 + 1 = 75, so p = 39.

58. The sum of required number of votes will be minimum when the number of votes for top four candidates will be as close as possible and the fifth candidate gets no vote. In that case the number of votes by top four candidates, in decreasing order will be 3752, 3751, 3749 and 3748.

Hence, the sum = 3752 + 0 = 3752.

59. This sum will be maximum for the person who got maximum number of votes in Round 2, i.e. 50% and just one less than 50% of votes cast in Round 3 (assuming winner got exactly 50% votes in Round 3)

This person is Shiela, and her total votes = 3160 + 5000 + 4999 = 13159.

60. If he/she gets the least number of votes among the people who moved to Round 2, also he/she gets the least number of votes among the people who moved to Round3, and he wins the Round3 with minimum number of votes. This person can be Pravesh and his total votes will be 3084 + 2 + 4001 = 7087.

61. The total number can be minimum for Parvesh who qualified the Round 1 with minimum votes, and if he gets 2 votes, minimum votes needed to reach Round 3 and zero votes in Round 3. Hence total votes

= 3084 + 2 + 0 = 3086.

For questions 62 to 65:

By the information given in the question, we can determine that the number of items purchased by Hasan, Ram, Sanjay, Sunil, Alam and Govind were 3, 4, 4, 4, 5 and 5 respectively.

From statement (ii), the amount spent by Govind was equal to or less than that by Hasan. Since Govind purchase 5 items and the minimum cost of 5 items was Rs. 2000, the amount spent by Govind was also Rs. 2000.

From statement (iv), the amount spent by Sunil

$$= \frac{4000 + 2000}{2} = 3000$$

Now, using statements (iii), (v) and (vi), the final table can be drawn as follows:

Person	No. of items	Total amount spent	Price of items purchased
Govind	5	2000	100, 200, 400, 600, 700
Sunil	4	3000	1100, 900, 600, 400
Alam	5	4000	100, 200, 1100, 1200, 1400
Hassan	3	2000	200, 700, 1100
Ram	4	2900/3000	200, 700, 900, 1100/1200
Sanjay	4	3000/2900	200, 700, 900, 1200/1100

62. Item priced Rs. 200 was purchased by maximum number of friends i.e. 5.

63. Sanjay spent either Rs. 2900 or Rs. 3000.

64. Statement (i) is wrong.

Statement (ii) is correct.

65. If Ram purchased the item priced Rs. 1100, the answer is 1.

If Ram did not purchase the item of Rs. 1100, then the answer is 0.

Hence, option (d) is the correct answer.

For questions 66 to 69:

From (1), Mr. Gupta bought either a dress or a Sweater.

From (2), either Mr. Haathi or Mr. Handa would have bought the bicycle.

From (3), Mr. Chowbey spent Rs. 1200 for the item priced at Rs. 1500.

From (6), Mr. Pandey spent Rs. 800 for the item which he purchased.

From (8), Mr. Sharma spent less than Rs. 800 (Rs. 600 or Rs. 75) and Mr. Gupta spent less than Mr. Sharma (Rs. 75 or Rs. 50)

From (7), Mr. Haathi, bought a dress for Rs. 75. Hence Mr. Gupta must have spent Rs. 50 for sweater. Also Mr. Sharma must have spent Rs. 600.

Now since, every one's paid price is known, Mr. Handa must have bought the bicycle for Rs. 1000 and from (2), the original price must have been Rs. 2000. From (4), the only original price and paid price pair which is different by Rs. 100, in Rs. 900 and Rs. 800 respectively. Hence, Mr. Pandey bought tires for Rs. 800.

From (10), since the paid price of telephone was more than the camera, therefore, the paid price of telephone was Rs. 1200 and that of the camera was Rs. 600.

From (9) now, the original price of the lowest paid price item, sweater, would not be the lowest. Hence its original price must be Rs. 300.

Also from (7), the original price of the dress was Rs. 200 (twice the value of Rs. 100 note).

The summary of all the above is captured in the table below:

		Items						Price Paid					
	Persons	Dress	Sweater	Camera	Telephone	Tires	Bicycle	Rs. 800	Rs. 600	Rs. 1200	Rs. 1000	Rs. 75	Rs. 50
	Mr. Gupta		✓										✓
	Mr. Pandey					✓		✓					
	Mr. Sharma			✓					✓				
	Mr. Chowbey				✓					✓			
	Mr. Haathi	✓										✓	
	Mr. Handa						✓				✓		
Original price	Rs. 200	✓											
	Rs. 1500				✓								
	Rs. 300		✓										
	Rs. 2000						✓						
	Rs. 900					✓							
	Rs. 1200			✓									

66. Mr. Sharma bought the camera.

67. Mr. Chowbey paid the highest amount.

68. Mr. Handa bought the bicycle.

69. Since, Rs. 1000 is paid for the item of Rs. 2000 so

$$\text{percentage discount} = \frac{2000 - 1000}{2000} \times 100 = 50\%.$$

Arrangement

SOLVED EXAMPLES

Directions for examples 1 to 4: Answer the questions based on the following information.

There are seven coconut trees in Baghban's garden. Baghban has named these trees as Amitabh, Hrithik, Chunky, Dilip, Fardeen, Feroz and Govinda. The trees are situated in a row in increasing order of their heights, not necessarily in the given order, either from left to right or from right to left. It is known that their heights (in feet) are seven consecutive natural numbers between 1 and 10, both inclusive. Further, following clues are given about their positions and heights:

I. Amitabh is 3 feet taller than Dilip.

II. Hrithik is situated in the middle of the row.

III. The absolute difference between the heights of Hrithik and Feroz, who is shorter between the two, is the same as the absolute difference between the heights of Dilip and Chunky, who is taller between the two.

IV. Feroz is shorter than Govinda.

1. The absolute difference between the heights of Fardeen and Hrithik is the same as the absolute difference between the heights of Dilip and

(1) Amitabh (2) Hrithik (3) Chunky (4) Fardeen

2. The absolute difference between the heights (in inches) of Govinda and Dilip is

(1) 12 (2) 24 (3) 48 (4) Cannot be determined

3. The greatest possible values of the height of Amitabh is greater than the least possible value of the height of Feroz by

(1) 5 feet (2) 6 feet (3) 7 feet (4) 8 feet

4. What is the average of possible heights of Dilip?

(1) 3 feet (2) 4 feet (3) 4.5 feet (4) Cannot be determined

For examples 1 to 4:

Denote the positions as 1, 2, 3, 4, 5, 6, 7 from left to right in increasing order of heights. We know that Hrithik is in position 4. Also Amitabh – Dilip = 3. Thus, Amitabh cannot come at position 7 since then Dilip would have to come at position 4, which is already occupied. Also Amitabh has to be greater than 3 or else Dilip would be negative. Thus, only positions for Amitabh are 5 and 6. Assume one of them and proceed.

If Amitabh is at position 6: Dilip is at positon 3.

Also Hrithik – Feroz = Chunky – Dilip.

Feroz being shorter than Hrithik can come at positions either 1 or 2. If Feroz is at position 1, Chunky has to be at position 6 which is not possible. Thus, Feroz can be only at position 2 and Chunky at position 5. Left positions are 1 and 7 and since Feroz is shorter than Govinda, Govinda is at position 7 and Fardeen at position 1.

If Amitabh is in position 5: Dilip is at position 2. Using the same logic as above, Feroz can be at position either 1 or 3 and accordingly Chunky will be at position either 5 or 3. Both of these is not possible. Thus, Amitabh cannot be in position 5.

Thus, final position:

Fardeen < Feroz < Dilip < Hrithik < Chunky < Amitabh < Govinda

1. 1 Amitabh

2. 3 Required difference = 4 feet = 48 inches.

7.2 ARRANGEMENT

3. 3 Greatest possible height of Amitabh = 9 ft.

Least possible height of Feroz = 2 ft.

∴ Difference = 7 ft.

4. 3 Possible heights of Dilip = 3 ft, 4 ft, 5 ft and 6 ft

∴ The average of possible heights of Dilip $= \frac{3+4+5+6}{4} = 4.5$ft.

Directions for examples 5 to 8: Answer the questions on the basis of the information given below.

Preeti along with her elder brother, Parth, Younger brother, Sanju, and her parents – Rajeev (father) and Neeru (mother), is sitting for a photoshoot. Each of the them plays exactly one game out of the 5 games, 3 ball games namely Basketball, Tennis and Cricket, and 2 non-ball games namely Chess and Badminton.

Some additional information is given below:

(i) Preeti is not sitting adjacent to her father.

(ii) No child is sitting adjacent to both the parents.

(iii) Exactly one of the parents plays a ball game.

(iv) One of the parents, who plays chess, is adjacent to two of his/her children.

(v) Cricket and chess players are sitting adjacent to each other.

(vi) The persons who play the non-ball games are not sitting adjacent to each other.

(vii) All males of the family are not sitting together.

(viii) The number of persons sitting to the right of the chess player is not more than that of those sitting on his/her left.

5. Based on the given information which of the following can be determined uniquely?

(1) The game played by father (2) Who plays badminton
(3) Who is sitting at the middle (4) Who plays cricket

6. If the elder son plays basketball, which game does younger son play?

(1) Cricket (2) Badminton
(3) Tennis (4) Cannot be determined

7. Which of the following statements will be required to determine the game played by father?

(1) Younger son plays badminton (2) Daughter plays tennis
(3) Daughter plays cricket (4) No additional information is required

8. Sitting position of how many of them can be determined uniquely?

(1) 2 (2) 3 (3) 1 (4) All of them

For examples 5 to 8:

From (ii), there are at least 2 persons between parents. Since one parent has children sitting on either sides, he/she cannot be at the edge. From (iv) one of the parents plays chess and is sitting at 2nd from either end. And the other parent is sitting at other end, and he/she plays one of the ball games, so from (vi) the person playing badminton is sitting adjacent to him/her. If the mother is sitting at one end, and daughter cannot sit with her father, so she will be sitting adjacent to her mother, and in that case 3 males will be sitting together, which is not possible. Hence father is sitting at one end, and daughter sits at middle position.

So the only possible arrangement is as follows:

Father (badminton player) Daughter Mother ____

5. 3 On the basis of the given information, the position of the person who is sitting at middle position can be determined.

6. 2 If the elder son plays basketball then he is sitting at one end and younger brother is at 2nd from other end and plays badminton.

7. 2 If daughter plays tennis then other person sitting with mother plays cricket and hence father plays basketball.

8. 2 Sitting position of exactly three persons can be determined uniquely.

Directions for examples 9 to 12: Answer the questions on the basis of the information given below.

Five friends Anurag, Vijender, Vipin, Parakram and Abhinav, nicknamed Sonu, Tinkle, Babbu, Monu and Gorkhi (not necessarily in that order) met after a long time. To celebrate their reunion each of them decided to treat all other friends at different cafeterias viz. Barista, CCD, Mocha, Mojo and Keventers. Each cafeteria serves a different drink from among Fruit juice, Pepsi, Vodka, Milk and Cold Coffee. Following additional information is given about them.

I. Anurag, who is not Sonu or Tinkle, didn't treat at Keventers.

II. Parakram, who is Gorkhi, didn't treat with Vodka or at CCD.

III. Monu, who is not Abhinav or Anurag, treated at Barista.

IV. Abhinav treated with a drink whose name started with the same alphabet as of the cafeteria in which it is served. The same holds true for one other friend, who is neither Vijender nor Gorkhi.

V. Vodka was served at Mojo, and Vipin treated with Pepsi.

VI. Each friend has a different nickname, treats at a different cafeteria and treats with a different drink.

9. Who among the following cannot be the person who gave a treat at CCD?

I. Babbu
II. Sonu
III. Abhinav
IV. Vijender

(1) I and III (2) II, III and IV (3) Only IV (4) None of these

10. If Anurag treated his friends with Cold Coffee, then with which drink did Sonu treat his friends?

(1) Vodka (2) Milk (3) Fruit juice (4) Cannot be determined

11. Which drink was served at Barista?

(1) Pepsi (2) Fruit Juice (3) Cold Coffee (4) Milk

12. How many of the following cafeterias could be the one in which Tinkle could give a treat?

I. Mocha
II. Mojo
III. CCD

(1) I and II (2) I and III (3) II and III (4) I, II and III

For examples 9 to 12:

From statement 1 and 3 Anurag is not Sonu, Tinkle or Monu. As Parakram is Gorkhi so Anurag is Babbu.

From statement 4 Cold Coffee is served at CCD and Milk at Mocha (as Vodka is served at Mojo) Vijender and Gorkhi do not have the name of the drink and the cafeteria starting with the same alphabet and Gorkhi didn't treat with Vodka. It implies Gorkhi treated with Fruit Juice and Vijender treated at Mojo with Vodka.

From all the additional information we can compile the following table .

Anurag	Vijender	Vipin	Parakram	Abhinav
Babbu	Sonu/Tinkle	Monu	Gorkhi	Sonu/Tinkle
Cold Coffee/Milk	Vodka	Pepsi	Fruit Juice	Cold Coffee/Milk
CCD/Mocha	Mojo	Barista	Keventers	CCD/Mocha

9. 3 At CCD any one among Anurag (Babbu) or Abhinav (Sonu or Tinkle) can treat but not Vijender.

10. 4 It cannot be determined whether Sonu is Vijender or Abhinav, so drink with which Sonu treats cannot be determined.

11. 1 Pepsi is served at Barista.

12. 4 Tinkle can give a treat in any one of the mentioned Cafeterias.

7.4 ARRANGEMENT

Directions for examples 13 to 16: Answer the questions on the basis of the information given below.

Seven persons namely P, Q, R, S, T, U and V, each of whom is a professor of a different subject from among Chemistry, Accounts, Electrical, Maths, IT, Biology and Geography, not necessarily in the same order, are standing in a row.

We have following additional information :

(i) The number of persons to the left of R is the same as the number of persons to the right of the Biology professor.

(ii) IT professor is standing at the fourth place to the right of V.

(iii) Biology professor is standing as many places to the left of P as S is standing to the right of Chemistry professor.

(iv) R is standing immediately right of T.

(v) Maths and Geography professors are standing at the first and sixth positions from the right end.

(vi) Electrical professor is at the fourth place to the right of Accounts professor.

13. Q can not be the professor of

(1) Biology (2) Chemistry (3) Electrical (4) Maths

14. If the number of professors standing between Q and T is same as the number of professors standing between U and P, then Q is a professor of

(1) Biology (2) Electrical

(3) Accounts (4) This arrangement is not possible

15. Which of the following pairs of professor can never stand adjacent to each other ?

(1) Q and T (2) R and P (3) U and S (4) S and T

16. How many different sitting arrangements are possible?

(1) 2 (2) 3 (3) 5 (4) more than 5

For examples 13 to 16:

By using statements (ii), (v) and (vi), we get the following arrangement:

	V					
ACC	Geo			Elec.	IT	Maths

From statements (i) and (iv), we arrive at the following cases:

	V		T	R		
ACC	Geo	Bio	Che	Elec.	IT	Maths

	V	T	R			
ACC	Geo	Che	Bio	Elec.	IT	Maths

Using statement (iii), the final arrangements are as follows:

Q/U	V	T	R	U/Q	S	P
ACC	Geo	Che	Bio	Elec.	IT	Maths

Q/U	V	T	R	S	P	U/Q
ACC	Geo	Che	Bio	Elec.	IT	Maths

Q/U	V	U/Q	T	R	P	S
ACC	Geo	Bio	Che	Elec.	IT	Maths

13. 2 Q cannot be the professor of Chemistry.

14. 3 If the number of persons standing between Q and T is same as the number of people standing between U and P, then Q is the professor of Accounts.

15. 4 S and T can never stand adjacent to each other.

16. 4 In each arrangement Q and U can interchange their positions hence total 6 arrangements.

Directions for examples 17 to 20: Answer the questions on the basis of the information given below.

Six boys Kaif, Prem, Rahul, Ravi, Ajay and Akash, and two girls Pooja and Aish are sitting around a dinning table with numbered chairs as follows:

1 2 3 4

8 7 6 5

Below are some additional facts about how they occupy their seats.

I. The two girls are sitting on opposite sides of the table but they are not sitting opposite to each other. Also neither of them is sitting on a corner seat.

II. Ravi and Prem are sitting on diagonally-opposite-corner seats.

III. Akash is sitting on seat number 4.

IV. Rahul and Kaif are sitting on the same side but not adjacent to each other.

17. On which seat is Ajay sitting?

(1) 2 (2) 8 (3) 7 (4) Cannot be determined

18. If Rahul and Pooja are sitting on opposite sides, on which seat is Aish sitting?

(1) 2 (2) 3 (3) 7 (4) Cannot be determined

19. Who is sitting on seat number 8?

(1) Rahul (2) Kaif (3) Ajay (4) Cannot be determined

20. Which of the following pairs of persons can never sit adjacent to each other?

(1) Ajay and Aish (2) Kaif and Pooja (3) Ravi and Aish (4) None of these

For examples 17 to 20:

According to given information, we can make the following table.

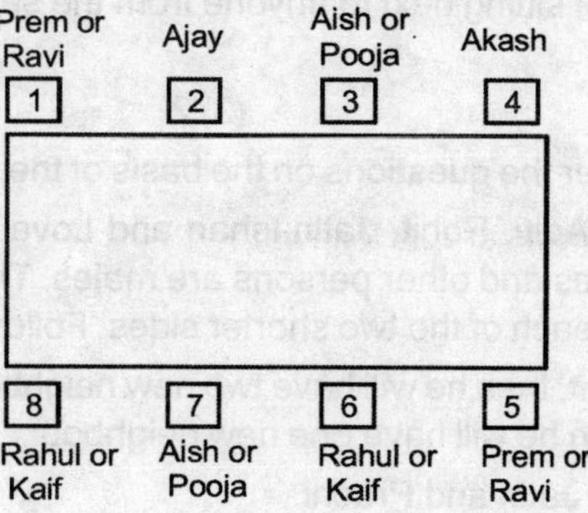

17. 1 Ajay occupies seat number 2.

18. 3 If Rahul and Pooja are on opposite sides, then Pooja can sit only on seat number 3. So, Aish will sit on seat number 7.

19. 4 Rahul or Kaif can occupy the seat number 8. So, the answer cannot be determined.

20. 3 Check the choices and see the table.

(1) Ajay and Aish can sit adjacent to each other.

(2) Kaif and Pooja can also sit adjacent to each other.

(3) Ravi and Aish can not sit adjacent to each other.

PRACTICE EXERCISE – 1

Directions for questions 1 to 4: Answer the questions on the basis of the information given below.

A news channel invited 8 people from KNU to be panelists on a debate and they were made to sit around a circular table. Four of them viz. Professor Brijesh along with his three students – Amit, Chirag and Pinky – are from sociology department. The other four viz. Professor Shailesh along with his three students – Nitin, Lokesh and Madhu – are from political science department.

Additional information :

1. Exactly two students are equidistant from both the professors.
2. Exactly one male student is sitting between the two girls.
3. No girl is sitting next to her professor.
4. Amit is sitting second to the right of Madhu.
5. Amit is not sitting to the immediate left of Brijesh.
6. Only Pinky and Madhu are girls.

1. If 3 people of same department are sitting together, then how many arrangements are possible?

(1) 3 (2) 4 (3) 5 (4) 6

2. Which of the following statement(s) is/are definitely true ?

(i) Madhu is sitting to the immediate left of Brijesh.

(ii) Amit is sitting next to Brijesh.

(iii) Pinky is an immediate neighbor of Shailesh.

(iv) Brijesh is sitting opposite Shailesh.

(1) Only (ii) (2) Only (i),(ii) & (iii) (3) Only (i) & (ii) (4) All of the above

3. Which of the following statement is sufficient to determine who is sitting opposite to Madhu?

(i) No person from sociology department is sitting next to Pinky.

(ii) Nitin and Chirag are sitting opposite to each other.

(iii) Nitin and Lokesh are sitting next to each other.

(1) Only (i) (2) Only (ii) (3) Either (i) or (ii) (4) Either (ii) or (iii)

4. If Pinky is the only person who is not sitting next to anyone from the same department as her, then in how many ways can all the persons sit?

(1) 4 (2) 1 (3) 2 (4) 6

Directions for questions 5 to 8: Answer the questions on the basis of the information given below.

Eight people – Prachi, Reema, Swati, Aditi, Rohit, Jatin,Ishan and Love – are sitting around a rectangular table. Prachi, Rima, Swati and Aditi are females and other persons are males. Three persons are sitting along each of the two longer sides and one person along each of the two shorter sides. Following information is also given:

1. If Jatin exchanges his seat with Rohit, then he will have two new neighbours, but if he exchanges his seat with the person sitting opposite to Rohit, then he will have one new neighbour.
2. Aditi is sitting equidistant from both Jatin and Prachi.
3. Reema is 4th to the right of Rohit.
4. Persons sitting on the shorter sides are of opposite gender and Aditi is one of them.
5. Love is sitting opposite to Reema.

5. Who is sitting to the immediate right of Jatin?

(1) Reema (2) Ishan (3) Swati (4) Either (1) or (3)

6. Who is definitely not a neighbour of Rohit?

(1) Aditi (2) Ishan (3) Prachi (4) Swati

7. For how many persons, can their neighbours be found out uniquely?

(1) Zero (2) Two (3) Four (4) More than four

8. If everyone moves to the seat just right of him/her, then which of the following pairs of persons can sit opposite to each other?
   (1) Jatin and Rohit (b) Jatin and Prachi (3) Swati and Love (4) Jatin and Love

Directions for questions 9 to 12: Answer the questions on the basis of the information given below.

Eight persons – A, B, C, D, E, F, G and H – are sitting in two rows, with four persons each, such that each person in a row faces exactly one person in the other row. It is also known that:

1. D is not sitting opposite to either F or C.
2. A is sitting opposite to G. G and C are sitting in different rows.
3. G and H are sitting in the same row; C and F are also sitting in the same row. G and H are not sitting adjacent to each other and the same is true for C and F.
4. A and C are not sitting at the end of the any row.
5. If any one of G and H is sitting at one of the ends, then he is sitting at the extreme right end of that row.
6. Neither C nor F is sitting opposite either G or H.

9. Who is sitting to the immediate right of C?
   (1) B (2) E (3) A (4) D
10. Who is sitting between B and E?
   (1) G (2) H (3) A (4) Cannot be determined
11. Who is sitting opposite to C?
   (1) G (2) B (3) E (4) Either (2) or (3)
12. Which of the following statements is/are required to determine the seating positions of each person?
   (i) C is sitting opposite to the person who is sitting just next to G.
   (ii) E is not sitting opposite to the person who is sitting just next to D.
   (iii) G is sitting next to E.
   (1) Only (iii) (2) Only (ii) (3) either (ii) or (iii) (4) Only (i)

Directions for questions 13 to 16: Answer the questions on the basis of the information given below.

Ten Members of Parliament (MPs) – Anant, Berman, Chauhan, Devendra, Enos, Farhan, George, Herman, Ishank and Jaitlay – were sitting around a circular table in such a way that the number of MPs facing away from the centre was not less than the number of MPs facing towards the centre. These MPs were from 4 different Parties from among BJP, INC, TMC and SP – there were 2 MPs from INC and SP each. All the MPs were sitting at an equal distance from their immediate neighbours. It was also known that:

(i) Devendra was sitting equidistant from George and Herman. The number of MP/MPs sitting between Devendra and George was an even number (consider zero as an even number).
(ii) The MPs sitting adjacent to Berman, a BJP MP, were from the same Party. Farhan, who was facing towards the centre, was sitting immediately right of Enos and second to the left of George. Both Enos and Farhan were facing either towards the centre or away from the centre.
(iii) Anant, a BJP MP, was facing towards the centre and was sitting fourth to the right of Chauhan, who was a SP MP and facing towards the centre. Enos and Jaitley were not INC MPs.
(iv) Three MPs were sitting between Enos and Jaitley and neither of them was sitting adjacent to Anant or Chauhan.
(v) INC MPs were sitting opposite each other and facing away from the centre. No INC MP was sitting adjacent to BJP MPs.
(vi) Farhan was a BJP MP.

13. How many TMC MPs were facing towards the centre?
   (1) 3 (2) 2 (3) 1 (4) None of these
14. Which of the following statements is/are true?
   (i) Berman was sitting second to the right of Herman.
   (ii) George, Herman and Enos were TMC MPs.
   (iii) Devendra and Ishank were facing each other.
   (1) Only (i) (2) Only (ii) (3) Only (iii) (4) Both (ii) and (iii)

7.8 ARRANGEMENT

15. Ishank was sitting

(1) second to the right of Farhan
(2) second to the left of Jaitley
(3) third to the left of Anand
(4) third to the right of Anand

16. Three of the following options follow a certain sitting arrangement. Which one of the following options does not follow that pattern?

(1) Chauhan – Berman – Jaitley
(2) Herman – Devendra – George
(3) Enos – Farhan – Anant
(4) Ishank – Jaitley – Herman

Directions for questions 17 to 20: Answer the questions on the basis of the information given below.

Salim, Sajid, Sunil and Sanjay visited Feroz one at a time in the following manner.

I. At least one person visited Feroz between Salim and Sajid.
II. At least one of Sunil and Sanjay visited Feroz before Salim.
III. Sunil did not visit Feroz between Sajid and Sanjay.

17. If Sajid was the last person to visit Feroz, who visited Feroz first?

(1) Salim
(2) Sanjay
(3) Sunil
(4) Cannot be determined

18. Who could not be the last person to visit Feroz?

(1) Salim
(2) Sajid
(3) Sunil
(4) Sanjay

19. In how many ways could the four people visit Feroz?

(1) 2
(2) 3
(3) 4
(4) 5

20. If Sanjay was the first to visit Feroz, who was the third to visit him?

(1) Salim
(2) Sajid
(3) Sunil
(4) Cannot be determined

Directions for questions 21 to 24: Answer the questions on the basis of the information given below.

There are seven coconut trees in Baghban's garden standing in a row. Baghban has named these trees as Amitabh, Hrithik, Chunky, Dilip, Fardeen, Feroz and Govinda. The trees are standing in increasing order of their heights from left to right, not necessarily in the given order. It is known that their heights (in feet) are seven consecutive integers lying between 1 and 10 (both inclusive). It is also known that:

I. Amitabh is 3 ft taller than Dilip.
II. Hrithik is standing in the middle of the row of seven trees.
III. The difference in the heights of Feroz and Hrithik, Feroz being shorter, is same as the difference in the heights of Chunky and Dilip, Chunky being taller.
IV. Feroz is shorter than Govinda.

21. Difference in heights of Fardeen and Hrithik is same as the difference between the heights of Dilip and which tree?

(1) Amitabh
(2) Hrithik
(3) Chunky
(4) Fardeen

22. Difference in heights of Govinda and Dilip (in inches) is

(1) 12 (2) 24 (3) 48 (4) Cannot be determined

23. The greatest possible height of Amitabh is greater than the least possible height of Feroz by

(1) 5 ft (2) 6 ft (3) 7 ft (4) 8 ft

24. What is the greatest possible height of Chunky?

(1) 7 ft (2) 8 ft (3) 9 ft (4) Cannot be determined

Directions for questions 25 to 27: Answer the questions on the basis of the information given below.

Eight persons – A, B, C, D, E, F, G, H – are sitting around a circular table facing the centre of the table. Each of them is wearing a T-shirt having 2 different colors out of red, blue, green, yellow and orange. It is also known that:

(a) No male member is wearing a T-shirt having one of its colors as orange.

(b) A, who is a girl and sitting between two persons who are wearing T-shirts having one of their colors as Red, is wearing a T-shirt having one of its colors as yellow.

(c) A, B, E and F are sitting diametrically opposite to C, D, G and H respectively.

(d) No pair of male members are sitting either adjacent to each other or opposite to each other.

(e) D, who is a male, is sitting to the immediate left of F and wearing a T-shirt having one of its colors as Green but the second one not as Blue. F is wearing a T-shirt having one of its colors as orange but the second one not as Red.

(f) G, who is wearing a T-shirt having colors as Red and Orange, is sitting to the left of B.

(g) H is wearing a T-shirt having colors as Yellow and Red. Yellow is one of the colors of T-shirts worn by exactly two persons.

25. The number of girls, out of the eight persons, cannot be more than

(1) 5 (2) 7 (3) 4 (4) 6

26. Which of the following is one of the colors of the T-shirt worn by D?

(1) Red (2) Orange (3) Yellow (4) Cannot be determined

27. Three persons with their names as three consecutive letters in the English-alphabet are sitting together. Out of these three, who is sitting between the remaing two?

(1) E (2) B (3) D (4) F

Directions for questions 28 to 31: Answer the questions on the basis of the information given below.

Seven friends – Ankit, Bhola, Chintu, Dolo, Ekta, Farhan and Govind – are standing in a row facing north. The ages of no two friends, out of the seven, are the same. It is also known that:

(i) The oldest friend has as many persons to his left as to his right.

(ii) The youngest and the second youngest friends are standing at the left and the right ends of the row respectively.

(iii) Farhan is younger than Chintu, who is standing to the immediate left of Ekta.

(iv) Exactly two persons are standing between Dolo and Govind, and Ekta is not one of them.

(v) Ankit is younger than Govind, who is not the oldest.

(vi) Ekta is not the second youngest.

(vii) Farhan is older than Ekta, but younger than Bhola.

28. Who is the oldest friend in the group?

(1) Dolo (2) Govind (3) Chintu (4) Ekta

29. How many persons are standing between Ekta and Govind?

(1) 1 (2) 2 (3) 3 (4) 4

30. Who among the following is definitely one of the persons standing adjacent to Dolo?

(1) Farhan (2) Govind (3) Chintu (4) Ekta

31. Who is standing at the right end of the row?

(1) Farhan (2) Govind (3) Chintu (4) Ekta

7.10 ARRANGEMENT

Directions for questions 32 to 35: Answer the questions on the basis of the information given below:

A dinner was hosted by Mr. and Mrs. Gupta for their son and two daughters along with their spouses. The eight of them sat around a rectangular table, three on each side and one on each end as illustrated in the diagram given below. From the given clues, answer the questions given below.

Males: Pankaj, Rahul, Bipin, Rakesh,

Females: Henny, Rekha, Naina, Teena

A. As the host, Rahul sat at the head of the table.

B. Henny noticed that each man sat between two women and no one sat next to his or her spouse.

C. Rakesh is married to Naina.

D. Bipin sat between Rekha and Mrs. Yadav.

E. Teena sat on her son's right.

F. Each of the three people on either side of the table had different surnames. One of the surnames was Bhandari.

Head

32. Who is sitting between Teena and Henny?

(1) Rahul (2) Bipin (3) Pankaj (4) Rakesh

33. Who among the following is Rahul Gupta's son?

(1) Bipin (2) Rakesh (3) Pankaj (4) Yadav

34. Who is sitting opposite Rakesh?

(1) Rekha (2) Pankaj (3) Henny (4) Bipin

35. Who among the following is Rekha's husband?

(1) Rahul (2) Pankaj (3) Rakesh (4) Bipin

PRACTICE EXERCISE – 2

Directions for questions 1 to 4: Answer the questions on the basis of the information given below:

A photo-shoot is to be done involving 9 people P, Q, R, S, T, U, V, W and X. They are sitting in a row from left to right, all facing the camera. Only 3 of them are formally dressed. Furthermore,

- P, U and V are males.
- S and X are females.
- Q is a formally dressed male while R is a formally dressed female.
- Males and females sit alternately in the row.

1. Which of the following statements provide sufficient information to determine, with respect to each and every person, whether the person is a male or a female and whether the person is formally dressed or not formally dressed?

(1) X is a formally dressed female. (2) W is a formally dressed female.

(3) P is a formally dressed male. (4) T is a formally dressed male.

2. If W is a male who is not formally dressed, then which of the following is/are necessarily false?

(1) P sits fifth from the left in the row. (2) Q sits seventh from the right in the row.

(3) W sits fourth from the left in the row. (4) S sits second from the right in the row.

3. Assume that T is a formally dressed female. If all the formally dressed persons must sit on the three rightmost seats, which of the following is an acceptable sitting sequences from left to right?

(1) PSUXVWRQT (2) VXUSPWTQR

(3) WVXPUSTQR (4) XPSUWVRQT

4. Let T be a male who is formally dressed. Photograph would not turn out to be good if three or more persons who are not formally dressed sit together. Which of the following information is sufficient to infer the position at which R sat (from left) in a photograph that turned out to be good?

(1) A formally dressed person sat first from the left.

(2) A formally dressed person sat fifth from the left.

(3) A formally dressed person sat fifth from the right.

(4) A formally dressed person sat third from the right.

Directions for questions 5 to 7: Answer the questions on the basis of the information given below.

Seven books, each on a different subject among Physics, Chemistry, Mathematics, Biology, English, Hindi and Sanskrit, are kept in a stack, not necessarily in this order. The books are numbered 1 to 7 from bottom to top. It is also known that:

(i) One has to remove at least 4 books from the top to reach the Chemistry book.

(ii) The number on the Physics book cannot be expressed as the arithmetic mean of any two numbers on the other books.

(iii) There are exactly three books between the English book and the Hindi book.

(iv) The Biology book is at one of the extreme ends of the stack.

(v) The Mathematics book occupies the 3rd position from one of the extreme ends of the stack.

5. The number of books between the books of Hindi and Chemistry is

(1) 0 (2) 1 (3) 2 (4) Either (1) or (3)

6. Had the books been numbered 1 to 7 from top to bottom, what would have been the sum of the numbers on the books of English and Hindi?

(1) 8 (2) 7 (3) 5 (4) 10

7. If the Biology book is at the bottom, and the numbers on the Physics and Sanskrit books are interchanged, what will be the new number on the Sanskrit book?

(1) 7 (2) 4 (3) 5 (4) 2

Directions for questions 8 to 10: Answer the questions on the basis of the information given below.

Eight persons are sitting at a rectangular table such that four persons are sitting along each of the longer sides of the table. Each person works in a different bank among PNB, SBI, HDFC, ICICI, CBI, BOB, BOI and Citi, and holds a different designation among IT Officer, Marketing Officer, Law Officer, Agricultural Officer, Rajbhasha Adhikari, Technical Officer, Finance Officer and HR Manager, not necessarily in the same order. It is also known that:

I. The Finance Officer, who works in BOI, is sitting to the immediate left of the HR Manager.

II. The Marketing Officer, who works in SBI, is sitting opposite the Technical Officer.

III. The Agricultural Officer, who works in ICICI, is sitting diagonally opposite the Rajbhasha Adhikari, who is sitting to the immediate left of the Technical Officer.

IV. The Law Officer, who works in HDFC, is sitting to the immediate left of the Marketing officer.

V. The persons who work in PNB and HDFC are sitting along the same side of the table.

VI. The Rajbhasha Adhikari, who works in CBI, is sitting at one of the extreme ends in his row.

8. Who is sitting to the immediate right of the Finance Officer?

(1) Agricultural Officer (2) Technical Officer (3) Marketing Officer (4) None of these

9. For how many persons can we definitely determine the banks in which they work?

(1) 8 (2) 6 (3) 4 (4) None of these

10. The person who is sitting opposite the Law Officer works in

(1) BOI (2) ICICI (3) BOB (4) Cannot be determined

Directions for questions 11 to 13: Answer the questions on the basis of the information given below.

Five persons – Jivan, Kamal, Lakhan, Monika and Nalin – stay on five different floors of a building – F1, F2, F3, F4 and F5 – from bottom to top, not necessarily in the same order. No two of them are of the same age. On September 6, 2013, each of them visited a different monument among Hawa Mahal, City Palace, Jantar Mantar, Jal Mahal and Rambagh Palace. It is also known that:

(i) The youngest person, who stays on the floor which is immediately below the floor of Lakhan, visited Rambagh Palace.

(ii) The person who stays on F5 visited Jantar Mantar.

(iii) There are two floors between the floors of the youngest and oldest persons.

(iv) The person who visited City Palace lives on F1.

(v) Kamal, who is older than exactly three persons, lives on a floor which is immediately below the floor of the youngest person and immediately above the floor of Jivan.

(vi) The person who lives on F5 is older than at least two persons.

(vii) Monika does not live on F1.

11. Which of the following statements is definitely not true?

(1) Kamal stays on F3 and visited Hawa Mahal.

(2) Jivan stays on F2 and visited Jal Mahal.

(3) Nalin is the youngest and visited Rambagh Palace.

(4) The oldest person stays on F1.

12. The monument visited by Kamal was

(1) Hawa Mahal

(2) Jal Mahal

(3) Jantar Mantar

(4) Either (1) or (2)

13. The number of floors between the floors of Lakhan and Nalin is

(1) 1 (2) 2

(3) 3 (4) None of these

Directions for questions 14 to 17: Answer the questions on the basis of the information given below.

Seven books, each on a different subject among Physics, Chemistry, Mathematics, Biology, English, Hindi and Sanskrit, are kept in a stack, not necessarily in this order. The books are numbered 1 to 7 from bottom to top. It is also known that:

(i) One has to remove at least 4 books from the top to reach the Chemistry book.

(ii) The number on the Physics book cannot be expressed as the arithmetic mean of any two numbers on the other books.

(iii) There are exactly three books between the English book and the Hindi book.

(iv) The Biology book is at one of the extreme ends of the stack.

(v) The Mathematics book occupies the 3rd position from one of the extreme ends of the stack.

14. The number of books between the books of Hindi and Chemistry is

(1) 0 (2) 1

(3) 2 (4) Either (1) or (3)

15. Had the books been numbered 1 to 7 from top to bottom, what would have been the sum of the numbers on the books of English and Hindi?

(1) 6 (2) 8 (3) 7 (4) 5

16. If the Biology book is at the bottom, and the numbers on the Physics and Sanskrit books are interchanged, what will be the new number on the Sanskrit book?

(1) 8 (2) 6 (3) 7 (4) 4

17. The number on Sanskrit book was

(1) 4 (2) 3 (3) 5 (4) 2

Directions for questions 18 to 21: Answer the questions on the basis of the information given below.

[CAT 1994]

A leading socialite decided to organize a dinner and invited a few of her friends. Only the host and the hostess were sitting at the opposite ends of a rectangular table, with three persons along each side. The pre-requisite for the seating arrangement was that each person must be seated such that atleast on one side it has a person of opposite sex. Maqbool is opposite Shobha, who is not the hostess. Ratan has a woman on his right and is sitting opposite a woman. Monisha is sitting to the hostess's right , next to Dhirubhai. One person is seated between Madhuri and Urmila who is not the hostess. The men were Maqbool, Ratan, Dhirubhai and Jackie, while the women were Madhuri, Urmila, Shobha and Monisha.

18. The eighth person present, Jackie, must be

I. the host

II. Seated to Shobha's right

III. Seated opposite Urmila

(1) I only (2) III only (3) I and II only (4) II and III only

19. Which of the following persons is definitely not seated next to a person of the same sex?

(1) Maqbool (2) Madhuri (3) Jackie (4) Shobha

20. If Ratan would have exchanged seats with a person four places to his left, which of the following would have been true after the exchange?

I. No one was seated between two persons of the opposite sex. (e.g. no man was seated between two women)

II. One side of the table consisted entirely of persons of the same sex.

III. Either the host or the hostess changed seats.

(1) I only (2) II only (3) I and II only (4) II and III only

21. If each person is placed directly opposite her spouse, which of the following pairs must be married?

(1) Ratan and Monisha (2) Madhuri and Dhirubhai

(3) Urmila and Jackie (4) Ratan and Madhuri

Directions for questions 22 to 24: Answer the questions on the basis of the information given below.

[CAT 1994]

Five of India's leading models are posing for a photograph promoting "World Peace and Understanding". But then, Rakesh Shreshtha the photographer is having a tough time getting them to stand in a straight line, because Aishwarya refuses to stand next to Sushmita since Sushmita had said something about her in a leading gossip magazine. Rachel and Anu want to stand together because they are "such good friends, y'know". Manpreet on the other hand cannot get along well with Rachel, because there is some talk about Rachel scheming to get a contract already awarded to Manpreet. Anu believes her friendly astrologer who has asked her to stand at the extreme right for all group photographs. Finally, Rakesh managed to pacify the girls and got a beautiful picture of five beautiful girls smiling beautifully in a beautiful straight line, promoting world peace.

22. If Aishwarya is standing at the extreme left, who is standing in the middle?

(1) Manpreet (2) Sushmita (3) Rachel (4) Cannot say

23. If Aishwarya stands at the extreme left, who is standing second from left?

(1) Cannot say (2) Sushmita (3) Rachel (4) Manpreet

24. If Anu's astrologer tells her to stand second from left and Aishwarya decides to stand second from right, then who is the girl standing at the extreme right?

(1) Rachel (2) Sushmita (3) Cannot say (4) Manpreet

Directions for questions 25 to 28: Answer the questions on the basis of the information given below.

[CAT 1994]

The primitive tribes – folk of the island of Lexicophobos have recently developed a language for themselves. Which has a very limited vocabulary. In fact, the words can be classified into only three types : the Bingoes, the Cingoes and the Dingoes.

The Bingoes type of words are : Grumbs, Harrumphs, Ihavitoo

The Cingoes type of words are : Ihavitoo, Jingongo, Koolodo

The Dingoes type of words are : Lovitoo, Metoo, Nana

They have also devised some rules of grammar:

Every sentence must have only five words.

Every sentence must have two Bingoes, one Cingo and two Dingoes.

If Grumbs is used in a sentence, Ihavitoo must also be used and vice versa.

Koolodo can be used in a sentence only if Lovitoo is used.

25. Which choice of words in a sentence is not possible, if no rules of grammar are to be violated?

(1) Grumbs and Harrumphs as the Bingoes and Ihavitoo as the Cingo.

(2) Harrumphs and Ihavitoo as the Bingoes.

(3) Grumbs and Ihavitoo as the Bingoes and Lovitoo and Nana as the Dingoes.

(4) Metoo and Nana as the Dingoes.

26. If Grumbs and Harrumphs are the Bingoes in a sentence, and no rule of grammar is violated, which of the following is / are true?

I. Ihavitoo is the Cingo.

II. Lovitoo is the Dingo.

III. Either Lovitoo or Metoo must be one of – or both – the Dingoes.

(1) I only (2) II only
(3) III only (4) I & III only

27. Which of the following is a possible sentence if no grammar rule is violated?

(1) Grumbs harrumphs ihavitoo lovitoo metoo. (2) Grumbs harrumphs ihavitoo jingongo lovitoo.
(3) Harrumphs ihavitoo jingongo lovitoo metoo. (4) Grumbs ihavitoo koolodo metoo nana.

28. If in a sentence Grumps is the Bingo and no rule of grammar is violated, which of the following cannot be true?

(1) Harrumphs must be a Bingo. (2) Ihavitoo must be a Bingo.
(3) Lovitoo may be used. (4) All three Bingoes are used.

Directions for questions 29 to 32: Answer the questions on the basis of the information given below.

[CAT 2017 Shift 2]

Eight friends: Ajit, Byomkesh, Gargi, Jayanta, Kikira, Manik, Prodosh and Tapesh are going to Delhi from Kolkata by a flight operated by Cheap Air. In the flight, sitting is arranged in 30 rows, numbered 1 to 30, each consisting of 6 seats, marked by letters A to F from left to right, respectively. Seats A to C are to the left of the aisle (the passage running from the front of the aircraft to the back), and seats D to F are to the right of the aisle. Seats A and F are by the windows and referred to as Window seats, C and D are by the aisle and are referred to as Aisle seats while B and E are referred to as Middle seats. Seats marked by consecutive letters are called consecutive seats (or seats next to each other). A seat number is a combination of the row number, followed by the letter indicating the position in the row; e.g., 1A is the left window seat in the first row, while 12E is the right middle seat in the 12th row.

Cheap Air charges Rs.1000 extra for any seats in Rows 1, 12 and 13 as those have extra legroom. For Rows 210, it charges Rs.500 extra for Window seats and Rs.300 extra for Aisle seats. For Rows 11 and 14 to 20, it charges Rs.200 extra for Window seats and Rs.400 extra for Aisle seats. All other seats are available at no extra charge.

The following are known:

1. The eight friends were seated in six different rows.
2. They occupied 3 Window seats, 4 Aisle seats and 1 Middle seat.
3. Seven of them had to pay extra amounts, totaling to Rs. 4600, for their choices of seat. One of them did not pay any additional amount for his/her choice of seat.
4. Jayanta, Ajit and Byomkesh were sitting in seats marked by the same letter, in consecutive rows in increasing order of row numbers; but all of them paid different amounts for their choices of seat. One of these amounts may be zero.
5. Gargi was sitting next to Kikira, and Manik was sitting next to Jayanta.
6. Prodosh and Tapesh were sitting in seats marked by the same letter, in consecutive rows in increasing order of row numbers; but they paid different amounts for their choices of seat. One of these amounts may be zero.

29. In which row was Manik sitting?

(1) 10 (2) 11 (3) 12 (4) 13

30. How much extra did Jayanta pay for his choice of seat?

(1) Rs. 300 (2) Rs. 400 (3) Rs. 500 (4) Rs. 1000

31. How much extra did Gargi pay for her choice of seat?

(1) 0 (2) Rs. 300 (3) Rs. 400 (4) Rs. 1000

32. Who among the following did not pay any extra amount for his/her choice of seat?

(1) Kikira (2) Manik (3) Gargi (4) Tapesh

Directions for questions 33 to 36: Answer the questions on the basis of the information given below.

[CAT 2017 Shift 2]

A high security research lab requires the researchers to set a pass key sequence Passed on the scan of the five fingers of their left hands. When an employee first joins the lab, her fingers are scanned in an order of her choice, and then when she wants to re-enter the facility, she has to scan the five fingers in the same sequence.

The lab authorities are considering some relaxations of the scan order requirements, since it is observed that some employees often get locked-out because they forget the sequence.

33. The lab has decided to allow a variation in the sequence of scans of the five fingers so that at most two scans (out of five) are out of place. For example, if the original sequence is Thumb (T), index finger (I), middle finger (M), ring finger (R) and little finger (L) then TLMRI is also allowed, but TMRLI is not.

How many different sequences of scans are allowed for any given person's original scan?

(1) 11 (2) 10 (3) 9 (4) 8

34. The lab has decided to allow variations of the original sequence so that input of the scanned sequence of five fingers is allowed to vary from the original sequence by one place for any of the fingers. Thus, for example, if TIMRL is the original sequence, then ITRML is also allowed, but LIMRT is not.

How many different sequences are allowed for any given person's original scan?

(1) 7 (2) 8 (3) 9 (4) 6

35. The lab has now decided to require six scans in the pass key sequence, where exactly one finger is scanned twice, and the other fingers are scanned exactly once, which can be done in any order. For example, a possible sequence is TIMTRL.

Suppose the lab allows a variation of the original sequence (of six inputs) where at most two scans (out of six) are out of place, as long as the finger originally scanned twice is scanned twice and other fingers are scanned once.

How many different sequences of scans are allowed for any given person's original scan?

(1) 14 (2) 13 (3) 15 (4) 12

36. The lab has now decided to require six scans in the pass key sequence, where exactly one finger is scanned twice, and the other fingers are scanned exactly once, which can be done in any order. For example, a possible sequence is TIMTRL.

Suppose the lab allows a variation of the original sequence (of six inputs) so that input in the form of scanned sequence of six fingers is allowed to vary from the original sequence by one place for any of the fingers, as long as the finger originally scanned twice is scanned twice and other fingers are scanned once.

How many different sequences of scans are allowed if the original scan sequence is LRLTIM?

(1) 8 (2) 11 (3) 13 (4) 14

Directions for questions 37 to 39: Answer the questions on the basis of the information given below.

[CAT 1994]

Five of India's leading models are posing for a photograph promoting "World Peace and Understanding". But then, Rakesh Shreshtha the photographer is having a tough time getting them to stand in a straight line, because Aishwarya refuses to stand next to Sushmita since Sushmita had said something about her in a leading gossip magazine. Rachel and Anu want to stand together because they are "such good friends, y'know". Manpreet on the other hand cannot get along well with Rachel, because there is some talk about Rachel scheming to get a contract already awarded to Manpreet. Anu believes her friendly astrologer who has asked her to stand at the extreme right for all group photographs. Finally, Rakesh managed to pacify the girls and got a beautiful picture of five beautiful girls smiling beautifully in a beautiful straight line, promoting world peace.

37. If Aishwarya is standing at the extreme left, who is standing in the middle?

(1) Manpreet (2) Sushmita (3) Rachel (4) Cannot say

38. If Aishwarya stands at the extreme left, who is standing second from left?

(1) Cannot say (2) Sushmita (3) Rachel (4) Manpreet

39. If Anu's astrologer tells her to stand second from left and Aishwarya decides to stand second from right, then who is the girl standing at the extreme right?

(1) Rachel (2) Sushmita (3) Cannot say (4) Manpreet

ANSWER KEYS

PRACTICE EXERCISE – 1

1. (4)	**2.** (3)	**3.** (2)	**4.** (3)	**5.** (4)	**6.** (4)	**7.** (2)	**8.** (3)	**9.** (3)	**10.** (1)
11. (4)	**12.** (2)	**13.** (2)	**14.** (2)	**15.** (3)	**16.** (4)	**17.** (3)	**18.** (4)	**19.** (4)	**20.** (3)
21. (1)	**22.** (3)	**23.** (3)	**24.** (2)	**25.** (2)	**26.** (1)	**27.** (3)	**28.** (1)	**29.** (3)	**30.** (4)
31. (2)	**32.** (4)	**33.** (3)	**34.** (4)	**35.** (2)					

PRACTICE EXERCISE – 2

1. (4)	**2.** (3)	**3.** (4)	**4.** (1)	**5.** (4)	**6.** (1)	**7.** (1)	**8.** (4)	**9.** (2)	**10.** (1)
11. (3)	**12.** (4)	**13.** (3)	**14.** (4)	**15.** (2)	**16.** (3)	**17.** (1)	**18.** (3)	**19.** (4)	**20.** (1)
21. (1)	**22.** (2)	**23.** (4)	**24.** (4)	**25.** (2)	**26.** (4)	**27.** (1)	**28.** (2)	**29.** (1)	**30.** (3)
31. (4)	**32.** (4)	**33.** (1)	**34.** (2)	**35.** (3)	**36.** (3)	**37.** (2)	**38.** (4)	**39.** (4)	

EXPLANATIONS

PRACTICE EXERCISE – 1

For questions 1 to 4:

From (2) there is one student between Pinky and Madhu, so they are sitting on alternate seats. From (4), Madhu will be 2nd to the right of Pinky and Amit will be 2nd to the right of Madhu.

By using (1), the two professors are either sitting opposite or sitting on alternate seats. Using these information and (3) as well, following 3 cases are possible –

Case - 1 **Case - 2**

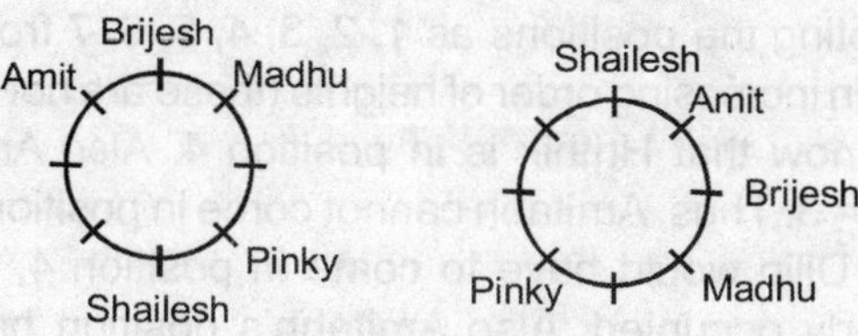

Case - 3

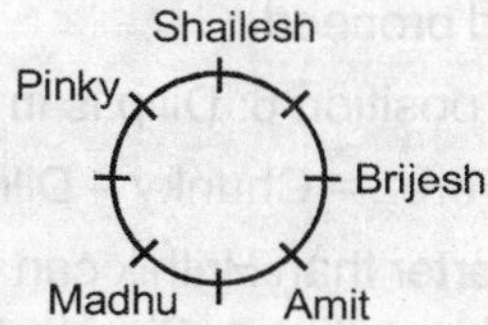

Because of (5), case3 will not be possible, as Amit is sitting to the immediate left of Brijesh in this case.

1. In case 1, if Chirag sits next to Amit, then Brijesh, Amit & Chirag will be adjacent. Lokesh and Nitin can sit on the remaining two seats, so 2 arrangements are possible.

If Chirag sits between 2 girls, then Nitin and Lokesh can again interchange their positions, and 2 arrangements possible.

In case 2, If Chirag sits between 2 girls, then Nitin and Lokesh can again interchange their positions, and 2 arrangements possible.

Total 6 arrangements are possible.

2. Only statements (i) & (ii) are definitely true in both cases.

3. (i) In case 1, depending upon who among Nitin and Lokesh is adjacent to Pinky, the other of two will be opposite to Madhu.

(ii) This is not possible in case 2.

In case 1, Lokesh will be opposite to Madhu

(iii) This points to case1, and more than 1 person can be opposite to Madhu.

4. In case 1, Chirag will be to the immediate right of Amit, and Nitin and Lokesh can interchange their positions, so there are 2 possible arrangements.

In case 2, Nitin and Lokesh will be on either side of Pinky. But Chirag will also have no neighbour from same department. Thus, case 2 is not possible.

For questions 5 to 8:

For (3) to be true, either of following is possible:

(a) both are sitting at middle of longer sides, but then Love cannot be sitting opposite to Reema

(b) both are sitting at shorter sides, which is also not possible because one seat is occupied by Aditi.

(c) both are sitting at the end of the two longer sides, which is possible.

To satisfy (1), Jatin will be sitting at the centre along the side which is opposite to the side along which Rohit is sitting. Since Aditi is on shorter side and equidistant from Jatin and Prachi, so Prachi will be sitting opposite to Jatin.

Following arrangements are possible:

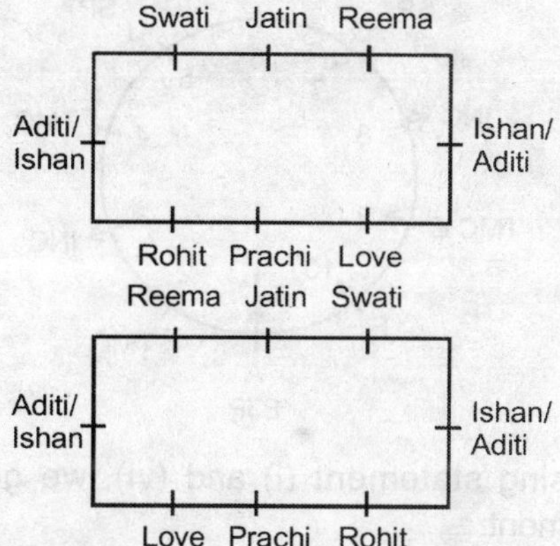

5. It can be either Swati or Reema

6. Swati is always opposite of Rohit

7. Only for Jatin and Prachi their both neighbours can be determined uniquely.

8. After the shift, Swati and Love will be opposite to each other in both the cases.

For questions 9 to 12:

From (2) (3) and (6) we get the following arrangements:

F/C	—	C/F	—
—	G/H	—	H/G

Since C is not at the end, F is sitting at the end. A is also not at any corner and sitting opposite to G, so H is sitting at the right end of the row. D is not sitting opposite to C or F so he is sitting opposite to H.

The following are the possible arrangements:

F	A	C	D
E/B	G	B/E	H

9. A is sitting immediately to the right of C.

10. G is sitting between B and E.

11. Either B or E is sitting opposite to C.

12. From statement (ii), E is not sitting opposite to C, so he is sitting at the left end of row.

For questions 13 to 16:

Denote all the names by their first letter. Using statements (iii), (iv) and (v) we get the following arrangement:

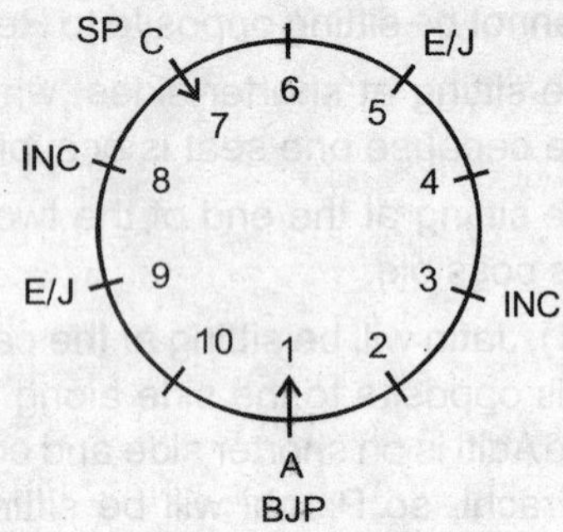

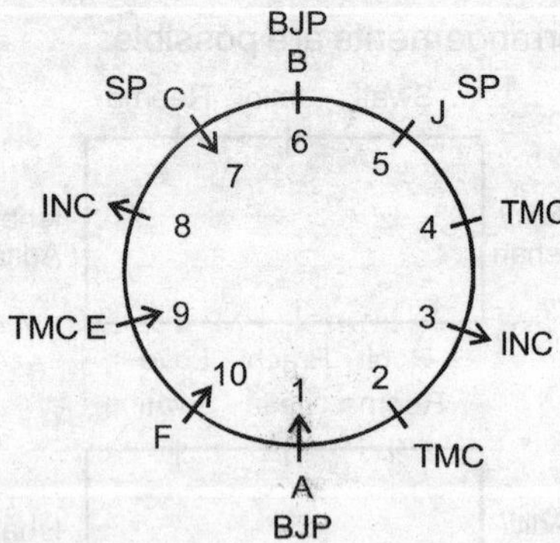

Now, using statement (i) and (vi), we get the final arrangement:

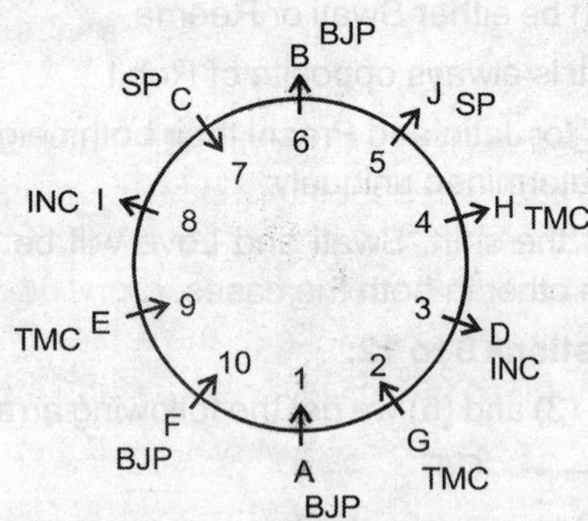

13. Two TMC MPs were facing towards the centre.

14. George, Herman and Enos were TMC MPs.

15. Ishank was sitting third to the left of Anant.

16. Ishant, Jaitley and Herman were not sitting at consecutive positions.

For questions 17 to 20:

The following five cases are possible:

	Case 1	Case 2	Case 3	Case 4	Case 5
First	Sunil	Sajid	Sajid	Sunil	Sanjay
Second	Salim	Sanjay	Sanjay	Sajid	Sajid
Third	Sanjay	Salim	Sunil	Sanjay	Sunil
Last	Sajid	Sunil	Salim	Salim	Salim

17. If Sajid is the last person to visit, then from Case 1 we can say that Sunil visited Feroz first.

18. Sanjay can never be the last person to visit Feroz.

19. Five ways

20. Sunil

For questions 21 to 24:

Denoting the positions as 1, 2, 3, 4, 5, 6, 7 from left to right in increasing order of heights (these are not heights), we know that Hrithik is in position 4. Also Amitabh – Dilip = 3. Thus, Amitabh cannot come in position 7 since then Dilip would have to come in position 4, which is already occupied. Also Amitabh's position has to be greater than 3 or else Dilip's position would be negative. Thus, only positions for Amitabh are 5 and 6. Assume one of them and proceed.

If Amitabh is in position 6: Dilip is in positon 3.

Also Hrithik – Feroz = Chunky – Dilip.

Feroz being shorter than Hrithik can come in positions 1 or 2. If Feroz is in position 1, Chunky has to be in position 6. Not possible. Thus, Feroz can be only in position 2 and Chunky in position 5. Left positions are 1 and 7 and since Feroz is shorter than Govinda, Govinda is in position 7 and Fardeen in position 1.

If Amitabh is in position 5: Dilip is in position 2. Using the same logic as above, Feroz can be in position 1 or 3 and accordingly Chunky will be in position 5 or 3. Both of these is not possible. Thus, Amitabh cannot be in position 5.

Thus, final position:

Fardeen < Feroz < Dilip < Hrithik < Chunky < Amitabh < Govinda

For questions 25 to 27:

Statement (c) implies that A is sitting opposite of C. Similarly, B, E and F are sitting in front of D, G and H respectively. By using statements (e) and (f), along with (c), two sitting arrangements are possible as follows:

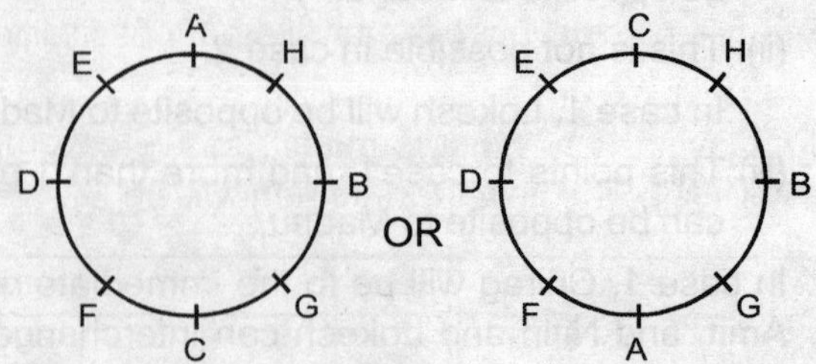

By using statements (b) and (e), we can deduce that as F is not wearing a T-shirt having one of its colors as red and thus, he cannot be a neighbor of A. Hence, we can negate the second arrangement.

25. D is definitely a male. By using statements (e) and (d), we can deduce that E, F and B are females. Using statements (a) and (f), we can see that G is a female. Hence, E, F, B, G and A are definitely females. C and H may be male or female. The number of females in the group cannot be more than 7.

26. According to statement (e), D is not wearing a T-shirt having one of its colors as blue. As he is a male, he is not wearing a T-shirt having one of its colors as orange either. By using statements (g) and (b), it's clear that D is not wearing a T-shirt having one of its colors as yellow, as A and H are already wearing T-shirts having one of their colors as yellow. Hence, D must be wearing a T-shirt having colors red and green.

27. E, D and F are sitting together and their names are also consecutive letters in the English-alphabet. Hence, D is sitting in between E and F.

For questions 28 to 31:

From statement (i) and (ii), the primary arrangement is as follows:

Youngest			Oldest			Second Youngest

From statement (iv) and (v), there are two persons between Dolo and Govind, and Govind is not the oldest. The various possibilities are

i.	Govind			Dolo			
ii.		Govind			Dolo		
iii.			Govind			Dolo	
iv.		Dolo			Govind		
v.			Dolo			Govind	
vi.				Dolo			Govind

From statement (iii) and (vii), it is clear that Chintu is neither the youngest nor the second youngest, hence will not stand at either of the ends.

Also, he is to the immediate left of Ekta, so he will not stand between Dolo and Govind.

From this information, we can rule out possibilities (ii), (iii), (iv) and (v).

Also, Govind is not the youngest, so we can rule out possibility (i). The new arrangement will be

	Chintu	Ekta	Dolo			Govind
Youngest			Oldest			Second Youngest

Now, among the remaining three persons, neither Bhola nor Farhan is the youngest. Hence, Ankit is the youngest.

The given information can be tabulated as shown below.

Order of the position of friends from left to right.

Ankit	Chintu	Ekta	Dolo	Farhan/ Bhola	Bhola/ Farhan	Govind
Youngest			Oldest			Second Youngest

28. Dolo is the oldest in the group.

29. Three people are standing between Ekta and Govind.

30. Ekta is certainly standing adjacent to Dolo.

31. Govind is standing at the right end of the row.

For questions 32 to 35:

The seating chart would be as shown in the diagram below. From Clue A, it is clear that one couple is Rahul Gupta, the father and Teena Gupta, his wife (clue E). Rakesh and Naina are a second couple (clue C). Since no one sat next to his or her spouse (clue B), Bipin is not married to Rekha implying that he is married to Henny.

Men and women alternated around the table (clue B), with Rahul Gupta at the head (clue A). Since the three people on each side of the table had different surnames (clue F), Mrs. Gupta and her son did not sit on the same side. By clue E, Teena sat to her son's right. Thus, Teena's son sat in position (5) and Teena sat in position (4).

Bipin then sat on the side opposite Teena, between Rekha and Mrs. Yadav (clue D) in position (7), and his last name is Bhandari (clue F). Then, by clue F, Rekha's last name is Gupta; her spouse Pankaj is the Gupta son. Since Rekha cannot sit next to her husband at the foot of the table, she sits at Bipin's left in position (8) and Mrs. Yadav sits at Bipin's right in position (6).

By elimination, Rakesh and Naina are the Yadavs. Rakesh Yadav sat opposite Bipin Bhandari (clue B) in position (3) and by elimination, Henny Bhandari sat between Rakesh and Rahul Gupta in position (2). Rahul Gupta, who sat at the head of the table, sat in position (1). In summary, going clockwise around the table:

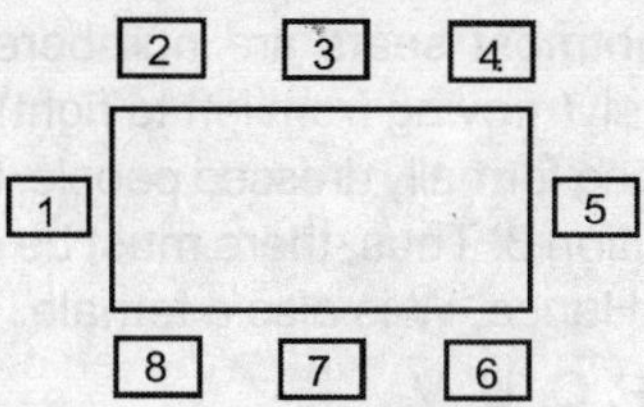

1. Rahul Gupta 2. Henny Bhandari

3. Rakesh Yadav 4. Teena Gupta

5. Pankaj Gupta 6. Naina Gupta

7. Bipin Bhandari 8. Rekha Gupta

32. Rakesh is sitting between Teena and Henny.

33. Pankaj is Rahul Gupta's son.

34. Bipin is sitting opposite Rakesh.

35. Pankaj is Rekha's husband.

PRACTICE EXERCISE – 2

For questions 1 to 4:

From the data given in the question the following table can be drawn:

	Formally Dressed	Non-formally Dressed
Males	Q	P, U, V
Females	R	S, X

Total formally dressed persons should be 3 in number. Thus, we must know about one more person who is formally dressed.

Since males and females sit alternately, total number of males / females should be 4 / 5 (in any order). We already know about 4 males and 3 females. Thus, the remaining two people T and W can either be both females or 1 male and 1 female.

1. If T is a formally dressed male, it can be concluded that P, U, V are males not formally dressed. S, X and W are females not formally dressed. It can also be concluded that there are 5 males and 4 females.
2. Since W is a male, T has to be female. Number of males = 5 and number of females = 4. If positions are numbered 1,2,3,4,5,6,7,8,9 from left to right; males sit at positions 1,3,5,7,9 and females sit at 2,4,6,8. Interpreting the options,

   In option (1), P is a male and hence he can be fifth from the left.

   In option (2), Q is a male and he can be seventh from right (or third from left).

   In option (3), W is a male and hence he cannot be fourth from left.

   In option (4), S is a female and she can be second from right (or eighth from left).

   Thus, option (3) is necessarily false.
3. Three rightmost seats are numbered 7, 8 and 9 respectively(moving from left to right). Q is the only male among formally dressed people, thus he should be at position 8. Thus, there must be 4 males and 5 females. Hence, W is also a female.

   Males = P, Q, U, V.

   Females = R, S, T, W, X.

   Males are seated at positions numbered 2, 4, 6 and 8.

   Females are seated at positions numbered 1, 3, 5 and 7.

   Options (1) and (2) are not acceptable because the sequence cannot start with a male. In option (4), P and U are both males, hence they cannot be together.
4. Working through the options, it can be observed that: If option (a) is provided then the only combination possible is:

   <u>FM</u> <u>NF</u> <u>NM</u> <u>FF</u> <u>NM</u> <u>NF</u> <u>FM</u> <u>NF</u> <u>NM</u>

   Where,

   FM = Formally dressed male

   NM = Non-formally dressed male

   NF = Non-formally dressed female

   FF = Formally dressed female

   Thus, R would be seated in the fourth position from the left.

   If option (2) is provided, then the following combinations could be possible:

   <u>NM</u> <u>FF</u> <u>NM</u> <u>NF</u> <u>FM</u> <u>NF</u> <u>FM</u> <u>NF</u> <u>NM</u>
   <u>NM</u> <u>NF</u> <u>FM</u> <u>NF</u> <u>FM</u> <u>NF</u> <u>NM</u> <u>FF</u> <u>NM</u>

   Thus, R could be seated either at the second position or the eighth position (from the left).

   [**Note:** There might be other cases possible but these two are enough to prove that option (2) is not sufficient]

   Option (3) is exactly the same as option (2) since, fifth from the left and fifth from the right are the same position.

   Thus, (3) is not sufficient.

   If option (4) is provided, then the following combinations could be possible:

   <u>FM</u> <u>NF</u> <u>NM</u> <u>FF</u> <u>NM</u> <u>NF</u> <u>FM</u> <u>NF</u> <u>NM</u>
   <u>NM</u> <u>FF</u> <u>NM</u> <u>NF</u> <u>FM</u> <u>NF</u> <u>FM</u> <u>NF</u> <u>NM</u>

   Thus, R could be seated either at the fourth or the second position (from the left).

   [**Note:** There might be other cases possible but these two are enough to prove that option (2) is not sufficient]

For questions 5 to 7:

From the statement (ii), it can be concluded that the number on the Physics book is either 1 or 7. From statement (iv) along with the inference drawn, it be concluded that the books at the top and bottom are Biology and Physics, not necessarily in this order. Now, from statement (iii), the numbers on the Hindi and English books have to be 2 and 6, not necessarily in this order. From statements (i) and (v), it can be deduced that the numbers on the book Chemistry, Sanskrit and Mathematics are 3, 4 and 5 respectively.

After collating above drawn conclusions, the order of the books in the stack is:

Numbering	Books
7	Biology/Physics
6	English/Hindi
5	Mathematics
4	Sanskrit
3	Chemistry
2	Hindi/English
1	Physics/Biology

5. The number of books between Hindi and Chemistry books is either 0 or 2.
6. The sum of the numbers on the English and the Hindi book would have remained unaltered, had the numbers on books been 1 to 7 from top to bottom. Hence, the sum of the numbers on the English book and the Hindi book will be (2 + 6) i.e. 8.
7. If the Biology book is at the bottom i.e. number on it is 1, then the number on the Physics book will be 7. Hence, in the event of interchange of numbers on the Physics and Sanskrit books, the number on the Sanskrit book will be 7.

For questions 8 to 10:

Consider the following table with marked positions.

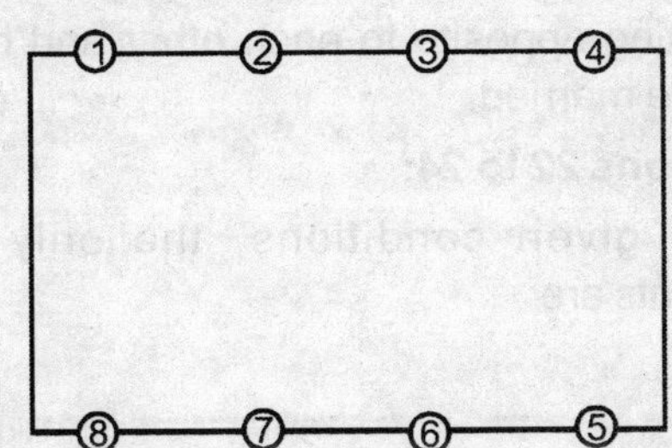

From statements (III) and (VI), Rajbhasa Adhikari is sitting on either chair 4 or chair 8. From statements (II), (IV) and (V), it can be deduced that the Law Officer, the Marketing Officer and the officer who works in PNB are sitting along the same side of the table. Now, from statements (I) and (III), it can be concluded that the Finance Officer, the HR Manager, the Technical Officer and the Rajbhasha Adhikari are sitting along the same side of the table. Therefore, IT Officer works in PNB.

Further analysis leads to the following arrangements.

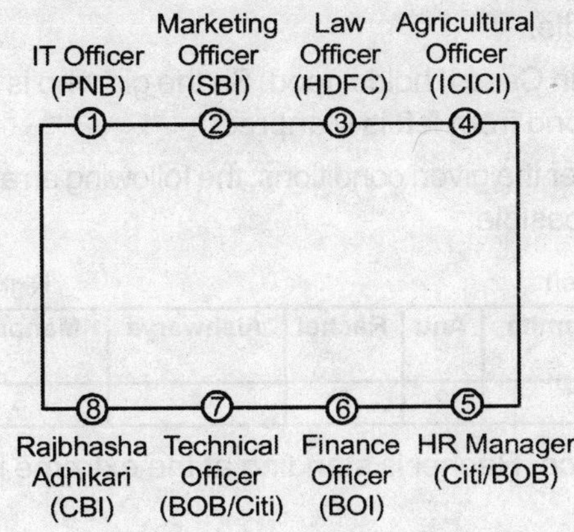

OR

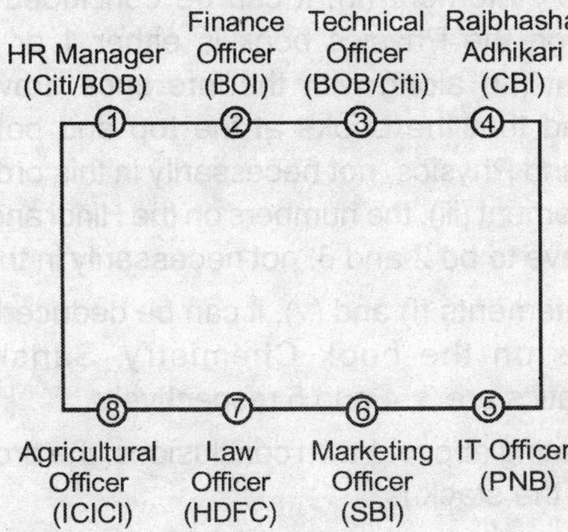

8. HR Manager is sitting to the immediate right of Finance officer.
9. For six persons, we can definitely determine the banks in which they work.
10. The person who is sitting opposite the Law Officer works in BOI.

For questions 11 to 13:

Let the ages of the five persons be A1 to A5 (in ascending order). From statements (v) and (i), it can be observed that Lakhan, the youngest person, Kamal and Jivan live on four consecutive floors from up to down. Now, from statement (iii), we can conclude that the oldest person lives on F1. From statement (vii), it can be deduced that Monika lives on F4 as she does not live on F1. Therefore, Nalin lives on F1.

From statement (v), Kamal is older than exactly three people, so his age must be A4. From statement (vi), the age of Lakhan must be greater than A2. Since Nalin is the oldest, the age of Lakhan must be A3.

Further analysis leads to the following table.

Floor	Name	Age	Monuments Visited
F5	Lakhan	A3	Jantar Mantar
F4	Monika	A1 (Youngest)	Rambagh Palace
F3	Kamal	A4	Hawa Mahal/Jal Mahal
F2	Jivan	A2	Jal Mahal/Hawa Mahal
F1	Nalin	A5 (Oldest)	City Palace

11. Nalin is not the youngest.
12. Kamal visited either Hawa Mahal or Jal Mahal.
13. The required number of floors is 3.

For questions 14 to 17:

From the statement (ii), it can be concluded that the number on the Physics book is either 1 or 7. From statement (iv) along with the inference drawn, it be concluded that the books at the top and bottom are Biology and Physics, not necessarily in this order. Now, from statement (iii), the numbers on the Hindi and English books have to be 2 and 6, not necessarily in this order.

From statements (i) and (v), it can be deduced that the numbers on the book Chemistry, Sanskrit and Mathematics are 3, 4 and 5 respectively.

After collating above drawn conclusions, the order of the books in the stack is:

Numbering	Books
7	Biology/Physics
6	English/Hindi
5	Mathematics
4	Sanskrit
3	Chemistry
2	Hindi/English
1	Physics/Biology

14. The number of books between Hindi and Chemistry books is either 0 or 2.

15. The sum of the numbers on the English and the Hindi book would have remained unaltered, had the numbers on books been 1 to 7 from top to bottom. Hence, the sum of the numbers on the English book and the Hindi book will be (2 + 6) i.e. 8.

16. If the Biology book is at the bottom i.e. number on it is 1, then the number on the Physics book will be 7. Hence, in the event of interchange of numbers on the Physics and Sanskrit books, the number on the Sanskrit book will be 7.

17. The number on Sanskrit book was 4.

For questions 18 to 21 : The correct seating arrangement can be depicted as shown below:

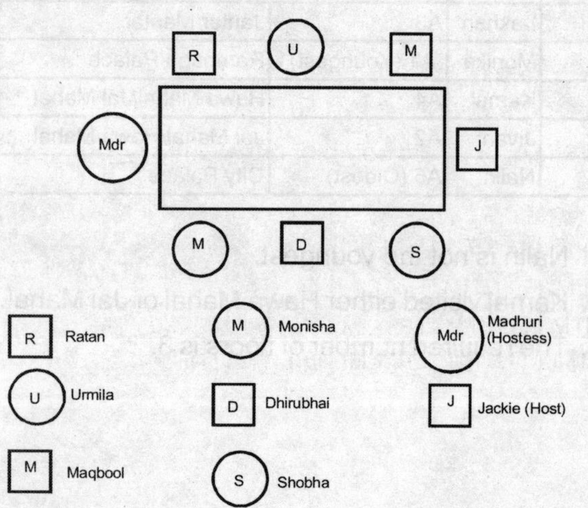

18. Jackie is the host and also sitting on Shobha's right. Hence (3) is the correct answer.

19. Shobha is sitting next to Jackie and Dhirubhai. So she is the only person who is not seated next to a person of the same sex.

20. If Ratan would have exchanged seat with a person four places to his left, which is Shobha, the following arrangement would exist.

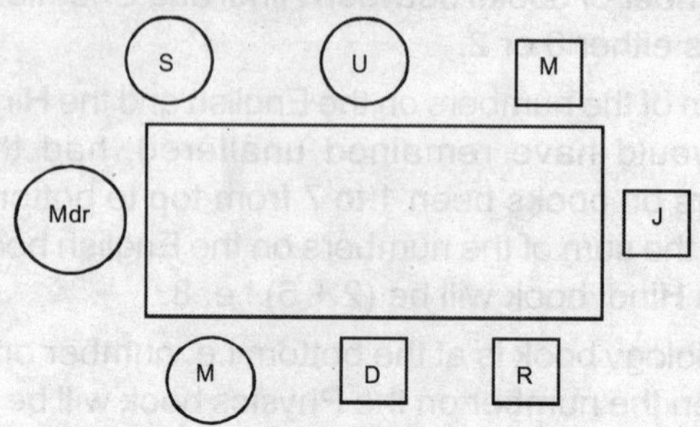

The first statement is hence true, since no man is sitting between two woman and no woman is sitting between two man. However statements II and III are not true. Hence the answer is (1).

21. Among the given choices, only Ratan & Monisha are sitting opposite to each other and hence they must be married.

For questions 22 to 24:

From the given conditions, the only possible arrangements are

Case I:

Left — Right

Sushmita	Manpreet	Aishwarya	Rachel	Anu
1	2	3	4	5

Case II:

Left — Right

Aishwarya	Manpreet	Sushmita	Rachel	Anu
1	2	3	4	5

22. If Aishwarya is standing at the extreme left, case II holds good. Hence Sushmita is standing in the middle.

23. Again Case II holds good. So the girl who is standing second from left is Manpreet.

24. Under the given conditions, the following arrangement is possible:

Left — Right

Sushmita	Anu	Rachel	Aishwarya	Manpreet
1	2	3	4	5

Hence, Rachel is standing at the extreme right.

25. All the sentences are possible except (2) as Grumbs have to be used with Ihavitoo and Grumbs cannot be used in any other type but Bingoes.

26. Since Grumbs and Harrumphs are the Bingoes and Grumbs has to always go with Ihavitoo, so we will have to use Ihavitoo as the Cingo. Since statement I is true, the answer can only be (1) or (4). So we will only evaluate the option (4). Since we have not used Koolodo as Cingo, we can use either Lovitoo or Metoo or both as Dingos. Hence, statement III is also true, so the answer is (4).

27. Option (2) uses two Cingo's instead of one, hence grammatically incorrect. Option (3) violates the same rule again and in addition it uses ihavitoo without using Grumbs. Option (4) again uses two Cingo's instead of one. Hence, the only option that is grammatically correct is (1).

28. If Grumps is the Bingo, then Ihavitoo must also be used. And since Ihavitoo is common to Bingo and Cingo, Ihavitoo must be used as a Cingo . Also no other Cingo can be used. So obviously Harrumphs must also be used as a Bingo. And since we are not using Koolodo as Cingo, we can use Lovitoo as Dingo. So (1), (3) and (4) can all be true. So (2) cannot be true.

For questions 29 to 32:

Since Jayanta, Ajit and Byomkesh are sitting in rows 10, 11, 12 respectively since only this combination of rows have 3 different consecutive amount for their choices of seat.

Possible combination

Aisle	Jayanta, 10 500	Ajit, 11 400	Byomkesh, 12 1000
Window	300	200	1000

Since, Manik is sitting next to Jayanta, so possible combinations for Manik is

Jayanta	Manik	Amount
Aisle, C	Auskem, D	500
Aisle, D	E, Middle	0
Window, A	Middle, B	0

Total amount = 4600

∴ Jayanta, Ajim, Byomkesh and Manik sits at Aisle seat, which costs them total of 24000.

Information gathered by details given:-

	Seat	Row	Extra amount paid
Ajit	Aisle	10	400
Byomkesh	Aisle	12	1000
Gargi	Middle	1/13	1000
Jayanta	Aisle	10	500
Kikira	Window	1/13	1000
Manik	Aisle	10	500
Prodosh	Window	20	200
Tapesh	Window	21	0
Total			4600

29. Since Jayanta is sitting in row 10, and Manik is next to Jayanta, therefore he is sitting in row 10.

30. Jayanta is sitting in row 10, seat C which is an Aisle seat, therefore she paid 500 extra.

31. Gargi was sitting at middle seat in either row 1 or 13, therefore she paid 1000 extra.

32. Tapesh sat in row 21, for which there extra amount.

33. Let original sequence be abcde.

Therefore, possible combinations could be:

bacde			
cbade	acbde		
dbcae	adcbe	abdce	
ebcda	aecdb	abedc	abced

⇒ 11 sequences.

34. Let original sequence be abcde.

Therefore, possible combinations could be:

bacde			
badce	acbed		
baced	acbde	abdce	abced

⇒ 8 sequences.

35. 5 + 4 + 3 + 2 + 1

⇒ 15 sequences.

36. Let original sequence be LRLTIM.

Therefore, possible combinations could be:

RLLTIM				
RLTLIM				
RLTLMI	LLRTIM			
RLLITM	LLRITM	LRTLIM		
RLLTMI	LLRTMI	LRTLMI	LRLITM	LRLTMI

For questions 37 to 39:

From the given conditions, the only possible arrangements are

Case I:

Left Right

Sushmita	Manpreet	Aishwarya	Rachel	Anu
1	2	3	4	5

Case II:

Left Right

Aishwarya	Manpreet	Sushmita	Rachel	Anu
1	2	3	4	5

37. If Aishwarya is standing at the extreme left, case II holds good. Hence Sushmita is standing in the middle.

38. Again Case II holds good. So the girl who is standing second from left is Manpreet.

39. Under the given conditions, the following arrangement is possible:

Left Right

Sushmita	Anu	Rachel	Aishwarya	Manpreet
1	2	3	4	5

Hence, Rachel is standing at the extreme right.

Grouping and Distribution

SOLVED EXAMPLES

Directions for examples 1 to 4: Answer the questions on the basis of the information given below.

There are four companies — CCA, T & T, Birla Tea and LLL – in Udyog Nager. The following information, recorded during the FY 2014-15, is known about these four companies:

I. The local sales of LLL were eleven times the profits of T & T.

II. The sum of exports of Birla Tea and LLL is equal to half the equity base of CCA.

III. The sum of equity base of Birla Tea and the local sales of T & T is equal to five times the exports of T & T.

IV. The profit of LLL = the local sales of CCA – the exports of Birla Tea.

V. The profit of CCA is equal to the average profits of T & T and LLL.

VI. The total profit of all the companies put together was Rs. 100 crore.

VII. The local sales of Biral Tea was 1.25 times the exports of CCA.

VIII. The equity base of T & T = Total exports of all four companies – Rs. 50 crore.

IX. The equity base of LLL = 7 × (Profit of LLL + Profit of Birla Tea – Profit of T & T).

The following are some additional information regarding the four aforementioned parameters for the given companies:

1. Local sales of LLL = Rs. 110 crore
2. Equity base of CCA = Rs. 500 crore
3. Local sales of Birla Tea = Rs. 100 crore
4. Equity base of Birla Tea = Rs. 450 crore
5. Exports of T & T = Rs. 120 crore
6. Profit of Birla Tea = Rs. 40 crore
7. Exports of Birla Tea = Rs. 100 crore

1. In FY 2014-15, the equity base of LLL was

(1) Rs. 500 crore (2) Rs. 400 crore

(3) Rs. 450 crore (4) Rs. 420 crore

2. In FY 2014-15, the profit of LLL was

(1) Rs. 30 crore (2) Rs. 40 crore

(3) Rs. 20 crore (4) Rs. 10 crore

3. In FY 2014-15, the equity base of CCA was greater than the equity base of T & T by

(1) 10% (2) 20%

(3) 25% (4) 50%

4. In FY 2014-15, the total local sales of all the four companies put together as a percentage of total equity base of all four companies put together was

(1) 36% (2) 28%

(3) 32% (4) 33%

8.2 GROUPING AND DISTRIBUTION

For examples 1 to 4:

From the additional data, we can draw the following table:

Terms	Companies			
(Rs. in crore)	CCA	T & T	Birla Tea	LLL
Equity base	500	D	450	G
Local sales	A	E	100	110
Export	B	120	100	H
Profit	C	F	40	I

Using the mother data,

(I) $F = \frac{110}{11} =$ Rs. 10 crore

(II) $100 + H = \frac{500}{2} \Rightarrow H =$ Rs. 150 crore

(III) $450 + E = 5 \times 120 \Rightarrow E =$ Rs. 150 crore

(IV) $I = A - 100$ ... (i)

(V) $C = \frac{F+I}{2}$

$\Rightarrow 2C = F + I$

$\Rightarrow 2C = 10 + I$ ... (ii)

(VI) $C + F + I + 40 = 100$

From equation (ii), we get

$C + 10 + (2C - 10) + 40 = 100$

$\Rightarrow 3C - 10 = 50$

$\Rightarrow C =$ Rs. 20 crore

$\therefore I =$ Rs. 30 crore and $A =$ Rs. 130 crore

(VII) $100 = 1.25 \times B$

$\Rightarrow B = \frac{100}{1.25} =$ Rs. 80 crore

(VIII) $D = 80 + 120 + 100 + 150 - 50 =$ Rs. 400

(IX) $G = 7 \times (I + 40 - F)$

$= 7 \times (30 + 40 - 10)$

$= 7 \times 60 =$ Rs. 420 crore

1. 4 Rs. 420 crore.

2. 1 Rs. 30 crore.

3. 3 Required percentage $= \left(\frac{500}{400} - 1\right) \times 100 = 25.$

4. 2 Total local sales of all companies

$= 130 + 150 + 100 + 110 =$ Rs. 490 crore

Total equity base of all companies

$= 500 + 400 + 450 + 420 =$ Rs. 1,770 crore

$\therefore$ Required percentage $= \frac{490}{1770} \times 100 \approx 28.$

Directions for examples 5 to 8: Answer the questions on the basis of the information given below.

Six ladies are travelling together in a train. They are sitting in one block with two rows facing each other, with three ladies in each row. Each of them has written a book in the subject of her interest, and everyone is reading a book written by one of the other ladies in the group. No two ladies are reading a book written by the same lady. It is also known that:

I. Aishwarya, who is sitting at a corner seat of a row, is reading the book on mathematics. She does not have interest in psychology.

II. Bipasha is reading a book written by the person sitting opposite her.

III. Champi, sitting between the ladies who have interest in mathematics and chemistry, is reading a book on biology.

IV. Dola, sitting opposite the lady who has interest in biology, is reading a book on geology.

V. The lady who has interest in mathematics is sitting opposite the lady who has interest in psychology.

VI. Geeta, sitting next to the lady who has interest in geology, is reading a book on chemistry.

VII. Farah, who is sitting at a corner seat of a row, is sitting next to the lady who has interest in astronomy.

5. Who is sitting opposite Champi?

(1) Aishwarya (2) Bipasha (3) Geeta (4) Dola

6. Which book is Ms. Farah reading?

(1) Psychology (2) Chemistry (3) Astronomy (4) Biology

7. Aishwarya is

(1) an astronomer (2) a geologist (3) a biologist (4) a psychologist

8. Which of the following pairs of ladies are not sitting opposite each other?

(1) Aishwarya – Dola (2) Bipasha – Champi (3) Geeta – Ms. Farah (4) None of these

For examples 5 to 8:

From statement III

Reading	Mathematics	Astronomy	Chemistry
Occupation			
Name			
Name		Champi	
Occupation	Chemistry		Mathematician
Reading		Biology	

From statement V

Reading	Mathematics	Astronomy	Chemistry
Occupation			Psychologist
Name			
Name		Champi	
Occupation	Chemistry		Mathematician
Reading		Biology	

From statement I, Aishwarya is in a corner and she is not a psychologist and is reading a mathematics' book. Hence the options are:

Reading	Mathematics		
Occupation			Psychologist
Name	Aishwarya		
Name	Aishwarya	Champi	
Occupation	Chemistry		Mathematician
Reading	Mathematics	Biology	

From Statement IV, Since Champi cannot be a biologist, the only option for Dola is in a corner, opposite Aishwarya,

Reading	Mathematics	Astronomy	Chemistry
Occupation	Biologist		Psychologist
Name	Aishwarya		
Name	Dola	Champi	
Occupation	Chemistry		Mathematician
Reading	Geology	Biology	

From statements VI/VII, Farah will be in one corner. Geeta will also be in a corner since she is sitting next to geologist. (We do not know the occupation of the middle-seat occupants only.

From statement II, Bipasha is in the middle-seat. Of the two occupations left (Geologist and Astronomer), Champi must be an astronomer to satisfy statement II

Reading	Mathematics	Astronomy	
Occupation	Biologist	Geologist	Psychologist
Name	Aishwarya	Bipasha	
Name	Dola	Champi	
Occupation	Chemistry	Astronomer	Mathematician
Reading	Geology	Biology	

Now from statements VI/VII, we have the final table.

Reading	Mathematics	Astronomy	Chemistry
Occupation	Biologist	Geologist	Psychologist
Name	Aishwarya	Bipasha	Geeta
Name	Dola	Champi	Farah
Occupation	Chemistry	Astronomer	Mathematician
Reading	Geology	Biology	Psychology

5. 2 By the table above, Bipasha is sitting opposite to Champi.

6. 1 By the table above, Ms. Farah is reading the book on Psychology.

7. 3 By the table above, Aishwarya is a biologist.

8. 4 By the table above, each of the given pair of ladies are sitting opposite to each other.

Directions for examples 9 to 12: Answer the questions on the basis of the information given below.

Six friends — George, John, Antony, Dhaanush, Sandeep and Ravi — are married to six different ladies — Arpita, Kamya, Jacklin, Nishita, Mamta and Deepika — not necessarily in the same order. Each of the six friends belongs to a different city from among Patiala, Delhi, Mumbai, Kolkata, Chennai and Bengalore. Each of them plays a different game from among Cricket, Football, Basketball, Billiards, TT and Badminton.

It is also known that:

I. Husbands of Jacklin, Mamta or Deepika do not play Football or Basketball.
II. The friend from Mumbai plays Cricket.
III. Ravi, who is from Bengalore, plays Football.
IV. Antony and Sandeep, neither of whom is from Mumbai, are married to Arpita and Nishita respectively.
V. The friends from Delhi and Kolkata play TT and Basketball respectively.
VI. Dhaanush is from Chennai.
VII. Antony plays Billiards.

9. The friend from Kolkata is married to

(1) Jacklin (2) Nishita (3) Arpita (4) Cannot be determined

10. The friend who plays Billiards is from

(1) Chennai (2) Patiala (3) Bengalore (4) Cannot be determined

11. Dhaanush plays

(1) Badminton (2) Football (3) Basketball (4) Cannot be determined

12. If Mamta's husband plays TT and Deepika is married to George, then Dhaanush's wife is

(1) Mamta (2) Kamya (3) Jacklin (4) None of these

For examples 9 to 12:

By the information given in the question the following table can be made:

Name	Wife	Place	Game
George		Delhi / Mumbai	TT / Cricket
John		Mumbai / Delhi	Cricket / TT
Antony	Arpita	Patiala	Billiards
Dhaanush		Chennai	Badminton
Sandeep	Nishita	Kolkata	Basketball
Ravi	Kamya	Bengalore	Football

9. 2 Nishita is married to the man from Kolkata.

10. 2 Antony plays Billiards and belongs to Patiala.

11. 1 Dhaanush plays Badminton.

12. 3 In this scenario Jacklin is Dhaanush's wife.

Directions for examples 13 to 16: Answer the questions on the basis of the information given below.

Four dogs, each of a different breed from amongst Airedale, Boxer, Collie and Doberman, participated in the 'Kennel Show' and obtained the top four ranks. Name of the dogs were Jack, Kelly, Lad and Max, not necessarily in the same order. Their owners are Ms Anubhuti, Ms Dewdrops, Ms Suchita and Ms Rakhi, again not necessarily in the given order.

Some additional information is given below:

I. Ms. Suchita's dog stood neither first nor second.
II. The Collie stood first.
III. Max stood second.
IV. Jack is an Airedale.
V. Ms Dewdrops' dog, the Doberman, ranked fourth.
VI. The name of Ms Rakhi's dog is Kelly.

13. The first rank was obtained by
(1) Ms Anubhuti's dog (2) Ms Rakhi's dog (3) Max (4) Jack

14. The breed of Ms. Suchita's dog was
(1) Collie (2) Boxer (3) Airedale (4) Dobermann

15. In which of the following statements, are the dogs correctly listed in the descending order of their rank (highest rank to lowest rank)?
I. Kelly; the Airedale; Ms Anubhuti's dog
II. The boxer; Ms Suchita's dog; Jack
III. Ms Anubhuti's dog; the Airedale; Lad
(1) I only (2) II only (3) III only (4) I and III

16. Which of the following conclusions can be drawn?
A. Max is a boxer.
B. The Doberman is Lad.
C. Jack wins the third prize.
(1) A and B (2) A and C (3) A, B and C (4) B and C

For examples 13 to 16:

The given information can be tabulated as shown below:

Prize	First	Second	Third	Fourth
Owner	Rakhi	Anubhuti	Suchita	Dewdrops
Breed	C	B	A	D
Name	Kelly	Max	Jack	Lad

13. 2 The first prize is won by ms. Rakhi's dog.

14. 3 The breed of ms. Suchita's dog is Airedale.

15. 3 Dogs are correctly listed in the descending order of their prizes in option (c).

16. 3 Conclusions A, B and C can be drawn on the basis of the given information.

8.6 GROUPING AND DISTRIBUTION

Directions for examples 17 to 20: Answer the questions on the basis of the information given below.

A house tax inspector, Choitram, evaluated the houses of Arpan, Bunty, Chhotu, Dinku and Eshwar. The house of each of them belong to a different category from among A, B, C, D, and E. The categories are based on the year of its completion, which are prior to 1970, 1970 to 1979, 1980 to 1989, 1990 to 1999 and 2000 onwards. Each of these houses are either self-occupied or tenanted, given out on rent.

Additional information are given:

I. Chhotu's house is one of the two houses which are tenanted.

II. Bunty's house was constructed earlier than that of Arpan's.

III. Eshwar's house is the newest and Dinku's house is the oldest. Neither of the two belongs to categories A or B.

IV. Bunty's house belongs to category D.

V. The tenanted houses belong to categories B and D.

VI. Chhotu built his house in 1987.

17. What is the correct sequence (oldest to newest) of houses in terms of year of construction?

(1) Dinku, Bunty, Arpan, Chhotu, Eshwar

(2) Dinku, Chhotu, Bunty, Arpan, Eshwar

(3) Dinku, Bunty, Chhotu, Arpan, Eshwar

(4) Dinku, Arpan, Bunty, Chhotu, Eshwar

18. Which of the following combinations of 'Person's house - Category' are necessarily correct?

I. Arpan's house – A

II. Dinku's house – C

III. Chhotu's house – B

(1) I and III only (2) II and III only (3) III only (4) All are correct

19. If Eshwar's house belongs to the category E, to which category Dinku's house belongs to?

(1) A (2) B (3) C (4) D

20. Which of the following is the correct sequence (newest to oldest) of self-occupied houses?

(1) Dinku, Arpan, Eshwar (2) Arpan, Dinku, Eshwar (3) Eshwar, Arpan, Dinku (4) Eshwar, Dinku, Arpan

For examples 17 to 20: The given information can be tabulated as shown below:

Name	Category	Year of construction	Self occupied / Tenanted
Arpan	A	1990 to 1999	Self occupied
Bunty	D	1970 to 1979	Tenanted
Chhotu	B	1980 to 1989	Tenanted
Dinku	C or E	Prior to 1970	Self occupied
Eshwar	C or E	2000 onwards	Self occupied

17. 3 From the above table, the correct sequence (oldest to newest) of houses in terms of year of construction is Dinku, Bunty, Chhotu, Arpan, Eshwar.

18. 1 From the above table, only I and III are correct.

19. 3 From the above table, if Eshwar's house belongs to the category E, then Dinku's house belongs to category C.

20. 3 From the above table, the correct sequence (newest to oldest) among self-occupied houses is Eshwar, Arpan, Dinku.

PRACTICE EXERCISE – 1

Directions for questions 1 to 4: Answer the questions on the basis of the information given below.

Six writers – A, B, C, D, E and F – made their contribution to literature in the form of at least one genre out of poem, novel and drama. Each one of them wrote in only one language. Two belonged to the 17th century, three to the 19th century and one to the 20th century. Four were recognized as great poets, three as great novelists, and three as great dramatists. One contributed to Bengali literature, One to Tamil, two to Hindi and two to Marathi. Of the two Marathi writers one contributed to poetry only and the other contributed to poetry, novel and drama. Only the Hindi and Tamil writers belonged to 19th century. One of the Hindi writers contributed to poetry and novel only, while the Tamil writer contributed to novels and drama only. The Bengali writer belonged to the 17th century and contributed to poetry only. A belonged to 20th century and was only a poet. B wrote drama only and C wrote in Marathi. D was a Hindi poet and novelist of 19th century, and F contributed to poetry only.

1. B wrote in

(1) Marathi (2) Hindi (3) Bengali (4) Tamil

2. Who was the Tamil writer?

(1) F (2) E (3) B (4) A

3. To which genre of literature did C contribute?

(1) Poetry (2) Novel (3) Drama (4) All the three

4. Who among the following belonged to 19th century?

(1) A (2) B (3) F (4) None of these

Directions for questions 5 to 8: Answer the questions on the basis of the information given below.

In Kannes film festival eight short films were screened back to back in eight slots. Each film was one hour in length and belonged to one of the two categories – Crime or environment. Four directors viz. Pratyush, Rakesh, Yash and Satyajit, each having exactly one film from each category, participated in this film festival.

Further information is given :

1. No director had both his films screened back to back.
2. Films of the same category were screened back to back only once.
3. First and the last films, screened, were on environment.
4. Yash's film on crime was screened after Rakesh's film on crime.
5. Satyajit's film on crime was not among the first four films screened.
6. Not more than 3 films were screened between the two films directed by Satyajit.
7. Only one film of Pratyush was screened before all the films directed by Rakesh and Yash.

5. For how many films can we determine its exact slot?

(1) Zero (2) One (3) Four (4) Six

6. What extra information is required to find out the exact order of screening of films?

(i) Pratyush and Rakesh's films on crime were screened back to back.

(ii) Satyajit's film on crime and Yash's film on environment were screened back to back.

(iii) Yash's film on crime was not screened in the second last slot.

(1) Only (i) alone (2) Only (ii) alone (3) Only (i) or (iii) alone (4) (i) and (iii) together

7. Which of the following is not a possible slot for Yash's film on environment?

(1) 2nd (2) 3rd (3) 4th (4) (1) and (2) both

8. Which of the following statement is definitely false?

(1) Film directed by Rakesh was not screened in 7th slot.

(2) Film directed by Yash was not screened in 2nd slot.

(3) Film directed by Pratyush was not screened in 1st slot.

(4) None of these

Directions for questions 9 to 12: Answer the questions on the basis of the information given below.

Six friends – Amit, Dan, Farhan, Golu, Sumit and Nitin – bought one item each from among mobile, Ipad, laptop, printer, pendrive and tablet not necessarily in the same order. Each item was of different brand from among Nokia, Samsung, Hp, Philips, LG and Apple. It is also known that:

1. Laptop is of Samsung brand.
2. Farhan bought the item of Philips brand but it was not a pendrive.
3. Nokia manufactures only Ipad and LG doesn't manufacture mobiles.
4. Amit bought a mobile.
5. Apple manufactures only mobiles, pendrives and tablets.
6. Golu bought either a tablet or a printer. Nitin did not buy a laptop.
7. No person bought an item of brand which had the same initial letter as his own name.

9. Which of the following is a correct combination of 'person – item bought – brand'?

(1) Amit – mobile – Apple (2) Nitin – laptop – Samsung (3) Sumit – Ipad – Nokia (4) More than one of the above

10. If it is known that no brand manufactures an item whose initial letter is same as the initial letter of the brand, then who bought the item of LG brand?

(1) Golu (2) Sumit (3) Dan (4) Amit

11. Who bought the printer?

(1) Farhan (2) Golu (3) Nitin (4) Cannot be determined

12. Which item did Dan purchase?

(1) Tablet (2) Laptop (3) Pendrive (4) Mobile

Directions for questions 13 to 16: Answer the questions on the basis of the information given below.

Vikas, a student, has prepared a weekly schedule for his exam preparations. He has to study four subjects – Maths, Physics, Chemistry and Economics. During a period of any seven consecutive days, he will study Maths and Physics on four days each, Chemistry on three days and Economics on two days. On Saturdays as well as Sundays he will study only one subject. On one of the weekdays, which span from Monday to Friday, he will study three subjects, one of which is Economics. On rest of the weekdays, he will study two subjects each.

Some additional information is also given :

1. He will not study any subject on three consecutive days.
2. He will not study Economics on two consecutive days.
3. He will study both Maths and Chemistry exactly once in a week on the same day.

A partial information of the schedule is given in the table below –

Days	Tuesday	Wednesday	Thursday	Friday	Saturday	Sunday	Monday
Subjects	Maths	Physics	Economics	Chemistry	-	Physics	Chemistry

13. Which subject does he study on Saturday?

(1) Maths (2) Physics (3) Chemistry (4) Economics

14. Which subject does he definitely study on Tuesday?

(1) Physics (2) Economics (3) Chemistry (4) None of these

15. Which of the following statement(s) is/are definitely true?

(1) Vikas will study both Maths and Economics on at least one day.

(2) Vikas will study both Physics and Economics on at least one day.

(3) Vikas will study both Chemistry and Economics on at least one day.

(4) More than one of the above.

16. On which day he could have studied both Maths and Physics?

(1) Monday (2) Tuesday (3) Thursday (4) Sunday

Directions for questions 17 to 20: Answer the questions on the basis of the information given below.

Each of the seven siblings – Anshu, Bhuvan, Crystal, Daksh, Eric, Foram and Giresh – participated in a different activity among Painting, Singing, Dancing, Debate, Essay Writing, Cooking and Gymnastics, not necessarily in the same order, during a talent hunt competition organized by their housing society. It is also known that:

(i) There is exactly one pair of twins among the seven and none of the twins participated in Gymnastics.

(ii) Bhuvan participated in Cooking and Anshu participated in Debate.

(iii) Those who participated in Singing, Dancing and Essay Writing are younger to Daksh, who is not the eldest among the seven.

(iv) Eric is younger to Crystal, who is younger to Foram.

(v) The eldest and the youngest of the siblings participated in Dancing and Debate, in no particular order.

(vi) The one who participated in Painting has exactly four siblings elder to him/her and the one who participated in Gymnastics has exactly four siblings younger to him/her.

Note: Twins to be considered equal in age.

17. In which of the following activities did Foram definitely not participate?

(1) Painting (2) Essay Writing (3) Singing (4) None of these

18. Who among the following is one of the twins?

(1) Eric (2) Foram (3) Giresh (4) Daksh

19. Who participated in Gymnastics?

(1) Giresh (2) Eric (3) Crystal (4) Daksh

20. Who participated in dancing?

(1) Eric (2) Foram (3) Giresh (4) Crystal

Directions for questions 21 to 24: Answer the questions on the basis of the information given below.

In Mohan Engineering College, there are four branches – Computers, Electronics, Mechanical and Civil –in engineering program. Each of the four boys Alok, Bimal, Chetan and Daniel is pursuing engineering in a different branch in the aforementioned college, and the same holds true four each of the four girls Parul, Qasa, Rita and Suman. These eight students come to college by four cars – Maruti, Palio, Skoda and Audi – with two students, one male and one female, in each car. Exactly one pair of students who are pursuing engineering in the same branch commute by the same car. Further, it is known :

(i) Suman, who commutes by Skoda and is not pursuing engineering in either Computers branch or Civil branch, is pursuing engineering in the same branch as that of either Bimal or Daniel.

(ii) Rita does not commute by Maruti and Qasa is pursuing engineering in Mechanical branch.

(iii) Chetan and Parul commute by different cars and those who are pursuing engineering in Civil branch commute by Maruti.

(iv) Bimal, who is pursuing engineering in Mechanical branch, commutes by Palio.

21. The boy who is pursuing engineering in Electronics branch commutes by

(1) Maruti (2) Skoda (3) Audi (4) Palio

22. Who are pursuing Civil engineering?

(1) Chetan and Parul (2) Alok and Rita (3) Alok and Parul (4) Daniel and Rita

23. Who commute by Audi?

(1) Alok and Rita (2) Chetan and Qasa (3) Daniel and Qasa (4) Chetan and Rita

24. Which of the following is a correct combination of 'branch – student – the car by which he/she commutes'?

(1) Electronics-Chetan-Audi

(2) Computers-Chetan-Skoda

(3) Electronics-Suman-Palio

(4) Mechanical-Qasa-Palio

Directions for questions 25 to 28: Answer the questions on the basis of the information given below.

Eight families – Bhatias, Guptas, Roys, Mittals, Saxenas, Aptes, Jains and Kriplanis – stay in an apartment, having six floors, numbered 1 to 6 from bottom to top with two flats each. There are six flats in one column, exactly one above another, and similarly six flats are in another column. It is also known that:

(1) There is at least one occupant on each floor.

(2) Guptas and Aptes live on the floor immediately above the floor on which Kriplanis live.

(3) There is only one family that lives in the flats below Bhatias flats in the same column.

(4) Jains and Bhatias flats are not in the same column. Roys live in a flat that is below Jain's flat in the same column.

(5) There are five families that live on the floors above the floor on which Mittals live.

(6) Only Bhatias occupy two flats and these are in the same column on two consecutive floors.

(7) The floor numbers on which Jains and Mittals, whose flats are in the same column, live add upto eight

(8) The number of flats occupied on floors below the floor on which Kriplanis live, is equal to four.

(9) Saxenas' flat is not in the same column in which both Guptas and Mittals flats are.

25. Which family occupies a flat below the Bhatias' flats in the same column?

(1) Mittals (2) Saxenas (3) Roys (4) Jains

26. Which of the following families does definitely not have any other family occupying a flat on their floor?

(1) Kriplani (2) Saxena (3) Jains (4) Roys

27. Which family/families lives/live on the 4th floor?

(1) Only Bhatias (2) Only Kriplanis (3) Both Aptes and Guptas (4) Both Bhatias and Kriplanis

28. Which family lives in a flat immediately below Jains' flat?

(1) Apte (2) Mittals (3) Guptas (4) That flat has no occupant

Directions for questions 29 to 32: Answer the questions on the basis of the information given below.

Each of the seven friends Amit, Boman, Chandu, Dhiru, Endra, Fenka and Gangu, having a different surname from among Chawla, Singh, Negi, Dhawan, Kohli, Yadav and Dhoni, not necessarily in this order, visited a different place from among Goa, Shimla, Mussoorie, Nanital, Darjiling, Dharamsala and Manali, not necessarily in this order. Each of them had a different car from among i10, Sx4, Polo, Alto, Indica V2, i20 and MXUV. Each car was of a different colour out of green, yellow, silver, white, orange, blue and red. It is also know that:

(i) Endra Singh's car was of silver colour, and the place visited by her was neither Mussoorie nor Shimla. Dhiru owned a white coloured i10.

(ii) The number of friends whose first name and surname start with the same letter was two.

(iii) Chandu went to Dharamsala in an orange coloured MXUV. Mr. Dhawan owned a Polo. The silver coloured car was neither i20 nor Alto.

(iv) The friend who owned a green Indica V2 visited Manali and his surname was not Yadav. Gangu and the friend who visited Goa had green and yellow coloured car respectively.

(v) Amit Kohli had red coloured car and he went to Nainital.

(vi) Mr. Yadav did not visit Goa.

29. All the seven friends created their email ids using their first name and surname. Which of the following ids could be the id of the person who visited Manali?

(1) Gangu.negi@gmail.com (2) Boman.yadav@gmail.com

(3) Gangu.yadav@gmail.com (4) Fenku.dhawan@gmail.com

30. Which of the following statement(s) is/are necessary to determine the surname, car, colour of car and the place visited by each of the seven friends?

(i) The surname of Boman was Yadav and he visited Shimla.

(ii) Amit had Alto car.

(1) Only (i) (2) Only (ii) (3) Either (i) or (ii) (4) Both (i) and (ii)

31. The place visited by Dhoni was

(1) Mussoorie (2) Shimla (3) Goa (4) Either (a) or (b)

32. For how many friends it was possible to determine their surname exactly?

(1) 4 (2) 5 (3) 6 (4) 7

Directions for questions 33 to 36: Answer the questions on the basis of the information given below.

Ten objects A, B, C, D, E, F, G, H, I and J are kept in four boxes. Box 1 and Box 2 have at least 3 objects each. Box 3 has at least 2 objects. Box 4 has at least 1 object. It is also known that:

(i) A and B are in the same box. C and F are in the same box which is neither Box 2 nor Box 3.

(ii) Out of C, D, H and J, no two objects are in the same box.

(iii) I is in Box 3. None of E, H and J is in Box 3.

33. If A and E are not in the same box and the number of objects in Box 2 and Box 3 are equal, then which of the following statements cannot be true?

(1) H is in Box 4. (2) E and F are in the same box.

(3) J and B are in the same box. (4) G and D are not in the same box.

34. All the objects from two out of the four boxes are collected and wrapped as a 'gift'. The 'gift' contains 3 objects, and does not have H. H and G are in the same box. How many of the following statements must be true?

I. B and E are not in the same box.

II. One of the objects in the 'gift' is D.

III. Box 1 has more objects than Box 2.

(1) 0 (2) 1 (3) 2 (4) 3

35. If the number of objects in Box 3 and Box 4 are found to be equal and E is in Box 1, then how many of the following statements must be true?

I. C and E are in the same box.

II. A and E are not in the same box.

III. A and H are in the same box.

IV. Exactly one out of C and G is in Box 4.

(1) 1 (2) 2 (3) 3 (4) 4

36. If C and F are in Box 4, then which of the following objects are in Box 3?

(1) I, D and G (2) I, D and E (3) I and D (4) I and G

Directions for questions 37 to 39: Answer the questions on the basis of the information given below.

A survey was conducted among 600 CAT 2012 aspirants to gauge the popularity of four different Test Series – T1, T2, T3 and T4. It was found that the number of aspirants who had joined T1, T2, T3 and T4 was 209, 217, 288 and 284 respectively. It is also known that:

(i) The number of aspirants who had joined T1, T2 and T3 but not T4 was equal to that of those who had joined T1, T2 and T4 but not T3, which, in turn, was 2 less than that of those who had joined all the four Test Series.

(ii) The number of aspirants who had joined only T1, only T2, only T3 and only T4 was 30, 30, 80 and 60 respectively.

(iii) The number of aspirants who had joined exactly three of the four Test Series was 100.

(iv) The number of aspirants who had joined both T1 and T3 but neither T2 nor T4 was 5 less than that of those who had joined both T1 and T4 but neither T2 nor T3.

(v) The number of aspirants who had joined both T3 and T4 but not T2 was equal to that of those who had joined both T3 and T4 but not T1.

(vi) The number of aspirants who had joined both T1 and T2 was 96 and that of those who had joined both T1 and T2 but neither T3 nor T4 was 28.

(vii) The number of aspirants who had joined both T3 and T4 but neither T1 nor T2 was 55.

37. How many aspirants had joined exactly two of the four Test Series?

(1) 201 (2) 191 (3) 221 (4) Cannot be determined

38. How many aspirants had joined both T3 and T4?

(1) 135 (2) 125 (3) 155 (4) 145

39. The number of aspirants who had not joined any of the four Test Series was

(1) 75 (2) 95 (3) 105 (4) 80

Directions for questions 40 to 43: Answer the questions on the basis of the information given below.

There are seven persons namely A, B, C, D, E, F and G, comprising 3 females and 4 males. Each of these seven persons was born on the seven different days of a week starting with Sunday. It is also known that:

I. No **male** was born on a day starting with the letter S.

II. D, **who** is not a female, is younger than both F and G.

III. No two females were born on the consecutive days of the week.

IV. F, who is not a male, is younger than A, who is a female. G is younger than F and elder than B.

V. C is younger than only one person.

40. Which of the following cannot be the day on which D was born?

(1) Friday (2) Thursday (3) Wednesday (4) None of these

41. Who among the following is definitely a male?

(1) B (2) G (3) E (4) None of these

42. If E was born on Saturday, then on which day of the week B was born?

(1) Wednesday (2) Thursday (3) Friday (4) Cannot be determined

43. C was born on

(1) Thursday (2) Monday (3) Wednesday (4) Tuesday

Directions for questions 44 to 47: Answer the questions on the basis of the information given below.

Arjun calls five of his friends - Julie, Sheila, Rano, Jamalo and Rita - from five different phones made by Samsung, Sony, Apple, Nokia and Micromax, not necessarily in the same order. He meets exactly one friend on each day, from Monday to Friday. The day he meets a friend, he does not call her that day, but calls exactly three other friends. He follows this from Monday to Friday, meeting each friend once and calling her thrice in a week. He neither meets nor calls any of these five friends on Saturday and Sunday. It is also known that:

(i) On Wednesday, he neither calls Julie nor the friend whom he calls from his Nokia phone.

(ii) He meets the friend whom he calls from his Apple phone on Friday, which is one of the three days on which he calls Sheila.

(iii) He calls Jamalo, whom he meets on Thursday, from his Sony phone, and two of the three days on which he calls her are the days on which he meets Sheila and Rita.

(iv) He does not use his Samsung phone, which he uses to call Rita, on either Tuesday or Thursday.

(v) Two of the three days on which he calls Julie are Monday and Thursday, and he does not use his Apple phone to call her.

(vi) One of the three days on which he calls Sheila is Tuesday, which is a day on which he does not use his Micromax cell phone to call any of the given friends.

44. The day on which he does not use his Micromax phone to call his given friends is

(1) Tuesday (2) Wednesday (3) Either (1) or (2) (4) Both (1) and (2)

45. The mobile phone that he does not use to call the given friends on the day he meets Rita is

(1) Nokia (2) Sony (3) Micromax (4) Apple

46. The friend whom he does not call on the day when he meets Sheila is

(1) Rita (2) Julie (3) Jamalo (4) Rano

47. The day on which he meets Rita is

(1) Thursday (2) Tuesday (3) Either (1) or (2) (4) Cannot be determined

PRACTICE EXERCISE – 2

Directions for questions 1 to 4: Answer the questions on the basis of the information given below.

A team is to be selected out of a group comprising five men, namely A, B, C, D and E, and six women, namely L, M, N, O, P and Q. In the group, A, B and N are lecturers; C, D, L, M and O are engineers; and the rest are doctors. It is also known that:

I. If at least one out of N and D is selected, B cannot be selected.

II. If L is selected, P must be selected and vice versa.

III. If any one out of A, L, or Q is selected, the other two must also be selected.

IV. D and L cannot be selected together.

V. If E is selected, M must be selected and vice versa.

VI. L and O cannot be selected together.

1. If the team consists of one lecturer, two engineers and three doctors, which of the following is the composition of the team?

(1) BELMPA (2) ALEDPQ (3) AELMPQ (4) ADEMPQ

2. If the team consists of two male lecturers, two female doctors and one engineer, which of the following is the composition of the team?

(1) ABLPQ (2) ABLEQ (3) AQBLO (4) ABLOP

3. If the team consists of two lecturers, two engineers, two doctors and not more than three women, which of the following is the composition of the team?

(1) ABELPQ (2) ABCLPQ (3) ABCLMQ (4) ABELNQ

4. The number of members in the team cannot be more than

(1) 9 (2) 8 (3) 7 (4) None of these

Directions for questions 5 to 7: Answer the questions on the basis of the information given below.

Each of the six friends – Aabhas, Barun, Charu, Deepak, Farooq and Govinda – holds a different designation from among MD, Actor, B.M., Footballer, Consultant, Doctor – with no two of them holding the same designation. Each of them lives in a different city from among Faridabad, Chennai, Delhi, Gurgaon, Kolkata and Bombay and owns a different car from among Corolla, Mercedes, Santro, Swift, Dicor and BMW. Each of the six cars is of a different colour out of Blue, White, Black, Yellow, Green and Red. It is also known that:

I. Aabhas stays in Faridabad and owns a Swift. The actor owns the Mercedes and stays in Delhi.

II. For exactly one of them, the initial letter of his name, his designation, his city, his car and the colour of the car is the same.

III. For exactly one of them, the initial letter for all the four parameters is different from the initial letter of his name.

IV. Except for the above two friends for every other friend exactly one out of designation, city, car, colour of the car starts with the same initial letters as their names.

V. The person having the black Corolla stays in Gurgaon.

VI. Dicor is Yellow in color, and Santro is owned by the Doctor and is not Green in colour.

VII. Deepak does not own Santro.

5. Which of the following is true about Charu?

(1) He owns Corolla (2) He lives in Chennai

(3) He is a Consultant (4) Both (1) and (2)

6. The designation of the person who stays in Kolkata is

(1) Doctor (2) MD

(3) Footballer (4) Cannot be determined

7. Which of the following is definitely true about the person who lives in Kolkata?

(1) He owns a yellow car (2) He is the Footballer

(3) He owns the Corolla (4) None of the above

Directions for question 8 to 11: Answer the questions on the basis of the information given below.

Seven professors – J, K, L, M, N, P and Q – teach vocational courses at a college named Pragatee. Each professor teaches during exactly one out of the three semesters – Fall, Spring and Winter. Further it is known that:

I. K teaches during the winter semester.
II. L and M teach during the same semester.
III. Q teaches during either the Fall semester or the Spring semester.
IV. The number of professors who teach during the Winter semester is twice of the number of professors who teach during the Fall semester.
V. N and Q teach during different semesters. The same is true for J and P.
VI. Exactly one professor teaches during the Spring semester.

8. If J teaches during the Spring semester, then during which semester does N teach?
(1) Winter (2) Fall (3) Spring (4) Either (1) or (2)

9. Each of the following contains a list of professors who can all teach during the same semester EXCEPT:
(1) J, K and M (2) J, L and M (3) K, L and P (4) K, P and Q

10. In which semester does M teach?
(1) Spring (2) Fall (3) Winter (4) Cannot be determined

11. If Q teaches in the Spring semester, who among the following definitely does not teach in winter semester?
(1) J (2) K (3) N (4) None of these

Directions for questions 12 to 14: Answer the questions on the basis of the information given below.

A team comprising of two male and three female members is to be formed from 10 persons namely A, B, C, D, E, F, G, H, I and J. It is known that B, D, E, H and J are females and the remaining persons are males.

Some more Information regarding the team formation is given below:

(i) B and D will not be together in any team.
(ii) A and J will not be together in any team.
(iii) F and E will always be together in any team.
(iv) If G is present in the team then D and I have to be present in the team.
(v) F and J will not be together in any team.
(vi) If D is present in the team then J has to be present in the same team.

12. How many teams could be formed if G is present in all the teams?
(1) 3 (2) 2 (3) 1 (4) 4

13. How many teams could be formed if B and J are present in all the teams?
(1) 2 (2) 1 (3) 3 (4) 4

14. If E and D are present in the team then which of the following persons will definitely be not present in the team?
(1) A (2) J (3) F (4) Data inconsistent

Directions for questions 15 to 18: Read the following information and answer the items that follow:

The number written on T-shirts of eight children are 1, 2, 3, 4, 5, 6, 7 and 8, with one number on a T-shirt. On a particular day, each of the eight children ate exactly one fruit out of three different types of fruits – apple, orange and mango. Each type of fruit is eaten by at least one child but not more than three children. The consecutive time slots of the day in which the eight children ate fruits were I, II, III, IV, V, VI, VII and VIII, in that order.

Additional Information Given:

A. No two fruits of the same type were eaten in any two consecutive time slots.
B. No two children with two consecutive numbers on their T-shirts ate either a mango or an apple.
C. Three children with three consecutive numbers on their T-shirts ate an orange each.
D. The children with T-shirts numbered 1 and 7 ate an apple and a mango respectively.

15. Which of the following fruits did child with T-shirt numbered 4 eat?
(1) Apple (2) Orange (3) Mango (4) Either (1) or (2) or (3)

16. If the time slots in which children with T-shirts numbered 3, 1 and 7 ate fruits were IV, V and III respectively, then which of the following MUST be false?

(1) The time slot in which child with T-shirt numbered 2 ate fruit was II.

(2) The time slot in which children with T-shirts numbered 4 and 5 ate fruits was VI and VII respectively.

(3) The time slot in which children with T-shirts numbered 2 and 5 ate fruits was VI and VIII respectively.

(4) The time slot in which children with T-shirts numbered 6 and 8 ate fruits was VI and VII respectively.

17. If the time slots in which children with T-shirts numbered 5 and 3 ate fruits were I and II respectively, then each of the following statements could be true, EXCEPT:

(1) The time slot in which child with T-shirt numbered 4 ate fruit was III.

(2) The time slots in which children with T-shirts numbered 6 and 8 ate fruits were III and IV respectively.

(3) The time slots in which children with T-shirts numbered 1 and 8 ate fruits were V and VI respectively.

(4) Both (2) and (3)

18. Which of the following sequences of fruits eaten by children with T-shirts numbered 2, 3, 5 and 8, in that order, is not possible?

(1) Orange, Orange, Mango and Apple

(2) Mango, Orange, Mango and Apple

(3) Orange, Orange, Apple and Apple

(4) Both (2) and (3)

Directions for questions 19 to 22: Answer the questions on the basis of the information given below:

There are ten students: A, B, C, D, E, F, G, H, J and K. At least five of them will register for Correspondence MBA course and at least five of them will register for Correspondence Java course. The following conditions apply:

I. At least four students register for both the courses.

II. A registers for either Correspondence Java course or Correspondence MBA course, but not both.

III. H registers for Correspondence Java course only.

IV. For at least one of the two courses, E and G both are registered.

V. K and B register for different course.

VI. D and C register for both the courses.

VII. If J registers for both the courses, then E and F will also register for both the courses.

19. If G registers for one of the two courses then what is the minimum number of students who register for Correspondence Java course?

(1) 5 (2) 6 (3) 7 (4) 8

20. If A and B register for different courses then what is the maximum number of students who register for Correspondence MBA course?

(1) 6 (2) 7 (3) 8 (4) 9

21. If 6 students register for Correspondence Java course, then which of the following could be a complete list of students registered for Correspondence Java course?

(1) A, C, D, E, F and H (2) A, C, D, E, H and K (3) B, C, D, E, F and H (4) C, D, E, H, J and K

22. If 7 students register for Correspondence MBA course, than which of the following could be the list of students registered for Correspondence MBA course?

I. A, B, C, D, E, F and G

II. B, C, D, E, F, J and G

III. C, D, E, F, G, J and K

IV. A, C, D, E, G, J and K

(1) II or III (2) I, II or III (3) II or IV (4) I, II, III or IV

Directions for questions 23 to 25: Answer the questions on the basis of the information given below.

The four major components of a PC are monitor, CPU, keyboard and mouse. Shobhit bought four pieces, all of different brands and prices, of each of the four components. The brands of monitor were Dell, Apple, HP and Samsung; the brands of CPU were NVIDIA, Sun, Qualcomm and Motorola; the brands of keyboard were BenQ, Intel, Roche and Kingston; and the brands of mouse were Logitech, Razer, Belkin and Toshiba. He used these components to assemble four PCs with the intention of selling them at some profit. The four costliest components in their respective categories were assembled together and the same was true for the four cheapest components. It is also known that:

(i) He fits Belkin mouse and BenQ keyboard in the same PC.

(ii) A Dell monitor is compatible only with a Toshiba mouse.

(iii) An Apple monitor is compatible only with an NVIDIA CPU.

(iv) An HP monitor is compatible only with a Belkin mouse and a Qualcomm CPU. A Samsung monitor is incompatible with a Motorola CPU.

(v) A Kingston keyboard is incompatible with monitors of both HP and Dell.

(vi) The Intel keyboard is the costliest among the four brands of keyboards.

(vii) The Qualcomm CPU is the cheapest among the four brands of CPUs.

(viii) The costliest mouse among the four is neither Razer nor Toshiba.

23. The monitor of which company is the costliest?

(1) HP (2) Dell (3) Samsung (4) Cannot be determined

24. Which of the following is a right combination?

(1) HP–Motorola–Intel–Belkin (2) Dell–Qualcomm–Roche–Toshiba
(3) Dell–Motorola–Roche–Toshiba (4) Apple–NVIDIA–BenQ–Logitech

25. Which brand of mouse is the costliest among the four?

(1) Belkin (2) Logitech (3) Toshiba (4) Cannot be determined

Directions for questions 26 to 29: Answer the questions on the basis of the information given below.

Eight persons – Chintu, Pintu, Mintu, Sintu, Tintu, Muddy, Jango and Charlie – belong to eight different professions – Doctor, Engineer, Actor, Professor, Architect, Scientist, Cricket-Coach and Singer, not necessarily in the same order. Each of the eight persons lives in a different city among Delhi, Chennai, Hyderabad, Mumbai, Nagpur, Muzaffarnagar, Bengaluru and Jaipur. It is also known that:

(i) Jango is the Singer.

(ii) Sintu, who lives in Chennai, is not the Professor.

(iii) Mintu, who lives in Mumbai, is the Architect.

(iv) Charlie, who lives in Hyderabad, is the Engineer.

(v) The Doctor, who lives in Jaipur, is not Tintu.

(vi) Pintu, who lives in neither Delhi nor Bengaluru, is the Cricket-Coach.

(vii) The actor, who is neither Tintu nor Muddy, lives in Nagpur.

26. Which of the following is a correct Profession-City combination?

(1) Professor – Muzaffarnagar (2) Scientist – Chennai
(3) Singer – Jaipur (4) Cricket-Coach – Delhi

27. For how many persons can we definitely determine both the profession and the city?

(1) 4 (2) 5 (3) 6 (4) 8

28. Who is the Doctor?

(1) Chintu (2) Muddy (3) Tintu (4) Cannot be determined

29. Who lives in Bengaluru?

(1) Tintu (2) Jango (3) Pintu (4) Cannot be determined

Directions for questions 30 to 32: Answer the questions on the basis of the information given below.

Five persons—Aman, Ishan, Jayant, Leela and Shradha—boarded five different trains— Rajdhani, Duronto, Double-decker, Shatabdi and Garib Rath—from five different stations—Delhi, Bengaluru, Mumbai, Chennai and Lucknow—for five different destinations—Kolkata, Pune, Hyderabad, Patna and Dehradun, not necessarily in this order. It is also known that:

(i) The destination of the person who boarded Rajdhani was Kolkata.
(ii) Aman boarded Double-decker and his destination was Pune.
(iii) Ishan boarded his train at Chennai and got down at Hyderabad.
(iv) The destination of the person who boarded Duronto was Patna.
(v) Leela and Shradha boarded their trains at Lucknow and Bengaluru respectively.
(vi) Leela neither boarded Shatabdi nor was her destination Kolkata.
(vii) The person who boarded his/her train at Bengaluru did not board Rajdhani.

30. Which of the following statements is definitely false?

(1) Shradha boarded Duronto and her destination was Patna.
(2) Aman boarded his train at Mumbai and his destination was Pune.
(3) Jayant boarded Garib Rath and his destination was Dehradun.
(4) Ishan boarded Shatabdi.

31. The train boarded by Jayant was

(a) Duronto (2) Garib Rath (3) Rajdhani (4) Shatabdi

32. The destination of Shradha was

(1) Patna (2) Dehradun (3) Kolkata (4) Either (1) or (2)

Directions for questions 33 to 35: Answer the questions on the basis of the information given below.

A group of nine friends, hailing from Noida, consisting of 3 couples, 2 bachelors and one bachelorette decided to visit Agra. They hired a nine-seater bus having three rows, with three seats in each row – two on the left and one on the right of the aisle. The seats were designated by the letters A to I of English alphabet. The seats, from left to right, in the 1st row were designated as A, B and C; in the 2nd row as D, E and F; and in the 3rd row as G, H and I. The bus picked them up from three locations – Noida City Centre, Botanical Garden and Atta Market – in the same order. It is also known that:

(i) Ajay, Shobhit, Samar, Lovenish and Gautam were males and Neeta, Seema, Garima and Karishma were females.
(ii) The couples were Samar-Seema, Ajay-Neeta and Shobhit-Garima.
(iii) Exactly five of the nine friends boarded the bus from Noida City Centre.
(iv) Exactly two of the nine friends boarded the bus from Botanical Garden and both were unmarried.
(v) Shobhit and Garima boarded the bus from Atta Market.
(vi) A couple always boarded the bus together and sat in two adjacent seats in a row.
(vii) Seats F and B were occupied by Lovenish and Samar respectively and Seats E and I were both occupied by females.

33. From which location did Samar and Seema board the bus?

(1) Noida City Centre (2) Botanical Garden (3) Atta Market (4) Cannot be determined

34. If one of the couples that boarded the bus along with Karishma sat in the same row as she did, then which of the following could be the seat of Garima?

(1) E (2) G (3) H (4) Either (2) or (3)

35. How many different friends could have sat on Seat G?

(1) 2 (2) 4 (3) 3 (4) 1

...OUPING AND DISTRIBUTION

...ections for questions 36 to 39: Answer the questions on the basis of the information given below.

Five persons—Aman, Ishan, Jayant, Leela and Shradha—boarded five different trains— Rajdhani, Duronto, Double-decker, Shatabdi and Garib Rath—from five different stations—Delhi, Bengaluru, Mumbai, Chennai and Lucknow—for five different destinations—Kolkata, Pune, Hyderabad, Patna and Dehradun, not necessarily in this order. It is also known that:

(i) The destination of the person who boarded Rajdhani was Kolkata.

(ii) Aman boarded Double-decker and his destination was Pune.

(iii) Ishan boarded his train at Chennai and got down at Hyderabad.

(iv) The destination of the person who boarded Duronto was Patna.

(v) Leela and Shradha boarded their trains at Lucknow and Bengaluru respectively.

(vi) Leela neither boarded Shatabdi nor was her destination Kolkata.

(vii) The person who board ed his/her train at Bengaluru did not board Rajdhani.

36. Which of the following statements is definitely false?

(1) Shradha boarded Duronto and her destination was Patna.

(2) Aman boarded his train at Mumbai and his destination was Pune.

(3) Jayant boarded Garib Rath and his destination was Dehradun.

(4) Ishan boarded Shatabdi.

37. The train boarded by Jayant was

(a) Duronto (2) Garib Rath (3) Rajdhani (4) Shatabdi

38. The destination of Shradha was

(1) Patna (2) Dehradun (3) Kolkata (4) Either (1) or (2)

39. If Jayant boarded the train at Mumbai station, then at which station did Aman board the train?

(1) Delhi (2) Lucknow (3) Bengaluru (4) Chennai

Directions for questions 40 to 43: Answer the questions on the basis of the information given below.

A group has to be selected from seven persons containing two women (Rehana and Kavya) and five men (Rohit, Rahul, Kamal, Nusarat and John). Rohit would not like to be in the group if Rahul is selected. Rahul and John want to be selected together in the group. Kavya would like to be in the group only if Kamal is also there. Kamal, if selected, would not like Nusarat in the group. Rohit would like to be in the group only if Nusarat is also there. Kamal insists that Rehana must be selected in case he is there in the group.

40. Which of the following is an acceptable combination of a group of three?

(1) Rohit, John, Kavya (2) Rahul, Kamal, Nusarat

(3) Rohit, Nusarat, Rahul (4) Rohit, Nusarat, Rehana

41. Which of the following is an acceptable combination of a group of four?

(1) Rohit, Nusarat, Rehana, John (2) Rahul, John, Kavya, Kamal

(3) Rahul, John, Rehana, Kamal (4) Rehana, Kamal, Rohit, Nusarat

42. Which of the following statements is true?

(1) Kavya and Rohit both can be selected in a group of four.

(2) A group of four can have both the women.

(3) A group of four can have four men.

(4) None of the above

43. If a group of five members has to be selected, then in how many ways is it possible such that Kamal is definitely a member of the group?

(1) 1 (2) 0 (3) 2 (4) 3

ANSWER KEYS

PRACTICE EXERCISE – 1

1. (2)	**2.** (2)	**3.** (4)	**4.** (2)	**5.** (2)	**6.** (3)	**7.** (1)	**8.** (4)	**9.** (3)	**10.** (1)
11. (4)	**12.** (2)	**13.** (1)	**14.** (4)	**15.** (1)	**16.** (2)	**17.** (1)	**18.** (3)	**19.** (4)	**20.** (1)
21. (3)	**22.** (3)	**23.** (3)	**24.** (2)	**25.** (2)	**26.** (3)	**27.** (4)	**28.** (3)	**29.** (1)	**30.** (4)
31. (4)	**32.** (2)	**33.** (4)	**34.** (3)	**35.** (2)	**36.** (3)	**37.** (1)	**38.** (1)	**39.** (1)	**40.** (3)
41. (2)	**42.** (4)	**43.** (2)	**44.** (4)	**45.** (3)	**46.** (4)	**47.** (2)			

PRACTICE EXERCISE – 2

1. (3)	**2.** (1)	**3.** (2)	**4.** (2)	**5.** (2)	**6.** (4)	**7.** (1)	**8.** (1)	**9.** (4)	**10.** (3)
11. (3)	**12.** (3)	**13.** (2)	**14.** (4)	**15.** (2)	**16.** (4)	**17.** (3)	**18.** (4)	**19.** (2)	**20.** (3)
21. (3)	**22.** (4)	**23.** (4)	**24.** (3)	**25.** (2)	**26.** (2)	**27.** (3)	**28.** (2)	**29.** (4)	**30.** (3)
31. (3)	**32.** (4)	**33.** (1)	**34.** (1)	**35.** (2)	**36.** (3)	**37.** (3)	**38.** (4)	**39.** (1)	**40.** (4)
41. (3)	**42.** (4)	**43.** (1)							

EXPLANATIONS

PRACTICE EXERCISE – 1

For questions 1 to 4:

17th century = 2

19th century = 3

20th century = 1

Poets = 4

Novelists = 3

Dramatist = 3

Bengali = 1

Hindi = 2

Marathi = 2

Tamil = 1

Using the given data

Writer	Century	Field	Language
A	20	Poetry	Marathi
B	19	Drama	Hindi
C	17	Poetry, Novel, Drama	Marathi
D	19	Novel, Poetry	Hindi
E	19	Novel, Drama	Tamil
F	17	Poetry	Bengali

1. B wrote in Hindi.
2. E was the Tamil writer.
3. C contributed to all the three genre.
4. B belonged to 19th century.

For questions 5 to 8:

From (2) & (3), the only possible arrangements for films on crime (C) & environment(E) are –

E C C E C E C E

E C E C E C C E

E C E C C E C E

From (7), atleast 4 films are screened between the films of Pratyush. If only these 4 films are screened between his films then either the films of Satyajit will be back to back or of same category, which cannot be possible. Hence there are 5 films screened between the two films of Pratyush.

IF Satyajit's film on crime is screened in 6th or 7th slot, then 1st condition will be violated for either Rakesh or Yash. Hence it can only be screened in 5th slot.

Taking all the conditions, the possible arrangements are–

Case 1 - $S_E\ P_C\ Y_E\ R_C\ S_C\ R_E\ Y_C\ P_E$

Case 2 - $S_E\ P_C\ R_C\ Y_E\ S_C\ R_E\ Y_C\ P_E$

Case 3 - $P_E\ R_C\ Y_C\ R_E\ S_C\ Y_E\ P_C\ S_E$

Where P_E means Pratyush's film on environment and so on.

5. We can determine exact slot for only Satyajit's film on crime.

6. From statement (i) and (iii), case 2 and case 3 are possible respectively.

7. Only second slot is not possible for Yash's film on environment.

8. Statement (a) & (b) are definitely true. Whereas statement (c) is possibly but not definitely false.

For questions 9 to 12:

From (7) Amit cannot buy the item of Apple and from statements 1, 2, 3 and 4, he cannot buy the item of LG, Nokia, Samsung and Philips. So he bought the item of HP brand. Golu bought the item of either LG or Apple. Nitin and Sumit cannot buy the item of Samsung so Dan bought Samsung laptop. Sumit bought Nokia Ipad and Nitin bought (Apple or LG) pendrive because Farhan did not buy pendrive.

Name	Product	Brand
Amit	Mobile	HP
Dan	Laptop	Samsung
Farhan	Printer/tablet	Philips
Golu	Tablet/printer	LG/Apple
Sumit	Ipad	Nokia
Nitin	Pendrive	Apple/LG

9. Sumit – Ipad – Nokia is a correct combination.

10. By the given condition, Farhan bought a tablet and Golu bought a printer. It is clear from the table above that since one of mobile, pendrive and tablet is of Apple brand, the pendrive belonging to Nitin has to be of Apple. Thus, Golu bought the item of LG brand.

11. Farhan or Golu can buy the printer.

12. Dan purchased laptop.

For questions 13 to 16:

He has to study Maths on Saturday, else there will be two days on which he will be studying both Maths and Chemistry. And it cannot be either Friday or Monday, because then he will be studying three subjects on that day, which is not possible, since Economics should be studied on the day he studies three subjects. Since he cannot study Economics on Wednesday or Friday, then the only days possible on which he can study three subjects are Monday, Tuesday and Thursday.

Following are the possible schedules which he can follow under the given conditions -

Days	Tuesday	Wednesday	Thursday	Friday	Saturday	Sunday	Monday
Subjects	Maths, Economics	Physics, Maths	Economics, Physics, Chemistry	Chemistry, Maths	Maths	Physics	Chemistry, Physics

Days	Tuesday	Wednesday	Thursday	Friday	Saturday	Sunday	Monday
Subjects	Maths, Physics, Economics	Physics, Chemistry	Economics, Maths	Chemistry, Physics	Maths	Physics	Chemistry, Maths

Days	Tuesday	Wednesday	Thursday	Friday	Saturday	Sunday	Monday
Subjects	Maths, Physics	Physics, Chemistry	Economics, Maths	Chemistry, Physics	Maths	Physics	Chemistry, Maths, Economics

13. He studies Maths on Saturday.

14. He definitely studies Maths on Tuesday.

15. Vikas will study both Maths and Economics on at least one day.

16. It can be either Tuesday or Wednesday.

For questions 17 to 20:

From statement (vi), positions of Painting and Gymnastics in the activity column can be fixed. From statement (iii), those who participated in Dancing, Singing and Essay Writing must be younger to Daksh and hence, the remaining positions in the activity column will be occupied by Cooking and Debate. Thus, Daksh must have participated in Gymnastics. From statement (v), the youngest sibling must have participated in Dancing and the eldest one in Debate. Crystal and Giresh are the twins and the two cases possible are shown below.

Activity	**Case I:**	**Case II:**
Dancing	Eric	Eric
Singing/ Essay writing	Crystal	Giresh
Painting	Giresh	Crystal
Essay writing/ Singing	Foram	Foram
Gymnastics	Daksh	Daksh
Cooking	Bhuvan	Bhuvan
Debate	Anshu	Anshu

17. Painting

18. Giresh

19. Daksh

20. Eric participated in dancing.

For questions 21 to 24:

From statement (i): Suman can pursue engineering in electronics or mechanical branch.

From statement (ii): Since Qasa is pursuing in Mechanical branch, Suman is pursuing engineering in Electronics branch. Rita does not commute by Maruti so she is not pursuing Civil engineering. Now, we can conclude that Rita is pursuing engineering in Computers and Parul in Civil. So, Parul commutes by Maruti.

From statement (iv): Bimal is pursuing Mechanical so Daniel is pursuing engineering in Electronics because Suman is pursuing engineering in the same branch as that of Bimal or Daniel.

Now, we can summarize the drawn conclusions in the table given below:

Alok	Maruti	Civil
Bimal	Palio	Mechanical
Chetan	Skoda	Computers
Daniel	Audi	Electronics
Parul	Maruti	Civil
Qasa	Audi	Mechanical
Rita	Palio	Computers
Suman	Skoda	Electronics

21. Daniel is pursuing engineering in electronics branch and he commutes by Audi.

22. Alok and Parul are pursuing civil engineering.

23. Daniel and Qasa commute by Audi.

24. Computers-Chetan-Skoda is a correct combination.

For questions 25 to 28:

From (5) and (7), Mittals are staying on either 3rd or 2nd floor.

Case (i): When Mittals are on 3rd floor.

Kriplanis must be on 4th floor and Guptas and Aptes is on the 5th floor. Bhatias' flats are in the column other than Mittal's, hence, Jains, Mittals and Roys flats are in the same column. But jains would live on 6th floor and condition (7) will be violated.

Case (ii): When Mittals are on 2nd floor.

Jains are on 6th floor. Kriplanis are on the 4th floor and Guptas and Aptes are on the 5th floor. From (8), two flats of Bhatias are on 3rd and 4th floor, and they are in different columns than that of column of Mittals' flat. So, Jains are in the same : as that of Mittals, and Roys are on 1st floor, in the same row. Saxenas are exactly below Bhatias, either on 1st or 2nd floor. From (9), Guptas' flat is immediately above Mittals' flat and Aptes' flat is immediately above Bhatias' flats.

The following two cases are possible:

Floor no	Row 1	Row 2
6		Jains
5	Aptes	Guptas
4	Bhatias	Kriplanis
3	Bhatias	
2	Saxenas	Mittals
1		Roys

Floor no	Row 1	Row 2
6		Jains
5	Aptes	Guptas
4	Bhatias	Kriplanis
3	Bhatias	
2		Mittals
1	Saxenas	Roys

25. Saxenas are staying below Bhatia's flat in the same column.

26. Jains do not have any other family occupying the other flat on their floor.

27. Both Bhatias and Kriplanis live on 4th floor.

28. Guptas live in the flat which is immediately below Jains' flat.

For questions 29 to 32: From statement (ii), The surname of Chandu will be Chawla and that of Dhiru will be either Dhawan or Dhoni. But it is given that Dhawan travelled in Polo and Dhiru owned white coloured i10, therefore the surname of Dhiru will be Dhoni.

From statement (vi), Amit couldn't have blue colour car. Further analysis leads to the following table:

Name	Place	Car	Colour of Car	Surname
Amit	Nainital	Alto/i20	Red	Kohli
Boman/Fenka	Goa	Polo	Yellow	Dhawan
Chandu	Dharmshala	MXUV	Orange	Chawla
Dhiru	Mussoorie/ Shimla	i10	White	Dhoni
Endra	Darjiling	Sx4	Silver	Singh
Fenku/Boman	Shimla/ Mussoorie	i20/Alto	Blue	Yadav
Gangu	Manali	Indica V2	Green	Negi

29. Gangu visited Manali. His mail id could be Gangu.negi@gmail.com.

30. Both statements are necessary.

31. The place visited by Dhoni was either Mussoorie or Shimla.

32. Surnames of five friends can be determined uniquely.

questions 33 to 36:

...he number of objects in Box 1 and Box 2 must be at least 3 each. There must be at least 2 objects in Box 3 as well. So the number of objects in Box 4 can be either 1 or 2.

The following cases of the distribution of objects are possible:

		Box 1	Box 2	Box 3	Box 4
Number of objects	Case 1	3	3	3	1
	Case 2	4	3	2	1
	Case 3	3	4	2	1
	Case 4	3	3	2	2

33. As the number of objects in Box 2 and Box 3 are the same, only Case 1 can be followed here.

Statement (ii) indicates that the only object in Box 4 would be one of C, D, H and J. But it cannot be C (Statement (i)).

Hence, E must be in either Box 1 or Box 2.

Also, A and B cannot be with I in Box 3 (Statement (ii) will be violated).

Hence, A and B must be in Box 2. Also, C and F must be in Box 1 with E.

The final distribution would look like:

Box 1	Box 2	Box 3	Box 4
E, C, F	A, B, H/J	I, D, G	J/H

Hence, G and D must be placed together in Box 3 along with I.

34. The information given in the question indicates that either Case 2 or Case 3 would be valid.

Since I is in Box 3 (Statement (iii)), there must be exactly 1 more object in Box 3. That object cannot be one of C, F, A, B (Statement (i)), H, G, J and E (Statement (iii)).

So that object is definitely D.

The only object in Box 4 (third object in 'gift') must be J.

C and F must be in Box 1 (Statement (i)) and H and G both must be in Box 2 (as C and H cannot be together).

The following two ways of distribution are possible:

	Box 1	Box 2	Box 3 (gift)	Box 4 (gift)
Way 1	C, F, A, B	E, G, H	I, D	J
Way 2	C, F, E	A, B, G, H	I, D	J

Statements I and II are always true; Statement III would not be true if distribution is done according to Way 2.

35. The information given in the question indicates that Case 4 would be valid here.

Both Box 3 and Box 4 must have two objects each. Since E is in Box 1 and exactly one out of C, H, J and D must also be in Box 1, we can conclude that both A and B must be in Box 2.

C and F are either in Box 1 or in Box 4. D must be placed in Box 3 with I as none of C, H and J can be in Box 3.

The following ways of distribution are possible:

	Box 1	Box 2	Box 3	Box 4
Way 1	E, C, F	A, B, H	I, D	G, J
Way 2	E, C, F	A, B, J	I, D	G, H
Way 3	E, G, H	A, B, J	I, D	C, F
Way 4	E, G, J	A, B, H	I, D	C, F

Statements II and IV are definitely true. Statements I and III may or may not be true.

36. Since two objects are in Box 4, there must be two objects in Box 3, one of them is I and the other is D.

For questions 37 to 39:

Let the number of aspirants who joined T1, T2 and T3 but not T4, that of those who had joined T3, T4 and T1 but not T2, that of those who had joined both T1 and T4 but neither T2 nor T3, that of those who had joined both T2 and T3 but neither T1 nor T4 and that of those who joined both T2 and T4 but neither T1 nor T3 be x, y, z, a and b respectively.

Now, the given information can be depicted as shown below.

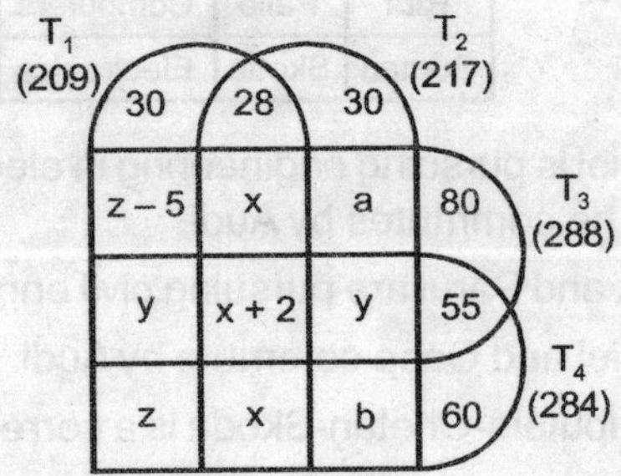

Now from statement (vi),

$28 + x + (x + 2) + x = 96 \Rightarrow x = 22$

From statement (iii),

$2x + 2y = 100 \Rightarrow y = 28$

Similarly, z = 30, a = 26, b = 37

Using the above conclusions, the final break-up of the aspirants across the four Test Series can be depicted as:

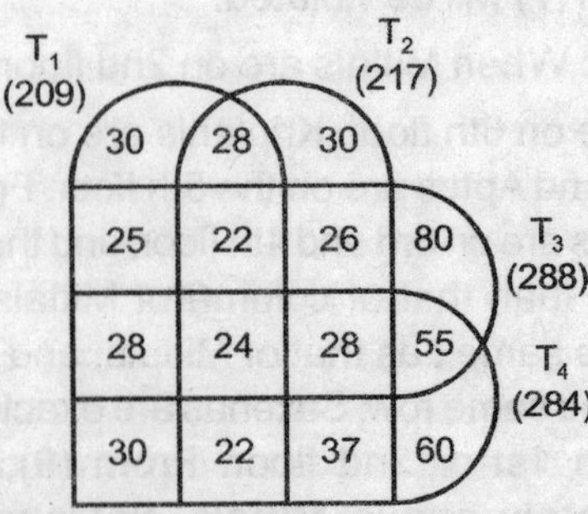

37. The number of aspirants who had joined exactly two test series

= 28 + 26 + 55 + 37 + 30 + 25 = 201.

38. The number of aspirants who had joined both T3 and T4 = 28 + 24 + 28 + 55 = 135.

39. From the diagram, we can calculate that the total number of aspirants who had joined at least one of the four Test Series was 525.

Hence, the required number of the aspirants = 600 – 525 = 75.

For questions 40 to 43:

From Additional Information I:

Two out of the three females were born on Sunday and Saturday.

From Additional Information II:

D is a male and is younger than F as well as G.

From Additional Information III:

A female was not born on Monday or Friday.

From Additional Information IV:

F is a female and is younger to only one female A; hence A is born on Sunday.

From Additional Information V:

C is born on Monday.

Therefore, using the Additional Information IV we can conclude that F is born on Tuesday and G is born on Wednesday.

40. Out of the given options, Wednesday cannot be the day on which D was born.

41. Since F is a female and is born on Tuesday and G is born on Wednesday, therefore G has to be a male as no two females were born on consecutive days of the week.

42. Either Thursday or Friday can be the day on which B was born.

Hence, option (4) is the correct choice.

43. C was born on Monday.

For questions 44 to 47:

From statement (iv), we can see that Arjun must have called Rita on Monday, Wednesday and Friday. Also from statement (iii), it is clear that he does not meet Rita on Friday. Hence Arjun must meet Rita on Tuesday. From statements (ii) and (v), we can deduce that Apple mobile is used to talk to Rano, and Arjun meets her on Friday. From statement (i), we can deduce that MicroMax and Nokia mobiles are used to talk to Julie and Sheila respectively.

As Arjun talks to Julie on Monday, he must meet her on Wednesday. So he meets Sheila on Monday. Hence, from statement (iii), it can be concluded that Arjun talks to Jamalo on Monday and Tuesday. Considering Arjun talks to each girl on exactly 3 days, we get the following table:

Friend	Phone	Monday	Tuesday	Wednesday	Thursday	Friday
Julie	Micromax	Call	×	Meet	Call	Call
Sheila	Nokia	Meet	Call	×	Call	Call
Rano	Apple	×	Call	Call	Call	Meet
Jamalo	Sony	Call	Call	Call	Meet	×
Rita	Samsung	Call	Meet	Call	×	Call

44. He does not talk to Julie on Tuesday or Wednesday.

45. He does not talk to Julie on Tuesday and does not use MicroMax mobile.

46. He meets Shiela on Monday, and does not call Shiela and Rano on that day.

47. He meets Rita on Tuesday.

PRACTICE EXERCISE – 2

For questions 1 to 4: According to the given information, we can draw the following table.

	Men					Women					
	A	B	C	D	E	L	M	N	O	P	Q
Lecturer	✓	✓						✓			
Engineer			✓	✓		✓	✓		✓		
Doctor					✓					✓	✓
With in the same group											
1						✓				✓	
2	✓					✓					✓
3					✓		✓				
Not in the same group											
1		×						×			
2		×		×							
3				×		×					
4						×			×		

1. As all the three doctors P, Q and E are selected, A and L will have to be selected due the presence of Q, and M due to presence of E. So, the composition of the team is AELMPQ.
2. As the team contains two male lecturers, A and B are selected. Due to the presence of A, L and Q have to be in the team. P's presence in the team will ensure L's presence. So, the composition of the team is ABLPQ.
3. If two doctors P and Q are selected, then L and A have to be selected. So P, Q and L are three women. So B has to be selected and the left one is only C. Hence, members of the team are ABCLPQ. If E and Q are considered as doctors, then the team will be ABELMQ (choice not given).
4. From statements (II), (III) and (IV) and (VI), it can be observed that to maximize the number of members in the team, L has to be selected. Now, from (IV) and (VI), it can be seen that in the event of L's selection, D and O cannot be selected. Also, from statement (I), out of B and N, only one can be selected. Except these three persons, all the other members can be selected together in the team. Hence, the maximum number of members in the team can be 8.

ions 5 to 7:

servation it can be analyzed that the person having the attributes starting with the first alphabet of his name is Barun.

The attribute starting with the first letter of the name of Govinda is the color of his car i.e. green, as no other color matches with the first alphabet of anybody's name.

Aabhas is the one who has no attribute starting with the first letter of his name because Aabhas cannot be an actor as the actor stays in Delhi.

Farooq has only two attributes starting with the first letter of his name, i.e. Faridabad and Footballer. Since Aabhas stays in Faridabad, Farooq is a Footballer.

Now, as Deepak, Farooq and Govinda cannot have a Santro, Charu must have the Santro.

Therefore, we can also conclude that Charu stays in Chennai.

Further analysis leads to the following cases:

Name	Profession	Car	Place	Color
Aabhas	MD/ Consultant	Swift	Faridabad	Red / White
Barun	B.M	BMW	Bombay	Blue
Charu	Doctor	Santro	Chennai	Red / White
Deepak	MD / Consultant	Dicor	Kolkata	Yellow
Farooq	Footballer	Corolla	Gurgaon	Black
Govinda	Actor	Mercedes	Delhi	Green

Or

Name	Profession	Car	Place	Color
Aabhas	MD/Consultant	Swift	Faridabad	
Barun	B.M	BMW	Bombay	Blue
Charu	Doctor	Santro	Chennai	
Deepak	Actor	Mercedes	Delhi	Red / White
Farooq	Footballer	Dicor	Kolkata	Yellow
Govinda	Consultant/MD	Corolla	Gurgaon	Black

5. Chennai
6. Cannot be determined because he can either be the MD or the Consultant.
7. The person who lives in Kolkata must owns Dicor (i.e. an yellow car).

For questions 8 to 11: By using the given information, we can arrive at the following six cases:

Case I:

J	K	L	M	N	P	Q
Spring	Winter	Winter	Winter	Winter	Fall	Fall

Case II:

J	K	L	M	N	P	Q
Fall	Winter	Winter	Winter	Winter	Spring	Fall

Case III:

J	K	L	M	N	P	Q
Fall	Winter	Winter	Winter	Spring	Winter	Fall

Case IV:

J	K	L	M	N	P	Q
Winter	Winter	Winter	Winter	Spring	Fall	Fall

Case V:

J	K	L	M	N	P	Q
Fall	Winter	Winter	Winter	Fall	Winter	Spring

Case VI:

J	K	L	M	N	P	Q
Winter	Winter	Winter	Winter	Fall	Fall	Spring

8. Given that J teaches during the spring semester, which implies that it is **Case I.**

   Therefore, N teaches during the winter semester.

   Hence, option (a) is the correct choice.
9. From the given six cases, it can be observed that the professors given in option (d) cannot teach during the same semester.
10. In all the 6 cases, M teaches during the winter semester. Hence, option (c) is the correct choice.
11. From cases V and VI, it can be seen that when Q teaches in spring semester, N cannot teach in the winter semester.

For questions 12 to 14:

12. If G is present in the team then D and I have to be present in the team. So that leaves us with the job of choosing two more females. Now, since D is present in the team therefore J has to be present in the team. So only possible team is G, I, D, J and H.
13. If B and J are present in all the teams then one more female and two more males are required to form the team. Possible team is B, H, J, C and I.
14. If E and D are present in the team then from statement (iii) F has to be present in the team. Also, from statement (vi), J must also be present in the same team because D is present but according to statement (v), F and J cannot be together in the same team. Hence, E and D can never be together in a team and thus it is not possible.

For questions 15 to 18:

Let an apple, an orange and a mango be denoted by A, O and M respectively.

From the additional information (2), (3) and (4), the following the following table lists down the three cases that are possible.

	Child Numbered							
	1	2	3	4	5	6	7	8
Case 1	A	O	O	O	M	A	M	A
Case 2	A	M	O	O	O	A	M	A
Case 3	A	M	A	O	O	O	M	A

15. In all the three cases, child numbered 4 will always eat an Orange.

16. Given that the time slots in which child numbered 3, 1 and 7 ate the fruit is IV, V and III respectively.

So, Case 3 is not possible as in case 3 children numbered 3 and 1 eat an apple and this violates the additional information (1).

Option (a): It is possible in the following manner

Child Numbered	1	2	3	4	5	6	7	8
Time slot	V	II	IV	VI	VII	VIII	III	I
Fruit	A	O	O	O	M	A	M	A

Option (b): It is possible as shown in the table given above.

Option (c): It is possible in the following manner

Child Numbered	1	2	3	4	5	6	7	8
Time slot	V	VI	IV	II	VIII	VII	III	I
Fruit	A	O	O	O	M	A	M	A

Option (d): It is not possible because in Case 1 as well as Case 2; child numbered 6 and 8 ate an apple each and this violates the additional information (1) given.

Hence, option (4) is the correct choice.

17. Given that the time slots in which child numbered 5 and 3 ate the fruits is I and II respectively.

This means that Case 2 is not possible.

Option (1): It is possible in the following manner

Child Numbered	1	2	3	4	5	6	7	8
Time slot	V	IV	II	III	I	VIII	VI	VII
Fruit	A	M	A	O	O	O	M	A

Option (2): It is possible in the following manner

Child Numbered	1	2	3	4	5	6	7	8
Time slot	VIII	V	II	VI	I	III	VII	IV
Fruit	A	M	A	O	O	O	M	A

Option (3): Is not possible because in Case 1 as well as Case 3, children numbered 1 and 8 ate an apple each and henceforth the mentioned two children cannot eat the fruit in time slots V and VI respectively as it violates the additional information (1).

Hence, option (3) is the correct choice.

18. Referring the first table that lists down all the three possible cases

Option (1): It is possible in Case 1

Option (2): It is not possible

Option (3): It is not possible

Hence, option (d) is the correct choice.

For questions 19 to 22:

19. By the question, we require minimum number of students. Either K or B will take Correspondence Java course. C, D and H also take Correspondence Java course. We need four students for both courses. So E and F will take correspondence Java course. Hence, there are six students who register for Correspondence Java course.

Alternate Method:

4 students (in both courses) + H + (K or B)

= 6 students.

20. By the question, we require maximum number of students who register for Correspondence MBA course. So, A and K will register for Correspondence MBA course. C, D, E, F and J will register for both courses. Also, G will register for Correspondence Java course. Hence, there are eight students who register for Correspondence MBA course.

Alternate Method:

10 – H (Java only) – (B) = 8 students.

21. It would be best to approach this question by checking the options.

Option (1): Either B or K has to register for Correspondence Java course. But none of them is in the list. Thus, it is not the right list.

Option (2): At least four students should register for both courses. But A, H, K cannot register for more than one course. Thus, it is not the right list.

Option (3): Either B or K will register for Correspondence Java course. So B is a part of the list. H is also a part of the list. C, D, E and F can register for both the courses. Hence, it could be the right list.

Option (4): Here, H and K can register for only one course. The other four students have to register for both the courses. If J registers for both the courses, then E and F necessarily register for both the courses. However, since F is not in the list, it is not the right list.

22. It would be best to approach this question by checking the options.

Statement I: If C, D, E and F register for both courses then A, B and G can register only for correspondence MBA course.

Thus, it could be the list.

Statement II: If C, D, E, F and J register for both courses then B and G can register only for correspondence MBA course.

Thus, it could be the list.

Statement III: If C, D, E, F and J register for both courses then G and K can register only for correspondence MBA course.

Thus, it could be the list.

Statement IV: If C, D, E and G register for both courses then A, J and K can register only for correspondence MBA course.

Thus, it could be the list.

For questions 23 to 25:

Using statements (i), (ii), (iii), and (iv), we can draw the following table.

Monitor	HP	Dell	Apple	Samsung
CPU	Qualcomm		NVIDIA	
Keyboard	BenQ			
Mouse	Belkin	Toshiba		

From statement (iv), Samsung monitor is incompatible with a Motorola CPU. Hence, the Motorola CPU must be assembled with Dell monitor. Consequently, Sun CPU must be assembled with Samsung monitor. From statements (ii), (v), (vi) and (viii), Roche keyboard must be assembled with Dell monitor.

The final table can be drawn as follows:

Monitor	HP	Dell	Apple	Samsung
CPU	Qualcomm	Motorola	NVIDIA	Sun
Keyboard	BenQ	Roche	Kingston/ Intel	intel/ Kingston
Mouse	Belkin	Toshiba	Logitech/ Razer	Razer/ Logitech

23. Since the costliest Keyboard of Intel can be attached to either Apple monitor or Samsung monitor, the costliest monitor could be either of Apple or Samsung.

24. Dell–Motorola–Roche–Toshiba is the correct combination.

25. The Belkin mouse must be the cheapest as it is assembled with the Qualcomm CPU. From statement (viii), we can say that Logitech mouse must be the costliest.

For questions 26 to 29:

From statements (i), (ii), (iii), (iv), and (vi), we can draw the following table.

Name	Profession	City
Chintu		
Pintu	Cricket-Coach	
Mintu	Architect	Mumbai
Sintu		Chennai
Tintu		
Muddy		
Jango	Singer	
Charlie	Engineer	Hyderabad

From statements (ii) and (vii), Chintu must be the Actor, who lives in Nagpur. From statement (v), Muddy must be the Doctor, who lives in Jaipur. From statement (ii), Tintu must be the Professor. Hence, Sintu must be the Scientist. From statement (vi), Pintu must be living in Muzaffarnagar.

The final table can be drawn as shown below.

Name	Profession	City
Chintu	Actor	Nagpur
Pintu	Cricket-Coach	Muzaffarnagar
Mintu	Architect	Mumbai
Sintu	Scientist	Chennai
Tintu	Professor	Delhi/Bengaluru
Muddy	Doctor	Jaipur
Jango	Singer	Bengaluru/Delhi
Charlie	Engineer	Hyderabad

26. The Scientist lives in Chennai.

27. We can definitely determine the profession and the city for 6 persons.

28. Muddy is the Doctor.

29. Either Tintu or Jango live in Bengaluru.

Thus, the exact person cannot be determined.

For questions 30 to 32:

Preliminary table on the basis of the given information can be drawn as shown below.

Person	Train	Boarding Station	Destination
Aman	Double Decker		Pune
Ishan		Chennai	Hyderabad
Jayant			
Leela		Lucknow	
Shradha		Bengaluru	

From statements (i), (v), (vi) and (vii), it can be deduced that Jayant boarded Rajdhani. Further analysis leads to the following table:

Person	Train	Boarding Station	Destination
Aman	Double Decker	Mumbai/Delhi	Pune
Ishan	Garib Rath/ Shatabdi	Chennai	Hyderabad
Jayant	Rajdhani	Mumbai/Delhi	Kolkata
Leela	Duronto/Garib Rath	Lucknow	Patna/ Dehradun
Shradha	Duronto/Garib Rath/Shatabdi	Bengaluru	Patna/ Dehradun

30. All the other statements except third are possible.

31. The train boarded by Jayant was Rajdhani.

32. The destination of Shradha was either Patna or Dehradun.

For questions 33 to 35:

From statements (i) and (ii), we can conclude that the couples were Samar-Seema, Ajay-Neeta and Shobhit-Garima. The bachelors were Gautam and Lovenish and the bachelorette was Karishma.

From statement (v), Shobhit and Garima boarded the bus from Atta market. From statement (iv), two unmarried persons boarded the bus from Botanical Garden. Therefore, the rest of the two couples, Samar-Seema and Ajay-Neeta, must have boarded the bus from Noida City Centre.

From statements (vii) and (vi), Seema and Karishma must have sat on seats A and I respectively. Consequently, Gautam must have occupied seat C.

The seating arrangement of the persons in the bus can be shown as:

Seema	Samar		Gautam
A	B		C
______	______	Aisle	Lovenish
D	E		F
______	______		Karishma
G	H		I

33. Samar and Seema boarded the bus from Noida City Centre.

34. Since Shobhit and Garima boarded the bus from Atta Market, they must not have been in the same row as Karishma. Hence, Shobhit and Garima must have sat on seats D and E. Since seat E was occupied by a female, Garima must have sat on it.

35. From the concluded seating arrangement, we can see that seats D, E, G and H were occupied by the couples – Ajay-Neeta and Shobhit-Garima. Any of the four could have sat on seat G.

For questions 36 to 39:

Preliminary table on the basis of the given information can be drawn as shown below.

Person	Train	Boarding Station	Destination
Aman	Double Decker		Pune
Ishan		Chennai	Hyderabad
Jayant			
Leela		Lucknow	
Shradha		Bengaluru	

From statements (i), (v), (vi) and (vii), it can be deduced that Jayant boarded Rajdhani. Further analysis leads to the following table:

Person	Train	Boarding Station	Destination
Aman	Double Decker	Mumbai/Delhi	Pune
Ishan	Garib Rath/ Shatabdi	Chennai	Hyderabad
Jayant	Rajdhani	Mumbai/Delhi	Kolkata
Leela	Duronto/Garib Rath	Lucknow	Patna/ Dehradun
Shradha	Duronto/Garib Rath/Shatabdi	Bengaluru	Patna/ Dehradun

36. All the other statements except third are possible.

37. The train boarded by Jayant was Rajdhani.

38. The destination of Shradha was either Patna or Dehradun.

39. If Jayant boarded the train at Mumbai station then Aman boarded the train at Delhi station.

40. Option (1) Violates the condition that Rahul and John want to be selected together.

Option (2) Violates the condition that Kamal cannot be in the group with Nusarat.

Option (3) Violates the condition that Rahul and John are to be selected together.

Option (4) Rohit, Nusarat, Rehana – is acceptable

41. Option (1) Violates the condition that John and Rahul are selected together.

Option (2) Violates the condition that Kamal has to be with Rehana.

Option (3) Rahul, John, Rehana, Kamal – is acceptable

Option (4) Violates the condition that Nusarat cannot be with Kamal.

42. Option (1) is not correct as if Kavya and Rohit both the selected then Rahul and John cannot be selected and Kamal and Rehana must be selected. If Kamal is selected then Nusarat cannot be selected but as Rohit is selected Nusarat must be selected which is contradictory.

Option (2) is also incorrect.

Both women $\Rightarrow$ Rehana and Kavya

Kavya $\Rightarrow$ Kamal

Now, one more male is required. He cannot be Rahul or John because they should necessarily be together. Rohit cannot exist in the group without Nusarat and Nusarat cannot exist because Kamal is already selected. Hence, a group of 4 having both women is also not possible.

Option (3) is not correct as Kamal should not be with Nusarat and Rohit cannot be with Rahul.

43. The only possible group:

Kamal, Kavya, Rehana, Rahul and John.

CHAPTER

Sports Based

SOLVED EXAMPLES

Directions for examples 1 to 4: Answer the questions on the basis of the information given below.

Four runners – Anurag, Brijesh, Chakri and Deepak – participated in a tournament, which comprises two races. No two of them secured the same position in either of the races. Only one athlete, out of the four, secured the same position place in both the races. Anurag did not secure last position in either of the races. Chakri beat Deepak in both the races. Brijesh secured first position in at least one of the two races. Anurag secured third position in at least one of the two races. Deepak secured the second position in one of the races and Chakri did the same in the other race.

1. The winner of a race was awarded 4 points, the runner-up was awarded 3 points, the third position holder was awarded 2 points and the last position holder was awarded 1 point. If the winner of the event was the athlete whose aggregate points in the two races was the maximum, then who won the tournament?

(1) Anurag (2) Brijesh

(3) Chakri (4) Deepak

2. The athlete(s) who secured a better position in the second race compared to that in the first race was/were

(1) Anurag (2) Both Chakri and Deepak

(3) Brijesh (4) Cannot be determined

3. For whom was the absolute difference between the positions secured in the two races the maximum?

(1) Anurag (2) Brijesh

(3) Chakri (4) Deepak

4. Who secured the same position in both the races?

(1) Brijesh (2) Anurag

(3) Chakri (4) Deepak

For examples 1 to 4:

Since Chakri always beat Deepak and Deepak secured the second position in one of the races, Chakri finished first and Deepak finished second in one of the races. Brijesh, therefore, won the race in which Chakri secure the second position. Since only one runner finished at the same position in both the races, Anurag must have finished at the same position in both the races as he did not secure the last position in either of the races.

The following are the standing of the runners in the two races:

Race A: Brijesh, Chakri, Anurag, Deepak.

Race B: Chakri, Deepak, Anurag, Brijesh.

1. 3 If the winner of the event was the athlete whose aggregate points in the two races was the maximum, then Chakri won the tournament

2. 4 We cannot find which race was first and which last. Hence answer to the question cannot be determined.

3. 2 The absolute difference between the positions secured in the two races was maximum for Brijesh.

4. 2 Anurag secured the same position in both the races.

9.2 SPORTS BASED

Directions for examples 5 to 8: Answer the questions on the basis of the information given below.

In the Wimbeldon Tennis tournament 2014, top 64 ranked, from 1 to 64, players participated. In the first round, the first match was played between the top ranked i.e. 1st ranked and the lowest ranked i.e. 64th ranked players, the second match was played between 2nd ranked and 63 ranked players and so on. In the next round, the winner of match 1 played with winner of match 32, winner of match 2 played with winner of match 31 and so on. This pattern continued in the subsequent rounds as well, till the final. When a lower ranked player beats a higher ranked player it's called an upset.

5. If there was no upset in the 1st and 3rd rounds and all matches in second round were upsets, the highest ranked player who could win the final was

(1) 16 (2) 24 (3)32 (4) None of these

6. If the player ranked 54 reached the semifinals, which of the following ranked player could have won the tournament?

(1) 22 (2) 59 (3) 38 (4) None of these

7. If the player ranked 16 reached the semifinals, what was the minimum number of upsets in the tournament?

(1) 2 (2) 3 (3) 4 (4) More than 4

8. If the winner, Federer, who was also the top ranked player, beats Berdych and Bhupathi in Quarterfinals and round 2 respectively, then what was the maximum possible sum of the ranks of Berdych and Bhupathi?

(1) 72 (2) 73 (3) 90 (4) 89

For examples 5 to 8:

5. 4 If all the matches were won by higher ranked player in the 1st round, top 32 ranked players must have advanced to the next round. And if all the matches in next round resulted in upsets, players ranked 17 to 32 must have advanced to the next round. So the highest rank player who could win the final was 17.

6. 4 He can meet player ranked 22 in 2nd round, and players ranked 59 and 38 in round 3. So they got eliminated before semifinal and could not reach the final.

7. 1 The number of upsets must have been minimum when only the matches involving player ranked 16 resulted in upsets. So he needed to upset the higher ranked players in 3rd round and Quarter finals.

8. 3 The lowest ranked player with Federer could play in 2nd round was 33rd, and the lowest ranked player with he could play in quarter finals was ranked 57th. So the maximum possible sum will be 90.

Directions for examples 9 to 12: Answer the questions on the basis of the information given below.

Six teams – East Bengal, Mohan Bagan, Dempo, KKR, Gymkhana and Roshnara – participated in hockey tournament, in which each team played against each of the other teams exactly once and the team with the highest number of points was declared the winner. In a match, the winner was awarded 2 points and the loser was awarded zero points. If a match ends in a draw, both teams were awarded one point each. The following table gives the partial information at the end of tournament based on final points earned by the six teams.

Team	Matches Win	Matches Drawn	Matches Lost	Points
Dempo		1		
Roshnara				4
Gymkhana				3
East Bengal		1		
Mohan Bagan				7
KKR				

Further, information is also known :

(i) East Bengal ended up with the maximum number of points, but Gymkhana did not end up with the minimum number of points.

(ii) No two teams ended up with the same number of points.

(iii) The match between Dempo and East Bengal ended in a draw.

(iv) Gymkhana lost its match against Dempo, but won against the team ended up with the minimum number of points.

(v) The number of draws in the tournament was not more than 2.

9. What was the absolute difference between the points earned by Dempo and KKR at the end of tournament?

(1) 2 (2) 3 (3) 4 (4) 5

10. The number of points with which East Bengal ended up was

(1) 8 (2) 9 (3) 10 (4) Either (1) or (2)

11. Which of the following statements will be sufficient to find the result of every match uniquely?

(1) The only team that lost against Gymkhana defeated Dempo.

(2) The team against which Gymkhana played a draw defeated KKR.

(3) Dempo defeated KKR.

(4) Both (a) and (c) are alone sufficient.

12. What was the total number of points earned by the six teams put together?

(1) 28 (2) 26 (3) 30 (4) Either (1) or (2)

For examples 9 to 12:

The sum of points awarded to the two teams involved in any match, irrespective of the result, is 2 and hence the sum of total points of all the teams was 15 × 2 = 30. As East Bengal ended up with maximum points and it was envolved in a draw, it must have ended with 9 points. Dempo had one draw, so its total points must have been an odd number. It could not be 3 or 7 as these were the points obtained by the other teams, and if it was 9, then Its total must have been highest, which was not possible. Since Dempo won at least one match, so its total must have been 5. Based on the above conclusions, the points of KKR must have been 2. Since Gymkhana won one of its match, hence it must have had one draw and would 3 loses.

Mohan Bagan played one draw and that was against Gymkhana, lost against East Bengal and won against the other three teams. Gymkhana won against KKR and lost against Dempo, East Bengal and Roshnara.

The three unknown results involved matches played amongst Dempo, KKR and Roshnara, with each team winning one match each and losing other.

9. 2 The required difference = 5 – 2 = 3.

10. 2 East Bengal ended up with 9 points.

11. 4 From (1): only KKR had lost against Gymkhana, and if it had beaten Dempo, then Dempo must have beaten Roshnara and Roshnara would have beaten KKR.

No extra information can be derived from (2)

From (3): we can determine the three unknown results

Hence both (1) and (3) alone are sufficient.

12. 3 Required answer is 30.

Directions for examples 13 to 16: Answer the questions based on the following information.

Three countries – India, Sri Lanka and Pakistan – participated in a T20 tournament, in which each team played with every other team twice. A T20 match comprises two innings (one played by each team), of 20 overs each. The RR of a team for an inning of a match is calculated by dividing the number of runs scored by the team in the inning by the number of overs allocated to an inning i.e. 20. The NRR of a team for a match is calculated by subtracting the opponent's RR from its own RR. The TNRR of a team is the total of NRR of that team in the four matches, in which it participated, put together. No match in the tournament ended in a tie/draw. It is also known that:

I. No two teams won the same number of matches in the tournament.

II. The TNRR of Sri Lanka, which scored a total of 943 runs in the tournament, was –6.95.

III. 175, 315 and 203 were the scores of some of the innings in the tournament.

IV. 15.05 was the RR of a team in an innings of a match in the tournament.

V. The highest RR of Pakistan in an inning was thrice its lowest RR in an inning in the tournament.

VI. India and Sri Lanka scored 336 and 308 respectively in the first match played between them and their scores were 270 and 222 (in that order) in the second.

VII. Sri Lanka won exactly one match, in which its NRR was 1.75, against Pakistan.

VIII. Pakistan, whose NRR in one of the matches was –7, was the only team that scored more than 300 twice.

13. In the tournament, what was the total runs scored by Pakistan in the four matches put together?

(1) 924 (2) 896 (3) 906 (4) 914

14. What was the NRR of Sri Lanka against Pakistan in the match that it lost?

(1) –4.9 (2) –5.1 (3) –3.9 (4) –2.45

15. What was the score of India against Pakistan in the match that it won?

(1) 245 (2) 175 (3) 280 (4) Cannot be determined

16. What was the minimum score of Pakistan in an innings of a match in the tournament?

(1) 175 (2) 240 (3) 105 (4) 217

For example 13 to 16:

Total number of matches held were 6, with each team playing 2 matches with the other 2 teams. From statement 1, we can deduce that the teams won 1, 2 and 3 matches.

From statements 3, 4, 6 and 8, we can conclude that Pakistan's scored 315 and 301 (i.e. 15.05 × 20) runs in two of its innings, 315 being its highest score. It must have won both these matches as India and Sri Lanka scored more than 300 only once when they played each other.

From statement 5, the lowest score in an innings by Pakistan = $\frac{315}{3} = 105$.

Using statements 2, 6 and 7, it can be said that Sri Lanka's total run difference inclusive of all the 4 matches it played = –6.95 × 20 = –139. And as we already know the margin of victory/defeat of the 3 matches played by Sri Lanka, the margin in its fourth match = –139 – [–28 – 48 + 35] = –98, i.e. Sri Lanka must have lost the 4th match by 98 runs against Pakistan.

Using statements 2, 3 and 7, we can deduce that Pakistan defeated Sri Lanka 301–203 and lost to it 175–210. Also, Pakistan lost to India 105-245. All of it can be summarized as follows:

i. India (?) - Pakistan (315): Pakistan won
ii. India (245) - Pakistan (105)
iii. India (336) - Sri Lanka (308)
iv. India (270) - Sri Lanka (222)
v. Pakistan (301) - Sri Lanka (203)
vi. Pakistan (175) - Sri Lanka (210)

13. 2 Total = 315 + 105 + 301 + 175 = 896

14. 1 Net run rate = $\frac{203-301}{20} = \frac{-98}{20} = -4.9$

15. 1

16. 3

Directions for examples 17 to 19: Answer the questions on the basis of the information given below.

Manky is given a puzzle called "Prime Game" by his mathematics teacher. He is required to determine a single digit, non-even prime number which is written on one out of the four cards namely "a", "b", "c" and "d". The four cards are lying on a table starting from his left to his right. Three out of the four cards have single digit, non-prime even numbers written on them. He can take help of a super computer "Param" which can be given a four-digit binary code as the input. The super computer multiplies each digit of the binary code to the respective number on the card from left to right.

For example:

If computer is given 1011 as the input then it completes multiplication in the following order:

1 × a + 0 × b + 1 × c + 1 × d

where a, b, c and d are the single digit distinct numbers written on cards "a", "b", "c" and "d" respectively.

The super computer then gives the above output in the decimal notation. Manky can see both the input as well as the output on the super computer.

In case an input has less than four digits in the binary system, prefix appropriate number of '0' to make the input a four digit number. For example, if an input is 11, then consider it as 0011.

17. One of the options below shows the set of values in decimal notation , whose binary equivalent as input to the computer would be sufficient to determine the prime number written on one of the cards. Which of the following is the required set of values ?

(1) 1, 2, 4 and 8 (2) 7, 5, 1 and 2 (3) 3, 2, 1 and 4 (4) 3, 3, 1 and 2

18. If Manky sends binary equivalent of 15 as input to the super computer and gets 25 as the output, then the prime number thus obtained by Manky is

(1) 3 (2) 5 (3) 2 (4) 7

19. If the number written on card 'd' is 5 and the decimal notation of the input is 14 then which of the following is the output?

(1) 20 (2) 22 (3) 24 (4) 18

For examples 17 to 19:

17. 1 Each binary code we send as input to the computer should be such that it gives number written on exactly 1 card.

If 0001 is given as input, computer will generate output as: $a \times 0 + b \times 0 + c \times 0 + 1 \times d = d$

If 0010 is given as input, computer will generate output as: $a \times 0 + b \times 0 + c \times 1 + 0 \times d = c$

If 0100 is given as input, computer will generate output as: $a \times 0 + b \times 1 + c \times 0 + 0 \times d = b$

If 1000 is given as input, computer will generate output as: $a \times 1 + b \times 0 + c \times 0 + 0 \times d = a$

Hence the above 4 binary code as input is sufficient to determine each of the number written on the 4 cards.

Decimal notation of 0001, 0010, 0100, and 1000 are 1, 2, 4 and 8 respectively.

18. 4 Binary equivalent of 15 is 1111.

If 1111 is send as input to the computer, it will generate the output as: $1 \times a + 1 \times b + 1 \times c + 1 \times d$

According to the question,

$a + b + c + d = 25.$

Since it's given that three numbers are even and one of them is prime.

The only possible combination is 4, 6, 7 and 8.

19. 4 The only possible non-prime even numbers are 4, 6 and 8.

So, when the input is 14, i.e. 1110, the output will be $(1 \times 4) + (1 \times 6) + (1 \times 8) + (0 \times 5) = 18$

Here, the order of 4, 6, 8 does not matter as in any case 0 will be multiplied by 5 only.

PRACTICE EXERCISE – 1

Directions for questions 1 to 4: Answer the questions on the basis of the information given below.

Four car drivers – A, B, C and D – were driving their cars on one of the tracks in a car zone, shown below. In the zone, there are two concentric circular tracks passing through either P or Q and one square track passing through R and S, as shown in the figure below where O is the center of the concentric circles.

Car Zone

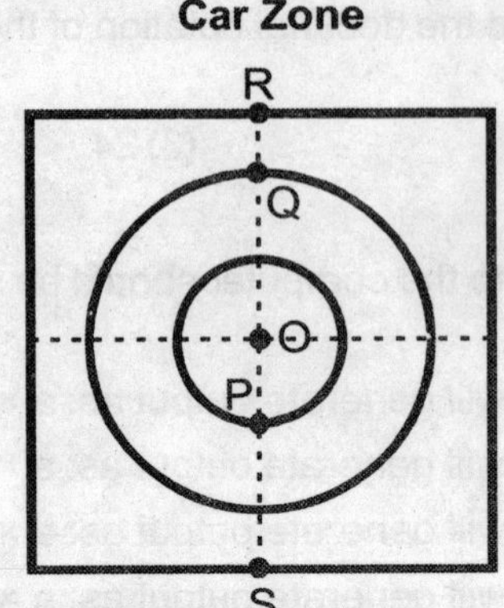

Following information is given:

I. The cars are such that their drivers cannot get to know whether they are moving or stationary. They cannot even judge the speed of their own cars.

II. However, the drivers can measure the speed of the other cars only with respect to themselves, whenever two or more cars are moving parallel to each other.

III. They move at a constant speed in either clockwise or anticlockwise direction.

When B passed from point P, he made the following observations at that instant:

A. A's car passed through point Q at a speed of 50 mph.

B. C's car passed through point R and D's car passed through point S.

C. C and D were moving in same directions at that particular instant, and their speed was 40 mph & 60 mph respectively.

1. If A, B, C, D are all moving in a clockwise direction and B's speed is 20 mph, what was the ratio of speed of A, B, C and D?

(1) 7 : 2 : 6 : 4 (2) 3 : 2 : 2 : 4 (3) 3 : 2 : 2 : 8 (4) 7 : 2 : 6 : 8

2. If both A and B are moving in the clockwise direction, what could be the possible value of the average of the speeds of these four cars?

(1) 37.5 mph (2) 22.5 mph (3) 27.5 mph (4) 47.5 mph

3. If A drove his car in the clockwise direction, and B in the anticlockwise direction and C observed that D's speed was 20mph with respect to him. What could be the speed of driver B?

(1) 75 mph (b) 50 mph (3) 65 mph (4) 80 mph

4. One out of A and B drove his car in the clockwise direction and the other in the anticlockwise direction. At the same instant when B passed through point P, a person E, who was standing at point O, observed that while passing through points R and S, C and D had the same speed with respect to him. Which of the following could also be observed by E?

(1) Three of these four cars had a speed of 10 mph.

(2) Three of these four cars had a speed of 50 mph.

(3) A's car was moving at exactly double the speed of either of C's or D's car.

(4) A's car was moving at more than double the speed of B's car.

Directions for questions 5 to 7: Answer the questions on the basis of the information given below.

Sixteen teams – named A to P in the English alphabet – participated in a football tournament named Diamond Cup. In the first round of the tournament, the teams were divided into two groups – X and Y – with eight teams in each group. In this round, a total of eight matches were played and all the teams played a match each; each team of Group X played against one of the teams of Group Y. Further information about the matches played in the first round is given below:

(i) The matches were numbered 1 to 8 according to the order in which they were played.

(ii) A, H and L were in the same group. The same was true for M, J and E.

(iii) H was in Group X.

(iv) P was in Group Y and played against F.

(v) The 6th match was played between M and C; the 8th match was played between H and J.

(vi) D was not in the group which had C, K and O. G was not in the group which had B, N and I.

(vii) B played its match before P's match and immediately after I's match.

(viii) G and K played the 1st match and 2nd match respectively.

(ix) L did not play the 1st, 3rd, 5th or 7th match.

5. If D and F played the 1st match and the 5th match respectively, then B played against

(1) A (2) L

(3) O (4) Either (1), (2) or (3)

6. If A played against I, then O could have played its match against how many teams?

(1) 2 (2) 3

(3) 4 (4) 5

7. If A played against I, then which of the following statements was definitely true?

(1) B played against L (2) M played its match before P's match

(3) Neither (1) nor (2) (4) Both (1) and (2)

Directions for questions 8 to 10: Answer the questions on the basis of the information given below.

Four teams—T1, T2, T3 and T4— participated in a tournament of 'Bat and trap', an English bat-and-ball pub game. In the tournament, each team played exactly one match with each of the other teams. The matches were played on six consecutive days of a week from Monday to Saturday. Two points were awarded to the winner of a match and no points to the loser. No match in the tournament resulted in a tie/draw. It is also known that:

I. T1 won only one match in the tournament and it was played on Monday.

II. The match played on Thursday was won by T4.

III. T3 won against T2 on Tuesday.

IV. T2, T3 and T4 definitely did not play on Wednesday, Monday and Saturday respectively.

V. T2 and T3 ended up with the same number of points at the end of the tournament.

8. How many points did T4 score in the tournament?

(1) 2 (2) 4

(3) 6 (4) Cannot be determined

9. T3 lost its match against

(1) T1 (2) T2

(3) T4 (4) Both T1 and T2

10. The match played on Friday was between

(1) T1 and T2 (2) T2 and T3

(3) T1 and T4 (4) T2 and T4

9.8 SPORTS BASED

Directions for questions 11 to 13: Answer the questions on the basis of the information given below.

A Cricket team of 11 players is to be formed from a group of 15 players—A, B, C, D, E, F, G, H, I, J, K, L, M, N and O. Among the players A, D, K, L, M, N and O are batsmen; B, C, E, F, G and H are bowlers; I and J are wicketkeepers. It is also known that:

I. The team must have at least 5 batsmen and exactly 1 wicketkeeper.

II. H can be selected only if B is selected.

III. F can be selected only if both G and N are selected.

IV. If I is selected, then F is also selected.

V. K and M cannot be selected together for the team. The same is true for B and G.

11. In how many ways can the team be formed?

(1) 3 (2) 4 (3) 5 (4) 6

12. If G is one of the bowlers in the team, then who will be the wicketkeeper?

(1) J (2) I

(3) Either (1) or (2) (4) No such team is possible

13. If H is selected, then who among the following cannot be selected in the team?

(1) O (2) N (3) G (4) J

Directions for questions 14 to 17: Answer the questions on the basis of the information given below.

Four teams—T1, T2, T3 and T4— participated in a tournament of 'Bat and trap', an English bat-and-ball pub game. In the tournament, each team played exactly one match with each of the other teams. The matches were played on six consecutive days of a week from Monday to Saturday. Two points were awarded to the winner of a match and no points to the loser. No match in the tournament resulted in a tie/draw. It is also known that:

I. T1 won only one match in the tournament and it was played on Monday.

II. The match played on Thursday was won by T4.

III. T3 won against T2 on Tuesday.

IV. T2, T3 and T4 definitely did not play on Wednesday, Monday and Saturday respectively.

V. T2 and T3 ended up with the same number of points at the end of the tournament.

14. How many points did T4 score in the tournament?

(1) 2 (2) 4 (3) 6 (4) Cannot be determined

15. T3 lost its match against

(1) T1 (2) T2 (3) T4 (4) Both T1 and T2

16. The match played on Friday was between

(1) T1 and T2 (2) T2 and T3 (3) T1 and T4 (4) T2 and T4

17. Who won the match played on Thursday?

(1) T1 (2) T2 (3) T3 (4) T4

Directions for questions 18 to 21: Answer the questions on the basis of the information given below.

Sixteen teams – A through P – participated in the Hockey World Cup,2013. The tournament was conducted in two stages. In the first stage, the teams were divided into two groups – teams A to H in group 1 and teams I to P in group 2. In the first stage, each team in a group played exactly one match against every other team in that group. At the end of the first stage, the top four teams from each group advanced to the second stage while the rest got eliminated. The second stage comprised three rounds – Quarterfinals, Semi-finals and Finals. A round involves one match for each team. The winner of a match in a round advanced to the next round, while the loser got eliminated. The team that remains undefeated in the second stage was declared the winner of the tournament.

At the end of the first stage, top four teams in each group were determined on the basis of total number of matches won by individual teams; in case, two or more teams in a group were ended up with the same number of wins, ties were resolved by a series of complex tie-breaking rules to determine the top four positions. The teams qualifying for the second stage from group 1 were A, B, C and D and those from group 2 were I, J, K and L. No match in the tournament ended in a draw/tie.

18. In the tournament, if E and L won the same number of matches and L was the winner of the tournament, then what was the sum of the number of matches won by E and that by L?

(1) 10 (2) 9 (3) 8 (4) 7

19. The number of matches won in the first stage by a team that advanced to the second stage could not be less than

(1) 1 (2) 2 (3) 3 (4) 4

20. How many of the following statements is/are true?

(i) Maximum number of teams which could have one win in the first stage was 6.

(ii) Maximum number of teams which could have three wins in the first stage was 12.

(iii) Number of teams which had exactly 2 wins in the second stage was 2.

(1) None (2) 1 (3) 2 (4) 3

21. The value of the total of number of matches won, in the first stage, by teams A, B, C and D together could not be more than

(1) 16 (2) 18 (3) 20 (4) 22

Directions for questions 22 to 24: The following questions relate to a game to be played by you and your friend. The game consists of a 4 x 4 board (see below) where each cell contains a positive integer. You and your friend make moves alternately. A move by any of the players consists of splitting the current board configuration into two equal halves and retaining one of them. In your moves you are allowed to split the board only vertically and to decide to retain either the left or the right half. Your friend, in his/her moves, can split the board only horizontally and can retain either the lower or the upper half. After two moves by each player a single cell will remain which can no longer be split and the number in that cell will be treated as the gain (in rupees) of the person who has started the game. A sample game is shown below.

[CAT 1990]

2	1	2	4
5	1	6	7
9	1	3	2
6	1	8	4

Initial Board

2	1		
5	1		
9	1		
6	1		

After your move (Retain left)

2	1		
5	1		

After your friends move (Retain upper)

	1		
	1		

After your move (Retain right)

	1		

After your friends move (Retain lower)

So your gain is Re.1. With the same initial board configuration as above and assuming that you have to make the first move, answer the following questions.

22. If you choose (retain right) (retain left) in your turns, the best move sequence for your friend to reduce your gain to a minimum will be

(1) (retain upper)(retain lower)

(2) (retain lower) (retain upper)

(3) (retain upper) (retain upper)

(4) (retain lower) (retain lower)

23. If both of you select your moves intelligently then at the end of the game your gain will be

(1) Rs.4 (2) Rs.3

(3) Rs.2 (4) None of these

24. If your first move is (retain right), then whatever moves your friend may select you can always force a gain of no less than

(1) Rs.3 (2) Rs.6

(3) Rs.4 (4) None of these

9.10 SPORTS BASED

Directions for questions 25 to 28: The pages of a book are numbered 0, 1, 2 ... upto M, M>0. There are four categories of instructions that direct a person in positioning the book at a page. The instruction types and their meanings are :

1. OPEN : Position the book at page No. 1
2. CLOSE : Position the book at page No. 0
3. FORWARD, n :From the current page move forward by n pages; if, in this process, page number M is reached, stop at M.
4. BACKWARD, n : From the current page, move backward by n pages; if in this process, page number 0 is reached, stop at page number 0.

In each of the following questions, you will find a sequence of instructions formed from the above categories. In each case, let n_1 be the page number before the instructions are executed and n_2 be the page number at which the book is positioned after the instructions are executed.

[CAT 1990]

25. FORWARD, 25 ; BACKWARD, 10.

Which of the following statements is true about the above set of instructions?

(1) $n_1 = n_2$ if M = 10 and $n_1 = 0$ (2) M = 20 provided $n_1 > 0$

(3) $n_1 > 30$ provided M = 900 (4) $n_1 = 37$ provided M = 25

26. BACKWARD, 5; FORWARD, 5. Which of the following statements is true about the above set of instructions?

(1) $n_1 = n_2$ provided $n_1 \geq 5$ (2) $n_1 = n_2$ provided $n_1 > 0$

(3) $n_2 = 5$ provided M > 0 (4) $n_1 > n_2$ provided M > 0

27. FORWARD, 10; FORWARD, 10. Which of the following statements about the above instructions is true?

(1) $n_2 - n_1 = 20$ only if $n_1 = 0$ (2) $n_2 - n_1 = 20$ if M > 20 and $n_1 = 1$

(3) $n_2 - n_1 = 10$ if M = 21 and $n_1 = 0$ (4) $n_2 > n_1$ if M > 0

28. FORWARD, 5; BACKWARD, 4. Which of the following statements about the above instructions is true?

(1) $n_2 = n_1 + 4$ Provided $1 < n_1 < 7$ (2) $n_2 = n_1$ provided M < 6

(3) $n_2 = n_1 + 1$ provided $M - n_1 > 5$ (4) $n_2 - n_1 < 0$ provided M > 0

Directions for questions 29 to 32: Answer the questions on the basis of the information given below.

[CAT 1993]

"Kya – Kya" is an island in the South Pacific. The inhabitants of "Kya – Kya" always answer any question with two sentences, one of which is always true and the other always false.

29. You find that your boat is stolen. You question three inhabitants of the island and they reply as follows:

John says, "I didn't do it. Mathew didn't do it."

Mathew says. "I didn't do it. Krishna didn't do it."

Krishna says. "I didn't do it. I don't know who did it."

Who stole your boat?

(1) John (2) Mathew (3) Krishna (4) None of them

30. There is only one pilot on the island. You interview three men, Koik, Lony and Mirna. You also notice that Koik is wearing a cap.

Mirna says, "Lony's father is the pilot. Lony is not the priest's son."

Koik says, "I am the priest. On this island, only priests can wear caps."

Lony says, "I am the priest's son. Koik is not the priest."

Which of the following is true?

(1) Lony is not Koik's son. (2) Koik is the pilot. (3) Mirna is the pilot. (4) Lony is the priest.

31. You are walking on the road and come to a fork. You ask the inhabitants Ram, Laxman and Lila. "Which road will take me to the village?"

Ram says, "I never speak to strangers. I am new to these parts."

Laxman says, "I am married to Lila. Take the left road."

Lila says, "I am married to Ram. He is not new to this place."

Which of the following is true?

(1) Left road takes you to the village. (2) Right road takes you to the village.
(3) Lila is married to Laxman. (4) None of these.

32. You want to speak to the chief of the village. You question three inhabitants. Amar, Bobby and Charles. Only Bobby is wearing a red shirt."

Amar says. "I am not Bobby's son. The chief wears a red shirt."

Bobby says, "I am Amar's father. Charles is the chief."

Charles says, "The chief is one among us. I am the chief."

Who is the chief?

(1) Amar (2) Bobby (3) Charles (4) None of them

Directions for questions 33 to 36: Answer the questions on the basis of the information given below.

[CAT 1993]

Swetha, Swarna, Sneha and Soumya are four sisters who have an agreement that they share all snacks equally among themselves. One day, uncle Prem gave a box of cookies to Swetha. Since the other sisters were not around, Swetha divided the cookies into four parts, ate her share and put the rest into the box. As she was closing the box, Swarna came in, She took all the cookies from the box and divided them into four equal parts. Swetha and Swarna ate one part each and put the rest into the box. Just then Sneha walked in. She took all the cookies from the box, divided them into four equal parts. The three of them ate their respective shares and put the rest into the box. Later, when Soumya came, she divided all the cookies into four equal parts and all the four sisters ate their respective shares. In total, Soumya ate 3 cookies.

33. How many cookies, in total, did Sneha eat?

(1) 30 (2) 12 (3) 15 (4) 6

34. How many cookies did uncle Prem give to Swetha?

(1) 128 (2) 156 (3) 256 (4) 192

35. How many cookies, in total, did Swetha eat?

(1) 32 (2) 142 (3) 72 (4) 71

36. How many cookies, in total, did Swarna eat?

(1) 9 (2) 30 (3) 39 (4) 78

Directions for questions 37 to 40: Answer the questions on the basis of the information given below.

[CAT 1994]

Bankatlal works x hours a day and rests y hours a day. This pattern continues for 1 week, with an exactly opposite pattern next week, and so on for four weeks. Every fifth week he has a different pattern. When he works longer than he rests, his wage per hour is twice what he earns per hour when he rests longer than he works.

The following are his daily working hours for the weeks numbered 1 to 13.

	1st week	5th week	9th week	13th week
Rest	2	3	4	-
Work	5	7	6	8

A week consists of six days and a month consists of 4 weeks.

37. If Bankatlal is paid Rs. 20 per working hour in the 1st week. What is his salary for the 1st month?

(1) Rs.1760 (2) Rs.1440 (3) Rs.1320 (4) Rs.1680

9.12 SPORTS BASED

38. Referring to the data given in Q.187, Bankatlal's average monthly salary at the end of the first four months will be

(1) Rs.1780 (2) Rs.2040 (3) Rs.1830 (4) Rs.1680

39. The new manager Khushaldas stipulated that Rs.5 be deducted for every hour of rest and Rs. 25 be paid per hour starting 9th week, then what will be the change in Bankatlal's salary for the 3rd month? (Hourly deductions are constant for all weeks starting 9th week)

(1) Rs.540 (2) Rs.480 (3) Rs.240 (4) Rs.120

40. Using the data in the previous questions, what will be the total earning of Bankatlal at the end of sixteen weeks.

(1) Rs.7320 (2) Rs.7800 (3) Rs.8400 (4) Rs.9600

Directionsfor questions 41 to 45: Answer the questions on the basis of the information given below.

[CAT 1995]

Machine M1 as well as machine M2 can independently produce either product P or product Q. The time taken by machines M1 and M2 (in minutes) to produce one unit of product P and product Q are given in the table below: (Each machine works 8 hour per day).

Product	M1	M2
P	10	8
Q	6	6

41. What is the maximum number of units that can be manufactured in one day?

(1) 140 (2) 160 (3) 120 (4) 180

42. If M1 works at half its normal efficiency, what is the maximum number of units produced, if at least one unit of each must be produced?

(1) 96 (2) 89 (3) 100 (4) 119

43. What is the least number of machine hours required to produce 30 pieces of P and 25 pieces of Q respectively?

(1) 6 hr 30 min (2) 7 hr 24 min (3) 6 hr 48 min (4) 4 hr 6 min

44. If the number of units of P is to be three times that of Q, what is the maximum idle time to maximize total units manufactured?

(1) 0 min (2) 24 min (3) 1 hr (4) 2 hr

45. If equal quantities of both are to be produced, then out of the four choices given below, the least efficient way would be

(1) 48 of each with 3 min idle

(2) 64 of each with 12 min idle

(3) 53 of each with 10 min idle

(4) 71 of each with 9 min idle

PRACTICE EXERCISE – 2

Direction for questions 1 to 3: Answer the questions on the basis of the information given below.

[CAT 1997]

A certain race is made up of three stretches: A, B and C, each 2 km long, and to be covered by a certain mode of transport. The following table gives these modes of transport for the stretches, and the minimum and maximum possible speeds (in km/hr) over these stretches. The speed over a particular stretch is assumed to be constant. The previous record for the race is 10 min.

		Min.	Max.
A	Car	40	60
B	Motorcycle	30	50
C	Bicycle	10	20

1. Anshuman travels at minimum speed by car over A and completes stretch B at the fastest speed. At what speed should he cover stretch C in order to break the previous record?
   (1) Maximum speed for C
   (2) Minimum speed for C
   (3) This is not possible
   (4) None of these
2. Mr Hare completes the first stretch at the minimum speed and takes the same time for stretch B. He takes 50% more time than the previous record to complete the race. What is Mr Hare's speed for the stretch C?
   (1) 10.9 km/hr
   (2) 13.3 km/hr
   (3) 17.1 km/hr
   (4) None of these
3. Mr Tortoise completes the race at an average speed of 20 km/hr. His average speed for the first two stretches is four times that for the last stretch. Find the speed over stretch C.
   (1) 15 km/hr
   (2) 12 km/hr
   (3) 10 km/hr
   (4) This is not possible

Directions for questions 4 to 6: Answer the questions on the basis of the information given below.

[CAT 1999]

A young girl Roopa leaves home with x flowers, goes to the bank of a nearby river. On the bank of the river, there are four places of worship, standing in a row. She dips all the x flowers into the river. The number of flowers doubles. Then she enters the first place of worship, offers y flowers to the deity. She dips the remaining flowers into the river, and again the number of flowers doubles. She goes to the second place of worship, offers y flowers to the deity. She dips the remaining flowers into the river, and again the number of flowers doubles. She goes to the third place of worship, offers y flowers to the deity. She dips the remaining flowers into the river, and again the number of flowers doubles. She goes to the fourth place of worship, offers y flowers to the deity. Now she is left with no flowers in hand.

4. If Roopa leaves home with 30 flowers, the number of flowers she offers to each deity is
   (1) 30
   (2) 31
   (3) 32
   (4) 33
5. The minimum number of flowers that could be offered to each deity is
   (1) 0
   (2) 15
   (3) 16
   (4) Cannot be determined
6. The minimum number of flowers with which Roopa leaves home is
   (1) 16
   (2) 15
   (3) 0
   (4) Cannot be determined

Directions for questions 7 to 9: Answer the questions on the basis of the information given below.

[CAT 1999]

Recently, Ghosh Babu spent his winter vacation on Kyakya Island. During the vacation, he visited the local casino where he came across a new card game. Two players, using a normal deck of 52 playing cards, play this game. One player is called the 'dealer' and the other is called the 'player'. First, the player picks a card at random from the deck. This is called the base card. The amount in rupees equal to the face value of the base card is called the base amount. The face values of ace, king, queen and jack are ten. For other cards the face value is the number on the card. Once the 'player' picks a card from the deck, the 'dealer' pays him the base amount. Then the 'dealer' picks a card from the deck and this card is called the top card. If the top card is of the same suit as the base card, the 'player' pays twice the base amount to the 'dealer'. If the top card is of the same colour as the base card (but not the same suit), then the 'player' pays the base amount to the 'dealer'. If the top card happens to be of a different colour than the base card, the 'dealer' pays the base amount to the 'player'.

Ghosh Babu played the game four times. First time he picked eight of clubs and the 'dealer' picked queen of clubs. Second time, he picked ten of hearts and the 'dealer' picked two of spades. Next time, Ghosh Babu picked six of diamonds and the 'dealer' picked ace of hearts. Lastly, he picked eight of spades and the 'dealer' picked jack of spades. Answer the following questions based on these four games.

7. If Ghosh Babu stopped playing the game when his gain would be maximized, the gain in Rs. would have been

(1) 12 (2) 20 (3) 16 (4) 4

8. The initial money Ghosh Babu had (before the beginning of the game sessions) was Rs. X. At no point did he have to borrow any money. What is the minimum possible value of X?

(1) 16 (2) 8 (3) 100 (4) 24

9. If the final amount of money that Ghosh Babu had with him was Rs. 100, what was the initial amount he had with him?

(1) 120 (2) 8 (3) 4 (4) 96

Directions for questions 10 and 11: Answer the questions on the basis of the information given below.

[CAT 2000]

There are three bottles of water — A, B, C, whose capacities are 5 L, 3 L, and 2 L respectively. For transferring water from one bottle to another and to drain out the bottles, there exists a piping system. The flow through these pipes is computer-controlled. The computer that controls the flow through these pipes can be fed with three types of instructions, as explained below.

Instruction type	Explanation of the instruction
Fill (X, Y)	Fill bottle labelled X from the water in bottle labelled Y, where the remaining capacity of X is less than or equal to the amount of water in Y.
Empty (X, Y)	Empty out the water in bottle labelled X into bottle labelled Y, where the amount of water in X is less than or equal to remaining capacity of Y.
Drain (X)	Drain out all the water contained in bottle labelled X.

Initially, A is full with water, and B and C are empty.

10. After executing a sequence of three instructions, bottle A contains one litre of water. The first and the third of these instructions are shown below.

First instruction: FILL (C, A)

Third instruction: FILL (C, A)

Then which of the following statements about the instructions is true?

(1) The second instruction is FILL (B, A).

(2) The second instruction is EMPTY (C, B).

(3) The second instruction transfers water from B to C.

(4) The second instruction involves using the water in bottle A.

11. Consider the same sequence of three instructions and the same initial state mentioned above. Three more instructions are added at the end of the above sequence to have A contain 4 L of water. In this total sequence of six instructions, the fourth one is DRAIN (A). This is the only DRAIN instruction in the entire sequence. At the end of the execution of the above sequence, how much water is contained in C?

(1) 1 L (2) 2 L (3) 0 (4) None of these

Directions for questions 12 to 16: Answer the questions on the basis of the information given below.

[CAT 2000]

Sixteen teams have been invited to participate in the ABC Gold Cup cricket tournament. The tournament is conducted in two stages. In the first stage, the teams are divided into two groups. Each group consists of eight teams, with each team playing every other team in its group exactly once. At the end of the first stage, the top four teams from each group advance to the second stage while the rest are eliminated. The second stage comprises of several rounds. A round involves one match for each team. The winner of a match in a round advances to the next round, while the loser is eliminated. The team that remains undefeated in the second stage is declared the winner and claims the Gold Cup.

The tournament rules are such that each match results in a winner and a loser with no possibility of a tie. In the first stage, a team earns one point for each win and no points for a loss. At the end of the first stage, teams in each group are ranked on the basis of total points to determine the qualifiers advancing to the next stage. Ties are resolved by a series of complex tie-breaking rules so that exactly four teams from each group advance to the next stage.

12. What is the total number of matches played in the tournament?

(1) 28 (2) 55 (3) 63 (4) 35

13. The minimum number of wins needed for a team in the first stage to guarantee its advancement to the next stage is

(1) 5 (2) 6 (3) 7 (4) 4

14. What is the highest number of wins for a team in the first stage in spite of which it would be eliminated at the end of first stage?

(1) 1 (2) 2 (3) 3 (4) 4

15. What is the number of rounds in the second stage of the tournament?

(1) 1 (2) 2 (3) 3 (4) 4

16. Which of the following statements is true?

(1) The winner will have more wins than any other team in the tournament.

(2) At the end of the first stage, no team eliminated from the tournament will have more wins than any of the teams qualifying for the second stage.

(3) It is possible that the winner will have the same number of wins in the entire tournament as a team eliminated at the end of the first stage.

(4) The number of teams with exactly one win in the second stage of the tournament is 4.

Directions for questions 17 to 20: Answer the questions on the basis of the information given below.

[CAT 2005]

In the table below is the listing of players, seeded from highest (#1) to lowest (#32), who are due to play in an Association of Tennis Players (ATP) tournament for women. This tournament has four knockout rounds before the final, i.e., first round, second round, quarterfinals, and semi-finals. In the first round, the highest seeded player plays the lowest seeded player (seed #32) which is designated match No. 1 of first round; the 2nd seeded player plays the 31st seeded player which is designated match No. 2 of the first round, and so on. Thus, for instance, match No. 16 of first round is to be played between 16th seeded player and the 17th seeded player. In the second round, the winner of match No. 1 of first round plays the winner of match No. 16 of first round and is designated match No. 1 of second round. Similarly, the winner of match No. 2 of first round plays the winner of match No. 15 of first round, and is designated match No. 2 of second round. Thus, for instance, match No. 8 of the second round is to be played between the winner of match No. 8 of first round and the winner of match No. 9 of first round. The same pattern is followed for later rounds as well.

Seed#	Name of Player	Seed#	Name of Player	Seed#	Name of Player
1	Maria Sharapova	12	Mary Pierce	23	Silvia Farina Elia
2	Lindsay Davenport	13	Anastasia Myskina	24	Tatiana Golovin
3	Amelie Mauresmo	14	Alicia Molik	25	Shinobu Asagoe
4	Kim Clijsters	15	Nathalie Dechy	26	Francesca Schiavone
5	Svetlana Kuznetsova	16	Elena Bovina	27	Nicole Vaidisova
6	Elena Dementieva	17	Jelena Jankovic	28	Gisela Dulko
7	Justine Henin	18	Ana Ivanovic	29	Flavia Pennetta
8	Serena Williams	19	Vera Zvonareva	30	Anna Chakvetadze
9	Nadia Petrova	20	Elena Likhovtseva	31	Al Sugiyama
10	Venus Williams	21	Daniela Hantuchova	32	Anna-lena Groenefeld
11	Patty Schnyder	22	Dinara Safina		

17. If there are no upsets (a lower seeded player beating a higher seeded player) in the first round, and only match Nos. 6, 7, and 8 of the second round result in upsets, then who would meet Lindsay Davenport in quarter finals, in case Davenport reaches quarter finals?

(1) Justine Henin (2) Nadia Petrova (3) Patty Schnyder (4) Venus Williams

18. If Elena Dementieva and Serena Williams lose in the second round, while Justine Henin and Nadia Petrova make it to the semi-finals, then who would play Maria Sharapova in the quarterfinals, in the event Sharapova reaches quarterfinals?

(1) Dinara Safina (2) Justine Henin (3) Nadia Petrova (4) Patty Schnyder

19. If, in the first round, all even numbered matches (and none of the odd numbered ones) result in upsets, and there are no upsets in the second round, then who could be the lowest seeded player facing Maria Sharapova in semi-finals?

(1) Anastasia Myskina (2) Flavia Pennetta (3) Nadia Petrova (4) Svetlana Kuznetsova

20. If the top eight seeds make it to the quarterfinals, then who, amongst the players listed below, would definitely not play against Maria Sharapova in the final, in case Sharapova reaches the final?

(1) Amelie Mauresmo (2) Elena Dementieva (3) Kim Clijsters (4) Lindsay Davenport

Directions for questions 21 to 24: Answer the questions on the basis of the information given below. **[CAT 2005]**

The year is 2089. Beijing, London, New York, and Paris are in contention to host the 2096 Olympics. The eventual winner is determined through several rounds of voting by members of the IOC with each member representing a different city. All the four cities in contention are also represented in IOC.

(1) In any round of voting, the city receiving the lowest number of votes in that round gets eliminated. The survivor after the last round of voting gets to host the event.

(2) A member is allowed to cast votes for at most two different cities in all rounds of voting combined. (Hence, a member becomes ineligible to cast a vote in a given round if both the cities (s)he voted for in earlier rounds are out of contention in that round of voting.)

(3) A member is also ineligible to cast a vote in a round if the city (s)he represents is in contention in that round of voting.

(4) As long as the member is eligible, (s)he must vote and vote for only one candidate city in any round of voting.

The following incomplete table shows the information on cities that received the maximum and minimum votes in different rounds, the number of votes cast in their favour, and the total votes that were cast in those rounds.

Round	Total votes	Maximum votes cast		Eliminated	
		City	No. of votes	City	No. of votes
1		London	30	New York	12
2	83	Paris	32	Beijing	21
3	75				

It is also known that:

- All those who voted for London and Paris in round, 1 continued to vote for the same cities in subsequent rounds as long as these cities were in contention. 75% of those who voted for Beijing in round 1, voted for Beijing in round 2 as well.
- Those who voted for New York in round 1, voted either for Beijing or Paris in round 2.
- The difference in votes cast for the two contending cities in the last round was 1.
- 50% of those who voted for Beijing in round 1, voted for Paris in round 3.

21. What percentage of members from among those who voted for New York in round 1, voted for Beijing in round 2?

(1) 33.33 (2) 50 (3) 66.67 (4) 75

22. What is the number of votes cast for Paris in round 1?

(1) 16 (2) 18 (3) 22 (4) 24

23. What percentage of members from among those who voted for Beijing in round 2 and were eligible to vote in round 3, voted for London?

(1) 33.33 (2) 38.10 (3) 50 (4) 66.67

24. Which of the following statements must be true?

I. IOC member from New York must have voted for Paris in round 2.

II. IOC member from Beijing voted for London in round 3.

(1) Only I (2) Only II (3) Both I and II (4) Neither I nor II

Directions for questions 25 to 29: Answer the questions on the basis of the information given below.

[CAT 2006]

Mathematicians are assigned a number called Erdös number (named after the famous mathematician, Paul Erdös). Only Paul Erdös himself has an Erdös number of zero. Any mathematician who has written a research paper with Erdös has an Erdös number of 1. For other mathematicians, the calculation of his/her Erdös number is illustrated below:

Suppose that a mathematician X has co-authored papers with several other mathematicians. From among them, mathematician Y has the smallest Erdös number. Let the Erdös number of Y be y. Then X has an Erdös number of y + 1. Hence any mathematician with no co-authorship chain connected to Erdös has an Erdös number of infinity.

In a seven day long mini-conference organized in memory of Paul Erdös, a close group of eight mathematicians, call them A, B, C, D, E, F, G and H, discussed some research problems. At the beginning of the conference, A was the only participant who had an infinite Erdös number. Nobody had an Erdös number less than that of F.

1. On the third day of the conference F co-authored a paper jointly with A and C. This reduced the average Erdös number of the group of eight mathematicians to 3. The Erdös numbers of B, D, E, G and H remained unchanged with the writing of this paper. Further, no other co-authorship among any three members would have reduced the average Erdös number of the group of eight to as low as 3.
2. At the end of the third day, five members of this group had identical Erdös numbers while the other three had Erdös numbers distinct from each other.
3. On the fifth day, E co-authored a paper with F which reduced the group's average Erdös number by 0.5. The Erdös numbers of the remaining six were unchanged with the writing of this paper.
4. No other paper was written during the conference.

25. How many participants in the conference did not change their Erdös number during the conference?

(1) 2 (2) 3 (3) 4 (4) 5 (5) Cannot be determined

26. The person having the largest Erdös number at the end of the conference must have had Erdös number (at that time):

(1) 5 (2) 7 (3) 9 (4) 14 (5) 15

27. How many participants had the same Erdös number at the beginning of the conference?

(1) 2 (2) 3 (3) 4 (4) 5 (5) Cannot be determined

28. The Erdös number of C at the end of the conference was:

(1) 1 (2) 2 (3) 3 (4) 4 (5) 5

29. The Erdös number of E at the beginning of the conference was:

(1) 2 (2) 5 (3) 6 (4) 7 (5) 8

Directions for questions 30 to 33: Answer the questions on the basis of the information given below.

[CAT 2017 Shift 1]

In a square layout of size 5 m × 5 m, 25 equal-sized square platforms of different heights are built. The heights (in metres) of individual plalforms are as shown below:

6	1	2	4	3
9	5	3	2	8
7	8	4	6	5
3	9	5	1	2
1	7	6	3	9

Individuals (all of same height) are seated on these platforms. We say an individual A can reach an individual B if all the three following conditions are met:

(i) A and B are in the same row or column

(ii) A is at a lower height than B

(iii) if there is/are any individual(s) between A and B, such individual(s) must be at a height lower than that of A.

Thus in the table given above, consider the individual seated at height 8 on 3rd row and 2nd column. He can be reached by four individuals. He can be reached by the individual on his left at height 7, by the two individuals on his right at heights of 4 and 6 and by the individual above at height 5.

Rows in the layout are numbered from top to bottom and columns are numbered from left to right.

30. How many individuals in this layout can be reached by just one individual?

(1) 3 (2) 5 (3) 7 (4) 8

31. Which of the following is true for any individual at a platform of height 1 m in this layout?

(1) They can he reached by all the individuals in their own row and column.

(2) They can be reached by at least 4 individuals.

(3) They can be reached by at least one individual.

(4) They cannot be reached by anyone.

32. We can find two individuals who cannot be reached by anyone in

(1) the last row.

(2) the fourth row.

(3) the fourth column.

(4) the middle column.

33. Which of the following statements is true about this layout?

(1) Each row has an individual who can be reached by 5 or more individuals.

(2) Each row has an individual who cannot be reached by anyone.

(3) Each row has at least two individuals who can be reached by an equal number of individuals.

(4) All individuals at the height of 9 m can be reached by at least 5 individuals.

Directions for questions 34 to 37: Answer the questions on the basis of the information given below.

In an 8 × 8 chessboard a queen placed anywhere can attack another piece if the piece is present in the same row, or in the same column or in any diagonal position in any possible 4 directions, provided there is no other piece in between in the path from the queen to that piece.

The columns are labelled a to h (left to right) and the rows are numbered 1 to 8 (bottom to top). The position of a piece is given by the combination of column and row labels. For example, position c5 means that the piece is in c^{th} column and 5th row.

Sub questions

[CAT 2017 Shift 2]

34. If the queen is at c5, and the other pieces at positions c2, g1, g3, g5 and a3, how many are under attack by the queen? There are no other pieces on the board.

(1) 2 (2) 3 (3) 4 (4) 5

35. If the other pieces are only at positions a1, a3, b4, d7, h7 and h8, then which of the following positions of the queen results in the maximum number of pieces being under attack?

(1) f8 (2) a7 (3) c1 (4) d3

36. If the other pieces are only at positions a1, a3, b4, d7, h7 and h8, then from how many positions the queen cannot attack any of the pieces?

(1) 0 (2) 3 (3) 4 (4) 6

37. Suppose the queen is the only piece on the board and it is at position d5.
In how many positions can another piece be placed on the board such that it is safe from attack from the queen?

(1) 32 (2) 33 (3) 36 (4) 37

Directions for questions 38 to 40: Answer the questions on the basis of the information given below.

Five teams participated in the recently played Premier Hockey League. As per the scheme of the tournament, every team has to play every other team 5 times, i.e. a total of 20 matches per team and then points were awarded for Win (W), Lose (L) and Tie (T). The following chart gives the number of matches won, matches lost and matches tied by five teams. The number of matches won, lost and tied by Assam is denoted by X, Y, Z.

Team	W	L	T
Haryana	2	15	3
Maharashtra	7	9	4
Punjab	6	12	2
Bengal	10	8	2
Assam	X	Y	Z

38. Find the value of X.

(1) 0 (2) 1 (3) 19 (4) 20

39. Find the value of Y.

(1) 0 (2) 1 (3) 19 (4) 20

40. Find the value of Z.

(1) 0 (2) 1 (3) 19 (4) 20

ANSWER KEYS

PRACTICE EXERCISE – 1

1. (3)	**2.** (1)	**3.** (2)	**4.** (4)	**5.** (4)	**6.** (2)	**7.** (1)	**8.** (1)	**9.** (3)	**10.** (4)
11. (4)	**12.** (3)	**13.** (3)	**14.** (1)	**15.** (3)	**16.** (4)	**17.** (4)	**18.** (1)	**19.** (2)	**20.** (3)
21. (4)	**22.** (3)	**23.** (2)	**24.** (1)	**25.** (1)	**26.** (1)	**27.** (2)	**28.** (3)	**29.** (2)	**30.** (2)
31. (1)	**32.** (2)	**33.** (3)	**34.** (1)	**35.** (4)	**36.** (3)	**37.** (2)	**38.** (3)	**39.** (4)	**40.** (4)
41. (2)	42. (4)	**43.** (1)	**44.** (1)	**45.** (3)					

PRACTICE EXERCISE – 2

1. (3)	**2.** (2)	**3.** (3)	**4.** (3)	**5.** (3)	**6.** (2)	**7.** (1)	**8.** (2)	**9.** (4)	**10.** (2)
11. (3)	**12.** (3)	**13.** (2)	**14.** (*)	**15.** (3)	**16.** (3)	**17.** (4)	**18.** (3)	**19.** (1)	**20.** (3)
21. (4)	**22.** (4)	**23.** (4)	**24.** (1)	**25.** (4)	**26.** (2)	**27.** (2)	**28.** (2)	**29.** (3)	**30.** (3)
31. (4)	**32.** (3)	**33.** (3)	**34.** (3)	**35.** (4)	**36.** (3)	**37.** (3)	**38.** (c)	**39.** (a)	**40.** (b)

EXPLANATIONS

PRACTICE EXERCISE – 1

1. If B's speed is 20 mph.
Then A's speed = 30 mph
C's speed = 20 mph
D's speed = 80 mph
Ratio of their speeds = 3 : 2 : 2 : 8.

2. At that instant A, B, C and D passed through the points P, Q, R and S. As they passed these points, all of them were moving parallel to each other. Let their speeds be V_a, V_b, V_c and V_d respectively.
At that instant A & B were moving in the same directions (both clockwise), so we must have.
$V_a + V_b = 50$ …(i)
Similarly C and D also moved in the same directions (either both in the clockwise direction or both in the anticlockwise direction) and their speeds with respect to B are 40 mph and 60 mph respectively.
Case I:

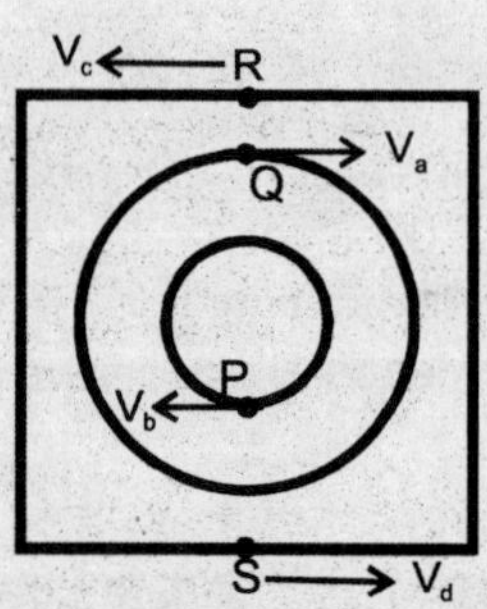

Fig. C & D, both anti-clockwise

If both C & D are moving in the anticlockwise direction, then
$V_c - V_b = \pm 40$ …(ii)
$V_b + V_d = 60$ …(iii)
Adding (i), (ii) and (iii)
$V_a + V_b + V_c + V_d = 150$ or 70
Therefore, the average of the speeds of these cars is: $\frac{150}{4}$ or $\frac{70}{4}$ i.e. 37.5 mph or 17.5 mph

Case II:

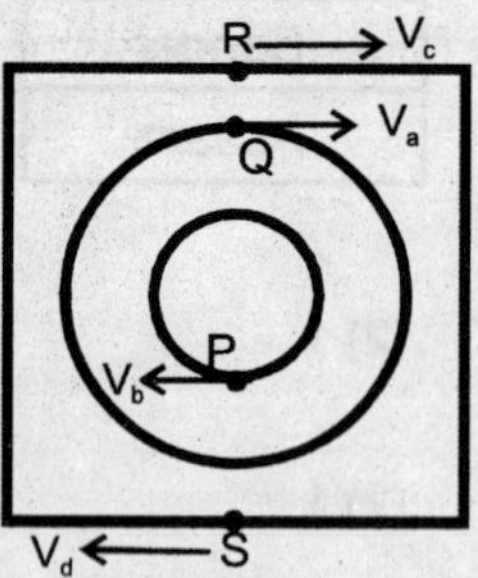

If both C & D are moving in the clockwise direction, then
$V_d - V_b = \pm 60$ …(iv)
$V_b + V_c = 40$ …(v)
Adding (i), (iv) and (v)
$v_a + v_b + v_c + v_d = 150$ or 30
But 30 is not possible as in that case $v_c + v_d = -20$ (speed cannot be negative)

$\Rightarrow$ Average speed = $\frac{150}{4}$ = 37.5 mph.

3. C observes that D is moving at a speed of 20 mph.

As C and D are moving in the same direction we must have:

$V_c + V_d = 20$

From this equation, the maximum values of either V_c OR V_d can be 20mph only irrespective of the direction of C & D ...(i)

Again, there are two cases:

Case I: Both C and D drive in the clockwise direction.

$V_b - V_c = +40$ ...(ii)

$V_b + V_d = 60$ ...(iii)

Case II: Both C and D drive in the anticlockwise direction.

$V_b - V_d = 60$ ...(iv)

$V_b + V_c = 40$ ...(v)

Case II is impossible.

As all the speeds are either positive or zero, equations (ii) and (iii) must be changed as following:

$V_b - V_c = 40$ or $V_b = V_c + 40$ ...(vi)

{since $V_c \leq 20$}

$V_b + V_d = 60$ or $V_b = 60 - V_d$ ...(vii)

{since $V_d \leq 20$}

From both equations, we get

$40 \leq V_b \leq 60$.

Out of the given options, only option (ii) lies in the given range. Hence (b) is the correct choice.

4. As E is stationary, the speeds observed by E, are the actual speeds of the cars. Let both the drivers C and D were driving with a speed of V mph. As C and D have the same speed, we need not find the solution under different cases as we did in the previous problems. We can write the following equations:

$V_a - V_b = \pm 50$ ...(i)

$V_b + V = 60$ ...(ii)

$V - V_b = \pm 40$ ...(iii)

Adding (ii) and (iii) we get:

$V = V_c = V_d = 50$ or 10...(iv)

Subtracting (iii) from (ii) we get:

$V_b = 10$ or 50 ...(v)

Putting both these values of V_b in (i), we get

$V_a = 50 \pm 50$ or 10 ± 50 i.e.

$V_a = 100, 0$ or $60, -40$

As V_a represents speed, it cannot be negative, hence $V_a = -40$ is discarded.

$V_a = 100, 0$ or 60 ... (vi)

From (iv), (v) and (vi) we observe that V_b and V_a do not have unique values rather they have more than one allowed value. As a result (V_a, V_b, V_c, V_d) can have any one of the following combinations of values:

Case I: (V_a, V_b, V_c, V_d) have values (0,50, 10,10)

OR

Case II: (V_a, V_b, V_c, V_d) have values (100,50, 10,10)

OR

Case III: (V_a, V_b, V_c, V_d) have values (60, 10, 50,50)

Options (a), (b) and (c) are not correct. If we check the options, only option (d) is correct. As $V_b = 10$ and $V_a = 60$ (more than double) is a possible combination of speeds.

For questions 5 to 7:

Using statements (ii), (iv), (v), and (vi), we can get the distribution of the teams in groups X and Y as:

Group	X	Y
Teams	F, A, H, L, C, K, O, G	P, J, M, E, D, B, N, I

From statements (iv), (v), (vii), (viii) and (ix), we can draw the table showing order in which the matches were played as:

Teams playing matches against each other		Match No.
X	Y	
F	P	
A		
H	J	8th
L		4th
C	M	6th
K		2nd
O		
G		1st

5. As F played the 5th match, P must have played the 5th match. As B played before P's match and immediately after I's match, B must have played either the 3rd match or the 4th match. L played the 4th match and one of the teams that played the 3rd match must have been either A or O. Hence, B played against either A, L or O.

6. From the table, it can be observed that O must have played either the 3rd, 5th or 7th match against either E, D, B or N. But from statement (vii), B didn't play the 3rd, 5th or 7th match. Hence, B could have played against 3 teams.

7. Since B was not part of the 3rd, 5th or 7th match, it must have played the 4th match against L.

For questions 8 to 10:

From statements (III) and (V), it can be concluded that both T2 and T3 ended up with either 2 or 4 points.

Case 1: When T2 and T3 scored 2 points each.

Since T3 won against T2, T3 must have lost its remaining matches and T4 must have won all its matches. Thus, T1 must have played on Monday against T3, but this was not the case as per the statement (IV). Hence, this case is invalid.

Case 2: When T2 and T3 scored 4 points each.

Since T2 lost against T3 on Tuesday, it must have won against T1 and T4. From statement (IV), T2 and T4 did not play on Wednesday and Saturday respectively. So T2 must have won its matches against T4 and T1 on Friday and Saturday respectively.

Further analysis leads to the following table.

Day	Match played between	Winner
Monday	T1 & T4	T1
Tuesday	T2 & T3	T3
Wednesday	T1 & T3	T3
Thursday	T3 & T4	T4
Friday	T2 & T4	T2
Saturday	T1 & T2	T2

8. T4 scored 2 points.
9. T3 lost against T4.
10. The match played on Friday was between T2 and T4.

For questions 11 to 13:

From statement (V), B and G cannot be together in the team. Therefore, there are three possible cases.

Case I: When B is selected.

F cannot be selected as F can only be selected when both G and N are selected. Thus, when B is selected, the team comprises exactly four bowlers. Also, J must be the wicketkeeper in the team, as selection of I ensures selection of F. Following table gives the possible compositions for the team.

Batsmen	Bowlers	Wicketkeeper
A, D, L, N, O, K/M	B, H, C, E	J

The number of ways in which the team can be formed $= 2 \times 1 \times 1 = 2$

Case II: When G is selected.

H cannot be selected as H can only be selected when B is selected. Thus, when G is selected, then again the team comprises exactly four bowlers. Following table gives the possible compositions for the team.

Batsmen	Bowlers	Wicketkeeper
A, D, L, N, O, K/M	G, F, C, E	I/J

The number of ways in which the team can be formed $= 2 \times 1 \times 2 = 4$.

Case III: When neither B nor G is selected.

When both B and G are not selected, then there is no possible composition for the team.

11. The total number of ways in which the team can be formed $= 2 + 4 = 6$.
12. If G is one of the bowlers in the team, then either of the two (i.e., I and J) can be selected as the wicketkeeper in the team.
13. If H is selected, G cannot be selected.

For questions 14 to 17:

From statements (III) and (V), it can be concluded that both T2 and T3 ended up with either 2 or 4 points.

Case 1: When T2 and T3 scored 2 points each.

Since T3 won against T2, T3 must have lost its remaining matches and T4 must have won all its matches. Thus, T1 must have played on Monday against T3, but this was not the case as per the statement (IV). Hence, this case is invalid.

Case 2: When T2 and T3 scored 4 points each.

Since T2 lost against T3 on Tuesday, it must have won against T1 and T4. From statement (IV), T2 and T4 did not play on Wednesday and Saturday respectively. So T2 must have won its matches against T4 and T1 on Friday and Saturday respectively.

Further analysis leads to the following table.

Day	Match played between	Winner
Monday	T1 & T4	T1
Tuesday	T2 & T3	T3
Wednesday	T1 & T3	T3
Thursday	T3 & T4	T4
Friday	T2 & T4	T2
Saturday	T1 & T2	T2

14. T4 scored 2 points.
15. T3 lost against T4.
16. The match played on Friday was between T2 and T4.
17. T4 won the match played on Thursday.
18. Since, L is the winner of the tournament, it must have won at least five matches. E is not qualified for second stage, it means E definitely won less than six matches.

    Only possible case is shown below:

    Number of matches won by E = Number of matches won by L = 5

    Hence, required number = 5 + 5 = 10.
19. Any team who had won two matches, there is a possibilities that the team will qualify for second stage. A possible case for the number of wins = 2 2 2 2 2 6 6 6.

20. Statement (i) is obviously true.

Three teams in group 1 and three teams in group 2 can win one match each in stage 1.

Statement (ii) is incorrect because maximum number of teams which could have three wins in the first stage would be 14.

Possible case: 3 3 3 3 3 3 3 7 i.e. seven teams in each group would have three wins in the first stage.

Statement (iii) is clearly correct.

Hence, statement (i) and (iii) are correct

21. Four teams cannot have six wins each hence maximum number of matches won in the first stage by teams A, B, C and D together would be 22

Possible case for number of wins: 2 1 1 2 4 6 6 6.

Required number = 4 + 6 + 6 + 6 = 22.

For questions 22 to 24:

22.

2	1	2	4
5	1	6	7
9	1	3	2
6	1	8	4

Initial Board

		2	4
		6	7
		3	2
		8	4

After your move (Retain right)

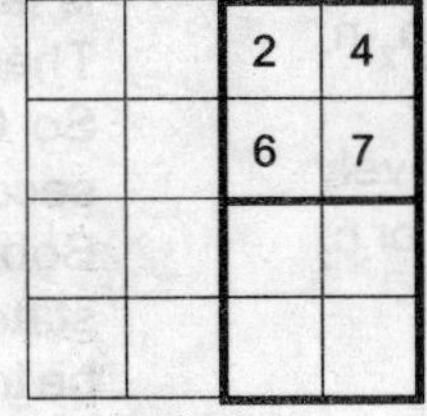

After your friends move (Retain upper)

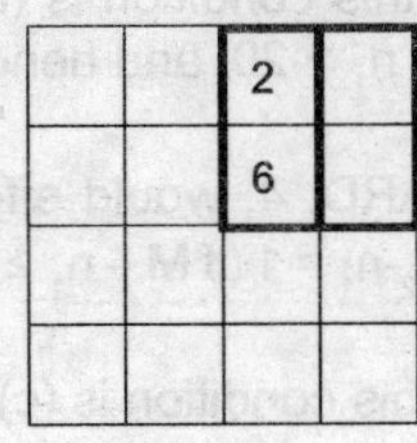

After your move (Retain left)

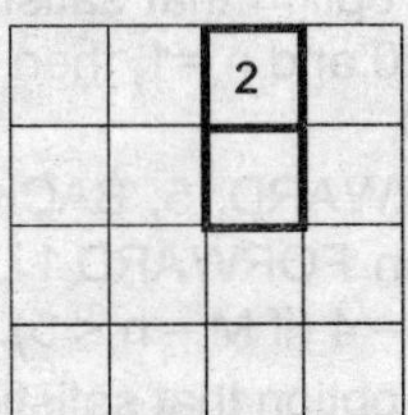

After your friends move (Retain upper)

Since you choose to retain right and then left in your next move, the cells that would hence be retained contain 2,6,3,8. (look at the second grid) Hence, to reduce your gain to minimum, your friend has to retain 2 at the end. So his strategy has to be retain upper and retain upper.

23. If both of you select the moves intelligently, you would both go for maximising your earnings.

In your first move you have to select either left or right and your friend has to then select either upper or lower. Hence the possibilities could be :

2	1	2	4
5	1	6	7
9	1	3	2
6	1	8	4

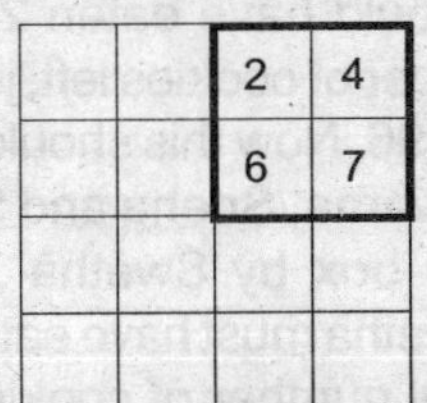

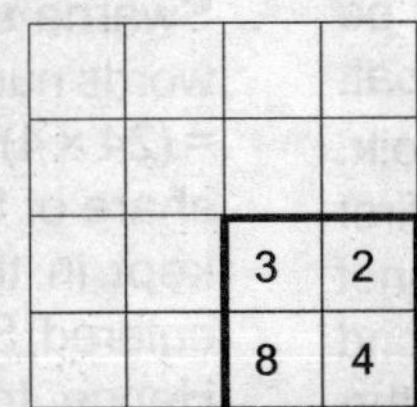

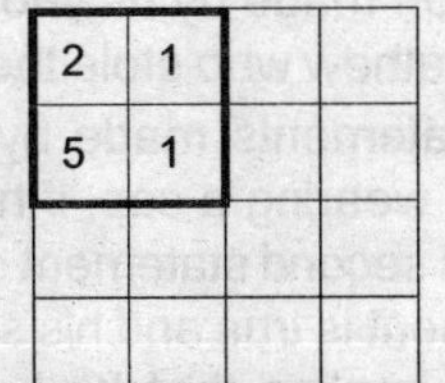

9	1		
6	1		

You Move	Your Friend Moves	Integers left for your 2nd move	Minimum gain ensured
(Retain Right)	(Retain Upper)	2, 4, 6, 7	4 (after you move retain right)
	(Retain Lower)	3, 2, 8, 4	3 (after you move retain left)
(Retain Left)	(Retain Upper)	2, 1, 5, 1	2 (after you move retain left)
	(Retain Lower)	9, 1, 6, 1	6 (after you move retain left)

So, if you move (retain right) you ensure a minimum gain of Rs.3 and if you move (retain left) you ensure a minimum gain of Rs.2. Hence if both of you play intelligently, you would first move retain right and ensure a minimum win of Rs.3, irrespective of what your friend moves.

24. If your first move is (retain right) then the grid will look the same as in Q82. Your friend may hence choose either (retain upper), which will leave you to choose from 2,4,6,7 or he may choose (retain lower), which will leave you to choose from 3,2,8,4. In case he takes the former move, you can then move (retain right) and hence force a minimum gain of 4. But in case he chooses the latter move, you can then move (retain move) and force a minimum gain of 3. In either case you can force a minimum gain of Rs.3

25. FORWARD 25, BACKWARD 10 would effectively mean FORWARD 15 i.e. n_2-n_1 = 15, (if M – n_1> 25) and n_2 = M – 10 (if M – n_1 < 25).
The only option satisfies is option (a).
So if M = 10 and n_1 = 0., then M – n_1 < 25 and so n_2 = 10 – 10 = 0. Hence, n_1= n_2.

26. BACKWARD, 5; FORWARD, 5 would effectively mean $n_1 = n_2$ (in case $n_1 \geq 5$) or $n_2 = 5$ (in case $n_1<5$). The only option that satisfies this is (a).

27. FORWARD, 10 ; FORWARD, 10 would effectively mean FORWARD 20 i.e. n_2-n_1 = 20, (if M – $n_1 \geq$ 20). or n_2 = M (if M – n_1 < 20).
The option that satisfies this condition is (b), as if M>20 and n_1=1, then M – n_1 > 20, and hence n_2-n_1 = 20.

28. FORWARD, 5; BACKWARD, 4, would effectively mean FORWARD 1 i.e. n_2-n_1 = 1 (if M – $n_1 \geq$ 5) or n_2 = M – 4 (if M – n_1< 5).
The option that satisfies this condition is (c).

For questions 29 to 32:

The best way to solve these kinds of questions is to assume that one of the statements is either true or false and thus figure out whether there is consistency in what everyone is saying.

29. Let us assume that John's first statement is true. So his second statement must be false. This implies that Mathew did it. This makes Mathew's first statement false. So the second statement has to be true. This implies that Krishna didn't do it. So Krishna's first statement is true and his second statement is false. Since all the statements are consistent with each other, the assumption made by us should be the correct one. So it is Mathew who stole the boat.

30. The key here are the statements made by Koik. Since we know that he is wearing a cap, if his first statement is false, then his second statement cannot be true. So his first statement is true and his second statement is false. This implies that Koik is the priest. This makes Lony's second statement false and so his first statement is true. So Lony is Koik's son. This makes Mirna's second statement false and so his first statement is true. So Lony's father is a pilot. Thus, Koik is the pilot.

31. The first statement of Ram is obviously false, as he is saying that he never speaks to a stranger, when he actually is. So he must be new to those parts. This makes the second statement of Lila false. So she should be married to Ram. This makes the first statement of Laxman false. So the left road should take you to the village.

32. If you observe Charle's statement carefully, you will figure out that his first statement is true and second statement is false. For instance, if his first statement is false, then his second statement cannot be true. There would be inconsistency in what he is talking. So Charles is not the chief. This makes Bobby's second statement false and first statement true. So Bobby is Amar's father and hence, Amar's first statement is false. So his second statement must be true. This implies that the chief is wearing the red shirt. So Bobby is the chief.

For questions 33 to 36:

Since Soumya was the last one to eat the cookies and she ate 3 cookies, the total number of cookies left when she entered the room = (3 × 4) = 12. This should be Soumya's share that was left in the box uneaten. Hence, just before Soumya entered, Swetha, Sneha and Swarna would have eaten their share of 12 cookies each. Total number of cookies left when Sneha entered = (12 × 4) = 48. This in turn should have been the combined share of Sneha and Soumya (24 × 2) that was left in the box uneaten. So just before Sneha entered, Swetha and Swarna should have eaten 24 cookies each. In other, words number of cookies left, just before Swarna entered = (24 × 4) = 96. Now this should have been the combined share of Swarna, Sneha and Soumya (3 × 32) that was kept in the box by Swetha . So just before Swarna entered, Swetha must have eaten her share of 32 cookies. Hence, total number of cookies given by Prem uncle = (32 × 4) = 128.

The situation is also shown in the following table:

		Number of cookies eaten					
		Swetha	Swarna	Sneha	Soumya	Not Eaten	Total
Girl entered	Soumya	3	3	3	3	-	12
	Sneha	12	12	12	-	12	48
	Swarna	24	24	-	-	(24×2) = 48	96
	Swetha	32	-	-	-	(32×3) = 96	128
	Total	71	39	15	3	-	-

33. Sneha ate 15 cookies, in total.

34. Prem uncle gave 128 cookies to Swetha.

35. Swetha ate 71 cookies, in total.

36. Swarna ate 39 cookies, in total.

For questions 37 to 40:

The data given in the question can be computed as :

37. From the first week data we can arrive at the following work pattern of Bankatlal for the 1st month.

First Month :

	1st week	2nd week	3rd week	4th week
Hours of rest	2	5	2	7
Working hrs.	5	2	5	3
Wage per hour	Rs.20	Rs.10	Rs.20	Rs.10
Total Wage per day	Rs.100	Rs.20	Rs.100	Rs.20
Total Wage per w eek	Rs.600	Rs.120	Rs.600	Rs.120

Thus his total wage = (600 + 120 + 600 + 120) = Rs.1440

38. Let us compile the data for 2nd, 3rd and 4th month.

Second Month :

	5th week	6th week	7th week	8th week
Hours of rest	3	7	3	7
Working hrs.	7	3	7	3
Wage per hour	Rs.20	Rs.10	Rs.20	Rs.10
Total Wage per day	Rs.140	Rs.30	Rs.140	Rs.30
Total Wage per w eek	Rs.840	Rs.180	Rs.840	Rs.180

Third Month :

	9th week	10th week	11th week	12th week
Hours of rest	4	6	4	6
Working hrs.	6	4	6	4
Wage per hour	Rs.20	Rs.10	Rs.20	Rs.10
Total Wage per day	Rs.120	Rs.40	Rs.120	Rs.40
Total Wage per w eek	Rs.720	Rs.240	Rs.720	Rs.240

Fourth Month :

	13th week	14th week	15th week	16th week
Hours of rest	0	8	0	8
Working hrs.	8	0	8	0
Wage per hour	Rs.20	Rs.10	Rs.20	Rs.10
Total Wage per day	Rs.160	0	Rs.160	0
Total Wage per w eek	Rs.960	0	Rs.960	0

Total wage for 1st month = Rs.1440

Total wage for 2nd month = (840 +180 +840 +180) = Rs.2040

Total wage for 3rd month = (720 + 240 + 720 + 240) = Rs.1920

Total wage for 4th month = (960+960) = Rs.1920

Total wage for the 4 months = (1440 + 2040 + 1920 + 1920) = 7320

Hence the average salary = $\frac{7320}{4}$ = Rs.1830.

39. Using the above data, we can revise the wage compilation for the third month as given below:

Third Month :

	9th week	10th week	11th week	12th week
Hours of rest	4	6	4	6
Working hrs.	6	4	6	4
Wage per hour or w ork	Rs.25	Rs.12.5	Rs.25	Rs.12.5
Fine per hour of rest	Rs.5	Rs.5	Rs.5	Rs.5
Total w age per day	Rs.150	Rs.50	Rs.150	Rs.50
Total fine per day	Rs.20	Rs.30	Rs.20	Rs.30
Effective w age per day	Rs.130	Rs.20	Rs.130	Rs.20
Total Wage per w eek	Rs.780	Rs.120	Rs.780	Rs.120

So now his third month age = (780 + 120 + 780 + 120) = Rs.1800.

Previously he used to earn Rs.1920 in the third month.

Hence change in Bankatlal's salary for the 3rd month = (1920 – 1800) = Rs.120.

40. For the fourth month, the new wage compilation will be as given below :
Fourth Month

	9th week	10th week	11th week	12th week
Hours of rest	0	8	0	8
Working hrs.	8	0	8	0
Wage per hour or work	Rs.25	Rs.12.5	Rs.25	Rs.12.5
Fine per hour of rest	Rs.5	Rs.5	Rs.5	Rs.5
Total wage per day	Rs.400	0	Rs.400	0
Total fine per day	0	Rs.40	0	Rs.40
Effective wage per day	Rs.400	-Rs.40	Rs.400	-Rs.40
Total Wage per week	Rs.2400	-Rs.240	Rs.2400	-Rs.240

So now his total wage for the 4th month = (2400 + 2400 – 240 – 240) = Rs.4320.

Since the calculations for the first two months are made as per the old scheme of things, this has already been computed.

Total wage for 1st month = Rs.1440

Total wage for 2nd month = Rs.2040

Calculation for the third and fourth month are as per new calculations and they are :

Total wage for 3rd month = Rs.1800

Total wage for 4th month = Rs.4320

Therefore, total salary for the four months = (1440 + 2040 + 1800 + 4320) = Rs.9600.

41. Since time taken to manufacture Q by both the machines is the least, we have to manufacture only Q in order to maximize the output for the day. In such a case, total number of units of Q produced by M1 = $\frac{(8 \times 60)}{6}$ = 80 units and that by M2 = $\frac{(8 \times 60)}{6}$ = 80 units. So the maximum number of units that can be produced in one day = (80 + 80) = 160 units.

42. If M1 works at half of its normal efficiency, time taken by M1 to manufacture 1 unit of P = 20 min and Q = 12 min. For producing maximum number of units, we have to produce Q on M2 first as it takes only 6 min per piece. Also since at least one unit of P has to be manufactured and it is more efficient to do so on M2, we would do that. So time taken to manufacture 1 unit of P on M2 = 8 min. Hence, time remaining on M2 = (480 – 8) = 472. In this remaining time number of units of Q that can be manufactured on M2 = $\frac{472}{6}$ = 78 (only completed units taken).

Now since it takes less time to manufacture Q on M1 as well, we will maximize Q on M1. Since 1 unit of number of units that can be produced = $\frac{(8 \times 60)}{12}$ = 40. Hence, the total number of units manufactured = (1 + 78 + 40) = 119 units.

43. In order to minimize time required, we will manufacture P on M2 and Q on M1. Number of machine hours required to manufacture 30 units of P on M2 = (30 × 8) = 240 min = 4 hr. Number of machine hours required to manufacture 25 units of Q on M1 = (25 × 6) = 150 min = 2.5 hr. So total time taken = (4 + 2.5) = 6.5 hr or 6 hr 30 min.

44. Since P has to be produced in more number than Q and since time taken to produce P is least on M2, to maximize the output utilize the entire time available on M2 for producing P. Number of units of P produced in this time = $\frac{(8 \times 60)}{8}$ = 60 units. Now since the number of units of Q should be one-third that of P, we should manufacture 20 units of Q. To manufacture this on M1, it would take (20 × 6) = 120 min. So there are still (480 – 120) = 360 min of M1 to be utilized. Now for every 3 units of P that is manufactured, we have to manufacture 1 unit of Q. To run one such cycle on M1, it would take (3 × 10 + 1 × 6) = 36 min. Hence in 360 min, we have 10 such cycles and utilize all the idle time of M1. Hence, to maximize the output under the given condition it is possible to have no idle time on any of the machines.

45. The least efficient way is the option that gives least production with highest idle time. So we can compare the options in the following two ways. Assume that production is constant (viz. LCM of 48, 64, 53 and 71) in all 4 options and compare the corresponding idle time. Or we can assume the idle time to be constant (viz. LCM of 3, 12, 10 and 9) in all 4 options and compare the corresponding production. The latter method is more preferable as finding LCM of idle time is easier. So LCM of 3, 12, 10, 9 = 180. If we assume that the idle time has to be 180 min, then as per option (a) we would get production = $\left(\frac{180}{3} \times 48\right)$ = 2,880 units, as per option (b), we would get production = $\left(\frac{180}{12} \times 64\right)$ = 960 units, as per option (c), production = $\left(\frac{180}{10} \times 53\right)$ = 954 units and as per option (d), production = $\left(\frac{180}{9} \times 71\right)$ = 1,420 units. Since option (c) gives the least production, it is the least efficient way.

PRACTICE EXERCISE – 2

1. If he travels at minimum speed over stretch A (i.e. 40 km/hr), the total time taken to cover this stretch

$= \frac{2}{40} = \frac{1}{20}$ hr = 3 min.

If he then travels at the fastest speed over stretch B (i.e. 50 km/hr), the total time taken to cover this

stretch = $\frac{2}{50} = \frac{1}{25}$ = 2.4 min.

Thus, total time taken over the first two stretches

= 3 + 2.4 = 5.4 min.

In order to break the previous record he will have to cover the third stretch in (10 – 5.4) = 4.6 min.

To do this he will have to cover the third stretch at

$\frac{2}{4.6}$ = 0.434 km per minute or 26.08 km/hr. But the

maximum speed over the stretch C is 20 km/hr. Hence, it is not possible for C to break the previous record.

2. The minimum speed in stretch A is 40 km/hr. If Mr Hare travels the first stretch at this speed, then

the time taken by him to cover this stretch = $\frac{2}{40}$

= 3 min. Also he takes 3 min to cover stretch B. And he covers the entire race in (1.5 × 10) = 15 min. This means that he should have taken (15 – 3 – 3) = 9 min to cover stretch C.

Hence, his speed over this stretch should be $\frac{2}{9}$

= 0.22 km per minute or 13.3 km/hr.

3. Let his average speed over the last stretch be x. Hence, his average speed for first two stretches = 4x.

So the total time taken to cover the three stretches

$= \frac{4}{4x} + \frac{2}{x}$

His average speed over the race is 20 km/hr.

Hence, the time taken to complete the race = $\frac{6}{20}$

Hence, we have the equation $\frac{4}{4x} + \frac{2}{x} = \frac{6}{20}$

Solving this equation, we get x = 10 km/hr.

For questions 4 to 6:

Place of worship	Number of flowers before offering	Number of flowers offered	Number of flowers left
1	(15/8)y	y	(7/8)y
2	(7/4) y	y	(3/4)y
3	(3/2) y	y	y/2
4	y	y	0

Starting from the fourth place of worship and moving backwards, we find that number of flowers before entering the first place of worship is $\frac{15}{8}$y.

4. Hence, number of flowers before doubling = $\frac{15}{16}$y

(but this is equal to 30)

Hence, y = 32

5. The minimum value of y so that $\frac{15}{16}$y is a whole number is 16.

Therefore, 16 is the minimum number of flowers that can be offered.

6. For y = 16, the value of $\frac{15}{16}$y = 15.

Hence, the minimum number of flowers with which Roopa leaves home is 15.

For questions 7 to 9:

Game	Opening balance	Player's pick		Dealer's pick		Closing balance
		Debit (–)	Credit (+)	Debit (–)	Credit (+)	
1	0	0	8	16	0	-8
2	-8	0	10	0	10	12
3	12	0	6	6	0	12
4	12	0	8	16	0	4

7. Hence, we see that the maximum gain is Rs. 12

8. Since the maximum negative that Ghosh Babu goes into is –8, he should begin with at least Rs. 8, so that he does not have to borrow any money at any point.

9. From the above table it is evident that in four games, Ghosh Babu makes a profit of Rs. 4. Hence, if the final amount left with Ghosh Babu is Rs. 100, the initial amount that he had would be Rs. 96.

10. The initial water in bottles A, B and C are 5 L, 0 L and 0 L respectively.

First instruction. FILL (C, A) means that 2 litres is transferred from A to C (leaving 3 litres A, and C is full)

Third instruction FILL (C, A) again means some water is transferred from A to C.

After the third instruction, 1 litre of water is left in bottle A.

Option (a) is not possible because if it were executed, there would not be any water left in A for executing the third instruction of FILL(C,A).

Option (b) is possible because C is emptied out and when third instruction is followed, of the 3 litres left in A (at the end of first instruction), two litres are transferred to C leaving only 1 litre in A.

Option (c) can be eliminated because, there was no water in B.

Option (d) is not possible because had it been executed, there would not be any water left in A for executing the third instruction.

11. The first four instructions are:

1st : FILL (C, A)

2nd : EMPTY (C, B)

3rd : FILL (C, A)

4th : DRAIN (A)

Fourth instruction drains off 1 liter from A and the quantities with A, B and C at the end of 3rd instruction is 1 L, 2 L and 2 L respectively.

Amount of water in the system after 4th instruction = 5 – 1 = 4 L

If at the end of the 6th instruction, all the 4 L are in A, then B and C will definitely be empty.

12. There shall be 8 teams in each group. Each team in a group shall be playing with every other team. Hence, total number of matches shall be $\frac{(7 \times 8)}{2} = 28$ in one group. Hence, in both the groups, there shall be 56 matches. This is for the first stage. Thereafter, there are 8 teams in knockout rounds from which one winner emerges, or 7 losers are identified.

Hence, 7 more matches, i.e. in all 63 matches.

13. In the first stage, there are 28 matches to be played by each group of 8 teams and eventually 4 from each group moved into second stage.

7 teams can win 4 matches each. Then, three of them will be eliminated on the basis of tiebreak rules. This doesn't assure any team a place in the second stage.

5 teams can win 5 matches each and there can be 3 more matches won by the remaining teams. Then, one of the teams winning 5 matches will be eliminated on the basis of tiebreak rules. This also doesn't assure any team a place in the second stage.

4 teams can win 6 matches and there can be 4 matches won by the remaining teams. This will guarantee a place for each team winning 6 matches a place in the second round.

14. In order to maximize the number of wins of a team which would be eliminated at the end of first stage, we minimize the number of wins in the bottom 3 teams. The bottom 3 teams will play ${}^3C_2 = 3$ matches among themselves (i.e. there will be 3 wins). So the remaining wins (28 – 3) = 25 must be divided among top 5 teams, such that the 5th ranked team wins the maximum and yet fail to qualify for the second round. This is possible if each of the top 5 teams win an equal number of matches, i.e. $\frac{25}{5} = 5$. Hence, the 5th ranked team can win a maximum of 5 matches and would get eliminated at the end of first stage on the basis of tiebreak rules.

*** Note:** The answer given in the answer key of 'CAT 2001 Bulletin' is incorrect. Ideal answer should be 5 wins.

15. There are 8 teams. Hence, there would be 7 matches in 3 rounds.

16. Statement 1 is false. Consider a case where the points scored by the top three teams were 7, 6 and 5. Rest of the 10 points were distributed equally among the remaining five teams with 2 points to each. Any one of these five teams could have won the tournament with total of 5 wins.

Statement 2 is false, as only the top four teams were advanced to the stage II.

Statement 3 is true. Consider a case where five different teams of the same group got 5 points each. Also, a team with 2 points in the different group of stage I won could have won the tournament with total of 5 points.

Statement 4 is false as the number of teams with exactly one win in stage II is 2.

17.

1	16
2	15
3	14
4	13
5	12
6	11
7	10
8	9

Winners after round two would be 1, 2, 3, 4, 5, 11, 10, 9 for 8 rounds respectively. As Lindsay is number two, she will play Venus Williams in quarter finals.

18. Elena is at number 6 and Serena is at number 8. If they lose, then table would be:

1	9
2	7
3	11
4	5

Maria is at number 1 and she will play the player at number 9. i.e., Nadia Petrova.

19.

1	32
2	31
3	30
4	29
5	28
6	27
7	26
8	25
9	24
10	23
11	22
12	21
13	20
14	19
15	18
16	17

Matches in bold letters had upsets.

Then, from the table, winners would be:

1, 31, 3, 29, 5, 27, 7, 25, 9, 23, 11, 21, 13, 19, 15 and 17.

So for the next round, table would look like:

1	17
31	15
3	19
29	13
5	21
27	11
7	23
25	9

Since, there was no upset in the second round, so the table in the next round would look like:

1	9
15	7
3	11
13	5

We are given Maria is in the semi-finals. As we are not sure what is the result of other games, table for the next round can be drawn as follows:

1	5/13
7/15	3/11

Hence, Anastasia will play with Maria Sharapova.

20.

1	8
2	7
3	6
4	5

In this case, Kim Clijster will either not reach semi-finals or she will play Maria in semi-finals.

Hence, she cannot play Maria in finals.

For questions 21 to 24:

L = London, Paris = P, New York= NY, Beijing = B

In round III, one of the two cities, either London or Paris will get 38 votes and the other 37. Further:

(1) The persons representing London, Paris, Beijing and New York can not vote as long as their own cities are in contention. In round I, New York gets eliminated and hence the representative from NY becomes eligible for voting in the II round hence increasing the total votes by 1. This means the total votes in the first round must be 83 – 1 = 82.

(2) After round II, the representative from Beijing votes in the III round. This should have increased the number of total votes by 1 and the total votes must have become 83 + 1 = 84.

We are given that the total votes in round III are 75 only. We conclude that 84 – 75 = 9 people who voted in round I and II have become ineligible for voting in round III.

(3) 9 people who have voted in round I and II become ineligible for voting in round III. The reason of their ineligibility is that till round I and II, they have already voted for two different cities which are not available for contention in round III. All of these 9 voters are those who voted for NY in round I and then voted for Beijing in round II.

(4) Beijing's vote in round II is 21. This includes 9 votes from people who voted for NY in the first round. So 21 – 9 = 12 people voted for Beijing in both round I and II.

(5) We are given that 75% of the people who voted for Beijing in round I, voted again for Beijing in round II as well. So, 16 people must have voted for Beijing in round I.

(6) In round I we have:

82 = L + P + B + NY

Or

82 = 30 + P + 16 + 12

Giving P = 24

(7) In round II, we have:

83 = L + 32 + 21, giving L = 30

(8) NY had 12 votes in round I. 9 of these votes went to B(see point 2 , again). The rest 3 went to P.

(9) 16 votes for B in round I. 12 of them still vote for B. The rest 4 voted for either L or P. L has the same number of votes in both the rounds I and II. This means in round II, these 4 votes must have gone to Paris only.

(10) The representative from NY did not vote in round I but has voted in round II. As L has the same people voting for it (30 votes in both the rounds I and II) and we know the exact break up of B in II. This NY-representative vote must go to Paris only. Further, in order to avoid ineligibility, this NY rep must vote for Paris only in round III also.

(11) Paris (in round II) break up is:

32 = 24 (from round I, who voted for Paris)

+ 4 (out of the 16, who voted for Beijing in round I)

+ 3(out of 12, who voted for NY in round I)

+ 1 (NY -Rep)

(12) Beijing gets eliminated in round II. So the rep of Beijing can vote in round III.

(13) 12 People (out of 21) who voted for Beijing in round II are still eligible for vote in round III.

(14) 50% of people who voted for Beijing in I (i.e. 8 People) voted for Paris in round III. These 8 People include 4 of those who voted for Paris in round II also. Therefore 4(out of 12 who voted for Beijing in round II and are still eligible for vote in round III) people have voted for Paris in round III.

(15) This implies that the rest 8(out of 12 who voted for Beijing in round II and are still eligible for vote in round III) can vote for London only. This makes London's vote = 30+ 8 or 38 in round III. Which implies that Paris got 37 votes.

(16) The Beijing Rep who is eligible to vote in round III must have voted for Paris only.

The following table sums up the Vote Pattern:

Round	Total Votes	London (L)	Paris(P)	Beijing (B)	New York (NY)
I	82	**30**	24	16	**12**
II	**83**	30	**32** = (24 + 4 + 3 + 1 of NY-rep)	**21** (12 + 9)	X
III	**75**	38 = (30 + 8)	37= (32 + 4 + 1 of B-rep)	X	X

(The data shown in **Bold** was already provided in the problem. The other data is deduced from the solution.)

21. Required percentage = $\frac{9}{12} \times 100 = 75\%$

22. As seen from the table, Paris got 24 votes.

23. Required percentage = $\frac{8}{12} \times 100 = 66.67\%$

24. Based on the table, IOC members from New York must have voted for Paris in Round II.

For questions 25 to 29:

As only Paul Erdös was having an Erdös number of zero, so the minimum Erdös number among A, B, C, D, E, F, G, H should be 1 or greater than one. At the end of the third day, F co-authored a paper with A and C. F had the minimum Erdös number among the 8 people. So if F's Erdös number is y, then A and C's Erdös number should change to (y + 1) after third day. As A and C decreased the average by maximum possible extent, it means C had the second-height Erdös number among all eight, as A had an Erdös number of infinity. Suppose Erdös numbers of A, B, C, D, E, F, G, H are y + 1, b, y + 1, c, d, e, y, g, h respectively at the end of third day.

$\therefore$ (y + 1 + b + y + 1 + c + d + e + y + g + h) = 24

= (3 × 8)

$\Rightarrow$ 3y + 2 + b + d + e + g + h = 24

When E co-authored with F, the average Erdös number reduced again, it means, E's Erdös number was not the same with A & C initially. As at the end of third day, 5 people had same Erdös number, they should be A, C and any 3 out of B, D, G, H. Suppose those 3 people are B, D, G. Then

(3y + 2 + y + 1 + y + 1 + y + 1 + e + h) = 24

$\Rightarrow$ 6y + h + e = 19…(i)

On the fifth day, E co-authored a paper with F and hence, Erdös number of E changed to (y + 1). Also the average decreased by 0.5 which means the total decreased by 4.

Hence, e - (y + 1) = 4

$\Rightarrow$ e – y = 5

Putting the value of e in equation (i), we get

$6y + h + (5 + y) = 19$

$\Rightarrow 7y + h = 14$

Only possible value of y = 1 as h cannot be zero.

So after 3rd round Erdös number of A, C, E, F were 2, 2, 6, 1 respectively.

25. Only A, C, E changed their Erdös number, rest 5 did not change their Erdös number.

26. At the end of conference 6 people including E were having an Erdös number of 2 and F was having 1 as Erdös number. So 8th person was having an Erdös number of $[20 – (2 \times 6 + 1)] = 7$

27. At the end of 3rd round, 5 people were having same Erdös number. A and C changed their Erdös number after coauthoring with F. So, the other 3 will have same Erdös number in the beginning.

28. 2

29. After co-authoring with F, E was having Erdös number of 2, which was 4 less than initial Erdös number of E. So answer is 2 + 4 = 6.

30. As per the rule given in question, the following circled places can be reached by only one individual:

	1	(2)	4	3
9	5	3	2	8
(7)	8	(4)	6	(5)
(3)	9	5	1	(2)
1	7	6	(3)	9

∴ 7 individuals can be reached by just one individuals.

31. Using (ii), '1' being the smallest number in given layout no individual can reach to the individual at a platform of height 1.

32. In fourth column only, the individuals sitting at platforms of height 2 and 1 cannot be reached by any individual.

33. (1) Row 1 doesn't have any individual who can be reached by 5 or more individual. Hence option (1) is FALSE.

(2) Row 3 doesn't have any individual who cannot be reached by anyone. Hence option (2) is FALSE.

(4) 9 in Row 2 can not be reached by 5 or more individual. Hence option (4) is also FALSE.

For questions 38 to 40:

Total matches played = 50

Total number of losses = 44 + Y

Total number of ties = $\frac{11+Z}{2}$

Total matches played = number of losses + number of ties

and total number of wins = Total number of losses

So, $50 = 44 + Y + \frac{11+Z}{2}$

$\Rightarrow 2Y + Z = 1$

Since Y and Z are non-negative integers.

Z = 1, Y = 0

So, X = 19.

38. As shown above the value of X = 19.

39. As shown above the value of Y = 0.

40. As shown above the value of Z = 1.

CHAPTER 10

Miscellaneous

SOLVED EXAMPLES

Directions for examples 1 to 4: Answer the questions on the basis of the information given below.

In a given season of F1 racing, 9 races are to be held. There are 8 teams with two drivers in each team and the points are awarded to the drivers in each race as per to the following table.

Rank	1st	2nd	3rd	4th	5th	6th	7th	8th	9th to 16th
Points	10	8	6	5	4	3	2	1	0

Two championships viz. 'Driver's Championship' and 'Constructor's Championship' take place simultaneously. 'Driver's Championship' is given to the player who has the maximum number of points at the end of the season. 'Constructor's Championship' is given to the team for which the sum of the points of two its drivers is the maximum. A driver is said to get the podium finish only when he is among the top 3 rankers in a race.

After the first 6 races, the point standings of the 16 drivers is as follows:

Driver	Team	Points
Alonso	Renault	54
Schumacher	Ferrari	39
Kimi	Mclaren	29
Fisichella	Renault	27
Montoya	Mclaren	22
Massa	Ferrari	22
Button	Honda	21
Barichello	Honda	10
Villeneuve	Red Bull	4
Webber	Williams	3
Roseberg	Williams	2
Coulthard	BMW Soubers	1
Heidfeld	Red Bull	0
Klien	BMW Soubers	0
Liuzzi	Toro Rosso	0
Scott Speed	Toro Rosso	0

1. If Alonso got the podium finish in each of the first 6 races, then what was the maximum number of races in which he had 2nd rank?

(1) 4 (2) 3 (3) 2 (4) 1

2. Apart from the first six races, Alonso got the podium finish in the 7th race as well. However, he was not allowed to participate in the subsequent races due to mechanical failure. At the end of the season, if Schumacher won the 'Driver's Championship', then which of the following could have been his lowest rank in any of the last three races?

(1) 5th (2) 6th (3) 7th (4) 4th

3. Which of the following statements CANNOT be true?
   (1) Renault and Ferrari had a tie for the 'Constructor's Championship'.
   (2) Alonso got the podium finish in each of the first 6 races out of which he did not have rank 1st in the 6th race.
   (3) Fisichella got the podium finish in the 9th race and Honda won the 'Constructor's Championship'.
   (4) Barichello got the podium finish in the 3rd race but he did not score any point in the 1st race.
4. If Schumacher ranked 9th in one of the first six races, then which of the following CANNOT be the points scored by him in any one of the first six races?
   (1) 3 (2) 2 (3) 1 (4) 0

For examples 1 to 4:

1. 2 Alonso finished on podium in each of the first six races and scores 54 points.
He can score 54 points as
10, 10, 10, 8, 8, 8 [in any order]
10, 10, 10, 10, 8, 6
So, he can get 2nd rank in at most 3 races.

2. 3 Alonso finishes the next race on podium.
$\Rightarrow$ his total points are 60 or 62 or 64.
For finding lowest rank obtained by Schumacher, we take Alonso's score as 60 (lowest among 60, 62, 64)
To win the championship Schumacher needs 61 points.
$\Rightarrow$ in the last three races he has to score 61 – 39 = 22 points.
For lowest rank 22 can be scored as 10, 10, 2 (in any order).
Hence, the lowest rank obtained by Schumacher is 7th (corresponding to 2 points).

3. 3 If Fisichella finishes on podium in race 9 (or in any of the last 3 races), the points scored by Renault will be 87 (or more).
Hence, even if Honda drivers take top two ranks in all three races they will end up with 85 points.
i.e. 31 + 3 (8 + 10) = 31 + 54 = 85 points.
Hence, in this case Honda won't be able to win the 'Constructor's Championship'.

4. 2 After first six races Schumacher's total points are 39.
He didn't score any point in 1 race. Hence effectively, he scored 39 points in 5 races and 0 points in 1 race.
If in any of the 5 races he scores 7th rank or 2 points, then in other four races he has to score 37 points, which is not possible in any combination.

Directions for examples 5 to 8: Answer the questions on the basis of the information given below.

From ISBT, buses ply on 6 different routes viz. 414, 413, 427, 966, 893 and 181 at an interval of 10 min, 10 min, 12 min, 15 min, 20 min and 30 min, not necessarily in that order, to four different destinations viz. Mehrauli, Badarpur, Uttam Nagar and Azadpur. There is at least one bus for each destination. Further information is also known:

i. Two buses to the same destination cannot start at the same time.
ii. If the timings of two buses plying different routes but heading towards the same destination clash, then the bus of the route number having the shorter time interval will skip this journey.
iii. Buses on two different routes ply between ISBT and Mehrauli.
iv. The difference between the time intervals of a route to Mehrauli and Uttam Nagar is equal to the difference between the time intervals of the two routes to Uttam Nagar.
v. Buses on a route to Mehrauli leaves after every 10 min.
vi. 414 leaves for Badarpur after every 30 min.
vii. Time intervals between two different routes heading towards the same destination cannot be equal.
viii. Buses on one of the routes to Uttam Nagar leave after every 15 min.
ix. Buses to any destination can leave from ISBT with an interval of at least one minute or an integral multiple of one minute.

5. If 427 leaves to Mehrauli after every 10 min, then in a given hour a minimum of how many buses can ply on route 427?

(1) 3 (2) 4 (3) 6 (4) 2

6. On a festival day, if frequency of all buses was increased by decreasing the time interval of all the routes by 5 min, then what can be the minimum time difference between any two buses plying to Mehrauli?

(1) 2 min (2) 5 min (3) 1 min (4) None of these

7. Which of the following statements is necessarily TRUE?

(1) A maximum of 3 buses can depart at a given time.

(2) Maximum of 11 buses can depart for Mehrauli in 1 hour.

(3) Maximum difference between the intervals of the buses plying to Uttam Nagar and Badarpur is 10 min.

(4) The difference between the time intervals of buses plying to Uttam Nagar is an integral multiple of 5 min.

8. If condition (iii) is not there, then what can be the minimum difference between the time intervals between the buses plying to Uttam Nagar?

(1) 2 min (2) 3 min (3) 4 min (4) 5 min.

For examples 5 to 8:

5. 1 A bus to Uttam Nagar departs after every 15 min.

One of the buses to Mehrauli leaves after every 10 min.

Other bus to Mehrauli can leave after every 12 min or 20 min

Let us assume bus on route no. 427 leaves after every 10 min between 9:00 a.m & 10:00 a.m i.e. at 9:00, 9:10, 9:20, 9:30, 9:40, 9:50 and 10:00 a.m.

12 min

If timings of buses plying after 12 & 10 min clash then the bus plying after every 12 min will go.

If timings of any of the buses plying after 12 min coincides with departure time of 427 then the next bus timings will clash only after 60 min(LCM of 12 & 10)

So maximum of 1 bus timings can clash with route no. 427 in a given hour.

Hence, a minimum 7 – 1 = 6 buses on route 427 can depart in an hour.

20 min

If timings of buses plying after 20 & 10 min clash then the bus plying after every 20 min will go.

If timings of any of the bus plying after 20 min coincides with departure time of 427 then the next bus timings will clash again after 20 min(LCM of 20 & 10)

If the timings of two buses clash at 9:00 AM then timings will again clash at 9:20, 9:40 and 10:00

Hence, a minimum 7 – 4 = 3 buses on route 427 can depart in an hour.

6. 3 If frequency of all buses increases by 5 min then new time intervals become 5, 5, 7, 10, 15 and 25 min.

So now one of the bus to Mehrauli departs after every 5 min. The Other bus can depart after every 7 min or 15 min.

The minimum time difference between buses plying after 5 and 7 min can be 1 min (GCD of 5 and 7).

7. 4 The difference in time intervals between a particular bus to Mehrauli and Uttam Nagar is same as the difference in time intervals between two buses plying towards Uttam Nagar.

Hence, time intervals between Buses for Mehrauli and Uttam Nagar can only be:

Mehrauli – 10 and 12 / 20

Uttam Nagar – 15 and 10 / 20

So the time interval between two different routes to Uttam Nagar is always a multiple of 5.

8. 1 If condition (iii) is waved off then there can be possibility of 3 buses plying to Uttam Nagar. Then 3 buses to Uttam Nagar can ply between intervals 10,12 and 15 mins or between intervals of 10,15, 20 mins.

So the minimum time interval can be in the first case i.e. when 3 buses ply after an interval of 10, 12, 15 mins.

Minimum difference between time interval = 12 – 10 = 2 minute.

10.4 MISCELLANEOUS

Directions for examples 9 to 12: Answer the questions based on the following information.

A group of eight athletes from South India are preparing to participate in the Shooting or Weight Lifting competitions in the Olympics 2016. Each athlete belongs to exactly one state out of Karnataka, Andhra Pradesh and Tamil Nadu, and there is at least one athlete from each state. All female athletes belong to Andhra Pradesh. The results after the first round of screening are as follows:

I. At least two athletes have qualified for Shooting competition, but not for the Weight Lifting competition.

II. At least two athletes have qualified for Weight Lifting competition, but not for the Shooting competition.

III. At least one athlete has qualified for both the competitions.

IV. Among the eight athletes, only athletes from Karnataka have qualified for Weight Lifting competition.

9. Which of the following statements CANNOT be true?

(1) The group includes more females than males.

(2) The group includes fewer athletes from Karnataka than those from Tamil Nadu.

(3) The group includes fewer athletes from Tamil Nadu than those from Andhra Pradesh.

(4) More athletes have qualified for Weight Lifting than Shooting.

10. If each athlete has qualified to compete in at least one of the two competitions, all of the following must be true EXCEPT:

(1) All athletes from Andhra Pradesh have qualified for Shooting.

(2) All athletes from Tamil Nadu have qualified for Shooting.

(3) All athletes from Karnataka have qualified for Weight Lifting.

(4) No athlete from Andhra Pradesh has qualified for Weight Lifting.

11. If four of the athletes are male and four of the athletes are female, all of the following must be true EXCEPT:

(1) One of the athletes is from Tamil Nadu.

(2) Four athletes are from Andhra Pradesh.

(3) Three athletes are from Karnataka.

(4) Four athletes have qualified for the Shooting competition.

12. If the group includes more athletes from Tamil Nadu than those from Karnataka, the number of male athletes who have qualified for the Shooting competition cannot be less than

(1) 0 (2) 1 (3) 2 (4) 3

For examples 9 to 12:

If all female athletes are from AP. Then all athletes from Karnataka and TN are male.

If only athletes from Karnataka have qualified for "Weight Lifting" competition. Then no athlete from AP or TN have qualified for "Weight Lifting" competition

Competition	S/Ⓦ	W/Ⓢ	S/ W
Qualified athletes	atleast 2	atleast 2	atleast 1

Here Weight Lifting — Karnataka, Andhra Pradesh — All females and Karnatak and Tamil Nadu — All males.

9. 1 Number of qualified athletes for Weight Lifting is at least 3. So at least 3 athletes are from Karnataka, all of whom are male. Atleast one athlete must be from TN and all athletes from TN are male. Thus, at least 4 athletes must be male. So it is not possible that there can be more females than males in the group.

10. 3 All athletes except those from Karnataka have qualified for "Shooting" but not for "Weight Lifting". However it is possible for a athlete from Karnataka to have qualified for "Shooting" but not "Weight Lifting". Hence nothing can be said for sure for "All Athletes from Karnataka".

11. 4 Since all females must be from AP, all athletes from Karnataka and TN must be male. There must be at least one athlete from each state, so one athlete must be from TN and 3 athletes must be from Karnataka. The remaining 4 must be from AP. Thus statements I, II and III must be true.

12. 3 At least 3 athletes must be from Karnataka. Since each region is represented at least once, one of the athlete must be from AP and remaining 4 must be from TN. One of the 3 athletes from Karnataka (all of whom are male) has qualified for "Shooting". All 4 from TN are male and at least one from TN has qualified for "Shooting". For minimum number of males, the female athlete from AP must have qualified for "Shooting" (As one of the two who qualified for "Shooting" but not for the Weight Lifting). Thus, a minimum of 2 male athletes (1 from Karnataka and other from TN) have qualified for "Shooting".

	AP	Karnataka		TN
Competition	S/(W)	W/(S),	S/ W	S/(W)
Minimum Qualified athletes	1	2	1	1

Directions for examples 13 to 16: Answer the questions based on the information given below.

Some lecturers belonging to four disciplines, viz. physics, chemistry, mathematics and biology were selected to take part in a conclave. All applicants shortlisted for the selection were classified into five age groups, namely:

Age Range	Age Group
Age less than 50	Young
50 ≤Age < 60	Middle aged
60 ≤ Age < 70	Senior
70 ≤ Age < 80	Stalwart
Age 80 and above	Retired

For the conclave, not more than two lecturers of a particular age group were shortlisted for representing a discipline. Initially, the maximum possible number of lecturers were shortlisted. However, only five more than half of them were selected and they finally participated in the conclave. The following observations about the selected lecturers were made:

I. If two lecturers were excluded from the retired lecturers, then the number of seniors and stalwarts, each is one less than the number in each of the other three age groups.

II. The total number of lecturers selected from diciplines physics, chemistry and biology put together was the square of an integer.

III. There was no biology lecturer who was middle aged or stalwart, and there was no physics lecturer who was a senior. Every other discipline was represented by at least one lecturer from each age group.

IV. Rocky and Platy were young physics lecturers.

13. If the number of physics lecturers was greater than the number of chemistry lecturers, then which of the following is NOT possible to determine?

(1) Number of middle aged physics lecturers.

(2) Number of retired physics lecturers.

(3) Number of middle-aged chemistry lecturers.

(4) Number of retired chemistry lecturers.

14. What can be said about the total number of physics and chemistry lecturers put together?

I. It was less than or equal to 12.

II. It was more than or equal to 12.

(1) Only I (2) Only II (3) Both I and II (4) Neither I nor II

15. If Kandy was the lone retired chemistry lecturer, then which of the following is definitely true?

(1) There was one middle aged physics lecturer.

(2) There were two middle-aged physics lecturers.

(3) There was one retired biology lecturer.

(4) There were two retired biology lecturers.

16. Which of the following was NOT possible?

(1) Two retired physics lecturers and two retired chemistry lecturers were selected for the conclave.

(2) One retired physics lecturer and two retired chemistry lecturers were selected for the conclave.

(3) One retired physics lecturer and one retired chemistry lecturer were selected for the conclave.

(4) Two retired physics lecturers and one retired chemistry lecturer were selected for the conclave.

For examples 13 to 16:

The maximum possible lecturers were short-listed. Since there are 5 age groups and 4 different disciplines and there can be at most two lecturers of a particular age group representing a particular discipline, the number of lecturers short-listed = 5 × 4 × 2 = 40.

The number of lecturers selected = 5 + 20 = 25.

From statement I: It is only possible that number of retired lecturers = 7
Young = Middle = 5, senior = Stalwarts = 4

From statement IV: Only 2 young physics lecturers are possible.

From statement II: Total number of lecturers of (Phy + Che + Bio) = 1, 4, 9, 16 and 25.

However, if number of lecturers of (Phy + Che + Bio) = 1, 4 or 9, then number of lecturers of Mathematics > 10, which is not possible.

If number of lecturers of (Phy + Che + Bio) = 25, then number of lecturers of Mathematics = 0, which is not possible.

Thus, number of lecturers of (Phy + Che + Bio) = 16

Hence, in Mathematics 9 lecturer were selected (1 from young group and 2 from other groups each.

	Physics	Chemistry	Math	Bio
Young (5)	2	1	1	1
Middle (5)			2	X
Senior (4)	X	1	2	1
Stalwart (4)	1	1	2	X
Retired (7)			2	

13. 4 Number of physics lecturers > number of chemistry lecturers.

Let there be 1 middle aged physics lecturer and 2 middle aged chemistry lecturers.

Then, maximum possible value of the number of physics lecturers = 2 + 1 + 1 + 2 = 6

Minimum possible value of the number of chemistry lecturers = 1 + 2 + 1 + 1 + 1 = 6

In this case number of physics lecturers can't be more than the number of chemistry lecturers.

So, it is not possible.

It is clear that there are 2 middle aged physics lecturers and 1 middle aged chemistry lecturer.

Number of physics lecturers (excluding the retired age group) = 2 + 2 + 1 = 5

Number of chemistry lecturers (excluding the retired age group) = 1 + 1 + 1 + 1 = 4

Now, if there is 1 retired physics lecturer then there must be 2 retired chemistry lecturer. In this case, total physics lecturers cannot be more than chemistry lecturer.

So, there must be 2 retired physics lecturers.

Hence, number of retired chemistry lecturers may be 1 or 2.

14. 2 Number of retired biology lecturers may be 1 or 2.

So, from above table it is clear that total number of physics and chemistry lecturers put together must be either 12 or 13.

15. 4 If there is only 1 retired chemistry lecturer, then there must be 2 retired physics lecturers and 2 retired biology lecturers.

16. 3 From the above table it is sure that there can't be one retired physics lecturer and retired chemistry lecturer because in this case there would be 4 retired biology lecturers, which is not possible.

Directions for examples 17 to 20: Answer the questions on the basis of the information given below.

There are ten students – A, B, C, D, E, F, G, H, J and K. At least five of them decide to enroll for Correspondence MBA course. Also, at least five of them decide to enroll for Correspondence Java course. The following conditions apply:

I. At least four students enroll for both the courses.
II. A enrolls for either Correspondence Java course or Correspondence MBA course, but not both.
III. H enrolls for Correspondence Java course only.
IV. K and B, each of whom enroll for one of the two courses, enroll for different course.
V. D and C enroll for both the courses.
VI. If J enrolls for both the courses, then E and F will also enroll for both the courses.

17. If G enrolls for one of the two courses, then what is the minimum number of students who enroll for Correspondence Java course?
(1) 5 (2) 6 (3) 7 (4) 8

18. If A and B enroll for different courses, then what is the maximum number of students who enroll for Correspondence MBA course?
(1) 6 (2) 7 (3) 8 (4) 9

19. If 6 students enroll for Correspondence Java course, then which of the following can be a complete list of the students who enroll for Correspondence Java course?
(1) A, C, D, E, F and H (2) A, C, D, E, H and K (3) B, C, D, E, F and H (4) C, D, E, H, J and K

20. If 7 students enroll for Correspondence MBA course, then which of the following can be a list of the students who enroll for Correspondence MBA course?
I. A, B, C, D, E, F and G
II. B, C, D, E, F, J and G
III. C, D, E, F, G, J and K
IV. A, C, D, E, G, J and K
(1) II or III (2) I, II or III (3) II or IV (4) I, II, III or IV

For examples 17 to 20:

17. 2 The required number = 4 students (in both courses) + H + (K or B) = 6 students.

18. 3 The required number = 10 – H (Java only) – (A/B) = 8 students.

19. 3 Check the options.

Option (1): Either B or K will register for Correspondence Java course. But none of them is in the list. So it is not a correct list.

Option (2): At least four students should register for both courses. But A, H, K cannot register for more than one course. So it is not the right list.

Option (3): Either B or K will register for Correspondence Java course. So B is the part of the list. H is also a part of the list. C, D, E and F can register for both the courses. Hence, it could be the right list.

Option (4): H and K can register for one course. The other four students should register for both the courses. If J registers for both the courses, then E and F necessarily register for both the courses. Since F is not in the list, it is not the right list.

20. 4 Check the statements.

Statement I: If C, D, E and F register for both courses, then A, B and G can register for correspondence MBA course.
So, it could be a list.

Statement II: If C, D, E, F and J register for both courses, then B and G can register for correspondence MBA course.
So, it could be a list.

Statement III: If C, D, E, F and J register for both courses, then G and K can register for correspondence MBA course.
So, it could be a list.

Statement IV: If C, D, E and G register for both courses, then A, J and K can register for correspondence MBA course.
So, it could be a list.

Hence, I, II, III or IV could be a list.

PRACTICE EXERCISE – 1

Directions for questions 1 to 4: Answer the questions on the basis of the information given below.

A vending machine, having five switches viz. 1, 2, 3, 4 and 5, when operated, dispenses Coca-cola, 7-up, Mirinda, Limca and Pepsi depending upon which switch is turned on. The machine is such that each switch dispenses two different drinks and each drink is dispensed by two different switches. If two or more switches are turned on, the common drink, if any, nullifies each other and will not come out at all. To get the drink that one wants, he/she has to turn on the right combination of switches, put in the money and press the delivery button.

Following information is also given:

Turning on switches:

I. 1 and 3, we get 7-up and Mirinda.

II. 2, 4 and 5, we get 7-up and Mirinda.

III. 1 and 2, we get Coca-cola and Pepsi.

IV. 1 and 4, we get Limca, Coca-cola, Mirinda and Pepsi.

V. 3, 4 and 5, we get Coca-cola and Pepsi.

VI. 2, 3 and 5, we get Limca, Coca-cola, Mirinda and Pepsi.

VII. Switches 1, 2, 3, 4 and 5 do not supply 7-up, Limca, Coca-cola, Mirinda and Pepsi respectively.

1. One of the drinks which is dispensed by turning on switch 1 is

(1) Limca (2) Coca-cola (3) Mirinda (4) 7-up

2. 7-up is one of the drinks that is dispensed by turning on switch

(1) switch 1 (2) switch 2 (3) switch 3 (4) switch 4

3. One of the drinks which is dispensed by turning on switch 2 is

(1) 7-up (2) Mirinda (3) Limca (4) Pepsi

4. What drinks are dispensed by turning on switches 2 and 3?

(1) Mirinda, Limca and 7-up

(2) Pepsi, Limca and 7-up

(3) Coca-cola and Mirinda

(4) Coca-cola, Mirinda, Pepsi and 7-up

Directions for questions 5 to 8: Answer the questions on the basis of the information given below.

Top seven chess players viz. Anand, Casporoz, Kramnik, Shashi, Michael, Topolov and Vladimir participated in a knock out tournament. These players were ranked from 1 to 7 respectively. Anand, who was the best player, was ranked 1. In the tournament, the winner of the first match played the second match of the tournament with the player whose rank was immediately higher to the rank of the loser of the first match and loser got knocked out. The winner of the second match played the third match of the tournament with the player whose rank was immediately higher to the rank of the loser of the second match and the loser of this match got knocked out. The same continued until exactly one player was left. It was also observed that:

1. No player played more than three matches and each player played at least one match.
2. Anand played exactly two matches.
3. The player with rank 5 did not participate in the last match of the tournament.

5. For which player, except Anand, can we exactly determine the number of matches that he played?

(1) Shashi

(2) Vladimir

(3) Topolov

(4) Not possible for any player

6. What was the sum of the ranks of the players who played the third match of the tournament?

(1) 6 (2) 8 (3) 5 (4) 7

7. Who could have beaten Michael in the tournament ?

(i) Anand

(ii) Casporoz

(iii) Kramnik

(iv) Shashi

(1) Only (ii) & (i) (b) Only (i) (3) Only (i) & (iii) (4) Only (ii)

8. How many matches did Topolov play in the tournament?

(1) 1 (2) 2 (3) 3 (4) Cannot be determined

Directions for questions 9 to 12: Answer the questions on the basis of the information given below.

In a company, there are four managers – Akash, Bharat, Chetna and Dimple – in marketing department, and four managers – Prakash, Kamal, Richa and Shilpa – in finance department. Akash, Bharat, Prakash and Kamal are male and others are female. Two teams, with four members each, are to be constitueted out of these eight persons to handle launch of two new products – Crux and Shivel. Also each team has two members from each department. Prakash and Bharat cannot not be in the same team. Chetna is a part of the team that is to handle launch of Crux and Richa is a part of the team that is to handle launch of Shivel.

9. If Bharat and Shilpa are in the same team, who among the following is definitely in their team?

(1) Richa (2) Chetna (3) Akash (4) None of these

10. If the team handling launch of Crux has exactly two males, then in how many ways can the other team be formed?

(1) 3 (2) 2 (3) 4 (4) 1

11. If one of the team has three males, then which of the following pairs of persons are definitely in the same team?

(i) Bharat and Chetna

(ii) Bharat andRicha

(iii) Prakash and Chetna

(iv) Prakash and Richa

(1) Only (i) (2) Only (iii) (3) Both (ii) & (iii) (4) Only (ii) and (iv)

12. If Prakash and Kamal are in different teams, then which of the following pairs of persons are definitely in the same team?

(i) Kamal and Richa

(ii) Chetna and Shilpa

(iii) Prakash and Dimple

(iv) Bharat and Akash

(1) Only (ii) (2) Only(ii) and (iii) (3) Only (i) (4) Only (iii) and (iv)

Directions for questions 13 to 16: Answer the questions on the basis of the information given below.

Each of the five siblings Nishit, Vasav, Richa, Akash and Pulkit pursues at least one out of the five activities namely Dancing, Singing, Guitar, Painting and Gardening. Further, the following information is known:

(1) There are exactly two activities, one of which is Guitar, that are pursued by both Akash and Vasav. But there is no activity which is pursued by both Pulkit and Akash.

(2) Gardening is pursued by the maximum number of siblings.

(3) None of them pursues both Singing and Guitar together.

(4) Pulkit pursues the same number of activities as pursued by Richa.

(5) Each of Dancing and Singing is pursued by three siblings. Each of Guitar and Painting is pursued by two siblings.

(6) Pulkit pursues only singing and Dancing and Nishit pursues all the activities except Guitar.

(7) The number of activities pursued by Vasav is not more than that pursued by Akash.

13. Who among the following pursues Painting?

(1) Akash (2) Vasav (3) Richa (4) Pulkit

14. How many activities are pursued by Akash?

(1) 2 (2) 3 (3) 4 (4) Either (1) or (2)

15. How many common activities are pursued by both Vasav and Nishit?

(1) 1 (2) 2 (3) 3 (4) Either (1) or (2)

16. Names of the siblings who pursue Singing are

(1) Vasav, Pulkit and Nishit (2) Nishit, Vasav and Akash
(3) Richa, Nishit and Akash (4) Richa, Nishit and Pulkit

Directions for questions 17 to 20: Answer the questions on the basis of the information given below.

In a face-off between India and Palistan, 5 soldiers from each side are facing each other, with one Indian soldier is facing exactly one Palistani soldier. Two of the Palistani soldiers are tribal terrorists, and one of the Indian soldiers is a traitor who has planted landmines on which two other Indian soldiers are standing. One soldier on each side is carrying a Bazooka. It is also known that:

I. Neither of those Palistani soldiers who are terrorists is facing the traitor.

II. Exactly one person is standing between the two Indian soldiers who are standing on the landmine. The same is true for the two Palistani soldiers who are terrorists.

III. The Palistani soldier standing between the soldiers who are terrorists is facing one of the Indian soldiers standing on landmines.

IV. The Indian soldier carrying the Bazooka, who is not the traitor, is the neighbor of only one soldier who is standing on the landmine.

V. One of the soldiers carrying the Bazooka is standing in the middle of its defense line and the other on the extreme end.

17. Which of the following statements is definitely true?

(1) One of the soldiers carrying the Bazooka is a terrorist and is standing in the middle of the defense line of Palistan.

(2) One of the soldiers carrying the Bazooka is a terrorist and is standing at one of the extreme ends of the defense line of Palistan.

(3) The Indian soldier carrying the Bazooka is standing in the middle of its defense line.

(4) The Indian soldier carrying the Bazooka is standing in the middle of the soldiers standing on landmine.

18. Who is not a neighbor of the soldiers standing on landmine?

(1) Traitor

(2) Soldier with the Bazooka

(3) A soldier who is neither a traitor nor carrying the Bazooka.

(4) Every Indian soldier is a neighbor of either one of them.

19. Which of the following pair of soldiers are facing each other?

(1) Terrorist with Bazooka and the traitor.

(2) One of the Indian soldier standing on landmine and a Palistani soldier with Bazooka.

(3) Terrorist without Bazooka and the Indian soldier with Bazooka.

(4) Indian soldier with Bazooka and a Palistani soldier who is neither a terrorist nor carrying the Bazooka.

20. Who among the following is standing opposite to the terrorist with Bazooka?

(1) Indian soldier with Bazooka.

(2) Indian soldier standing on the landmine.

(3) The traitor

(4) None of the above

Directions for questions 21 to 24: Answer the questions based on the following information.

Each of the six writers – A, B, C, D, E and F – writes books belonging to one or more genre out of poem, novel and drama. Each one of them writes in only one language. Two of them were born in the 1970s, three in the 1980s and one in the 1990s. Four of them are poets; three of them are novelists; and three of them are dramatists. Two write in Hindi, two in Marathi, one in Bengali and one in Tamil. Only the Hindi and Tamil writers were born in the 1980s. The Tamil writer writes novels and drama but not poetry. The Bengali writer, who was born in the 1970s, writes only poetry. A, who was born in the 1990s, writes only poetry. B writes only drama. C writes in Marathi. D, who was born in the 1980s, writes only poetry and novels in Hindi. F writes only poetry.

21. B writes in

(1) Marathi (2) Hindi (3) Bengali (4) Tamil

22. Who writes in Tamil?

(1) F (2) E (3) B (4) A

23. C writes

(1) Poetry (2) Novel (3) Drama (4) All of these

24. Who among the following was born in the 1980s?

(1) A (2) B (3) F (4) None of these

Directions for questions 25 to 28: Answer the questions based on the following information.

The following are the details of symptoms related to four diseases - G,L,T and Z.

(i) A patient with disease G exhibits rash and fever, along with either sore throat or headache but not both.

(ii) A patient with disease L exhibits rash and fever but neither sore throat nor headache.

(iii) A patient with disease T always exhibits sore throat and headache, and sometimes either rash or fever or both.

(iv) A patient with disease Z always exhibits headache, and sometimes either fever or sore throat or both, but never rash.

(v) A patient cannot have more than one disease out of the four at the same time.

25. If a patient exhibits sore throat and fever, then which of the following is definitely true about the patient?

(1) She has disease Z.

(2) She does not have disease G.

(3) She does not have disease L.

(4) She does not have disease T.

26. If a patient, who has one of the four diseases, does not exhibit rash, then which of the following is definitely true about the patient?

(1) She exhibits headache.

(2) She exhibits sore throat.

(3) She has disease T.

(4) She has disease Z.

27. If a patient, who has one of the four diseases, exhibits neither fever nor sore throat, then which of the following statements is/are definitely true about the patient?

I. She exhibits headache.

II. She has disease Z.

III. She exhibits rash.

(1) I only (2) I and II (3) III only (4) II and III

28. If a patient exhibits three symptoms out of the given four symptoms, then she definitely does not have

(1) Disease G (2) Disease T (3) Disease L (4) Disease Z

10.12 MISCELLANEOUS

Directions for questions 29 to 32: Answer the questions on the basis of the information given below.

Nine friends – A, B, C, D, E, F, H, I and J – joined a fitness center. The fitness center is closed on Monday. At the fitness center, a week starts from Tuesday and ends on Sunday. On each of the six days of a particular week, exactly three persons, out of the nine, visited the fitness center such that each person visited the fitness center on at least one day of that week. There are exactly four persons who visited the fitness center on more than two days. It is also known that:

(I) Both D and E visited the fitness center on three of the first four days of the week.

(II) H visits the fitness center only on those days when both A and B visit the fitness center.

(III) Each of B, I and J visited the centre only once and on different days of the week.

(IV) C and F always visit the fitness center on the same day of the week.

(V) None of the persons visited the fitness center on three consecutive days of the week.

29. Which of the following persons visited the fitness center on exactly three days?

(1) H (2) A (3) C (4) Cannot be determined

30. If A did not visit the fitness center on Sunday and J visited the fitness center only on Friday, which of the following can be the day on which I visited the fitness center?

(1) Wednesday (2) Thursday (3) Saturday (4) Sunday

31. If E and I visited the fitness center on Sunday and Friday respectively, on which day did J visit the fitness center?

(1) Tuesday (2) Wednesday (3) Thursday (4) Saturday

32. Which of the following can visit the fitness center on four days?

(1) A (2) E (3) F (4) C

Directions for questions 33 to 36: Answer the questions on the basis of the information given below.

Production department of a multinational company houses seven typists, all of them are working on a project. The given diagrams depict their performance over a four days period. In each diagram, the four corner figures show the percentage of total lines typed on that day by the top four typists of the day whereas the middle circle denotes the total number of lines typed by the remaining three typists put together on that day. No two typists typed the same number of lines on any of the given four days. A typist may not type even a single line on a given day. HR also computed two parameters for each typist: Performance Variance (PV), is the positive difference between the sum of the maximum and minimum number of lines typed by a typist over the period of 4 days and the sum of the lines typed on the remaining two days; Sigma, is the mean (average) of the two middle quantities when a typist's number of lines, typed across 4 days, is arranged in non-decreasing order.

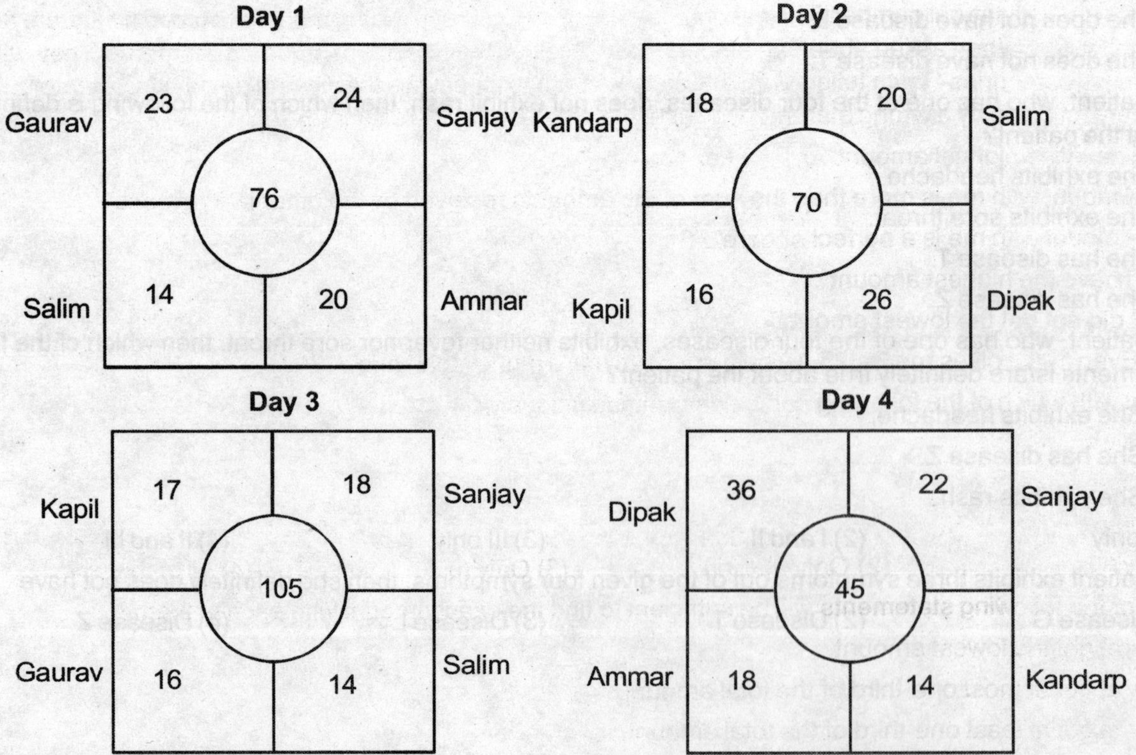

33. Given that the Sigma for all typists is an integer, for how many of them is it not possible to calculate the exact value of it?

(1) 0 (2) 2 (3) 4 (4) More than 4

34. For which of the given typists, can the value of PV be 0?

(1) Salim (2) Sanjay (3) Salim and Sanjay (4) None of them

35. During the given period, how many typists did definitely type more number of pages than what Kapil did?

(1) 1 (2) 2 (3) 3 (4) More than 3

36. For which typist was the difference between minimum and maximum possible Sigma the least?

(1) Sanjay (2) Salim (3) Gaurav (4) Kandarp

Directions for questions 37 to 40: Answer the questions on the basis of the information given below.

There are three friends — Saptarsh, Rushat and Trivendra — each has some red and white balls.

I. Saptarsh has atleast one red ball and twice as many white balls as red balls.

II. Rushat has atleast one red ball and three times as many white balls as red balls.

III. Trivendra has atleast one red ball and three more white balls than red balls.

IV. When I tell you the number of balls we have altogether (the number is less than 25), you will know how many balls I have, but not how many balls each of the others has", said one of the friends.

37. The number of balls with the three friends put together cannot be more than

(1) 12 (2) 19 (3) 24 (4) Cannot be determined

38. Who is the speaker?

(1) Saptarsh (2) Rushat (3) Trivendra (4) Cannot be determined

39. The number of balls with Saptarsh cannot be more than

(1) 3 (2) 9 (3) 6 (4) Cannot be determined

40. How many balls does Rushat have?

(1) 8 (2) 12 (3) 4 (4) Cannot be determined

Directions for questions 41 to 44: Answer the questions on the basis of the information given below.

Five hundred rupees were divided among three friends – Atul, Bharat and Chirag. The amount received by each of them is a distinct three-digit natural number. The maximum amount, out of these three amounts, is a perfect square and has the same digit twice. When asked about the amount, they received, each of them made 2 statements. They belong to either of the two categories- Truth teller or an Alternator. A truth teller always tells the truth and an alternator makes a true statement followed by a wrong statement or vice versa. Following were their replies –

Atul – "I have the highest amount".

– "Amount with me is more than the sum of the amounts received by the other two persons".

Bharat – "Amount with me is a perfect square".

– "I have the highest amount".

Chirag – "I did not get the lowest amount".

– "Even if Atul gives me Rs.25, I would not have more money than him".

41. Amount with which of the following can be determined uniquely?

(i) Atul

(ii) Bharat

(iii) Chirag

(1) Only (ii) (2) Only (i) & (ii) (3) Only (i) (4) All of them

42. Which of the following statements will be sufficient to find the exact amount with each of them?

(1) Bharat got the lowest amount.

(2) Bharat got at most one-third of the total amount.

(3) Chirag got at least one-third of the total amount.

(4) Atul got less than the half of the total amount.

43. How many of them are truth tellers?

(1) One (2) Two (3) Zero (4) Cannot be determined

44. If the absolute difference between the amount received by exactly two of them is a perfect cube, then how much amount (in Rs.) did Chirag get?

(1) 131 (2) 175 (3) 161 (4) Not possible

Directions for questions 45 to 48: Answer the questions on the basis of the information given below.

1. P, Q, R, S, T, V and W are seven members of a family.
2. Each one of them has a different profession, from among Doctor, Teacher, Lawyer, Engineer, Architect, Chartered Accountant and Banker, and a different income.
3. There are two married couples in the family.
4. R is the Doctor and earns more than the Engineer as well as the Lawyer.
5. T is married to the Chartered Accountant and she earns the least.
6. No lady is either Lawyer or Engineer.
7. Q, the Teacher, earns less than P, the Banker. W is married to Q and he earns more than S as well as P.
8. V is not a Lawyer. The Chartered Accountant earns less than the Lawyer but more than the Banker.

45. Who earns the maximum in the family?

(1) V (2) W (3) R (4) S

46. What is P's position from the top when they are arranged in descending order of their incomes?

(1) Second (2) Fourth (3) Third (4) Fifth

47. What is the profession of V?

(1) Engineer

(2) Chartered Accountant

(3) Engineer or Chartered Accountant

(4) Data inadequate

48. At least how many male members are there in the family?

(1) Two (2) Three (3) Four (4) Five

PRACTICE EXERCISE – 2

Directions for questions 1 to 4: Answer the questions on the basis of the information given below.

A cube, having two red faces, two blue faces and two green faces, is cut into 216 smaller and identical cubes.

1. The number of cubes with both red and green coloured faces cannot be more than

(1) 22 (2) 16 (3) 24 (4) 18

2. What is the maximum and minimum respective value of the number of smaller cubes that have all the three colours on them?

(1) 8, 4 (2) 6,4 (3) 8,2 (4) 8,0

3. If one of unpainted faces of all the smaller cubes is painted with red color, then what is the minimum possible number of smaller cubes now that have all three colours on them?

(1) 8 (2) 12 (3) 14 (4) 16

4. The number of smaller cubes that have exactly one colour on them cannot be more than

(1) 108 (2) 96 (3) 144 (4) 134

Directions for questions 5 to 8: Answer the questions on the basis of the information given below.

Four friends namely Dinesh, Jatin, Prakash and Vivek, each of whom has a different coloured car from among red, blue, green and yellow, not necessarily in the same order, belong to three categories of persons (at least one from each category) – truth teller, alternator and liar. A truth teller always speaks the truth; an alternator makes a true statement followed by a false one or vice versa; and a liar always speaks a lie. It is known that out of the four, two are alternators. When these four persons were enquired regarding the colors of their cars, each of them made two statements, the details of which are as follows:

Prakash : The color of my car is either red or blue. The red colored car is either Dinesh's or mine.

Vivek : The color of my car is neither red nor blue. The yellow colored car is neither Jatin's nor mine.

Dinesh : The color of Vivek's car is yellow. Jatin is a truth teller.

Jatin : The color of my car is yellow. The color of Dinesh's car is not green.

5. Who among the following cannot be a truth teller?

(1) Vivek (2) Dinesh (3) Jatin (4) Prakash

6. If the color of Vivek's car is blue, then the color of whose car is green?

(1) Jatin (2) Prakash (3) Dinesh (4) Cannot be determined

7. If the color of Prakash's car is Red, then the color of whose car is yellow?

(1) Vivek (2) Jatin (3) Dinesh (4) Cannot be determined

8. Who among the following cannot be the liar?

(1) Dinesh (2) Vivek (3) Jatin (4) Prakash

Directions for questions 9 to 12: Answer the questions independently.

[CAT 2001]

9. At a village mela, the following six nautankis (plays) are scheduled as shown in the table below.

No.	Nautanki	Duration	Show Times
1	Sati Savitri	1 hr	9 a.m. and 2 p.m.
2	Joru ka Ghulam	1 hr	10.30 a.m . and 11: 30 a.m.
3	Sundar Kand	30 min	10 am and 11 a.m.
4	Veer Abhimanyu	1 hr	10 a.m. and 11a.m.
5	Reshma aur Shera	1 hr	9.30 a.m., 12 noon and 2 p.m.
6	Jhansi ki Rani	30 min	11 a.m. and 1: 30 pm

You wish to see all the six nautankis. Further, you wish to ensure that you get a lunch break from 12.30 p.m. to 1.30 p.m. Which of the following ways can you do this?

(1) Sati Savitri is viewed first; Sundar Kand is viewed third, and Jhansi ki Rani is viewed last

(2) Sati Savitri is viewed last; Veer Abhimanyu is viewed third, and Reshma aur Shera is viewed first

(3) Sati Savitri is viewed first; Sundar Kand is viewed third, and Joru ka Ghulam is viewed fourth

(4) Veer Abhimanyu is viewed third; Reshma aur Shera is viewed fourth, and Jahansi ki Rani is viewed fifth

10. Mrs Ranga has three children and has difficulty remembering their ages and months of their birth. The clue below may help her remember.

- The boy, who was born in June, is 7 years old.
- One of the children is 4 years old but it was not Anshuman.
- Vaibhav is older than Suprita.
- One of the children was born in September, but it was not Vaibhav.
- Suprita's birthday is in April.
- The youngest child is only 2-year-old.

Based on the above clues, which one of the following statements is true?

(1) Vaibhav is the oldest, followed by Anshuman who was born in September, and the youngest is Suprita who was born in April

(2) Anshuman is the oldest being born in June, followed by Suprita who is 4-year-old, and the youngest is Vaibhav who is 2-year-old

(3) Vaibhav is the oldest being 7-year-old, followed by Suprita who was born in April, and the youngest is Anshuman who was born in September

(4) Suprita is the oldest who was born in April, followed by Vaibhav who was born in June, and Anshuman who was born in September

11. The Bannerjees, the Sharmas, and the Pattabhiramans each have a tradition of eating Sunday lunch as a family. Each family serves a special meal at a certain time of day. Each family has a particular set of chinaware used for this meal. Use the clues below to answer the following question.

- The Sharma family eats at noon.
- The family that serves fried brinjal uses blue chinaware.
- The Bannerjee family eats at 2 o'clock.
- The family that serves sambar does not use red chinaware.
- The family that eats at 1 o'clock serves fried brinjal.
- The Pattabhiraman family does not use white chinaware.
- The family that eats last likes makkai-ki-roti.

Which one of the following statements is true?

(1) The Bannerjees eat makkai-ki-roti at 2 o'clock, the Sharmas eat fried brinjal at 12 o'clock and the Pattabhiramans eat sambar from red chinaware

(2) The Sharmas eat sambar served in white chinaware, the Pattabhiramans eat fried brinjal at 1 o'clock, and the Bannerjees eat makkai-ki-roti served in blue chinaware

(3) The Sharmas eat sambar at noon, the Pattabhiramans eat fried brinjal served in blue chinaware, and the Bannerjees eat makkai-ki-roti served in red chinaware

(4) The Bannerjees eat makkai-ki-roti served in white chinaware, the Sharmas eat fried brinjal at 12 o'clock and the Pattabhiramans eat sambar from red chinaware

12. While Balbir had his back turned, a dog ran into his butcher shop, snatched a piece of meat off the counter and ran out. Balbir was mad when he realised what had happened. He asked three other shopkeepers, who had seen the dog, to describe it. The shopkeepers really did not want to help Balbir. So each of them made a statement which contained one truth and one lie.

- Shopkeeper number 1 said: "The dog had black hair and a long tail."
- Shopkeeper number 2 said: "The dog had a short tail and wore a collar."
- Shopkeeper number 3 said: "The dog had white hair and no collar."

Based on the above statements, which of the following could be a correct description?

(1) The dog had white hair, short tail and no collar

(2) The dog had white hair, long tail and a collar

(3) The dog had black hair, long tail and a collar

(4) The dog had black hair, long tail and no collar

Directions for questions 13 to 18: Answer the questions independently.

[CAT 2002]

Four students — Ashish, Dhanraj, Felix and Sameer sat for the Common Entrance Exam for Management (CEEM). One student got admission offers from three NIMs (National Institutes of Management), another from two NIMs, the third from one NIM, while the fourth got none. Below are some of the facts about who got admission offers from how many NIMs and what is their educational background.

I. The one who is an engineer didn't get as many admissions as Ashish.

II. The one who got offer for admissions in two NIMs isn't Dhanraj nor is he a chartered accountant.

III. Sameer is an economist.

IV. Dhanraj isn't an engineer and received more admission offers than Ashish.

V. The doctor got the most number of admission offers.

13. Which one of the following statements is necessarily true?

(1) Ashish is a chartered accountant and got offer for admission in three NIMs.

(2) Dhanraj is a doctor and got admission offer in one NIM.

(3) Sameer is an economist who got admission offers in two NIMs.

(4) Felix who is not an engineer did not get any offer for admission.

14. Five boys went to a store to buy sweets. One boy had Rs. 40. Another boy had Rs. 30. Two other boys had Rs. 20 each. The remaining boy had Rs. 10. Below are some more facts about the initial and final cash positions.

I. Alam started with more than Jugraj.

II. Sandeep spent Rs. 1.50 more than Daljeet.

III. Ganesh started with more money than just only one other person.

IV. Daljeet started with $\frac{2}{3}$ of what Sandeep started with.

V. Alam spent the most, but did not end with the least.

VI. Jugraj spent the least and ended with more than Alam or Daljeet.

VII. Ganesh spent Rs.3.50.

VIII. Alam spent 10 times more than what Ganesh did.

In the choices given below, all statements except one are false. Which one of the following statements can be true?

(1) Alam started with Rs. 40 and ended with Rs. 9.50

(2) Sandeep started with Rs. 30 and ended with Re. 1

(3) Ganesh started with Rs. 20 and ended with Rs. 4

(4) Jugraj started with Rs. 10 and ended with Rs. 7

15. In a hospital there were 200 diabetes, 150 hyperglycaemia and 150 gastro-enteritis patients. Of these, 80 patients were treated for both diabetices and hyperglycaemia. Sixty patients were treated for gastro-enteritis and hyperglycaemia, while 70 were treated for diabetes and gastro-enteritis. Some of these patients have all the three diseases. Dr. Dennis treats patients with only gastro-enteritis. Dr. Paul is a generalist. Therefore, he can treat patients with multiple diseases. Patients always prefer a specialist for their disease. If Dr. Dennis had 80 patients, then the other three doctors can be arranged in terms of the number of patients treated as:

(1) Paul > Gerard > Hormis (2) Paul > Hormis > Gerard

(3) Gerard > Paul > Hormis (4) None of these

16. Three children won the prizes in the Bournvita Quiz contest. They are from the schools: Loyola, Convent and Little Flowers, which are located at different cities. Below are some of the facts about the schools, the children and the city they are from.

I. One of the children is Bipin.

II. Loyola School's contestant did not come first.

III. Little Flower's contestant was named Riaz.

IV. Convent School is not in Hyderabad.

V. The contestant from Pune took third place.

VI. The contestant from Pune is not from Loyola School.

VII. The contestant from Bangalore did not come first.

VIII. Convent School's contestant's name is not Balbir.

Which of the following statements is true?

(1) 1st prize: Riaz (Little Flowers), 2nd prize: Bipin (Convent), 3rd prize: Balbir (Loyola)

(2) 1st prize: Bipin (Convent), 2nd prize: Riaz (Little Flowers), 3rd prize: Balbir (Loyola)

(3) 1st prize: Riaz (Little Flowers), 2nd prize: Balbir (Loyola), 3rd prize: Bipin (Convent)

(4) 1st prize: Bipin (Convent), 2nd prize: Balbir (Loyola), 3rd prize: Riaz (Little Flowers)

17. Two boys are playing on a ground. Both the boys are less than 10 years old. Age of the younger boy is equal to the cube root of the product of the age of the two boys. If we place the digit representing the age of the younger boy to the left of the digit representing the age of the elder boy, we get the age of father of the younger boy. Similarly, if we place the digit representing the age of the elder boy to the left of the digit representing the age of the younger boy and divide the figure by 2, we get the age of mother of the younger boy. The mother of the younger boy is younger to his father by 3 years. Then, what is the age of the younger boy?

(1) 3 (2) 4 (3) 2 (4) None of these

18. Flights A and B are scheduled from an airport within the next one hour. All the booked passengers of the two flights are waiting in the boarding hall after check-in. The hall has a seating capacity of 200, out of which 10% remained vacant. 40% of the waiting passengers are ladies. When boarding announcement came, passengers of flight A left the hall and boarded the flight. Seating capacity of each flight is two-third of the passengers who waited in the waiting hall for both the flights put together. Half the passengers who boarded flight A are women. After boarding for flight A, 60% of the waiting hall seats became empty. For every twenty of those who are still waiting in the hall for flight B, there is one air hostess in flight A. What is the ratio of empty seats in flight B to the number of air hostesses in flight A?

(1) 10 : 1 (2) 5 : 1 (3) 20 : 1 (4) 1 : 1

Directions for questions 19 to 22: Answer the questions on the basis of the information given below.

[CAT 2002]

A country has the following types of traffic signals.

3 red lights = stop

2 red lights = turn left

1 red light = turn right

3 green lights = go at 100 km/hr speed

2 green lights = go at 40 km/hr speed

1 green light = go at 20 km/hr speed

A motorist starts at a point on a road and follows all traffic signals. His car is heading towards the north. He encounters the following signals (the time mentioned in each case below is applicable after crossing the previous signal).

Starting point - 1 green light

After half an hour, 1st signal - 2 red and 2 green lights

After 15 min, 2nd signal - 1 red light

After half an hour, 3rd signal - 1 red and 3 green lights

After 24 min, 4th signal - 2 red and 2 green lights

After 15 min, 5th signal - 3 red lights

19. The total distance travelled by the motorist from the starting point till the last signal is

(1) 90 km (2) 100 km (3) 120 km (4) None of these

20. What is the position (radial distance) of the most motorist when he reaches the last signal?

(1) 45 km directly north of the starting point

(2) 30 km directly to the east of the starting point

(3) 50 km away to the north-east of the starting point

(4) 45 km away to the north-west of the starting point

21. After the starting point if the 1st signal were 1 red and 2 green lights, what would be the final position of the motorist?

(1) 30 km to the west and 20 km to the south

(2) 30 km to the west and 40 km to the north

(3) 50 km to the east and 40 km to the north

(4) Directly 30 km to the east

22. If at the starting point, the car was heading towards south, what would be the final position of the motorist?

(1) 30 km to the east and 40 km to the south

(2) 50 km to the east and 40 km to the south

(3) 30 km to the west and 40 km to the south

(4) 50 km to the west and 20 km to the north

Directions for questions 23 to 25: Answer the questions on the basis of the information given below.

[CAT 2003]

The seven basic symbols in a certain numeral system and their respective values are as follows:
I = 1, V = 5, X = 10, L = 50, C = 100, D = 500 and M = 1000

In general, the symbols in the numeral system are read from left to right, starting with the symbol representing the largest value; the same symbol cannot occur continuously more than three times; the value of the numeral is the sum of the values of the symbols. For example, XXVII = 10 + 10 + 5 + 1 + 1 = 27. An exception to the left-to-right reading occurs when a symbol is followed immediately by a symbol of greater value; then the smaller value is subtracted from the larger.

For example, XLVI = (50 – 10) + 5 + 1 = 46.

23. The value of the numeral MDCCLXXXVII is

(1) 1687 (2) 1787 (3) 1887 (4) 1987

24. The value of the numeral MCMXCIX is

(1) 1999 (2) 1899 (3) 1989 (4) 1889

25. Which of the following represent the numeral for 1995?

I. MCMLXXV II. MCMXCV III. MVD IV. MVM

(1) Only I and II (2) Only III and IV (3) Only II and IV (4) Only IV

Directions for questions 26 to 28: Answer the questions on the basis of the information given below.

[CAT 2003]

Two binary operations $\oplus$ and $*$ are defined over the set {a, e, f, g, h} as per the following tables:

$\oplus$	a	e	f	g	h
a	a	e	f	g	h
e	e	f	g	h	a
f	f	g	h	a	e
g	g	h	a	e	f
h	h	a	e	f	g

$*$	a	e	f	g	h
a	a	a	a	a	a
e	a	e	f	g	h
f	a	f	h	e	g
g	a	g	e	h	f
h	a	h	g	f	e

Thus, according to the first table $f \oplus g = a$, while according to the second table $g * h = f$, and so on. Also, let $f^2 = f * f$, $g^3 = g * g * g$, and so on.

26. What is the smallest positive integer n such that $g^n = e$?

(1) 4 (2) 5 (3) 2 (4) 3

27. Upon simplification, $f \oplus [f * \{f \oplus (f * f)\}]$ equals

(1) e (2) f (3) g (4) h

28. Upon simplification, $\{a^{10} * (f^{10} \oplus g^9)\} \oplus e^8$ equals

(1) e (2) f (3) g (4) h

Directions for questions 29 to 32: Answer the questions on the basis of the information given below.

[CAT 2003]

Recently, the answers of a test held nationwide were leaked to a group of unscrupulous people. The investigative agency has arrested the mastermind and nine other people A, B, C, D, E, F, G, H and I in this matter. Interrogating them, the following facts have been obtained regarding their operation. Initially the mastermind obtains the correct answer-key. All the others create their answer-key in the following manner. They obtain the answer-key from one or two people who already possess the same. These people are called his/her 'sources'. If the person has two sources, then he/she compares the answer-keys obtained from both sources. If the key to a question from both sources is identical, it is copied, otherwise it is left blank. If the person has only one source, he/she copies the source's answers into his/her copy. Finally, each person compulsorily replaces one of the answers (not a blank one) with a wrong answer in his/her answer key.

The paper contained 200 questions; so the investigative agency has ruled out the possibility of two or more of them introducing wrong answers to the same question. The investigative agency has a copy of the correct answer key and has tabulated the following data. These data represent question numbers.

Name	Wrong Answer(s)	Blank Answer(s)
A	46	—
B	96	46, 90, 25
C	27, 56	17, 46, 90
D	17	—
E	46, 90	—
F	14, 46	92, 90
G	25	—
H	46, 92	—
I	27	17, 46, 90

29. Which one among the following must have two sources?

(1) A (2) B (3) C (4) D

30. How many people (excluding the mastermind) needed to make answer-keys before C could make his answer-key?

(1) 2 (2) 3 (3) 4 (4) 5

31. Both G and H were sources to

(1) F (2) B (3) I (4) None of the nine

32. Which of the following statements is true?

(1) C introduced the wrong answer to question 27.

(2) E introduced the wrong answer to question 46.

(3) F introduced the wrong answer to question 14.

(4) H introduced the wrong answer to question 46.

33. Which of the following two groups of people had identical sources?

I. A, D and G

II. E and H

(1) Only I (2) Only II (3) Neither I nor II (4) Both I and II

Directions for questions 34 to 37: Answer the questions on the basis of the following information.

[CAT 2003]

Seven faculty members at a management institute frequent a lounge for strong coffee and stimulating conversation. On being asked about their visit to the lounge last Friday we got the following responses.

JC: I came in first, and the next two persons to enter were SS and SM. When I left the lounge, JP and VR were present in the lounge. DG left with me.

JP: When I entered the lounge with VR, JC was sitting there. There was someone else, but I cannot remember who it was.

SM: I went to the lounge for a short while, and met JC, SS and DG in the lounge that day.

SS: I left immediately after SM left.

DG: I met JC, SS, SM, JP and VR during my first visit to the lounge, I went back to my office with JC. When I went to the lounge the second time, JP and VR were there.

PK: I had some urgent work, so I did not sit in the lounge that day, but just collected my coffee and left. JP and DG were the only people in the lounge while I was there.

VR: No comments.

34. Based on the responses, which of the two, JP or DG, entered the lounge first?

(1) JP

(2) DG

(3) Both entered together

(4) Cannot be determined

35. Who was sitting with JC when JP entered the lounge?

(1) SS (2) SM (3) DG (4) PK

36. How many of the seven members did VR meet on Friday in the lounge?

(1) 2 (2) 3 (3) 4 (4) 5

37. Who were the last two faculty members to leave the lounge?

(1) JC and DG (2) PK and DG (3) JP and PK (4) JP and DG

Directions for questions 38 to 41: Answer the questions on the basis of the information given below.

[CAT 2004]

Coach John sat with the score cards of Indian players from the 3 games in a one-day cricket tournament where the same set of players played for India and all the major batsmen got out. John summarized the batting performance through three diagrams, one for each game. In each diagram, the three outer triangles communicate the number of runs scored by the three top scores from India, where K, R, S, V, and Y represent Kaif, Rahul, Saurav, Virender, and Yuvraj respectively. The middle triangle in each diagram denotes the percentage of the total score that was scored by the top three Indian scorers in that game. No two players score the same number of runs in the same game. John also calculated two batting indices for each player based on his scores in the tournaments; the R-index of a batsman is the difference between his highest and lowest scores in the 3 games while the M-index is the middle number, if his scores are arranged in a non-increasing order.

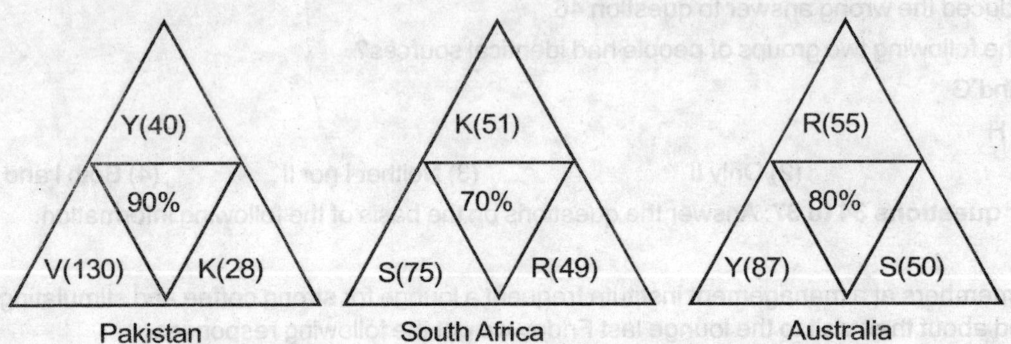

38. For how many Indian players is it possible to calculate the exact M-index?

(1) 0 (2) 1 (3) 2 (4) More than 2

39. Among the players mentioned, who can have the lowest R-index from the tournament?

(1) Only Kaif, Rahul or Yuvraj (2) Only Kaif or Rahul

(3) Only Kaif or Yuvraj (4) Only Kaif

40. How many players among those listed definitely scored less than Yuvraj in the tournament?

(1) 0 (2) 1 (3) 2 (4) More than 2

41. Which of the players had the best M-index from the tournament?

(1) Rahul (2) Saurav (3) Virender (4) Yuvraj

Directions for questions 42 to 45: Answer the questions on the basis of the information given below.

[CAT 2004]

The year was 2006. All six teams in Pool A of World Cup hockey, play each other exactly once. Each win earns a team three points, a draw earns one point and a loss earns zero points. The two teams with the highest points qualify for the semifinals. In case of a tie, the team with the highest goal difference (Goal For - Goals Against) qualifies.

In the opening match, Spain lost to Germany. After the second round (after each team played two matches), the pool table looked as shown below.

Pool A

Teams	Games Played	Won	Drawn	Lost	Goals For	Goals Against	Points
Germany	2	2	0	0	3	1	6
Argentina	2	2	0	0	2	0	6
Spain	2	1	0	1	5	2	3
Pakistan	2	1	0	1	2	1	3
New Zealand	2	0	0	2	1	6	0
South Africa	2	0	0	2	1	4	0

In the third round, Spain played Pakistan, Argentina played Germany, and New Zealand played South Africa. All the third round matches were drawn. The following are some results from the fourth and fifth round matches

(1) Spain won both the fourth and fifth round matches.

(2) Both Argentina and Germany won their fifth round matches by 3 goals to 0.

(3) Pakistan won both the fourth and fifth round matches by 1 goal to 0.

42. Which one of the following statements is true about matches played in the first two rounds?

(1) Germany beat New Zealand by 1 goal to 0.

(2) Spain beat New Zealand by 4 goals to 0.

(3) Spain beat South Africa by 2 goals to 0.

(4) Germany beat South Africa by 2 goals to 1.

43. Which one of the following statements is true about matches played in the first two rounds?

(1) Pakistan beat South Africa by 2 goals to 1.

(2) Argentina beat Pakistan by 1 goal to 0.

(3) Germany beat Pakistan by 2 goals to 1.

(4) Germany beat Spain by 2 goals to 1.

44. If Pakistan qualified as one of the two teams from Pool A, which was the other team that qualified?

(1) Argentina (2) Germany (3) Spain (4) Cannot be determined

45. Which team finished at the top of the pool after five rounds of matches?

(1) Argentina (2) Germany (3) Spain (4) Cannot be determined

Directions for questions 46 to 49: Answer the questions on the basis of the information given below:

[CAT 2005]

Help Distress (HD) is an NGO involved in providing assistance to people suffering from natural disasters. Currently, it has 37 volunteers. They are involved in three projects: Tsunami Relief (TR) in Tamil Nadu, Flood Relief (FR in Maharashtra, and Earthquake Relief (ER) in Gujarat. Each volunteer working with Help Distress has to be involved in at least one relief work project.

- A maximum number of volunteers are involved in the FR project. Among them, the number of volunteers involved in FR project alone is equal to the volunteers having additional involvement in the ER project.
- The number of volunteers involved in the ER project alone is double the number of volunteers involved in all the three projects.
- 17 volunteers are involved in the TR project.
- The number of volunteers involved in the TR project alone is one less than the number of volunteers involved in ER project alone.
- Ten volunteers involved in the TR project are also involved in at least one more project.

46. Based on the information given above, the minimum number of volunteers involved in both FR and TR projects, but not in the ER project is

(1) 1 (2) 3 (3) 4 (4) 5

47. Which of the following additional information would enable to find the exact number of volunteers involved in various projects?

(1) Twenty volunteers are involved in FR.

(2) Four volunteers are involved in all the three projects.

(3) Twenty three volunteers are involved in exactly one project.

(4) No need for any additional information.

48. After some time, the volunteers who were involved in all the three projects were asked to withdraw from one project. As a result, one of the volunteers opted out of the TR project, and one opted out of the ER project, while the remaining ones involved in all the three projects opted out of the FR project. Which of the following statements, then, necessarily follows?

(1) The lowest number of volunteers is now in TR project.

(2) More volunteers are now in FR project as compared to ER project.

(3) More volunteers are now in TR project as compared to ER project.

(4) None of the above.

49. After the withdrawal of volunteers, as indicated in Question 89, some new volunteers joined the NGO. Each one of them was allotted only one project in a manner such that, the number of volunteers working in one project alone for each of the three projects became identical. At that point, it was also found that the number of volunteers involved in FR and ER projects was the same as the number of volunteers involved in TR and ER projects. Which of the projects now has the highest number of volunteers?

(1) ER (2) FR (3) TR (4) Cannot be determined

ANSWER KEYS

PRACTICE EXERCISE – 1

1. (3)	**2.** (3)	**3.** (2)	**4.** (4)	**5.** (1)	**6.** (2)	**7.** (2)	**8.** (4)	**9.** (4)	**10.** (1)
11. (3)	**12.** (1)	**13.** (1)	**14.** (2)	**15.** (2)	**16.** (4)	**17.** (1)	**18.** (4)	**19.** (3)	**20.** (4)
21. (2)	**22.** (2)	**23.** (4)	**24.** (2)	**25.** (3)	**26.** (1)	**27.** (2)	**28.** (3)	**29.** (3)	**30.** (4)
31. (1)	**32.** (2)	**33.** (4)	**34.** (3)	**35.** (2)	**36.** (1)	**37.** (2)	**38.** (1)	**39.** (3)	**40.** (4)
41. (3)	**42.** (3)	**43.** (4)	**44.** (2)	**45.** (3)	**46.** (4)	**47.** (4)	**48.** (2)		

PRACTICE EXERCISE – 2

1. (3)	**2.** (3)	**3.** (2)	**4.** (1)	**5.** (2)	**6.** (4)	**7.** (4)	**8.** (4)	**9.** (3)	**10.** (3)
11. (3)	**12.** (2)	**13.** (3)	**14.** (4)	**15.** (4)	**16.** (3)	**17.** (3)	**18.** (1)	**19.** (1)	**20.** (3)
21. (3)	**22.** (3)	**23.** (2)	**24.** (1)	**25.** (3)	**26.** (1)	**27.** (4)	**28.** (1)	**29.** (2)	**30.** (3)
31. (4)	**32.** (3)	**33.** (4)	**34.** (2)	**35.** (3)	**36.** (2)	**37.** (4)	**38.** (3)	**39.** (1)	**40.** (2)
41. (2)	**42.** (4)	**43.** (2)	**44.** (4)	**45.** (4)	**46.** (3)	**47.** (1)	**48.** (2)	**49.** (4)	

EXPLANATIONS

PRACTICE EXERCISE – 1

For questions 1 to 4:

Step 1: From the data given we can analyse and classify the information as shown below.

Switch	Can supply any two of the following (We do not yet know which two)
1	Limca, Coca-cola, Mirinda, Pepsi
2	7-up, Coca-cola, Mirinda, Pepsi
3	7-up, Limca, Mirinda, Pepsi
4	7-up, Limca, Coca-cola, Pepsi
5	7-up, Limca, Coca-cola, Mirinda

We also note that if the switches are turned on, the common drinks are nullified.

⇒ (1) When two switches are turned on and if there is no overlapping, 4 different items would come out.
(2) When two switches are turned on and if there is one common item, two different items would come out.
(3) By the condition given it is seen that no two switches are giving both identical items.

Step 2: Now we will form the final table that gives the exact switch-item combination from I. 1 and 3 give 7-up and Mirinda. From the above table, it is seen that 1 just cannot supply 7-up. Hence 7-up has to definitely come from switch 3. Hence Mirinda has to definitely come from switch 1.

From III, 1 and 2 give Coca-cola and Pepsi. Hence, it means that Mirinda of switch 1 which has not come out as it was cancelled by switch 2. Hence switch 2 definitely gives Mirinda. Therefore, switch 2 must account for Mirinda and one of Coca-cola and Pepsi but not both. It follows that switch 1 must account for one of Coca-cola and Pepsi but not both.

From IV, switches 1 and 4 give Limca, Coca-cola, Mirinda and Pepsi. This means there is nothing common between these two switches. (Hence 4 items have come out). This means that switch 4 definitely has Limca because Mirinda is near to 1. This also means that switch 4 has either Pepsi or Coca-cola but not both.

We see that 2, 3 and 5 together give Limca, Coca-cola, Mirinda and Pepsi. Since we already know that switch 3 contains 7-up which has not come out, 7-up must be present in switch 5. Since Mirinda has come out from 2, it means that 3 and 5 do not have Mirinda.

From II, we see that 2, 4 and 5 give 7-up and Mirinda. This means that Limca from 4 has been cancelled by Limca from some other switch. Since 2 cannot have Limca, Limca must be present in switch 5.

From VI again, 2, 3 and 5 give Limca, Coca-cola, Mirinda and Pepsi. Hence, 3 cannot have Limca. So 3 has Pepsi for sure.

So the final table is:

Switch	Supplies
1	Mirinda, Pepsi
2	Coca-cola, Mirinda
3	7-up, Pepsi
4	Limca, Coca-cola
5	7-up, Limca

Now all the questions can be solved directly.

1. Mirinda is one of the drinks that would be supplied by turning on switch 1.
2. 7-up is one of the drinks that would be supplied by turning on switch 3.
3. Mirinda is one of the drinks that would be supplied by turning on switch 2.
4. Coca-cola, Mirinda, Pepsi and 7-up are supplied by turning on switches 2 and 3.

For questions 5 to 8:

Loser is knocked out of tournament, so every player will lose one match except the winner of the tournament. So there will be 6 matches in the tournament. Since loser is replaced by higher ranked player, Anand would have played last two matches only, because rank 1 player cannot be replaced by anyone. Since last rank player cannot replace anyone so he would have definitely played first match.

Rank 1 must have played match number 5 and 6 only. Rank 2 must have played match 4, as he was replaced by rank 1 in 5th match. Rank 2 must have played maximum three matches i.e. match number 2, 3 and 4; which means he replaced rank 3. So rank1 cannot play against rank 3 in his last match.

If rank 1 plays against rank 6 in his last match then he would have played rank 7 in 5th match but it is not possible because rank 7 can play maximum three matches i.e. match number 1, 2 and 3. In the question it is also given that rank 5 player did not play in the last match.

So rank 1 can play against rank 4 in the last match. And the following possibilities arise.

The tables below give the ranks of two players in each match starting from first match.

Ist match →	7-3	7-3	7-3
IInd match →	6-3	6-3	7-2
IIIrd match →	5-3	6-2	6-2
IVth match →	5-2	5-2	5-2
Vth match →	5-1	5-1	5-1
VIth match →	4-1	4-1	4-1

5. The number of matches is one for rank 4 player in all the possibilities. For every other player, except Anand, the number of matches played is not unique in all the possibilities.

6. The sum of ranks of two player in match number 3 will be 8 (6 + 2) or (5 + 3).
7. Only Anand could have beaten Michael in the tournament.
8. Topolov can play either 1 or 2 matches.
9. If Bharat and Shilpa are in team Crux then their team will be Bharat, Shilpa, Chetna & Kamal

   If they are in team Shivel then their team can be either – Bharat, Shilpa, Richa & Akash or it can be Bharat, Shilpa, Richa & Dimple. So no one is part of their team in all the three possibilities.
10. If the team Crux will have two males then team Shivel will also have two males and two females. And the possible combination in this team are-

    Richa, Bharat, Akash & Shilpa

    Richa, Bharat, Kamal & Dimple

    Richa, Prakash, Akash, Dimple
11. One team will have three males and one female, while other team will have one male and three females. And the possible combinations are –

    (1) Team Crux – Chetna, Akash, Kamal, Prakash & Team Shivel – Richa, Bharat, Shilpa, Dimple

    (2) Team Crux – Chetna, Prakash, Shilpa, Dimple & Team Shivel – Richa, Bharat, Akash, Kamal

    So Prakash & Chetna are always in same team so as Bharat & Richa
12. If Prakash and Kamal are in different teams then Kamal and bharat will be in same team. And in that case teams can be formed in following ways –

    (1) Team Crux – Chetna, Prakash, Shilpa, Dimple & Team Shivel – Richa, Bharat, Akash, Kamal

    (2) Team Crux – Chetna, Akash, Prakash, Shilpa & Team Shivel – Richa, Kamal, bharat, Dimple

    (3) Team Crux – Chetna, Kamal, Bharat, Shilpa & Team Shivel – Richa, Prakash, Dimple, Akash

    So only Chetna & Shilpa are always together in all the cases.

For questions 13 to 16:

From statements (2) and (5), Gardening is pursue by either 4 or 5 siblings. Using (6), Pulkit does not pursue Gardening, hence it is pursued by 4 siblings, all except Pulkit. From statements (1) and (5), Guitar is pursued only by Akash and Vasav, and the other activity which both Akash and Vasav pursue is Gardening.

From statements (3) and (5), Singing is pursued by Pulkit, Nishit and Richa. From statement (4), Richa pursue only Singing and Gardening. So Singing is pursued by Pulkit, Nishit and Richa. Since Akash and Pulkit do not pursue same activity, so Vasav pursues Dancing, along with Pulkit and Nishit.

Using statement (7), Vasav cannot pursue Painting, otherwise he will pursue 4 activities, which will be more than that pursued by Akash, i.e 2. Hence Akash and Nishit pursue Painting.

Activity	Siblings pursuing the activity
Dancing	Pulkit, Nishit, Vasav
Singing	Pulkit, Nishit, Richa
Guitar	Akash, Vasav
Painting	Nishit, Akash
Gardening	Nishit, Richa, Akash, Vasav

13. Akash pursues Painting
14. Akash pursues three activities
15. The common activities pursued by Vasav and Nishit are Gardening and Dancing
16. Singing are pursued by Richa, Nishit and Pulkit.

For questions 17 to 20:

Using statements II and III, we have the following two possibilities

Pakistan	———	Terrorist	———	Terrorist	———
India	Mine	———	Mine	———	———

Pakistan	———	———	Terrorist	———	Terrorist
India	———	Mine	———	Mine	———

Using statements IV, we can rule out the first possibility and using statement I, we get the following argument

Pakistan	———	———	Terrorist	———	Terrorist
India	Terrorist	Mine	———	Mine	Bazooka

Using statement V, we get the final arrangement as–

Pakistan	———	———	Terrorist	———	Terrorist
India	Terrorist	Mine	———	Mine	Bazooka

17. From the arrangement, we can say that only option (a) true.
18. The traitor, the soldier with Bazooka, and the soldier who is neither a traitor nor carrying the Bazooka are all neighbours of either of the soldier standing on the mine.

For questions 21 to 24:

Number of poets born in 1970s = 2

Number of poets born in 1980s = 3

Number of poets born in 1990s = 1

Poets = 4

Novelists = 3

Dramatist = 3

Bengali = 1

Hindi = 2

Marathi = 2

Tamil = 1

Using the given data

	Decade	Field	Language
A	1990s	Poetry	Marathi
B	1980s	Drama	Hindi
C	1970s	Poetry, Novel, Drama	Marathi
D	1980s	Novel, Poetry	Hindi
E	1980s	Novel, Drama	Tamil
F	1970s	Poetry	Bengali

For questions 25 to 28:

According to the given information, we can draw the following table.

	Rash	Fever	Headache	Sore throat
G	√	√	√	×
L	√	√	×	×
T	Possible	Possible	√	√
Z	×	Possible	√	Possible

Or

	Rash	Fever	Headache	Sore throat
G	√	√	×	√
L	√	√	×	×
T	Possible	Possible	√	√
Z	×	Possible	√	Possible

25. As patient exhibits sore throat and fever, she does not have disease L.

26. As patient does not exhibits rash, she must have either Z or T. Hence, she definitely exhibits headache.

27. As the patient exhibits neither fever nor sore throat, she must have disease Z. Hence, she definitely exhibits headache.

28. The required disease is L as a patient suffering for it exhibits exactly two symptoms.

For questions 29 to 32:

From statement (I) and (II), A, B, D, E and H could have attended the fitness center in one of the following ways:

	(i)	(ii)	(iii)	(iv)	(v)	(vi)	(vii)	(viii)
Tue	DE_	DE_	DE_	DE_	DE_	DE_	DE_	DE_
Wed	DE_		D_ _	E_ _	DE_		D_ _	E_ _
Thu		DE_	E_ _	D_ _		DE_	E_ _	D_ _
Fri	DE_	DE_	DE_	DE_	DE_	DE_	DE_	DE_
Sat	ABH	ABH	ABH	ABH				
Sun					ABH	ABH	ABH	ABH

Case (i), (ii), (v) and (vi) would violate the condition that exactly four persons visit the fitness center on more than two days.

Hence, the final possible scenarios are as follows:

	(i)	(ii)	(iii)	(iv)
Tue	DE_	DE_	DE_	DE_
Wed	DCF	ECF	DCF	ECF
Thu	ECF	DCF	ECF	DCF
Fri	DE_	DE_	DE_	DE_
Sat	ABH	ABH	CF_	CF_
Sun	CF_	CF_	ABH	ABH

Since, B, I and J visit the center only once and on different days of the week, one of the remaining spots in each of the four cases will be filled by one of A, D and E.

29. C, F, D and E are the only people who could have visited the center on exactly three days. Out of these, C and F definitely visited the center on exactly three days.

30. In the second table above cases (ii) and (iv) are no longer possible. It can also be seen that A would visit the center on Monday. Thus, I visits the center on Sunday.

31. If E and I visit the fitness center on Sunday and Friday respectively then, J visits the center on Tuesday.

32. D and E are the only ones who can visit the center on four days.

For questions 33 to 36: From the given information, we can find the number of lines typed per day by the given persons.

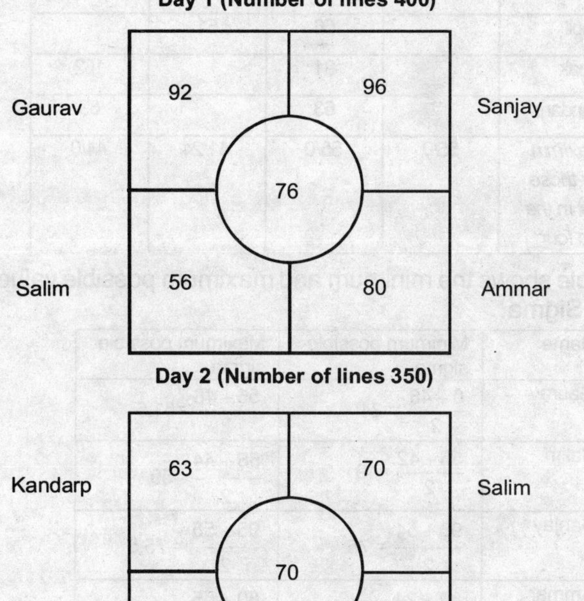

Day 3 (Number of lines 300)

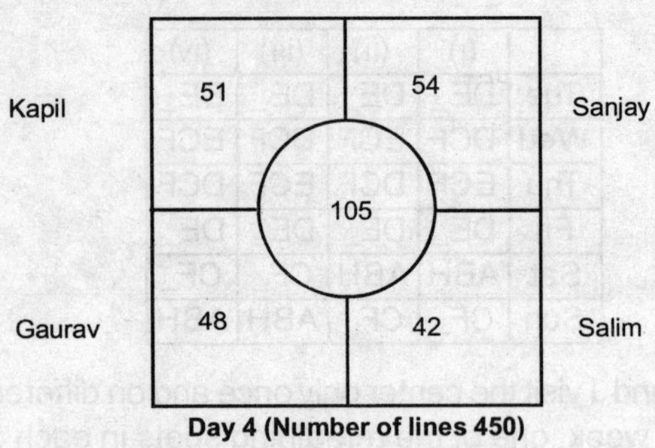

Day 4 (Number of lines 450)

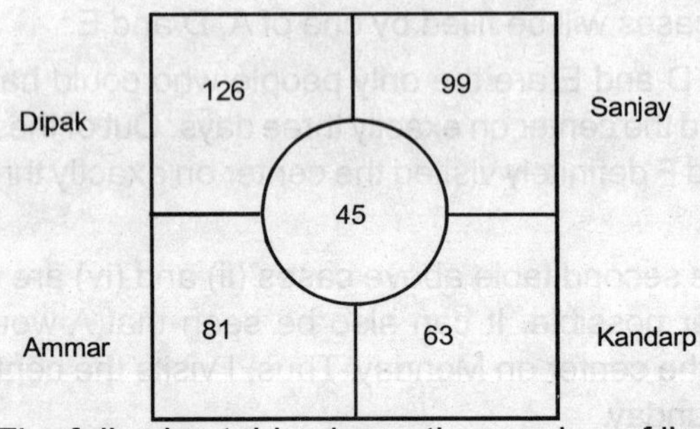

The following table shows the number of lines typed by the seven typist during the four days period:

Name	Day 1 (Total = 400)	Day 2 (Total = 350)	Day 3 (Total = 300)	Day 4 (Total = 450)
Gaurav	92		48	
Salim	56	70	42	
Sanjay	96		54	99
Ammar	80			81
Kapil		56	51	
Dipak		91		162
Kandarp		63		63
Max/min for those not in the top four	55/0	55/0	41/24	44/0

Table shows the minimum and maximum possible values of Sigma.

Name	Minimum possible sigma	Maximum possible sigma
Gaurav	$\frac{0+48}{2} = 24$	$\frac{55+48}{2} = 51.5$
Salim	$\frac{56+42}{2} = 49$	$\frac{56+44}{2} = 50$
Sanjay	$\frac{96+54}{2} = 75$	$\frac{96+55}{2} = 75.5$
Ammar	$\frac{80+24}{2} = 52$	$\frac{80+55}{2} = 67.5$
Kapil	$\frac{51+0}{2} = 25.5$	$\frac{51+55}{2} = 53$
Kandarp	$\frac{63+24}{2} = 43.5$	$\frac{63+55}{2} = 59$
Dipak	$\frac{91+24}{2} = 57.5$	$\frac{91+55}{2} = 73$

33. Only in case of Sanjay, there lies only one integer between the highest and lowest possible values of Sigma, and thus only for him the a unique value of Sigma can be calculated. Hence, there are six typist for whom value of Sigma cannot be calculated.

34. For both Sanjay and Salim, PV can be zero as shown in the following table.

Name	Day 1	Day 2	Day 3	Day 4	PV
Salim	56	70	42	28	0
Sanjay	96	51	54	99	0

35. Maximum lines that Kapil can type was (55 + 56 + 51 + 44 = 206). From the table, it can be seen that Sanjay and Dipak definitely typed more number of pages than what Kapil did.

36. From the table, it can be seen that the difference for Sanjay is the least, which is 0.5.

For question 37 to 40:

From (I) Saptarsh has at least 3 balls and the number of balls can be 3, 6, 9 12, 15, 18, 21 ...

From (II) Rushat has at least 4 balls and the sequence can be 4, 8, 12, 16, 20, ...

From (III) Trivendra has at least 5 balls and the sequence can be 5, 7, 9, 11, 13, 15 ....

The total number of balls is at least 12 and atmost 24.

If total number of balls is even, then Saptarsh will have an odd number of balls and vice versa.

Make different combinations

The total cannot be 13 because no numbers gives a sum of 13.

Total cannot be 12, 14, 15 and 17 because the number of balls with each person; which will contradict statement (IV).

Total cannot be 18, 20, 21, 22, 23 or 24, because then number of balls could be known for anybody; which contradicts statement (IV). So the total number of balls with the three is either 16 or 19. Following are the possible compositions:

16 = 3 + 8 + 5 = 3 + 4 + 9

19 = 6 + 8 + 5 = 6 + 4 + 9

If the total is 19 then Saptarsh much have even number of balls which is less than 19 – (4 + 5) = 10.

Therefore, Saptarsh much have either 3 or 6 balls. Rushat and Trivendra together have 13 balls. Rushat can have either 4 or 8 balls. Trivendra can have either 9 or 5 balls.

∴ The number of balls with Rushat and Trivendra cannot be known. Speaker is Saptarsh.

37. The number of ball with the three cannot be more than 19.

38. Speaker is Saptarsh.

39. The number of ball with Saptarsh cannot be more than 6.

40. The number of balls with Rushat cannot be calculated.

For questions 41 to 44:

The person, who gets the highest amount, will get at least one third of the total amount, and since each of them got Rs. 100 or more so highest amount can be Rs. 300. As highest received amount is a perfect square and has two digits repeated, the only possible value is Rs. 225.

These three persons are either truth teller or alternator, so at least one statement of each will be true. If second statement of Atul is true then he will have more amount than Rs. 250 and definitely have the highest amount. This contradicts the above conclusion that highest amount is Rs. 225. So second statement made by Atul is false, hence his first statement is true. So he received the highest amount i.e. Rs. 225.

If Atul got highest amount then second statement made by Bharat is false, so Bharat's first statement will be true. Hence, amount with Bharat is a perfect square. So he can received any of the following amounts i.e. Rs. 100/121/144/169.

This gives us possible amount with Chirag – Rs. 175/ 154/ 131/106 in same order corresponding to the amount with Bharat. So second statement made by Chirag is definitely true but his 1st statement can be either true or false.

41. Amount only with Atul can be determined uniquely.

42. (a) There are two cases where Bharat gets the lowest amount

(b) There are 3 cases possible

(d) This is there in all 4 cases

Only with statement (c) we get unique distribution, that is, Bharat got Rs. 100 and Chirag got Rs. 175.

43. Atul and Bharat are alternators and Chirag can be either truth teller or alternator. So we cannot determine that how many truth tellers there are.

44. This is possible when Bharat got Rs. 100 and difference between his and Atul's amount will be Rs. 125 i.e. a perfect cube. Hence, Chirag will get Rs. 175.

For questions 45 to 48:

The given information can be summarized as shown below:

P → Banker

Q → Teacher

R → Doctor

S → Lawyer / Engineer / CA

T → Architect

V → Engineer / CA

W → Lawyer / Engineer

Arrangement on the basis of their income:

T(–)	< Q(–)	< P	< S/V	< W/S	< V/W	< R
Architect	Teacher	Banker	CA	Lawyer	Engineer	Doctor

(–) represents sure-shot female members.

45. R earns maximum in the family.

46. P's position is fifth from the top.

47. V is either Engineer or CA.

48. There are at least three male members (S, V and W) are in the family.

PRACTICE EXERCISE – 2

1. The number of cubes with both red and green colours on them will be maximum when the faces of cube, to be painted with same colours, are opposite to each other. All the cubes on corner will have both and red, and blue as well, i.e. 8. Number of cubes with exactly two faces painted, one each in red and green will be = 4 × (6 – 2) = 16. So total will be 24.

2. The number of cubes with all three colours on them will be maximum when the faces of cubes, to be painted with same colour, are opposite to each other. All the corners will have three different colours, that is 8 small cubes.

The number of cubes with all three colours on them will be minimum when the faces of cubes, to be painted with same colour, are adjacent faces. Only two corners will have three different colours.

3. The number of cubes with all three colours on them will include the cubes –

(i) which already had three colours on them

(ii) which had blue and green painted on it

The sum of these two will be minimum when red is painted on two opposite faces. And blue and green are painted on faces which are adjacent.

Number of cubes of type (i) will be 4 and of type (ii) will be 4+4 = 8. So the total is 4+8 = 12.

4. The number will be maximum when the faces of cubes, to be painted with same colour, are adjacent faces.

The number of cubes with one colour painted on only one face = $6 \times (6-2)^2 = 96$

The number of cubes with one colour on two faces

= 3 × (6 – 2) = 12

Total number of cubes will be 96 + 12 = 108.

For questions 5 to 8:

Dinesh cannot be a truth teller, in that case Vivek and Jatin both will have yellow car, which is not possible. Also if Prakash's 2nd statement is true then 1st will also be true.

If Dinesh's first statement is false and 2nd is true, then other conditions will be contradictory. If Dinesh's 1st statement is true and 2nd is false, then Jatin's 1st statement and Vivek's 2nd statement will be false. If Jatin's 2nd statement is true then, Vivek has to be a liar, in which case he will have either red or blue car, which is false. So Jatin will be a liar if Dinesh is an alternator. So Dinesh will have green car, and from Vivek's 1st statement he will have yellow car. Prakash will be the truth teller and hence he will have red car, from his 2nd statement.

Dinesh can be a liar. If Jatin's 1st statement is truth the nother conditions will be contradictory. So Jatin's 1st statement will be false and 2nd will be true. Then Vivek's 2nd statement will be true. Now two case are possible in this as well –

i) If Vivek's 1st statement is true then he will have green car. Then Prakash's 2nd statement will be false and 1st true, and hence he will have blue car.

ii) If Vivek's 1st statement is false then Prakash will be truth teller. Prakash will have red car and Vivek will have blue car. Dinesh will have yellow and Jatin will have green.

	Case I	Case II	Case III	Case IV	Case V
Prakash	TT, Red	Alt, Blue	TT, Red	Alt, Green	Alt, Yellow
Vivek	Alt, Yellow	TT, Green	Alt, Blue	L, Blue	TT, Green
Dinesh	Alt, Green	L, Yellow	L, Yellow	Alt, Red	L, Red
Jatin	L, Blue	Alt, Red	Alt, Green	TT, Yellow	Alt, Blue

(Note: TT is truth teller, Alt is alternator, L is liar)

5. Dinesh cannot be truth teller.

6. If the colour of Vivek's car is blue, then either Prakash's or Jatin's car is green.

7. Case I and Case III, in both cases Prakash has red car. Yellow car can be with Vivek or Dinesh.

8. Prakash is not the liar in any of the case.

9. Sati-Savitri starts at the earliest.

So we view it first.

(1) *Sati-Savitri* — 9.00 a.m. to 10.00 a.m.

(2) *Veer Abhimanu* — 10.00 a.m. to 11.00 a.m.

(3) *Jhansi Ki Rani/Sundar Kand* — 11.00 a.m. to 11.30 a.m.

(4) *Joru Ka Ghulam* — 11.30 a.m. to 12.30 p.m.

Now lunch break from 12.30 p.m. to 1.30 p.m.

At 1.30 p.m. he can takes the show of only *Jhansi Ki Rani* so it cannot be viewed at 3rd.

(5) *Jhansi Ki Rani* — 1.30 p.m. to 2.00 p.m.

(6) *Reshma aur Shera* 2.00 p.m. to 3.00 p.m.

Hence, option (c) is best.

10. Three children Vaibhav, Suprita and Anshuman.

Vaibhav > Suprita

↓

(Born in April)

One of children is born in September, but it is not Vaibhav, so it has to be Anshuman.

So Vaibhav is born in June and is 7-year-old. Vaibhav is 7-year-old and Anshuman is not 4-year-old.

So Suprita is 4-year-old.

Youngest child is 2-year-old and it has to be Anshuman.

Vaibhav > Suprita > Anshuman

(June, 7 years) (April, 4 years) (Sept., 2-year-old)

Hence, (c) is the answer.

11. We can find out the time for lunch of respective families from the table below:

Family/Time	12:00	1:00	2:00
Sharma	✓		
Banerjee			✓
Pattabhiraman	✓		

Fried brinjal → Chinaware

Sambar → White Chinaware

Makkai-ki-roti → Red Chinaware

The family that eats at 1 o'clock serves fried brinjal, hence Pattabhiraman serves fried brinjal.

The family that eats last like makkai-ki-roti so Banaerjees like makkai-ki-roti. Sharmas are left with sambar.

Sharma - 12:00 - Sambar - White

Pattabhiraman - 1:00 - Fried brinjal - Blue

Bannerjees - 2:00 - Makkai-ki-roti - Red

Hence, (c) is the best option.

12. We have two possible cases:

Case I:

	F	T
Shopkeeper 1:	Black hair	Long tail
	F	T
Shopkeeper 2:	Short tail	Wore a collar
	T	F
Shopkeeper 3:	White hair	No collar

Case II:

	T	F
Shop keeper 1: Black hair		Long tail
	T	F
Shop keeper 2:	Short tail	Wore a collar
	F	T
Shop keeper 3:	White hair	No collar

Hence, we see only option (b) is correct.

13. Statement I tells us that

(1) Ashish is not an engineer, (2) Ashish got more offers than the engineers.

Hence, Ashish did not have 0 offers.

After this the following table can be achieved.

Profession	Names	Offers				
		3	2	1	0	X Profession
CA	Ashish	×	×	✓	×	X Engineer
MD	Dhanraj	✓	×	×	×	X Engineer
Economist	Sameer	×	✓	×	×	
Engineer		×	×	×	✓	

From statement IV, Dhanraj is not at 0 and 1.

14. Option (3) is ruled out by statement VII.

Option (1) is ruled out by statements VII and VIII.

From statement IV, Sandeep had Rs. 30 to start and Daljeet Rs. 20.

From statement II, option (2) is not possible as Sandeep was left with Re 1, he spent Rs. 29. But according to (2) he spent Rs. 1.50 more than Daljeet. But Daljeet had only Rs. 20. Hence option (4) is correct.

15. Data insufficient, please check the question.

16. Statements V and VI rule out options (1) and (2). Since contestants from Bangalore and Pune did not come first, school from Hyderabad can come first. Convent is not in Hyderabad which rules out option (4).

17. The only two possible combinations are:

Younger	Older
2	4
3	9

Cubes of natural numbers are 1, 8, 27, 64, ...

Here, 64 and above are not possible as the age will go above 10 years.

If younger boy is 2 years old, then older boy is 4 years

old. Then, Father's age is 24 years and Mother's age is $\frac{42}{2} = 21$ years.

Also, 24 – 21 = 3

$\therefore$ Age of younger boy = 2 years

18.

Total seats in the hall	200
Seats vacant	20
Total waiting	180
Ladies	72
Seating capacity of flight	$\frac{2}{3} \times 180 = 120$

Number of people in flight A = 100

For flight B = 180 – 100 = 80

Thus, airhostess for A = $\frac{80}{20} = 4$

Empty seats in flight B = 120 – 80 = 40

40 : 4 = 10 : 1

19.

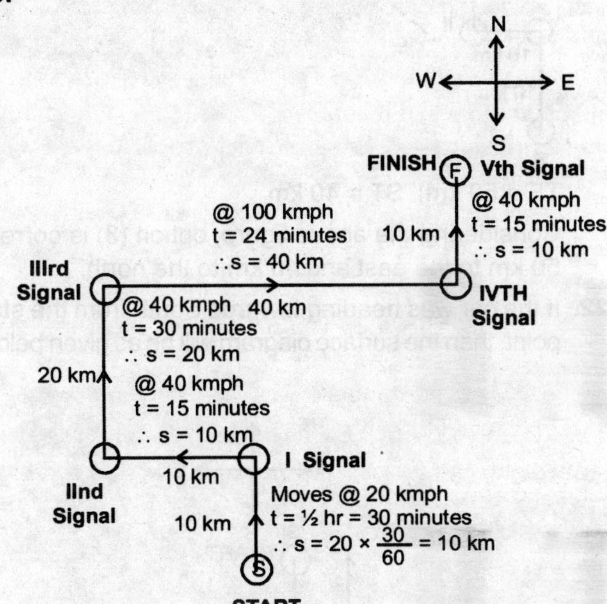

Note: s = Distance covered; v = Velocity (km/hr)

t = Time taken; $s = v \times t$

The total distance travelled by the motorist from the starting point till last signal = 10 + 10 + 20 + 40 + 10 = 90 km.

20.

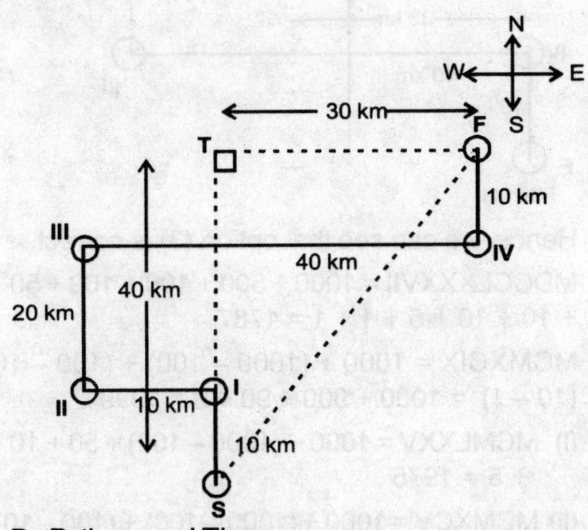

By Pythagoras' Theorem,

$$SF = \sqrt{ST^2 + TF^2} = \sqrt{40^2 + 30^2} = \sqrt{2500} = 50 \text{ km}$$

21. For the case when 1st signal were 1 red and 2 green lights, the surface diagram will be as given below.

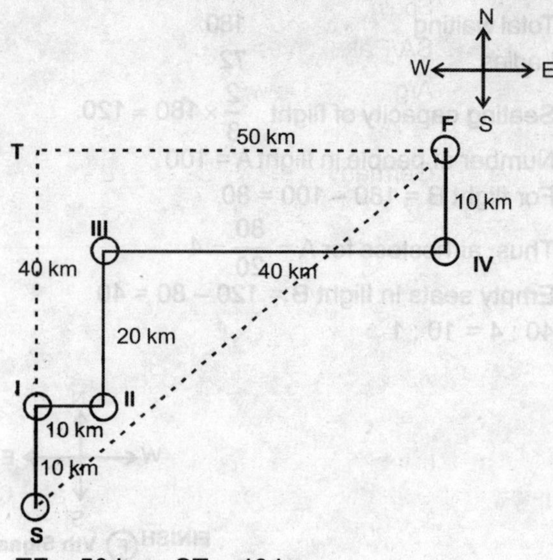

TF = 50 km; ST = 40 km

Considering the above figure, option (3) is correct, 50 km to the east and 40 km to the north.

22. If the car was heading towards South from the start point, then the surface diagram will be as given below.

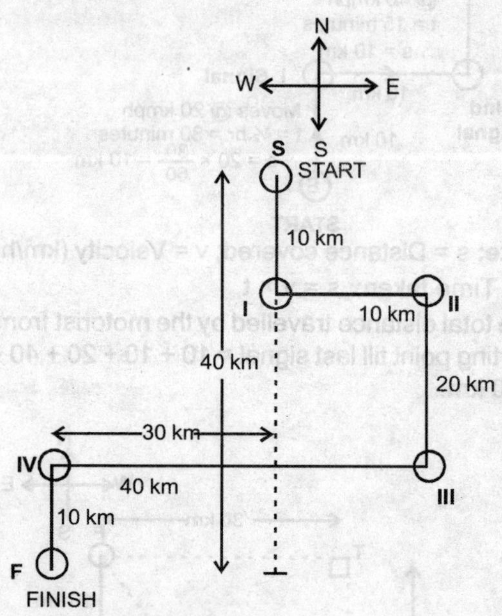

Hence, we can see that option (3) is correct.

23. MDCCLXXXVII = 1000 + 500 + 100 + 100 + 50 + 10 + 10 + 10 + 5 + 1 + 1 = 1787

24. MCMXCIX = 1000 + (1000 – 100) + (100 – 10) + (10 – 1) = 1000 + 900 + 90 + 9 = 1999

25. (I) MCMLXXV = 1000 + (1000 – 100) + 50 + 10 + 10 + 5 = 1975

(II) MCMXCV = 1000 + (1000 – 100) + (100 – 10) + 5 = 1995

(III) MVD = 1000 + (500 – 5) = 1495

(IV) MVM = 1000 + (1000 – 5) = 1995

Therefore, the answer is (II) and (IV), i.e. option (3).

26. $g^2 = g * g = h$

$g^3 = g^2 * g = h * g = f$

$g^4 = g^3 * g = f * g = e$

$\therefore n = 4$

27. $f \oplus [f * \{f \oplus (f * f)\}]$

$= f \oplus [f * \{f \oplus h\}]$

$= f \oplus [f * e\}]$

$= f \oplus [f]]$

$= h$

28. $e^8 = e^2 * e^2 * e^2$

$= e * e * e$

$= e$

If we observe a $_*$ anything = a

$\therefore a^{10} = a$

$\therefore \{a^{10} * (f^{10} \oplus g^9)\} \oplus e^8$

$= a \oplus e = e$

For questions 29 to 32:

If a person copies from one source, he must have the same blank answers as the source and exactly one wrong answer more than the source (as the copier has introduced one wrong answer on his own). If the person copies from two sources, the distinct wrong answers from the two sources would be left blank by the copier and the same wrong answers in the two sources would be copied as it is.

29. A and D have only one source since they have only one wrong answer each.

C may have copied from only one source i.e. I and hence, only B has two sources.

30. I did it before C since 27 is the wrong choice for I. Similarly, A, D and E made keys before C. Hence, 4 people made their keys before C.

31. Both G and H can't be sources to any of F, B or I and hence, (4) is the correct option.

32. F introduced wrong answer to question 14, because nobody else has done question 14 wrong.

33. A, D and G have one distinct wrong answer and no blank answers. So they must have the same source. E and H also have a common wrong answer and no blanks.

Hence, both the groups had identical sources.

For questions 34 to 37:

JC came in first and the next 2 people were SS and SM. When he left, DG left with him. JP and VR stayed behind.

Entry	Exit	Met
JC → SS → SM	JC and DG	JP and VR
JP and VR together		JC and one more person

SS left immediately after SM.

PK only met JP and DG.

The key to this question is that when JP and VR entered apart from JC there was only one other person. This could not have been SS or SM as they came and left together. Hence, this would have to be DG.

Hence, DG came 4th, before JP and is the answer to both 143 and 144.

Now for Qs 145, we need to see how many people VR met. Both SS and SM had already left and JC and DG were sitting. He entered with JP eliminating 2 and 5 from our answer choices. Since PK did not meet VR, the answer is 3 and not 4.

For questions 38 to 41: Go through the following table.

	Pakistan	South Africa	Australia
K	28	51	≤ 48
R	≤ 22	49	55
S	≤ 22	75	50
V	130	< 49	≤ 48
Y	40	< 49	87
Top 3 batsmen	198	175	192
India Total	220	250	240

For questions 42 to 45:

Germany has won both their matches, so possible winning combinations in first two rounds is

R1 : Won 1 - 0 and R2: Won 2 - 1

Or

R1 : Won 2 - 1 and R2: Won 1 - 0.

Argentina must have won R1 and R2 by 1 - 0.

If Germany won by 2 - 1 in R1 vs Spain, Spain won in R2 by 4 - 0, and if Germany won 1 - 0 in R1, then Spain won 5 - 1 in R2.

Since only New Zealand and South Africa conceded 4 or more than 4 goals, then Spain must have played either one in R2.

If Spain won 4 - 0 in R2 vs South Africa, then South Africa must win R1 by 1 - 0, which is a contradiction to the fact that South Africa has lost both R1 and R2. Also, Spain can never win 5 -1 vs South Africa in R2 (goals conceded by South Africa is 4).

Therefore, Spain won against New Zealand in R2.

Germany:

R1	vs	Spain	Won 2 -1 or 1 - 0
R2	vs	SA/Pak	Won 1 - 0 or 2 - 1
R3	vs	Arg	Draw

Spain:

R1	vs	Germany	Lost 1 - 2 or 0 - 1
R2	vs	NZ	Won 4 - 0 or 5 - 1
R3	vs	Pak	Draw

New Zealand:

R1	vs	Arg/Pak	Lost 1 - 2 or 0 - 1
R2	vs	Spain	Lost 0 - 4 or 1 - 5
R3	vs	SA	Draw

Looking at the table, the only possible outcomes for Pakistan in the first two rounds are 2 -0 win and 0 - 1 loss.

In R1, New Zealand cannot lose 1 - 2 since Argentina conceded no goals and Pakistan's only loss was by a margin 0 - 1. Therefore, NZ lost R1 0 - 1. This score is possible only if its opponent is Argentina. Consequently, NZ lost 1 - 5 in R2 vs Spain. Hence, Spain must have lost 0 - 1 to Germany.

The above information can be finally summarised as:

Germany:

R1	vs	Spain	Won 1 - 0
R2	vs	SA	Won 2 - 1
R3	vs	Arg	Draw

Spain:

R1	vs	Germany	Lost 0 - 1
R2	vs	NZ	Won 5 - 1
R3	vs	Pak	Draw

New Zealand:

R1	vs	Arg	Lost 0 - 1
R2	vs	Spain	Lost 1 - 5
R3	vs	SA	Draw

Pakistan:

R1	vs	SA	Won 2 -0
R2	vs	Arg	Lost 0 - 1
R3	vs	Spain	Draw

Argentina:

R1	vs	NZ	Won 1 - 0
R2	vs	Pak	Won 1 - 0
R3	vs	Germany	Draw

South Africa:

R1	vs	Pak	Lost 0 - 2
R2	vs	Germany	Lost 1 - 2
R3	vs	NZ	Draw

Additional information for Q.44-45:

* The given data set for rounds 4 and 5 appears to be inconsistent because from statements (a), (b) and (c) it is evident that four teams namely Spain, Argentina, Germany and Pakistan won their fifth round matches whereas the maximum possible wins in any round is only 3.

For questions 46 to 49:

- 17 in TR

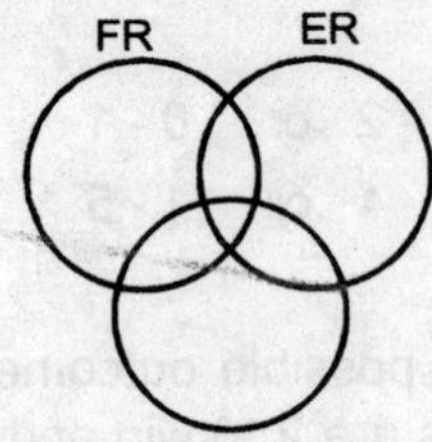

- 10 in TR also in at least one more ⇒ 7 in TR alone

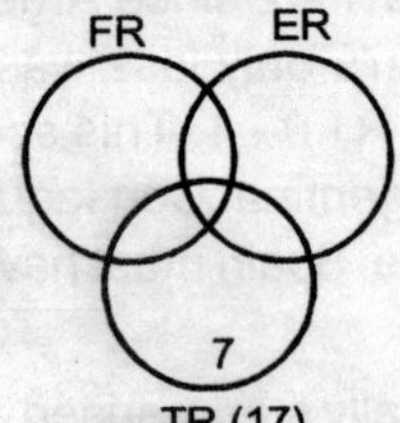

- TR alone = one less than ER alone ⇒ ER alone = 8
- ER alone = double of all 3 ⇒ In all three $= \frac{8}{2} = 4$

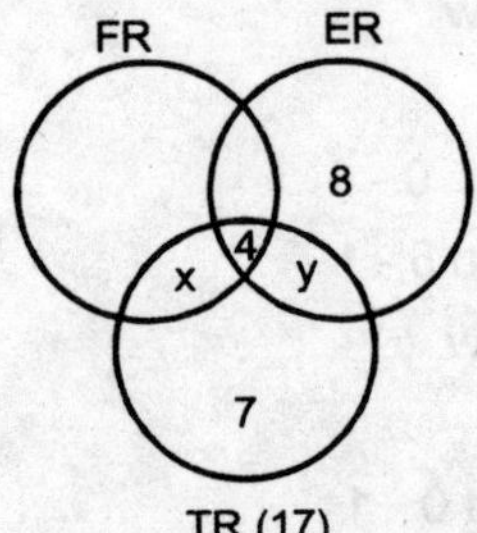

- FR alone = (FR and ER)

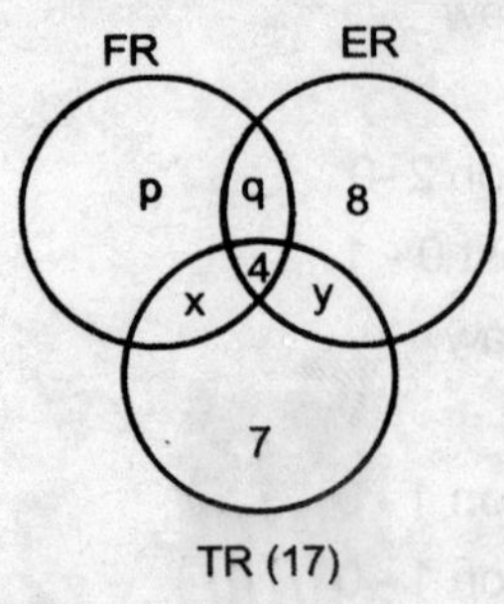

$\Rightarrow p = q + 4$ ...(1)

Total = 37

$[7 + 8 + p + (x + y + q) + 4]$

$= 37 \quad [p + q = 12]$

$\Rightarrow p - a = 4 \Rightarrow p = 8$ and $q = 4$

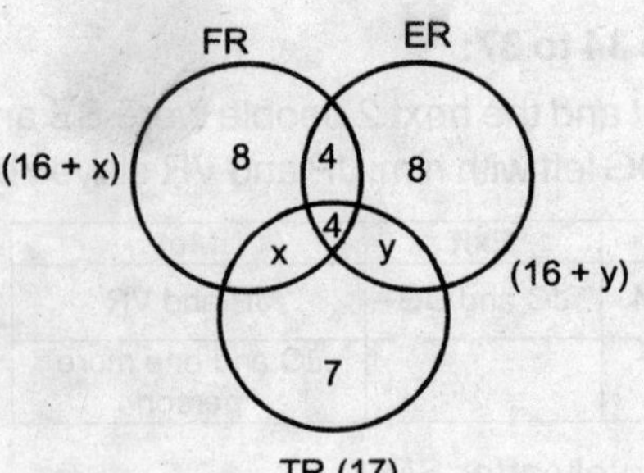

Now, total number of FR is maximum

$\Rightarrow 8 + 4 + 4 + x > 8 + 4 + 4 + y$

$\Rightarrow x > y$ and $x + y = 6$

as $n(TR) = 17$

$= x + y + 4 + 7$

$\Rightarrow x = \{4, 5, 6\}$

$y = \{0, 1, 2\}$

46. Both FR and TR but not ER

$= x$

Minimum $x = 4$

47. Option (2) and option (3) are superfluous. They are not required.

Option (1), if given, would tell us the value of $x = 4$ and hence $y = 2$.

48. Out of 4 who are in all three projects, 2 move out of FR and one-one move out of ER and TR.

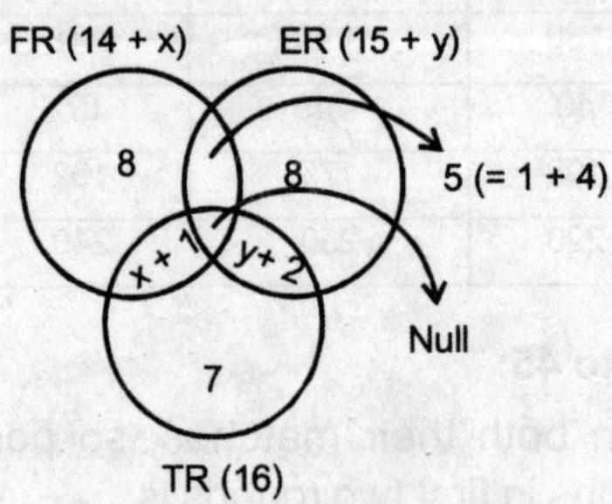

Minimum in FR = 14 + x = 14 + 4 = 18

Maximum in ER = 15 + y = 15 + 2 = 17

$$\left\{\begin{array}{c}\text{As} \\ x = \{4, 5, 6\} \\ y = \{0, 1, 2\}\end{array}\right\}$$

Hence, option (2).

49. FR and ER = 5

ER and TR = y + 2

$\Rightarrow 5 = y + 2$

$\Rightarrow y = 3;$

which is not a possible value as y is 0, 1, or 2 only.

⇒ option (4)

Inconsistent data.

CAT 2019 SOLVED PAPER (SLOT-1)

Section I: VRC

Question Numbers (1 to 5): The passage below is accompanied by a set of five questions. Choose the best answer to each question.

Contemporary internet shopping conjures a perfect storm of choice anxiety. Research has consistently held that people who are presented with a few options make better, easier decisions than those presented with many. . . . Helping consumers figure out what to buy amid an endless sea of choice online has become a cottage industry unto itself. Many brands and retailers now wield marketing buzzwords such as curation, differentiation, and discovery as they attempt to sell an assortment of stuff targeted to their ideal customer. Companies find such shoppers through the data gold mine of digital advertising, which can catalog people by gender, income level, personal interests, and more. Since Americans have lost the ability to sort through the sheer volume of the consumer choices available to them, a ghost now has to be in the retail machine, whether it's an algorithm, an influencer, or some snazzy ad tech to help a product follow you around the internet. Indeed, choice fatigue is one reason so many people gravitate toward lifestyle influencers on Instagram—the relentlessly chic young moms and perpetually vacationing 20-somethings—who present an aspirational worldview, and then recommend the products and services that help achieve it. . . .

For a relatively new class of consumer-products start-ups, there's another method entirely. Instead of making sense of a sea of existing stuff, these companies claim to disrupt stuff as Americans know it. Casper (mattresses), Glossier (makeup), Away (suitcases), and many others have sprouted up to offer consumers freedom from choice: The companies have a few aesthetically pleasing and supposedly highly functional options, usually at mid-range prices. They're selling nice things, but maybe more importantly, they're selling a confidence in those things, and an ability to opt out of the stuff rat race. . . .

One-thousand-dollar mattresses and $300 suitcases might solve choice anxiety for a certain tier of consumer, but the companies that sell them, along with those that attempt to massage the larger stuff economy into something navigable, are still just working within a consumer market that's broken in systemic ways. The presence of so much stuff in America might be more valuable if it were more evenly distributed, but stuff's creators tend to focus their energy on those who already have plenty. As options have expanded for people with disposable income, the opportunity to buy even basic things such as fresh food or quality diapers has contracted for much of America's lower classes.

For start-ups that promise accessible simplicity, their very structure still might eventually push them toward overwhelming variety. Most of these companies are based on hundreds of millions of dollars of venture capital, the investors of which tend to expect a steep growth rate that can't be achieved by selling one great mattress or one great sneaker. Casper has expanded into bedroom furniture and bed linens. Glossier, after years of marketing itself as no-makeup makeup that requires little skill to apply, recently launched a full line of glittering color cosmetics. There may be no way to opt out of stuff by buying into the right thing.

1. Which one of the following best sums up the overall purpose of the examples of Casper and Glossier in the passage?

1. They are exceptions to a dominant trend in consumer markets.
2. They are increasing the purchasing power of poor Americans.
3. They are facilitating a uniform distribution of commodities in the market.
4. They might transform into what they were exceptions to.

2. A new food brand plans to launch a series of products in the American market. Which of the following product plans is most likely to be supported by the author of the passage?

1. A range of 10 products priced between $5 and $10.
2. A range of 25 products priced between $10 and $25.
3. A range of 10 products priced between $10 and $25.
4. A range of 25 products priced between $5 and $10.

3. Which of the following hypothetical statements would add the least depth to the author's prediction of the fate of start-ups offering few product options?

1. Start-ups with few product options are no exception to the American consumer market that is deeply divided along class lines.
2. An exponential surge in their sales enables start-ups to meet their desired profit goals without expanding their product catalogue.
3. With Casper and Glossier venturing into new product ranges, their regular customers start losing trust in the companies and their products.
4. With the motive of promoting certain rival companies, the government decides to double the tax-rates for these start-ups.

4. Based on the passage, all of the following can be inferred about consumer behaviour EXCEPT that:

1. too many options have made it difficult for consumers to trust products.
2. consumers tend to prefer products by start-ups over those by established companies.
3. consumers are susceptible to marketing images that they see on social media.
4. having too many product options can be overwhelming for consumers.

5. All of the following, IF TRUE, would weaken the author's claims EXCEPT:

1. the annual sales growth of companies with fewer product options were higher than that of companies which curated their products for target consumers.
2. product options increased market competition, bringing down the prices of commodities, which, in turn, increased purchasing power of the poor.
3. the empowerment felt by purchasers in buying a commodity were directly proportional to the number of options they could choose from.
4. the annual sale of companies that hired lifestyle influencers on Instagram for marketing their products were 40% less than those that did not.

Question Numbers (6 to 10): The passage below is accompanied by a set of five questions. Choose the best answer to each question.

In the past, credit for telling the tale of Aladdin has often gone to Antoine Galland . . . the first European translator of . . . Arabian Nights [which] started as a series of translations of an incomplete manuscript of a medieval Arabic story collection. . . But, though those tales were of medieval origin, Aladdin may be a more recent invention. Scholars have not found a manuscript of the story that predates the version published in 1712 by Galland, who wrote in his diary that he first heard the tale from a Syrian storyteller from Aleppo named Hanna Diyab . . .

Despite the fantastical elements of the story, scholars now think the main character may actually be based on a real person's real experiences. . . . Though Galland never credited Diyab in his published translations of the Arabian Nights stories, Diyab wrote something of his own: a travelogue penned in the mid-18th century. In it, he recalls telling Galland the story of Aladdin [and] describes his own hard-knocks upbringing and the way he marveled at the extravagance of Versailles. The descriptions he uses were very similar to the descriptions of the lavish palace that ended up in Galland's version of the Aladdin story. [Therefore, author Paulo Lemos] Horta believes that "Aladdin might be the young Arab Maronite from Aleppo, marveling at the jewels and riches of Versailles." . . .

For 300 years, scholars thought that the rags-to-riches story of Aladdin might have been inspired by the plots of French fairy tales that came out around the same time, or that the story was invented in that 18th century period as a byproduct of French Orientalism, a fascination with stereotypical exotic Middle Eastern luxuries that was prevalent then. The idea that Diyab might have based it on his own life — the experiences of a Middle Eastern man encountering the French, not vice-versa — flips the script. [According to Horta,] "Diyab was ideally placed to embody the overlapping world of East and West, blending the storytelling traditions of his homeland with his youthful observations of the wonder of 18th-century France." . . .

To the scholars who study the tale, its narrative drama isn't the only reason storytellers keep finding reason to return to Aladdin. It reflects not only "a history of the French and the Middle East, but also [a story about] Middle Easterners coming to Paris and that speaks to our world today," as Horta puts it. "The day Diyab told the story of Aladdin to Galland, there were riots due to food shortages during the winter and spring of 1708 to 1709, and Diyab was sensitive to those people in a way that Galland is not. When you read this diary, you see this solidarity among the Arabs who were in Paris at the time. . . . There is little in the writings of Galland that would suggest that he was capable of developing a character like Aladdin with sympathy, but Diyab's memoir reveals a narrator adept at capturing the distinctive psychology of a young protagonist, as well as recognizing the kinds of injustices and opportunities that can transform the path of any youthful adventurer."

6. Which of the following is the primary reason for why storytellers are still fascinated by the story of Aladdin?

1. The traveller's experience that inspired the tale of Aladdin resonates even today.
2. The tale of Aladdin documents the history of Europe and Middle East.
3. The archetype of the rags-to-riches story of Aladdin makes it popular even today.
4. The story of Aladdin is evidence of the eighteenth century French Orientalist attitude.

7. Which of the following, if true, would invalidate the inversion that the phrase "flips the script" refers to?

1. The description of opulence in Hanna Diyab's and Antoine Galland's narratives bore no resemblance to each other.
2. Diyab's travelogue described the affluence of the French city of Bordeaux, instead of Versailles.
3. Galland acknowledged in the published translations of Arabian Nights that he heard the story of Aladdin from Diyab.
4. The French fairy tales of the eighteenth century did not have rags-to-riches plot lines like that of the tale of Aladdin.

8. The author of the passage is most likely to agree with which of the following explanations for the origins of the story of Aladdin?

1. The story of Aladdin has its origins in an undiscovered, incomplete manuscript of a medieval Arabic collection of stories.
2. Basing it on his own life experiences, Diyab transmitted the story of Aladdin to Galland who included it in Arabian Nights.
3. Galland received the story of Aladdin from Diyab who, in turn, found it in an incomplete medieval manuscript.
4. Galland derived the story of Aladdin from Diyab's travelogue in which he recounts his fascination with the wealth of Versailles.

9. All of the following serve as evidence for the character of Aladdin being based on Hanna Diyab EXCEPT:

1. Diyab's narration of the original story to Galland.
2. Diyab's humble origins and class struggles, as recounted in his travelogue.
3. Diyab's cosmopolitanism and cross-cultural experience.
4. Diyab's description of the wealth of Versailles in his travelogue.

10. Which of the following does not contribute to the passage's claim about the authorship of Aladdin?

1. Galland's acknowledgment of Diyab in his diary.
2. The depiction of the affluence of Versailles in Diyab's travelogue.
3. The story-line of many French fairy tales of the 18th century.
4. The narrative sensibility of Diyab's travelogue.

Question Numbers (11 to 15): The passage below is accompanied by a set of five questions. Choose the best answer to each question.

As defined by the geographer Yi-Fu Tuan, topophilia is the affective bond between people and place. His 1974 book set forth a wide-ranging exploration of how the emotive ties with the material environment vary greatly from person to person and in intensity, subtlety, and mode of expression. Factors influencing one's depth of response to the environment include cultural background, gender, race, and historical circumstance, and Tuan also argued that there is a biological and sensory element. Topophilia might not be the strongest of human emotions—indeed, many people feel utterly indifferent toward the environments that shape their lives—but when activated it has the power to elevate a place to become the carrier of emotionally charged events or to be perceived as a symbol.

Aesthetic appreciation is one way in which people respond to the environment. A brilliantly colored rainbow after gloomy afternoon showers, a busy city street alive with human interaction—one might experience the beauty of such landscapes that had seemed quite ordinary only moments before or that are being newly discovered. This is quite the opposite of a second topophilic bond, namely that of the acquired taste for certain landscapes and places that one knows well. When a place is home, or when a space has become the locus of memories or the means of gaining a livelihood, it frequently evokes a deeper set of attachments than those predicated purely on the visual. A third response to the environment also depends on the human senses but may be tactile and olfactory, namely a delight in the feel and smell of air, water, and the earth.

Topophilia—and its very close conceptual twin, sense of place—is an experience that, however elusive, has inspired recent architects and planners. Most notably, new urbanism seeks to counter the perceived placelessness of modern suburbs and the decline of central cities through neo-traditional design motifs. Although motivated by good intentions, such attempts to create places rich in meaning are perhaps bound to disappoint. As Tuan noted, purely aesthetic responses often are suddenly revealed, but their intensity rarely is long-lasting. Topophilia is difficult to design for and impossible to quantify, and its most articulate interpreters have been self-reflective philosophers such as Henry David Thoreau, evoking a marvelously intricate sense of place at Walden Pond, and Tuan, describing his deep affinity for the desert.

Topophilia connotes a positive relationship, but it often is useful to explore the darker affiliations between people and place. Patriotism, literally meaning the love of one's terra patria or homeland, has long been cultivated by governing elites for a range of nationalist projects, including war preparation and ethnic cleansing. Residents of upscale residential developments have disclosed how important it is to maintain their community's distinct identity, often by casting themselves in a superior social position and by reinforcing class and racial differences. And just as a beloved landscape is suddenly revealed, so too may landscapes of fear cast a dark shadow over a place that makes one feel a sense of dread or anxiety—or topophobia.

11. Which one of the following comes closest in meaning to the author's understanding of topophilia?

1. The tendency of many cultures to represent their land as "motherland" or "fatherland" may be seen as an expression of their topophilia
2. The French are not overly patriotic, but they will refuse to use English as far as possible, even when they know it well.
3. Scientists have found that most creatures, including humans, are either born with or cultivate a strong sense of topography.
4. Nomadic societies are known to have the least affinity for the lands through which they traverse because they tend to be topophobic.

12. Which one of the following best captures the meaning of the statement, "Topophilia is difficult to design for and impossible to quantify . . ."?

1. The deep anomie of modern urbanisation led to new urbanism's intricate sense of place.
2. People's responses to their environment are usually subjective and so cannot be rendered in design.
3. Philosopher-architects are uniquely suited to develop topophilic design.
4. Architects have to objectively quantify spaces and hence cannot be topophilic.

13. Which of the following statements, if true, could be seen as not contradicting the arguments in the passage?

1. The most important, even fundamental, response to our environment is our tactile and olfactory response.
2. Patriotism, usually seen as a positive feeling, is presented by the author as a darker form of topophilia.
3. Generally speaking, in a given culture, the ties of the people to their environment vary little in significance or intensity.
4. New Urbanism succeeded in those designs where architects collaborated with their clients.

14. In the last paragraph, the author uses the example of "Residents of upscale residential developments" to illustrate the:

1. social exclusivism practised by such residents in order to enforce a sense of racial or class superiority.
2. introduction of nationalist projects by such elites to produce a sense of dread or topophobia.
3. manner in which environments are designed to minimise the social exclusion of their clientele.
4. sensitive response to race and class problems in upscale residential developments.

15. The word "topophobia" in the passage is used:

1. to represent a feeling of dread towards particular spaces and places.
2. as a metaphor expressing the failure of the homeland to accommodate non-citizens.
3. to signify the fear of studying the complex discipline of topography.
4. to signify feelings of fear or anxiety towards topophilic people.

Question Numbers (16 to 19): The passage below is accompanied by a set of four questions. Choose the best answer to each question.

Scientists recently discovered that Emperor Penguins—one of Antarctica's most celebrated species—employ a particularly unusual technique for surviving the daily chill. As detailed in an article published today in the journal Biology Letters, the birds minimize heat loss by keeping the outer surface of their plumage below the temperature of the surrounding air. At the same time, the penguins' thick plumage insulates their body and keeps it toasty. . . .

The researchers analyzed thermographic images . . . taken over roughly a month during June 2008. During that period, the average air temperature was

0.32 degrees Fahrenheit. At the same time, the majority of the plumage covering the penguins' bodies was even colder: the surface of their warmest body part, their feet, was an average 1.76 degrees Fahrenheit, but the plumage on their heads, chests and backs were -1.84, -7.24 and -9.76 degrees Fahrenheit respectively. Overall, nearly the entire outer surface of the penguins' bodies was below freezing at all times, except for their eyes and beaks. The scientists also used a computer simulation to determine how much heat was lost or gained from each part of the body—and discovered that by keeping their outer surface below air temperature, the birds might paradoxically be able to draw very slight amounts of heat from the air around them. The key to their trick is the difference between two different types of heat transfer: radiation and convection.

The penguins do lose internal body heat to the surrounding air through thermal radiation, just as our bodies do on a cold day. Because their bodies (but not surface plumage) are warmer than the surrounding air, heat gradually radiates outward over time, moving from a warmer material to a colder one. To maintain body temperature while losing heat, penguins, like all warm-blooded animals, rely on the metabolism of food. The penguins, though, have an additional strategy. Since their outer plumage is even colder than the air, the simulation showed that they might gain back a little of this heat through thermal convection—the transfer of heat via the movement of a fluid (in this case, the air). As the cold Antarctic air cycles around their bodies, slightly warmer air comes into contact with the plumage and donates minute amounts of heat back to the penguins, then cycles away at a slightly colder temperature.

Most of this heat, the researchers note, probably doesn't make it all the way through the plumage and back to the penguins' bodies, but it could make a slight difference. At the very least, the method by which a penguin's plumage wicks heat from the bitterly cold air that surrounds it helps to cancel out some of the heat that's radiating from its interior. And given the Emperors' unusually demanding breeding cycle, every bit of warmth counts. . . . Since [penguins trek as far as 75 miles to the coast to breed and male penguins] don't eat anything during [the incubation period of 64 days], conserving calories by giving up as little heat as possible is absolutely crucial.

16. Which of the following best explains the purpose of the word "paradoxically" as used by the author?

1. Keeping their body colder helps penguins keep their plumage warmer.
2. Heat gain through radiation happens despite the heat loss through convection.
3. Keeping a part of their body colder helps penguins keep their bodies warmer.
4. Heat loss through radiation happens despite the heat gain through convection.

17. In the last sentence of paragraph 3, "slightly warmer air" and "at a slightly colder temperature" refer to ______ AND ______ respectively:

1. the cold Antarctic air whose temperature is higher than that of the plumage AND the fall in temperature of the Antarctic air after it has transmitted some heat to the plumage.
2. the air inside penguins' bodies kept warm because of metabolism of food AND the fall in temperature of the body air after it transfers some heat to the plumage.
3. the air trapped in the plumage which is warmer than the Antarctic air AND the fall in temperature of the trapped plumage air after it radiates out some heat.
4. the cold Antarctic air which becomes warmer because of the heat radiated out from penguins' bodies AND the fall in temperature of the surrounding air after thermal convection.

18. Which of the following can be responsible for Emperor Penguins losing body heat?

1. Food metabolism.
2. Thermal convection.
3. Reproduction process.
4. Plumage.

19. All of the following, if true, would negate the findings of the study reported in the passage EXCEPT:

1. the temperature of the plumage on the penguins' heads, chests and backs were found to be 1.84, 7.24 and 9.76 degrees Fahrenheit respectively.
2. the penguins' plumage were made of a material that did not allow any heat transfer through convection or radiation.
3. the average temperature of the feet of penguins in the month of June 2008 were found to be 2.76 degrees Fahrenheit.
4. the average air temperature recorded during the month of June 2008 in the area of study were – 10 degrees Fahrenheit.

Question Numbers (20 to 24): The passage below is accompanied by a set of five questions. Choose the best answer to each question.

"Free of the taint of manufacture" – that phrase, in particular, is heavily loaded with the ideology of what the Victorian socialist William Morris called the "anti-scrape", or an anti-capitalist conservationism (not conservatism) that solaced itself with the vision of a pre-industrial golden age. In Britain, folk may often appear a cosy, fossilised form, but when you look more closely, the idea of folk – who has the right to sing it, dance it, invoke it, collect it, belong to it or appropriate it for political or cultural ends – has always been contested territory. . . .

In our own time, though, the word "folk" . . . has achieved the rare distinction of occupying fashionable and unfashionable status simultaneously. Just as the effusive floral prints of the radical William Morris now cover genteel sofas, so the revolutionary intentions of many folk historians and revivalists have led to music that is commonly regarded as parochial and conservative. And yet – as newspaper columns periodically rejoice – folk is hip again, influencing artists, clothing and furniture designers, celebrated at music festivals, awards ceremonies and on TV, reissued on countless record labels. Folk is a sonic "shabby chic", containing elements of the uncanny and eerie, as well as an antique veneer, a whiff of Britain's heathen dark ages. The very obscurity and anonymity of folk music's origins open up space for rampant imaginative fancies. . . .

[Cecil Sharp, who wrote about this subject, believed that] folk songs existed in constant transformation, a living example of an art form in a perpetual state of renewal. "One man sings a song, and then others sing it after him, changing what they do not like" is the most concise summary of his conclusions on its origins. He compared each rendition of a ballad to an acorn falling from an oak tree; every subsequent iteration sows the song anew. But there is tension in newness. In the late 1960s, purists were suspicious of folk songs recast in rock idioms. Electrification, however, comes in many forms. For the early-20th-century composers such as Vaughan Williams and Holst, there were thunderbolts of inspiration from oriental mysticism, angular modernism and the body blow of the first world war, as well as input from the rediscovered folk tradition itself.

For the second wave of folk revivalists, such as Ewan MacColl and AL Lloyd, starting in the 40s, the vital spark was communism's dream of a post-revolutionary New Jerusalem. For their younger successors in the 60s, who thronged the folk clubs set up by the old guard, the lyrical freedom of Dylan and the unchained melodies of psychedelia created the conditions for folk-rock's own golden age, a brief Indian summer that lasted from about 1969 to 1971. . . . Four decades on, even that progressive period has become just one more era ripe for fashionable emulation and pastiche. The idea of a folk tradition being exclusively confined to oral transmission has become a much looser, less severely guarded concept. Recorded music and television, for today's metropolitan generation, are where the equivalent of folk memories are seeded. . . .

20. The primary purpose of the reference to William Morris and his floral prints is to show:

1. that despite its archaic origins, folk continues to remain a popular tradition.
2. that what is once regarded as radical in folk, can later be seen as conformist.
3. the pervasive influence of folk on contemporary art, culture, and fashion.
4. that what was once derided as genteel is now considered revolutionary.

21. All of the following are causes for plurality and diversity within the British folk tradition EXCEPT:

1. that British folk forms can be traced to the remote past of the country.
2. paradoxically, folk forms are both popular and unpopular.
3. the fluidity of folk forms owing to their history of oral mode of transmission.
4. that British folk continues to have traces of pagan influence from the dark ages.

22. Which of the following statements about folk revivalism of the 1940s and 1960s cannot be inferred from the passage?

1. Freedom and rebellion were popular themes during the second wave of folk revivalism.
2. It reinforced Cecil Sharp's observation about folk's constant transformation.
3. Electrification of music would not have happened without the influence of rock music.
4. Even though it led to folk-rock's golden age, it wasn't entirely free from critique.

23. The author says that folk "may often appear a cosy, fossilised form" because:

1. folk is a sonic "shabby chic" with an antique veneer.
2. of its nostalgic association with a pre-industrial past.
3. it has been arrogated for various political and cultural purposes.
4. the notion of folk has led to several debates and disagreements.

24. At a conference on folk forms, the author of the passage is least likely to agree with which one of the following views?

1. The power of folk resides in its contradictory ability to influence and be influenced by the present while remaining rooted in the past.
2. Folk forms, despite their archaic origins, remain intellectually relevant in contemporary times.
3. The plurality and democratising impulse of folk forms emanate from the improvisation that its practitioners bring to it.
4. Folk forms, in their ability to constantly adapt to the changing world, exhibit an unusual poise and homogeneity with each change.

25. The four sentences (labelled 1, 2, 3, 4) given below, when properly sequenced would yield a coherent paragraph. Decide on the proper sequence of the order of the sentences and key in the sequence of the four numbers as your answer.

1. Metaphors may map to similar meanings across languages, but their subtle differences can have a profound effect on our understanding of the world.
2. Latin scholars point out carpe diem is a horticultural metaphor that, particularly seen in the context of its source, is more accurately translated as "plucking the day," evoking the plucking and gathering of ripening fruits or flowers, enjoying a moment that is rooted in the sensory experience of nature, unrelated to the force implied in seizing.
3. The phrase carpe diem, which is often translated as "seize the day and its accompanying philosophy, has gone on to inspire countless people in how they live their lives and motivates us to see the world a little differently from the norm
4. It's an example of one of the more telling ways that we mistranslate metaphors from one language to another, revealing in the process our hidden assumptions about what we really value.

26. Five sentences related to a topic are given below. Four of them can be put together to form a meaningful and coherent short paragraph. Identify the odd one out. Choose its number as your answer and key it in.

1. One argument is that actors that do not fit within a single, well-defined category may suffer an "illegitimacy discount".
2. Others believe that complex identities confuse audiences about an organization's role or purpose.
3. Some organizations have complex and multidimensional identities that span or combine categories, while other organizations possess narrow identities.
4. Identity is one of the most important features of organizations, but there exist opposing views among sociologists about how identity affects organizational performance.
5. Those who think that complex identities are beneficial point to the strategic advantages of ambiguity, and organizations' potential to differentiate themselves from competitors.

27. The passage given below is followed by four alternate summaries. Choose the option that best captures the essence of the passage.

Physics is a pure science that seeks to understand the behavior of matter without regard to whether it will afford any practical benefit. Engineering is the correlative applied science in which physical theories are put to some specific use, such as building a bridge or a nuclear reactor. Engineers obviously rely heavily on the discoveries of physicists, but an engineer's knowledge of the world is not the same as the physicist's knowledge. In fact, an engineer's know-how will often depend on physical theories that, from the point of view of pure physics, are false. There are some reasons for this. First, theories that are false in the purest and strictest sense are still sometimes very good approximations to the true ones, and often have the added virtue of being much easier to work with. Second, sometimes the true theories apply only under highly idealized conditions which can only be created under controlled experimental situations. The engineer finds that in the real world, theories rejected by physicists yield more accurate predictions than the ones that they accept.

1. Though engineering draws heavily from pure science, it contributes to knowledge, by incorporating the constraints and conditions in the real world.
2. Engineering and physics fundamentally differ on matters like building a bridge or a nuclear reactor.
3. The unique task of the engineer is to identify, understand, and interpret the design constraints to produce a successful result.
4. The relationship between pure and applied science is strictly linear, with the pure science directing applied science, and never the other way round.

28. The four sentences (labelled 1, 2, 3, 4) given below, when properly sequenced would yield a coherent paragraph. Decide on the proper sequence of the order of the sentences and key in the sequence of the four numbers as your answer.

1. If you've seen a little line of text on websites that says something like "customers who bought this also enjoyed that" you have experienced this collaborative filtering firsthand.
2. The problem with these algorithms is that they don't take into account a host of nuances and circumstances that might interfere with their accuracy.
3. If you just bought a gardening book for your cousin, you might get a flurry of links to books about gardening, recommended just for you! – the algorithm has no way of knowing you hate gardening and only bought the book as a gift.
4. Collaborative filtering is a mathematical algorithm by which correlations and co-occurrences of behaviors are tracked and then used to make recommendations.

29. Five sentences related to a topic are given below in a jumbled order. Four of them form a coherent and unified paragraph. Identify the odd sentence that does not go with the four. Key in the number of the option that you choose.

1. 'Stat' signaled something measurable, while 'matic' advertised free labour; but 'tron', above all, indicated control.
2. It was a totem of high modernism, the intellectual and cultural mode that decreed no process or phenomenon was too complex to be grasped, managed and optimized.
3. Like the heraldic shields of ancient knights, these morphemes were painted onto the names of scientific technologies to proclaim one's history and achievements to friends and enemies alike.
4. The historian Robert Proctor at Stanford University calls the suffix '-tron', along with '-matic' and '-stat', embodied symbols.
5. To gain the suffix was to acquire a proud and optimistic emblem of the electronic and atomic age.

30. The four sentences (labelled 1, 2, 3, 4) given below, when properly sequenced would yield a coherent paragraph. Decide on the proper sequence of the order of the sentences and key in the sequence of the four numbers as your answer.

1. We'll all live under mob rule until then, which doesn't help anyone.
2. Perhaps we need to learn to condense the feedback we receive online so that 100 replies carry the same weight as just one.
3. As we grow more comfortable with social media conversations being part of the way we interact every day, we are going to have to learn how to deal with legitimate criticism.
4. A new norm will arise where it is considered unacceptable to reply with the same point that dozens of others have already.

31. The passage given below is followed by four alternate summaries. Choose the option that best captures the essence of the passage.

Vance Packard's The Hidden Persuaders alerted the public to the psychoanalytical techniques used by the advertising industry. Its premise was that advertising agencies were using depth interviews to identify hidden consumer motivations, which were then used to entice consumers to buy goods. Critics and reporters often wrongly assumed that Packard was writing mainly about subliminal advertising. Packard never mentioned the word subliminal, however, and devoted very little space to discussions of "subthreshold" effects. Instead, his views largely aligned with the notion that individuals do not always have access to their conscious thoughts and can be persuaded by supraliminal messages without their knowledge.

1. Packard held that advertising as a 'hidden persuasion' builds on peoples' conscious thoughts and awareness, by understanding the hidden motivations of consumers and works at the subliminal level.
2. Packard argued that advertising as a 'hidden persuasion' works at the supraliminal level, wherein the people targeted are aware of being persuaded, after understanding the hidden motivations of consumers and works.
3. Packard held that advertising as a 'hidden persuasion' understands the hidden motivations of consumers and works at the supraliminal level, though the people targeted have no awareness of being persuaded.
4. Packard argued that advertising as a 'hidden persuasion' understands the hidden motivations of consumers and works at the subliminal level, on the subconscious level of the awareness of the people targeted.

32. The four sentences (labelled 1, 2, 3, 4) given below, when properly sequenced would yield a coherent paragraph. Decide on the proper sequence of the order of the sentences and key in the sequence of the four numbers as your answer.

1. People with dyslexia have difficulty with print-reading, and people with autism spectrum disorder have difficulty with mind-reading.
2. An example of a lost cognitive instinct is mind-reading: our capacity to think of ourselves and others as having beliefs, desires, thoughts and feelings.
3. Mind-reading looks increasingly like literacy, a skill we know for sure is not in our genes, since scripts have been around for only 5,000-6,000 years.
4. Print-reading, like mind-reading varies across cultures, depends heavily on certain parts of the brain, and is subject to developmental disorders.

33. Five sentences related to a topic are given below. Four of them can be put together to form a meaningful and coherent short paragraph. Identify the odd one out. Choose its number as your answer and key it in.

1. His idea to use sign language was not a completely new idea as Native Americans used hand gestures to communicate with other tribes.
2. Ancient Greek philosopher Aristotle, for example, observed that men who are deaf are incapable of speech.
3. People who were born deaf were denied the right to sign a will as they were "presumed to understand nothing; because it is not possible that they have been able to learn to read or write."
4. Pushback against this prejudice began in the 16th century when Pedro Ponce de León created a formal sign language for the hearing impaired.
5. For millennia, people with hearing impairments encountered marginalization because it was believed that language could only be learned by hearing the spoken word.

34. The passage given below is followed by four alternate summaries. Choose the option that best captures the essence of the passage.

A distinguishing feature of language is our ability to refer to absent things, known as displaced reference. A speaker can bring distant referents to mind in the absence of any obvious stimuli. Thoughts, not limited to the here and now, can pop into our heads for unfathomable reasons. This ability to think about distant things necessarily precedes the ability to talk about them. Thought precedes meaningful referential communication. A prerequisite for the emergence of human-like meaningful symbols is that the mental categories they relate to can be invoked even in the absence of immediate stimuli.

1. Thoughts are essential to communication and only humans have the ability to think about objects not present in their surroundings.
2. The ability to think about objects not present in our environment precedes the development of human communication.
3. Thoughts precede all speech acts and these thoughts pop up in our heads even in the absence of any stimulus.
4. Displaced reference is particular to humans and thoughts pop into our heads for no real reason.

Section II: DI & LR

Question Numbers (35 to 38): Answer the questions on the basis of the information given below.

The Ministry of Home Affairs is analysing crimes committed by foreigners in different states and union territories (UT) of India. All cases refer to the ones registered against foreigners in 2016.

The number of cases – classified into three categories: IPC crimes, SLL crimes and other crimes – for nine states/UTs are shown in the figure below. These nine belong to the top ten states/UTs in terms of the total number of cases registered. The remaining state (among top ten) is West Bengal, where all the 520 cases registered were SLL crimes.

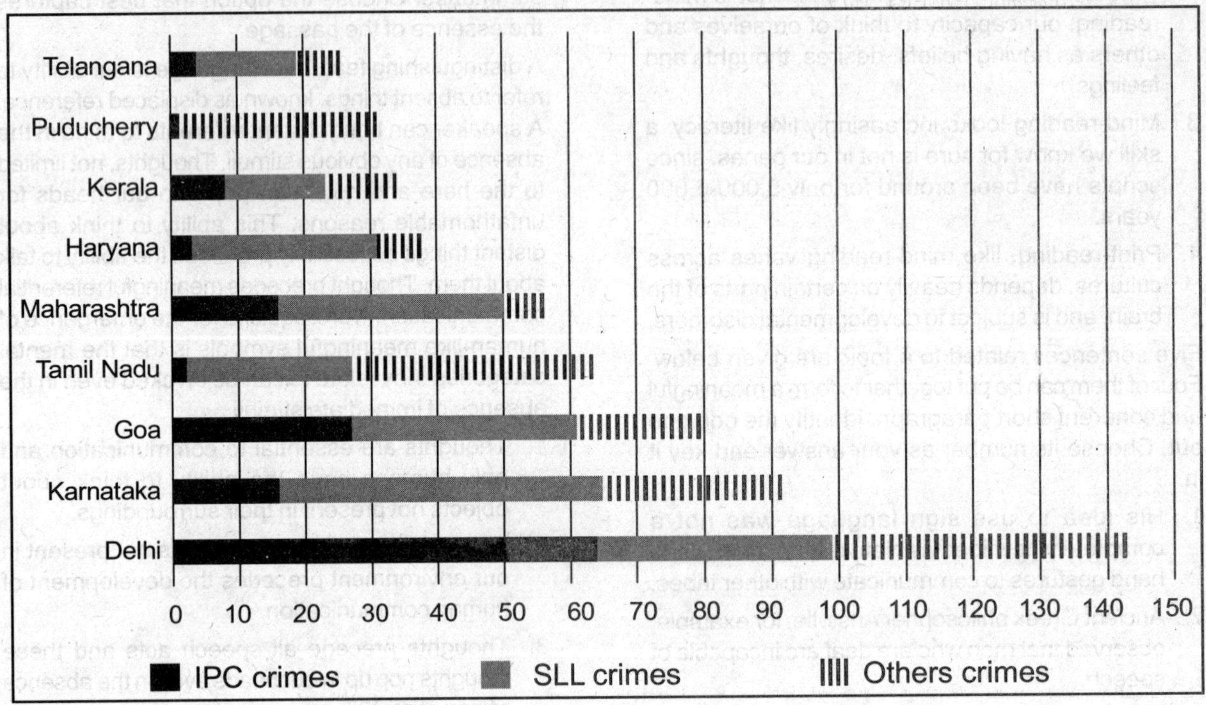

The table below shows the ranks of the ten states/UTs mentioned above among ALL states/UTs of India in terms of the number of cases registered in each of the three category of crimes. A state/UT is given rank r for a category of crimes if there are (r-1) states/UTs having a larger number of cases registered in that category of crimes. For example, if two states have the same number of cases in a category, and exactly three other states/UTs have larger numbers of cases registered in the same category, then both the states are given rank 4 in that category. Missing ranks in the table are denoted by *.

	IPC Crimes	SLL Crimes	Other Crimes
Delhi	*	*	*
Goa	*	4	*
Haryana	8	6	*
Karnataka	3	2	*
Kerala	*	9	*
Maharashtra	3	4	8
Puducherry	13	29	*
Tamil Nadu	11	7	*
Telangana	6	9	8
West Bengal	17	*	16

35. What is the rank of Kerala in the 'IPC crimes' category?

36. In the two states where the highest total number of cases are registered, the ratio of the total number of cases in IPC crimes to the total number in SLL crimes is closest to

(1) 19 : 20 (2) 1 : 9

(3) 3 : 2 (4) 11 : 10

37. Which of the following is DEFINITELY true about the ranks of states/UT in the 'other crimes' category?

i) Tamil Nadu: 2

ii) Puducherry: 3

(1) both i) and ii)

(2) only ii)

(3) neither i), nor ii)

(4) only i)

38. What is the sum of the ranks of Delhi in the three categories of crimes?

Question Numbers (39 to 42): Answer the questions on the basis of the information given below.

The following table represents addition of two six-digit numbers given in the first and the second rows, while the sum is given in the third row. In the representation, each of the digits 0, 1, 2, 3, 4, 5, 6, 7, 8, 9 has been coded with one letter among A, B, C, D, E, F, G, H, J, K, with distinct letters representing distinct digits.

	B	H	A	A	G	F
+	A	H	J	F	K	F
A	A	F	G	C	A	F

39. Which digit does the letter A represent?

40. Which digit does the letter B represent?

41. Which among the digits 3, 4, 6 and 7 cannot be represented by the letter D?

42. Which among the digits 4, 6, 7 and 8 cannot be represented by the letter G?

Question Numbers (43 to 46): Answer the questions on the basis of the information given below.

A new game show on TV has 100 boxes numbered 1, 2, . . ., 100 in a row, each containing a mystery prize. The prizes are items of different types, a, b, c, . . . , in decreasing order of value. The most expensive item is of type a, a diamond ring, and there is exactly one of these. You are told that the number of items at least doubles as you move to the next type. For example, there would be at least twice as many items of type b as of type a, at least twice as many items of type c as of type b and so on. There is no particular order in which the prizes are placed in the boxes.

43. What is the minimum possible number of different types of prizes?

44. What is the maximum possible number of different types of prizes?

45. Which of the following is not possible?

(1) There are exactly 75 items of type e.

(2) There are exactly 45 items of type c.

(3) There are exactly 30 items of type b.

(4) There are exactly 60 items of type d.

46. You ask for the type of item in box 45. Instead of being given a direct answer, you are told that there are 31 items of the same type as box 45 in boxes 1 to 44 and 43 items of the same type as box 45 in boxes 46 to 100.

What is the maximum possible number of different types of items?

(1) 5 (2) 4

(3) 3 (4) 6

Question Numbers (47 to 50): Answer the questions on the basis of the information given below.

Princess, Queen, Rani and Samragni were the four finalists in a dance competition. Ashman, Badal, Gagan and Dyu were the four music composers who individually assigned items to the dancers. Each dancer had to individually perform in two dance items assigned by the different composers. The first items performed by the four dancers were all assigned by different music composers. No dancer performed her second item before the performance of the first item by any other dancers. The dancers performed their second items in the same sequence of their performance of their first items.

The following additional facts are known.

i) No composer who assigned item to Princess, assigned any item to Queen.

ii) No composer who assigned item to Rani, assigned any item to Samragni.

iii) The first performance was by Princess; this item was assigned by Badal.

iv) The last performance was by Rani; this item was assigned by Gagan.

v) The items assigned by Ashman were performed consecutively. The number of performances between items assigned by each of the remaining composers was the same.

47. Which of the following is true?

(1) The second performance was composed by Dyu.

(2) The second performance was composed by Gagan.

(3) The third performance was composed by Ashman.

(4) The third performance was composed by Dyu.

48. Which of the following is FALSE?

(1) Queen did not perform in any item composed by Gagan.

(2) Rani did not perform in any item composed by Badal.

(3) Samragni did not perform in any item composed by Ashman.

(4) Princess did not perform in any item composed by Dyu.

49. The sixth performance was composed by:

(1) Badal (2) Dyu

(3) Ashman (4) Gagan

50. Which pair of performances were composed by the same composer?

(1) The second and the sixth

(2) The first and the seventh

(3) The third and the seventh

(4) The first and the sixth

Question Numbers (51 to 54): Answer the questions on the basis of the information given below.

Six players – Tanzi, Umeza, Wangdu, Xyla, Yonita and Zeneca competed in an archery tournament. The tournament had three compulsory rounds, Rounds 1 to 3. In each round every player shot an arrow at a target. Hitting the centre of the target (called bull's eye) fetched the highest score of 5. The only other possible scores that a player could achieve were 4, 3, 2 and 1. Every bull's eye score in the first three rounds gave a player one additional chance to shoot in the bonus rounds, Rounds 4 to 6. The possible scores in Rounds 4 to 6 were identical to the first three.

A player's total score in the tournament was the sum of his/her scores in all rounds played by him/her. The table below presents partial information on points scored by the players after completion of the tournament. In the table, NP means that the player did not participate in that round, while a hyphen means that the player participated in that round and the score information is missing.

	Round-1	Round-2	Round-3	Round-4	Round-5	Round-6
Tanzi	-	4	-	5	NP	NP
Umeza	-	-	-	1	2	NP
Wangdu	-	4	-	NP	NP	NP
Xyla	-	-	-	1	5	-
Yonita	-	-	3	5	NP	NP
Zeneca	-	-	-	5	5	NP

The following facts are also known.

1. Tanzi, Umeza and Yonita had the same total score.
2. Total scores for all players, except one, were in multiples of three.
3. The highest total score was one more than double of the lowest total score.
4. The number of players hitting bull's eye in Round 2 was double of that in Round 3.
5. Tanzi and Zeneca had the same score in Round 1 but different scores in Round 3.

51. What was the highest total score?

(1) 23 (2) 25

(3) 21 (4) 24

52. What was Zeneca's total score?

(1) 23 (2) 22

(3) 24 (4) 21

53. Which of the following statements is true?

(1) Zeneca's score was 23.

(2) Xyla was the highest scorer.

(3) Xyla's score was 23.

(4) Zeneca was the highest scorer.

54. What was Tanzi's score in Round 3?

(1) 1 (2) 3

(3) 5 (4) 4

Question Numbers (55 to 58): Answer the questions on the basis of the information given below.

The figure below shows the street map for a certain region with the street intersections marked from a through l. A person standing at an intersection can see along straight lines to other intersections that are in her line of sight and all other people standing at these intersections. For example, a person standing at intersection g can see all people standing at intersections b, c, e, f, h, and k. In particular, the person standing at intersection g can see the person standing at intersection e irrespective of whether there is a person standing at intersection f.

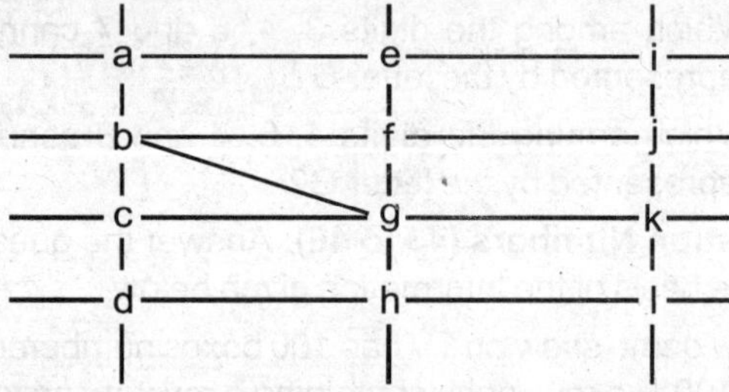

Six people U, V, W, X, Y, and Z, are standing at different intersections. No two people are standing at the same intersection.

The following additional facts are known.

1. X, U, and Z are standing at the three corners of a triangle formed by three street segments.
2. X can see only U and Z.
3. Y can see only U and W.
4. U sees V standing in the next intersection behind Z.
5. W cannot see V or Z.
6. No one among the six is standing at intersection d.

55. Who is standing at intersection a?

(1) W (2) V

(3) Y (4) No one

56. Who can V see?

(1) U and Z only (2) Z only

(3) U only (4) U, W and Z only

57. What is the minimum number of street segments that X must cross to reach Y?

(1) 1 (2) 4

(3) 3 (4) 2

58. Should a new person stand at intersection d, who among the six would she see?

(1) W and X only (2) V and X only

(3) U and W only (4) U and Z only

Question Numbers (59 to 62): Answer the questions on the basis of the information given below.

A supermarket has to place 12 items (coded A to L) in shelves numbered 1 to 16. Five of these items are types of biscuits, three are types of candies and the rest are types of savouries. Only one item can be kept in a shelf. Items are to be placed such that all items of same type are clustered together with no empty shelf between items of the same type and at least one empty shelf between two different types of items. At most two empty shelves can have consecutive numbers.

The following additional facts are known.

1. A and B are to be placed in consecutively numbered shelves in increasing order.
2. I and J are to be placed in consecutively numbered shelves both higher numbered than the shelves in which A and B are kept.
3. D, E and F are savouries and are to be placed in consecutively numbered shelves in increasing order after all the biscuits and candies.
4. K is to be placed in shelf number 16.
5. L and J are items of the same type, while H is an item of a different type.
6. C is a candy and is to be placed in a shelf preceded by two empty shelves.
7. L is to be placed in a shelf preceded by exactly one empty shelf.

59. In how many different ways can the items be arranged on the shelves?

(1) 8 (2) 4

(3) 2 (4) 1

60. Which of the following items is not a type of biscuit?

(1) A (2) L

(3) G (4) B

61. Which of the following can represent the numbers of the empty shelves in a possible arrangement?

(1) 1, 2, 8, 12 (2) 1, 2, 6, 12

(3) 1, 5, 6, 12 (4) 1, 7, 11, 12

62. Which of the following statements is necessarily true?

(1) All biscuits are kept before candies.

(2) All candies are kept before biscuits.

(3) There are at least four shelves between items B and C.

(4) There are two empty shelves between the biscuits and the candies.

Question Numbers (63 to 66): Answer the questions on the basis of the information given below.

Five vendors are being considered for a service. The evaluation committee evaluated each vendor on six aspects – Cost, Customer Service, Features, Quality, Reach, and Reliability. Each of these evaluations are on a scale of 0 (worst) to 100 (perfect). The evaluation scores on these aspects are shown in the radar chart. For example, Vendor 1 obtains a score of 52 on Reliability, Vendor 2 obtains a score of 45 on Features and Vendor 3 obtains a score of 90 on Cost.

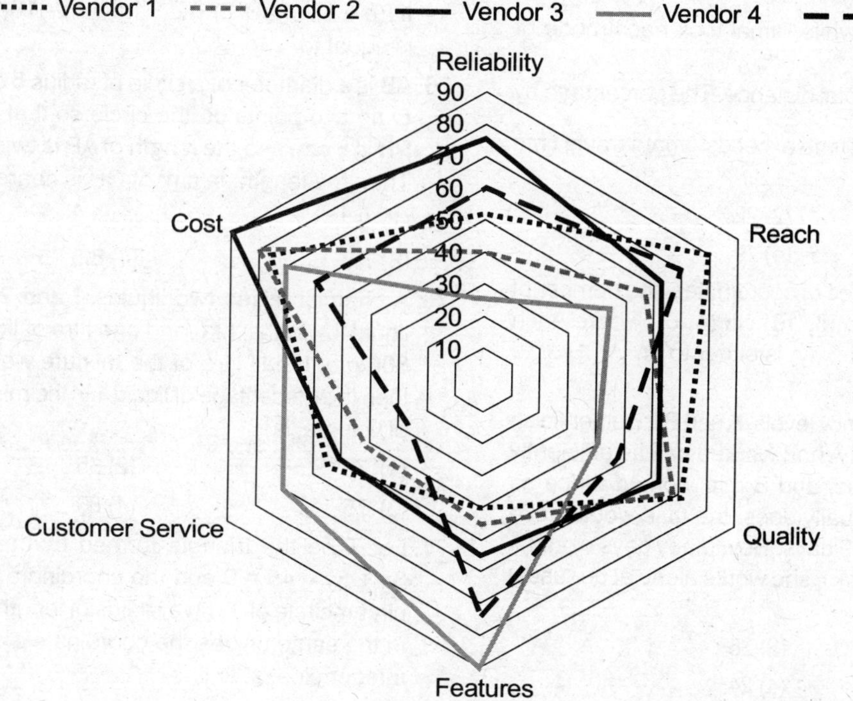

63. On which aspect is the median score of the five vendors the least?

(1) Quality (2) Cost
(3) Reliability (4) Customer Service

64. A vendor's final score is the average of their scores on all six aspects. Which vendor has the highest final score?

(1) Vendor 1 (2) Vendor 4
(3) Vendor 3 (4) Vendor 2

65. List of all the vendors who are among the top two scorers on the maximum number of aspects is:

(1) Vendor 1 and Vendor 5
(2) Vendor 1 and Vendor 2
(3) Vendor 2, Vendor 3 and Vendor 4
(4) Vendor 2 and Vendor 5

66. List of all the vendors who are among the top three vendors on all six aspects is:

(1) Vendor 3
(2) Vendor 1 and Vendor 3
(3) None of the Vendors
(4) Vendor 1

Section III: QA

67. Corners are cut off from an equilateral triangle T to produce a regular hexagon H. Then, the ratio of the area of H to the area of T is

(1) 2 : 3 (2) 4 : 5
(3) 3 : 4 (4) 5 : 6

68. Let x and y be positive real numbers such that $\log_5 (x + y) + \log_5 (x - y) = 3$, and $\log_2 y - \log_2 x = 1 - \log_2 3$. Then xy equals

(1) 25 (2) 100
(3) 150 (4) 250

69. One can use three different transports which move at 10, 20, and 30 kmph, respectively. To reach from A to B, Amal took each mode of transport $\frac{1}{3}$ of his total journey time, while Bimal took each mode of transport $\frac{1}{3}$ of the total distance. The percentage by which Bimal's travel time exceeds Amal's travel time is nearest to

(1) 21 (2) 22
(3) 20 (4) 19

70. With rectangular axes of coordinates, the number of paths from (1, 1) to (8, 10) via (4, 6), where each step from any point (x, y) is either to (x, y + 1) or to (x + 1, y), is

71. At their usual efficiency levels, A and B together finish a task in 12 days. If A had worked half as efficiently as she usually does, and B had worked thrice as efficiently as he usually does, the task would have been completed in 9 days. How many days would A take to finish the task if she works alone at her usual efficiency?

(1) 18 (2) 36
(3) 12 (4) 24

72. Meena scores 40% in an examination and after review, even though her score is increased by 50%, she fails by 35 marks. If her post-review score is increased by 20%, she will have 7 marks more than the passing score. The percentage score needed for passing the examination is

(1) 70 (2) 60
(3) 75 (4) 80

73. In a race of three horses, the first beat the second by 11 metres and the third by 90 metres. If the second beat the third by 80 metres, what was the length, in metres, of the racecourse?

74. Consider a function f satisfying $f(x + y) = f(x) f(y)$ where x, y are positive integers, and $f(1) = 2$. If $f(a + 1) + f(a + 2) + ... + f(a + n) = 16(2^n - 1)$ then a is equal to

75. AB is a diameter of a circle of radius 5 cm. Let P and Q be two points on the circle so that the length of PB is 6 cm, and the length of AP is twice that of AQ. Then the length, in cm, of QB is nearest to

(1) 9.1 (2) 9.3
(3) 7.8 (4) 8.5

76. A chemist mixes two liquids 1 and 2. One litre of liquid 1 weighs 1 kg and one litre of liquid 2 weighs 800 gm. If half litre of the mixture weighs 480 gm, then the percentage of liquid 1 in the mixture, in terms of volume, is

(1) 70 (2) 85
(3) 75 (4) 80

77. Let T be the triangle formed by the straight line $3x + 5y - 45 = 0$ and the coordinate axes. Let the circumcircle of T have radius of length L, measured in the same unit as the coordinate axes. Then, the integer closest to L is

78. On selling a pen at 5% loss and a book at 15% gain, Karim gains Rs. 7. If he sells the pen at 5% gain and the book at 10% gain, he gains Rs. 13. What is the cost price of the book in Rupees?

(1) 80 (2) 85

(3) 95 (4) 100

79. The income of Amala is 20% more than that of Bimala and 20% less than that of Kamala. If Kamala's income goes down by 4% and Bimala's goes up by 10%, then the percentage by which Kamala's income would exceed Bimala's is nearest to

(1) 29 (2) 31

(3) 28 (4) 32

80. The product of the distinct roots of $|x^2 - x - 6| = x + 2$ is

(1) –24 (2) –16

(3) –8 (4) –4

81. Two cars travel the same distance starting at 10:00 am and 11:00 am, respectively, on the same day. They reach their common destination at the same point of time. If the first car travelled for at least 6 hours, then the highest possible value of the percentage by which the speed of the second car could exceed that of the first car is

(1) 20 (2) 25

(3) 30 (4) 10

82. The number of solutions to the equation $|x|(6x^2 + 1) = 5x^2$ is

83. The wheels of bicycles A and B have radii 30 cm and 40 cm, respectively. While traveling a certain distance, each wheel of A required 5000 more revolutions than each wheel of B. If bicycle B traveled this distance in 45 minutes, then its speed, in km per hour, was

(1) 18π (2) 12π

(3) 16π (4) 14π

84. For any positive integer n, let f(n) = n(n + 1) if n is even, and f(n) = n + 3 if n is odd.

If m is a positive integer such that 8f(m + 1) – f(m) = 2, then m equals

85. The product of two positive numbers is 616. If the ratio of the difference of their cubes to the cube of their difference is 157:3, then the sum of the two numbers is

(1) 85 (2) 95

(3) 58 (4) 50

86. The number of the real roots of the equation $2\cos(x(x + 1)) = 2^x + 2^{-x}$ is

(1) 1 (2) 0

(3) infinite (4) 2

87. If $a_1 + a_2 + a_3 + ... + a_n = 3(2^{n+1} - 2)$, for every $n \geq 1$, then a_{11} equals

88. In a circle of radius 11 cm, CD is a diameter and AB is a chord of length 20.5 cm. If AB and CD intersect at a point E inside the circle and CE has length 7 cm, then the difference of the lengths of BE and AE, in cm, is

(1) 3.5 (2) 1.5

(3) 2.5 (4) 0.5

89. A person invested a total amount of Rs 15 lakh. A part of it was invested in a fixed deposit earning 6% annual interest, and the remaining amount was invested in two other deposits in the ratio 2 : 1, earning annual interest at the rates of 4% and 3%, respectively. If the total annual interest income is Rs 76000 then the amount (in Rs lakh) invested in the fixed deposit was

90. If m and n are integers such that $(\sqrt{2})^{19} 3^4 4^2 9^m 8^n = 3^n 16^m (\sqrt[4]{64})$ then m is

(1) –24 (2) –16

(3) –12 (4) –20

91. Let S be the set of all points (x, y) in the x-y plane such that $|x| + |y| \leq 2$ and $|x| \geq 1$. Then, the area, in square units, of the region represented by S equals

92. A club has 256 members of whom 144 can play football, 123 can play tennis, and 132 can play cricket. Moreover, 58 members can play both football and tennis, 25 can play both cricket and tennis, while 63 can play both football and cricket. If every member can play at least one game, then the number of members who can play only tennis is

(1) 32 (2) 43

(3) 38 (4) 45

93. Three men and eight machines can finish a job in half the time taken by three machines and eight men to finish the same job. If two machines can finish the job in 13 days, then how many men can finish the job in 13 days?

94. Amala, Bina, and Gouri invest money in the ratio 3 : 4 : 5 in fixed deposits having respective annual interest rates in the ratio 6 : 5 : 4. What is their total interest income (in Rs) after a year, if Bina's interest income exceeds Amala's by Rs 250?

(1) 7000 (2) 6000

(3) 7250 (4) 6350

95. If $a_1, a_2, \ldots$ are in A.P., then

$$\frac{1}{\sqrt{a_1}+\sqrt{a_2}}+\frac{1}{\sqrt{a_2}+\sqrt{a_3}}+\ldots+\frac{1}{\sqrt{a_n}+\sqrt{a_{n+1}}}$$

is equal to

(1) $\frac{n-1}{\sqrt{a_1}+\sqrt{a_{n-1}}}$ (2) $\frac{n-1}{\sqrt{a_1}+\sqrt{a_n}}$

(3) $\frac{n}{\sqrt{a_1}+\sqrt{a_{n+1}}}$ (4) $\frac{n}{\sqrt{a_1}-\sqrt{a_{n+1}}}$

96. Ramesh and Gautam are among 22 students who write an examination. Ramesh scores 82.5. The average score of the 21 students other than Gautam is 62. The average score of all the 22 students is one more than the average score of the 21 students other than Ramesh. The score of Gautam is

(1) 51 (2) 53

(3) 48 (4) 49

97. If the rectangular faces of a brick have their diagonals in the ratio $3 : 2\sqrt{3} : \sqrt{15}$, then the ratio of the length of the shortest edge of the brick to that of its longest edge is

(1) $\sqrt{2} : \sqrt{3}$ (2) $2 : \sqrt{5}$

(3) $\sqrt{3} : 2$ (4) $1 : \sqrt{3}$

98. In a class, 60% of the students are girls and the rest are boys. There are 30 more girls than boys. If 68% of the students, including 30 boys, pass an examination, the percentage of the girls who do not pass is

99. If the population of a town is p in the beginning of any year then it becomes 3 + 2p in the beginning of the next year. If the population in the beginning of 2019 is 1000, then the population in the beginning of 2034 will be

(1) $(1003)2^{15} - 3$ (2) $(997)2^{14} + 3$

(3) $(997)^{15} - 3$ (4) $(1003)^{15} + 6$

100. If $(5.55)^x = (0.555)^y = 1000$, then the value of $\frac{1}{x}-\frac{1}{y}$ is

(1) 1 (2) $\frac{2}{3}$

(3) $\frac{1}{3}$ (4) 3

ANSWERS

1. (4)	**2.** (1)	**3.** (2)	**4.** (2)	**5.** (1)	**6.** (1)	**7.** (1)	**8.** (2)	**9.** (1)	**10.** (3)
11. (1)	**12.** (2)	**13.** (2)	**14.** (1)	**15.** (1)	**16.** (3)	**17.** (1)	**18.** (3)	**19.** (3)	**20.** (2)
21. (2)	**22.** (3)	**23.** (2)	**24.** (4)	**25.** (3241)	**26.** (1)	**27.** (1)	**28.** (4123)	**29.** (2)	**30.** (3241)
31. (3)	**32.** (2341)	**33.** (2)	**34.** (2)	**35.** (5)	**36.** (2)	**37.** (1)	**38.** (5)	**39.** (1)	**40.** (9)
41. (7)	**42.** (6)	**43.** (2)	**44.** (6)	**45.** (2)	**46.** (1)	**47.** (1)	**48.** (1)	**49.** (1)	**50.** (4)
51. (2)	**52.** (3)	**53.** (2)	**54.** (1)	**55.** (4)	**56.** (1)	**57.** (4)	**58.** (1)	**59.** (1)	**60.** (3)
61. (2)	**62.** (3)	**63.** (4)	**64.** (3)	**65.** (1)	**66.** (1)	**67.** (1)	**68.** (3)	**69.** (2)	**70.** (3920)
71. (1)	**72.** (1)	**73.** (880)	**74.** (3)	**75.** (1)	**76.** (4)	**77.** (9)	**78.** (1)	**79.** (2)	**80.** (2)
81. (1)	**82.** (5)	**83.** (3)	**84.** (10)	**85.** (4)	**86.** (1)	**87.** (6144)	**88.** (4)	**89.** (9)	**90.** (3)
91. (2)	**92.** (2)	**93.** (13)	**94.** (3)	**95.** (3)	**96.** (1)	**97.** (4)	**98.** (20)	**99.** (1)	**100.** (3)

EXPLANATIONS

1. In order to answer this question, we need to refer to the last paragraph of the passage. Consider the lines, 'For start-ups that promise accessible simplicity, their very structure still might eventually push them toward overwhelming variety......' Thus, the fourth option provides the right answer. While option 1 is only partially correct, options 2 and 3 are factually inconsistent with the information provided in the passage.

2. The central premise of the author's argument is two-fold:

1. Fewer choices effectively result in better, easier decisions
2. The creators of new products continue to focus on those who already have plenty while access to basic necessities has shrunk even further for the lower classes.

Hence, the author is likely to support any scheme that offers a limited range of products at low prices. This makes the choice, *A range of 10 products priced between $5 and $10* the right answer.

3. In the last paragraph of the passage, the author states that starts-ups offering limited products also have revenue considerations and will have to eventually increase the range of products being offered, just like Casper and Glossier have done. The question asks you to identify the option that will add the least depth to the author's argument (in other words, a statement that weakens the argument).

Option 1 which states that *start-ups with few product options are no exception to the American consumer market that is deeply divided along class lines* adds depth to the author's argument since it contends that there is nothing unique about start-ups. They are bound to fail or will have to change. Another option which states that *with the motive of promoting certain rival companies, the government decides to double the tax-rates for these start-ups* also predicts that start-ups are likely to fail, adding weight to author's argument about their fate mentioned in the last para.

Option 2 adds least depth because it brings out a point that will not lead start-ups to offer more product varieties, after all they are experiencing a surge in revenue without expanding their product catalogue. This actually contradicts the author's prediction.

The third statement strengthens the author's perspective and is thus negated.

4. In this question we need to identify the inference that can't be made based on the information provided in the passage. The statement *having too many product options can be overwhelming for consumers* can be easily inferred from the initial lines of the passage.

Similarly, *consumers are susceptible to marketing images that they see on social media* can be inferred from the lines, 'Indeed, choice fatigue is one reason so many people gravitate toward lifestyle influencers on Instagram....'

The statement *too many options have made it difficult for consumers to trust products* can be inferred from 'They're selling nice things, but maybe more importantly, they're selling a confidence in those things, and an ability to opt out of the stuff rat race. . . .'.

Thus, the only statement that can't be inferred is *'consumers tend to prefer products by start-ups over those by established companies.'*

5. Throughout the passage, the author is in favor of offering limited choices to customers. This particular option demonstrates that offering fewer products can bring positive results. Thus, it strengthens the author's content and is the right answer.

The other options directly contradict the information provided in the passage and weaken the author's claims.

6. As can be inferred from the passage, the main reason for scholars' fascination with the story of Aladdin is that the experiences of the author are reflected in the story. The story of Aladdin, in a way, is a reflection of the author's life. This is what makes it so interesting. Therefore, the correct answer is option 1. Documentation of history and the concept of Orientalism is not necessarily something that would keep the interest alive. This negates options 2 and 4. Similarly, the concept of rags-to-riches is showcased in various stories. So, option 3 is also out of scope.

7. Scholars initially thought that the plot of Aladdin must have been inspired by 18th century French fairy tales, but to quote the author, "The idea that Diyab might have based it on his own life — the experiences of a Middle Eastern man encountering the French, not vice-versa — flips the script."

In other words, the story of Aladdin was not inspired by the French fairy tales but that Diyab was the actual author. By invalidating the inversion, the question wants us to not give the credit to Diyab

Option 4 is negated because by pointing out the dissimilarity between Aladdin and the French fairy tales, it gives the credit to Diyab.

Option 2 is negated because even though Diyab described Bordeaux, he still saw the luxury and opulence of France.

Option 3 also gives the credit to Diyab, so it is not invalidating the inversion.

Option 1 is the right choice because, if the narratives bore no resemblance, then it disputes the evidence that Diyab ever narrated the story to Galland, as Galland claims in his diary. This would contradict, at least to some extent, the author's claim that Diyab was the inspiration for the character of Aladdin.

8. Options 1, 3 and 4 are out of scope and cannot be considered. The origin of the story of Aladdin was based on Diyab's life experiences. He transmitted this story to Galland who made it a part of Arabian Nights. Therefore, the correct answer is option 2.

9. Diyab's travelogue serves as evidence for the character of Aladdin being based on him. This negates options 2 and 4. Moreover, the second-last paragraph of the passage is suggestive of Diyab's cosmopolitanism and cross-cultural experience. So, option 3 is also negated. Refer to the following lines from the first paragraph of the passage, "Galland, who wrote in his diary that he first heard the tale from a Syrian storyteller from Aleppo named Hanna Diyab". There is no evidence of Diyab's narration of the story to Galland. This makes option 1 the correct answer.

10. Diyab and his life experiences have the authorship of the story of Aladdin. Since this is reflected in options 1, 2 and 4, they cannot be considered. This makes option 3 the correct answer as it proposes an entirely different theory to the authorship.

11. As per the passage, 'topophilia' has positive connotations and evokes feelings of love, affection and a strong emotional bond. Thus, all options that talk about lack of affinity or poor emotional connect can be negated. Thus, the statements '*Nomadic societies are known to have the least affinity for the lands through which they traverse because they tend to be topophobic*' and '*The French are not overly patriotic, but they will refuse to use English as far as possible, even when they know it well*' can be easily negated. There is no discussion regarding 'topography' in the passage. Hence, the correct answer is '*The tendency of many cultures to represent their land as "motherland" or "fatherland" may be seen as an expression of their topophilia.*'

12. Refer the lines *Topophilia is difficult to design for and impossible to quantify, and its most articulate interpreters have been self-reflective philosophers such as Henry David Thoreau, evoking a marvelously intricate sense of place at Walden Pond, and Tuan, describing his deep affinity for the desert.* Thus, there is an element of subjectiveness that underlies all topophilic expression. Hence, option 2 is the right answer.

13. This is a slightly difficult question. We have to read the options carefully and look for the one that is not against what the author has to say.

Option 1 is contradictory because the author says that olfactory response is the third most important factor, while the option says that it is the most important factor.

Option 3 can be ruled out because the author says in the first paragraph: the emotive ties with the material environment vary greatly from person to person and in intensity, subtlety, and mode of expression. The author says, 'vary greatly', while the option says, 'vary little'.

Refer the lines - *"As Tuan noted, purely aesthetic responses often are suddenly revealed, but their intensity rarely is long-lasting. Topophilia is difficult to design for and impossible to quantify..."* However, the option says that New Urbanism succeeded in those designs where architects collaborated with their clients. Thus, option 4 can also be negated.

Option 2 can be seen in the last paragraph and is parallel to what the author has to say. This is not contradicting the author's argument, and hence it is the right choice.

14. This example has been discussed in the last paragraph of the passage where the author is talking about the darker applications of topophilia while exploring the affiliations between people and places. This immediately negates statements 3 and 4 - *manner in which environments are designed to minimize the social exclusion of their clientele* and *sensitive response to race and class problems in upscale residential developments.* There is no discussion regarding nationalist projects of the elites. Hence, option 1 is the right answer.

15. The answer to this question can be found in the last lines of the passage - And just as a beloved landscape is suddenly revealed, so too may landscapes of fear cast a dark shadow over a place that makes one feel a sense of dread or anxiety—or topophobia.

16. This is a simple question. Just go through the relevant section of the passage - *"...by keeping their outer surface below air temperature, the birds might paradoxically be able to draw very slight amounts of heat from the air around them..."* Option 3 captures this precisely.

17. It is already given that the sentence can be found in the last part of the third paragraph. Let's see the context: *As the cold Antarctic air cycles around their bodies, slightly warmer air comes into contact with the plumage and donates minute amounts of heat back to the penguins, then cycles away at a slightly colder temperature.*
We know that the outer plumage of the penguins is even colder than the air, thus, the first blank refers to the cold air whose temperature is higher than that of the plumage and the second blank refers to the fall in temperature after some heat has been transmitted to the plumage.

18. We know that the plumage is responsible for maintaining body heat; it is the central idea of the passage. Food metabolism, too, helps generate heat, the passage says that clearly. We are left with two choices, thermal convection and reproduction process. The passage says that thermal convection helps them gain heat ("the simulation showed that they might gain back a little of this heat through thermal convection"). Thus, we see that thermal convection, food metabolism, and plumage all are responsible for heat gain, not heat loss. We are left with choice 3 as the right answer.
Choice 3 can be inferred from the following lines of the passage: "And given the Emperors' unusually demanding breeding cycle, every bit of warmth counts...". This suggests that the reproduction process results in heat loss.

19. The passage says that the outer air temperature is warmer than the plumage temperature, but if the outer air temperature becomes colder than the plumage temperature, as option 4 says, the author's argument would be invalidated, because the heat transfer from the outer colder air to the relatively warmer plumage will not happen.
Similarly, the plumage has to be colder than the outer Antarctic air, but in choice 1 the plumage is warmer than the outer Antarctic air, so this too would weaken the author's argument in the passage.
In option 2; thermal convection helps the penguins get some heat, if the plumage is not allowing thermal convection to take place, there would be no gain of warmth, thus this too weakens the argument.
Only option 3 does not weaken the argument. The passage says that the feet are the warmest part of the body of a penguin. If you make them a little warmer, they will still remain the warmest part of the body. Hence, it is the answer.

20. This is a simple question whose answer can be easily inferred from the following lines - *Just as the effusive floral prints of the radical William Morris now cover genteel sofas, so the revolutionary intentions of many folk historians and revivalists have led to music that is commonly regarded as parochial and conservative.* Option 4 distorts the idea by reversing its order.

21. This question can be answered by reading the options closely. A long history and varied influences will contribute to the diversity of an art form. Similarly, the presence of fluidity and oral traditions will also introduce diversity. However, the popularity and unpopularity of any art form has no correlation with the presence of diversity. Hence, this is the correct answer.

22. The question asks us to select an option that cannot be inferred from the passage. The statement that is made in the passage is: "In the late 1960s, purists were suspicious of folk songs recast in rock idioms. Electrification, however, comes in many forms." In other words, electrification need not always come through rock alone. It might come from any other form of music as well. Thus, this option surely cannot be inferred.
"...the lyrical freedom of Bob Dylan..." this phrase supports option 1.
Option 2 can be inferred because Cecil Sharp talks about folk music's ability to adapt. The music of 40s and 60s demonstrates that adaptation.
The passage says that in the late 1960s, Purists were suspicious of folk songs recast in rock idioms, this suggests that it had critics. Thus, option 4 can be inferred.

23. Fossilized refers to something belonging to/associated with the past. Out of the options given, only the second option comes close in meaning. The other options don't correlate with the word fossilized.

24. The author appreciates how folk forms have been used by modern musicians and the fusion of folk with other forms of music throughout the passage.

Hence, he is likely to agree with all options except 4 because it says that folk music exhibits unusual homogeneity.

If there is homogeneity, then the idea of adapting and infusing with other kinds of music is not valid. Thus, the author will not agree with this.

25. Sentence 3 introduces the phrase 'carpe diem' so it comes in beginning. It is followed by statement 2 which further explains the meaning of the phrase. 4 and 1 form a mandatory pair as they talk about metaphors. Thus, the correct sequence is 3241.

26. Statement 4 is the introductory statement as it introduces the concept of complex identities. It will be followed by statement 3 as it further explains the phenomena of complex identities. Statements 2 and 5 form a pair because as they discuss two conflicting ideas of complex identities. Only statement 1 is the odd one out.

27. The passage discusses the difference between pure and applied science and the difference between the knowledge of an engineer and that of a physicist. This is not captured by option 2. Option 4 cannot be considered as it is untrue. Option 3 has no mention of pure science, so it cannot be considered. So, the correct answer is option 1 as it clearly captures the essence of the passage.

28. Sentence 4 is clearly the introductory line as it introduces the concept of collaborative filtering. Sentence 1 further discusses the experience of collaborative filtering, so it comes after 4. 2 and 3 form a mandatory pair as they throw light on the problems in collaborative filtering. So, the correct sequence is 4123.

29. 4 is the introductory sentence as it introduces 'suffix'. The author then talks about what these symbols mean in statement 1. This is followed by statement 5 which talks about gaining suffix. It is followed by statement 3 which throws light on how these symbols are painted on the names of scientific technologies. Statement 2 does not fit entirely with the context of the passage and is hence the odd one out.

30. Statement 3 acts as an introductory statement as it talks about dealing with legitimate criticism. It is followed by statement 2. Statement 4 and 1 form a mandatory pair, which is evident from the phrase "until then". So, the correct sequence is 3241.

31. Choices with respect to supraliminal and subliminal have a clear difference. Also, the passage mentions that Packard believed in supraliminal images, not subliminal. This makes options 1 and 4 incorrect. The passage mentions that people are not aware, which is also indicated in option 3. Thus, the correct answer is option 3.

32. Statement 2 is clearly the introductory line as it introduces the concept of mind-reading. It is followed by 3 which further elaborates on the concept. Statements 4 and 1 form a mandatory pair as they talk about the concept of print-reading, which is very similar to mind-reading. Thus, the correct sequence is 2341.

33. The five sentences discuss the issue of hearing impairments and marginalization because of this. Statements 5, 4, 1 and 3 revolve around the same concept. Sentence 2 seems a little out of context. Thus, the correct answer is option 2.

34. Option 1 cannot be considered because it mentions information that has not been described in the passage. Options 3 and 4 are untrue as they distort the information provided in the passage, so they cannot be considered. Option 2 does not have any distortions and clearly captures the essence of the passage. Thus, the correct answer is option 2.

35. Can simply observe from given graph that Kerala has rank 5 in IPC crimes, (Delhi, Karnataka, Goa, Maharashtra are ranked above it)

36. Two highest crime states are Delhi and West Bangal

	Delhi	W-B
IPC	64	0
SLL	34	520

$$\text{Ratio of IPC to SLL} = \frac{64+0}{34+520} = 1:9$$

37. Can observe from the graph that in "other crimes"

Delhi > Tamil Nadu > Puducherry > Karnataka

So option 1 is correct, where Tamil Nadu rank = 2, Puducherry = 3

38.

IPC	SLL	Other Crimes
1	3	1
(Observed from graph)	(WB = 1, Karnataka = 2, Delhi/Maharashtra = 3)	(Observed from graph)

∴ Sum of Ranks = 1 + 3 + 1 = 5

For questions 39 to 42:

We need to find the values of A, B, C, D, E, F, G, H, J and K which are distinct digits among 0 to 9 such that :-

		B	H	A	A	G	F
+		A	H	J	F	K	F
	A	A	F	G	C	A	F

The value of F must be 0 since F + F = F can hold only if F = 0

The value of H must be 5 since H + H = F and F = 0

Now, since, 1 will be carried forward by the sum of H(5) + H(5) = F(0), therefore, A has to be 1 and B must be 9, only then B + A = AA

Modified table will now look like,

		9	5	1	1	G	0
+		1	5	J	0	K	0
	1	1	0	G	C	I	0

Unknown variables :- J, G, C, K

Unused digits :- 2, 3, 4, 6, 7, 8

Clearly, the sum of G + K must be 11, So 1 will be carried forward and therefore, C = 2.

Possible combinations for (G, K) = (3, 8), (8, 3), (4, 7) and (7, 4)

Case I :- (G, K) = (3, 8)

		9	5	1	1	3	0
+		1	5	J	0	8	0
	1	1	0	3	2	I	0

This case is not possible, since J has to be 2 but C = 2

Case II :- (G, K) = (8, 3)

		9	5	1	1	8	0
+		1	5	J = 7	0	3	0
	1	1	0	8	2	1	0

This case is possible.

A = 1, B = 9, C = 2, F = 0, G = 8, H = 5, J = 7, K = 3.

Case III :- (G, K) = (4, 7)

		9	5	1	1	4	0
+		1	5	J = 3	0	7	0
	1	1	0	4	2	1	0

This case is possible

A = 1, B = 9, C = 2, F = 0, G = 4, H = 5, J = 3, K = 7

Case IV :- (G, K) = (7, 4)

		9	5	1	1	7	0
+		1	5	J = 6	0	4	0
	1	1	0	7	2	1	0

This case is possible

A = 1, B = 9, C = 2, F = 0, G = 7, H = 5, J = 6, K = 4.

39. Letter A represent digit 1

40. Letter B represent digit 9

41. Digit 7 cannot be represented by D, as in all cases 7 is already represented by some other letter.

42. Letter G cannot be represented by digit 6.

43. It is given that the most expensive item is a diamond ring of type a and there is exactly one of these. Since the item b should be at least twice. The minimum number of items will be obtained when a = 1 and b = 99, which means there are only two different types of items.

44. It is given that the most expensive item is a diamond ring of type a and there is exactly one of these. Since the number of items of type b should be at least twice of that of a and the number of items of type c should be at least twice of that of b and so on. So the maximum number of different types of items of a, b and c will be obtained when a = 1, b = 2, c = 4, d = 8, e = 16, f = 69. Hence the maximum number of different types of items will be 6.

If the number of items is 7, then the minimum number of prizes should be 1 + 2 + 4 + 8 + 16 + 32 + 64 = 127 which is more than 100. Hence, 6 is the answer.

45. Option 1: There are exactly 75 items of type e.

a = 1, b = 2, c = 4, d = 8, e = 85. Here the maximum value of e = 85. Hence it can take the value 75.

An example of such case is a = 1, b = 2, c = 4, d = 18, e = 75

Option 2: There are exactly 45 items of type c.

Since the value of d should be at least 90, it means that d is not present because 45 + 90 will be more than 100(maximum number of items). Only a, b and c are present.

The maximum value of b = 22 and a = 1, but 45 + 22 + 1 = 68, which is less than 100. So this case is not possible.

Option 3: There are exactly 30 items of type b.

a = 1, b = 30 and c = 69. Hence this case is also possible.

Option 4: There are exactly 60 items of type d.

d = 60, c = 30, b = 9 and a = 1. a + b + c + d = 100. Hence, this case is possible.

2 is the answer.

46. The total number of items from 1 to 100, which are of same type as in box 45 = 31 + 1 + 43 = 75

Now to maximize the number of items, a = 1, b = 2, c = 4, d = 18 and e = 75(given)

There can be maximum 5 types of items.

If we consider number of items to be 6, then minimum number of items of 5th type will be 16,

1 + 2 + 4 + 8 + 16 + 75 = 106 which is more than 100.

Direction 47 to 50 :-

From statement (iii) and (iv) we get

	First item				Second item			
	I	II	III	IV	I	II	III	IV
Finalists	Princess							Rani
Composer	Badal		G			B		Gagan

By statement (V), since items assigned by Ashman were performed consecutively and first items performed by the four dancers were all assigned by different music composers therefore, fourth performance of first item and 1st performance of second items was assigned by Ashman.

Also, the number of performances between the items assigned by each of the remaining composers was the same, which is possible only if 4 performances happen between the items assigned.

	First item				Second item			
	I	II	III	IV	I	II	III	IV
Finalists	Princess							Rani
Composer	Badal	Dyu	Gagan	Ashman	Ashman	Badal	Dyu	Gagan

It is given that dancers performed their second items in the same sequence of their performance of their first items, i.e., princess performed first in both dance items and Rani performed the last.

Also by statement (i) and (ii), we get the final table as.

	First item				Second item			
	I	II	III	IV	I	II	III	IV
Finalists	Princess	Samragiri	Queen	Rani	Princess	Samragni	Queen	Rani
Composers	Badal	Dyu	Gagan	Ashman	Ashman	Badal	Dyu	Gagan

47. The second performance was composed by Dyu, is true.

48. Statement Queen didn't perform in any item composed by Gagan, is false

49. The sixth performance was composed by Badal.

50. The first and the sixth pair of performances were composed by the same composer.

For questios 51 to 54:

	Round-1	Round-2	Round-3	Round-4	Round-5	Round-6
Tanzi	-	4	-	5	NP	NP
Umeza	-	-	-	1	2	NP
Wangdu	-	4	-	NP	NP	NP
Xyla	-	-	-	1	5	-
Yonita	-	-	3	5	NP	NP
Zeneca	-	-	-	5	5	NP

It is given that every bull's eye score in the first three rounds gave a player one additional chance to shoot in the bonus rounds, Rounds 4 to 6, which means Tanzi scored Bull's eye only once in the first 3 rounds because she participated only once in round 4 to 6. Similarly, Umeza scored Bull's eye exactly 2 times in the first 3 rounds. Wangdu did not score Bull's eye in the first three rounds and so on.

Now from 1, Tanzi, Umeza and Yonita had the same total score.

So, Total score of Tanzi will be 4 + 5 + 5 + a = 14 + a, (She scored Bull's eye(a score of 5) in exactly one round and a is the unknown score)

Total score of Umeza = 1 + 2 + 5 + 5 + b = 13 + b (She scored Bull's eye(a score of 5) in exactly 2 rounds and b is the unknown score)

Total score of Yonita = 3 + 5 + 5 + c = 13 + c (She scored Bull's eye(a score of 5) in exactly one round and c is the unknown score)

Now 14 + a = 13 + b = 13 + c,

Also it is given that total scores for all players, except one, were in multiples of three, so these three will have to be a multiple of 3.

So, (a, b, c) can be either (1, 2, 2) or (4, 5, 5) in the same order. But the value (5, 5) for b and c is not possible. (Umeza scored Bull's eye in exactly 2 rounds and Yonita in exactly 1 round)

Hence, a = 1, b = 2 and c = 2. So, each of Tanzi, Umeza and Yonita had total score of 15.

Tabulating the data, we have

	Round-1	Round-2	Round-3	Round-4	Round-5	Round-6	Total
Tanzi	1/5	4	1/5	5	NP	NP	15
Umeza	5/5/2	5/5/2	5/5/2	1	2	NP	15
Wangdu	1/2/3/4	4	1/2/3/4	NP	NP	NP	6-12
Xyla	5	5	5	1	5	1/2/3/4/5	22-26
Yonita	2/5	2/5	3	5	NP	NP	15
Zeneca	-	-	-	5	5	NP	-

From 5, Tanzi and Zeneca had the same score in Round 1 but different scores in Round 3.

Zeneca score Bull's eye 2 times in round 1 to 3. If Tanzi scored 1 in round 1, then Zeneca also has to score 1 in round 1, which means both Tanzi and Zeneca scores in round 3 will be 5, which violates 5. Hence Tanzi scored 5 in round 1 and Zeneca also scored the same in round 1.

So the new table is:

	Round-1	Round-2	Round-3	Round-4	Round-5	Round-6	Total
Tanzi	5	4	1	5	NP	NP	15
Umeza	5/5/2	5/5/2	5/5/2	1	2	NP	15
Wangdu	1/2/3/4	4	1/2/3/4	NP	NP	NP	6-12
Xyla	5	5	5	1	5	1/2/3/4/5	22-26
Yonita	2/5	2/5	3	5	NP	NP	15
Zeneca	5	5/(2/34)	5/(2/3/4)	5	5	NP	-

From 4, the number of players hitting bull's eye in Round 2 was double of that in Round 3.

So, in round 3 either 1 or 2 Bull's eye can be scored and in round 2, 2 or 4 Bull's eye can be scored.

Case 1: If only 1 Bull's eye is scored in the round 3, then in round 3 Umeza will score 2 and Zeneca will score 2/3/4 in round 3, which means both will score 5 in round 2. So, minimum Bull's eye in round 2 will be 3. (Umeza, Zeneca, and Xyla). Hence, this case is rejected.

Case 2: 2 Bull's eye were scored in round 3 and 4 Bull's eye were scored in round 2. So in round 2 Umeza, Yonita and Zeneca scored 5. This can be tabulated as:

	Round-1	Round-2	Round-3	Round-4	Round-5	Round-6	Total
Tanzi	5	4	1	5	NP	NP	15
Umeza	5/2	5	5/2	1	2	NP	15
Wangdu	1/2/3/4	4	1/2/3/4	NP	NP	NP	6-12
Xyla	5	5	5	1	5	1/2/3/4/5	22-26
Yonita	2	5	3	5	NP	NP	15
Zeneca	5	5	(2/3/4)	5	5	NP	-

In round 3, 2 Bull's eye can only be scored by Xyla and Umeza.

	Round-1	Round-2	Round-3	Round-4	Round-5	Round-6	Total
Tanzi	5	4	1	5	NP	NP	15
Umeza	2	5	5	1	2	NP	15
Wangdu	1/2/3/4	4	1/2/3/4	NP	NP	NP	6-12
Xyla	5	5	5	1	5	1/2/3/4/5	22-26
Yonita	2	5	3	5	NP	NP	15
Zeneca	5	5	(2/3/4)	5	5	NP	22-24

The highest scorer can be either Xyla or Zeneca. The lowest scorer will be Wangdu.

Let Zeneca is the highest scorer.

From 3, the highest total score was one more than double of the lowest total score. So the only possible score for Zeneca is 23 and that for Wangdu is 11. (11 × 2 + 1 = 23)

But this will violate condition 2, since both Zeneca and Wangdu do not have their scores as multiples of three in this case.

Hence, Xyla will be the highest scorer. The only possible total score for Xyla will be 25, and that for Wangdu is 12(4 + 4 + 4). (12 × 2 + 1 = 25)

Since Xyla already has non-multiple of 3 as total score. Zeneca will have 24 as the total score. The complete table is:

	Round-1	Round-2	Round-3	Round-4	Round-5	Round-6	Total
Tanzi	5	4	1	5	NP	NP	15
Umeza	2	5	5	1	2	NP	15
Wangdu	4	4	4	NP	NP	NP	12
Xyla	5	5	5	1	5	4	25
Yonita	2	5	3	5	NP	NP	15
Zeneca	5	5	4	5	5	NP	24

51. The highest score is 25.

52. Zeneca total score is 24.

53. Xyla was the highest scorer.

54. Tanzi scored 1 in round 3.

For questios 55 to 58:

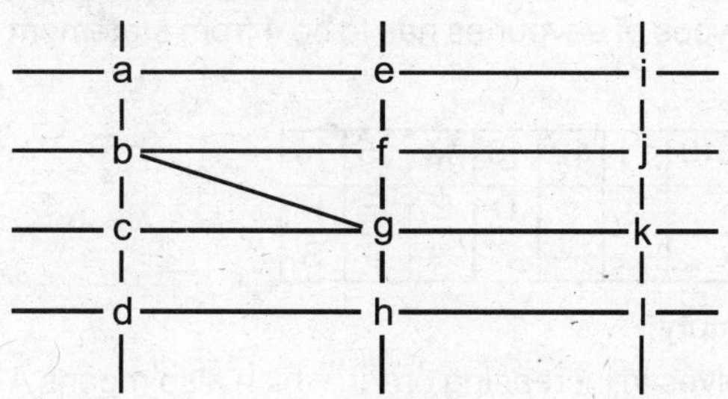

From 1, X, U, and Z are standing at the three corners of a triangle formed by three street segments.

From 2, X can see only U and Z.

From 4, U sees V standing in the next intersection behind Z. Also, no one among the six is standing at intersection d.

Only cases possible are:

1.

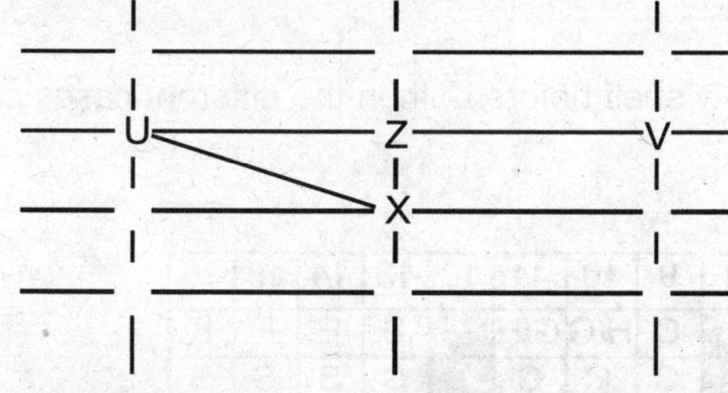

W cannot see V or Z. So, W can only be at the intersection a. Since Y can see only U and W, Y can only be at c where X can see him. Hence this case is rejected.

2.

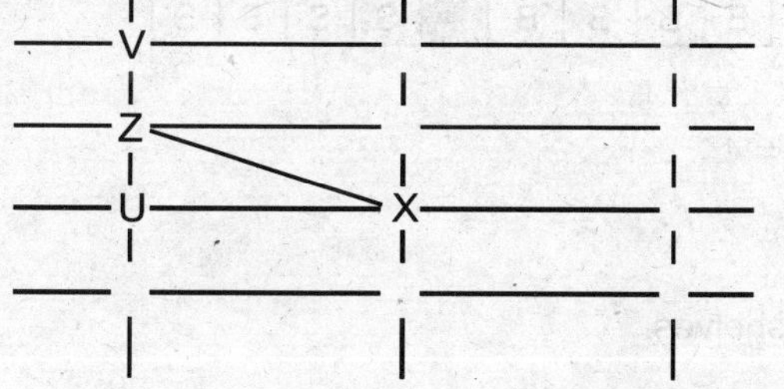

Y can only see U and W. Y cannot be placed anywhere. Hence this case is also rejected.

3.

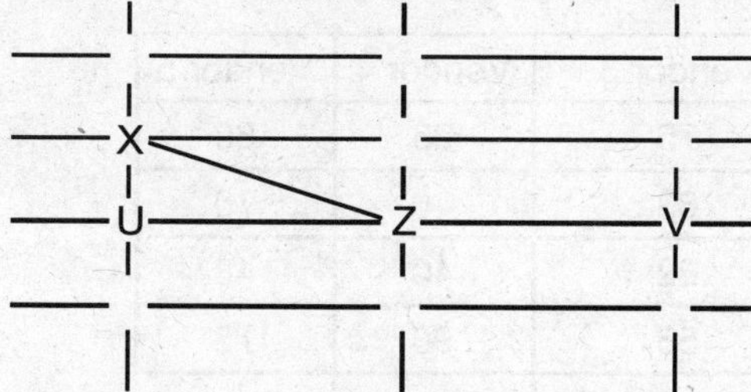

Y can only see U and W. Y cannot be placed anywhere. Hence this case is also rejected.

4.

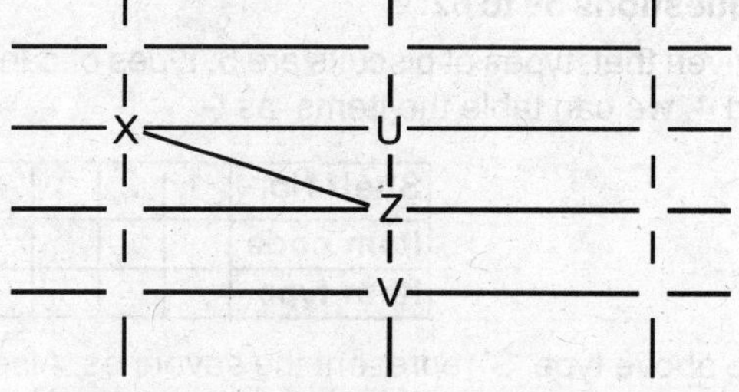

W cannot see V or Z. W can only be placed at i. Y can see only U and W. Y can only be placed at j or e, where he can see more people than U and W. Hence this case is also rejected.

5.

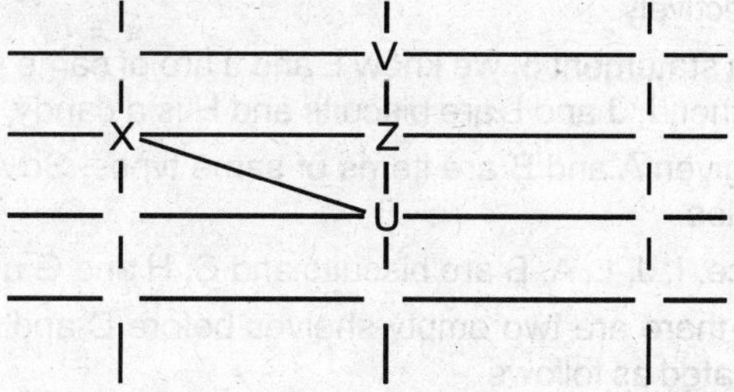

W cannot see V or Z. Y can only see U and W. Hence W and Y can only be placed as shown:

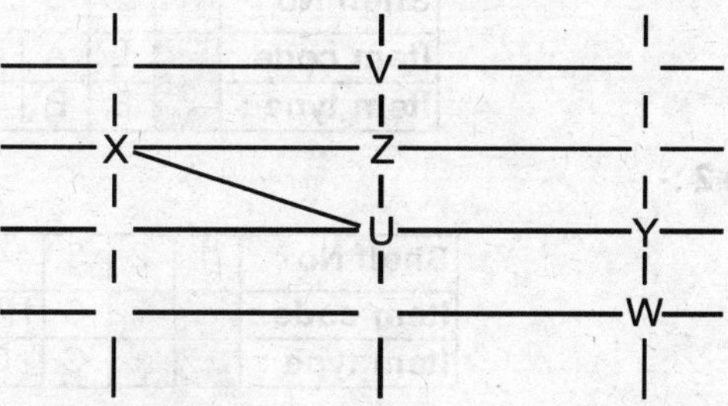

55. No one is standing at the intersection a. Hence (4) is the answer.

56. V can see U and Z only. Hence (1) is the answer.

57. To reach Y, X has to go from b to g and g to k, i.e. 2 streets.

58. If a new person stands at d(left down corner), they can see W and X only. Hence (1) is the answer.

For questions 59 to 62:

It is given that, types of biscuits are 5, types of candies are 3, therefore, types of savouries has to be 4 from statement 3 and 4, we can table the items as :-

Shelf No.	1	2	3	4	5	6	7	8	9	10	11	12	13	14	15	16
Item code													D	E	F	K
Item type													S	S	S	S

In the above type 'S' represent the savouries. Also, shelf 12 has to be empty

From statement 1, A and B are to placed in consecutively numbered shelves in increasing order, which also means A and B are of same kind, i.e, either biscuits or candies.

From statement 6 and 7 , C is a candy and is to be placed in a shelf preceded by two empty shelves and L is to be placed in a shelf preceded by exactly one empty shelf. Hence C and L are items of different types i.e., candy and biscuit respectively.

From statement 5, we know L and J are of same type and H is an items of a different type since I and J are clustered together, I, J and L are biscuits and H is a candy. So C, H are candies and I, J, L are biscuits.

It is given A and B are items of same types. So A, B should be biscuits because if they are candies there will be 4 candies.

Hence, I, J, L, A, B are biscuits and C, H and G are candies.

Now there are two empty shelves before C and exactly one empty shelf before L, then the different cases can be tabulated as follows :-

Case 1 :-

Shelf No :	1	2	3	4	5	6	7	8	9	10	11	12	13	14	15	16
Item code :		L	A	B	I/J	J/I			C	H/G	G/H		D	E	F	K
Item type :		B	B	B	B	B			C	C	C		S	S	S	S

Case 2 :-

Shelf No :	1	2	3	4	5	6	7	8	9	10	11	12	13	14	15	16
Item code :			C	H/G	G/H		L	A	B	I/J	J/I		D	E	F	K
Item type :			C	C	C		B	B	B	B	B		S	S	S	S

59. The number of arrangements for the first case = 2 × 2 = 4.

The number of arrangements for the second case = 2 × 2 = 4

The total number of arrangements = 4 + 4 = 8

60. G is not a type of biscuit.

61. 1, 2, 6, 12 can be the possible arrangement of the empty shelves.

62. There are atleast four shelves between items B and C.

For questios 63 to 66:

The data can be tabulated as follows (approximately):

Parameters	Vendor 1	Vendor 2	Vendor 3	Vendor 4	Vendor 5
Reliability	52	40	75	26	60
Reach	80	58	63	46	70
Quality	72	69	62	40	48
Features	40	45	56	90	75
Customer Services	55	41	50	70	28
Cost	77	81	90	71	50

63. Customer Services: 28,41,50,55,70 (The median is 50)

Cost: 50,71,77,81,90 (The median is 77)

Reliability: 26, 40, 52, 60, 75 (The median is 52)

Quality: 40, 48, 62, 69, 72 (The median is 62)

Hence the customer services have the lowest median.

64. The average of the vendor will be highest which has highest total score. Hence vendor 3 has the highest average.

65. Top 3 on Reliability: Vendor 3, Vendor 5

Top 3 on Reach: Vendor 1, Vendor 5

Top 3 on Quality: Vendor 1, Vendor 2

Top 3 on Features: Vendor 4, Vendor 5

Top 3 on Customer Services: Vendor 4, Vendor 1

Top 3 on Cost: Vendor 3, Vendor 2

Vendor 1: 3 times, Vendor 2: Only once, Vendor 3: 2 times, Vendor 4: 2 times, Vendor 5: 3 times

Here, vendor 1 and 5 comes 3 times. Hence B is the answer.

66. Top 3 on Reliability: Vendor 3, Vendor 5, Vendor 1

Top 3 on Reach: Vendor 1, Vendor 5, Vendor 3

Top 3 on Quality: Vendor 1, Vendor 2, Vendor 3

Top 3 on Features: Vendor 4, Vendor 5, Vendor 3

Top 3 on Customer Services: Vendor 4, Vendor 1, Vendor 3

Top 3 on Cost: Vendor 3, Vendor 2, Vendor 1

Only Vendor 3 ranks among top 3 in all the six parameters.

67.

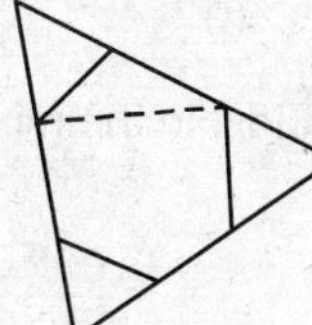

If the corners of the triangle are folded inside the hexagon, half of the area would be covered.

$$\therefore \frac{\Delta H}{\Delta T} = \frac{\Delta H}{\Delta H + \frac{\Delta H}{2}} = \frac{2}{3}$$

68. $\text{Log}_5 (x + y) + \log_5 (x - y) = 3$

$\Rightarrow \log_5 (x + y) (x - y) = 3.$

$\Rightarrow \log (x^2 - y^2) = 3 \log 5$

$\Rightarrow x^2 - y^2 = 5^3$ ...(1)

$\log_2 y - \log_2 x = 1 - \log_2 3$

$$\Rightarrow \log_2 \frac{y}{x} = \log_2 2 - \log_2 3$$

$$\Rightarrow \log_2 \frac{y}{x} = \log_2 \frac{2}{3}$$

$$\Rightarrow \frac{y}{x} = \frac{2}{3} \quad \text{...(2)}$$

Substitute the value of y from (2) in (1) and get,

$$\Rightarrow x^2 - \left(\frac{2x}{3}\right)^2 = 5^3$$

$$\Rightarrow x^2 \frac{5}{9} = 5^3$$

$\Rightarrow x = 15$ and $y = 10$

$\therefore xy = 150.$

69. Assume time taken by Amal = t

Then, the distance A and B = $d = \frac{t}{3}(10 + 20 + 30)$

$= 20t$

Total time taken by Bimal

$$= \frac{20t}{3}\left(\frac{1}{10} + \frac{1}{20} + \frac{1}{30}\right)$$

$$= \frac{20t}{3}\left(\frac{6+3+2}{60}\right) = \frac{11t}{9}$$

Hence, the time taken by Bimal will exceed Amal

$$\text{by} = \frac{\frac{11t}{9} - t}{t} \times 100 = 22.22\%$$

70. Paths from (1, 1) to (8, 10) via, (4, 6)

Means No. of paths from (1, 1) to (4, 6) multiplied by no. of paths from (4,6) to (8, 10)

Moving from (1, 1) to (4, 6) we have to take (4 – 1) + (6 – 1) steps = 8 steps, out of which '3' are horizontal and 5 are vertical. If we select '3' out of 8 steps, and assign them to horizontal, them all vertical steps are already assigned.

$\therefore$ No. of paths = ${}^8C_3 \times {}^8C_4 = 3920.$

71. Let A completes 'a' units of work in a day and B completes 'b' units of work in a day and the total work = 1 unit.

Hence, 12(a + b) = 1 and, ...(1)

$$9\left(\frac{a}{2} + 3b\right) = 1 \quad \text{...(2)}$$

Using both equations, we get

$$12(a + b) = 9\left(\frac{a}{2} + 3b\right)$$

$\Rightarrow 4a + 4b = \frac{3a}{2} + 9b. \Rightarrow a = 2b$

Substituting the value of b in equation (1),

$\Rightarrow 12\left(\frac{3a}{2}\right) = 1.$

$\therefore$ Number of days required = 18.

72. Let the maximum marks = 100a, then Meena got 40a.

After increasing her score by 50%, she will get

$\Rightarrow 40a\left(1 + \frac{50}{100}\right) = 60a.$

Given:- Passing score = 60a + 35.

Post review score after 20% increase

= 60a × 1.2 = 72a

$\Rightarrow$ 60a + 35 + 7 = 72a

$\Rightarrow$ 12a = 42

$\Rightarrow$ a = 3.5

$\therefore$ maximum marks = 350.

Passing marks = 210 + 35 = 245.

and, passing percentage = $\frac{245 \times 100}{350} = 70\%.$

73. Let the length of race course = x and the speed of three horses be a, b and c respectively.

Hence, $\frac{x}{a} = \frac{x - 11}{b}$ ... (1)

and, $\frac{x}{a} = \frac{x - 90}{c}$ ... (2)

Also, $\frac{x}{b} = \frac{x - 80}{c}$ ... (3)

From (1) and (2) we get, $\frac{x - 11}{b} = \frac{x - 90}{c}$ ... (4)

Dividing (3) and (4) we get, $\frac{x - 11}{x} = \frac{x - 90}{x - 80}$

$\Rightarrow (x - 11)(x - 80) = x(x - 90)$

$\Rightarrow 91x - 90x = 880$

$\Rightarrow x = 880$

74. Given f(x + y) = f(x) f(y) and f(1) = 2

$\Rightarrow f(a + 1) + f(a + 2) + ... + f(a + n) = 16(2^n - 1)$

Now f(2) = f(1 + 1) = f(1) f(1) = 4

f(3) = f(2 + 1) = f(2) f(1) = 8

f(4) = f(3 + 1) = f(3) f(1) = 16

$\therefore f(x) = 2^x$

Now, $f(a + 1) + f(a + 2) + ... + f(a + n) = 16(2^n - 1)$

on putting n = 1 in the equation, we get

f(a + 1) = 16

$\Rightarrow$ f(a) f(1) = 16

$\Rightarrow 2^a . 2 = 16$

$\Rightarrow$ a = 3.

75.

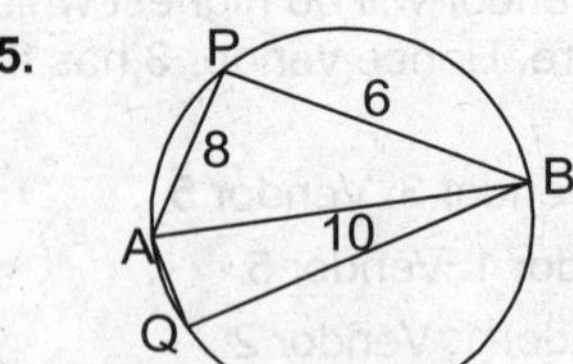

APB are vertices of a right angled triangle.

$\therefore AP = \sqrt{10^2 - 6^2} = 8$

$\therefore$ AQ = 4

$\Rightarrow QB = \sqrt{10^2 - 4^2} = \sqrt{84} \simeq 9.1$

76. The weight/volume (g/L) for liquid 1 = 1000

The weight/volume (g/L) for liquid 2 = 800

The weight/volume (g/L) of the mixture = $\frac{480}{\left(\frac{1}{2}\right)} = 960$

using alligation the ratio of liquid 1 and liquid 2 in the mixture = $\frac{(960 - 800)}{(1000 - 960)} = \frac{160}{40} = 4$.

Hence, the percentage of liquid 1 in the mixture

$= \frac{4 \times 100}{4 + 1} = 80$

77. Equation of straight line = 3x + 5y – 45 = 0

It intersects 'X' axis when y = 0, $\Rightarrow$ at the point (15, 0)

It intersects Y axis, when x = 0, $\Rightarrow$ at the point (0, 9)

Diameter of circumcircle = length of hypotenuse

$= \sqrt{15^2 + 9^2}$

$\therefore$ Radius = $\frac{\sqrt{225 + 81}}{2} \simeq 9$

78. Let cost price of pen and book be x and y respectively. Then selling price of pen and book will be 0.95x and 1.15y respectively.

$(0.95x + 1.15y) - (x + y) = 7$ ... (1)

and

$(x1.05 + 1.10y) - (x + y) = 13$ ... (2)

Solving (1) and (2) we get,

$0.15y - 0.05x = 7$

$0.10y + 0.05x = 13$

$\Rightarrow \boxed{y = 80}$.

79. Let income of Bimala = 100

Then, Amala's income = 100 × 1.2 = 120.

Kamala's income = $\frac{120 \times 100}{80} = 150$.

Kamala income down by 4% = 144.

Bimala's income goes up by 10% = 110.

∴ Percentage by which Kamala's income would exceed Bimala's income

$= \frac{144 - 110}{110} \times 100 = 30.91\% \approx 31\%$

80. Given :- $|x^2 - x - 6| = x + 2$

$\Rightarrow |(x - 3)(x + 2)| = x + 2$

For $x < -2$, $(3 - x)(-x - 2) = x + 2$

$\Rightarrow x - 3 = 1 \Rightarrow x = 4$ (Not possible, as $x < -2$)

For $-2 \le x < 3$, $(3 - x)(x + 2) = (x + 2)$

$\Rightarrow x = 2, -2$

For $x \ge 3$, $(x - 3)(x + 2) = x + 2$

$\Rightarrow x = 4$

Hence the product = 4 × 2 × (–2) = –16

81. Let the speed of cars be a and b and the distance = d.

Minimum time taken by 1st car = 6 hours

For maximum difference in time taken by both of them, car 1 has to start at 10 : 00 AM and car 2 has to start at 11 : 00 AM

Hence, car 2 will take 5 hours.

Hence $a = \frac{d}{6}$ and $b = \frac{d}{5}$.

∴ The speed of car 2 will exceed the speed of car

1 by $\frac{\frac{d}{5} - \frac{d}{6}}{\frac{d}{6}} \times 100 = \frac{\frac{d}{30}}{\frac{d}{6}} \times 100 = 20\%$.

82. $|x|(6x^2 + 1) = 5x^2$

For $x < 0$, $(-x)(6x^2 + 1) = 5x^2$

$\Rightarrow 6x^3 + x + 5x^2 = 0$

$\Rightarrow x(6x^2 + 5x + 1) = 0$

$\Rightarrow x(6x^2 + 3x + 2x + 1) = 0$

$\Rightarrow x(3x + 1)(2x + 1) = 0$

$x = 0, \frac{-1}{3}, \frac{-1}{2}$

For $x > 0$, $(x)(6x^2 + 1) = 5x^2$

$\Rightarrow 6x^3 + x - 5x^2 = 0$

$\Rightarrow x(6x^2 + 1 - 5x) = 0$

$\Rightarrow x(6x^2 - 3x - 2x + 1) = 0$

$\Rightarrow x(2x - 1)(3x - 1) = 0$

$\therefore x = 0, x = \frac{1}{2}, \frac{1}{3}$

Hence, the total number of solutions = 5.

83. Distance covered by A in 1 revolution = $2\pi \times 30 = 60\pi$

Distance covered by B in 1 revolution = $2\pi \times 40 = 80\pi$

Now, $(5000 + n)(60\pi) = 80\pi n$

$\Rightarrow 15000 = 4n - 3n$

$\Rightarrow n = 15000$

Then distance travelled by B = $15000 \times 80\pi$ cm $= 12\pi$ km

Hence the speed = $\frac{12\pi \times 60}{45} = 16\pi$

84. Let us assume that m is even, then, m + 1 will be odd and $\Rightarrow 8f(m + 1) - f(m) = 2$

$\Rightarrow 8(m + 1 + 3) - m(m + 1) = 2$

$\Rightarrow 8m + 32 - m^2 - m = 2$

$\Rightarrow m^2 - 7m - 30 = 0$

$\Rightarrow m = 10, -3.$

Rejecting the negative value, we get m = 10.

85. Let two positive numbers be x and y.

Given :- $xy = 616$ and $\frac{x^3 - y^3}{(x - y)^3} = \frac{157}{3}$.

To find :- $x + y = ?$

$\Rightarrow \frac{x^3 - y^3}{(x - y)^3} = \frac{(x - y)^3 + 3xy(x - y)}{(x - y)^3}$

$\Rightarrow \frac{x^3 - y^3}{(x - y)^3} = \frac{(x - y)^2 + 3xy}{(x - y)^2}$

$\Rightarrow \dfrac{x^3 - y^3}{(x-y)^3} \dfrac{x^2 + y^2 - 2xy + 3xy}{x^2 + y^2 - 2xy}$.

$\Rightarrow \dfrac{x^2 + y^2 + xy}{x^2 + y^2 - 2xy} = \dfrac{157}{3}$

$\Rightarrow 3[x^2 + y^2] + 3 \times xy = 157\,[x^2 + y^2] - 2(xy) + 157$

$\Rightarrow 3(x^2 + y^2) + 1848 = 157\,(x^2 + y^2) - 193424$

$\Rightarrow 195272 = 154\,(x^2 + y^2)$

$\Rightarrow 1268 = x^2 + y^2$

Now, use $(x + y)^2 = x^2 + y^2 + 2xy$

$= 1268 + 2 \times 616 = (x + y)^2$

$\Rightarrow 2500 = (x + y)^2$

$\Rightarrow x + y = 50$ (Since, x and y are positive numbers)

86. $2 \cos (x (x + 1)) = 2^x + 2^{-x}$

The maximum value of L.H.S is 2 when cos (x (x + 1)) is 1 and the minimum value of R.H.S is 2.

Hence, L.H.S and R.H.S can only be equal when both sides are 2.

For L.H.S, $\cos (x (x + 1)) = 1$

$\Rightarrow x(x + 1) = 0$

$\Rightarrow x = 0, -1$.

For R.H.S minimum value, x = 0.

Hence, only one solution x = 0.

87. Given $a_1 + a_2 + a_3 + ... + a_n$

$= 3\,(2^{n+1} - 2), n \geq 1$

11th term of series $= a_{11}$

= Sum of 11 terms – Sum of 10 terms

$= 3(2^{12} - 2) - 3(2^{11} - 2)$

$= 3[2^{12} - 2 - 2^{11} + 2]$

$= 3[2^{12} - 2^{11}]$

$= 3 \times 2^{11}$

$= 6144$.

88.

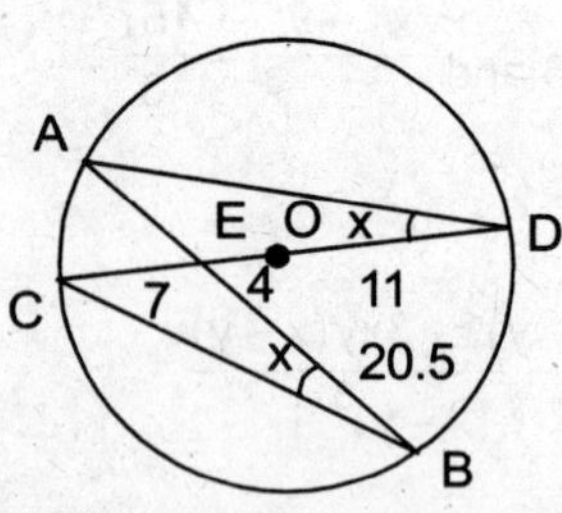

DE = 4, EC = 7, AB = 20.5

CD = 22

|BE – AE| = ?

In figure AE × BE = CE × DE (P tolemy Theorem)

$\Rightarrow 7 \times 15 = x(20.5 - x)$

(Let AE = x)

$\Rightarrow 210 = x(41 - 2x)$

$\Rightarrow 2x^2 - 41x + 210 = 0$

$\Rightarrow x = 10$ or 10.5

AE = 10 or AE = 10.5

Hence, BE = 20.5 – 10 = 10.5 or

BE = 20.5 – 10.5 = 10

Required difference = 10.5 – 10 = 0.5

89. Let the amount invested in the ratio 2 : 1 was 200 x and 100 x, then the fixed deposit investment = 1500000 – 300 x.

Hence, the interest $= 200x \times \dfrac{4}{100} = 8x$ and,

$100x \times \dfrac{3}{100} = 3x$

Interest from the fixed deposit

$= (1500000 - 300x)\dfrac{6}{100} = 90000 - 18x$

Hence the total interest $= 90000 - 18x + 8x + 3x$

$= 90000 - 7x$

$\Rightarrow 90000 - 7x = 76000$

$\Rightarrow 7x = 14000$

$\Rightarrow x = 2000$

Hence the fixed deposit investment

$= 15000000 - 300 \times 2000$

= 9,00,000

= 9 lakhs.

90. $(\sqrt{2})^{19} 3^4\, 4^2\, 9^m\, 8^n = 3^n\, 16^m (\sqrt[4]{64})$

$\Rightarrow 2^{\frac{19}{2}}\, 3^4\, 2^4\, 3^{2m}\, 2^{3n} = 3^n\, 2^{4m}\, (64)^{\frac{1}{4}}$

$\Rightarrow \left(2^{\frac{19}{2}+4+3n}\right)\left(3^{4+2m}\right) = 3^n\, 2^{4m}\, 2^{\frac{3}{2}}$.

$\Rightarrow 2^{\frac{27}{2}+3n}\, 3^{4+2m} = 3^n\, 2^{4m+\frac{3}{2}}$

$\therefore \dfrac{27}{2} + 3n = 4m + \dfrac{3}{2}$ ...(1)

and $4 + 2m = n$ ...(2)

Solving (1) and (2), we get,

m = –12

91. $|x| + |y| \le 2$, $|x| \ge 1$

we have to find the shaded area

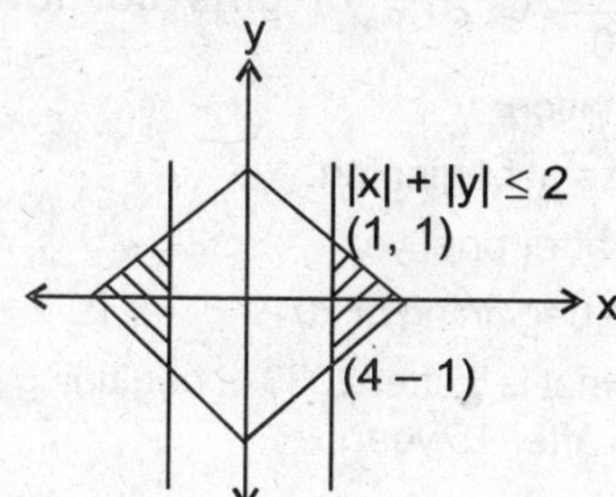

$= 2 \times \frac{1}{2} \times 2 \times 1$

$= \boxed{2}$ sq. units

92.

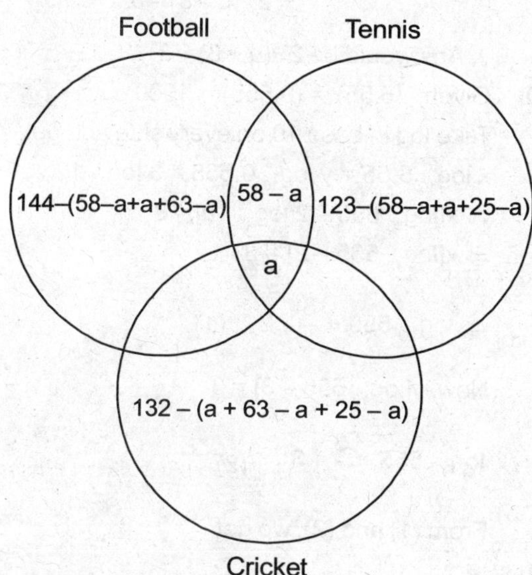

All players total = 256

$\Rightarrow 256 = 144 + 123 + 132 - (58 + 25 + 63) + a$

$\Rightarrow 256 = 399 - 146 - 2a$

$\Rightarrow 256 = 253 + a$

$\Rightarrow \boxed{a = 3}$

$\therefore$ only Tennis = 123 – 58 – 25 + 3

= 123 – 80 = 43

93. Let 'W' be work, M be efficiency of men, 'm' be efficiency of machines

3M + 8m = 2(8M + 3m) ... (1)

2m = 13 days

from eqⁿ (1) : 3M + 8m = 16M + 6m

$\Rightarrow \boxed{2m = 13M}$

If '2' machines complete work in 13 days

⇒ 13 Men will complete the work in 13 days.

94. Let the investment of Amala, Bina and Gouri be 300x, 400x and 500x, hence the interest incomes will be $(300x)\frac{6}{100} = 18x$, $(400x)\frac{5}{100} = 20x$ and $(500x)\frac{4}{100} = 20x$ respectively.

Given, Bina's interest income exceeds Amala by. $20x - 18x = 2x = 250 \Rightarrow x = 125$.

Now, total interest income = 18x + 20x + 20x

= 58x = 58 × 125 = 7250.

95. Given:- $a_1, a_2, \ldots\ldots$ are in A.P.

therefore, $a_1 = a_1$

$a_2 = a_1 + d$

$a_3 = a_2 + d$

and so on.

where d is the common difference.

Now consider

$$\frac{1}{\sqrt{a_1}+\sqrt{a_2}} + \frac{1}{\sqrt{a_2}+\sqrt{a_3}} + \ldots + \frac{1}{\sqrt{a_n}+\sqrt{a_{n+1}}}$$

Rationalise each term and get,

$$\Rightarrow \frac{\sqrt{a_1}-\sqrt{a_2}}{a_1-a_2} + \frac{\sqrt{a_2}-\sqrt{a_3}}{a_2-a_3} + \ldots + \frac{\sqrt{a_n}-\sqrt{a_{n+1}}}{a_n-a_{n+1}}$$

$$\Rightarrow \frac{-1}{d}\left[\sqrt{a_1}-\sqrt{a_2}+\sqrt{a_2}-\sqrt{a_3}+\ldots+\sqrt{a_n}-\sqrt{a_{n+1}}\right]$$

$$\Rightarrow \frac{-1}{d}\left[\sqrt{a_1}-\sqrt{a_{n+1}}\right]$$

$$\Rightarrow \frac{-1}{d}\left[\frac{a_1-a_{n+1}}{\sqrt{a_1}+\sqrt{a_{n+1}}}\right] \text{ [rationalise again]}$$

$$\Rightarrow \frac{n}{\sqrt{a_1}+\sqrt{a_{n+1}}}.$$

96. Let the score of Ramesh and Gautam be denoted by S_R and S_G respectively.

Given:- $S_R = 82.5$ and,

$$\frac{\text{sum of scores of 20 students} + S_R}{21} = 62$$

⇒ sum of scores of 20 students = 62 × 21 – 82.5

= 1219.5

Average score of 21 students other than Ramesh

$$= \frac{1219.5 + S_G}{21}$$

Average score of 22 students

$= \frac{1219.5 + 82.5 + S_G}{22}$

Given:- $\frac{1219.5 + 82.5 + S_G}{22} = 1 + \frac{1219.5 + S_G}{21}$

$\Rightarrow (1302 + S_G) \times 21 = (1240.5 + S_G)22$

$\Rightarrow 27342 - 27291 = S_G$

$\Rightarrow 51 = G$

97. Rectangular faces have diagonals

$3 : 2\sqrt{3} : \sqrt{15}$

Let's take sides in a ratio such that this case can be observed.

$\Rightarrow \sqrt{l^2 + b^2} : \sqrt{b^2 + h^2} : \sqrt{l^2 + h^2} = 3 : 2\sqrt{3} : 15$

or $l^2 + b^2 = 9$,

$b^2 + h^2 = 12$, $l^2 + h^2 = 15$

$\Rightarrow l^2 = 6$, $b^2 = 3$, $h^2 = 9$.

$\therefore$ shortest to longest edge $= \sqrt{\frac{3}{9}} = 1 : \sqrt{3}$

98. Let there be x students in the class

Girls = x × 0.6

Boys = x × 0.4

Given:- There are 30 more girls than boys i.e.,

$\Rightarrow x(0.6) = (x \times 0.4) + 30$

$\Rightarrow x(0.2) = 30$

$\Rightarrow x = 150$

68% pass the examination ⇒102 students

since, 102 students, includes 30 boys, therefore, 72 will be Girls who passed.

Girls who do not pass = (150 × 0.6) – 72 = 18

$\therefore \frac{18 \times 100}{90} = 20\%$ of girls do not pass the examination.

99. popl^n = p at beginning,

3 + 2p after one year

1000 in beginning of 2019

Then what is it after 2033 or beginning of 2014 that means after 15 years

year 1	year 2	year 3	year3
p	3 + 2p	2(3 + 2p) + 3	2(4p + 9) + 3
		= 4p + 9	= 8p + 21
		= 4(p + 3) – 3	= 8(p + 3) – 3
		$= 2^2(p+3) - 3$	$= 2^3(p+3) - 3$

$\therefore$ Ans would be $2^{15}(p + 3) - 3$

100. Given;- $(5.55)^x = (0.555)^y = 1000$

Take log in base 10 on every side and get,

$x \log_{10} 5.55 = y \log_{10} 0.555 = 3 \log_{10} 10$.

$\Rightarrow x[\log_{10} 555 - 2 \log_{10} 10] = 3$

$\Rightarrow x[\log_{10} 555 - 2] = 3$

$\Rightarrow \log_{10} 555 = \frac{3}{x} + 2$ ... (1)

Now, $y[\log_{10} 555 - 3] = 3$

$\log_{10} 555 = \frac{3}{y} + 3$ ... (2)

From (1) and (2), we get

$\Rightarrow \frac{3}{x} + 2 = \frac{3}{y} + 3 \Rightarrow \frac{3}{x} - \frac{3}{y} = 1 \Rightarrow \frac{1}{x} - \frac{1}{y} = \frac{1}{3}$.